THE
unofficial **GUIDE**®
ᴛᴼ Ireland

2ND EDITION

THE
unofficial GUIDE®
TO Ireland

2ND EDITION

STEPHEN BREWER

Published by:
John Wiley & Sons, Inc.
111 River Street
Hoboken, NJ 07030-5774

Produced by Menasha Ridge Press

Cover design by Michael J. Freeland

Interior design by Vertigo Design

For information on our other products and services or to obtain technical support, please contact our Customer Care Department within the United States at 800-762-2974, outside the United States at 317-572-3993, or by fax at 317-572-4002.

John Wiley & Sons, Inc., also publishes its books in a variety of electronic formats. Some content that appears in print may not be available in electronic formats.

ISBN 978-0-470-28568-8

Manufactured in the United States of America

5 4 3 2

CONTENTS

LIST *of* MAPS

ACKNOWLEDGMENTS

I WISH TO THANK ALL MY IRISH FRIENDS AND RELATIVES who shared stories, advice, and inspiration: Gerry Madigan and Hal Erbe, wise and always ready to talk about home; Annie Callan, a fine poet and advisor; Emmet Kelleher and Suzanne Rowan Kelleher, warm, charming, and first-rate conversationalists; and my Coyne cousins, a pleasure to be with and dispensers of good advice on what to say and not to say in a pub. Thanks, too, to the many, many fine folks I met along the way who were on hand with help, humor, and hospitality. Here in the States, I am deeply grateful to Molly Merkle, Ritchey Halphen, Steve Jones, and Annie Long at Menasha Ridge Press, along with copyeditor Andy Sloan, proofreaders Terri Fredrickson and Vanessa Rusch Thomas, and indexer Ann Cassar.

This book is dedicated to the Leonard sisters, Mary and Patricia, who never lost the lilt and magic of the old country and whom I will always miss.

—*Stephen Brewer*

ABOUT *the* AUTHOR

STEPHEN BREWER is a writer and editor who loves his home and friends in New York City but is just as happy traveling. He is the author of several other guidebooks, including *The Unofficial Guide to England*, *Frommer's Best Day Trips from London*, and *Frommer's Venice Day by Day*, and is the coauthor of the forthcoming *Frommer's Italy Day by Day*.

INTRODUCTION

WELCOME *to* IRELAND

TALK. THE IRISH HAVE A NAME FOR IT—*cráic*—and these days it's often about the new prosperity that's falling over Ireland. And while Ireland's doing well (though the *cráic* is also about how the good times are slowing down a bit), the unprecedented wealth, as well as the newness that comes with it, may bring to mind the lines of the Irish poet William Butler Yeats: "All changed, changed utterly."

It's not, though—changed, that is. Not really. The essence of being in Ireland is still about taking the first sip of a freshly poured Guinness and wondering how beer could be so much better here than it is back home. Or noticing that a craggy, purple-shaded, heather-covered landscape looks just like the backdrop of an MGM musical, or trying to determine how many shades of green are contained within one valley. The pleasure of being in Ireland is still about sitting in a pub and listening to a discussion about the Troubles, fishing rights, and road improvements (all mixed into one monologue) out of one ear and the strains of a fiddle out of the other. Or finding a comfortable spot next to a crackling fire at your castle hotel or bed-and-breakfast and feeling that you've come back to a familiar place. Ireland has a way of evoking nostalgia for the old country, even in visitors who don't have a trace of Irish blood coursing through their veins.

Ireland will throw a few surprises your way, too. As you travel around the country, you will sit down to some of the best meals you've ever had. The ingredients aren't necessarily exotic—just good Kerry lamb or Dublin Bay scallops, for example—but are prepared with a finesse that should put to rest forever the bad jokes about Irish cuisine. With the peace dividends comes the chance to discover Northern Ireland, where yes, signs of the Troubles are still in evidence, but the Giants Causeway and other natural phenomena have a way of reminding us that nature is going to be a force long after we're gone.

In *The Unofficial Guide to Ireland,* we show you how to get the most out of your visit. We point out what's right and what's wrong about hotels and restaurants, tell you what paintings to look for, and lead you to tours that will give you an insider's view of a city or take you to a patch of wilderness you'd never find on your own. For a highly selective list of our favorite places in Ireland, see the Not to Be Missed lists at the beginning of each chapter. Our advice should make your trip more enjoyable (and save you time and money, too), but follow your own travel instincts as well. Make discoveries, make friends (not hard to do in Ireland), let yourself be drawn into a session of *cráic.* We'll help you with the basics, but only you can embrace the welcome that Ireland will extend to you.

ABOUT *this* GUIDE

WHY "UNOFFICIAL"?

MOST TRAVEL GUIDES TO IRELAND follow the usual tracks of the typical tourist—automatically sending everyone to the well-known towns and sights without offering any information about how to get the most out of the visit, recommending restaurants and hotels indiscriminately, and failing to recognize the limits of human endurance in sightseeing. This guide is different: we appreciate the fact that you'll want to be discerning about hotels and restaurants, to spend your time doing what you really want to do, and to see what you want to see.

Accordingly, we help you make choices that will maximize your trip to Ireland. We tell you what we think of certain tourist traps, why you should spend time in one place and not in another, what rooms to ask for in hotels, what to order (and what not to order) in restaurants, what the options are if you want to stay off the beaten track, and how to spend a little less money on some meals and hotels so you can splurge a little when you want to (and we give you suggestions of places worthy of a splurge). We complain about rip-offs, advise you on bargains, and steer you out of the madness of the crowds for a break now and then. We also give you the kinds of details—from historical background to juicy tidbits—that will make you appreciate Ireland all the more.

We're well aware that you probably only have a week or two to spend in Ireland, so we've done the footwork to help you prepare and strategize to get the most out of your time. We lead you to hotels that offer the best deals and the most pleasant surroundings, good restaurants in varying price ranges, and the sights you won't want to miss plus tips for visiting them when they are least crowded. In laying out our visits, we take things easy (the way we think you'll want to), and we have gone to considerable effort to ensure that the quality of your travels in Ireland will be high and the irritation quotient low. We've tried to anticipate the special needs of older people, families with young children, families with teenagers, solo travelers, people with disabilities, and those who have a particular passion for literature, sports, architecture, shopping, painting, antiques, or whatever.

Please remember that prices and admission hours change constantly; we have listed the most up-to-date information we can get, but it never hurts to double-check times in particular (if prices of attractions change, it is generally not by much). Most of all, whether you're visiting Ireland for the first time or the twentieth, traveling on pleasure or business, we trust we will help you better enjoy the experience.

ABOUT UNOFFICIAL GUIDES

READERS CARE ABOUT AUTHORS' OPINIONS. Authors, after all, are supposed to know what they are talking about. This, coupled with the fact that the traveler wants quick answers (as opposed to endless alternatives), dictates that travel authors be explicit, prescriptive, and above all, direct. The *Unofficial Guides* try to be just that. We spell out alternatives and recommend specific courses of action. We simplify complicated destinations and attractions to allow the traveler to feel in control in the most unfamiliar environments. Our objective is not to give the most information or all the information, but the most accessible, useful information. Of course, many hotels, restaurants, and attractions are so closely woven into the fabric of Ireland that it would be a disservice to omit them from our guide solely because we can't recommend them. So we've included all the famous haunts, giving our opinion of and experience with them, in the hopes that you will approach (or avoid) these institutions armed with the necessary intelligence.

SPECIAL FEATURES

- Vital information about traveling abroad
- Friendly introductions to Irish towns and cities
- Listings that are keyed to your interests, so you can pick and choose
- Advice on how to avoid the worst crowds, traffic, and excessive costs
- Recommendations for lesser-known sights that are off the well-beaten tourist path but no less worthwhile
- Maps that make it easy to find places you want to visit—and places you want to avoid
- Hotel and restaurant selections that help you narrow down your choices quickly, according to your needs and preferences
- Candid opinions of hotels, sights, and restaurants that are overrated—and those that are especially worthwhile
- A table of contents and detailed index to help you find things fast

---

WHAT YOU WON'T GET

- Long, useless lists where everything looks the same
- Information that gets you to your destination at the worst possible time
- Information without advice on how to use it

An *Unofficial Guide* is a critical reference work; we focus on a travel destination that appears to be especially complex. Our authors and researchers are completely independent from the attractions, restaurants, and hotels we describe. *The Unofficial Guide to Ireland* is designed for individuals and families traveling for fun as well as for business, and it will be especially helpful to those hopping "across the pond" for the first time. It's directed at value-conscious adults who seek a cost-effective but not Spartan travel style.

HOW THIS GUIDE WAS RESEARCHED AND WRITTEN

IN PREPARING THIS BOOK, we took nothing for granted. Each hotel, restaurant, shop, and attraction was visited by trained observers who conducted detailed evaluations and rated each according to formal criteria. Team members conducted interviews with tourists of all ages to determine what they enjoyed most and least during their visits to Ireland.

Although our observers are independent and impartial, they are otherwise ordinary travelers. Like you, they have visited Ireland as tourists or business travelers, noting their satisfaction or dissatisfaction. The primary difference between the average tourist and the trained evaluator is the evaluator's skills in organization, preparation, and observation. Observer teams use detailed checklists to analyze hotel rooms, restaurants, nightclubs, and attractions. Finally, evaluator ratings and observations are integrated with tourist reactions and the opinions of patrons for a comprehensive profile of each feature and service.

In compiling this guide, we recognize that a tourist's age, background, and interests will strongly influence his or her taste in Ireland's wide array of attractions and will account for a preference for one sight or museum over another. Our sole objective is to provide the reader with sufficient description, critical evaluation, and pertinent data to make knowledgeable decisions according to individual tastes.

LETTERS, COMMENTS, AND QUESTIONS FROM READERS

WE EXPECT TO LEARN FROM our mistakes, as well as from the input of our readers, and to improve with each new book and edition. Many of those who use the *Unofficial Guides* write to us asking questions, making comments, or sharing their own discoveries and lessons learned. New hotels, restaurants, and attractions are opening all the time in Ireland, and if there's something new you'd like us to check out, let us know about it. We appreciate all such input, and we encourage our readers to continue writing. Readers' comments and observations will be frequently incorporated in revised editions of *The Unofficial Guide to Ireland* and will contribute immeasurably to its improvement.

How to Write the Author

Stephen Brewer
The Unofficial Guide to Ireland
P.O. Box 43673
Birmingham, AL 35243

When you write, be sure to put your return address on your letter as well as on the envelope—sometimes envelopes and letters get separated. Remember, our work takes us out of the office for long periods of time, so forgive us if our response is delayed.

HOW THIS GUIDE IS ORGANIZED: BY REGION AND BY SUBJECT

WE HAVE ORGANIZED THIS GUIDE by region—not by any sort of official, government-designated regional organization, but by manageably sized geographic areas that we use to help you plan your travels through Ireland. We then organize each region by the major (and the most appealing) cities and towns that you can use as a base. Within our coverage of each place, you'll find detailed coverage on the following:

PLANNING YOUR VISIT   This section includes local informational resources and seasonal events that may help you decide when to visit.

ARRIVING AND GETTING ORIENTED   Here we give information on reaching the city by air (when relevant), train, car (including where to park), and bus.

GETTING AROUND   In larger destinations where walking is not an option, we give detailed descriptions of how to use the bus network, subway, or other public transportation.

HOTELS   This section provides profiles of our hotel picks; you can peruse them and book ahead if you wish.

EXPLORING   Here we lead you through a town, city, or region, pointing out the sights (including those of secondary interest but still worth a quick visit) and providing detailed profiles of all the major sightseeing attractions. You'll also find a section on tours, with our choices for the best guided tours to help you become acquainted with a particular destination.

DINING   Provides our choices of the most pleasant places to eat.

ireland

Some Do's and Don'ts When Visiting Ireland

- **Don't** try to intervene in football (soccer) arguments or those about hurling or Gaelic football—these are very serious subjects, and no one really cares what an outsider thinks about them.

- **Don't** think you'll endear yourself to the Irish by complaining about the rain. They tend to like it.

- **Do** be prepared to talk about the weather, and be prepared for a daily forecast that includes showers, fog, periods of sunshine, spells of daytime darkness, and gales.

- **Don't** tell anyone that his or her accent sounds British.

- **Don't** think British pounds are acceptable as currency in the Republic.

- **Do** listen. Not only do the Irish have a lot to say, but they have a nice way of saying it.

- **Do** read. The Irish are still producing great literature; step into any bookshop and stock up on some volumes to enjoy long after you've left Ireland.

ENTERTAINMENT AND NIGHTLIFE   We lead you to theaters, concert halls, pubs, discos, and other venues.

SHOPPING   Here we focus on where to find items that are unique to a particular place.

EXERCISE AND RECREATION   This section provides ideas on where to exercise—we often lead you to walking and biking trails, of which Ireland has so many.

We discuss these categories in greater depth in Part Two, Arriving (page 55). Below and following are the regions that make up our coverage of Ireland.

Dublin

The capital of the Republic is an easy place to be—despite the traffic that clogs the streets and the cranes that pierce the sky these days. Prosperity has brought new shops, restaurants, nightlife, hotels, and a burst of cosmopolitan vitality. But there's no need to sing the lament "Me darlin', Dublin's dead and gone." In many ways, the city is still as mellow as the gray stone of its cathedrals and other landmarks and the verdant hues of its parks and greens. You can get around on foot, stepping in and out of the country's great museums and landmarks, and come time to rest, find a snug corner in one of the city's thousand-odd pubs. We guide you through all the major attractions, as well as our favorite minor ones, and give you a selection of hotels, restaurants, shops, and clubs, making sure you enjoy this lovely city as much as we do.

The South of Ireland

Southern Ireland is surprisingly urbane. **Kilkenny** is one of Ireland's most lovely cities, and **Cork** is one of its most lively. **Cobh** and **Kinsale** have long been linked to the sea and are well steeped in episodes of the Irish past. Even when you think you're deep in the countryside, you'll see a remarkable medieval monument (none more haunting than the **Rock of Cashel**) or two rising above the green landscapes.

The Southwest of Ireland

Kenmare, the **Dingle Peninsula, Killarney National Park,** the **Ring of Kerry**—the place-names here read like a list of the most beautiful spots in Ireland. To get the most out of this scenery-endowed region, settle into the welcoming guesthouses of Kenmare and Dingle Town, and from there follow our lead off the beaten path to enjoy cliff-hugging coast roads and mountain trails.

The Lower Shannon

The Shannon, the longest river in the British Isles, flows into the Atlantic Ocean through a wide estuary. The green landscapes that roll away from the river are littered with castles (the most famous is **Bunratty**), pretty towns and villages (the prettiest is **Adare**), some of Ireland's grandest hotels, and one of Ireland's largest cities, **Limerick.**

The West of Ireland

The West of Ireland is a land of rugged seascapes, mountains, bogs, and moors. The region is *Gaeltacht* (Irish speaking) in many parts; cradles some of Ireland's most remarkable landscapes, including the **Burren** and **Connemara;** and is home to one of its most hospitable cities, **Galway.**

The Northwest of Ireland

It's easy to bypass the desolate landscapes of **counties Donegal and Sligo.** But to do so would mean missing a lot: places such as **Slieve League,** the tallest, and certainly most dramatic, sea cliffs in Europe; the heather-covered mountains of **Glenveagh National Park;** the pre-historic tombs that surround **Sligo Town;** and the dramatic headlands where the region dips into the North Sea.

Northern Ireland

Derry and **Belfast** still bear the marks of the Troubles, most visibly in the wall murals that are now attractions in both cities, but things have changed with the peace dividends. The talk in Belfast these days is about revival; the surprise for the visitor is just how appealing these places are. The impression is magnified along the **Antrim Coast,** where nature conjures up magic like the **Giants Causeway.**

An **OVERVIEW** of **IRISH HISTORY**

THE FIRST INHABITANTS

SCIENTIFIC OPINION IS INCONSISTENT, but it seems likely that humans first arrived in Ireland around the late 8000s BC. These people were Mesolithic, and the artifacts they left behind (mostly flint) make it clear that they lived a nomadic life, fishing and hunting.

Neolithic people begin to appear in Ireland in about 3000 BC. Unlike the earlier inhabitants, these people farmed. Armed with stone axes, they could easily cut down trees and build dwellings. With tilled fields and crops, permanent settlements took root, leading to relatively stable communities.

These inhabitants also left behind a remarkable variety of megalithic stone monuments: hundreds of court, portal, and passage tombs. Many of these bear fascinating engraved designs. Newgrange and Knowth, just north of Dublin (see page 178), are two of the most spectacular and moving examples. Later inhabitants came to think that their creators were faeries, or little people, a belief that is still (to a degree) alive today.

The Bronze Age (1750–500 BC) witnessed the introduction of metalworking, a vast improvement over stone. Bronze, copper, and gold objects were fashioned, and by the late Bronze Age (800 BC) the industry was well established.

- **Late 8000s BC**   Mesolithic people first appear in Ireland
- **3000 BC**   Neolithic people arrive
- **1750–500 BC**   The Bronze Age

THE CELTS ARRIVE

THE CELTS ARRIVED IN IRELAND in successive waves, beginning around 500 BC, and immediately began to plant their culture on the new soil in every possible way. The influence of their most important clan, the Gaels, lives on in many ways today, especially in the Gaelic language.

The Celts came to Ireland equipped with the ability to produce iron. They brought with them iron weapons and tools, which gave them an advantage over those who produced bronze, as iron is much stronger and tougher. They also brought with them a lively culture of song and poetry.

The Celts were never interested in a unified government. Many tribes existed, loosely allied to several kings. Despite their casual organization, which would seem to invite invasion, the Romans never conquered the Celts in Ireland.

- **500 BC**   Celt settlements begins
- **55 BC**   Romans conquer the Celts in England
- **AD 100**   The Gaels appear in Ireland

CHRISTIANITY COMES TO IRELAND

TRADITION HAS IT THAT PRIESTS came to Ireland before St. Patrick, but when we think of the birth of Christianity in Ireland, it is Patrick whom we think of. The saint, whose actual name was Maewyn Succat, was kidnapped from his home in Britain and transported to Ireland, where he spent seven years working as a slave. He escaped, went back to Britain, then returned to Ireland in AD 432 to convert the Irish to Christianity. He preached throughout the country, often at Celtic religious festivals, and he became incredibly popular, even among the Celts. Many legends rose around him, the most familiar contending that he drove the snakes out of Ireland—not literal reptiles, but, rather, pagan religion—and that he used the shamrock to explain the Trinity. Patrick, who died on March 17, AD 461, also helped found many schools and monasteries. He later became the patron saint of Ireland.

Many monasteries existed by the sixth and seventh centuries AD, and Ireland had become a major center of Christianity. Scholars from abroad flocked to the monasteries, where they preserved religious and classical texts. Many devoted themselves to illustrating, or illuminating, manuscripts, especially the initial letters, which were elaborately designed. The Book of Kells (see page 124), now at Dublin's Trinity College, is perhaps the most famous example.

- **AD 432**   St. Patrick arrives in Ireland to convert the Celts
- **AD 461**   St. Patrick dies
- **AD 500–800**   Ireland becomes one of Europe's major centers of Christianity

THE VIKING INVASIONS

THE VIKINGS FIRST SWEPT into Ireland in AD 795 and continued to arrive in successive waves. They founded Ireland's first towns along the east coast, among them Dublin and Waterford. Though the Vikings continued to plunder and pillage, they also began an economic relationship with the Irish. Gradually the two groups became traders, and commercial towns sprang up in the countryside.

The Vikings mercilessly attacked the monasteries; the monks had no means of defending themselves and were easy prey. Unable to read, the Vikings saw nothing of value in the manuscripts the monks had produced, preferring gold altarpieces and the jewel-encrusted covers of the manuscripts. Thus came down to us, almost by mistake, masterpieces of classical literature and religious thought.

The Irish defeated the Vikings' High King, Brian Boru, at the Battle of Clontarf in AD 1014. With the departure of the Vikings, Ireland experienced a period of relative prosperity and peace, though the country was attractive to foreign powers. An Irishman, Dermot MacMurrough, wanted to rule all of Ireland and asked Henry II, the Norman king of England, for aid. He sent Richard de Clare, Earl of Pembroke, known as Strongbow, to MacMurrough's aid. Henry was a hands-on ruler, controlling towns, kings, and churches. For the first time, England took an active interest in Ireland.

- **AD 795**   Viking invasions begin
- **AD 841**   A Viking band settles in Ireland, building Dublin
- **AD 1014** High King of Ireland Brian Boru defeats a Viking army at the Battle of Clontarf near Dublin

THE NORMAN INVASION

FROM 1167 UNTIL 1169, Anglo-Normans swept into Ireland. Henry II arrived in 1171, proclaiming Ireland to be under Anglo-Norman rule and giving his troops land. They built a chain of fortresses to protect their possessions, and they built new towns. Many Anglo-Normans married Irish women and gradually adopted Irish culture. Attempts were made to oust the invaders, but none were successful. By 1250 the Anglo-Normans occupied almost all of Ireland. They had a more sophisticated social system than the Irish did, and they organized cities and government to their liking.

- **1066**   William the Conqueror conquers England in the Battle of Hastings
- **1167–69**   The Anglo-Normans sweep into Ireland
- **1171**   King Henry II proclaims Ireland under Anglo-Norman rule and seizes Dublin
- **1348–1350**   The Black Death arrives, killing a third of Dublin's population

THE FLIGHT OF THE EARLS

EVENTUALLY THE ENGLISH KINGS lost interest in Ireland, being preoccupied with their own wars. Yet in 1366 they passed the Statutes of Kilkenny, outlawing all of Gaelic culture, including the Gaelic language.

The Earls of Kildare rebelled against Henry VIII in 1534. When Henry squashed the revolt, he executed the earls and took their land, giving it to English colonists. This scenario would repeat itself over and over again for centuries, with the Irish fighting against English landowners. At the Battle of Yellow Ford in 1598, the nobleman

Hugh O'Neill led a revolt against the English and won, but the Irish were soundly defeated by the British in the Battle of Kinsale in 1601. O'Neill and other Ulster nobles later sailed to the Continent in an exodus known as the Flight of the Earls, abandoning their homes and their culture.

• **1366**	The Statutes of Kilkenny outlaw Gaelic culture
• **1534**	The Earls of Kildare rebel against King Henry VIII; they fail and are executed
• **1558–1603**	Ireland is divided into counties
• **1598**	A Gaelic revolt led by Hugh O'Neill is successful
• **1601**	The Battle of Kinsale squashes the revolt
• **1607**	O'Neill and other nobles leave Ireland behind and sail to the Continent; the old Gaelic order sails with them

ENGLISH COLONIZATION

JAMES I SAW IRELAND as an opportunity for his countrymen, and he sent more than 20,000 English and Scottish planters onto land that had been confiscated.

Although there was disparity between the poor and the gentry, these groups were united by their Catholic faith, and in 1642 they rallied together in the Confederation of Kilkenny against Oliver Cromwell, the ruler of England, and his Protestant Parliament.

Cromwell savagely retaliated by invading Ireland (1649–50) with more than 20,000 men. They tortured and murdered, destroyed villages, and sent thousands into slavery. By 1652, all Irish resistance had ceased. In 1653, Catholic landowners were exiled to the rocky west coast.

The Irish spirit was never really broken, however. In 1688–89, the Catholic James II came to Ireland and with an army tried to regain his crown. He surrounded Londonderry, but the city withstood a siege of 105 days.

In 1690, in the Battle of the Boyne, James and his army met the troops of the Protestant William III of Orange. James was defeated, and *Orange* became associated with the pro-Protestant, pro-English sentiment.

The Penal Laws closed the century. They made it illegal to take part in anything having to do with Gaelic culture—playing certain musical instruments or speaking the language were punishable offenses. The laws also made it illegal to buy land or hold office, and contact with priests was forbidden, as was Catholic education.

• **1642**	In the Confederation of Kilkenny, Catholics form an alliance to defend their rights and their religion

• **1649–1650**	Oliver Cromwell invades Ireland with 20,000 troops and conquers the country savagely—murdering, plundering, raping, and seizing millions of acres of land
• **1653**	The Cromwellian Settlement strips landowners of their belongings and forces them to move west of the River Shannon
• **1660**	King Charles II is restored to the throne and returns land to some landowners
• **1688–89**	Catholic King James II assembles an army in Ireland to retake the crown; he fails after a standoff in Londonderry
• **1690**	James II fails again, this time defeated by the army of Protestant King William III of Orange at the Battle of the Boyne
• **1704**	The English Penal Laws strip Irish Catholics of most of their rights

THE IRISH REBELLION

IN 1798, IRISH REBELS—both Catholic and Protestant—banded together against the British. Their goal was to use the word *Irishman* instead of *Catholic* or *Protestant*. More than 30,000 died before the British ended the revolt.

England found the solution to the problem in the Act of Union in 1801. Ireland became united with Great Britain, the Irish Parliament was dissolved, and Catholics were prohibited from the British Parliament.

• **1798**	The United Irishmen revolt against Britain, but their rebellion is quashed; more than 30,000 die
• **1801**	The Act of Union dissolves the Irish Parliament

THE GREAT POTATO FAMINE

IN 1845, RURAL IRELAND'S primary food, the potato, suddenly began to rot in the ground. The cause was the fungus *Phytophthora*. Over the next four years, as the blight became worse and worse, it destroyed the country's entire crop, and more than a million people died of starvation and illness. A huge number fled the country, emigrating to America, England, Canada, and Australia.

The British initially ignored the masses of starving, ill, and dead; the aid that was eventually offered—such as the opening of workhouses, with their savage conditions—was often ineffective. After the Famine ended in 1849, mass emigration continued, mostly to America but to England, Europe, Canada, and Australia as well. By 1921, Ireland's population was half what it had been before the blight.

The effects of the Famine lingered for more than 20 years. Emigration continued unabated, reducing the population still more. The rural poor were poorer than ever, and landowners had trouble collecting rents. Continuing anger at the British spawned a number of movements and organizations aimed at promoting all things Irish and breaking away from English control.

> - **1845–49** The Great Potato Famine devastates Ireland, killing more than 1 million people and forcing 1 million–plus to emigrate

REBELLION AND HOME RULE

THE IRISH REPUBLICAN BROTHERHOOD, founded in Dublin in 1858, grew quickly, both at home and abroad (its American counterpart, the Fenian Brotherhood, was formed the next year). Its aim was to promote Ireland's freedom by damaging English interests, and it published newspapers to spread its message. Some groups were formed to promote pride. The Gaelic Athletic Association's goal was to foster pride in Irish sports. The Gaelic League attempted to revive interest in the speaking and study of Irish to bring back pride in the Irish heritage. The Sinn Féin (We Ourselves) movement was connected to the Irish Republican Brotherhood. Home rule was an ever-present goal.

Two home-rule bills were defeated in 1886 and 1893. When the third was being debated in Parliament, World War I broke out. The bill was passed, but it was not put into effect until the end of the war.

> - **1858** The Irish Republican Brotherhood, later to become the Irish Republican Army (IRA), forms in Dublin; its U.S. wing, the Fenian Brotherhood, forms in New York in 1859
> - **1879–1882** Reforms return land to those who work it
> - **1884** To foster pride in Irish sports, the Gaelic Athletic Association is formed
> - **1886** First Home Rule Bill, intended to give Ireland some independence, is rejected
> - **1893** The Gaelic League is formed to promote pride in traditional poetry, literature, and music
> - **1893** Second Home Rule Bill is rejected
> - **1905–08** The Sinn Féin (We Ourselves) movement is founded
> - **1914** Third Home Rule Act is signed by King George V
> - **1914–18** World War I

THE EASTER RISING

WHEN WORLD WAR I BROKE OUT, revolution was still in the air. An uprising finally took place on Easter Monday in 1916, when Patrick

Pearse, James Connolly, and others proclaimed the existence of an Irish Republic and occupied the General Post Office in Dublin. The British acted swiftly, alarmed about a rebellion so close to home while they were fighting a war in Europe, and sent in British troops. A fierce battle went on for six days; then Pearse, Connolly, and their cohorts were captured, tried, and executed.

> • **1916**   On Easter Monday, April 24, Patrick Pearse and James Connolly proclaim Ireland independent and occupy the General Post Office; the rebels are arrested or killed

THE WAR OF INDEPENDENCE

FOLLOWING THE EASTER REBELLION, Éamon de Valera, an Irish-American teacher, returned to Ireland to reestablish the Sinn Féin party, and Michael Collins joined the Irish Volunteers (a paramilitary organization that the Irish Republican Brotherhood had gradually commandeered), renamed the Irish Republican Army (IRA) in 1919. The two men continued the nationalist movement.

De Valera's party won a huge victory in 1918 and established the first Dáil (independent Parliament) in Dublin. For two years, Britain tried to quash the Irish nationalists. In 1920, Collins ordered 14 British operatives murdered while they slept. England retaliated by shooting into a football crowd in Dublin, killing 12. A truce was eventually declared. In 1921, King George V opened the Parliament in Belfast, pleading for the end of the strife.

> • **1917**   Sinn Féin is reorganized under Éamon de Valera
> • **1918**   Sinn Féin candidates win 73 seats in the general election
> • **1921**   The Anglo-Irish Treaty partitions Ireland into the Irish Free State and Northern Ireland, both parts of the British Commonwealth
> • **1922**   A constitution is written for the Irish Free State

The Anglo-Irish Treaty (1921) partitioned Ireland into two separate nations, with 26 counties forming the Irish Free State and 6 counties remaining part of the United Kingdom. Many republicans objected to the terms of the treaty. After it was passed in the Dáil, de Valera stepped down as president. Civil war quickly broke out between the government and the republicans. Serious fighting lasted in the capital for a week, until de Valera's supporters were ordered to surrender. De Valera escaped to the southwest; Collins was killed in an ambush.

The Civil War influenced politics in Ireland for decades. De Valera founded Fianna Fáil (Warriors of Ireland). The party won the election of 1932, and de Valera governed for 17 years.

- **1922–23**   Ireland enters a civil war that lasts a year; the IRA bitterly opposes dividing Ireland into two countries
- **1932**   Éamon de Valera leads Fianna Fáil to victory
- **1937**   The Free State forms a new constitution, and the name of the country becomes Éire
- **1948**   The Republic severs constitutional ties to England
- **1949**   Éire becomes the Republic of Ireland
- **1955**   The Republic of Ireland joins the United Nations

THE TROUBLES

THE DISPARITY BETWEEN the economies of the Republic and Northern Ireland became more and more pronounced in the 1960s. Religious and economic tension also mounted in the North: Northern Ireland was 55% Protestant and 45% Catholic, and the Protestant majority was far better off economically. Much of the tension was between those who wanted to remain part of the United Kingdom and those who wanted to be part of a unified Ireland.

- **1967**   The Civil Rights Association of Northern Ireland forms to demand reform in local politics
- **1969**   British troops are sent to Northern Ireland to maintain peace when violence breaks out
- **1972**   Riots take place in Derry on "Bloody Sunday"; England imposes direct rule
- **1994**   Peace talks begin when the IRA announces a cease-fire
- **1996**   The IRA begins shooting and bombing again, and rioting begins, the most violent in 15 years
- **1997**   The IRA announces a new cease-fire
- **1998**   The Good Friday Peace Agreement is reached
- **2000**   The IRA states that it will decommission its arms
- **2000**   International weapons inspectors supervise the full disarmament of the IRA

In 1967, the Northern Ireland Civil Rights Movement demonstrated for better housing and jobs for the Catholic minority. In response, Protestants marched through Catholic neighborhoods to show their dominance. Bloody riots followed.

In 1969, when England sent in troops to help maintain peace, the IRA considered them an occupying army, and for the next two decades Northern Ireland was a war zone. About 3,000 people were killed. In 1972, police opened fire on a peaceful gathering in Derry, killing 12 on what has come to be known as Bloody Sunday. In retaliation, the IRA began a bombing campaign in England. Secret negotiations in the 1990s eventually led to the 1994 IRA cease-fire. In 1998, on Good Friday, a peace agreement was signed in Belfast.

- **1990**   Mary Robinson becomes Ireland's first woman president
- **1992**   Ireland becomes a charter member of the new European Union
- **1993**   Homosexuality is decriminalized
- **1995**   Divorce becomes legal, but under very restricted circumstances
- **2000**   Ireland's economy continues to grow
- **2002**   Immigration to Ireland reaches record highs, and many of the "newcomers" are Irish returning home

IRELAND TODAY

MANY OF THE CONFLICTS that have plagued Ireland through the centuries still exist. Some believe that Northern Ireland should be united with the Republic, while others favor the status quo. Sharp divisions also continue between Catholics and Protestants. The big force these days, though, is economic growth and prosperity. For much of the 1990s and into the current millennium, Ireland's economy has been one of the fastest growing in the world. With the boom have come new construction, improvements, and enormous fortunes—and, as happens with such growth, a great disparity between the poor and the rich.

The **BEST** of **IRELAND**

THE BEST ABBEYS AND OTHER RELIGIOUS SITES

Book of Kells
Location   Dublin
For more information   "Exploring Dublin," page 124
ONE OF THE WORLD'S MOST EXQUISITE manuscripts—believed to be the work of ninth-century monks at the great scriptorium of the monastic community of St. Colomba, on the island of Iona off Scotland—resided in the Colomban monastery at Kells, north of Dublin, for most of the Middle Ages and now occupies pride of place in the Long Library of Trinity College.

Glendalough Abbey
Location   Wicklow Mountains, outside Dublin
For more information   "Day Trips from Dublin," page 179
THESE STONE STRUCTURES on the floor of a peaceful valley once composed one of Europe's great centers of learning, founded by St. Kevin. The complex's remains present a satisfying look at what religious communities were like in the days when the faithful and those hungry for sustenance and learning found their way to monasteries like this throughout Ireland.

Jerpoint Abbey

Location   Outside Kilkenny

For more information   The South of Ireland, page 192

THESE REMAINS of a 12th-century monastery, built for the Benedictine order but handed over to the Cistercians a century later, are lost in time in a bucolic setting.

Kells Priory

Location   Outside Kilkenny

For more information   The South of Ireland, page 198

ONE OF IRELAND'S LARGEST medieval ruins, a monastery that once housed hundreds of monks, rises from the banks of the King's River.

Kilmacduagh

Location   Outside Gort

For more information   The West of Ireland, page 318

NOW IN RUIN on a plain at the edge of the Burren, Kilmacduagh flourished for almost 1,000 years. A round tower from the 11th century leans a bit but is remarkably intact, as are the walls of the now-roofless cathedral.

Kylemore Abbey and Garden

Location   Outside Letterfrack, near Connemara

For more information   The West of Ireland, page 334

NOW THE HOME of an order of Irish Benedictine nuns and an exclusive boarding school for girls, this faux-Gothic castle, surrounded by lavish grounds, lies at the foot of the craggy Twelve Bens Mountains. Built in the 19th century as a private retreat for a British industrialist, Kylemore is more secular than religious, though a small chapel that's built like a cathedral in miniature is one of Ireland's most distinctive churches.

Rock of Cashel

Location   Near Cashel

For more information   The South of Ireland, page 203

THIS GIANT ROCK topped with medieval remains is a spectacular sight. Early Irish kings settled it as early as the fourth century AD, and the Catholic Church presided here until the late 18th century, leaving behind some of Ireland's most magnificent Romanesque ruins. The extensive lore attached to the rock includes a visit from St. Patrick, who allegedly held up a shamrock to explain the mystery of the Trinity, endowing Ireland with its enduring emblem.

St. Patrick's Cathedral

Location   Dublin

For more information   "Exploring Dublin," page 140

BUILT ON THE SITE where St. Patrick is said to have preached in the fifth century AD, St. Patrick's—the largest church in Ireland and the flagship of the Church of Ireland—is littered with the tombs of Irish notables, including *Gulliver's Travels* author Jonathan Swift.

Skellig Michael
Location   County Kerry
For more information   The Southwest of Ireland, page 254
EARLY-CHRISTIAN MONKS retreated to this conical-shaped island some 13 kilometers (8 miles) off the Iveragh Peninsula about 1,000 years ago, where their church, oratory, and beehive-shaped cells have survived pounding surf and brutal winds.

THE BEST OF ANCIENT IRELAND
Carrowmore and Carrowkeel
Location   Around Sligo
For more information   The Northwest of Ireland, page 354
THE 40 OR SO PASSAGE tombs dug into the hillside at Carrowmore comprise the largest prehistoric burial site in the British Isles. At Carrowkeel, just to the east, 14 burial chambers are set high above Lough Arrow.

Hill of Tara
Location   North of Dublin
For more information   "Day Trips from Dublin," page 177
THE SEAT OF THE HIGH KINGS of Ireland was, from the pre-Christian era to as late as the 11th century, an assembly point for tribal and religious leaders from throughout the country.

Newgrange
Location   North of Dublin
For more information   "Day Trips from Dublin," page 178
THESE 6,000-YEAR-OLD passage tombs, covered by a mound 100 meters (330 feet) across and constructed with some 250,000 tons of stones, appear to have done double duty as a burial place and an observatory. On each of five days on and around the winter solstice, the main chamber is brilliantly illuminated by sunlight for 20 minutes.

THE BEST OF IRELAND FOR NATURAL BEAUTY
The Antrim Coast
Location   Northeast of Derry
For more information   Northern Ireland, page 413
THE GIANTS CAUSEWAY, a sweep of cylindrical basalt outcroppings that extend far out to sea, enhances the allure of this coast; the Glens of Antrim, nine densely wooded river valleys, are etched out of the surrounding mountains.

The Beara Peninsula
Location   Outside Kenmare
For more information   The Southwest of Ireland, page 245
ONE OF SEVERAL craggy peninsulas that stretch into the Atlantic Ocean in Southwest Ireland, the Beara remains relatively remote and unspoiled. In addition to magnificent sea views, there are desolate moors and purple peaks, best viewed on a drive across Healy Pass.

The Burren

Location   Western County Clare
For more information   The West of Ireland, page 310

THE BURREN (from *boireann,* Gaelic for "rocky land") is a plain of limestone that covers some 1,600 hectares (4,000 acres). This natural wonderland—home to rare butterflies, puffins, goats, and hare—becomes a sea of color when plants flower in profusion from cracks in the limestone.

Cliffs of Moher

Location   West of Ennis
For more information   The West of Ireland, page 305

RISING SOME 230 METERS (700 feet) out of the sea, the cliffs provide an eight-kilometer (five-mile) swath of spectacular scenery. The Aran Islands float in mist in the distance, and the surf rushes ceaselessly ashore.

Connemara

Location   North of Galway
For more information   The West of Ireland, page 332

CONNEMARA IS MOUNTAINOUS in some parts, covered with prairielike moors in others, and dotted with forests of pine and fir that surround rushing streams and glittering lakes. The largest of the lakes—in fact, the second largest lake in Ireland—is 175-square-kilometer (65-square-mile) Lough Corrib. Some 2,000 hectares (4,942 acres) of this beautiful and evocative landscape are preserved as Connemara National Park.

The Dingle Peninsula

Location   The Southwest
For more information   The Southwest of Ireland, page 270

STRETCHING SOME 50 KILOMETERS (30 miles) from the mainland into the Atlantic surf, the westernmost tip of Ireland is a spine of rugged mountains, rocky cliffs, and soft sands. A sense of otherworldliness prevail heres, enhanced by thick mists, good stout, and traditional Irish tunes.

Glenveagh National Park

Location   Northwest of Letterkenny
For more information   The Northwest of Ireland, page 375

HERE, HEATHS AND WOODLANDS climb the slopes of the Derryveagh Mountains. Capping the park is Errigal Mountain, a pyramid-shaped peak that is covered with snow for much of the year.

Howth Head

Location   Outside Dublin
For more information   "Day Trips from Dublin," page 174s

THOUGH ONLY 20 MINUTES by train from central Dublin, this rocky headland provides stunning views of the sea, the mountains, and the Eye of Ireland, an islet just offshore, all from an 8.5-kilometer (5-mile) path.

Inishowen Peninsula

Location Northeast of Letterkenny
For more information The Northwest of Ireland, page 374

THE LARGEST OF THE northern peninsulas ends at Malin Head, the northernmost tip of Ireland. Views are also spectacular from the Gap of Mamore, a mountain pass that climbs to 250 meters (820 feet).

Killarney National Park

Location Outside Killarney
For more information The Southwest of Ireland, page 258

THIS WILDERNESS OF heather-covered mountains, lush forests, and shimmering lakes is protected as a 10,000-hectare (25,000-acre) national park. Some of the most enchanting scenery is in the Gap of Dunloe, accessible only on foot, horseback, or bike; here, enormous boulders litter a pass that cuts through MacGillycuddy's Reeks, Ireland's highest mountains.

Slieve League

Location North of Donegal
For more information The Northwest of Ireland, page 371

THE TALLEST SEA CLIFFS in Europe—and one the most dramatic spectacles in all of Ireland—rise some 600 meters (2,000 feet) out of the raging surf.

Wicklow Mountains

Location Outside Dublin
For more information "Day Trips from Dublin," page 178

IN THESE GENTLE MOUNTAINS, dense forests cover the slopes, and rushing streams sprint through valleys into clear lakes. The Wicklows are all the more appealing because they cradle one of Ireland's grandest estates, Powerscourt, and one of its most romantic monastic ruins, Glendalough.

THE BEST MUSEUMS

Chester Beatty Library and Gallery of Oriental Art

Location Dublin
For more information "Exploring Dublin," page 125

A REMARKABLE COLLECTION of sacred texts, illuminated manuscripts, and miniature paintings from the great religions of the world includes cuneiform clay tablets; ancient Biblical papyri; 270 copies of the Koran, paintings from India's Mughal era; and some of the earliest bound books, dating from the Renaissance.

Crawford Municipal Art Gallery

Location Cork
For more information The South of Ireland, page 215

ONE OF IRELAND'S BEST collections of art includes a number of casts of Greek and Roman sculptures and canvases by Irish artists.

Dublin City Gallery–The Hugh Lane

Location   Dublin
For more information   "Exploring Dublin," page 130
THE GRANDEST DWELLING on Parnell Square houses an exquisite collection of 19th- to early-20th-century artworks by painters of the French Barbizon and Impressionist schools, works by Jack Yeats and other Irish artists, and stained-glass panels by Irish artisans Harry Clark and Evie Hone.

Hunt Museum

Location   Limerick
For more information   The Lower Shannon, page 289
LIMERICK'S ELEGANT 18th-century Customs House displays an amazing collection of Celtic and medieval artifacts second only to that on display in the National Museum in Dublin, as well as 18th-century ceramics, 19th- and 20th-century paintings by Renoir and Picasso, and other decorative arts that span the centuries.

National Gallery of Ireland

Location   Dublin
For more information   "Exploring Dublin," page 135
IRELAND'S NATIONAL COLLECTION of European art is small but immensely satisfying, not overwhelming but still boasting an impressive number of masterpieces. Caravaggio's *The Taking of Christ,* Vermeer's *Lady Writing a Letter with Her Maid,* and Jack Yeats's *The Liffey Swim* are among the works represented.

National Museum of Ireland

Location   Dublin
For more information   "Exploring Dublin," page 136
IRELAND'S TREASURE TROVE of artifacts from 6,000 BC to the 20th century includes a cache of Irish gold—scepters, jewelry, crosses, a boat from the first century—as well as remnants of the centuries of Viking occupation and an in-depth and highly evocative collection devoted to the Easter Rebellion of 1916.

Ulster Museum

Location   Belfast
For more information   Northern Ireland, page 396
THE MOST COMPREHENSIVE museum in Northern Ireland is devoted to history, the natural sciences, and art. Holdings include one of the world's leading collections of African arts and crafts; an exhibit that takes an unflinching look at the Troubles and the developments that led to the formation of the North as a separate entity; and masterpieces by Gainsborough, Reynolds, and other painters.

THE BEST CASTLES

Blarney Castle

Location   Outside Cork

For more information The South of Ireland, page 213

BLARNEY BASICALLY MEANS "NONSENSE," and you'll encounter a lot of it in this ruin of the onetime stronghold of the McCarthy clan. The highlight of a tour is being held by the legs as you dangle precariously backward to kiss the Stone of Eloquence, aka the Blarney Stone. Just as rewarding is a stroll through the colorful gardens to admire the romantic towers and crumbling walls of the castle.

Bunratty Castle and Folk Park

Location Bunratty, County Clare
For more information The Lower Shannon, page 295

IRELAND'S MOST INTACT MEDIEVAL CASTLE is also one of the country's most visited tourist attractions. Despite its crowds and commercial buzz, the castle is a pleasure to visit, beautifully restored down to its last medieval timber and filled with stunning 15th-to-17th-century furnishings.

Donegal Castle

Location Donegal Town
For more information The Northwest of Ireland, page 368

STANDING MIGHTILY IN THE CENTER OF TOWN, Donegal Castle is partly in ruin but incorporates the splendid and beautifully restored 15th-century fortified house that was the residence of the O'Donnell clan. The turrets and gables that lend the castle its distinctive appearance, along with the grounds, enclosed behind high walls, rise high above Donegal Town.

Dunluce Castle

Location Antrim Coast
For more information Northern Ireland, page 415

A 14TH-CENTURY CASTLE complex clings to the edge of oceanside cliffs, high above the pounding surf. Indeed, much of the castle has fallen into the sea, but this former stronghold of the powerful MacDonnell clan still romantically evokes life in the Middle Ages.

Glenveagh Castle

Location Glenveagh National Park
For more information The Northwest of Ireland, page 376

ONE OF THE MOST DELIGHTFUL historic homes in Ireland, Glenveagh looks like a Hollywood stage set and has served as a retreat for Greta Garbo and many other glamorous celebs over the years. Perched on the shores of Lough Beagh and surrounded by formal gardens and heath-covered mountainsides, the castle was the creation of John George Adair, a notorious 19th-century landlord, but owes much of its charm to wealthy and refined American Henry P. McIlhenny of Tabasco fame.

Kilkenny Castle

Location Kilkenny
For more information The South of Ireland, page 198

A FORMIDABLE CASTLE has dominated Kilkenny ever since Strongbow, an Anglo-Norman warrior and settler, built a wooden fortress here in 1172. Most of the stone castle rising from the banks of the Kilkenny River dates to the 14th century, and it was once the seat of the Irish Parliament. Generations of Butlers, who lived in Kilkenny Castle from the Middle Ages well into the 20th century, look down from the walls of the Long Gallery.

King John's Castle
Location   Limerick
For more information   The Lower Shannon, page 290
ONE OF IRELAND'S most intact medieval monuments, this imposing 13th-century fortress on an island in the heart of the city is especially impressive when viewed from across the rivers that surround it. Costumed craftspeople plying their trades enliven the castle courtyard and enrich a visit.

Knappogue Castle and Walled Gardens
Location   Outside Limerick
For more information   The Lower Shannon, page 297
THE LOVINGLY RESTORED 15th-century home of the McNamara clan is filled with a remarkable collection of medieval furnishings.

Malahide Castle
Location   Malahide, outside Dublin
For more information   "Day Trips from Dublin," page 176
THE HOME OF THE TALBOT CLAN for more than 800 years, Malahide has enough turrets and towers to be solidly medieval, but the well-furnished home shows off the domestic habits of the aristocracy well into the 20th century. One hundred hectares (250 acres) of parkland shelter the Talbot Botanic Garden, one of Ireland's finest collections of exotic flora.

Parke's Castle
Location   Outside Sligo
For more information   The Northwest of Ireland, page 365
MORE OF A FORTIFIED MANOR HOUSE than a castle per se, this tall, handsome manor of light stone and sturdy timbers is formidable nonetheless. A great hall and other drafty rooms surround a courtyard and overlook Lough Gill, the lake that so inspired poet W. B. Yeats.

Ross Castle
Location   Killarney, County Kerry
For more information   The Southwest of Ireland, page 261
ONE OF THE MANY natural and man-made attractions in and around Killarney National Park rises from the waters of Lough Leane. The medieval walls glimmer romantically in the lake waters, and a fine collection of splendid 16th- and 17th-century furniture warms up the dank and dark rooms of this mighty stronghold, which has been besieged on more than one occasion.

THE BEST PLACES TO ENCOUNTER IRISH HISTORY

Bogside

Location Derry

For more information Northern Ireland, page 407

THE CATHOLIC NEIGHBORHOOD beneath Derry's city walls has been largely rebuilt since the violence of the past decades, but political murals are stunning reminders of the recent turbulence. One of the most poignant symbols from the neighborhood's history is the huge sign painted on the end of a building that announces, YOU ARE NOW ENTERING FREE DERRY, capturing the quest for independence that ignited the Troubles.

Charles Fort

Location Kinsale

For more information The South of Ireland, page 233

THIS MIGHTY STAR-SHAPED BASTION has been protecting Kinsale Harbour since 1677, with a strategic position and miles of thick walls that seem to make it impregnable.

Cobh, the Queenstown Story

Location Cobh

For more information The South of Ireland, page 228

COBH WAS ONCE IRELAND'S major port for emigration, and millions embarked from here between 1750 and the mid–20th century. Extensive exhibits trace conditions in Ireland and life aboard the outgoing ships, as well as the sinkings of the *Titanic*, which called here in 1912 just days before hitting an iceberg and sinking, and the *Lusitania*, torpedoed off nearby Kinsale Head by the Germans in 1915.

Derrynane House

Location Caherdaniel, County Kerry

For more information The Southwest of Ireland, page 252

DANIEL O'CONNELL, who owned this estate, won for Catholics the full rights of citizenship in 1829 and founded the grassroots Catholic Association to promote education and representation. The so-called Liberator is very much a presence in the old rooms, many of which he remodeled with his own hands.

Falls Road and Shankill Road

Location Belfast

For more information Northern Ireland, page 393

NO OTHER CITY IN WESTERN EUROPE, with the possible exception of Derry, has been as war-torn as Belfast in recent decades, and remnants of the divisiveness are much in evidence. In the Catholic neighborhood around Falls Road, you'll pass the Sinn Féin offices and endless murals, then go through the so-called peace wall to Milltown Cemetery, where hunger striker Bobby Sands and other IRA members are buried. In the Protestant Shankill Road neighborhood, murals include Union Jack motifs and even elaborate portrayals of the victory of Protestant William of Orange over Catholic King James II in the Battle of the Boyne in 1690.

Kilmainham Gaol
Location Dublin
For more information "Exploring Dublin," page 134
THIS FORMIDABLE PRISON, opened in 1798 and closed in 1927, now serves as a testament to Irish revolutionary history. Displays and commentaries provide background on 18th- and 19th-century revolutionary heroes such as Robert Emmet and Charles Stewart Parnell, the 19th-century nationalist leader and member of the Irish Parliament. Most gripping are those exhibits recounting the 1916 Easter Rising, when the Irish Republican Brotherhood mounted an armed revolt in Dublin, for which the British executed 15 of the leaders, many of them here at Kilmainham.

THE BEST LITERARY AND MUSICAL EXPERIENCES

Doolin
Location County Clare
For more information The West of Ireland, page 307
THIS SMALL VILLAGE on the rugged coast of northern County Clare is known throughout the world for traditional Irish music that attracts droves of enthusiasts. You'll hear the tunes that make the village famous in three homey pubs.

Dublin Literary Pub Crawl
Location Dublin
For more information "Exploring Dublin," page 113
AT ONE TIME OR ANOTHER, most Dublin writers found inspiration at the bottom of a pint glass in the hundreds of pubs around the city, and you can follow in their footsteps to enjoy the *cráic* and literary ambience of four famous writerly haunts.

Dublin Writers Museum
Location Dublin
For more information "Exploring Dublin," page 132
EXTENSIVE LETTERS, manuscripts, photos, news clippings, audio recordings, and other fascinating memorabilia honor Oscar Wilde, James Joyce, Samuel Beckett, Jonathan Swift, and scores of other writers who have been both stifled and inspired by Dublin.

Marsh's Library
Location Dublin
For more information "Exploring Dublin," page 135
IRELAND'S OLDEST PUBLIC LIBRARY, founded in 1701, is an atmospheric repository of rare manuscripts and books from the 16th through 18th centuries. Scholars were once locked into mesh cages to view these precious volumes.

Music Pub Crawl
Location Dublin
For more information "Exploring Dublin," page 114
EVENING EXPEDITIONS depart from Oliver St. John Gogarty's on Fleet Street and make calls at three pubs, where you'll hear an assortment of instruments, Irish ballads, and discussion about the fine points of Irish music—all while you enjoy a pint or two.

Shaw Birthplace
Location Dublin
For more information "Exploring Dublin," page 141
AT THE CHILDHOOD HOME of George Bernard Shaw, one of the greatest playwrights of the late 19th and early 20th centuries, you can peer into the cramped, overfurnished parlors, the primitive kitchen, and the wee bedroom on the landing where the playwright slept as a youth.

Yeats Country
Location In and around Sligo
For more information The Northwest of Ireland, page 364
ADMIRERS OF THIS MOST IRISH of poets can examine first editions and letters in the Sligo County Museum, gaze upon the Isle of Innisfree from the shores of Lough Gill, and pay homage at Yeats's simple grave in the cemetery at Drumcliff.

kids THE BEST OF IRELAND FOR KIDS

Bunratty Castle and Folk Park
Location Bunratty, County Clare
For more information The Lower Shannon, page 295
THE GREAT HALL, drawbridge, and turrets fulfill just about every kid's fantasy of what a medieval castle should like. In the adjoining Folk Park, young visitors will enjoy stepping in and out of laborers', farmers', and fishing families' cottages; watching water mills; speaking with blacksmiths and millers; and in other ways partaking in scenes of the Irish life of yesteryear.

Carrick-a-Rede Bridge
Location Antrim Coast
For more information Northern Ireland, page 415
CROSSING THIS CONCOCTION of rope and planks that sways a dizzying height above the sea is a heck of a lot of fun, a memorable experience that kids and their parents will long remember.

Church of St. Anne Shandon
Location Cork
For more information The South of Ireland, page 214
AT CORK'S MOST FAMOUS LANDMARK, visitors can climb into the pepperpot steeple and take turns playing a tune on the six-ton Bells of Shandon.

Craggaunowen

Location   Near Quin, County Clare

For more information   The Lower Shannon, page 296

A PREHISTORIC THEME PARK with re-creations of ring forts, fortified island dwellings, and other fragments of Ireland's long past appeals a lot more to kids than to their parents, but a day among costumed Celts and Iron Age farmers can provide relief from more-serious sightseeing.

Dublin Zoo

Location   Phoenix Park, Dublin

For more information   "Exploring Dublin," page 143

RECENT RENOVATIONS have made the world's third oldest zoo much more pleasant to visit. The most popular denizens of the many cageless environments are the lions, whose frolicking cubs often put on a good show.

Fota Wildlife Park

Location   Fota Island, County Cork

For more information   The South of Ireland, page 224

ONLY LOW ELECTRONIC FENCES separate visitors from free-roaming flamingos, giraffes, and 90 other species of creatures exotic to Ireland. Other residents include Irish natives such as the white-tailed sea eagle.

Fungie

Location   Dingle

For more information   The Southwest of Ireland, page 266

THE BOTTLE-NOSED DOLPHIN who has dwelled in Dingle Harbour since 1983 never fails to make an appearance for boatloads of admirers.

King John's Castle

Location   King's Island, Limerick

For more information   The Lower Shannon, page 290

THIS IMPOSING 13TH-CENTURY FORTRESS, one of Ireland's most intact medieval monuments, houses extensive archaeological treasures that might bore the young ones. But they will love the rampart walks and the reconstructed medieval courtyard, where costumed craftspeople and merchants ply their trades.

Malahide Castle

Location   Malahide, outside Dublin

For more information   "Day Trips from Dublin," page 176

FOR YOUNG VISITORS, a reward for their patience on the guided tours of the castle is a visit to the Fry Model Railway, where dozens of trains chug through fantasy landscapes, and Tara's Dollhouse, filled with delightful miniatures. Youngsters can run and play to their hearts' content in the extensive parklands.

National Transport Museum of Ireland

Location   Grounds of Howth Castle, outside Dublin

For more information   "Day Trips from Dublin," page 175
BUSES, TRUCKS, AND TRAMS—60 vintage vehicles in all—will evoke a sense of wonderment in visitors accustomed to the comparatively mundane-looking vehicles that clog the road today. Even vehicles that look surprisingly like their modern-day descendants, such the generations of double-decker buses and trams, delight young visitors.

Ulster Folk and Transport Museum
Location   Outside Belfast
For more information   Northern Ireland, page 394
TWO FASCINATING COLLECTIONS await visitors to this vast 70-hectare (176-acre) museum compound, an assemblage of old structures and a showcase of cars, planes, and other modes of transport, all built in Ireland. Youngsters will especially enjoy the folk park, where the costumed staff demonstrates spinning and other crafts.

THE BEST CASTLE HOTELS, GUESTHOUSES, AND INNS

Adare Manor
Location   Adare Village, County Limerick
For more information   The Lower Shannon, page 276
THE NEO-GOTHIC MANOR HOUSE of the Earls of Dunraven, on the banks of the River Maigue, is one of Ireland's finest hotels. Two staff members for every guest ensure top-notch service. The extensive grounds are graced not only with a golf course but also the romantic ruins of a castle and monastery.

Ballynahinch Castle
Location   Recess, County Galway
For more information   The West of Ireland, page 336
THIS 18TH-CENTURY MANOR on the banks of the Ballynahinch River is surrounded by forests and mountain pastures. Fishing, walking, and other activities await just outside the front door. Beautifully furnished accommodations are complemented by the best dining room in Connemara.

Bushmills Inn
Location   Bushmills, County Antrim
For more information   Northern Ireland, page 413
AT ONE OF IRELAND'S most beloved and character-rich inns, turf fires burn beneath old beams, and guests relax in charming lounges and accommodations that are tastefully oriented to solid comfort.

Frewin
Location   Ramelton, County Donegal
For more information   The Northwest of Ireland, page 372
A VICTORIAN RECTORY is filled with a collection of antiques, memorabilia, books, Persian carpets, and old prints—all handsomely displayed in warm, uncluttered lounges and commodious guest rooms.

Glenview House

Location   Midleton, County Cork
For more information   The South of Ireland, page 222

KEN AND BETH SHERRARD set the gold standard for a stay in an Irish country home, with their Georgian farmhouse set amid lovely grounds. The Sherrards' gracious hospitality includes a bountiful breakfast of eggs from Beth's hens as well as fresh fruit and home-baked breads.

Glin Castle

Location   Glin, County Limerick
For more information   The Lower Shannon, page 277

KNIGHT AND NOTED ART HISTORIAN Desmond FitzGerald and his wife offer noble hospitality at their treasure-filled ancestral seat on the banks of the River Shannon.

Greenmount House

Location   Dingle, County Kerry
For more information   The Southwest of Ireland, page 264

THIS HILLSIDE PERCH overlooking the Dingle and its bay is almost legendary on the Irish B&B circuit, and it seems to improve with each passing year. The suitelike rooms enjoy airy and lovely views, and the day begins with a lavish breakfast in the conservatory.

Markree Castle

Location   Collooney, County Sligo
For more information   The Northwest of Ireland, page 352

THIS 1640 CASTLE on a 400-hectare (1,000-acre) estate is delightfully quirky, with massive staircases, a galleried and paneled great hall, roaring fires, and ample comfort in the guest rooms, no two of which are alike.

Rathmullan House

Location   Rathmullan, County Donegal
For more information   The Northwest of Ireland, page 373

A FINE 19TH-CENTURY MANSION overlooking the sea is quietly luxurious but relaxed, with an inviting drawing room and library and distinctive accommodations in the old house, plus a tasteful and appealing new wing.

Shelburne Lodge

Location   Kenmare, County Kerry
For more information   The Southwest of Ireland, page 242

AN 18TH-CENTURY STONE FARMHOUSE at the edge of town is surrounded by stunning grounds and decorated with taste and style, providing a good base for exploring the Southwest.

Temple House

Location   Ballymote, County Sligo
For more information   The Northwest of Ireland, page 353

THIS GRAND GEORGIAN MANSION, one of Ireland's largest homes still in private hands, is a delightful country retreat complete with handsome sitting rooms, huge guest rooms filled with comfy old family furniture, and Wellingtons by the door for those who want to wander through the wooded grounds or down to the dock for a row.

THE BEST CITY LODGINGS

The Clarence

Location   Dublin

For more information   "Hotels in Dublin," page 106

WHO KNEW? U2, the Irish rock band that owns this refurbished old hostelry on the banks of the River Liffey, runs a first-rate hotel, too. They've created a stylish and soothing retreat with light oak paneling, Shaker-style furnishings, state-of-the-art entertainment systems, and many other amenities.

The Fitzwilliam

Location   Dublin

For more information   "Hotels in Dublin," page 107

LARGE, LIGHT-FILLED public areas and guest rooms face either St. Stephen's Green or a roof garden at the rear of the hotel. Clean lines, neutral tones, and natural fabrics create attractive and extremely restful surroundings in the city center.

Hayfield Manor

Location   Cork

For more information   The South of Ireland, page 209

BUILT IN 1996 in the style of a grand Georgian country house, Hayfield Manor serves up more old-world ambience than the real McCoy ever could. Heavy paneling, a grand staircase, and plush guest rooms provide the ultimate in traditional comfort.

Merrion Hotel

Location   Dublin

For more information   "Hotels in Dublin," page 109

DUBLIN'S MOST LUXURIOUS HOTEL consists of four Georgian town houses and, beyond the large formal gardens, a stylish contemporary wing. One of the country's most extensive private collections of 19th- and 20th-century Irish art hangs in the public lounges, while large and gracious guest rooms are swathed in yards of luxurious Irish fabrics and outfitted with other comforts geared to spoiling guests.

Number 31

Location   Dublin

For more information   "Hotels in Dublin," page 110

AT ONE OF DUBLIN'S MOST distinctive hostelries, extremely comfortable rooms occupy a contemporary coach house and Georgian terrace house. A sunken conversation pit surrounds a fireplace where an aromatic peat fire burns, and a memorable breakfast is served in a conservatory overlooking a rooftop garden.

The Shelbourne
Location   Dublin
For more information   Dublin, page 111
THE LIGHTS FROM THE TALL WINDOWS of Dublin's most famous hostelry are once again shining bright over St. Stephen's Green after a cellar-to-attic renovation. Once more, the city has a choice place to stay.

Ten Square
Location   Belfast
For more information   Northern Ireland, page 387
THE FIRST AND STILL THE BEST of Belfast's ever-growing stable of small luxury hotels manages to be both showy and relaxing, with handsome public areas and luxurious guest rooms you won't want to leave.

THE BEST FOOD-AND-DRINK EXPERIENCES

Ballymaloe House
Location   Shanagarry, Midleton, County Cork
For more information   The South of Ireland, page 226
BALLYMALOE, in the capable hands of the Allen family of culinary stars, has a well-deserved reputation for turning the freshest ingredients into masterpieces of modern Irish cuisine and serving them in the refined surroundings of one of Ireland's most renowned country-house hotels.

Chart House
Location   Dingle, County Kerry
For more information   The Southwest of Ireland, page 266
A HANDSOME STONE BUILDING near the bay provides sophisticated yet informal surroundings for superb meals created with the bounty of local waters and Kerry farms.

Crown Liquor Saloon
Location   Belfast
For more information   Northern Ireland, page 400
THIS VICTORIAN SHOWCASE of mirrors and carved wood is a lovely place to enjoy a pint and a plate of oysters or other light fare.

Deane's Restaurant
Location   Belfast
For more information   Northern Ireland, page 398
ONE OF IRELAND'S FINEST RESTAURANTS, recently and brilliantly revamped, delivers a memorable dining experience, enlivened with subtle Asian influences.

English Market
Location   Cork
For more information   The South of Ireland, page 216
YOU HAVEN'T EXPERIENCED real Cork life until you taken a leisurely stroll through this vast covered hall, which dates back to 1881. More than

140 stalls brim with Irish produce, fish, and meat, making it easy to see why Cork is one of Ireland's culinary capitals. Grab a bite at one of the bustling counters, or enjoy a meal upstairs in the Farmgate Café, with a bird's-eye view of the proceedings below.

Guinness Storehouse

Location   Dublin
For more information   "Exploring Dublin," page 133

DUBLIN'S MOST FAMOUS tourist attraction is this shrine to Ireland's favorite beverage. A tour through a renovated fermentation plant, built around a five-story glass atrium shaped like a pint and filled with displays on how Guinness is made, ends with a free sample in the top-floor Gravity Bar.

Jacobs on the Mall

Location   Cork
For more information   The South of Ireland, page 218

A FORMER TURKISH BATH is the setting for a memorable meal of modern Irish cuisine, with an emphasis on the freshest local ingredients.

Jacob's Ladder

Location   Dublin
For more information   "Dining in Dublin," page 154

WITHIN THIS SERIES of upstairs rooms overlooking Trinity College through tall windows, excellent service and Adrian Roche's careful preparations (with an emphasis on seafood) enhance the feeling that you are enjoying a special experience high above the city.

James Street South

Location   Belfast
For more information   Northern Ireland, page 399

MINIMALIST ENVIRONS strike just the right note in suggesting that the emphasis here is on the exquisite preparations of chef Niall McKenna. Expertly served, lunch or dinner in this place is always a special occasion.

L'Ecrivain

Location   Dublin
For more information   "Dining in Dublin," page 154

ONE OF IRELAND'S few restaurants to have earned a Michelin star continually lives up to its reputation with a traditional-yet-innovative approach to meat and seafood classics, served in light and airy surroundings.

Nick's Warehouse

Location   Belfast
For more information   Northern Ireland, page 399

THIS WARM AND WELCOMING eatery, in a warehouse district on an alley near St. Anne's Cathedral, shows just how satisfying simple modern Irish cuisine can be, especially when complemented by a bottle or glass from the extensive wine list.

Nimmo's

Location   Galway
For more information   The West of Ireland, page 327
AN OLD STONE HOUSE on a quay beside the River Corrib provides a romantic setting for a heavily timbered wine bar and a charming candlelit upstairs restaurant, where hearty fish soup and succulent roast lamb do justice to the ambience.

Old Bushmills Distillery

Location   Bushmills, County Antrim
For more information   Northern Ireland, page 417
WHAT MAKES A TOUR of Bushmills more satisfying than a visit to any other Irish distillery is the quality of the product—generally regarded as the best Irish whiskey—and the fact that this is a working plant. You'll actually see workers mashing and bottling, which adds a bit of veracity to the guides' lectures on how whiskey is made.

Out of the Blue

Location   Dingle, County Kerry
For more information   The Southwest of Ireland, page 268
BOATS THAT DOCK just outside the door supply the ingredients for delicious chowders and heavenly sauced fish dishes, served in a crowded little shack on the waterfront.

Restaurant Patrick Guilbaud

Location   Dublin
For more information   "Dining in Dublin," page 157
LOVELY WORKS by Irish painters enliven this simple and elegant room overlooking the gardens of the Merrion Hotel, where French classics are enlivened with an Irish flair.

PART ONE

PLANNING *your* VISIT *to* IRELAND

How FAR *in* ADVANCE SHOULD YOU PLAN?

YOUR ORGANIZED, BLACKBERRY-DRIVEN FRIENDS ARE RIGHT: advance planning has definite advantages. Airline fares are generally (but not always) lower if you book at least a month in advance, and many lower-priced air-and-hotel packages require advance booking. Advance planning is an especially good idea if you're visiting Ireland in the summer. First of all, airfares are highest then and flights are well booked, so if you wait until the last moment, only the highest-priced seats will be available. Second, hotels in Dublin, Dingle, Galway, and many other popular places in Ireland fill up quickly in the summer—remember, many summer resorts are as popular with vacationing Irish and other Europeans as they are with visitors from America and elsewhere. Hotels, too, will often put last-minute guests in their most expensive rooms.

Of course, even spur-of-the-moment travelers will have to admit that the more time you have to plan your trip before it actually begins, the better prepared you'll be. You'll have more leisure time to read up on the places you want to visit, plan the logistics of your trip, and contact the friends of friends you might want to visit.

But what if you just can't plan in advance—or don't want to? Take heart. Advance planning is not as important outside of the busy summer months and at Christmastime, when many Irish return home. In fact, at times waiting to book can have definite advantages. Eager to fill empty seats, airlines often offer extremely low fares during the winter (usually January through March) and sometimes run special flight and hotel packages. Hotels try to lure guests with special weekend rates; three-nights-for-two specials; bed, breakfast, and dinner packages; and many other attractive offers.

WHEN *to* GO

THINK "RAIN" WHENEVER YOU GO TO IRELAND. OK, that said, don't think about rain, because the predictably unpredictable Irish weather should not keep you from going to Ireland. Then think about where you want to go.

Dublin doesn't really have a tourist season, so prices don't necessarily come down outside of summer. The city's indoor attractions can keep you just as occupied and content in winter as in summer, and the fire-warmed pubs, lively concert halls, and treasure-filled museum galleries seem especially well suited to winter visits. What's more, transatlantic airfares are much lower in winter, putting Dublin within reach for a long weekend from the eastern United States.

unofficial **TIP**
If you plan on seeing more of Ireland than city life—and you should—think May, September, and October. Long twilights make May especially attractive; the scent of peat fires and the feel of autumn in the air will win you over to Ireland in September and October.

The pleasures of the Irish countryside can wane with the colder months. Outside Dublin, Cork, Galway, and other major cities, many hotels, restaurants, and attractions close "for the season" in late October and don't open again until March or April, when more than flowers begin to bloom. Hotels and restaurants are in full swing from mid-April through September or October. Summer days in Ireland are long, especially from late May through late July, giving you hours of extra light for country drives and walks (the lovely Irish gloaming can last well past 11 p.m.). The downside is that the Irish and their visitors alike take advantage of the season to descend on beaches and mountain glades, sometimes taking the bucolic blush off even the most lovely spot.

PRICES

IN GENERAL, DUBLIN HOTEL and restaurant prices are on par with those in New York and other expensive cities in North America and Europe. Hotel rates are lower outside of Dublin, but a meal in a good restaurant is fairly expensive anywhere in Ireland. You can blame the tax man in part for the high bill: value-added tax, or VAT (see page 49), is 21% on wine and 13.5% on food. Admission prices for the country's top attractions are also fairly steep.

Prices in Dublin don't necessarily vary with the seasons. Elsewhere in Ireland the high season is roughly from Easter to mid-September, with prices hitting highs in July and August. You're likely to find better deals on hotels during the "shoulder seasons" of mid-September to mid-December and January to March, but many hotels, especially in smaller towns and in the countryside, close in November and don't open again until March or April.

To give you a very rough idea of what things cost in Ireland, here's a list of some approximate prices in dollars:

Bus or shuttle to and from airport in Dublin	$18
Double room at a medium-range hotel in Dublin	$175–$250
Meal for one in an upscale Dublin restaurant (without wine)	$40–$60
Pub meal	$20–$30
Admission to top attractions throughout the country	$8–$25

WEATHER

RAIN IS A CONSTANT IN IRELAND—even summer months can be showery, and they aren't really that warm. Extremes of climate are rare, and temperatures don't often fall below freezing or soar to uncomfortable levels.

Dublin's Average Temperatures and Rainfall

TEMPERATURE	(FAHRENHEIT)	(CELSIUS)	RAINFALL (INCHES)	(CENTIMETERS)
January	36–46°	2.2–7.7°	2.6	6.6
February	37–48°	2.7–8.8°	2.2	5.6
March	37–49°	2.7–9.4°	2	5.1
April	38–52°	3.3–11°	1.8	4.6
May	42–57°	5.5–13.8°	2.4	6.1
June	46–62°	7.7–16.6°	2.2	5.6
July	51–66°	10.5–18.8°	2.8	7.1
August	50–65°	10–18.3°	2.9	7.4
September	48–62°	8.8–16.6°	2.8	7.1
October	44–60°	6.6–15.5°	2.8	7.1
November	39–49°	3.6–9.4°	2.9	7.4
December	38–47°	3.3–8.3°	2.9	7.4

AIRFARE DEALS *and* PACKAGE TOURS

START WITH YOUR LOCAL TRAVEL AGENT

THE WEB IS RENDERING THE SERVICES of travel agents redundant, but don't give up on these professionals yet. A good agent can save you time and money by booking your flights, scouting out special package deals, reserving hotels, arranging car rentals, and arranging rail tickets and rail passes. If you don't already have a travel agent, ask your friends if they can recommend one. Or contact the American Society of Travel Agents, 1101 King Street, Suite 200, Alexandria, VA 22314; ☎ 703-739-2782; **www.asta.org.** Ask the travel agent if he or she has experience with booking trips to Ireland or has visited the country—if the answer is no, find someone else.

When you meet with the agent, you'll need to provide the dates of your trip and at least a rudimentary budget. With the information you provide, the agent can make suggestions about specific flights and hotels and make the reservations for you. You are not charged for the travel agent's services—although this could change in the future, now that agents no longer receive the same kinds of commissions from airlines and hotels.

CHECK THE TRAVEL SECTION OF YOUR LOCAL NEWSPAPER

ONE OF YOUR BEST SOURCES of information on package tours to Ireland is the travel section of your local paper. Ireland—especially Dublin—is a favorite destination of North Americans, and to serve this lucrative market there are frequently special money-saving deals that combine airfare and hotel costs. Blackout dates and a host of restrictions generally accompany these offers. Do a little research before you book a flight or package. Call the tour operator and ask questions: What is and is not included in the deals they're offering? What restrictions apply? Will you receive a refund if you cancel? What are the hotels included in the package? (Then check out the property on the Web.)

SURF THE WEB

WITH ALL THE INFORMATION available on the Internet, more and more travelers are acting as their own travel agents. Using the Web you can find and book special airfares, surf for discounted hotel rooms (see page 86 for specific hotel Web sites), order Eurail Passes, and much more.

unofficial **TIP**
Special low prices and seasonal deals are often available only on the Web.

Many travel-related Web sites offer reservations and tickets for airlines, plus reservations and purchase capabilities for hotels and car-rental companies. Some to check out include **Travelocity** (**www.travelocity.com**), **Expedia Travel** (**www.expedia.com**), **Yahoo! Travel** (**travel.yahoo.com/destinations**), **Cheap Tickets** (**www.cheaptickets.com**), and **Orbitz** (**www.orbitz.com**). You can find some of the lowest prices on **Hotwire** (**www.hotwire.com**), but there's a catch—you provide the dates you want to travel, Hotwire comes up with a fare, and you purchase the ticket—but you don't know departure times or the airlines until you've finalized the purchase. Similarly, you can get some great deals on **Priceline** (**www.priceline.com**)—with this outfit's most popular and inexpensive booking option, you provide the price you want to pay, along with your credit card info, but if your price is accepted, your card is charged before you know your departure times or airlines.

It's also useful to check out the Web sites of airlines that fly to Ireland (see facing page for a list). Frequently they post special discounts only available through online reservations. Some airlines will send you weekly e-newsletters and special last-minute e-fares, including specials for weekend travel from major North American hubs to Ireland. The airlines are also among your best sources for finding package tours to Ireland.

Check the sites below for air-and-hotel-package options:

- Aer Lingus Vacation Store   (**www.aerlingusvacationstore.com**)
- American Airlines Vacations   (**www.aavacations.com**)
- British Airways Holidays   (**www.baholidays.com**)
- Continental Airlines Vacations   (**continental.covacations.com**)
- Delta Vacations   (**www.deltavacations.com**)
- Northwest Airlines WorldVacations (**www.nwaworldvacations.com**)
- United Airlines Vacations   (**www.unitedvacations.com**)

The following airlines serve Dublin. Many have nonstop service into Shannon; Continental Airlines has nonstop service from New York to Belfast; and British Airways offers connections through London and Manchester to Dublin, Shannon, Belfast, and Cork

AIRLINE CONTACT INFORMATION FROM NORTH AMERICA		
Aer Lingus	☎ 800-474-7424	**www.flyaerlingus.com**
Air Canada	☎ 888-247-2262	**www.aircanada.com**
Air New Zealand	☎ 800-262-2468	**www.airnz.co.uk**
American Airlines	☎ 800-433-7300	**www.aa.com**
British Airways	☎ 800-247-9297	**www.ba.com**
Continental Airlines	☎ 800-231-0856	**www.continental.com**
Delta Air Lines	☎ 800-241-4141	**www.delta.com**
United Airlines	☎ 800-538 2929	**www.united.com**

You can, of course, call an airline directly—but you may get a better deal by using the Web. If you do call the airline, have your travel dates handy and be prepared to ask questions: "Will this flight cost less if I fly on a different day of the week or at a different time?" and "What is the cancellation policy if I can't use tickets I've already paid for on my credit card?" Your goal is to get the lowest fare to your destination. You can be direct and simply ask what the lowest fare is from your city to Dublin, Shannon, or Belfast, and if flying into one is considerably cheaper than flying into another. Chances are that the service representative will tell you; if he or she won't, hang up and try again.

unofficial **TIP**
If you've done some comparison shopping on the Web, an airline will usually match the lowest fare you've already found for specific flights.

Sometimes, you might find it less expensive to fly to London from major hubs in the eastern United States and continue on to Ireland from there. Ireland-based **Ryanair** (☎ 01-609-7800; **www.ryanair.com**) operates especially inexpensive flights from Britain to Dublin, Shannon, Cork, and other Irish airports; British Airways and Aer Lingus often match the low fares.

SUGGESTED TOUR OPERATORS

ESCORTED TOURS DIFFER FROM package tours in several fundamental ways. A package tour generally includes your airfare and hotel, but you are left on your own for everything else. Escorted tours offer full-service itineraries that generally include transfers to your hotel(s), some meals, sightseeing, nightlife, and more. Dozens of companies offer escorted tours to Dublin and other destinations in Ireland. A good travel agent can help you find a tour that suits your particular interests. It's also a good idea to scan the travel section in your local paper for tour possibilities.

It's important to know the basics of what is and isn't offered on an escorted tour before you sign up. Here are some questions you might want to ask:

- When do you pay, and how much?
- Will the trip be canceled if not enough people sign up? If so, what must you do to get a refund?
- How big will the group be? What are the age groups? Singles or couples? Men, women, or both?
- What's the daily schedule? Is it reasonable or so jam-packed that you won't have time to breathe?
- What are the accommodations? (Ask for the names and check these out on your own. Some tour operators use large, anonymous hotels in unappealing parts of town.)

Don't assume that anything not specifically spelled out is included in your fee. For example, you may have to pay to get yourself to or from the airport, or admission to attractions may not be included.

Cosmos (**www.cosmos.com**), **Trafalgar Tours** (**www.trafalgartours .com**), and **Maupintour** (**www.maupintour.com**) all offer escorted tours to Dublin and the rest of Ireland. For more information about specific offerings, check out their Web sites, and call or write with questions. *Remember:* Be a wise consumer.

Other companies provide flights, hotels, and ground transportation but leave you to do touring on your own. The advantage is that you sometimes get fairly good rates along with independence and the assurance of having the trip arranged before you leave home. Consider **Sceptre Tours** (**www.sceptretours.com**), which specializes in England and Ireland. In planning your itinerary, the company allows you to select from a long list of bed-and-breakfasts throughout Ireland and provides a rental car.

GATHERING INFORMATION

IRISH TOURIST BOARD OFFICES

FOR GENERAL INFORMATION ABOUT IRELAND, contact an office of the **Irish Tourist Board** at one of the following addresses:

IN THE UNITED STATES

Irish Tourist Board
345 Park Avenue
New York, NY 10154
☎ 800-223-6470 or 212-418-0800
[Vm 212-371-9052
www.discoverireland.com

Northern Ireland Tourist Board
551 Fifth Avenue, Suite 701
New York, NY 10176
☎ 800-326-0036 or 212-922-0101
[Vm 212-922-0099
www.discovernorthernireland.com

IN CANADA

Irish Tourist Board
2 Bloor Street West, Suite 1501
Toronto, ON M4W 3E2
☎ 800-223-6470 or 416-925-6368
[Vm 416-929-6783
www.discoverireland.com

Northern Ireland Tourist Board
2 Bloor Street West, Suite 1501
Toronto, ON M4W 3E2
☎ 800-576-8174 or 416-925-6368
[Vm 416-925-6033
www.discovernorthernireland.com

IN IRELAND

Irish Tourist Board–Bord Fáilte
Baggot Street Bridge
Dublin 2
☎ 01-602-4000
[Vm 01-602-4100
www.discoverireland.ie

Northern Ireland Tourist Board
16 Nassau Street
Dublin 2
☎ 01-679-1977
[Vm 01-679-1863
www.discovernorthernireland.com

IN NORTHERN IRELAND

Irish Tourist Board
53 Castle Street
Belfast BT1 1GH
☎ 028-9032-7888
[Vm 028-9024-0201
www.discoverireland.com/ire

Northern Ireland Tourist Board
59 North Street
Belfast BT1 1NB
☎ 028-9023-1221
[Vm 028-9024-0960
www.discovernorthernireland.co.uk

TOURIST INFORMATION CENTRES

YOUR BEST SOURCE OF UP-TO-DATE INFORMATION in any city or town is the Tourist Information Centre. You'll find addresses for them in every "Planning Your Visit to . . . " section in this guidebook. Tourist Information Centres are always centrally located, usually in the busiest areas of a city or town. In larger cities, you'll often find a branch in the train station. What are they good for? First and foremost, this being Ireland, for the chance to ask the friendly personnel any questions you might have. In general, you'll find that these people are eager to help visitors. Handouts, sometimes free, sometimes costing a few euros, usually include easy-to-use maps and guides to the city or town. You'll also find racks of brochures on local attractions. Something might catch your fancy, but remember that the brochures are advertisements—the fact that they are in a Tourist Information Centre doesn't automatically mean they are worth your time or money. There will often be a currency-exchange window in the center, along with a convenient hotel-booking service. For hotel booking there's usually a fee (10% of room cost) that is refunded when you pay for your room. Some Tourist Information Centres have small bookstores stocked with books of local interest, regional maps and guides, and souvenirs.

unofficial **TIP**
Many Tourist Information Centres offer free or low-cost guided walks of a city or town; join one of these informative tours if you have the time.

WEB SITES FOR FURTHER RESEARCH

THE WEB IS AN INVALUABLE TOOL when it comes to travel research, so even if you don't have Internet access at home we suggest you arrange to spend some time in front of a computer, perhaps one of those available for free use at local libraries. Web sites typically contain the most up-to-date information (provided that the site is well maintained)—hotels, for instance, list current prices and discounts (and provide pictures of their rooms), and attractions provide current prices and opening and closing times. We list Web sites whenever possible throughout this guide.

The following Web sites should provide you with enough info, as well as links to other sites, to keep you glued to your computer for weeks. We also recommend contacting the Web sites for visitors centers in cities, towns, national parks, and other places we list throughout this guide—you'll find a wealth of information specific to the places you most want to visit.

- **www.dublintouristboard.com** Contains up-to-the-minute info on events, hotels, restaurants, sightseeing, exhibits, and more.
- **www.ireland.com** The online edition of the *Irish Times,* the country's most esteemed newspaper. Try reading it before you go to get a taste of what's happening in Ireland today.
- **www.timeout.com** *Time Out* magazine's Web site posts detailed information on what's currently happening in Dublin.
- **www.entertainment.ie** Find up-to-date listings of events and exhibitions.
- **www.visitdublin.com** A plethora of information about Dublin can be found here, ranging from news about galleries and concerts to facts about car rentals and tours.
- **belfast.world-guides.com** Locate information on most facets of travel to Belfast: accommodations, weather, attractions, and more. An excellent source if you are traveling to Northern Ireland.

WHAT *to* PACK

AS LITTLE AS POSSIBLE. Resist the urge to cram your entire closet into your luggage. Take just *one suitcase,* preferably the kind with wheels. Augment that with a backpack or a zip-pered, waterproof carryall. Add a practical purse or bag that you can sling over your shoulder and use every day.

Keep in mind that not all Irish hotels have elevators or porters. In smaller, less expensive hotels and B&Bs, you're going to be lugging your own bags. Remember, too, that airlines now allow only one carry-on bag plus a purse or briefcase or laptop. They are strict about this, and you will have to go through various security checkpoints before boarding with your luggage.

unofficial **TIP**
Leave all your electric and electronic doodads at home; if you lug them with you, they'll have to fit in your luggage, and when in Ireland you will have to get a special adapter plug to use or recharge them.

In the wake of September 11, 2001, airlines now confiscate all sharp objects, no matter how innocuous, if they are in your carry-on luggage. This includes tiny scissors, hypodermic needles (unless you have a note from your doctor explaining why you need one), corkscrews, any kind of knife, and sporting equipment.

The amount of liquids, gels, and aerosols that airline passengers may carry on board is also severely restricted. These substances must be in three-ounce or smaller containers and placed in a single quart-size, zip-top clear plastic bag (each traveler can use only one), which must be removed and placed on the conveyor belt for x-ray screening. There are exceptions for baby formula and medicines. For more information, go to the **Transportation Security Administration** Web site at **www.tsa.gov/travelers/airtravel.**

PASSPORTS AND VISAS

IF YOU ARE AN AMERICAN, Canadian, Australian, or New Zealand tourist visiting Ireland for less than three months, a valid passport is the only legal form of identification you'll need to enter the country. Visas are required for any stay longer than three months. The Web site of the **U.S. State Department Bureau of Consular Affairs** (**travel .state.gov**) provides exhaustive information about

unofficial **TIP**
Make a copy of the information page of your passport, and keep it in your luggage in order to expedite replacement in case the passport gets lost or stolen.

passports (including a downloadable application), customs, and other government-regulated aspects of travel for U.S. citizens. Alternatively, call the **National Passport Information Center** at ☎ 877-487-2778.

Consulates and Embassies

Irish consulates abroad (see next page for a list) can advise you on obtaining visas for work or study in Ireland and address other legal and administrative questions prior to your trip.

If your passport gets lost or stolen or you need some other kind of special assistance while you're traveling in Ireland, the embassies at the bottom of the next page, both located in Dublin, will be able to help you or direct you to the resources you need.

CONSULATES

IN THE UNITED STATES
Irish Consulate General
Chase Building
345 Park Avenue, 17th Floor
New York, NY 10154-0037
☎ 212-319-2555; **fax** 202-980-9475
congenny@aol.com

Irish Consulate General
Ireland House
535 Boylston Street
Boston, MA 02116
☎ 617-267-9330; **fax** 617-267-6375
irlcons@aol.com

Irish Consulate General
400 North Michigan Avenue
Chicago, IL 60611
☎ 312-337-1868; **fax** 312-337-1954
irishconsulate@sbcglobal.net

Irish Consulate General
44 Montgomery Street
San Francisco, CA 94104
☎ 415-392-4214; **fax** 415-392-0885
irishcgsf@earthlink.net

Irish Embassy
2234 Massachusetts Avenue NW
Washington, D.C. 20008-2849
☎ 202-462-3939; **fax** 202-232-5993
washingtonembassy@dfi.ie

Honorary Consul
6186 Squire Lane
Reno, NV 89509
☎ 775-829-0221; **fax** 775-829-0221
bbrady@nybell.net

Honorary Consul
65 Broadview Drive
St. Louis, MO 63105
☎ 314-381-5112; **fax** 314-398-5189

Honorary Consul
2711 Wesleyan Road

Houston, TX 77027
☎ 713-961-5263; **fax** 970-925-7900

Honorary Consul
2511 NE 31st Court
Lighthouse Point
Fort Lauderdale, FL 33064
☎ 954-785-3427; **fax** 954-974-7524

Honorary Consul
191 Peachtree Street NE, 21st Floor
Atlanta, GA 30303
☎ 404 332 6401; **fax** 404-332-4299

IN CANADA
Embassy of Ireland
130 Albert Street, Suite 1105
Ottawa, ON K1P 5G4
☎ 613-223-6281; **fax** 613-233-5835
embassyofireland@rogers.com

Honorary Consul
100 West Pender Street, Tenth Floor
Vancouver, BC V6B 1R8
☎ 604-683-9233; **fax** 604-683-8402
irishconsul@telus.net

Honorary Consul General
20 Toronto Street, Suite 1210
Toronto, ON M5C 2B8
☎ 416-366-9300; **fax** 416-947-0584

Honorary Consul General
3803-8A Street SW
Calgary, AB T2T 3B6
☎ 403-243-2970; **fax** 403-287-1023

Honorary Consul
13 Glenmeadow Crescent
St. Albert, AB T8N 3AT
☎ 780-458-0810; **fax** 780-458-6483

Honorary Consul General
1590 Dr. Penrose Avenue
Montréal, QC H3G 1C5
☎ 514-848-7389; **fax** 514-848-4514

EMBASSIES

THE UNITED STATES
42 Elgin Road, Ballsbridge
Dublin 4
☎ 01-668-8777; **FAX** 01-668-9946
webmasterireland@state.gov

CANADA
65–68 St. Stephen's Green, 4th Floor
Dublin 2
☎ 01-678-1988; **FAX** 01-417-4101
dubln@international.gc.ca

HOW TO DRESS

GIVEN THE UNPREDICTABILITY of Irish weather, think layers. Bring mix-and-match coordinates that you can shed or add to as needed. A sweater will be welcome in any season, as will a waterproof coat or jacket with a hood and an umbrella (many hotels supply these to guests). A comfortable and casual pair of waterproof walking shoes is handy for city walks and country treks. If traveling to Ireland in the winter months, bring protection against the damp chill: gloves, a scarf, and a warm coat.

A Word on Tourist Garb

The Irish are pretty casual about their clothes, so wearing a pair of blue jeans while sightseeing will not set you apart as a gauche tourist. In better restaurants and at cultural events, a "smart but casual" dress code generally applies: slacks and footwear other than running shoes are usually the norm for men, a dress or good slacks and a nice blouse for women. (There are still a few places where gentlemen are required to wear a coat and tie, but not many.)

SPECIAL CONSIDERATIONS

TRAVELING WITH CHILDREN

THE RATING SYSTEM in our attraction profiles attempts to gauge suitability for children and adults of various ages, but keep in mind that all children have different interests and differing levels of tolerance for museums and other sights. All in all, though, we find that kids love Ireland—the common language provides a level of comfort, there are enough castles and suits of armor around to satisfy their romantic notions of days of yore, and a ride on a double-decker bus can be sheer heaven.

unofficial **TIP**
If you're traveling as a family, you can usually buy money-saving family tickets at major attractions. These tickets are available for two adults and two children (three children in some cases).

You'll find kid-friendly amusements throughout Ireland. Audio guides are available at many attractions, making them more fun and interesting for children age 9 and up. Kids under age 5 get in free almost everywhere. Finally, remember that kids get jet lag, too, so you'll want to plan your first day accordingly.

DISABLED ACCESS IN IRELAND

MANY IRISH ATTRACTIONS, as well as hotels and restaurants, are accessible to disabled visitors in wheelchairs, but portions of some historic properties cannot be changed to accommodate chairs. Larger and newer hotels, plus many smaller properties, provide special rooms designed for the disabled. We provide information on access for the disabled in our listings, but call ahead to find out what, if any, arrangements have been made for wheelchairs.

To make your trip pleasurable rather than a struggle, plan ahead by checking out these resources:

In Ireland and Northern Ireland

- The **Irish Wheelchair Association** (Áras Chuchulainn, Blackheath Drive, Clontarf, Dublin 3; ☎ 01-833-8241; **www.iwa.ie**) has information about holiday destinations for travelers with disabilities, as well as other helpful items.

- The **Irish Rail** (**www.irishrail.ie**) provides services and information for travelers with disabilities.

- In Northern Ireland, **Disability Action** (Portside Business Park, 189 Airport Road West, Belfast BT3 9ED; ☎ 028-9029-7880; **www.disabilityaction.org**) lists facilities for the disabled.

- At any **Northern Ireland Tourist Board offices,** pick up *Information Guide to Accessible Accommodation.*

- The **National Rehabilitation Board of Ireland** (24–25 Clyde Road, Ballsbridge, Dublin 4; ☎ 01-608-0400) publishes *Guide to Accessible Accommodation in Ireland,* helpful in finding lodging.

In the United States

- **Access-Able Travel Source** (☎ 303-232-2979; **www.accessable .com**) has a wealth of information about traveling with disabilities.

- **Accessible Journeys** (☎ 800-846-4537 or 610-521-0339; **www .disabilitytravel.com**) caters to mature travelers, slow walkers, wheelchair travelers, and their families and friends. The company specializes in accessible travel planning, group tours, and cruises.

- **Flying Wheels Travel** (☎ 507-451-5005; **www.flyingwheelstravel .com**) specializes in travel for persons with physical disabilities. The company offers a range of escorted tours.

SENIOR TRAVELERS

IF YOU'RE A SENIOR who gets around fairly well, Ireland won't present any particular problems for you. If you have mobility or health issues, though, be aware that not all hotels, particularly less expensive B&Bs, have elevators. Before reserving a hotel room, ask whether or not you'll have access to an elevator or if other facilities for travelers with disabilities are available.

Being a senior may entitle you to some travel bargains, such as reduced admission at theaters, museums, and other attractions. Always ask, even if a reduction isn't posted.

The following sources can provide information on discounts and other benefits for seniors:

- **AARP** (601 E Street NW, Washington, DC 20049; ☎ 888-687-2277; **www.aarp.org**) offers member discounts on car rentals and hotels.

- **Elderhostel** (75 Federal Street, Boston, MA 02110-1941; ☎ 877-426-8056; **www.elderhostel.org**) offers people 55 and older a variety of university-based education programs in Dublin and through-out Ireland. These courses are value-packed, hassle-free ways to learn while traveling. Package prices include airfare, accommodations, meals, tuition, tips, and insurance. And you'll be glad to know that there are no grades. Recent programs have included "Definitive Ireland," "Discovering the West of Ireland," "Medieval and Gaelic Ireland: A Celebration," "Walking Southwest Ireland's Coast and Country," "Theater and Art in Dublin," and "Celebrating Irish Mythology."

- **Grand Circle Travel** (347 Congress Street, Boston, MA 02210; ☎ 800-321-2835; **www.gct.com**) provides escorted tours for older travelers. Call for a copy of the publication "101 Tips for the Mature Traveler" or order online at the Web site above.

GAY AND LESBIAN TRAVELERS

HOMOSEXUALITY WAS NOT DECRIMINALIZED in Ireland until 1993 (in the North, not until 1982), and this largely conservative, predominantly Catholic country is still not terribly gay friendly. Gay and lesbian travelers should keep in mind that public expressions of affection may easily attract unwanted attention—gay bashing is not unheard of, even in Dublin.

That said, there's a growing gay community in Dublin and in other, more-liberal cities such as Galway. You can find gay-oriented activities in the monthly newspaper *Gay Community News* (**GCN**), available at some bookstores. *In Dublin,* the city's main events guide, devotes several pages to gay information, and two recent Dublin publications, *Free!* and *Scene City,* highlight gay venues. On the Web, *Gay Ireland Online* (**www.gay-ireland.com**) and **Outhouse** (**www.outhouse .ie**) provide listings, organization info, and discussion forums.

The following resources have knowledgeable staffers who can assist gay and lesbian travelers in Dublin and the rest of Ireland:

- **National Lesbian and Gay Federation (NLGF)** 2 Scarlet Row, Dublin 1; ☎ 01-671-0939; **nlgf@tinet.ie**
- **Outhouse Community Resource Centre** 105 Capel Street, Dublin 1; ☎ 01-873-4932; **www.outhouse.ie**
- **Gay Switchboard Dublin** Carmichael House, North Brunswick Street, Dublin 7; ☎ 01-872-1055; **www.gayswitchboard.ie**
- **Lesbian Line Dublin** Carmichael Centre, North Brunswick Street, Dublin 7; ☎ 01-872-9911

In the United States

- **International Gay and Lesbian Travel Association (IGLTA)** ☎ 800-448-8550 or 954-776-2626; **iglta@iglta.org; www.iglta.org**. Provides a wealth of information on gay travel.
- **Now, Voyager** ☎ 800-255-6951; **www.nowvoyager.com.** A gay-owned and -operated travel service.

OTHER TRAVEL CONCERNS

ELECTRICITY

LEAVE ALL BUT THE MOST ESSENTIAL electric gadgets and appliances at home. The electricity supply in Ireland is 220-volt AC, which will blow out any American 110-volt appliance unless it is plugged into a transformer. Irish outlets are made for large three-prong plugs, so in addition to the transformer, you will need to get an adapter, available at any hardware store, chemist (drugstore), supermarket, or gadget store. *Don't plug in anything until you've checked the voltage on the transformer!* It should be set to "Input AC 110-volt, output AC 220-volt."

HEALTH

CHECK YOUR EXISTING INSURANCE to see if it covers medical services abroad. If it doesn't, consider purchasing a policy from a company that offers health coverage for travelers, such as **Travelex,** ☎ 800-228-9792, **www.travelex.com; MEDEX International,** ☎ 800-537-2029 or 410-453-6300, **www.medexassist.com;** or **Travel Assistance International,** ☎ 800-821-2828, **www.travelassistance.com.**

MONEY

THE CURRENCY OF THE REPUBLIC OF IRELAND is the euro (€). For this book, we've assumed an exchange rate of €1 to $1.60 U.S. Euro notes come in denominations of €500, €200, €100, €50, €10, and €5. A euro is divided into 100 euro cents. Coins come in denominations of €2, €1, €0.50, €0.20, €0.10, €0.05, €0.02, and €0.01.

> ***unofficial* TIP**
> Coins cannot easily be changed into foreign cash, so spend them while you're in Ireland; better still, donate them on your way home to the **UNICEF Change Collection** program sponsored by most airlines.

As part of the United Kingdom, Northern Ireland continues to use British pounds (£), one of which converts to about $2. The pound is divided into 100 pence (p).

There are no longer any £1 notes. There are red £50s, purple £20s, brown £10s, and green £5s. Coins are divided into £2, £1, 50p, 20p, 10p, 5p, 2p, and 1p.

Check any major newspaper's business section for current exchange rates, or go to **www.travlang.com** or **www.x-rates.com.**

ATMs, Banks, and *Bureaux de Change*

There are ATMs all over Dublin and in cities and towns throughout the country that are large enough to have a bank branch. This is your best bet for getting the optimum rate when you withdraw money. Remember, you can't access your credit-card funds from an ATM without a PIN (personal identification number).

Weekday hours for banks are generally 9:30 a.m. to 4:30 p.m. All banks are closed on public holidays, but many branches have 24-hour banking lobbies with ATMs and/or ATMs on the street outside. Banks and *bureaux de change* (exchange centers) will exchange money at a competitive rate but charge a commission (typically 1% to 3% of the total transaction). All U.K. bureaux de change and other money-changing establishments are required to clearly display exchange rates as well as full details on any fees and rates of commission. Before exchanging your money, always check to see the exchange rate, how much commission will be charged, and whether any additional fees apply.

unofficial **TIP**
Bureaux de change are found in major tourist sections of Dublin (some are open 24 hours). Steer clear of those that offer good exchange rates but charge a heavy commission (up to 8%).

Value-added Tax (VAT)

In the Republic, the VAT is 13.5% for restaurants, hotels, car rentals, and the like; the VAT on wine, gifts, and souvenirs is 21%. In Northern Ireland, the VAT is 17.5%; food, children's clothing, and books are exempt. If you are not a citizen of a country in the European Union, you can often get a refund on this tax (see page 92). VAT is usually added directly to an item's sticker price, except for some merchandise sold in some small shops and some services. Check before you book a hotel to see if the quoted price includes VAT.

TELEPHONE, E-MAIL, AND POST OFFICES

Telephones

Three types of public pay phones are available: those that take only coins (increasingly rare), those that accept only phone cards, and those that take both. You can buy phone cards from newsstands and post offices. At coin-operated phones, insert your coins before dialing.

LOCAL AND INTERNATIONAL CODES The country code for the Republic is **353;** for Northern Ireland it is **44.** To call Ireland from the United States, dial 011-353 or 011-44, the area or city code, and then the six-, seven-, or eight-digit phone number. You will notice that area codes in Ireland always include an initial 0, as in 01 for Dublin. If you're calling from the U.S. or somewhere else overseas or are in Ireland and dialing a number within the same area code, do not use the 0; however, when calling another area code from within Ireland, do include the 0.

To make an international call from Ireland, dial the international access code (00), then the country code, then the area code, and finally the local number. Or call through one of the following long-distance access codes: **AT&T,** ☎ 800-550-000; **Sprint,** ☎ 800-552-001; or **Verizon,** ☎ 800-55-1001.

Some Important Numbers

00 International dialing code; that is, if calling outside Ireland, dial 00 + 1 for U.S. and Canada, 61 for Australia, 64 for New Zealand, and the like

IN THE REPUBLIC

10 General operator

999 Emergency for police, fire, or ambulance

1190 U.K. and Irish directory assistance

1198 International directory assistance

114 International operator

IN NORTHERN IRELAND

100 General operator

999 Emergency for police, fire, or ambulance

192 U.K. and Irish directory assistance

153 International directory assistance

155 International operator

CELL PHONES Within Ireland you can use any cell phone compatible with the GSM (Global System for Mobile Communications) network. However, you'll pay less in roaming charges by swapping out your phone's SIM (subscriber-information module, or "smart card") with a prepaid one that has an Ireland phone number (available at electronics stores or through online retailers). Be aware that some wireless providers configure their phones to work only with the SIMs they supply, so check whether your phone is locked or unlocked before you buy. You can also rent a GSM cell phone for use in Ireland, either before you leave home or once you arrive. For more information, contact **Cellular Abroad** (☎ 800-287-5072; **www.cellularabroad.com**), (**InTouch USA** (☎ 800-872-7626 or 703-222-7161; **www.intouchglobal.com**), or **Road-Post** (☎ 888-290-1616 or 905-272-5665; **www.roadpost.com**).

E-mail

You'll find Internet cafes in Irish cities, although they can be few and far between in the countryside. If you're in dire need of a computer to check or send e-mail, go to the local library.

If you have a laptop that can take advantage of it, a wireless connection will provide you with a high-speed connection without cable or a phone line. Ireland has been a little slow on the uptake with Wi-Fi, though many hotels now provide wireless access for guests.

Post Offices

Mail is called *the post* in Ireland. *Postboxes* (mailboxes) are green with POST lettered on them in the Republic, red and green with ROYAL

MAIL lettered on them in Northern Ireland. Post offices are generally open Monday through Friday, 9 a.m. to 5:30 p.m., and Saturday, 9 a.m. to 12:30 p.m.

CALENDAR of
SPECIAL EVENTS

IRELAND HAS MANY TRADITIONAL EVENTS and festivals throughout the year. Good resources for checking events and dates before you leave home are **www.discoverireland.ie** and **www.tourismireland.com.** If you're spending a major portion of your trip in Dublin, log on to the **Dublin Tourist Board**'s Web site, **www.visitdublin.com,** or **www .dublintown.com.** As you're traveling through the rest of Ireland, stop in at Tourist Information Centres to find out what's going on.

January

FUNDERLAND Royal Dublin Society, Ballsbridge, Dublin 4; ☎ 061-419988; **www.funfair.ie.** A yearly indoor fair, with carnival stalls, exciting rides, and family entertainment.

YEATS WINTER SCHOOL Sligo Park Hotel, Sligo Town; ☎ 071-42693; **www.yeats-sligo.com.** A relaxing weekend in late January with lectures and a tour of Yeats Country.

February

ANTIQUES AND COLLECTIBLES FAIR Newman House, 85 St. Stephen's Green, Dublin 2; fax 01-670-8295; **antiquesfairsireland@esatclear.ie.** Four consecutive Sundays.

JAMESON DUBLIN INTERNATIONAL FILM FESTIVAL Temple Bar, Dublin. The Irish Film Centre (see page 121) and other venues screen the best of Irish and international cinema. Contact Dublin International Film Festival, Temple Lane, Cecilia Street, Dublin 2; ☎ 01-635-0290; **www.dubliniff.com.**

SIX NATIONS RUGBY TOURNAMENT Lansdowne Road, Ballsbridge, County Dublin. Athletes from Ireland, the U.K., France, and Italy participate in this annual tourney. Contact Irish Rugby Football Union, 62 Lansdowne Road, Dublin 4; ☎ 01-668-4601; fax 01-660-5640.

March

BRIDGE HOUSE IRISH FESTIVAL Bridge House Hotel and Leisure Centre, Tullamore, County Offaly; ☎ 506-22000; **www.bridgehouse.com.** The biggest indoor festival in Ireland, with Irish song and dance.

ST. PATRICK'S DAY PARADES Throughout Ireland.

ST. PATRICK'S DUBLIN FESTIVAL Fireworks, dance, street theater, sports, carnival acts, and music ending in a spectacular parade; ☎ 01-676-3205; fax 01-676-3208; **www.stpatricksday.ie.**

April

PAN CELTIC FESTIVAL Kilkenny, County Donegal; ☎ 056-51500; **www.panceltic.com.** Celts from all over the British Isles gather for song, dance, cultural events, and nature walks.

WORLD IRISH DANCING CHAMPIONSHIPS Waterfront Hotel, Belfast; ☎ 01-475-2220; fax 01-475-1053; **cirg@tinet.ie.** Thousands come from around the world to take part in this competition.

May

BELFAST CITY MARATHON Six thousand runners compete in this 26-mile event, which starts and finishes at Maysfield Leisure Centre; ☎ 028-9027-0345.

COUNTY WICKLOW GARDENS FESTIVAL On certain days, heritage properties and gardens are open to the public; ☎ 0404-20070; **www .visitwicklow.ie.**

MAY DAY RACES Down Royal Racecourse, Maze, Lisburn, County Antrim; ☎ 028-9262-1256; **www.downroyal.com.** An important event in the horse-racing calendar.

June

AIB MUSIC FESTIVAL IN GREAT IRISH HOUSES A ten-day festival of classical music performed by Irish and international artists in stately buildings and mansions; ☎ 01-278-1528; fax 01-278-1529.

BLOOMSDAY FESTIVAL A celebration of James Joyce's *Ulysses* and its central character Leopold Bloom. Contact the James Joyce Centre, 34 North Great George's Street, Dublin 1; ☎ 01-878-8547; fax 01-878-8488; **www.jamesjoyce.ie.** June 16.

BUDWEISER IRISH DERBY The Curragh, County Kildare; ☎ 045-441205; fax 045-441442. This horse race is one of the stars of European racing. Fans converge from around the world in fancy dress, men in jackets and women in hats (think of the Ascot Day scene in *My Fair Lady*). Buy tickets in advance at **www.curragh.ie.**

KILLARNEY SUMMERFEST Fitzgerald Stadium, Killarney, County Kerry. This rock festival is one of Ireland's summer highlights. The big-name performers have included Sheryl Crow and Bryan Adams. For tickets contact **www.ticketmaster.ie.**

WATERFORD MARITIME FESTIVAL Quays of Waterford City. This four-day celebration takes place over the June bank holiday. The highlight is a powerboat race from Waterford to Swansea, Wales. Boats from the Irish, British, French, and Dutch naval fleets gather in Waterford Harbour. Other highlights are kayak races and concerts.

July

BATTLE OF THE BOYNE COMMEMORATION Belfast and other northern cities. This event, often called Orangeman's Day, commemorates a historic battle between two 17th-century kings. Protestants all over Northern Ireland celebrate and parade. Contact the House of Orange, 65 Dublin Road, Belfast BT2 7HE; ☎ 028-9032-2801. July 12.

GALWAY ARTS FESTIVAL AND RACES Galway City and Racecourse; ☎ 091-566577; fax 091-562655; **www.galwayartsfestival.ie.** Celebrates all manner of arts, with hundreds of participating writers, artists, and performers from around the world. The Galway Races follow, with five more days of racing and entertainment. Mid-July.

LUGHNASA FAIR Carrickfergus Castle, County Antrim; ☎ 028-4336-6455. A 12th-century Norman castle provides the setting for this fair. Enjoy medieval games, observe people dressed in period costumes, and sample traditional food and crafts. Late July.

OXYGEN Punchestown Racecourse, County Kildare. One of the largest and most popular rock festivals. To buy tickets, log on to **www.ticketmaster.ie.** Early July.

August

KERRYGOLD HORSE SHOW RDS Showgrounds, Ballsbridge, Dublin 4; ☎ 01-668-0866; fax 01-660-4014; **www.rds.ie.** This event draws a fashionable crowd and is considered the most important equestrian and social event on Ireland's calendar. Early August.

KILKENNY ARTS FESTIVAL Kilkenny Town; ☎ 056-52175; fax 056-51704; **www.kilkennyarts.ie.** This festival celebrates all the arts, from classical and traditional music to poetry readings.

LISDOONVARNA MATCHMAKING FESTIVAL Tralee, County Kerry; ☎ 065-707-4005; **www.matchmakerireland.com.** The idea is one that's sure to be a hit—bring a bunch of singles together and ply them with beer and music. The latter is some of the best you'll hear in Ireland.

PUCK FAIR Killorglin, County Kerry; ☎ 066-976-2366; **www.puckfair.ie.** A wild goat is captured, garlanded, and declared king in this three-day festival, one of Ireland's oldest.

ROSE OF TRALEE INTERNATIONAL FESTIVAL Tralee, County Kerry; ☎ 066-712-1322; fax 066-22654; **www.roseoftralee.ie.** This famous five-day festival includes concerts, horse races, and a talent pageant culminating in the selection of the Rose of Tralee.

September

ALL-IRELAND HURLING AND GAELIC FOOTBALL FINALS Croke Park, Dublin 3; ☎ 01-836-3222; fax 01-836-6420. The finals of hurling and Gaelic football, hugely important in Ireland. Buy tickets at **www.ticketmaster.ie.**

FLEADH CHEOIL NAH ÉIREANN Listowel, County Kerry; ☎ 01-280-0295; fax 01-280-3759; **www.comhaltas.com.** Since 1951, Ireland's most important celebration of traditional music. Late August.

GALWAY INTERNATIONAL OYSTER FESTIVAL Galway and environs; ☎ 091-522066; fax 091-527282; **www.galwayoysterfest.com.** A true feast for oyster lovers, with an oyster-opening championship, a golf tournament, traditional music, and more. Late September.

IRISH ANTIQUE DEALERS' FAIR RDS Showgrounds, Ballsbridge, Dublin 4; ☎ 01-285-9294. The most important antiques fair in Ireland; hundreds of dealers participate. Late September.

NATIONAL HERITAGE WEEK Throughout the country hundreds of events are held, including lectures, music, walks, and more. ☎ 01-647-2455; **www.heritageireland.ie.** Early September.

October

BABORÓ INTERNATIONAL ARTS FESTIVAL FOR CHILDREN Galway; ☎ 091-509705; fax 091-562655; **www.baboro.ie.** Children ages 3 to 12 can enjoy music, dance, and more. Late October.

BELFAST FESTIVAL AT QUEENS Queens University, Belfast; ☎ 028-9066-7687; fax 028-9066-5577; **www.belfastfestival.com.** An outstanding celebration of the arts—music, film, and more.

DUBLIN CITY MARATHON This popular run takes place on the last Monday in October. ☎ 01-626-3746; **www.dublincitymarathon.ie.**

DUBLIN THEATRE FESTIVAL Theaters throughout Dublin; ☎ 01-677-8439; fax 01-679-7709; **www.dublintheatrefestival.com.** Features new plays by major Irish and international companies. Early October.

GUINNESS CORK JAZZ FESTIVAL Cork City; ☎ 021-427-8979; fax 021-427-0463; **www.corkjazzfestival.com.** International acts play around town, in pubs, hotels, and concert halls. Late October.

KINSALE INTERNATIONAL GOURMET FESTIVAL ☎ 021-477-4026. Kinsale, known as the center of action for Irish foodies, struts its culinary might with special menus throughout area restaurants.

MURPHY'S CORK INTERNATIONAL FILM FESTIVAL Cinemas in Cork; ☎ 021-427-1711; fax 021-427-5945. Ireland's premier film festival offers features, documentaries, and shorts.

WEXFORD FESTIVAL Opera Theatre Royal, Wexford City; ☎ 053-22400; fax 053-424289; **www.wexfordopera.com.** Λ delightfully refreshing informal festival known for its productions of little-known 18th- and 19th-century works as well as recitals and classical music.

December

LEOPARDSTOWN NATIONAL HUNT FESTIVAL Leopardstown Racecourse, Foxrock, Dublin 18; ☎ 01-289-2888; fax 01-289-2634; **www.leopardstown .com.** Three days of thoroughbred racing. Late December.

WOODFORD MUMMERS Feile Woodford, County Galway; ☎ 059-49248. A celebration of traditional music, song, dance, and mime performed in period costume. Late December.

PART TWO

ARRIVING

ARRIVING *by* AIR

THE MAIN POINT OF ENTRY for most visitors from overseas to Ireland is **Dublin Airport,** although many travelers arrive at **Shannon Airport,** in the west of the country. **Belfast Airport,** in Northern Ireland, also handles international flights. **Cork Airport,** in the southwest, is the second-busiest in Ireland, after Dublin, handling many flights from other parts of Europe. For more about airlines flying from the United States and Canada, see page 39 and the following page.

PASSPORT CONTROL AND CUSTOMS

ON THE PLANE YOU WILL RECEIVE a landing card on which you'll provide your name, address, passport number, and the address of where you'll be staying. Present this completed form and your passport at Passport Control upon deplaning. Your passport will be stamped with a visitor's visa that, in most cases, allows you to stay in the country for up to three months. From here, proceed on to pick up your luggage and then go to Customs.

At the Customs area there are two choices: Nothing to Declare (the Green Channel) and Goods to Declare (the Red Channel). Limits on imports for visitors entering Ireland from outside the European Union include 200 cigarettes, 50 cigars, or 250 grams (8.8 ounces) of loose tobacco; 2 liters (2.1 quarts) of still table wine, 1 liter of liquor (more than 22% alcohol content), or 2 liters of liquor (less than 22%); and 2 fluid ounces of perfume. The total value of goods brought in must not exceed €175. You may not bring in controlled drugs (any medication you have should be in its original bottle with your name on it), firearms and/or ammunition, plants and vegetables, fresh meats, or any kind of animal. If you fall within the limits above, go through the Nothing to Declare area. Otherwise, go through the Goods to Declare area, where a Customs official will assess the amount of duty to be paid.

DUBLIN AIRPORT

THE REPUBLIC'S PRIMARY AIR GATEWAY, **Dublin Airport** (☎ 01-814-1111; **www.dublinairport.com**) is eight miles north of the city. Most travelers from North America arrive in Dublin on **Aer Lingus** (with nonstop flights from Baltimore, Boston, Chicago, Los Angeles, New York, and San Francisco); **Air Canada** (from major Canadian cities); **American** (nonstop flights from Boston, Chicago, and New York); **British Airways** (from Boston, Chicago, Miami, Newark, New York, Philadelphia, San Francisco, Seattle, and Washington D.C., all with a change of planes in London or Manchester, England); and **Delta** (nonstop flights from Atlanta, New York, and many other American cities).

The airport, which is about to expand into a new international terminal, has a tourist office, shops, bank and currency-exchange facilities including ATMs, a post office, a pharmacy, bars and restaurants, and desks for car rentals.

Getting into Dublin from the Airport

Dublin Bus's **Airlink** coach service will take you from the airport into the city. The 747 route runs from the airport to O'Connell Street (in the center of the city) and Busáras (the central bus station); Monday through Saturday, 5:45 a.m. to 11:30 p.m.; Sunday, 7:15 a.m. to 11:30 p.m. Buses run every 10 minutes Monday through Saturday and every 20 minutes on Sunday. The 748 runs from the airport to Busáras, Tara Street (DART station), Aston Quay (in the center of the city), and the Heuston Rail Station; Monday through Saturday, 6:50 a.m. to 9:30 p.m.; Sunday, 7 a.m. to 10:05 p.m. Buses run every 30 minutes. The fare on both routes is €6 for adults, €3 for children; tickets can be purchased from an Airlink desk in the arrivals lounge.

You can also get into the city center on **Aircoach,** with 24-hour service to St. Stephen's Green, Merrion Square, Ballsbridge, and other districts where many hotels are located; the fare is €7; ☎ 01-844-7118; **www.aircoach.ie.** Dublin Bus, the city bus service, also runs regular service from the airport to O'Connell Street, Busáras, and other city-center points, from 6 a.m. to 11 p.m.; the fare is €6.

Taxis line up outside the Arrivals lounge. A ride into the city will cost about €25.

SHANNON AIRPORT

THE GATEWAY TO THE WEST OF IRELAND is **Shannon Airport** (**www.shannonairport.com**). Nonstop service from North America includes flights on **Aer Lingus** (from Boston, Chicago, Los Angeles, and New York), **American** (from Boston, Chicago, and New York), **Continental** (from Newark), and **Delta** (from Atlanta). Shannon also handles many connecting flights on these airlines from Dublin, as well as flights from London (including **Aer Lingus, British Airways,** and **Ryanair**). Bus service runs from the airport to Ennis, Galway, Cork, and Limerick, with connections to many other towns in the west of Ireland; for more information on continuing on from Shannon by bus, contact **Bus Éireann** (☎ 01-836-6111; **www.buseireann.ie**).

BELFAST INTERNATIONAL AIRPORT

THIS AIRPORT (**www.belfastairport.com/en**), in Northern Ireland's capital city, handles nonstop **Continental** flights from Newark.

All of the above airports also handle flights from the Continent, and travelers from North America can connect to Dublin, Shannon, and Belfast from Paris (Air France, **www.airfrance.com**); Frankfurt (Lufthansa, **www.lufthansa.com**); Amsterdam (KLM, **www.klm.com**), and Madrid (Iberia, **www.iberia.com**), among other cities. **Cork Airport** (**www.cork-airport.com**) also handles flights from the Continent, on Air France, Aer Lingus, British Airways, KLM, and Ryanair.

ARRIVING *by* FERRY

CAR AND PASSENGER FERRIES cross the Irish Sea from Great Britain and France to Ireland. Many travelers make the crossing on **Irish Ferries** (☎ 8180-300-400; **www.irishferries.com**), which travels from Holyhead, Wales, to Dún Laoghaire, eight miles south of Dublin, and Pembroke, Wales, to Rosslare, County Wexford. Other lines and routes are:

- **The Isle of Man Steam Packet Company–Sea Cat** (☎ 0870-552-3523 in Great Britain or 01-800-80-50-55 in Ireland; **www.steam-packet.com**) sails from Liverpool to Dublin and from Heysham and Troon in Scotland to Belfast.
- **P&O Irish Sea Ferries** (☎ 561-563-2856 in the United States, 0870-242-4777 in Great Britain, and 01-638-3333 in Ireland; **www.poirishsea.com**) links Cairnryan, Scotland, and Larne, County Antrim, in Northern Ireland. P&O ferries also travel between Liverpool and Dublin.
- **Stena Line** (☎ 01-204-7777; **www.stenaline.com**) travels from Holyhead, Wales, to Dún Laoghaire, eight miles south of Dublin.

GETTING *around in* IRELAND

TRAVELING BY TRAIN

THE RAIL SYSTEM IN THE REPUBLIC is run by **Iarnród Éireann** (**Irish Rail,** ☎ 01-850-366222 or 01-836-6222; **www.irishrail.ie**), while **Northern Ireland Railways** (**NIR,** ☎ 028-9066-6630; **www.nirailways.co.uk**) operates trains in the North. Many rail routes originate in Dublin and depart from Heuston and Connolly stations.

The trip from Dublin to Belfast takes just two hours (on speedy Enterprise service; about €40), while slower service to Cork takes about three hours and costs from €40; to Galway, also about three hours, from €27; to Limerick, two hours, from €35; and Waterford, three hours, from €23.

You can buy tickets at any station window and pay with cash or credit card. A one-way trip is called a *single;* a round-trip is called a *return.* Trains are divided into first and second classes. First class costs about one-third more than second class. What are the advantages? First class offers seats that are larger and more comfortable, and in some cases more-personalized service, with small perks such as free newspapers or free tea and coffee. Both first- and second-class passengers use the same cafe cars or, on longer hauls, restaurant cars. Vendors come through on many trains selling beverages and snacks. Make sure you arrive early when you are traveling, because many trains fill up and you'll be left standing.

TRAVELING BY CAR

Car Rentals

Americans and Canadians renting cars in Ireland will need a driver's license that they've had for at least a year, plus a credit card. Renters usually must be 23 years old (21 in some instances); some companies will not rent to drivers 70 or older. Major rental companies include:

Alamo	☎ 800-462-5266	**www.alamo.com**
Auto-Europe	☎ 888-223-5555	**www.autoeurope.com**
Avis	☎ 800-230-4898	**www.avis.com**
Budget	☎ 800-527-0700	**www.budget.com**
Europcar	☎ 800-800-6000	**www.europcar.ie**
Hertz	☎ 800-654-8881	**www.hertz.com**
National	☎ 800-227-3876	**www.nationalcar.com**

unofficial **TIP**
If you plan on starting your trip in Dublin, wait to pick up your car until you have completed the Dublin portion of your trip and you're ready to tour the rest of the country. Driving in Dublin is difficult, and you're much better off traveling on public transportation.

When you make your reservation, ask if the quoted price includes the VAT (value-added tax) and unlimited mileage. VAT on car rentals in the Republic is 13.5%, 17.5% in Northern Ireland. Then find out what insurance options are included. Many credit-card companies do not automatically cover collision-damage insurance as they do for car rentals in other countries. (MasterCard Platinum is one of the few cards that do include the Collision Damage Waiver, though this is subject to change.) As a result of this policy, you must pay a hefty surcharge (about €15 a day) for collision-damage insurance on top of any personal-liability insurance you choose to purchase. Check with the rental-car company to see which cards cover the collision-damage waiver, and then verify this with the credit-card company. Some rental-car agencies in Ireland will charge you for collision-damage insurance unless you can produce a letter from a credit-card company stating that the company includes the collision-damage waiver with the use of its card.

Also keep an eye out of the terms of the insurance you buy to make sure you will not be required to pay a heavy deductible in case of an accident. With some standard policies you will be required to pay $500 or much more before the insurance coverage goes into effect; often, for a few dollars more per day, you can purchase a no-deductible clause, under the terms of which the insurance will begin paying from the first cent of the charges.

You can rent a car before you go at any of the agencies listed at left; in addition, some airlines offer package deals that include car rental. Remember, you'll probably get a better deal if you rent the car at least seven days in advance.

> *unofficial* **TIP**
> If you are visiting Ireland outside of the busy summer months, you can often bargain for a good rate on a rental car. Make sure you arrive at a price that includes all insurance charges (including collision-damage waiver and no-deductible), all taxes, and any drop-off charges.

 ## Roads and Roundabouts

What drivers in the United States would call a freeway the Irish call a *motorway* (indicated on maps by *M* plus a number). You needn't get too hung up on this designation, though, because there are very few motorways in Ireland—and fewer in the Republic than in the North, though many miles of new motorway are under construction all across the country. A two-way road is called a *single carriageway*, and a four-lane divided highway (two lanes in each direction) is a *dual carriageway*. Roads in the countryside are full of twists and turns and are often barely wide enough for two cars to pass. *Roundabouts* are traffic junctions where several roads meet at one traffic circle. On a roundabout, the cars to your right (that is, already on the roundabout) always have the right of way.

Drive Times

Traffic can add considerably to travel times, but as a rule of thumb, count on: Dublin to Belfast, two and a half hours; Dublin to Cork, four and a half hours; Dublin to Galway, three hours; Dublin to Limerick, two hours.

Road Emergencies

If you have an accident, you must report it to the Gardaí (police) before leaving the scene. You can contact the Gardaí from any telephone by dialing 999 (the Irish equivalent of 911), which will put you in touch with the fire service, ambulance, and coastal rescue as well.

Rules of the Road

Here's some general information you'll need to know when driving in Ireland:

- In the Republic, distances and speed limits are shown in kilometers and kilometers per hour; in Northern Ireland, they are given in miles. If you need to translate from the metric system, a kilometer is 0.62 miles, and a mile is 1.62 kilometers. Speed limits are usually 30 miles per hour (48 kilometers per hour) in towns, 40 mph (65 kph) on some town roads where posted, 60 mph (97 kph) on most single carriageways, and 70 mph (113 kph) on dual carriageways and motorways.

ALSO KEEP THESE RULES IN MIND:

- Always drive on the left side of the road.
- Road signs are usually the standard international signs.
- Using seat belts, front and back, is required by law. If you have children, make sure that the correct seat belts or car seats are available before you rent a vehicle.
- Children under the age of 12 may not sit in the front seat.
- At roundabouts (traffic circles), give way to traffic coming from the right.
- You can pass other vehicles only on the right.
- Parking in the center of most big towns is difficult and expensive. Make sure you read all posted restrictions, or park in a lot. Be sure to carry a lot of change.
- You must stop for pedestrians in striped (zebra) crossings. Pedestrians have the right of way.
- Don't drink if you are driving. Drivers with blood-alcohol levels higher than .08% are subject to imprisonment. Police carry Breathalyzers.
- It's illegal to talk on a cell phone while driving.

You are also required to notify the rental-car agency of an accident.

Buying Gasoline

Gasoline is called *petrol*. Petrol stations are self-service, and major credit cards are usually accepted; prices rise and fall (they mostly rise these days). Petrol is purchased by the liter (3.78 liters equals 1 U.S. gallon). Expect to pay a little more than a euro or more per liter, or at least €5 (£3.50 in the North) per gallon, for unleaded petrol.

TRAVELING BY BUS AND COACH

THE PRIMARY LONG-DISTANCE COACH company in the Republic is **Bus Éireann** (☎ 091-562000; **www.buseireann.ie**). The company serves all regions, with some service to just about every town and village, though service to many smaller places is infrequent at best.

Driving on the Left

With a little practice and common sense, you will soon become used to driving on the left side of the road. After all, the Irish do it every day. Here are a few tips to make the adjustment safer and easier:

- If you're uncomfortable driving a car with a manual transmission (with which most cars in Ireland are equipped), pay the extra for an automatic. You'll have enough on your mind adjusting to driving on the left.

- Make sure you are well rested when you get behind the wheel for the first time, as you'll need to keep your wits about you. Rather than picking up a car after flying all night, consider getting a good night's sleep and overcoming jet lag first.

- Once you pick up the car, practice. Even before turning on the ignition, get used to the gearshift—remember, you'll be using your left hand to shift gears, and you're probably used to shifting with your right hand, if you're used to shifting at all. Take a practice spin around the car park (parking lot), and don't set out until you feel comfortable.

- Be extremely cautious making turns. It's easy to forget that everything here is reversed: oncoming traffic will be coming from your right. Chances are, out of habit you will look left for oncoming traffic, as you're used to doing at home.

- When you're driving on a two-lane road, make sure the center line is on your right. This way, you'll know you're on the correct side of the road.

Because the Irish bus system is so much more extensive than the train system, you may find yourself traveling by coach more in Ireland than you would in other European countries. Or you may travel by train to a major city—from Dublin to Cork or Galway, for instance—and continue by coach from there. The Bus Éireann Web site provides detailed information on schedules and prices. Also included is information on multiday passes, which provide unlimited travel for a certain number of days—8 days of travel within 15 days for €228, for example. **Ulsterbus** (☎ 028-9033-3000; **www.translink.co.uk**) operates the bus network in Northern Ireland.

Rail and Bus Passes

Several money-saving passes are available, but remember: no pass is going to save you money if you don't use it. Before purchasing any kind of travel pass, think about how much moving around you are going to do, and then do some research to determine how much you will be spending on transportation if you buy individual tickets (the Web sites we list for train and bus travel make it easy to do this).

- **BritRail Pass + Ireland** If you're planning on traveling through the United Kingdom and Ireland, this might be just the ticket—it provides unlimited travel in Britain, Northern Ireland, and the Republic of Ireland, plus a round-trip ferry crossing. For more information, contact BritRail, ☎ 800-BRITRAIL; **www.britrail.net.**

- **Emerald Card** and **Irish Explorer** These passes combine travel on rail and bus services; the Emerald Card covers travel in the Republic and Northern Ireland, while Irish Explorer is good for travel only in the Republic. For more information, contact Bus Éireann, ☎ 091-562000; **www.buseireann.ie.**

- **Eurail Pass** This come in many varieties, including passes good all over Europe, including the Republic of Ireland, and a pass good only for travel within the Republic. Note that Eurail Passes are not good for travel in Northern Ireland or anywhere else in the United Kingdom, and the passes must be purchased before you leave home. For more information, contact RailEurope, ☎ 877-257-2887; **www.raileurope.com.**

- **Irish Rover** Good for train travel within both the Republic and Northern Ireland. For more information, contact Iarnród Éireann (Irish Rail), ☎ 1850-366222 or 01-836-6222; **www.irishrail.ie.**

TRAVELING BY AIR

IN ADDITION TO THE SIZABLE AIRPORTS in Dublin, Shannon, Cork, and Belfast, some other Irish airports include **Derry Airport** (**www.cityofderryairport.com**), **Donegal Regional Airport** (**www.donegal airport.ie**), **Galway Airport** (**www.galwayairport.com**), **Kerry Airport** (**www.kerryairport.ie**), **Knock Airport** (**www.knockairport.com**), **Sligo Regional Airport** (**www.sligoairport.com**), and **Waterford Regional Airport** (**www.flywaterford.com**). **Aer Lingus** (☎ 01-705-3333; **www.aer lingus.com**) and **Aer Arann** (☎ 1890-462726; **www.aerarann.ie**) service most of these. Keep in mind, though, that Ireland is a relatively small country and distances between cities aren't great, so you can often get to your destination as quickly and easily by land as by air.

TOURS *and* EXPLORING

SO MUCH TO SEE AND DO IN IRELAND . . . how are you going to fit it all in? You're not. But we're here to help. The secret of successful sightseeing is to be selective. When there's so much to see, it's important to choose wisely where you will spend your sightseeing hours (and your euros and pounds, with admission prices to major attractions in Ireland being pretty expensive).

In this guide, we tell you about the various tours available in a city, town, or region that we think will best help you get a sense of a place. Then we profile what we consider to be the major attractions. We rate each attraction to tell you how appealing we think it is to tourists of all ages. Along with a description that includes advice on what not to miss at an attraction and how best to enjoy it, we also provide all the practical information you need, such as addresses, admission prices, opening hours, and so on. From the information presented you should be able to decide whether or not the attraction is something that interests you or not (some people love visiting Irish country houses; others couldn't care less).

The attraction profiles are found in the Exploring section of each featured city, town, or region. In these sections we also often give you a brief walking tour and some idea of how to get to know a place; plus, we mention secondary sights that are maybe worth a visit or just a glance. If an attraction is not profiled, it's not a major sight. In the Tours sections we provide details on our favorite tours of the cities, towns, and regions we cover.

TOURING ON YOUR OWN OR WITH AN ESCORTED TOUR

THIS IS PURELY A MATTER of individual preference. If you choose not to rent a car, you'll find it difficult to tour the countryside and visit remote sights on your own. Public transportation to many remote parts of Ireland is often infrequent, and some major attractions are miles from the nearest train station or bus stop.

Escorted tours do all the logistical work for you: a coach or minivan takes you to the attraction, and someone explains it all to you. On page 40 we provide the names of some well-regarded companies that offer escorted tours around Ireland. You can find specific itineraries and other details by visiting their Web sites.

WALKING TOURS

A WALKING TOUR IS ONE of the most enjoyable ways to see a city and learn more about its history. The historic hearts of most Irish cities are compact and full of architectural and historical treasures that add to their charm, character, and fascination. Part of the fun is simply listening to the tour guide. The Irish love to show off their history and usually do so with intelligence, wit, and enthusiasm.

unofficial **TIP**
Most tourist-information offices in Ireland provide information on local walking tours, so take advantage of them.

BUS TOURS

ANOTHER GOOD WAY to introduce yourself to a place is by taking a guided bus tour. All major tourist towns and cities offer bus tours, often by a company called **City Sightseeing** (☎ 01-872-9010 or **www .city-sightseeing.com;** this company recently acquired **Guide Friday,** which you may have used on previous trips to Ireland). These tours usually make a circuit of all the major sights in about an hour, but the real advantage of them is the "hop on, hop off" service that allows you to get off, visit an attraction, and board another bus. The kind and quality of commentary varies from company to company and is sometimes canned—opt for live commentary if you can.

Bus Éireann (☎ 091-562000; **www.buseireann.ie**) also offers city tours, as well as day tours to nearby sights. Some itineraries include Dublin to Glendalough, Powerscourt Gardens, and Wicklow; Newgrange, the Boyne Valley, and Kilkenny City; Galway to Connemara and the Burren and Cliffs of Moher; and Sligo to Donegal.

Throughout this book, we list what we consider to be the best tours in the Exploring section of each featured city, town, or region.

SIGHTSEEING SAVINGS

THE HERITAGE CARD is good for entry at some 100 properties in the Republic that are maintained by the Irish Office of Public Works. Whether or not the pass will save you money depends on how much touring you plan to do, of course, but chances are it will. Just as a sample of possibilities, **Kilmainham Gaol, Kilkenny Castle,** the **Blasket Centre, Muckross House,** and **Glenveagh Castle** are among our choices for must-see sights in Ireland, and admission to all is included with the card. The cost is €21 adults, €16 seniors, €8 children and students, and €55 families of up to two adults and four children. You can buy the pass at participating sights; by mail from Heritage Card Officer, Visitor Services, Office of Public Works, Unit 20, Lakeside Retail Park, Clairmorris, County Mayo, Ireland; by calling ☎ 01-647-6592; or online at **www.heritageireland.com,** where you'll also find more information about the card.

EXPLORING IRELAND *on* FOUR WHEELS, TWO WHEELS, *and* TWO FEET

IRELAND IS BEST ENJOYED AT A SLOW PACE—on a country road in a car or, for a real taste of the countryside, on one of the many hiking paths and biking routes that crisscross the country. In addition to the resources on the following pages, see the Walks and Drives and Exploring sections included with our coverage of each region.

ESSENTIAL GEAR

HOWEVER YOU PLAN on getting around Ireland, equip yourself with a good map and, especially if you're walking, a compass. Even the most traveled routes are often poorly and confusingly marked, and walking paths often cross private lands on which signs are few and far between. You'll find a good selection of detailed maps ideal for overland walks and off-the-beaten path drives at **EastWest Mapping,** an online retailer specializing in maps of Ireland, at **homepage .tinet.ie/~eastwest;** EastWest also lists walking routes and provides links to walking resources. **Ordnance Survey Ireland (OSI)** and the **Ordnance Survey of Northern Ireland (OSNI)** compile small- and large-scale maps, 1:50,000 and 1:25,000, that usually indicate walking routes. You can find them at better bookshops throughout Ireland, with especially good selections at the **National Map Centre** (34 Angier Street, Dublin 2; ☎ 01-476-0487; **www.irishmaps.ie**) and the **OSNI** shop (Colby House, Stranmills Road, Belfast BT9 5B1; ☎ 028-9025-5768; **www.osni.gov.uk**).

WALKING AND BIKING IN IRELAND

IRELAND IS A COUNTRY WELL GEARED to hiking and biking, and the Irish are increasingly enthusiastic about both. Hundreds of paths and many resources are available to hikers and bikers. Below and in the regional coverage in this guide you'll find recommendations for routes of particular beauty and interest, but for every one we list there are dozens of others. Check with the tourist office in any region you visit for information on local routes. In addition, browse through the resources of the following organizations.

For Walkers

- **Go Walking Ireland** (**www.gowalkingireland.com**) lists recommended walks and also provides information on camping and other outdoor activities.

- **Hill-Walking in Ireland** (**www.simonstewart.ie**), an excellent Web resource for walks throughout Ireland, provides links to other hiking and climbing organizations.

- The **Irish Ramblers Club** (**www.theramblers.ie**) and **Wayfarers Association** (**www.wayfarerassociation.org**) are Dublin-based clubs that organize walks in the surrounding countryside. Both groups also provide information on walks throughout the country.

- The **Irish Tourist Board** (**www.discoverireland.com**) offers a decent overview of opportunities in the Republic in *Walking Ireland.* The **Northern Irish Tourist Board** (**www.discovernorthernireland.com**) publishes a similar booklet, *An Information Guide to Walking.* Contents are published online as well as in the booklets.

- The **Mountaineering Council of Ireland** (☎ 01-450-7376; **www.mountaineering.ie**) is an activist organization that promotes the interests of walkers in Ireland. The Web site provides information on paths throughout Ireland, with links to hiking associations and other resources.

- **Walking Ireland** (**www.walkingireland.com**), the Web presence of the Walking Centre in Clifden, County Galway, provides detailed information on walks throughout Ireland, with an emphasis on walks in and around Connemara.

- *Walking World Ireland* is a bimonthly magazine that covers all the ins and outs for enthusiasts, with excellent information on routes and events; look for it in bookshops, on newsstands, and at outdoor-equipment shops.

For Cyclists

- Cyclists who don't want to lug their bikes and gear across the Atlantic can rent from outfits that include **Eurotrek Raleigh** (Longmile Road, Dublin 12; ☎ 01-465-9659; **www.raleigh.ie**) and **Rent-A-Bike Ireland** (1 Patrick Street, Limerick, County Limerick; ☎ 061-416983; **www.irelandrentalbike.com**). Both work with a network of dealers who rent bikes throughout Ireland, so you can pick up your bike at one location and drop it off at another; service is readily available. Expect to pay about €20 per day for a standard rental.
- The **Irish Tourist Board** offers a limited amount of information on cycling in the Republic, with a listing of routes; you can browse the offerings at **www.discoverireland.com.**
- The **Northern Ireland Tourist Board** publishes *Cycling in Northern Ireland,* a fairly comprehensive booklet on biking routes for short- and long-distance rides in Northern Ireland, as well as other resources; contact the office for a copy (see page 41), or find the same information at **www.discovernorthernireland.com.**

WALKING AND BIKING HOLIDAYS

MOST WALKING AND BIKING ROUTES in Ireland are well traveled by groups organized by tour companies specializing in hiking and biking holidays. These outfits can provide an excellent introduction to exploring the country in these ways, and they'll take care of logistics such as transportation to and from routes and accommodations. The outfits offer guided tours, on which one or two guides will accompany you and usually offer plentiful advice and good company, as well as self-guided tours, in which an organization maps out a route and takes care of details such as daily baggage transfer to and from accommodations. The following are based in Ireland, so you can count on the staff knowing the terrain well:

- **Go Ireland (www.goactivities.com;** ☎ 066-976-2094) organizes hiking and biking expeditions throughout Ireland.
- **Irish Cycling Safaris (www.cyclingsafaris.com;** ☎ 01-260-0749) offers both hiking and biking expeditions, with an emphasis on the Southwest.
- **Irish Ways Walking Holidays (www.irishways.com;** ☎ 055-27479) provides guided tours and independent trips through most regions of Ireland, with an emphasis on scenic locales such as Connemara, the Antrim Coast, and the Wicklow Mountains.

WALKING FESTIVALS

LEAVE IT TO THE IRISH to turn a walk into a big social event. You'll encounter these festivals throughout the country in all but the dreariest winter months. Lasting one to several days, they usually combine walks through appealing countryside with refreshment, traditional-music sessions, often meals, and always a lot of conversation. Check with local tourist offices for news of upcoming festivals, or contact the **Irish Tourist Board** (**www.discoverireland.com**) or the **Northern Ireland Tourist Board** (**www.discovernorthernireland.com**).

GREAT WALKS

IN THE EXPLORING SECTIONS of this guide, you'll find detailed information on walks in each region of Ireland that are particularly scenic and enjoyable. You can travel many of these routes, or at least parts of them, on a bicycle. A sampling of some of the best routes in Ireland include:

BEARA WAY This 200-kilometer (120-mile) route circumnavigates the Beara Peninsula, one of Ireland's most beautiful coastal spots. Even a short walk along the Beara Way, such as the section around Eyeries Point, will introduce you to stunning views of the coasts and mountains of the Southwest. See page 249.

CAUSEWAY COAST WAY You can walk the northern coast from Portstewart to Ballycastle on this well-maintained path. The most spectacular scenery is around Giants Causeway, a remarkable swath of stone columns stretching into the sea. See page 386.

CROAGH PATRICK A walk up this cone-shaped mountain at the northern edge of Connemara is rewarding not only for the views from the top but also for the human spectacle—pilgrims often make the climb barefoot to pay homage to St. Patrick, who is said to have spent 40 days atop the peak. See page 313.

DINGLE WAY This 150-kilometer (90-mile) route around the Dingle Peninsula affords spectacular scenery at every bend in the path. You need only walk along the section at Slea Head to get a taste of the coastal scenery, or take a much more strenuous walk up Brandon Peak to enjoy wild mountainous terrain. See page 249.

GLENARIFF FOREST PARK Well-maintained trails in this park in the Glens of Antrim—nine forested valleys near the Antrim Coast—follow the Inver and Glenariff rivers. See page 386.

GLENVEAGH NATIONAL PARK You can enjoy the beauty of this remote and spectacularly beautiful park on even a short walk, such as one along the Derrylahan Nature Trail. A more ambitious climb takes you through the moors and bogs on the flanks of Errigal Mountain at the edge of the park. See pages 358 and 375.

HOWTH PENINSULA A walk around the stunning headland would be remarkable, and popular, even if the peninsula and town of the same name weren't so easily accessible from Dublin, via DART. Seabirds, seals, and stunning views of the sea and mountains add to the illusion of remoteness, and the seaside town and fishing port of Howth is a pleasant place to spend time before or after a walk. See page 116.

MUCKROSS Walking the shores of Muckross Lake, in the heart of Killarney National Park, introduces you to the woods, mountain views, streams, and wildlife that are among the delights of one of Ireland's most beautiful national parks. See page 250.

SLIEVE LEAGUE The highest sea cliffs in Europe provide a highly dramatic setting for an unforgettable coastal walk, all the more so when the route comes to landmarks such as One Man's Pass, a narrow passage with steep drops on either side. The biggest thrill, though, is the spectacle of the near-vertical cliff faces that rise some 600 meters (2,000 feet) out of the raging surf. See pages 358 and 371.

THE WICKLOW WAY This well-traveled route traverses forested mountain slopes, mountain valleys, and bogs for some 130 kilometers (78 miles) between the southern suburbs of Dublin and County Wexford. An especially popular and scenic portion of the route leads you past the monastic ruins at Glendalough, along the shores of the two lakes that surround it, and into the surrounding mountains. See page 117.

GREAT DRIVES

SET OUT IN ALMOST ANY DIRECTION anywhere in Ireland, and you're likely to drive through scenery that will awe you, or at least catch your interest. You'll find drives that are particularly scenic in the Walks and Drives and Exploring sections in our regional coverage throughout this guide. Here are some routes and driving destinations that are especially worth seeking out:

ACHILL ISLAND Ireland's largest island is also one of its most accessible, reached by a bridge near the town of Westport. Once on the island, follow the Atlantic Drive to golden beaches, craggy sea cliffs, and view-filled summits. See pages 344 and 345.

THE BEARA PENINSULA Southwestern Ireland meets the sea in a string of long peninsulas on which mountains drop down to the water. The Beara is relatively unspoiled and, with such spots as moor-clad Healy Pass, one of the most scenic. See page 245.

BLACKWATER VALLEY AND ROCK OF CASHEL You can visit one of Ireland's most spectacular religious monuments on a drive filled with lovely river views in the Blackwater Valley and the highland scenery of the Knockmealdown Mountains. See page 195.

THE CAUSEWAY COAST This spectacular drive along the narrow, winding Antrim Coast Road is filled with scenery and points of interest: green mountainsides, stone coastal villages, the natural wonder of Giants Causeway, and man-made attractions such as medieval Dunluce Castle and the revered Bushmills Distillery are among the sights awaiting you. See page 387.

THE DINGLE PENINSULA The cliff-top drive west from Dingle Town affords more than stunning sea views—the mysterious Blasket

Islands loom just offshore, and the coast is littered with Iron Age and early-Christian remains. See page 270.

GLENVEAGH NATIONAL PARK AND SURROUNDINGS Some of Ireland's wildest scenery is in and around Glenveagh National Park, where some surprisingly sophisticated pleasures, such as the art collection at Glebe House, await you as well. See pages 360 and 375.

LAKES OF CONNEMARA Lough Corrib and Lough Mask, two of the largest lakes in Ireland, are surrounded by the stark moors and mountains of Connemara. You'll find civilization in Cong and other appealing villages. See page 315.

THE NORTHERN HEADLANDS The craggy coast of Northwest Ireland is a string of long bays and peninsulas. You can follow these until you've had your fill of sea views. Mountain slopes, green valleys, and heather-surrounded lakes also contribute to the scenery. See page 359.

WICKLOW MOUNTAINS A drive through these mountains just south of Dublin takes you through bogs, into valleys glittering with lakes and littered with the ruins of the medieval abbey at Glendalough, and to the highest village in Ireland, Roundwood. See page 119.

YEATS COUNTRY The poet W. B. Yeats and his brother, the painter Jack Yeats, took inspiration from the mountain, lake, and coastal scenery around Sligo Town. You can enjoy this scenery on a drive around Lough Gill and out to Rosses Point.

THE NATIONAL PARKS

THE REPUBLIC'S SIX NATIONAL PARKS encompass some of Ireland's most beautiful scenery and provide easy access to wilderness regions for hikers and other outdoor enthusiasts. All have visitor centers that offer guided nature tours and provide a wealth of information on activities. For information on these parks, visit the Web site of the National Parks and Wildlife Service, **www.npws.ie.**

THE BURREN NATIONAL PARK The Burren covers some 1,600 hectares (4,000 acres) of Ireland's most uninhabitable land, a swath of limestone in western County Clare—"a savage land, yielding neither water enough to drown a man, nor tree to hang him, nor soil enough to bury," as Oliver Cromwell put it. Even so, the Burren becomes a sea of color in spring and summer, as plants blown from the Arctic and the Mediterranean flower in profusion from cracks in the limestone.

CONNEMARA NATIONAL PARK Connemara preserves an enchanting landscape of bogs, heather-covered moors, and the slopes of the Twelve Bens Mountains in County Galway. On nature trails and guided walks, visitors encounter the birds, Connemara ponies, and other diverse creatures that add to the charm of this beautiful place.

GLENVEAGH NATIONAL PARK In a remote part of County Donegal, Glenveagh encompasses 10,000 hectares (24,000 acres) of lakes and streams glittering among heaths and woodlands that climb the slopes of the Derryveagh Mountains, presenting some of the most beautiful and dramatic landscapes in Ireland. At the heart of the park is one of Ireland's most appealing historic homes, Glenveagh Castle.

KILLARNEY NATIONAL PARK One of many beautiful spots in County Kerry, Killarney has long and justifiably been admired for its spectacular panoramas of mountains (MacGillycuddy's Reeks, Ireland's tallest peaks, are here), lakes, and forests, all of which can be enjoyed on well-marked walking trails.

BALLYCROY NATIONAL PARK In County Mayo, Ballycroy rises and falls from the Atlantic shorelines up the slopes of the Nephin Beg Mountains. Many trails traverse an eerie and unique landscape of saltwater bogs.

WICKLOW MOUNTAINS NATIONAL PARK Just south of Dublin in County Wicklow, this park provides a quick retreat from city life, with moors and forest-clad mountains. The Wicklow Way, a 132-kilometer-long (80-mile-long) walking path, runs through the park, traversing valleys, skirting lakes, climbing mountains, and passing the ruins of the medieval Glendalough monastery.

OTHER OUTDOOR PURSUITS

Bird-watching

Ireland provides a convenient stopover for migrating birds, with many excellent venues for bird-watching throughout the year. You can keep up with the best places to see what birds when by visiting the Web sites of major Irish birding groups. In the Republic, these are **Irish Birding** (**www.irishbirding.com**) and **Birdwatch Ireland** (**www .birdwatchireland.ie**), and in the North, **The Royal Society for the Protection of Birds** (**www.rspb.org.uk/nireland**) and **Birdwatch Northern Ireland** (**www.birdwatch-ni.co.uk**).

Fishing

Irish seas and freshwater lakes and streams provide some of Europe's finest angling. In the Republic, a license is required only for salmon and sea-trout fishing and costs €17 a day and €21 for three days; a rod license, required for all fishing in Northern Ireland, begins at €5 a day, and in addition you will require a permit, beginning at €5 for three days. You can usually buy the necessary licenses from angling outfitters. In the Republic, contact the **Central Fisheries Board** (Balnagowan House, Mobhi Boreen, Glasnevin, Dublin 9; ☎ 01-884-2600; **www.cfb.ie**) and the **Irish Tourist Board** (**www.discoverireland.com**), which publishes a booklet, *The Angler's Guide*. In Northern Ireland, contact the **Department of Culture, Arts, and Leisure** (Interpoint Centre, York Street, Belfast BT4 3PW; ☎ 028-9052-3121) and the **Northern Ireland Tourist Board** (**www.discovernorthernireland.com**), which publishes *An Information Guide to Game Fishing.* These booklets are available at most tourist offices, which can also usually provide a list of local outfitters, guides, deep-sea-fishing excursion operators, and other contacts.

Golf

It's only fitting that in this country where the lush landscapes often resemble a golf green, golfing is a major activity and attraction. In the Exercise and Recreation sections throughout this guide, you will find information on some of Ireland's top courses. You'll also find a wealth of information on golf courses in Ireland at the Web sites of the **Irish Tourist Board** (**www.discoverireland.com**) and the **Northern Ireland Tourist Board** (**www.discovernorthernireland.com**). Companies that offer golf packages, including play on some of Ireland's finest courses, accommodations, and ground transportation from about $2,500 a week, include **Specialty Ireland** (☎ 053-39962; **www.specialtyireland.com**) and **Atlanticgolf** (in the United States, ☎ 800-542-6224 or 203-363-1003).

You'll find that even the finest and most exclusive courses are open to the public at least some days of the week, and that greens fees are relatively reasonable, anywhere from about €50 to €100 for 18 holes at the top courses, depending on the season, the day of the week, and the section of the course you choose to play.

Ireland's top courses include:

ADARE MANOR GOLF COURSE Sprawling across the grounds of the former estate of the Earls of Dunraven, Adare Manor is now one of Ireland's finest manor-house hotels. As if that provenance isn't romantic enough, the Robert Trent Jones course encompasses the ruins of a medieval castle and monastery. Adare, County Limerick; ☎ 061-395-044; **www.adaremanorgolfclub.ie.** 18 holes.

BALLYBUNION GOLF CLUB On the Atlantic at the mouth of the River Shannon, Ballybunion is one of the most beautiful and highly regarded courses in the world, with a section designed by Robert Trent Jones. Sandhill Road, Ballybunion, County Kerry; ☎ 068-27611. 36 holes, open to public only on weekdays.

THE K CLUB Designed by Arnold Palmer, this challenging and beautiful course is on the banks of the River Liffey west of Dublin. Kildare Country Club, Straffan, County Kildare; ☎ 01-627-333; **www.kclub.ie.** 18 holes.

OLD HEAD Old Head occupies, somewhat controversially, a spectacular peninsula in County Cork and is one of the world's most scenic courses. Kinsale, County Cork; ☎ 021-778-444; **www.oldheadgolflinks.com.** 18 holes.

PORTMARNOCK GOLF CLUB This is a legendary course on the sea, only 13 kilometers (8 miles) from the center of Dublin. Portmarnock,

County Dublin; ☎ 01-846-2968; **www.portmarnockgolfclub.ie.** 27 holes.

ROYAL COUNTY DOWN This is said to be one of the toughest and most beautiful courses in the world. Golf Links Road, Newcastle, BT33 0AN, County Down, Northern Ireland; ☎ 028-4372-2419; **www.royal countydown.ie.** 36 holes.

ROYAL PORTRUSH Royal Portrush is a favorite of many Irish golfers and host to the British Open. Dunluce Road, Portrush, BT56 8JQ, County Antrim, Northern Ireland; ☎ 028-7082-2311; **www.royalport rushgolfclub.com.** 36 holes.

Horseback Riding

Horse riding, as the Irish call it, is quite popular, and many stables rent to the public for rides along beaches and through other beautiful terrain. The **Irish Tourist Board** (**www.discoverireland.com**) and the **Northern Ireland Tourist Board** (**www.discovernorthernireland.com**) provide information on horseback riding, although you can more easily find local stables through the **Association of Irish Riding Establishments** (☎ 045-431-584), which lists accredited riding facilities throughout the country. For rides in particularly scenic terrain, contact **Horseriding Ireland** (**www.horseridingireland.com**), a network of riding facilities in Connemara, Killarney, Sligo, and Donegal.

Sailing and Kayaking

Ireland's many inlets lend themselves to sea kayaking, and the bays that etch the coast are ideal for sailing. You'll find marinas and leisure ports up and down the coasts, from Malahide and Howth around Dublin to Kinsale, Bantry, Kenmare, Westport, and Sligo on the West Coast. Kayak and sailboat instruction and rentals are available in most ports, and you can get detailed listings, with links to many clubs around the country, from the **Irish Canoe Union** (**www .irishcanoeunion.com**) and the **Irish Sailing Association** (3 Park Road, Dún Laoghaire, County Dublin; ☎ 01-280-0239; **www.sailing.ie**).

GREAT ITINERARIES

DRIVING IN IRELAND is not without its perils (see "Traveling by Car," page 58), but it's nonetheless the best way, and often the only way, to explore the country. Public transportation will get you to the major cities, but venturing beyond often leaves you at the whim of infrequent bus service. If you decide to get behind the wheel, here are some routes to follow; see also the Walks and Drives and Exploring sections of each part of this guide for detailed drives and hikes. Should you wish to stick to public transportation, focus on the most vibrant of Ireland's cities—Cork, Galway, Sligo, Derry, and Belfast—and from them piece together excursions on local buses (not always easy to do) or take organized day trips. And however you travel round Ireland, enjoy—the pleasures that await you are almost boundless.

ITINERARY I

Into the South

You can get a nice introduction to rural Ireland without venturing too far from Dublin. In fact, this route begins with a trip through the mountains that begin right at the city's outskirts.

DAY 1 Head south from Dublin, stopping at **Powerscourt,** an 18th-century house with elaborate gardens, then at **Glendalough,** a medieval abbey set deep in the Wicklow Mountains. From there it's only about a two-hour drive to **Kilkenny,** where you'll settle in for two nights.

DAY 2 It's a pleasure to explore Ireland's finest medieval city, with its mighty riverside castle, on foot. In the afternoon, take a short drive south to **Jerpoint Abbey,** where the remains of a 12th-century monastery are set in a remote valley. Return to Kilkenny in time for a meal at one of the city's excellent restaurants and a traditional-music session in a pub.

DAY 3 A full day of driving takes you east to the **Rock of Cashel,** a magnificent fortress and church complex set atop a rock overlooking the flat plains of Tipperary. From here, continue through the town of **Cahir** and through the **Vee Gap,** a scenic pass over the Knockmealdown Mountains. This brings you to **Lismore,** dominated by a huge castle that is home to the Duke of Devonshire. Follow the winding waterside route along the Blackwater River to the busy port of **Youghal,** then along N25 to **Midleton;** make one of the country hotels around this busy market town your base for two nights.

DAY 4 You won't need to venture too far for a day of memorable sightseeing. Stops include **Fota Island,** for its beautiful classical-style house and adjoining wildlife park. A very short drive from there south around the estuaries of Cork Harbour brings you to **Cobh,** where *Cobh, the Queenstown Story* celebrates this port's colorful maritime history, including its role as the point of embarkation for millions of emigrants.

DAY 5 A drive of just half an hour east from Midleton brings you to **Cork.** Stash the car, settle into a hotel for a two-night stay, and spend the rest of the day exploring this colorful and attractive city on foot. Enjoy an evening meal at one of the many restaurants that have earned the city a reputation as a culinary capital, and attend a concert or other event on the city's lively cultural roster.

DAY 6 Easy excursions can take you to nearby sights such as **Blarney Castle,** home of the famously kissable stone, and, more worthwhile, to **Kinsale,** a pleasant port town with seaside walks and a mighty fort.

itinerary 1: into the south of ireland

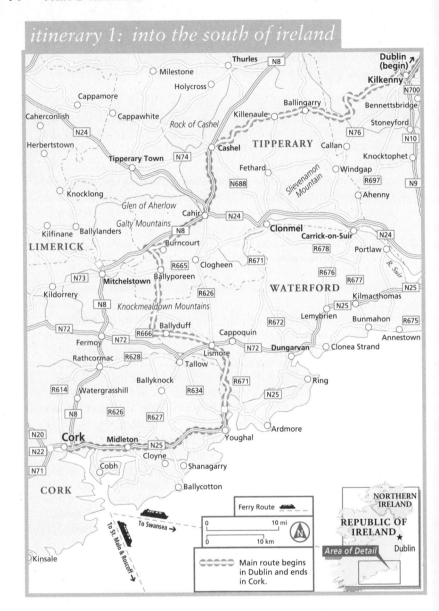

DAY 7 You can return to Dublin speedily on any number of routes. One option is to begin the trip on N25 north to **Waterford,** where you can visit the famous crystal factory and shop.

ITINERARY 2
Into the Southwest

In the Southwest, a bounty of magnificent scenery is compressed into a relatively small area. You can either add this itinerary to the one above or simply take the N8 south from Dublin to Cork, a trip of less than four hours, and begin a tour there.

DAY 1 After settling into a hotel in **Cork,** walk around this delightful city. A stroll through the **English Market** will whet your appetite for a meal at one of the city's many fine restaurants.

DAY 2 Spend the day exploring Cork and your pick of the nearby sights to the east—the **Old Midleton Distillery, Fota House and Wildlife Park,** and **Cobh.**

DAY 3 It's time to move on, but not far, to the pleasant port of **Kinsale.** En route, stop at **Blarney Castle.** You'll have the rest of the day and evening to explore Kinsale. Weather permitting, follow the **Scilly Walk** along the harbor to the **Bulman,** an atmospheric seaside pub warmed by fires, and to **Charles Fort.**

DAY 4 Head east to **Bantry,** paying a visit to one of Ireland's finest historic homes, **Bantry House.** From there, follow the lovely drive around Bantry Bay to **Glengarriff.** You have a choice here: you can either make a circuit of the unspoiled **Beara Peninsula** for some stunning seascapes or cross the peninsula over **Healy Pass** for a panorama of moors and heather-covered mountains—hands-down one of the most gorgeous drives in Ireland. Just beyond is **Kenmare,** where you'll find a nice selection of appealing guesthouses.

DAY 5 You'll want to spend a little time just soaking in the pleasant small-town atmosphere of Kenmare. If you're up for a longish drive, make the circuit of the **Iveragh Peninsula,** better known as the **Ring of Kerry.** But if you didn't explore the Beara Peninsula the day before, do that instead—the scenery is just as grand or even grander, and the roads are much less traveled.

DAY 6 Follow the scenic route, the so-called "tunnel road," into **Killarney National Park,** stopping at **Ladies View** for a panorama of lakes and mountains and sights such as **Muckross House** and **Ross Castle.** At Killarney, head west into the **Gap of Dunloe,** a rocky pass through the tall mountains known as **MacGillycuddy's Reeks.** This scenery-filled day ends with a drive past the beaches on the south side of the Dingle Peninsula to **Dingle Town.**

DAY 7 Spend the day exploring the **Dingle Peninsula,** the westernmost tip of Ireland. Sights include the **Blasket Centre,** celebrating the life of the inhabitants of the remote Blasket Islands, and **Gallus Oratory,** a remarkably well-preserved church from the early days of Christianity. Best of all are the views of the rugged scenery and the sea from **Slea Head,** just to the west of Dingle Town.

itinerary 2: into the southwest of ireland

Main route
Alternate route

CLARE Shannon Airport ✈
To Adare (end) →

River Shannon Kilrush Tarbert Ferryport
R551 Tarbert
ATLANTIC OCEAN Ballybunion R552
Mouth of the Shannon LIMERICK
Kerry Head Listowel
Ballyheige N69
Ballyheige Bay R551 N21
Tralee Bay Fenit Spa **Tralee** KERRY
Mt. Brandon Blennerville Connor Pass Kanturk
Ballyferriter DINGLE PENINSULA Camp Slieve Mish Mountains N23 ✈ **Farranfore Airport**
Dunquin Ventry Annascaul Castlemaine
Dingle Inch R561 Farranfore N22 R579
R559 Killorglin R563
Slea Head *Dingle Bay* R562 **Killarney**
Great Blasket Island Glenbeigh *Caragh Lough* Killarney National Park N72 *Blackwater River*
Valentia Island **Gap of Dunloe** *Lough Leane* Muckross House Millstreet
Ring of Kerry Carrauntoohil ▲ **KERRY** *Lough Guitane* N22
N70 IVERAGH PENINSULA Ladies' View R569 Macroom
Cahirciveen N71 Kilgarvan
R565 N567 MacGillycuddy's Reeks R584 Lee River N22
R566 *Lough Currane* Sneem *Ring of Kerry* **Kenmare**
Ballinskelligs Waterville Parknasilla *Shehy Mountain*
Skellig Rock Caherdaniel *Kenmare River* N571 R573 CORK *Bandon River*
Ballinskelligs Bay N571 *Caha Mountains* Glengarriff To Cork (begin) →
Allihies *Beara Peninsula* *Whiddy Island* **Bantry**
R575 R572 *Bere Island* Durrus R600 **Clonakilty**
Sheep's Head Peninsula R591 **Skibbereen** Rosscarbery
Dunmanus Bay Schull R592 Ballydehob Castletownshend
Crookhaven Baltimore
Toormore Bay *Roaringwater Bay* Cape Clear Island Sherkin Island

NORTHERN IRELAND
Dublin ★
REPUBLIC OF IRELAND
COUNTY KERRY

0 ___ 10 mi
0 ___ 10 km

DAY 8 Cross the spine of the Dingle Peninsula on **Connor Pass,** a view-a-minute mountain route that drops down to **Tralee.** From here, head north to **Glin** on the banks of the River Shannon, and follow the river east toward **Adare,** one of the prettiest villages in Ireland.

DAY 9 From Adare, head east back to Dublin, with a stop in **Limerick,** or continue north into the West, following Itinerary 3.

ITINERARY 3
Into the West

This route begins near Shannon Airport, the point of arrival for many visitors to Ireland. If you are coming from Dublin, follow Route N7 across Ireland to Limerick, a trip of about three hours—but add a couple of hours to the schedule and take the N8 so you can include a stop at the Rock of Cashel.

DAY 1 Ennis and **Adare,** just north and south of Limerick, respectively, are good bases from which to explore the surrounding region. Both are appealing low-key towns in which you'll enjoy spending time, and from both you can easily visit the city of Limerick and sights such as **Bunratty Castle.**

DAY 2 An easy drive brings you to the coast and the **Cliffs of Moher,** which are among Ireland's great natural wonders. These cliffs lie at the edge of one of the country's strangest landscapes: the **Burren,** a stark expanse of limestone riddled with prehistoric remains. Seaside **Doolin** is a pleasant stopover, all the more so because this small and otherwise unremarkable village is known around the world for its traditional music.

DAYS 3 AND 4 A short drive around Galway Bay brings you to **Galway,** one of Ireland's liveliest and most colorful cities. Spend two days here enjoying the pleasant buzz on the streets, the sound of spoken Irish, and some good music, and making several pleasant excursions—a day trip to the **Aran Islands,** time permitting, or a boat trip into **Lough Corrib.**

DAYS 5 AND 6 Just north of Galway lies the majestic landscape of the **Connemara,** mountainous in some parts, covered with prairielike moors in others, and dotted with forests of pine and fir that surround rushing streams and glittering lakes. You might want to treat yourself to stay at a retreat such as **Ballynahinch Castle,** or use the pleasant seaside town of **Clifden** or the village of **Cong** as your base. The best place to experience the wild splendor of this part of the world is in **Connemara National Park,** which is laced with excellent hiking trails.

DAY 7 You'll encounter more gorgeous scenery as you continue north through the **Kylemore Valley,** past **Kylemore Abbey,** and around conically shaped **Crough Patrick** to the appealing town of **Westport.**

DAY 8 You can return south to Shannon from Westport in about three hours or continue into the Northwest following Itinerary 4.

ITINERARY 4
Into the Northwest

The Northwest is rugged, bounded by rough seas and desolate

itinerary 3: into the west of ireland

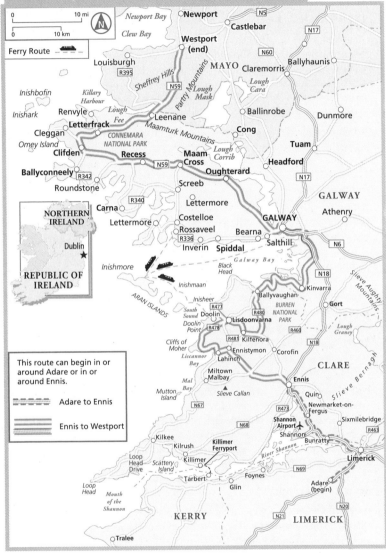

mountain landscapes. If you're coming from Dublin, plan on a drive of about three hours to **Sligo Town.**

DAY 1 After settling into Sligo Town or, better yet, into one of the distinctive lodgings in the nearby countryside, take a walk along the animated streets that run down to the River Garavogue. Step into the **County Museum,** for a look at manuscripts by the poet William Butler Yeats and canvases by his brother, Jack Yeats.

DAY 2 In the near vicinity of Sligo Town are two prehistoric sites: the passage tombs at **Carrowmore** and **Carrowkeel.** This is also Yeats country, and you can pay homage to the poet with a drive around **Lough Gill,** where the Isle of Innisfree inspired the poet's line "I will arise now and go, and go to Innisfree," and with a visit to **Drumcliff,** where Yeats is buried in the shadow of **Ben Bulben** mountain.

DAY 3 Break up the drive north with a walk around **Donegal Town,** dominated by its castle, and then pass through the busy fishing port of **Killybegs** to **Slieve League,** a majestic swath of tall cliffs that soar vertically out of the surf. If the weather's good, take time out for a short but hair-raising hike along the top of the cliffs. From here, head east and settle into one of several pleasant hotels in the countryside outside **Letterkenny.**

DAY 4 A short excursion takes you west into the wonders of **Glenveagh National Park,** where enchanting **Glenveagh Castle** is set amid the moor-clad hillsides of the Derryveagh Mountains. You might want to make a stop en route at **Glebe House,** a Regency manor filled with an outstanding collection of European art. You can explore the rugged **North Sea** coast on any number of headlands or in **Ards Forest Park,** whose trails traverse marshes, forested valleys, and the coast.

DAY 5 A day of exploring can include the sights you couldn't fit into the schedule the day before (you might want to spend that entire day in Glenveagh National Park and devote this day to driving along the coast). Venture east from Letterkenny onto the mountainous **Inishowen Peninsula,** the northernmost point in Ireland.

DAY 6 It's about a five-hour drive south to either Dublin or Shannon. If you're planning to continue east into Northern Ireland, follow Itinerary 5 in reverse, beginning in **Derry.**

ITINERARY 5
Northern Ireland

Peace has brought with it the chance to discover just how rich in natural beauty and urban pleasures the North is. **Belfast** is only two hours north of Dublin by car, though you might want to take a bit longer and leave the busy M1 for stops at the **Hill of Tara,** seat of the ancient kings of Ireland, and **Newgrange,** one of the world's most impressive prehistoric burial grounds.

DAY 1 After settling into a Belfast hotel for a two-night stay, hit the streets and walk through the city center. Along with the Victorian grandeur of the place, you can't help but notice the upbeat buzz of this city that's moving toward a better future. You'll have a choice of excellent

itinerary 4: into the northwest of ireland

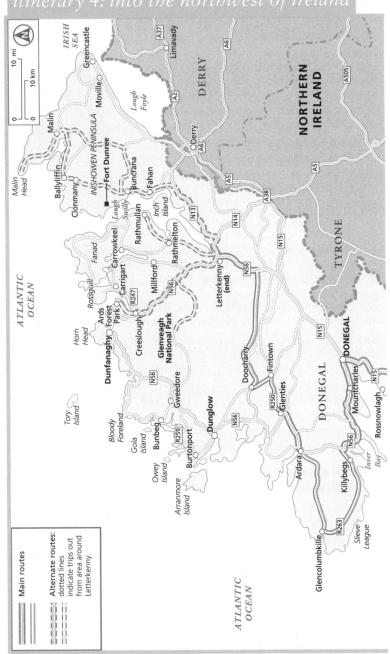

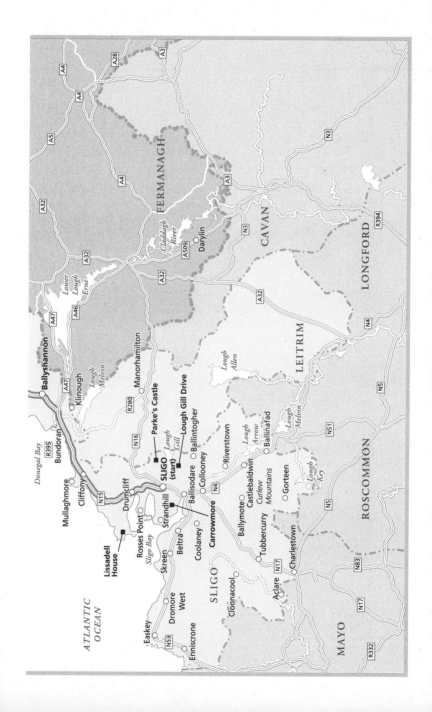

itinerary 5: into northern ireland

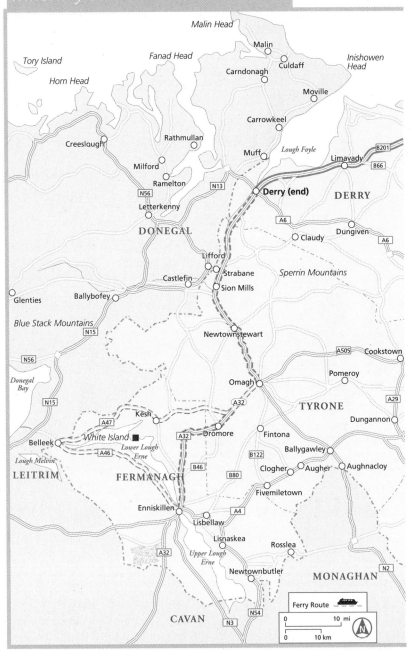

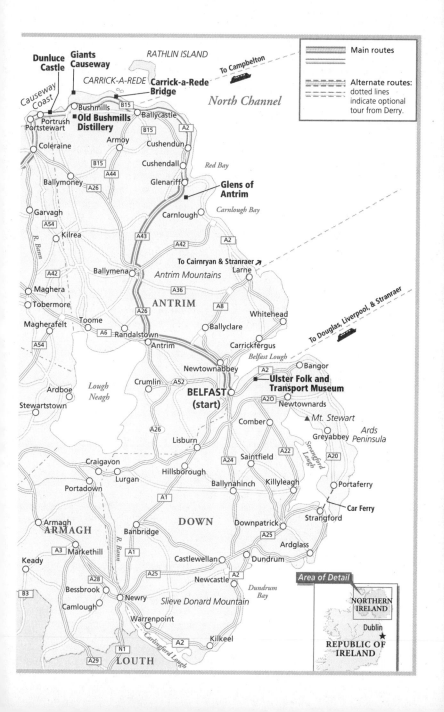

Main routes

Alternate routes: dotted lines indicate optional tour from Derry.

RATHLIN ISLAND

To Campbelton

North Channel

Dunluce Castle

Giants Causeway

Causeway Coast

CARRICK-A-REDE

Carrick-a-Rede Bridge

Bushmills

Old Bushmills Distillery

B15

Ballycastle

Portrush
Portstewart

Coleraine

Armoy

Cushendun

A2

B15

Ballymoney

A44

Cushendall

Red Bay

B15

A26

Garvagh

Glenariff

Glens of Antrim

A54

Carnlough

Carnlough Bay

Kilrea

A43

A42

A2

Ballymena

A42

Antrim Mountains

To Cairnryan & Stranraer ↗

Larne

Maghera

A36

Tobermore

ANTRIM

A8

Whitehead

Magherafelt

Toome

A26

A6

Ballyclare

To Douglas, Liverpool, & Stranraer

A54

Randalstown

Antrim

Carrickfergus

Ardboe

Lough Neagh

Newtownabbey

Belfast Lough

Bangor

A2

Crumlin

A52

Ulster Folk and Transport Museum

Stewartstown

BELFAST (start)

A20

Newtownards

Comber

▲ Mt. Stewart

Ards Peninsula

A26

Lisburn

Greyabbey

A24

Saintfield

A22

A20

Craigavon

Hillsborough

Killyleagh

Portaferry

Portadown

Lurgan

Ballynahinch

Car Ferry

A1

Strangford

Armagh

DOWN

Downpatrick

Strangford

ARMAGH

Banbridge

A25

Ardglass

A3

Markethill

A1

Castlewellan

Dundrum

Keady

A28

A25

A2

Newcastle

Dundrum Bay

Bessbrook

Slieve Donard Mountain

Camlough

Newry

B3

Warrenpoint

A2

Kilkeel

N1

Carlingford Lough

A2

A29

LOUTH

Area of Detail

NORTHERN IRELAND

Dublin ★

REPUBLIC OF IRELAND

and exciting dinner spots, and you'll enjoy fine entertainment at the **Grand Opera House** and other venues.

DAY 2 Your explorations of the city should extend south to the pleasant **Stranmills** neighborhood around the **Botanic Gardens,** the **Ulster Museum,** and **Queen's University.** You should also take a bus or taxi tour of the **Falls Road** and **Shankill Road** neighborhoods, epicenters of the Troubles in the recent past. If you have kids in tow, consider a half-day visit to the **Ulster Folk and Transport Museum,** just northeast of the city.

DAY 3 An incredibly scenic drive takes you north through the forested **Glens of Antrim** to the **Antrim Coast.** Slow down the pace for visits to **Dunluce Castle,** the **Old Bushmills Distillery,** the **Giants Causeway,** and **Carrick-a-Rede Bridge.** If the weather's good, follow at least a small section of the path that follows the coast. You can press on to Derry at the end of the day, but you might want to settle in for the night in **Portrush** or **Bushmills.**

DAY 4 A day in **Derry** allows you to explore this walled city at your leisure. The first order of business is to walk the walls, a 1.5-kilometer (1-mile) circuit that will provide a bird's-eye views of the sights. Your explorations should take you into **Bogside,** the Catholic neighborhood beneath the walls where political murals recall the violence of decades past.

DAY 5 You might want to continue into the Northwest (see Itinerary 4) or, if you're heading back south, take in the green hills that surround the **Loughs of Erne** en route, with stops in the pleasant town of **Enniskillen** and at **Castle Coole.**

PART THREE

LODGING, DINING, *and* SHOPPING

▌ HOTELS *in* IRELAND

LODGING IN IRELAND comes in many varieties: urban luxury hotels, castles, country houses, country inns, guesthouses, and bed-and-breakfasts. You can also expect to pay a bit for all this—lodging is as expensive as everything else is in Ireland these days. In general, expect to pay at least €100 to €150 (£60 to £80 in the North) for a double; of course, you can easily pay a lot more than that. Bed-and-breakfasts are often a bit less expensive than that, but just a bit.

WHAT TO EXPECT

LUXURY CITY HOTELS Hoteliers in Dublin, Belfast, and other Irish cities seem to be engaged in a contest to see who can provide the most luxurious, atmospheric lodgings, going overboard to equip rooms and suites with every possible creature comfort.

CHAIN HOTELS Novotel, InterContinental, Best Western, Hilton, and Westin are among the many chains that operate in Ireland. Predictable, yes, but that's a quality some travelers value.

GUESTHOUSES These are often large private homes that have been converted to inns, usually providing character-filled and comfortable accommodations but not the full services of a hotel.

CASTLE HOTELS Converting historic castles into hotels is an Irish specialty, and **Dromoland, Ashford,** and **Adare Manor** set the gold standard for luxury within stone walls. Some castles have forfeited character for standardized comfort, providing a strange hybrid: chain hotels with turrets. Others are charmingly idiosyncratic, right down to the drafts in the hallways. The **Irish Landmark Trust** can put you up in castles and other distinctive properties around the country (25 Eustace Street, Dublin 2; ☎ 01-670-4733; **www.irishlandmark.com.**

COUNTRY-HOUSE HOTELS Formerly private estates, often set within landscaped grounds, these places work hard to make guests feel like the lord and lady of the manor. You can usually expect pleasant lounges, and many have well-decorated rooms with private baths.

BED-AND-BREAKFASTS Long the mainstay of the budget-travel circuit, B&Bs are essentially private homes that take in guests—though these days some B&Bs are independent of a home. Some are filled with more chintz than your great-auntie ever dreamed of, but many are quite attractive and increasingly offer amenities such as TV, private bathrooms, and direct-dial telephones. B&Bs are still, however, usually less expensive than hotels and guesthouses.

SELF-CATERING ACCOMMODATIONS These range from apartments to cottages, always providing equipped kitchens. Well suited for families and groups, they usually rent by the week. The **Irish Tourist Board** and the **Northern Ireland Tourist Board** (see page 41) can provide information on self-catering accommodations.

FARM STAYS Many Irish farmers have learned that catering to city folk who want a rural experience beats a lot of other kinds of farm chores. These are essentially B&Bs in the countryside; some serve meals made from produce grown on the property. For listings, contact **Irish Farm Holidays** at **www.irishfarmholidays.com.**

SOME OTHER WEB RESOURCES

FOR A COMPREHENSIVE LISTING of Irish lodging, click your way through the following Web resources. But remember that these are just listings, and they do not provide you with critical reviews (for those, see the hotel reviews throughout this book). The **Irish Tourist Board** Web site, **www.ireland.ie,** can help you find any kind of accommodation anywhere in Ireland, from B&Bs to luxury hotels. *Be Our Guest* (**www.irelandhotels.com**), published by the Irish Hotel Federation and available in print from the Irish Tourist Board, provides information on hotels, castles, and other accommodations. **Ireland's Blue Book** (**www.irelands-blue-book.ie**) will introduce you to manor houses, castles, convents, and other significant buildings where you can stay. **Hidden Ireland** (**www.hidden-ireland.com**) lists B&Bs and guesthouses that are especially appealing; in fact, you would do well to stay at as many of the places listed as you can.

ROOM RATES

ROOM RATES CHANGE with the seasons and as occupancy rates rise and fall. If a hotel is close to full, don't expect to find any kind of rate reduction; if it's close to empty, though, you may be able to negotiate a discount. Innkeepers, wisely, are usually more willing to discount an expensive room than a cheap room. So you may be able to snatch the €200 suite for €120 but not get much leeway on the €100 room.

Here are some other money-saving options to consider:

- Expensive hotels catering to business travelers are most crowded on weekdays and usually offer substantial discounts for weekend stays.
- You may be able to save 20% or more by traveling off-season (mid-October to mid-December and January to March).
- Some of the best hotel rates of all, especially in Dublin, are found with air–hotel packages.
- The major travel-booking Web sites listed in Part One, Planning Your Visit to Ireland (see page 38), offer hotel-reservation services. Other Web sites are devoted entirely to lodging, including the following: **Hotel Reservations Network** lists bargain rates at hotels in Dublin, Belfast, Cork, and Limerick; **www.180096hotel .com. InnSite** provides B&B listings for inns around the globe, including Ireland; **www.inn site.com.** And **TravelWeb,** focusing on chains such as Hyatt and Hilton, offers weekend deals at many leading chains; **www.travelweb.com.**
- And finally, never be afraid to ask for the lowest rate—call and ask if special rates might apply or if rates are lower for longer stays.

unofficial **TIP**
Do not arrive in Dublin without a hotel reservation at any time of year, or anywhere in Ireland if you're traveling from mid-May to September (high season). In the fall, winter, and early spring, you will probably be able to find rooms on the spot, although many B&Bs and guesthouses are closed in winter.

Confirming a Room

Hotels do not consider a room reservation confirmed until they receive partial payment, usually for the first night. You can almost always confirm your reservations immediately with a credit card; otherwise, you must mail in your payment using an International Money Order, available at most banks. Before you reserve your room, ask about the cancellation policy. At some hotels you can get your money back if you cancel a room with 24 hours' notice; others require you to notify the hotel five or more days in advance. After you've reserved the room, request a written confirmation by fax, e-mail, or post.

unofficial **TIP**
Some smaller B&Bs, especially those in country villages, do not accept credit cards, so make sure you have enough cash if staying at a B&B is in your plans.

HOTEL RATINGS

PRICES IN OUR LISTINGS include value-added tax (VAT), 13.5% in the Republic and 17.5% in Northern Ireland, and refer to the starting price for a standard single and a standard double room. Prices for deluxe, executive, triple-occupancy, and family rooms, as well as suites and rooms with special features (such as four-poster beds, fireplaces, and balconies), may be significantly higher, but not necessarily; if the hotel's not full, ask if you can have a room with deluxe features for the price of a standard. Remember that prices are flexible and change all the time; you may find that a hotel charges more than the listed price and, just as often, less. Also keep in mind that these are

TIPS AND VAT

A word on tipping: €1 or €2 a bag for bellhops, €3 a night for the house-keeper, and more if service is extraordinary. In general, the quoted room rate includes the VAT (value-added tax), 13.5% in the Republic and 17.5% in Northern Ireland. Be sure to ask if the VAT is included so you won't get an unpleasant surprise when you're checking out.

standard rates; you may be able to get a better price with a Web offer, special package, or weekend rate—or just by asking.

OVERALL RATINGS We have distinguished properties according to the relative quality, tastefulness, state of repair, cleanliness, and size of standard rooms, grouping them into classifications denoted by stars. The overall star ratings in this guide do not correspond to ratings awarded by the Irish Tourist Board, the Northern Ireland Tourist Board, or other travel critics. Overall ratings are presented to show the difference we perceive between one property and another. They are assigned without regard to location or to whether a property has restaurants, recreational facilities, entertainment, or other extras.

★★★★★	Superior	Tasteful and luxurious by any standard
★★★★	Extremely Nice	Above average in appointments and design; very comfortable
★★★	Nice	Average but quite comfortable
★★	Adequate	Plain but meets all essential needs
★	Budget	Spartan; not aesthetically pleasing, but clean

QUALITY RATINGS In addition to overall ratings (which delineate broad categories), we also employ quality ratings. These apply to room quality only and describe the property's standard accommodations. Our rating scale is ★ to ★★★★★, with ★★★★★ as the best possible rating and ★ as the worst.

VALUE RATINGS We also provide a value rating to give you some sense of the quality of a room in relation to its cost. As before, the ratings are based on the quality of room for the money and do not take into account location, services, or amenities:

★★★★★	An exceptional bargain
★★★★	A good deal
★★★	Fairly priced (you get exactly what you pay for)
★★	Somewhat overpriced
★	Significantly overpriced

A ★★½ room at €100 may have the same value rating as a ★★★★★ room at €180, but that does not mean that the rooms will be of comparable quality. Regardless of whether it's a good deal or not, a ★★½ room is still a ★★½ room.

DINING *in* IRELAND

STEREOTYPICAL IRISH FOOD—potatoes accompanied by potatoes with a garnish of cabbage—has been the brunt of jokes for centuries. Happily, Irish cooking gets more varied and interesting by the day. In fact, dining in Ireland can be a real treat, when even old-fashioned stews are being reinvented as part of modern Irish cuisine.

Fish and seafood are fresh and plentiful, bread is almost always baked on the premises, and Irish cheeses give French *fromages* a run for their money. Irish cooking remains straightforward, relying on farm-raised lamb, pork, and poultry; garden-fresh vegetables; fish just out of the sea; and wild game, among other high-quality ingredients. Ethnic food is scarce, even in Dublin, though many Irish chefs infuse their creations with spices to provide a hint of exoticism.

THE COST FACTOR

A MEAL IN IRELAND IS, on the whole, less expensive than it would be in London or New York, but it probably costs more than you're used to paying if you live elsewhere. It's hard to find a good three-course meal with a bottle of wine for less than €40 a head, and you'll often pay more. There are ways to cut costs, though. Many restaurants offer lunch specials and early-bird dinner specials; if you're willing to dine before 7 p.m., you can enjoy a very nice meal in some of Ireland's better restaurants for about €30 to €35 per person. Pub meals are usually reasonably priced, as are those at casual eateries such as wine bars and cafes. With drinks making up a large part of many bills, look for house wines, or order by the glass if that's all you want. Don't feel obliged to order bottled water (almost always marked up heavily) if tap water will please you just as well. If you're traveling with children but don't see a kids' menu, ask if a child-sized portion can be prepared.

Prices usually include the 13.5% VAT. In many restaurants, a service charge of 12% to 15% is added to the bill, so examine your menu and your bill to see if it has already been added. If service is not included, it will be mentioned in some obvious manner on the bill. The normal range for tipping in restaurants is 12% to 20%, and because service is usually excellent, you probably won't mind paying it.

RATING OUR FAVORITE RESTAURANTS

WE HAVE DEVELOPED DETAILED PROFILES for the best and (in our opinion) most interesting restaurants all over Ireland. Each profile features an easily scanned heading that allows you to check out at a glance the restaurant's name and cuisine, the star rating, quality rating, and value rating we've assigned it, and the cost, along with a description of the dining experience you can expect to have.

CUISINE This is actually less straightforward than it sounds. In some cases we've used the broader terms (for example, "French" or "Italian") but added descriptions to give a clearer idea of the fare (for example, "Provençal" or "Southern Italian"). Don't hold us, or the chefs, to too strict a style, but we do ensure that we give you some idea of what type of cuisine to expect. Irish restaurants stick to mainstream cooking—you'll notice that the cuisine in many is labeled as "Irish" or "Modern Irish."

OVERALL RATING The overall rating encompasses the entire dining experience, including style, service, and ambience, in addition to the taste, presentation, and quality of the food. Five stars is the highest rating possible and denotes the best of everything. Four-star restaurants are exceptional, three-star restaurants well above average. Two-star restaurants are so-so. One star is used to indicate a forgettable restaurant that demonstrates an unusual capability in some area of specialization—for example, an otherwise unmemorable place that serves fresh fish.

COST Our expense description provides a comparative sense of how much a complete meal—for our purposes, an appetizer, entree, and dessert—will cost. Drinks and tips are excluded.

Inexpensive	Less than €20 (£14) per person
Moderate	€20–€35 (£14–£25) per person
Expensive	More than €35 (£25) per person

QUALITY RATING Food quality is rated on a scale of one to five stars, five being the best rating attainable. The quality rating is based on the taste, freshness of ingredients, preparation, presentation, and creativity of food served. There is no consideration of price. If you want the best food available and cost is not an issue, you need look no further than the quality ratings.

VALUE RATING If, on the other hand, you are looking for both quality and value, then you should check the value rating:

★★★★★	Exceptional value; a real bargain
★★★★	Good value
★★★	Fair value; you get exactly what you pay for
★★	Somewhat overpriced
★	Significantly overpriced

PAYMENT We've listed the type of payment accepted at each restaurant using the following codes: AE for American Express (and American Express Optima), D for Discover, DC for Diners Club, MC for MasterCard, and V for Visa.

WHO'S INCLUDED Our list is highly selective. We try to include the most noteworthy restaurants, and these needn't be expensive or fancy. The omission of a particular establishment does not necessarily indicate that the restaurant is bad, only that we felt it didn't rank among the best we wanted to offer our readers in a particular place.

SHOPPING *in* IRELAND

IT'S WORTH NOTING that many Irish are flying to New York these days for weekend shopping sprees. From this you can rightfully conclude that goods in Ireland are expensive. Rather than bargains, you will find high-quality, distinctively Irish goods—especially china, crystal, lace and linen, and woolen goods.

WISE BUYS IN IRELAND

THE FOLLOWING ITEMS are worth buying in Ireland because of their high quality or their unavailability in the United States.

Antiques

You'll find antiques shops in the old districts of every major city and town; see our shopping sections throughout this guide for tips on the places where you are most likely to pick up a bargain. There are fewer bargains to be had these days, but you can still come upon some finds—good china, prints, jewelry, and bric-a-brac are market mainstays and can be quite a find.

Crystal and China

Waterford crystal is widely available throughout Ireland, including the factory shops in Waterford. Prices are set, so you won't find many bargains, but you will find a much greater selection here in Ireland than you will abroad. You'll also encounter fine china from **Belleek** and other Irish houses.

Books

In general, the Irish are avid readers, and almost every town of any size has one or two excellent bookshops, some selling contemporary editions and others used and rare volumes. Staffers tend to be knowledgeable about the stock and are willing to make recommendations.

Designer Clothing

John Rocha, Jen Kelly, and other Irish designers are making names for themselves with distinctive, high-quality fashions. Most are well represented in the better Dublin shops, and also at the **Kilkenny Design Centre** in Kilkenny City.

Knits and Woolens

You'll encounter well-crafted, often handwoven goods throughout Ireland. Some of the names to look for are **Avoca Handweavers** (which branches out from its sumptuous wovens into all things Irish), **Blarney Woollen Mills,** and **Dublin Woollen Mills.** These are the big names, but you will also encounter many shops that sell exceptional sweaters, scarves, and other pieces hand-knit locally, often very well priced. Many shops will knit Aran sweaters to your specifications.

Pottery

Ireland is renowned for its beautifully crafted and glazed pottery, including pieces by internationally acclaimed artisans **Stephen Pearse** and **Louis Mulcahy;** you'll encounter their work, and that of others, in Dublin and in heavily touristed places such as Dingle and Killarney.

TIME TO SHOP

STORES IN IRELAND TEND TO OPEN at 9 a.m. and close at 6 or 6:30 p.m., with one weekly late closing at 8 or 9 p.m. While Sunday is still relatively sacrosanct for shopkeepers, some stores on the major shopping streets now open for a half day, from noon to 5 or 6 p.m. Street markets generally come to life on weekends, although you'll find weekday markets in Dublin, Cork, Belfast, and other cities.

PAYING UP

unofficial **TIP**
The **Tax Free for Tourists Network** makes getting a VAT refund a lot easier. Participating stores (look for a sticker in the window) will issue you a refund check at the time of purchase. For more information, visit **www.globalrefund.com.**

MOST SHOPS TAKE ALL MAJOR CREDIT CARDS (note that some small shops in small towns and villages may not). The credit card is a good way to go, as you'll have a record of your purchases and the exchange rate will be fair. The rate used will be that on the day that the purchase clears the credit-card company or bank.

AS FOR VAT

VALUE-ADDED TAX (VAT), which varies in the Republic, is 13.5% on hotel and restaurant bills and car rentals, as well as on many household items, and 21% for gifts and souvenirs. In Northern Ireland, VAT is 17.5% across the board. VAT is usually included in an item's sticker price, but in a few places it may be an add-on.

VAT Refunds

If you do not live in a country in the European Union, you may qualify for a VAT refund, provided you spend at least €155 at any one store. Keep the invoice, then present it to the VAT desk at the airport (don't pass it—you'll usually come to it before you go through passport control). Mail the stamped invoice back to the store within 90 days of your purchase, and the store will send you a refund check.

SALESPEOPLE'S ATTITUDES AND BEHAVIOR

YOU'LL PROBABLY BE SURPRISED at just how pleasant and helpful salespeople are in Ireland. A new crop of service workers, many from Eastern Europe and elsewhere in the EU, have adopted Irish courtesy, so shopping or dealing with hotel and restaurant staffs can be a real pleasure.

PART FOUR

DUBLIN

YOU MAY WELL COME TO DUBLIN equipped with few notions of what to expect other than a ditty running through your head ("In Dublin's Fair City, Where the Girls Are So Pretty . . . ") and literary visions of Leopold Bloom and Stephen Daedalus roaming damp streets. You'll leave, though, with many more impressions tucked away, most of them as pleasant as the sight of the slow-moving River Liffey, the first gulp of a really good pint of Guinness, and the sensation of a gentle mist on your face. Walking across the city center on a leisurely stroll, you'll encounter Celtic crosses, Georgian fanlights, James Joyce's handwritten manuscripts, and Renoir canvases. You'll enjoy the city on less lofty planes, too. You'll have pleasant encounters, pass many pubs, and, everywhere you go, hear the lovely lilt of what your grandparents may have always referred to as the old country. As the Irish say, you'll think Dublin is "spot on."

The **NEIGHBORHOODS**

DUBLIN POSTAL CODES are pretty straightforward. The two you will encounter most often are **Dublin 1,** the center of town north of the River Liffey, and **Dublin 2,** the center of town south of the Liffey. We break Dublin into neighborhoods that take the concept a little further to make getting around the city even easier. To explore each of these neighborhoods on foot, see "Dublin Walks," page 115.

 CENTRAL DUBLIN, NORTH OF THE LIFFEY

HERE YOU'LL FIND what many Dubliners still consider to be the city center, comprising **O'Connell Street** and the streets and squares around it. Some of the city's most beloved cultural institutions are here, including the **Abbey** and **Gate theaters,** and the **Dublin City Gallery–The Hugh Lane,** as well as the big shops lining O'Connell and Henry streets.

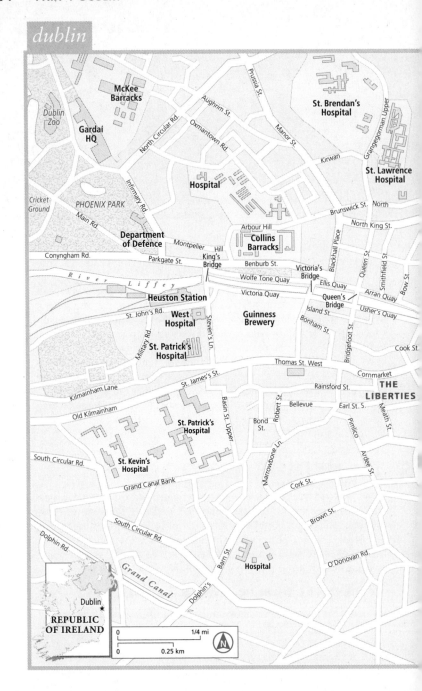

dublin

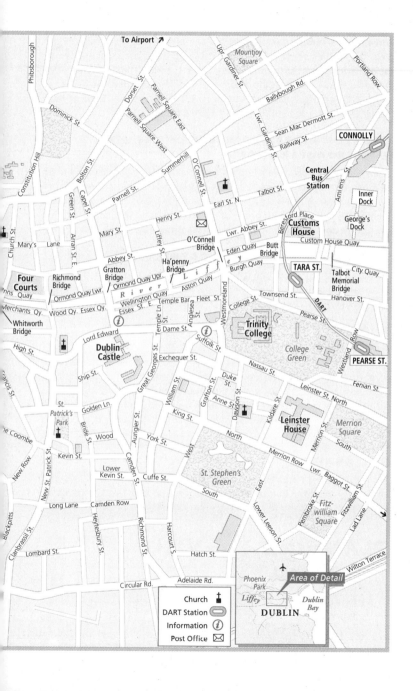

To Airport ↗

Phibsborough

Mountjoy Square

Upr. Gardiner St.

Dominick St.

Dorset St.

Parnell Square East

Parnell Square West

Ballybough Rd.

Constitution Hill

Bolton St.

Summerhill

Lwr. Gardiner St.

Sean Mac Dermott St.

Railway St.

Portland Row

CONNOLLY

Green St.

Capel St.

Parnell St.

O'Connell St.

Talbot St.

Central Bus Station

Amiens St.

Inner Dock

Church St.

Arran St. E.

Mary St.

Henry St.

Earl St. N.

Beresford Place

Customs House

George's Dock

Mary's Lane

Liffey St.

O'Connell Bridge

Lwr. Abbey St.

Custom House Quay

Abbey St.

Ha'penny Bridge

Eden Quay

Butt Bridge

TARA ST.

Talbot Memorial Bridge

City Quay

Four Courts

Richmond Bridge

Gratton Bridge

Ormond Quay Upr.

Liffey

Burgh Quay

Hanover St.

Inns Quay

Ormond Quay Lwr.

River

Wellington Quay

Aston Quay

Westmoreland

Townsend St.

DART

Merchants Qy.

Wood Qy. Essex Qy.

Essex St. E.

Temple Bar

Fleet St.

College St.

Pearse St.

Whitworth Bridge

ℹ

Temple Ln.

Anglesea St.

PEARSE ST.

High St.

Lord Edward

Dame St.

ℹ

Suffolk St.

Trinity College

College Green

Westland Row

Dublin Castle

Great Georges St.

Exchequer St.

Nassau St.

Fenian St.

Ship St.

Duke St.

Leinster St. North

Francis St.

St. Patrick's Park

Golden Ln.

Bride St.

Aungier St.

William St.

Grafton St.

Anne St.

Dawson St.

Kildare St.

Leinster House

Merrion Square North

Kevin St.

Wood

King St.

York St.

West

North

Merrion Row

Merrion Square South

New Row

New St. Patrick St.

Lower Kevin St.

Camden St.

Cuffe St.

St. Stephen's Green

East

Lwr. Baggot St.

Pembroke St.

Fitz-william Square

Fitzwilliam St.

Lad Lane

The Coombe

Long Lane

Camden Row

Richmond St.

Harcourt S.

South

Lower Leeson St.

Blackpitts

Clanbrassil St.

Lombard St.

Heytesbury St.

Hatch St.

Wilton Terrace

Circular Rd.

Adelaide Rd.

Phoenix Park

Area of Detail

Liffey

Dublin Bay

Church ✝

DART Station ⬭

Information ℹ

Post Office ✉

DUBLIN

TRINITY COLLEGE AND TEMPLE BAR

IRELAND'S OLDEST AND MOST HALLOWED UNIVERSITY, **Trinity College,** and **Temple Bar,** the city's raucous nightlife quarter, are both near the south banks of the River Liffey. Between the student population in one and the barely-of-age pub crawlers in the other, this neighborhood is decidedly youthful. You'll come here to drink, to dine, and, on a more serious note, to see the exquisite **Book of Kells** (see page 124), on display in the **Trinity Library.**

GRAFTON STREET, ST. STEPHEN'S GREEN, AND GEORGIAN DUBLIN

EXPENSIVE SHOPS AND ELEGANT GEORGIAN HOUSES surround **St. Stephen's Green,** creating what upwardly mobile Dubliners consider to be their center of town—that is, as opposed to the other center of town around O'Connell Street, north of the river. Also in this neighborhood are the **National Gallery** and the **National Museum.**

DUBLIN CASTLE AND THE CATHEDRALS

DUBLIN CASTLE STANDS at the edge of some of the city's oldest and most sacred ground. Here, the city's two cathedrals, **Christ Church** and **St. Patrick's,** are remnants of Dublin's medieval beginnings.

PHOENIX PARK, THE LIBERTIES, AND KILMAINHAM

IN MEANDERING NEIGHBORHOODS of terrace houses and factories west of the city center are some of the city's most visited attractions. Foremost among these is the **Guinness Storehouse** (see page 133), although places such as the **Kilmainham Gaol** and the **National Museum of Ireland**'s collection of **Decorative Arts at Collins Barracks** warrant a trip out here, too, as do the verdant precincts of **Phoenix Park.**

BALLSBRIDGE

THIS IS A LEAFY RESIDENTIAL neighborhood at the southern edge of the city center. Amid the fine houses on tree-lined streets are many embassies, corporate headquarters, and hotels.

PLANNING *Your* VISIT *to* DUBLIN

LOCATED IN AN OLD CHURCH on an atmospheric lane in the city center, **Dublin Tourism** itself seems like an attraction. The staff is quite eager to answer any questions visitors might have, and although the place is mainly a souvenir shop, it also distributes free maps and helpful pamphlets. You'll want the *Event Guide,* which covers entertainment and

NOT TO BE MISSED IN DUBLIN

Book of Kells (page 124)

Chester Beatty Library and Gallery of Oriental Art (page 125)

Christ Church Cathedral (page 129)

Dublin City Gallery–The Hugh Lane (page 130)

Dublin Writers Museum (page 132)

Kilmainham Gaol (page 134)

National Gallery of Ireland (page 135)

National Museum of Ireland (page 136)

Number 29 (page 138)

St. Patrick's Cathedral (page 140)

activities around town. Especially helpful is the Dublin Bus desk, where you can pick up a route map, buy tickets, and ask the staff how to get where you want to go. The center also books hotel rooms (for a fee), provides rail and long-distance bus information, and operates a pleasant cafe. The main office (Suffolk Street, *Trinity College and Temple Bar;* ☎ 01-605-7700; **www.visitdublin.com**) is open July through August, Monday through Saturday, 9 a.m. to 7 p.m. and Sunday, 10:30 a.m. to 3 p.m.; September through June, Monday through Saturday, 9 a.m. to 5:30 p.m. and Sunday, 10:30 a.m. to 3 p.m. Dublin Tourism also maintains offices on O'Connell Street (Central Dublin): Monday through Saturday, 9 a.m. to 5 p.m.; Lower Baggot Street (near St. Stephen's Green): Monday through Friday, 9:30 a.m. to noon and 12:30 to 5 p.m.; Dublin Airport: daily, 8 a.m. to 10 p.m.; Dún Laoghaire (at the ferry terminal): Monday through Saturday, 10 a.m. to 1 p.m. and 2 to 6 p.m.

unofficial **TIP**
Do some math before plunking down your euros for a Dublin Pass—you might be better off paying for individual admissions. Some of the places that you might want to visit and that are included on the pass are expensive (such as the **Guinness Storehouse** and the **Old Jameson Distillery**), but others are free.

THE DUBLIN PASS

THE PRICE OF THIS PASS includes admission to many sights in Dublin, plus the privilege of going to the head of the line. The pass is available at Dublin Tourism offices. One day: €31 adults, €17 children; two days: €49 adults, €29 children; three days: €59 adults, €34 children; six days: €89 adults, €44 children. If you decide to purchase the pass and are flying into Dublin, buy it when you arrive at Dublin Airport, because airport transfers on Aircoach are also included. Ask about seasonal promotions, such as the 15% discounts that are sometimes available in the winter and spring. For more information, check with Dublin Tourism or go to **www.dublinpass.com**.

GETTING *around* DUBLIN

BY FOOT

THIS IS AN EASY AND PLEASANT way to get around Dublin. Most sights within the city center (starting on page 115) are within easy walking distance from one another. Exercise extreme caution when crossing a street, because directions are reversed here—driving is in the left lane—and your instincts are geared to traffic moving on the right. Always look right before stepping into a street (your instinct will be to look left first), and for the greatest safety, cross only at signals or so-called zebra crossings, where diagonal white lines indicate that pedestrians have the right of way.

BY BUS

THE GREEN BUSES OF DUBLIN BUS, the main provider of transportation within Dublin, cover an extensive network serving every corner of the city. Many routes run along O'Connell Street on the North Side and Dame Street on the South Side. A bus that has AN LAR (Gaelic for "City Center") posted on the sign in front will most likely take you to O'Connell Street and probably to Dame Street and somewhere on or around St. Stephen's Green. Fares vary with distances traveled, beginning at €1.05; pay the driver in exact change. Passes are available for one day of travel (€6), three days (€11.50), five days (€18.50), and seven days (€23).

unofficial **TIP**
Because you can reach most places in the city center fairly easily on foot, you may want to purchase only a one-day Dublin Bus pass, to use when you venture out to outlying sights such as the Guinness Storehouse and Kilmainham Gaol.

Buses run Monday through Saturday, from 6 a.m. to 11:30 p.m., and on Sunday, 10 a.m. to 6 p.m. For more information and to pick up schedules and route maps, visit the Dublin Bus office at Dublin Tourism; drop into Dublin Bus (59 Upper O'Connell Street, ☎ 01-872-0000); or visit **www.dublinbus.ie.**

BY DART

A SUBURBAN LIGHT-RAIL SERVICE, **Dublin Area Rapid Transit (DART)** follows the shores of Dublin Bay, from Greystone in the south to Malahide in the north. DART also links parts of the city center, with stops at Pearse and Tara streets on the South Side and Connolly Station on the North Side. Fares vary with distances traveled, beginning at €1.50; buy a ticket at windows in some stations or from machines, which accept cash and debit and credit cards. Service runs Monday through Saturday, 7 a.m. to midnight and Sunday, 9:30 a.m. to 11 p.m. DART is a handy way to make excursions to outlying places such as Howth and Dún Laoghaire (see "Day Trips from Dublin," page 172). For more information, call ☎ 1850-366222, or visit **www.irishrail.ie.**

BY LUAS

THIS STREETCAR SYSTEM links central Dublin with surrounding areas, and it also provides a handy way to get from Heuston Station to the O'Connell Street area and Connolly Station. The system is a bit frustrating because it is not citywide. There are two Luas lines, one from St. Stephen's Green to Sandyford in the southern suburbs and one from Connolly Station to Tallaght in the southwest suburbs, but the two don't intersect—meaning, for instance, that you can't get from Heuston or Connolly Stations to St. Stephen's Green on Luas. Plus, the trams run on city streets, not necessarily alleviating congestion. Fares begin at €1.50 (that's what it costs to travel between Heuston and Connolly stations), and tickets are available from machines at each stop; these accept cash and debit and credit cards. For more information, call ☎ 01-703-2029, or go to **www.luas.ie**.

BY TAXI

YOU'LL FIND TAXI RANKS around the city center, especially near the larger hotels. Fares aren't cheap, though—expect to pay about €10 to get from St. Stephen's Green to O'Connell Street. To call a cab, try **Access** or **Metro** (☎ 01-668-333) or **VIP** (☎ 01-478-3333).

BY CAR

DON'T EVEN THINK OF IT. Traffic is terrible, the one-way grid is confounding, and parking is sometimes hard to find. If for some reason you choose to bring a car into the city center, stash it in a car park and leave it there. You'll find handy facilities at St. Stephen's Green West on the South Side and Abbey Street on the North Side for about €2 an hour, up to about €20 for 24 hours. Some hotels provide garages, as noted in our hotel listings.

HOTELS *in* DUBLIN

GOOD NEWS ON THE DUBLIN HOTEL FRONT: rooms are plentiful; you have a wide choice of places to stay, from modest B&Bs to sophisticated contemporary showcases; and prices have not yet caught up with those in New York, London, and other cities that draw visitors from around the world. That said, here are some do's and don'ts to keep in mind:

- *Do* expect good service and clean surroundings. These are hallmarks of Irish hospitality, so don't settle for less.
- *Do* check weekend packages (often providing a room for two nights and a dinner) and other special rates; hotel Web sites are the best places to find them. Some chain hotels and the more expensive lodgings offer good-value weekend rates; you might consider spending the weekend in luxury and then moving down a notch or two during the week.

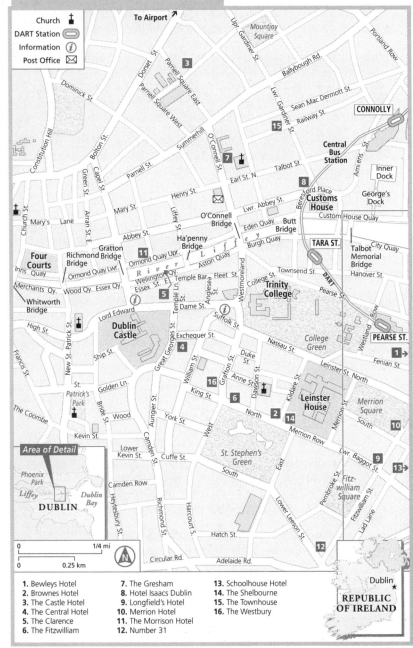

dublin accommodations

Church ✝
DART Station ⬭
Information ⓘ
Post Office ✉

To Airport ↗

1. Bewleys Hotel
2. Brownes Hotel
3. The Castle Hotel
4. The Central Hotel
5. The Clarence
6. The Fitzwilliam
7. The Gresham
8. Hotel Isaacs Dublin
9. Longfield's Hotel
10. Merrion Hotel
11. The Morrison Hotel
12. Number 31
13. Schoolhouse Hotel
14. The Shelbourne
15. The Townhouse
16. The Westbury

How Hotels Compare in Dublin

HOTEL	OVERALL	QUALITY	VALUE	PRICE
The Fitzwilliam	★★★★½	★★★★½	★★★★	€265–€450
Merrion Hotel	★★★★½	★★★★½	★★★	From €450
The Clarence	★★★★	★★★★½	★★★★	From €209
The Morrison Hotel	★★★★	★★★★½	★★★	€195–€240
Number 31	★★★★	★★★★	★★★★½	€110–€150
The Westbury	★★★★	★★★★	★★★½	From €239
Bewleys Hotel	★★★½	★★★½	★★★★½	€119
Brownes Hotel	★★★	★★★★	★★★	€165–€270
The Shelbourne	★★★	★★★★	★★★	From €240
Schoolhouse Hotel	★★★	★★★½	★★★	€189–€219
Central Hotel	★★★	★★★	★★★★	€78–€88
The Gresham	★★★	★★★	★★★	€140–€300
Longfield's Hotel	★★★	★★★	★★★	€80–€100
The Castle Hotel	★★★	★★½	★★★★	€75–€110
Hotel Isaacs Dublin	★★★	★★½	★★★★	From €105
The Townhouse	★★	★★★	★★★★	€70–€115

- *Don't* bring a car. Only a few city-center hotels provide parking, fees are high (about €20 a day), traffic is awful, and you can get around easily on foot and via public transportation.
- *Do* make sure breakfast and all taxes and service fees are included in the price you are quoted; these extras can add a lot to your bill.

CHOOSING YOUR LOCALE

CENTRAL DUBLIN IS SMALL ENOUGH that just about any city-center hotel will put you within easy reach of most major attractions. Hotels in the **Central Dublin** vicinity are close to Connolly Station, O'Connell Street shopping, and the Abbey and Gate theaters. Those in the **Trinity College and Temple Bar** neighborhood are in the heart of the action—handy when you want to pop round the corner for a pint, annoying when you have to step around a pile of unconscious, inebriated youths from Northern Europe. Hotels in the **Grafton Street, St. Stephen's Green,** and **Georgian Dublin** areas tend to have the toniest addresses, on and off the streets of Georgian Dublin; many, in fact, occupy charmingly historic houses. This neighborhood is convenient, too: many of Dublin's best restaurants are in this part of town, as are the fashionable Grafton Street shops and sights such as the National Gallery of Ireland. A hotel in the **Dublin Castle** and **Cathedrals** neighborhood is convenient to Christ Church and other historic landmarks and within close range of Temple Bar, while staying in **Ballsbridge** removes you from the action—you'll have to take a bus or DART to get to most places you want to go.

THE CHAINS

MANY INTERNATIONAL HOTEL GROUPS have followed the clarion call of Dublin's new prosperity and opened up shop in Dublin. To the standard list of comforts and amenities, all add the stamp of Irish hospitality.

COMFORT INN SMITHFIELD This international chain has a special flair here, with large, pleasantly neutral rooms overlooking Smithfield Plaza, just off the Liffey quays near the Jameson Distillery. 96 units, from €89; Smithfield Village, Dublin 7, *Central Dublin;* ☎ 01-485-0900; fax 01-485-0910; **www.comfortinndublincity.com;** Luas: Smithfield.

CONRAD HOTEL This commanding brick-and-glass presence on a corner of St. Stephen's Green has recently been spiffed up, bringing its small guest rooms up to a high standard of comfort. 191 units, from about €200. Earlsfort Terrace, Dublin 2, *St. Stephen's Green;* ☎ 01-676-5555; fax 01-676-5424; **www.conradhotels.com;** buses 10, 11, 13, 14, 15, 44, 46A, 47, 48, 86.

DAYS INN TALBOT STREET A chain with chic: contemporary furnishings, mellow lighting, lots of blond wood, a patio, and a handy central location off O'Connell Street near shops and transportation. 60 units, from about €90. 95–98 Talbot Street, Dublin 1, *Central Dublin;* ☎ 01-874-9202; fax 01-874-9672; **www.daysinntalbot.com;** all city-center buses.

FOUR SEASONS Over-the-top luxury (acres of glittering marble) belie the fact that this huge-but-hushed hostelry is part of a chain. One of Dublin's finest hotels, tucked away from the city center on the grounds of the Royal Dublin Showgrounds, with an indoor pool and many other amenities. 193 units, from about €300; Simmonscourt Road, Dublin 4, *Ballsbridge;* ☎ 01-665-4000; fax 01-665-4099; **www .fourseasons.com/dublin;** buses 5, 7, 7A, 8, 18, 45.

HILTON DUBLIN Views over the Grand Canal and a swath of greenery are the most appealing features of this rather bland business hotel just minutes away from the city center. 189 units, from about €140. Charlemont Place, Dublin 2; ☎ 01-402-9988; fax 01-402-9966; **dublin .hilton.com;** Luas: Grand Canal.

JURYS INN CHRISTCHURCH A convenient base for exploring central Dublin, with bland but large, great-value rooms. 182 units, from about €110; Christ Church Place, Dublin 8, *Dublin Castle and the Cathedrals;* ☎ 01-454-0000; fax 01-454-0012; **www.jurysinn.com;** buses 21A, 50, 50A, 78, 78A, 78B. Other Jurys are scattered around the capital: **Jurys**

Inn Custom House (Custom House Quay, Dublin 1, *Central Dublin;* ☎ 01-607-5000) and **Jurys Inn Parnell Street** (Moore Street Plaza, Parnell Street, Dublin 1, *Central Dublin;* ☎ 01-878-4900).

RADISSON SAS ROYAL This Scandinavian hotel group brings contemporary style and comfort to the edge of the city center. 150 units, from about €190; Golden Lane, Dublin 8, *St. Stephen's Green;* ☎ 01-898-2900; fax 01-898-2901; **royal.dublin.radissonsas.com;** all city-center buses.

THE WESTIN DUBLIN An imposing 19th-century bank building lends such features as a grand facade and distinctive public spaces (including the Mint bar, tucked away in the former bank vaults). This is the most grown-up place to stay near Temple Bar. 164 units, from about €215. College Green, Dublin 2, *Trinity College and Temple Bar;* ☎ 01-645-1000; fax 01-645-1234; **www.westin.com/dublin;** buses 5, 7A, 10, 11, 11A, 11B, 13A, 13B.

CHEAP BEDS: DORMS AND HOSTELS

kids **MERCER COURT** The home of students at the Royal College of Surgeons opens its doors to summertime visitors, providing extremely comfortable singles and doubles with private baths and a prime Grafton Street–area location. Amenities include continental breakfast, lounges, and parking at a rate of €7 a day. Singles from about €68, doubles from about €98. Lower Mercer Street, Dublin 2, *Grafton Street;* ☎ 01-474-4120; fax 01-672-9926; **www.mercer court.ie;** all city-center buses.

TRINITY COLLEGE Some of the most popular and inexpensive lodgings in Dublin are the summer-only dorm rooms at Trinity College. All are singles or doubles, some have private baths, and all enjoy the leafy campus and fantastic location. What other accommodation can boast the Book of Kells as an amenity? These rooms, available from mid-June to late September, are no secret, so book well in advance. Singles from about €59.95, doubles from about €39.95 per person. Accommodation Office, Trinity College; ☎ 01-896-1177; fax 01-671-1267; **www.tcd.ie.** All city-center buses.

Dublin is well endowed with hostels. Many are clean, chipper, and centrally located and offer dormitory beds as well as doubles and family rooms. Several are centrally located near Connolly Station, which puts them within easy reach of sights and transportation.

AVALON HOUSE A brick Victorian beauty just west of St. Stephen's Green welcomes hostelers of all ages in pleasant rooms that range from singles to dorms and family rooms. Lounges and a communal kitchen provide friendly environs, and amenities include Wi-Fi and a good breakfast. Singles and doubles from about €34; dormitory beds from about €14; family rooms from €65. 55 Aungier Street, Dublin 2, *St. Stephen's Green;* ☎ 01-475-0001; fax 01-475-0303; **www.avalon-house .ie;** all city-center buses.

GLOBETROTTERS Dorms are the only accommodations here, but they are clean, attractive, and equipped with good beds and powerful showers; plus, a tasty breakfast is included. The attractive premises share a Japanese garden with the Townhouse B&B (see page 111). Dormitory beds from about €20. 46–48 Lower Gardiner Street, Dublin 1, *Central Dublin;* ☎ 01-878-8088; **www.globetrottersdublin.com;** Luas: Connolly.

ISAACS HOSTEL Dublin's most popular hostel enhances its functional accommodations with a garden, in-house restaurant, lounge, and free breakfast and Wi-Fi. Singles and doubles from about €31; dormitory beds from about €14. 2–5 Frenchman's Lane, Dublin 1, *Central Dublin;* ☎ 01-855-6215; fax 01-855-6574; **www.isaacs.ie;** Luas: Connolly.

JACOBS INN A roof terrace, big sunny rooms with functional and attractive furnishings, and free Wi-Fi, movies, and breakfast make this well-run establishment, part of the Isaacs hotel and hostel empire, an especially good value. Singles and doubles from about €39; dormitory beds from about €14. 28 Talbot Place, Dublin 1, *Central Dublin;* ☎ 01-855-5660; fax 01-855-5664; **www.isaacs.ie;** Luas: Connolly.

HOTEL PROFILES
Bewleys Hotel ★★★½

QUALITY ★★★½	VALUE ★★★★½	€119

Merrion Road, Dublin 4, *Ballsbridge;* ☎ 01-668-1111; fax 01-668-1999; ballsbridge@bewleyshotels.com; www.bewleyshotels.com

Location Ballsbridge. **Buses** 7, 45; DART: Sandymount. **Amenities and services** 304 units; Internet access, hair dryers, in-room safes, in-room tea and coffee facilities, irons and ironing boards, restaurant, trouser press. **Elevator** Yes. **Parking** On property; €1.50 for an hour, €8 per day. **Price** Full Irish breakfast, €8.95; à la carte breakfast also available. **Credit cards** AE, DC, MC, V.

BALLSBRIDGE IS AN ATTRACTIVE Dublin neighborhood, a bastion of tree-shaded streets lined with swanky homes, embassies, and corporate headquarters. The out-of-city-center location makes the neighborhood less than ideal as a place to stay, but if you're trying to save euros, you may want to make an exception for Bewleys. This snazzy outlet in a small but popular chain occupies an old school to which a new wing has been seamlessly attached, providing comfortable, no-nonsense accommodations at a very good price. Bewleys is an especially good choice for guests traveling with children—family suites have living areas with pullout couches and kitchenettes, and sleep up to two adults and three children; plus, the grounds provide a place where little ones can run off steam. The excellent in-house restaurant, O'Connell's, is run by Tom O'Connell, part of the culinarily inspired clan that operates Ballymaloe, the famous cooking school, restaurant, and hotel, and offers good-value meals. You'll find other Bewleys in Newland's Cross west of the city center (☎ 01-464-0140), in outlying

Leopardstown (☎ 01-293-5000), and at Dublin Airport (☎ 01-871-1000); the Ballsbridge Bewleys is the most convenient to the city center.

Brownes Hotel ★★★

QUALITY ★★★★	VALUE ★★★	€165–€270

22 St. Stephen's Green, Dublin 2, *St. Stephen's Green;* **☎ 01-638-3939; fax 01-638-3900; info@brownesdublin.com; www.brownesdublin.com**

Location On St. Stephen's Green. **Buses** 10, 11A, 11B, 13, 20B; Luas: St. Stephen's Green; DART: Pearse. **Amenities and services** 11 units; bar, CD players, cable TV, Internet access, restaurant. **Elevator** Yes. **Parking** In nearby car parks, about €25 per day. **Price** Continental breakfast, €12.50; full Irish breakfast, €20. **Credit cards** AE, MC, V.

THIS SMALL, RATHER QUIRKY HOTEL in a Georgian mansion has the genuine feel of a private home, a handy location on the north side of St. Stephen's Green, and luxurious quarters that are the most comfortable of the many town-house hotels in this part of Dublin. A small but skilled staff adeptly sees to the needs of guests. The hotel has no public lounges, but the spacious rooms adeptly serve as sitting rooms as well as bedrooms, with comfortable reading chairs and writing desks. Retaining marble fireplaces, ornate plasterwork, and other original detailing, they are stylishly and comfortably furnished. (If you splurge on the junior suite, you can sleep in a king-size Murphy bed once owned by Marilyn Monroe.) Rooms in front overlook the green through double-glazed windows.

The Castle Hotel ★★★

QUALITY ★★½	VALUE ★★★★	€75–€110

3–4 Great Denmark Street, Dublin 1, *Central Dublin;* **☎ 01-874-6949; www.castle-hotel.ie**

Location On the north side of town, near O'Connell Street and Parnell Square. **Buses** All city-center buses. **Amenities and services** 50 units; in-room tea and coffee facilities, room service for breakfast (€5 extra), bar. **Elevator** Yes. **Parking** In nearby car park, about €10 a day. **Price** Most rates include breakfast. **Credit cards** AE, DC, MC, V.

ONE OF DUBLIN'S OLDEST HOTELS, welcoming guests since 1809, the Castle is an economy version of the Shelbourne—or so you might care to think of this inviting place, wrapped as it is in tradition, Irish hospitality, and charming old surroundings. Here, some of the woodwork and furnishings are a little worse for the wear, but the Castle is lovely, with small but serviceable rooms and an excellent location near the Gate Theatre, O'Connell Street shops, the Dublin City Gallery–The Hugh Lane, and other north-of-the-Liffey attractions. The establishment seems hell-bent on preserving the neighborhood's Georgian heritage and has expanded its holdings to the nearby St. George and Walton's, also excellent and traditional places to rest your head in this part of Dublin.

Central Hotel ★★★

QUALITY ★★★	VALUE ★★★★	€ 78–€ 88

**Exchequer Street, Dublin 2, *Dublin Castle;* ☎ 01-679-7302;
fax 01-679-7303; info@centralhoteldublin.com;
www.centralhoteldublin.com**

Location City center, between Grafton Street and Dublin Castle **Buses** All city-center buses. **Amenities and services** 70 units; in-room tea and coffee facilities, Wi-Fi in most rooms and all public areas, 2 bars, restaurant. **Elevator** Yes. **Parking** In nearby car parks, about €20 a day. **Price** Includes full Irish breakfast. **Credit cards** AE, DC, MC, V.

THE STERLING ATTRIBUTES of this old-fashioned hostelry include its self-proclaimed location, right in the middle of town, steps from Grafton Street and Temple Bar. Another great reason to stay here is to be just an elevator ride away from the in-house Library Bar, a cozy lair of roaring fires and comfy couches that is one of Dublin's best places for a relaxing drink (see page 163). Then there are the rooms, perfectly comfortable and snugly decked out with Irish pine and handsome fabrics, along with Wi-Fi and other handy modern touches.

 The Clarence ★★★★

QUALITY ★★★★½	VALUE ★★★★	FROM € 209

**6–8 Wellington Quay, Dublin 2, *Temple Bar;* ☎ 01-407-0800;
fax 01-407-0820; reservations@theclarence.ie; www.theclarence.ie**

Location On the River Liffey, at the edge of Temple Bar. **Buses** 51B, 51C, 68, 69, 79. **Amenities and services** 48 units; bar, bathrobes, DVD/CD players, hair dryers, high-speed Internet access, in-room entertainment, laundry and dry cleaning, minibars, 24-hour room service, 2 telephone lines. **Elevator** Yes. **Parking** Valet, €25 per day. **Price** Continental breakfast, €12.50; Irish breakfast, €27.50; many special offers available, including dinner and bed-and-breakfast packages. **Credit cards** AE, DC, MC, V.

AN OLD DUBLIN HOSTELRY that had fallen on hard times by the 1990s, the Clarence is now owned by the Irish rock band U2. One doesn't necessarily equate rockers with sensible comfort, but that is exactly what this lovely hotel achieves, and it adds a big dose of "coolness," too. The decor complements the original Arts and Crafts details: light oak paneling, Shaker-style furnishings, and gentle neutral tones create a soothing environment throughout the public areas and guest rooms. Thoughtful lighting, large writing desks, state-of-the-art entertainment systems, and fine towels and bed linens all create a retreat that you will find hard to leave—all the more so given that most rooms have nice outlooks (rooms in front of the hotel overlook the river, while the quieter rear-facing rooms look across the rooftops of old Dublin) and many on the top floor open to small balconies. The Octagon Bar and the Study are popular meeting places, and the Tea

Room (see page 157) is one of Dublin's finest restaurants. As adult as the Clarence is, it still welcomes kids, catering to them with milk and cookies, video games, and other amenities.

The Fitzwilliam ★★★★½

QUALITY ★★★★½	VALUE ★★★★	€265–€450

St. Stephen's Green, Dublin 2, *St. Stephen's Green;* ☎ **01-478-7000; fax 01-478-7878; enq@fitzwilliamhotel.com; www.fitzwilliamhotel.com**

Location On St. Stephen's Green. **Buses** 10, 11A, 11B, 13, 20B; Luas: St. Stephen's Green; DART: Pearse. **Amenities and services** 128 units; bar, beauty salon, gym, CD players, cafe, concierge, in-room entertainment, in-room tea and coffee facilities, Internet access, restaurant, roof garden, spa treatments, 2 telephones. **Elevator** Yes. **Parking** In nearby car parks, about €25 per day. **Price** Breakfast included in some rates; many special offers and packages available. **Credit cards** AE, DC, MC, V.

SIR TERRENCE CONRAN, the British purveyor of contemporary good taste, designed the interiors of this attractive hotel, and he had good space to work with—large, light-filled public areas and guest rooms face either St. Stephen's Green or a roof garden at the rear of the hotel. Sir Terrence's stamp is much in evidence where clean lines, neutral tones, and natural fabrics create stylish and restful surroundings. Many amenities and thoughtful touches, such as large tubs, separate showers, fluffy towels and bathrobes, and fresh-cut flowers, ensure a great deal of comfort. While the views over the green are wonderful, those of the large roof garden are extremely pleasant, too, and provide a sense of escape from the city hub-bub. Many rooms take advantage of these outlooks from small balconies. Citron Café serves light meals, Inn on the Green is the snug bar, and Thornton's is one of the city's finest restaurants.

The Gresham ★★★

QUALITY ★★★	VALUE ★★★	€140–€300

23 Upper O'Connell Street, Dublin 1, *Central Dublin;* ☎ **01-874-6881; fax 01-878-7175; info@thegresham.com; www.gresham-hotels.com**

Location In city center, north of the River Liffey. **Buses** All city-center buses; DART: Tara Street. **Amenities and services** 288 units; bars, fitness center, laundry service, lobby lounge, restaurant, some smoking rooms. **Elevator** Yes. **Parking** On premises, €12.50 per day. **Price** Some rates include full Irish breakfast; special offers available. **Credit cards** AE, DC, MC, V.

ONE OF DUBLIN'S MOST FAMOUS HOTELS lives up to its reputation in a series of grand public rooms, especially the sprawling lobby lounge and a stylish restaurant, 23. The lobby lounge is a popular and extremely appealing meeting place in downtown Dublin, and maybe the second-best place in town (after the Shelbourne; see page 111) for afternoon tea; here you can sit on plush couches, enjoy tea, and watch the passersby on busy O'Connell Street. Recent renovations have brought guest rooms back up to snuff. Decor ranges from business-traveler conventional to stylishly neutral, but all rooms are comfortable and equipped with new bathrooms. Since rooms vary a bit in style, ask to see a few—the best are those with views through tall windows over O'Connell Street.

Hotel Isaacs Dublin ★★★

QUALITY	★★½	VALUE	★★★★	FROM	€105

Store Street, Dublin 1, *Central Dublin*; ☎ 01-813-4700; fax 01-836-5390; hotel@isaacs.ie; www.isaacs.ie

Location Central Dublin, near O'Connell Street and Connolly Street train station. **Buses** 27A, 27B, 53A; Luas and DART: Connolly Station. **Amenities and services** 90 units; air-conditioning in some rooms, bar, e-mail facilities, garden, hair dryers, in-room safes, in-room tea and coffee facilities, irons and ironing boards, nonsmoking rooms, restaurant, trouser press. **Elevator** Yes. **Parking** In nearby car parks, about €20 per day. **Price** Many special rates available, some including breakfast; otherwise, breakfast available from about €10. **Credit cards** MC, V.

THE MOST IMPORTANT THING to know about this outlet of an Irish chain is that you should book far, far in advance, because it's no secret that these are some of the best-value lodgings in town. The grandiose lobby suggests the place is a bit fancier than it really is, but the guest rooms are surprisingly attractive (in a generic hotel/motel sort of way), plus they are immaculate and equipped with shiny tile bathrooms. Rooms facing the street can be noisy, and the pleasant staff always seems a bit overworked, but there are more pluses here than minuses. A leafy courtyard is a nice oasis in this hectic neighborhood; a restaurant, bar, and Internet cafe supply the essentials; and the O'Connell Street shops, as well as the airport bus and other transportation links, are just a few blocks away. Keep in mind that it's probably the hotel you want and not the adjacent hostel of the same name.

Longfield's Hotel ★★★

QUALITY	★★★	VALUE	★★★★	€80–€100

10 Lower Fitzwilliam Street, Dublin 2, *Georgian Dublin*; ☎ 01-676-1367; fax 01-676-1542; info@longfields.ie; www.longfields.ie

Location Between Fitzwilliam and Merrion squares. **Buses** 11, 11A, 11B, 13B. **Amenities and services** 26 units; bar service, in-room tea and coffee facilities, Wi-Fi, restaurant. **Elevator** Yes. **Parking** In nearby car parks, about €20 a day. **Price** Includes full Irish breakfast. **Credit cards** AE, DC, MC, V.

AN OLD-WORLD AMBIENCE PREVAILS in these two interconnected houses in the heart of Georgian Dublin. Traditional furnishings, high ceilings, and old-fashioned wallpaper lend an air of nonfussy comfort to the lounges and bedrooms and do justice to the surroundings. A little more fussiness might be in order, though: plumbing does not always operate at top form, and soiled bedspreads and worn carpets aren't acceptable, though the hotel is dong some refurbishing. Bedrooms vary considerably in size (some are large enough to accommodate four-poster beds, while those on the top floor are quite small), and most bathrooms are equipped with showers only. Number 10 restaurant, handily located on the ground floor of the hotel, is excellent.

Merrion Hotel ★★★★½

QUALITY ★★★★½	VALUE ★★★	FROM €450

Upper Merrion Street, Dublin 2, *Georgian Dublin*; ☎ 01-603-0600; fax 01-603-0700; info@merrionhotel.com; www.merrionhotel.com

Location In Georgian Dublin, near government buildings. **Buses** 5, 7A, 13A. **Amenities and services** 142 units; babysitting, bar, broadband Internet access, CD players, concierge, gym, hair dryers, in-room fax machines, in-room safes, laundry service, minibars, 2 restaurants, satellite and cable TV, spa, steam room, swimming pool, 3 telephones in each room, trouser press, 24-hour room service. **Elevator** Yes. **Parking** Free valet. **Price** Continental breakfast, €22; Irish breakfast, €27; many special offers available. **Credit cards** AE, DC, MC, V.

WHAT MAY WELL BE DUBLIN'S most luxurious hotel consists of four Georgian town houses and, beyond large formal gardens, a stylish contemporary wing. One of the country's most extensive private collections of 19th- and 20th-century Irish art hangs in the public lounges, where fires burn beneath original ornate plasterwork, and the efficient staff seems to appear out of thin air to provide superb service. Large and gracious guest rooms are traditionally yet stylishly furnished and swathed in yards of luxurious Irish fabrics; the bathrooms are nothing short of glamorous, equipped with huge walk-in showers. A beautiful swimming pool and excellent spa lend a resortlike air to the urbane surroundings. The Merrion manages to pull off all this pampering without pretense, creating a truly great hotel. Should you be lucky enough to stay here, have a meal in the hotel dining room, Restaurant Patrick Guilbaud (page 157), which—not surprisingly, given where it is—is the best in town.

The Morrison Hotel ★★★★

QUALITY ★★★★½	VALUE ★★★	€195–€240

Ormond Quay, Dublin 1, *Central Dublin*; ☎ 01-887-2400; fax 01-878-3185; sales@morrisonhotel.ie; www.morrisonhotel.ie

Location On the north side of the River Liffey. **Buses** 70, 80; Luas: Jervis. **Amenities and services** 148 units; CD players, in-room safes, Wi-Fi, minibars, restaurant, cafe, 2 bars, room service, spa. **Elevator** Yes. **Parking** In nearby car park, about €20 a day. **Price** À la carte breakfast from about €7; many special offers available. **Credit cards** AE, DC, MC, V.

THE "COOL" QUOTIENT is not necessarily the best criterion for a good hotel, but this creation of Irish designer John Rocha proves that a hotel can be stylish, edgy, and extremely comfortable all at the same time. Rocha had the good sense to expend his theatrics in the glamorous and colorful public rooms (including the excellent Halo restaurant; see page 153) and to use a spare hand in the guest quarters, many of which have river views. There, minimalist surroundings of modern furniture, natural fabrics, and warm tones of cream and brown create environments that are both sooth-ing and exciting—it's a pleasure to kick off your shoes and bask in the ambience (or soak in one of the deep tubs). When you're ready to hit the streets, you'll discover the advantages of this location north of the Liffey: O'Connell Street shops are a short stroll away, as are many of the muse-ums and other attractions south of the river, yet you are comfortably removed from the noisy antics of Temple Bar just across the river.

Number 31 ★★★★

QUALITY ★★★★	VALUE ★★★★½	€110–€150

31 Leeson Close, Dublin 2, *Georgian Dublin*; ☎ 01-676-5011; fax 01-676-2929; number31@iol.ie; www.number31.ie

Location South of St. Stephen's Green. **Buses** 11, 11A, 11B, 13, 13A. **Amenities and services** 20 rooms; garden, in-room tea and coffee facilities, lounge. **Elevator** No. **Parking** Free private car park. **Price** Includes full Irish breakfast. **Credit cards** AE, MC, V.

NOEL AND DEIRDRE COMER'S distinctive and extremely appealing guest-house (composed of a coach house and a Georgian terrace house, separated by a lush garden) should be among the top choices for a place to stay in central Dublin. The coach house bears the mark of a previous owner, Sam Stephenson, one of Ireland's leading 20th-century architects. The stunning interior is pleasantly contemporary, with a sunken conversation pit sur-rounding a fireplace where aromatic peat is usually burning. Brick walls are painted in soothing tones of white and cream, tile floors are covered with kilims, windows are tall, and a conservatory breakfast room opens to a roof garden. The five rooms in this wing have an informal feel to them, with low wooden ceilings and, in several, small sitting areas that open to private patios. The large, high-ceilinged rooms in the Georgian house, reached through the rear garden or a separate entrance on Fitzwilliam Street, are decorated in an uncluttered traditional style with contemporary touches; those facing the garden are blessedly quiet. Breakfast, which includes treats such as homemade potato cakes and cranberry bread, is as memorable as the other ingredients of a stay in this wonderful place.

Schoolhouse Hotel ★★★

QUALITY ★★★½	VALUE ★★★	€189–€219

28 Northumberland Road, Dublin 4, *Ballsbridge*; ☎ 01-667-5014; fax 01-676-5015; reservations@schoolhouse.com; www.schoolhousehotel.com

Location In Ballsbridge, but at the edge of the city center. **Buses** 7, 45. **DART:** Grand Canal Dock. **Amenities and services** 31 units; room service, in-room tea and coffee facilities, Internet access, Wi-Fi, bar, restaurant. **Elevator** Yes. **Parking** Free. **Price** Includes full Irish breakfast; special offers available on the Web site. **Credit cards** AE, DC, MC, V.

THIS CONVERTED VICTORIAN SCHOOL is one of Dublin's better-kept secrets—tucked away in a leafy neighborhood on the banks of the canal near the Docklands but only a ten-minute walk from St. Stephen's Green. Rooms are snugly done up with king-size beds, thick duvets, and handsome traditional furnishings; bathrooms are large and well equipped with big tubs and excellent showers. The former refectory now does duty as a pleasant restaurant and bar that spill out onto a pleasant patio, making it hard to tear yourself away from the premises after a day of sightseeing.

The Shelbourne   ★★★

QUALITY ★★★★	VALUE ★★★	FROM €240

26 St. Stephen's Green, Dublin 2, *St. Stephen's Green*; ☎ 01-663-4500; fax 01-661-6006; look@marriott.com; www.marriott.co.uk

Location In the heart of Dublin, facing St. Stephen's Green. All city-center buses. **Amenities and services** 265 units; in-room tea and coffee facilities, Wi-Fi, 24-hour room service, business center, 2 bars, 2 restaurants, health club, indoor pool, spa, loads of ambience. **Elevator** Yes. **Parking** In nearby car parks, about €20 a day. **Price** Most rates include lavish buffet breakfast. **Credit cards** AE, DC, MC, V.

DUBLIN LOST A BIT OF ITS SOUL when the most famous hostelry in town closed for renovation several years ago, and now that lights from the tall windows of the 18th-century edifice are once again shining bright over St. Stephen's Green, the city once again has a social center at its heart. The premises where the Irish Constitution was drafted is still the gathering spot for politicians, journalists, theater and literary folk, and other members of the city elite, who keep the Lord Mayor's Lounge, the Horseshoe Bar, and the elegant Saddle Room (one of the capital's best tables) constantly busy. Marriott has taken over the hotel but left much of the old-world flair intact; the best rooms are those in the old wing, overlooking the green, although units in a new wing are tastefully done as well, in plush, traditional style, with excellent beds and sumptuous bathrooms. A pool, glitzy health club, and spa are other new additions to what remains the best address in old Dublin.

The Townhouse   ★★

QUALITY ★★★	VALUE ★★★★	€70–€115

47–48 Lower Gardiner Street, Dublin 1, *Central Dublin*; ☎ 01-878-8808; fax 01-878-8787; info@townhouseofdublin.com; www.townhouseofdublin.com

Location Central Dublin, near train and bus stations. **Buses** 27A, 27B, 53A; DART: Connolly Station. **Amenities and services** 30 units; garden, hair dryers, in-room tea and coffee facilities, lounge. **Elevator** Yes. **Parking** In nearby car parks, about €20 a day. **Price** Includes full Irish breakfast. **Credit cards** MC, V.

A CONVENIENT LOCATION near the bus and train stations and the very reasonable rates account for the appeal of this popular bed-and-breakfast that sprawls through two Georgian houses (the former homes of two 19th-century playwrights, Lafcadio Hearn and Dion Boucicault) plus a new extension. While the lounge and the rooms in the older wings bear the mark of this heritage with dark and rather gloomy decor, the rooms in the new wing are surprisingly contemporary and chic—the wood floors, handsome furnishings, fluffy duvets, and well-appointed bathrooms would pass muster in a more expensive hotel. The reasonable rates may help you overcome a few drawbacks: rooms facing busy Gardiner Street can be noisy, and apart from the convenience of being near the airport link and other transportation, the busy, traffic-ridden neighborhood is not as appealing as others in Dublin.

The Westbury ★★★★

QUALITY ★★★★	VALUE ★★★½	FROM €239

Grafton Street, Dublin 2, *Grafton Street;* ☎ **01-679-1122; fax 01-679-7078; westbury@jurysdoyle.com; www.jurysdoyle.com**

Location In city center, off Grafton Street and near St. Stephen's Green. **Buses** 10, 11A, 11B, 13, 20B. **Amenities and services** 210 units; babysitting, bar, business services, concierge, gym, in-room entertainment, in-room safes, Wi-Fi, laundry, minibars, restaurant. **Elevator** Yes. **Parking** On property, free. **Price** Most rates include buffet breakfast; many special offers available. **Credit cards** AE, DC, MC, V.

THIS MODERN, RATHER NONDESCRIPT building announces itself as one of Dublin's poshest hostelries by its privileged location, on a cul-de-sac just off Grafton Street. For many guests, the elegant lobby and well-appointed suites and guest rooms are the ultimate in graciousness. Bright, spacious, and beautifully furnished in traditional style with large desks and comfortable lounge chairs, they are sumptuous and appealing. The 25 so-called executive rooms are especially large; depending on availability, you can upgrade to these for a relatively small extra charge. An attentive staff takes very good care of guests, ensuring that business execs and leisure travelers alike have everything they need. The only element lacking at the Westbury is pizzazz; a new crop of hotels provide similar levels of comfort with a little more dazzle.

EXPLORING DUBLIN

DUBLIN IS COMPACT—a pleasure to explore on foot and easy to navigate by public transportation. However you get around, the city will keep you entertained, enthralled even, but won't overwhelm you.

TOURS OF DUBLIN

THESE TOURS SHOW OFF THE BEST sides of Dublin and treat you to a uniquely Irish gift for gab. Many tours can fill up quickly during summer months, so book as far in advance as you can.

DUBLIN CITY SIGHTSEEING AND DUBLIN CITY TOURS Both outfits operate hop-on, hop-off schemes, with stops at 14 or so major attractions around the city and either canned or live commentary (the latter usually sounds as canned as the taped version). The convenience of these tours, which are virtually identical, is that you can ride around town, enjoying the view from an open-top bus, and get off whenever you feel like visiting a sight. Tickets are good for 24 hours. You can cram quite a bit of sightseeing into a full day or, better, an afternoon and the following morning (this gives you a chance to rest up between bouts). The tours include stops outside the city center—at Guinness Storehouse, Kilmainham Gaol, and Phoenix Park, among other attractions—so concentrate on those to get the most bang for your euro; you can reach the city-center sights on foot. Buy tickets from Dublin Tourism, from vendors at some of the well-marked stops, or on the buses. City Sightseeing Tours start at 14 Upper O'Connell Street and cost €16 for adults, €14 for seniors and students, €7 for children ages 5 to 15, free for children under age 5, €39 for families; ☎ 01-872-9010 or **www.city-sightseeing.com.** Dublin City Tours start at 59 Upper O'Connell Street and cost €13 for adults, €13 for seniors and students, €6 children under age 14; ☎ 01-873-4222 or **www .dublinbus.ie/sightseeing.**

DUBLIN LITERARY PUB CRAWL Dublin produced three Nobel Prize–winning authors—Samuel Beckett, George Bernard Shaw, and William Butler Yeats—as well as many literary geniuses who were not so rewarded (James Joyce and Brendan Behan come to mind). At one time or another, most Dublin writers found inspiration at the bottom of a pint glass in the hundreds of pubs around the city, and you can follow in their footsteps to enjoy the *cráic* and literary ambience of four famous writerly haunts. Visits are accompanied by recitations and a bit of song. Tours start at the Duke Pub, 9 Duke Street, Dublin 2, *Temple Bar;* April through November, Monday through Saturday, 7:30 p.m., Sunday, 12:30 p.m.; December through March, Thursday through Sunday, 7:30 p.m.; €12 adults, €10 students; ☎ 01-670-5602 to reserve or go to **www.dublinpubcrawl.com.**

HISTORICAL WALKING TOURS OF DUBLIN Walking through Dublin with these locals who know their history inside and out is a pleasure, and it's one of the best ways to get to know the city. Tours concentrate on some places you might otherwise rush by to get to leafier precincts or more-appealing streets: the Old Parliament House, City Hall, and the like. The guides are history buffs and graduates of Trinity College, and as they speak about the 1916 Easter Uprising and other events with flare and ease, they put the complexities of Irish and Dublin history into welcome perspective. The two-hour tours meet at the front gate of Trinity College, College Green, Dublin 2; May through September, daily, 11 a.m. and 3 p.m.; April and October, daily, 11 a.m.; November through March, Friday through Sunday, 11 a.m. You can purchase tickets at the meeting point: €12 adults, €10 seniors and students, free for children under 14. For more information, call ☎ 01-87-688-9412 or go to **www.historicalinsights.ie.**

MUSIC PUB CRAWL Want to spend some time in Dublin pubs? Hear some good traditional music? Learn about those strange instruments you see folks playing? Know the stories behind some of the songs you hear around Ireland? Then sign on to one of these pleasant expeditions departing from Oliver St. John Gogarty's (the upstairs bar) on Fleet Street. Two good-natured musicians take you to three pubs, play an assortment of instruments, sing a lot, and talk knowledgeably about the fine points of Irish music. Tours last about two and a half hours. All in all, a really good way to spend—or start—an evening. April through October, 7:30 p.m. daily; November through March, 7:30 p.m. Thursdays, Fridays, and Saturdays; €12 adults, €10 students; ☎ 01-478-0193 or reserve at the Dublin Tourism Office.

1916 REBELLION WALKING TOUR Even if you've come to Dublin for nothing but a pub crawl, you can't help but encounter evidence of the 1916 Rebellion, when the Irish took up arms against the British on Easter Monday. British troops suppressed the so-called Easter Rising after six days and executed many of the leaders (see Kilmainham Gaol, page 134), but the uprising set the stage for Irish independence in 1919. Historians Lorcan Collins and Conor Kostick bring the events and the broad scope of Irish history into focus on these wonderful two-hour walk-and-talk events through Central Dublin, stopping at such landmarks as the Central Post Office (still bullet-ridden). Tours leave from the International Bar, 23 Wicklow Street, Dublin 2, and run March through October, Monday through Saturday, 11:30 a.m., Sunday, 1 p.m.; €12. Show up at least ten minutes before the tour starts; **www.1916rising.com.**

PAT LIDDY WALKING TOURS Pat Liddy is a well-respected Dublin historian who has compiled excellent tours of the capital, led by a well-trained corps of enthusiastic and knowledgeable guides. Themes include Georgian Dublin, medieval Dublin, Victorian Dublin, and so on. If you wish to set your own pace, you can also download Pat's podcasts from his Web site. Tours leave from Dublin Tourism on Suffolk Street and last about two hours. From €12 adults, €10 seniors and students; ☎ 01-831-1109; **www.walkingtours.ie.**

VIKING SPLASH TOURS Driving around Dublin in a World War II–era amphibious vehicle is sort of silly. So is wearing a Viking helmet and roaring at passersby. Or splashing into a canal and floating past the apartments of rock stars. But the Viking folks pepper these antics with amusing and excellent commentary on city landmarks and history, and they deserve credit for proving that a tour can be informative without being stuffy. You'll probably learn more on one of the excellent walking tours other outfits offer, but you might not have as much fun. Tours last 75 minutes and run every half hour: February, Wednesday through Sunday, 10 a.m. to 4 p.m.; March through October, daily, 9:30 a.m. to 5 p.m.; and November, Tuesday through Sunday, 10 a.m. to 4 p.m.; €20 adults, €18 seniors and students, €10 children, free for children under 12. Tours depart from St. Patrick's Cathedral and St. Stephen's Green; 64–65 Patrick Street, Dublin 8; ☎ 01-707-6000; www.vikingsplash.ie.

DUBLIN WALKS

WALKING IS THE EASIEST WAY to get around Dublin and, given the number of fascinating places to see, a pleasure, even when holding an umbrella. Here's a look at the various neighborhoods and what to see on a walk through each of them. (For more on Dublin neighborhoods, see page 93.)

 ### A Walk up O'Connell Street

To those who live here, known as Northsiders, this is the real Dublin, and O'Connell Street is the heart of the city. (Southsiders will make that claim about Grafton Street and St. Stephen's Green.) Begin your walk at the foot of O'Connell Street, on the River Liffey at **O'Connell Street Bridge.** A statue of Daniel O'Connell (1775–1847), a statesman and fighter for Catholic emancipation in Ireland, stands just a little ways up the street. Just east along the river is what may still be the most impressive building in Dublin, the copper-domed **Custom House,** completed in 1791. The handsome columned facade, adorned with symbolic statuary representing Irish transportation and trade, still evokes pride and, overlooking a wide stretch of the Liffey, is an evocative reminder of the city's seafaring past.

While the Custom House shines as an emblem of the heights civic architecture achieved in the past, the **Monument of Light** in the middle of O'Connell Street reveals the utter banality that urban planners thrust upon us these days. The 120-meter (396-foot) steel pole is usually called the Spire and has inspired many rude names as well; one of the few that can be repeated in polite company is "stiletto in the ghetto." The **Abbey Theatre,** home of the Irish National Theatre, is just to the east, down Abbey Street (see page 159). Just north on O'Connell Street is the **General Post Office,** which became far more famous than its usual business warranted in 1916, when the building became the Republican command center of the Easter Rising. Rebels stormed the building, issued the Proclamation of the Irish Republic, and held out against British troops for five days. Bullet holes still riddle the facade, and you can follow the events of the uprising (which led to the Anglo-Irish Treaty and independence for 26 counties of the Irish Free State in 1921) on the painting cycle in the lobby (open Monday through Saturday, 8 a.m. to 8 p.m.).

Henry Street, just beyond the post office, is one of a number of pedestrian-only thoroughfares in this part of town. It leads to a European-looking outdoor market on **Moore Street;** the stalls here (open Monday through Saturday, 8 a.m. to 6 p.m.) are far more colorful than their neighbors, the chain stores and shopping centers that

Walks and Drives around Dublin

From the capital, it's easy to get away from it all into seascape, mountain wilderness, and history-filled countryside.

GREAT WALKS

HOWTH HEAD

Only 15 minutes from central Dublin yet more like a seaside village than a sub-urb, Howth is justifiably popular with Dubliners in search of a breath of sea air or a splash in the chilly waters of the Irish Sea. Walkers can get even more of a sense of getting away from urban life on the paths that skirt the shorelines and climb the summits of the Howth Peninsula (also see page 174).

The DART station is at the edge of **Howth Harbour,** a busy port that shelters fishing fleets and pleasure craft. A cliff path begins near the **East Pier;** once you round the **Nose of Howth,** you will soon find yourself in a remote-seeming seascape that combines heather-covered moors and a rocky coast that is home to huge colonies of seabirds and seals. A walk of about half an hour will bring you to **Baily Lighthouse** on the southern side of the peninsula. If you want to extend the walk to a half-day's excursion, you can follow the sea as far as the **Martello Tower,** 1 of 27 such watchtowers the British built along the east coast of Ireland in the early 19th century to help thwart a possible French invasion. From there, make the climb to **Ben of Howth,** the peninsula's 170-meter (510-foot) summit from which views extend to the Wicklow Mountains to the south and the Mourne Mountains to the north, then descend the side of the summit back toward Howth.

BRAY HEAD

An especially beautiful and dramatic stretch of coastal scenery lies between **Bray** and **Greystones,** south of Dublin. Both towns are suburban, and both also have the flair of popular seaside retreats, with beaches and boardwalk-type amuse-ments. Both towns are on the DART line from Dublin; for the best views, take the train to its terminus at Greystones, walk north to Bray, and catch a DART train back to Dublin there. Linking Greystones and Bray is a well-trodden ten-kilometer (six-mile) coastal path, full of views across **Dublin Bay** to **Howth Head, Bray Head,** and the twin summits of **Little Sugar Loaf** and **Great Sugar**

line Henry Street. A few steps east off O'Connell on Cathedral Street is **St. Mary's Pro-Cathedral,** the principal Catholic church of Dublin but never designated as a cathedral (that honor goes to two Church of Ireland outposts across the river, St. Patrick's and Christ Church). St. Mary's is severely classical and templelike in its design, a suitable setting for a Latin mass, which is sung by the famed Palestrina Choir every Sunday at 11 a.m. (the church is open daily, 8 a.m. to 6 p.m.).

Loaf to the west. Leave the coastal path for a short climb up the heather-covered hillsides of Bray Head to a viewpoint with a stunning outlook. You can reward yourself at the end of the walk with a dip in the sea at **Bray Beach** or with a tip of the elbow in any number of pubs in Bray.

ALONG THE WICKLOW WAY

The Wicklow Way, one of Ireland's finest walking paths, extends for 137 kilometers (85 miles), from **Marlay Park** on the south side of Dublin through the Wicklow Mountains to the village of **Clonegall** in County Carlow. Several companies and clubs in Dublin organize walks along the way, allowing you a chance to experience the moor-and-mountain scenery on a day's excursion (see page 179). If you want to get a taste of the way on your own, you can take the number 16 bus from O'Connell Street to Marlay Park and then follow the way into **Kilmashogue Wood** and up the flanks of **Kilmashogue Mountain;** enjoy the views over Dublin Bay from one of the viewpoints, and backtrack to Marlay Park. For a more rewarding walk, drive or take the bus to **Glendalough,** and from there follow the way as it passes the **Upper** and **Lower lakes,** the **Pollnass Waterfall,** and the beautiful monastic remains (see page 179). The **Wicklow Mountains National Park Visitor Centre** at Glendalough provides maps and information on walking the way and other trails.

GREAT DRIVES

THE BOYNE VALLEY

A relatively easy day's outing from Dublin exposes you to millennia of Irish history—from the fields where the Battle of the Boyne was fought in 1690 to the 5,000-year-old passage tombs at **Newgrange** to the seat of the medieval High Kings of Ireland at the **Hill of Tara.**

Leave Dublin to the north on M1 and follow this busy motorway about 32 kilometers (18 miles) to the turnoff for **Drogheda,** where you will pick up R132 east across the River Boyne to the Battle of the Boyne site. Here, in 1690, the armies of the Protestant William of Orange defeated the forces of the Catholic James I. Excellent signage at the site will lead you to **King William's**

Continued on next page

Another place that is sacred to Dubliners is the recently renovated **Gresham Hotel,** the best address on O'Connell Street and famous as a spot to enjoy a cup of tea while watching the parade of strollers and shoppers on the avenue (see hotel profile on page 107). O'Connell Street ends at **Parnell Square,** named for Charles Stewart Parnell, a 19th-century champion of home rule who was brought down in scandal-ridden tatters when he was named in divorce proceedings against his

Walks and Drives around Dublin (continued)

GREAT DRIVES (CONTINUED)

THE BOYNE VALLEY (CONTINUED)

Glen, where William's soldiers hid and launched their victorious surprise attack on James's armies, and to **Townley Hall Estate,** where walks through the forest lead you to overlooks of the valley where the battle was waged.

Some eight kilometers (five miles) west on N51 is **Slane,** a pretty village built around a castle and overlooked by the Hill of Slane, on which St. Patrick allegedly lit his paschal fire in AD 433, defying pagan King Laoghaire. Allegedly, the king allowed Patrick to preach Christianity after the saint brandished a shamrock to explain the mysteries of the Holy Trinity.

Newgrange (see page 178) is just three kilometers (two miles) south of Slane. This 5,000-year-old passage tomb is one of several prehistoric tombs and other archaeological sites collectively known as Brú na Bóinne, where the visitors center provides insight into the significance of some of the world's most impressive prehistoric structures.

Follow N51 12 kilometers (7.5 miles) west to Navan, and from there take R163 2 kilometers (1 mile) south to **Kells.** A round tower and the small, charming **St. Kevin's Church** are what remains of the great monastic complex that St. Colomba founded here in the sixth century AD. It is widely believed that Scottish monks brought the celebrated illuminated manuscript known as the **Book of Kells** to this monastic settlement, from which it was removed to Trinity College in Dublin and where it now resides in splendor (see page 124).

From Navan it's about ten kilometers (six miles) southeast on N3 to the **Hill of Tara** (see page 177), seat of the High Kings of Ireland through the pre-Christian centuries to as late as the 11th century. A climb up the grassy knoll towering over the site affords fine views of the surrounding plains.

A final stop on this history-filled itinerary is **Trim,** 15 kilometers (9 miles) west of the Hill of Tara on R154. Trim Castle is one of Ireland's finest medieval ruins, a huge Anglo-Norman complex that King Edward III fortified heavily in the 14th century. Oliver Cromwell attacked and destroyed the town and castle in 1649. Remnants include the keep, the turrets, portions of the outer wall, the nave and chancel of the cathedral, and, on the opposite banks of the River Boyne, the ruins of the Hospital of St. John the Baptist.

mistress, Kitty O'Shea. This handsome square does the so-called Uncrowned King of Ireland justice as Dublin's cultural bastion. Fine old buildings on and around the square house the **Gate Theatre,** founded in 1929 and one of Europe's most respected stages (see page 159); the **Dublin City Gallery–The Hugh Lane** (see page 130); and the **Dublin Writers Museum** (see page 132). On the north side of the square is the **Garden**

You can make a speedy return to Dublin from Trim on R154 and N3, a trip of about 50 kilometers (30 miles).

THROUGH THE WICKLOW MOUNTAINS

These mountains begin to rise in the southern suburbs of Dublin, providing city folks with a nearby retreat. In fact, the Wicklows encompass some of Ireland's most rugged scenery and also cradle monastic ruins and some charming villages.

Leave Dublin and head south on the M1, but you won't go far before you come to **Enniskerry,** a pretty village surrounding a square and a large 19th-century Gothic Revival church, but best known for **Powerscourt,** probably Ireland's most magnificent house and garden (see page 180).

From Enniskerry follow R755 through the forested mountains to **Roundwood,** notable not only for the mountain scenery that surrounds it but also for the fact that, at 250 meters (800 feet) above sea level, this small collection of houses surrounding a market square is the highest village in Ireland.

More spectacular scenery unfolds as you follow R759 and R115 deep into **Wicklow Mountains National Park** and through a pass in the mountain ridges known as **Sally Gap.** The road follows heather-covered hillsides through stands of pine and extensive bogs where peat is still cut for fuel. This stretch of road then passes high above **Glenmacnass,** a deep, impossibly green valley, at the end of which is the attractive village of **Laragh,** then **Glendalough** (see page 179). One of Ireland's most impressive medieval monastic communities, it is beautifully set in a valley beside a set of twin lakes.

You may want to return to Dublin by retracing your steps, so you can enjoy the scenery around Sally Gap again. Or head west on R756 and R758 for about 30 kilometers (18 miles), following the shores of **Blessington Lakes,** (actually one large reservoir, **Poulaphouca,** which provides Dublin with its water). The village of **Blessington,** on the lakeshore, comprises an attractive assemblage of Georgian houses. From there you can return to Dublin on N81, a trip of about 50 kilometers (30 miles).

of Remembrance, a lovely and moving tribute to all those who have died fighting for Irish freedom.

Trinity College and Temple Bar

These two landmarks represent two sides of Dublin—or do they? **Temple Bar** is the haunt of inebriated youth and **Trinity College** is the

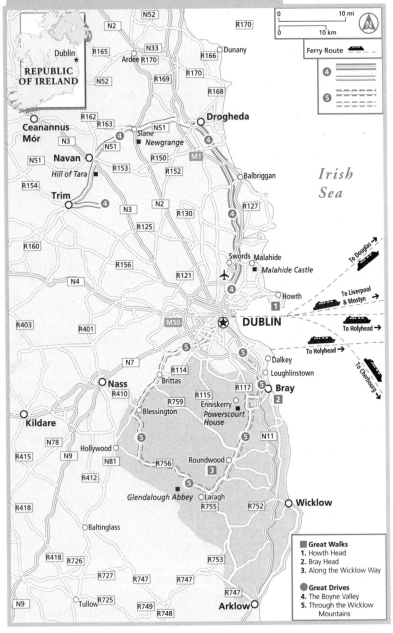

Dublin

REPUBLIC OF IRELAND

N52
R170
N2
R165
N33
R166 Dunany
Ardee R170
R169
R170
N52
R168
R162
R163
Drogheda
Ceanannus Mór
N3
Slane N51
Newgrange
N51 M1
Navan
R153
R150
Hill of Tara
R152
Balbriggan
N51
R154
Trim
N3
N2
R130
R127
R125
R160
R156
R121
Swords Malahide
R403
Malahide Castle
Irish Sea
To Douglas
N4
To Liverpool & Mostyn
Howth **1**
To Holyhead
M50
DUBLIN
To Holyhead
To Cherbourg
N7
R114
Dalkey
Brittas
Loughlinstown
Nass
R117
Bray **2**
R410
R115
R759 Enniskerry
Blessington *Powerscourt House*
Kildare
N78
N81
N11
Hollywood
R756 Roundwood **3**
N9
R415
R412
Glendalough Abbey Laragh
R418
R755 R752 Wicklow
Baltinglass
R418 R726
R753
R727 R747 R747
N9 R725 R747
Tullow R749 R748
Arklow

Ferry Route
4
5

■ Great Walks
1. Howth Head
2. Bray Head
3. Along the Wicklow Way

● Great Drives
4. The Boyne Valley
5. Through the Wicklow Mountains

0   10 mi
0   10 km

haunt of ineb . . . well, youth at Trinity study hard, too, and do so in a famous and markedly lovely institution founded by Queen Elizabeth I in 1592. Oscar Wilde, J. M. Synge, Jonathan Swift, Bram Stoker, and Samuel Beckett are among the alumni, and behind the college's walls are 40 acres of greens, atmospheric structures, and one of the world's most famous volumes, the **Book of Kells** (see page 124).

Temple Bar lies just beyond the college gates, on the other side of the **Bank of Ireland.** This handsome building was the seat of the Irish Parliament until 1801, when that body voted itself out of existence with passage of the Act of Union, transferring government rule to London. You can still visit the chamber of the **House of Lords,** richly paneled, hung with tapestries depicting the Battle of the Boyne and the Siege of Derry, and illuminated with a splendid Waterford chandelier. (Open to the public Monday through Friday, 10 a.m. to 4 p.m.; free guided tours on Tuesday at 10:30 a.m., 11:30 a.m., and 1:45 p.m.). Busy, traffic-choked **Dame Street** leads west from College Green. From here you can catch a bus to just about anywhere in Dublin, hear music in the wonderfully Victorian **Olympia Theatre,** and easily escape the noise and the bustle by following any of the alleylike streets north into the neighborhood known as Temple Bar.

In recent years, young merrymakers from throughout Europe have been drawn to this old riverside quarter like bees to honey, with encouragement from restaurateurs and pub owners. Saving the neighborhood from complete debauchery are several cultural institutions on and around **Meeting House Square.** Most popular is the **Irish Film Centre,** where the cinemas, bar-cafe, and bookstore are always packed with film enthusiasts (see page 147). The center occasionally screens films outdoors in the square on summer evenings, providing some of Dublin's favorite free entertainment. Also free, and facing each other from opposite sides of the square, are the **Gallery of Photography,** which exhibits works by Irish and international photographers (see page 143) and the **National Photographic Archive,** which rotates its collection of historic Irish images (Monday through Friday, 10 a.m. to 5 p.m., Saturday, 10 a.m. to 2 p.m.; ☎ 01-603-0371).

From the north side of Temple Bar, pass through Merchant's Gate onto Wellington Quay, where **Ha'Penny Bridge** beckons you to cross the Liffey; this span has connected the two sides of the city since 1816 and those who used it once paid the eponymous toll.

Into Georgian Dublin

Grafton Street, just south of Trinity College, is first and foremost a statement about Ireland's newfound prosperity: this pedestrian way is a road well traveled by shoppers who step in and out of expensive boutiques and pop into **Bewley's** for a cup of tea (see page 145). At the north end of the street is a reminder of a more humble Dublin: a statue of **Molly Malone,** the comely 17th-century fishmonger who also plied a nighttime trade and inspired the song "In Dublin's Fair City, Where the Girls Are So Pretty . . . ." (Dubliners refer to the statue of the unfortunate lass wheeling her load of mussels and cockles as "The Tart with the Cart.") About halfway up Grafton Street, a narrow lane leads west to the former town house of the Viscount Powerscourt, whose country seat was the magnificent **Powerscourt** in County Wicklow (see page 180). The viscount would no doubt be vexed by the fact that his 18th-century Palladian-style mansion, made of limestone quarried from his estate, is now the centerpiece of the **Powerscourt Townhouse Centre,** a posh shopping mall.

Grafton Street ends at **St. Stephen's Green,** 11 hectares (27 acres) of lawns and formal gardens surrounding a lake. Once used for hangings, the park is these days a lovely place for a stroll and a rest on a bench; you'll find yourself in the good company of James Joyce, W. B. Yeats, the Countess Markievicz, and other Irish luminaries, commemorated with busts and statures. The north side of the Green (which is how Dubliners refer to it) was known as Beaux Walk well into the 20th century, when it was still a row of gentlemen's clubs. One of these male bastions is now the pleasant **Brownes Hotel** (see page 105). A little ways down the street is the most popular hostelry and gathering spot on the Green, the **Shelbourne,** and down from that, the **Huguenot Cemetery,** a small burial ground that ensures its interred a good address for eternity.

Just to the east of the Green are **Merrion Street** and **Merrion Square,** elegant remnants of 18th-century Georgian Dublin. You can tour two of the fine houses that line these squares and streets, the **Oscar Wilde House,** at 1 Merrion Square (see page 139), and **Number 29,** east of Merrion Square on Fitzwilliam Street (see page 138). It's quite satisfying simply to admire the houses, with their large fanlights and brightly colored doors, from the pavement, as you can do repeatedly on the long stretch of **Fitzwilliam Street** known as the "Georgian Mile."

Between the west side of Merrion Square and Kildare Street is "official" Dublin, where government offices and museums (including the **National Gallery** and the **National Museum;** see pages 135 and 136, respectively) abut one another in all their limestone pomp. **Leinster House,** tucked between Merrion Square West and Kildare Street, inspired James Hoban's designs for the White House in Washington, D.C.; this formidable mansion, built for the Duke of Leinster in 1745, also serves a governmental function—it's the seat of the Oireachtas, the Irish legislature. The duke set a trend, and this part of Dublin soon attracted well-to-do residents who built the Georgian-style town houses that line the streets and squares today. You may want to settle for a view of the exterior; tours are given when the houses (the Dáil, or lower house, and Seanad, or senate) are in session, but if you're not Irish, your embassy or consulate needs to make the arrangements; for more information, call the Events Desk at ☎ 01-618-3781, e-mail **event.desk@oireachtas.ie,** or visit **www.oireachtas.ie.** Trinity College is at the north end of Kildare Street.

Dublin Castle and the Cathedrals

Dublin Castle, off Dame Street at the west end of Temple Bar, seems purposely built to separate that raucous quarter from some of Dublin's holiest ground, Christ Church and St. Patrick's cathedrals. You can get a taste for the might and glory of the castle (see page 129) just by looking at its formidable stone walls. But do take the time to step into nearby **City Hall,** built as the Royal Exchange and completed in 1779, and admire the domed rotunda surrounded by columns, the mosaic floor, and the frescoes depicting fact and fiction (legend and actual events) in Irish history

unofficial **TIP**
Seeing all these far-flung attractions in one outing is beyond the scope of even the most energetic walker. Consider the advantages of a hop-on, hop-off bus tour, which whisks you from one attraction to the next, allowing you to spend as much time as you want at each (see page 112).

(Dame Street, ☎ 01-672-2204; Monday through Friday, 10 a.m. to 5 p.m.; Saturday and Sunday, 2 to 5 p.m.; free admission).

Castle Street leads uphill to **Christ Church Cathedral** (page 129) and its neighbor, **Dublinia and the Viking World** (page 131). Between the old stones of the one and the ersatz re-creations of the other, you'll learn a bit about medieval Dublin—more of which is in evidence in the delightful **St. Patrick's Cathedral** (page 140), just to the north up St. Nicholas Street.

Phoenix Park, the Liberties, and Kilmainham

To the west of St. Patrick's Cathedral lies a slice of Dublin life that many visitors see little of: a real neighborhood. **The Liberties,** settled by Huguenots in the 17th century, was appallingly poor through much of the 19th and 20th centuries, and the area is still less prosperous than other parts of Dublin. Oddly, the glossy **Guinness Storehouse** (see page 133), Dublin's most popular tourist attraction, is out here, just off Thomas Street. Should you feel up to the trek, the **Royal Hospital Kilmainham–Irish Museum of Modern Art** (see page 140) and **Kilmainham Gaol** (see page 134), which so eloquently pays tribute to Irish nationalism, are farther west, along James and Old Kilmainham streets. Across the River Liffey is **Collins Barracks,** housing the National Museum of Ireland's decorative-arts collections (see page 137). **Phoenix Park,** with 1,750 acres that stretch five kilometers (three miles) along the banks of the river to compose Europe's largest public park, is just to the west of the Barracks, and the **Old Jameson Distillery** (see page 138) is just to the east. The massive assemblage on the quays east of the Jameson premises is **Four Courts,** which rose along the Liffey at the end of the 18th century, was shelled and burned in the 1916 Easter Uprising, and today houses the city's busy municipal court system.

There's no real reason to step inside, and indeed many handcuffed visitors would rather not be darkening the massive doorways.

PARKS

CENTRAL DUBLIN IS GRACED with some delightful spots of greenery. The most central is **St. Stephen's Green**, which, for all its busyness, is a delightful spot, with some secluded corners that include a heavenly scented Garden for the Blind. **Iveagh Gardens,** just to the south, is much less frequented and is even rustic by comparison, with a little waterfall and refreshing grotto. **Merrion Square,** east of the Green and the national museums complex around Kildare Street, is a beautifully tended oasis of green lawns and colorful flowerbeds that provide a nice counterpoint to the brightly doors of the fine Georgian houses that surround the park. **Fitzwilliam Square,** another Georgian greensward south of Merrion Square, is a pleasure to look at through the iron rails but is off-limits to us plebeians—the park is the private domain of the tenants of the surrounding houses. One of the most welcome spots of greenery in Dublin is the garden in the **Dublin Castle complex**—a refuge from the somber exterior and the pompousness of the staterooms. If you step into the adjoining **Chester Beatty Library,** and you should, find your way to the rooftop Zen garden, the capital's ultimate outdoor getaway.

ATTRACTIONS IN DUBLIN

 Book of Kells ★★★★

| APPEAL BY AGE | PRESCHOOL ★ | GRADE SCHOOL ★★★ | TEENS ★★★ |
| YOUNG ADULTS ★★★★ | | OVER 30 ★★★★ | SENIORS ★★★★ |

College Green, Trinity College, Dublin 2, *Trinity College and Temple Bar;* ☎ 01-608-1661; www.tcd.ie/library/heritage

Type of attraction Illustrated manuscript. **Buses** 5, 7A, 8, 15A, 15B, 15C, 46, 55, 62, 63, 83, 84; DART: Tara Street. **Admission** €8 adults, €7 seniors and students, free for children under age 12, €16 for families of up to 2 adults and 4 children. **Hours** May–September, Monday–Saturday, 9:30 a.m.–5 p.m.; Sunday, 9:30 a.m.–4:30 p.m.; October–April, Monday–Saturday, 9:30 a.m.–5 p.m.; Sunday, noon–4:30 p.m. **When to go** Midweek and early in the day to avoid crowds. **Special comments** You can buy a combination ticket for admission to the Book of Kells and the Dublin Experience (see page 143), a sound-and-light show in Davis Theatre, also on the campus. **How much time to allow** 2 hours.

DESCRIPTION AND COMMENTS The Book of Kells is one of the world's most exquisite manuscripts. Scholars are still debating where the book was crafted, though many believe that it is the work of ninth-century monks working in the great scriptorium at the monastic community of St. Colomba, on the island of Iona off Scotland. For most of the Middle Ages, the 680-page book, in which the four gospels of the New

Testament are illustrated with elaborate designs that show the influence of Eastern Christianity and Celtic cultures, was in the Colomban monastery at Kells, north of Dublin. The manuscript now occupies pride of place in the Long Library of Trinity College. Two sets of facing pages, one set displaying text and the other ornamental illumination, are shown at one time, and viewing them often requires standing in long lines; you catch only a brief glimpse of the treasures as the crowd presses forward. Nearby, fairly elaborate displays chronicle the restoration and conservation of the text and reproduce some of the most elaborate pages, such as the one showing the symbol of Christ, the XPI monogram. The crush is less pressing around two other medieval manuscripts, the ninth-century Book of Armagh, a copy of the New Testament, and the seventh-century Book of Durrow; while these two less-noted volumes are mules to the show pony, they are exquisite and can be appreciated at your leisure.

TOURING TIPS Take time to admire your surroundings. The library, also known as the Long Room, is an exquisite expanse of paneling and shelving beneath a barrel-vaulted ceiling. Glass cases running down the center of the room display the letters of Robert Emmet, expelled from Trinity for his anti-British convictions and executed in 1803 for acting on those sentiments. Marble busts of Jonathan Swift and other famous Trinity alumni oversee the comings and goings in the busy room.

Chester Beatty Library and Gallery of Oriental Art ★★★★½

| APPEAL BY AGE | PRESCHOOL ★ | GRADE SCHOOL ★★ | TEENS ★★★★ |
| YOUNG ADULTS ★★★ | OVER 30 ★★★★½ | | SENIORS ★★★★½ |

Clock Tower Building, Dublin Castle, Dublin 2, *Dublin Castle and the Cathedrals;* ☎ 01-407-0750; www.cbl.ie

Type of attraction Library and art gallery. Buses 50, 51B, 54A, 56A, 77, 77A, 78A, 123. Admission Free. Hours May–September, Tuesday–Friday, 10 a.m.–5 p.m.; Saturday, 11 a.m.–5 p.m.; Sunday, 1–5 p.m.; October–April, Tuesday–Friday, 10 a.m.–5 p.m., Saturday, 11 a.m.–5 p.m.; Sunday, 1–5 p.m. When to go Anytime. Special comments The library cafe, the Silk Road, serves excellent Middle Eastern food. How much time to allow 2–3 hours.

DESCRIPTION AND COMMENTS Sir Alfred Chester Beatty (1875–1968) was an American who became a British subject (and later an honorary Irish citizen) after making his fortune as a mining entrepreneur. He spent much of his life collecting sacred texts, illuminated manuscripts, and miniature paintings from the great religions of the world. The library he established in Dublin in 1953 is one of those rare places where visitors pause in wonder in front of case after case of these rare artifacts, perhaps the greatest such collection in the world. Holdings include cuneiform clay tablets, ancient Biblical papyri, 270 copies of the Koran, paintings from India's Mughal era, and some of the earliest bound books, dating from the Renaissance. It's a comment on the greatness of this place that the

dublin attractions

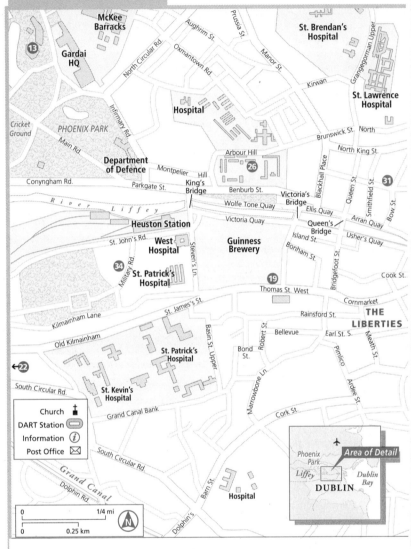

1. Abbey Theatre
2. The Ark
3. Bank of Ireland
4. Book of Kells
5. Casino at Marino
6. Chester Beatty Library and
   Gallery of Oriental Art
7. Christ Church Cathedral
8. Custom House

9. Dublin Castle
10. Dublin City Gallery–
    The Hugh Lane
11. Dublin Experience
12. Dublin Writers Museum
13. Dublin Zoo
14. Dublinia and the Viking World
15. Four Courts
16. Gallery of Photography

17. Gate Theatre
18. General Post Office
19. Guinness Storehouse
20. Irish-Jewish Museum
21. James Joyce Centre
22. Kilmainham Gaol
23. Marsh's Library
24. National Gallery of
    Ireland

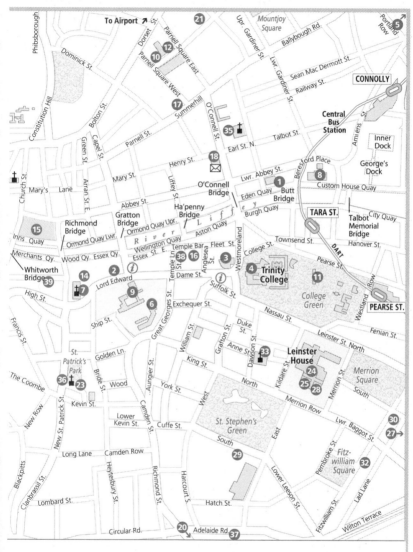

How Attractions Compare in Dublin

ATTRACTION	DESCRIPTION	AUTHOR'S RATING
Chester Beatty Library and Gallery of Oriental Art	Library and art gallery	★★★★½
Dublin City Gallery–The Hugh Lane	Museum of 19th-, 20th-, and 21st-century art	★★★★½
Kilmainham Gaol	Historic prison	★★★★½
National Gallery of Ireland–Archaeology and History	Ireland's premier collection of art	★★★★½
National Museum of Ireland	Treasure trove of Irish artifacts	★★★★½
Book of Kells	Illustrated manuscript	★★★★
National Gallery of Ireland–Collins Barracks	Museum of decorative arts	★★★★
Dublin Writers Museum	Museum honoring writers who lived in Dublin	★★★★
Marsh's Library	Ireland's first public library	★★★★
Number 29	Historic home	★★★★
Oscar Wilde House	Home of famous author	★★★★
St. Patrick's Cathedral	Church	★★★★
Royal Hospital Kilmainham–Irish Museum of Modern Art	Historic building and art museum	★★★½
Shaw Birthplace	Home of famous author	★★★½
Dublin Castle	Fortified compound that was center of British rule in Ireland	★★★
James Joyce Centre	Museum and learning center devoted to James Joyce	★★½
Christ Church Cathedral	Church	★★
Dublinia and the Viking World	Historical re-creation	★★
Guinness Storehouse	Brewery	★★
Old Jameson Distillery	Museum in a historic distillery	★★

prints of the old masters, including many by Albrecht Dürer, are overshadowed by the sheer magnitude of the rest of the collection.

TOURING TIPS The library is on the grounds of Dublin Castle and close enough to Trinity College and the Book of Kells that you can easily combine a visit to both on a mission to see old manuscripts.

Christ Church Cathedral ★★

APPEAL BY AGE	PRESCHOOL ★	GRADE SCHOOL ★★	TEENS ★★
YOUNG ADULTS ★★	OVER 30 ★★★		SENIORS ★★★

Christ Church Place, Dublin 8, *Dublin Castle and the Cathedrals;*
☎ 01-677-8099; www.cccdub.ie

Type of attraction Church. **Buses** 21A, 50, 50A, 78, 78A, 78B. **Admission** €6, €5 for seniors and students; free for children accompanied by adults; reduced rates for those who have paid admission to Dublinia. **Hours** June–August, daily, 9 a.m.–6 p.m.; September–May, daily, Monday–Friday, 9:45 a.m.–5 or 6 p.m. **When to go** Try to visit during Evensong: Sunday at 3:30 p.m., Wednesday and Thursday at 6 p.m., and Saturday at 5 p.m. **Special comments** Save your time and money for a visit to nearby St. Patrick's Cathedral. **How much time to allow** 1 hour.

DESCRIPTION AND COMMENTS A Victorian restoration, funded by whiskey magnate Henry Roe, took much of the life out of the 12th-century stone edifice that rose on the site of an 11th-century wooden Danish church—all but demolishing the medieval craftsmanship that graced this hilltop throughout much of Dublin's long history. The flying buttresses remain, adding a wonderful sense of drama to the hilltop church; some stonework and quaint carvings in the nave, transepts, and choir, plus the wonderfully spooky old crypt, remain as well. A brief tour must include a stop at the tomb of Strongbow, the 12th-century Norman warrior who conquered Ireland for Henry II and who founded the cathedral. There is some speculation that the primary inhabitant of the tomb and the figure depicted in stone is actually the Earl of Drogheda and that Strongbow's organs were placed here when his original resting place was destroyed in the 14th century; it's also been suggested that the half figure next to the tomb is Strongbow's son, legless because Strongbow cut the lad in half when he proved to be cowardly in battle (a Dark Ages example of the "spare the rod, spoil the child" approach to parenting). One of the effigies in the Chapel of St. Laurence is said to be Strongbow's wife. Adding to the allure of the dank crypt are the mummies of a cat and a rat, allegedly trapped in an organ pipe midchase in the 1860s.

TOURING TIPS The far more interesting St. Patrick's Cathedral, another bastion of Irish Protestantism, is just to the north, so you can easily visit both on one round of churchgoing; you can also easily combine a visit to Christ Church with a stop at Dublinia, connected to the cathedral by a bridge.

Dublin Castle ★★★

APPEAL BY AGE	PRESCHOOL ★★	GRADE SCHOOL ★★★	TEENS ★★★
YOUNG ADULTS ★★★	OVER 30 ★★★		SENIORS ★★★

Dublin Castle Dame Street, Dublin 2, *Dublin Castle and the Cathedrals;*
☎ 01-645-8813; www.dublincastle.ie

Type of attraction Castle. **Buses** 50, 50A, 54, 54A, 65, 65B, 77. **Admission** €4.50 adults, €3.50 seniors, €2 students; free for children under 12. **Hours** Monday–Friday, 10 a.m.–4:45 p.m.; Saturday–Sunday, 2–4:45 p.m. **When to go** The short weekend hours create a bit of a crush, so try to plan a weekday visit. **Special comments** Tours fill up quickly, and the admissions process is a bit disorganized; if you're eager to see the place, arrive early and plan to wait. **How much time to allow** 1 hour.

DESCRIPTION AND COMMENTS The former seat of British government in Ireland is appropriately somber and formidable, dating mostly from the 13th century, with even earlier foundations. Tours show off staterooms, the chapel, and parts of the royal apartments, but the place is better suited to the state functions it now hosts than to an entertaining tour. All the glittering crystal and silver is a bit stuffy and really sort of gauche—you'll see more interesting interiors in castles and great houses elsewhere in Ireland. Oldest is best here, and the Norman tower, now housing a dull police museum, is a fascinating bit of medieval Dublin, as are the ongoing excavations that reveal the castle's Viking underpinnings.

TOURING TIPS The castle cafe is a homey place to sit and enjoy a slice of shepherd's pie or some fish-and-chips and a glass from the decent wine selection. The wonderful Chester Beatty Library is on the grounds, so be sure to leave time to tour that collection (see page 125).

Dublin City Gallery–The Hugh Lane ★★★★½

APPEAL BY AGE	PRESCHOOL ★★	GRADE SCHOOL ★★★	TEENS ★★★
YOUNG ADULTS ★★★★	OVER 30 ★★★★½		SENIORS ★★★★½

Parnell Square North, Dublin 1, *Central Dublin;* ☎ **01-222-5550;** **www.hughlane.ie**

Type of attraction Museum of 19th-century, 20th-century, and contemporary art. **Buses** 11, 13, 16, 16A, 22, 22A. **Admission** Free. **Hours** Tuesday–Thursday, 10 a.m.– 6 p.m.; Friday–Saturday, 10 a.m.–5 p.m.; Sunday, 11 a.m.–5 p.m. **When to go** Weekday mornings, when the galleries are not particularly crowded. **Special comments** Guided tours are conducted Sunday at 1:30 p.m. At noon on Sunday, the gallery hosts free concerts presenting classical works as well as pieces commissioned for the series. Postcards and a good selection of art books are for sale in the bookshop, and the contemporary-style cafe overlooking a garden is one of the best places in this part of town for lunch or a snack. **How much time to allow** About 2 hours.

DESCRIPTION AND COMMENTS The grandest dwelling on Parnell Square, built for the Earl of Charlemont in 1762 and thoughtfully expanded over the years, houses an exquisite collection of 19th- to early-20th-century art as well as contemporary works by Irish and international artists. It's only fitting that these handsome rooms still display fine art—the earl was a great collector, amassing Titians and other masterpieces. Much of the collection now hanging here is that of Hugh Lane, an aristocratic connoisseur who went down with the *Lusitania* after it was torpedoed by the Germans off the Irish coast in 1915. You can savor lovely works of the French Barbizon and Impressionist schools such as Renoir's *Les*

Parapluies and Monet's *Waterloo Bridge.* Note that some of the dazzlers are moved back and forth to the National Gallery in London by an ongoing arrangement that leaves a few empty spaces on the gallery walls, but most of the paintings do remain here. The museum also exhibits many works by Irish artists, including canvases by the painter Jack Yeats, brother of the poet W. B. Yeats, and stained-glass panels by Irish artisans Harry Clark and Evie Hone. One of the museum's most stunning holdings is the studio of the 20th-century Irish painter Francis Bacon, moved here in its entirety from a London mews and painstakingly preserved, with the used paint tubes, rags, slashed canvases, and other clutter perfectly intact.

TOURING TIPS The Gallery is part of a cultural enclave in this part of Dublin; it can be included in an itinerary that would also include the Dublin Writers Museum and the James Joyce Centre.

kids Dublinia and the Viking World   ★★

APPEAL BY AGE	PRESCHOOL ★★★	GRADE SCHOOL ★★★★	TEENS ★★★
YOUNG ADULTS ★★★		OVER 30 ★★	SENIORS ★★

**St. Michael's Hill, Dublin 8, *Dublin Castle and the Cathedrals;*
☎ 01-679-4611; www.dublinia.ie**

Type of attraction Historical re-creation. **Buses** 50, 78A, 123. **Admission** €6.25 adults, €3.75 children, €5 seniors, €5.25 students, €17 families of up to 2 adults and 3 children. Visitors receive discounted admission to Christ Church Cathedral. **Hours** April–September, daily, 10 a.m.–5 p.m.; October–March, Monday–Friday, 11 a.m.–4 p.m., and Saturday–Sunday, 10 a.m.–4 p.m. **When to go** Weekdays, if possible; the place swarms with kids on weekends. **Special comments** Children enjoy putting on medieval costumes and engaging in activities. **How much time to allow** At least 1 hour, more if you'll be explaining the exhibits to young companions.

DESCRIPTION AND COMMENTS Neither fish nor fowl, this place is not really a museum but not flashy enough to be first-rate entertainment. The prototype for this theme-park approach to history is the Jorvick Centre in York, England, where visitors travel through Viking times. Here, in a 19th-century Gothic annex to Christ Church Cathedral, theatrical exhibits re-create everyday life in Viking and medieval Dublin with models of the early city, re-created streetscapes and medieval markets, and many costumed mannequins, all accompanied by sounds and the occasional odor. Kids especially will enjoy the scenes, and even adults will leave the premises a little more enlightened about who did what when in historic Dublin (the name means "Black Pool," by the way). Even so, the experience could be a lot more engaging were the theatrics a bit more sophisticated and less reliant on text panels. Interestingly, the old-fashioned approach best succeeds here: the museum of Viking artifacts is excellent, and the skeleton of a middle-aged woman buried in a shallow grave near the former city walls brings a genuine touch of real life to the show. Satisfying, too, is the view of Dublin from the adjoining St. Michael's tower.

TOURING TIPS A charming bridge links Dublinia to Christ Church Cathedral, which you can enter at a reduced price if you show your Dublinia receipt.

Dublin Writers Museum ★★★★

APPEAL BY AGE	PRESCHOOL ★	GRADE SCHOOL ★★	TEENS ★★
YOUNG ADULTS ★★★	OVER 30 ★★★★		SENIORS ★★★★

18 Parnell Square, Dublin 1, *Central Dublin*; ☎ 01-872-2077; www.writersmuseum.com

Type of attraction Museum honoring writers who lived in Dublin. **Buses** 11, 13, 16, 16A, 22, 22A. **Admission** €7.25 adults, €4.55 children, €6.10 seniors and students, €21 families; combined tickets with either the James Joyce Museum or the Shaw Birthplace: €12.50 adults, €7.70 children, €10.30 seniors and students, €33.50 families. **Hours** January–May and September–December, Monday–Saturday, 10 a.m.–5 p.m.; Sunday, 11 a.m.–5 p.m.; June–August, Monday–Friday, 10 a.m.–6 p.m.; Saturday, 10 a.m.–5 p.m.; Sunday, 11 a.m.–5 p.m. **When to go** The museum is a perfect place to spend a rainy afternoon. **Special comments** The cafe also serves an international school and is filled with European students sipping coffee (at the rear of the museum); a bookstore carries a small but admirable collection of works by Dublin writers. Chapter One, among Dublin's top restaurants, is on the ground floor. **How much time to allow** At least 2 hours.

DESCRIPTION AND COMMENTS The fairly steep price of admission buys hours of pleasurable browsing through extensive letters, manuscripts, photos, news clippings, audio recordings, and some other fascinating memorabilia—such as the lorgnette of Lady Augusta Gregory (patron of W. B. Yeats) and a postcard from Brendan Behan, then living in California ("great place for a piss-up"). A lively audio tour and the varied nature of the displays can accelerate whatever mild enthusiasm visitors might have for Oscar Wilde, James Joyce, Samuel Beckett, Jonathan Swift, and scores of other writers (most of whom appeared to have been both stifled and inspired by Dublin) into full-throttle fascination. While there have been many Dublin writers who left much behind, the museum's large collections are not overwhelming. They are tidily arranged in two salons of the Georgian mansion that was once home to a scion of the Jameson whiskey family—one room brings visitors up to the end of the 19th century, and the other is devoted to the 20th century. Oddly, the museum's homage to writers stops at about the midcentury mark, reflecting either a lack of space or a critical comment on the contemporary scene.

TOURING TIPS You can continue a literary pilgrimage at the James Joyce Centre, a couple of blocks away on North Great George's Street.

Guinness Storehouse ★★

APPEAL BY AGE	PRESCHOOL ★	GRADE SCHOOL ★★★	TEENS ★★★
YOUNG ADULTS ★★★★		OVER 30 ★★★★	SENIORS ★★★★

St. James's Gate, Dublin 8, *The Liberties*; ☎ 01-408-4800; www.guinness-storehouse.com

Type of attraction Brewery. **Buses** 51B, 78A, 90, 123. **Admission** €14 adults, €10 seniors and students over age 18, €8 students under age 18, €5 children ages 6–12, free for children under age 6, €30 families of up to 2 adults and 4 children; adult tickets are reduced by 10% when booked online. **Hours** July–August, daily, 9:30 a.m.–7 p.m.; September–June, daily, 9:30 a.m.–5 p.m. **When to go** In the morning to beat the crowd; the Gravity Bar is especially pleasant on summer evenings. **Special comments** A very large shop sells T-shirts, key chains, and many other items emblazoned with the Guinness logo. **How much time to allow** 2 hours.

DESCRIPTION AND COMMENTS It's not surprising that Dublin's most famous tourist attraction is this shrine to Ireland's favorite beverage. What is surprising is that so many people are willing to pay so much to see what amounts to so little. Visitors do not see the actual brewery, but instead are treated to an unabashed display of self-promotion housed in a renovated fermentation plant. Arranged around a five-story glass atrium shaped like a pint are flashy high-tech exhibits showing how Guinness and the barrels that store it are made. The sophisticated displays, with lots of flashing lights, rushing water, and sound effects, are certainly impressive, but it's all a bit overdone. Guinness is, after all, a brewery—they're making beer here, not splitting the atom. The most engaging bits of paraphernalia are the advertising posters by John Gilroy, a spinmaster of the 1930s and '40s who sold millions of pints of beer with charming illustrations of toucans and other animals, accompanied by such lines as "Guinness Is Good for You" and "It's a Lovely Day for a Guinness." In good weather, you will find it is indeed a lovely day for a Guinness when you step into the top-floor Gravity Bar, where you will be treated to a free pint and a 360-degree view of Dublin. Enjoy it, because this is one of the most expensive pints you'll ever quaff.

TOURING TIPS You might want to combine a Guinness visit with stops at some of the other attractions in this part of town, including Collins Barracks and Kilmainham Gaol; if you're primed to pay homage to other Irish spirits, the Old Jameson Distillery is also nearby.

James Joyce Centre ★★½

APPEAL BY AGE	PRESCHOOL ★	GRADE SCHOOL ★★	TEENS ★★
YOUNG ADULTS ★★		OVER 30 ★★½	SENIORS ★★½

35 North Great George's Street, *Central Dublin*; ☎ 01-878-8547; www.jamesjoyce.ie

Type of attraction Museum and learning center devoted to James Joyce. **Buses** 3, 10, 11, 13, 16, 19, 22, 123. **Admission** €5 adults, €4 students and seniors, free for children under age 12. **Hours** Tuesday–Saturday, 10 a.m.–5 p.m. **When to go** Anytime; the center is rarely crowded. **Special comments** The center has a bookstore and a cafe. **How much time to allow** About 2 hours; more if you are a Joyce enthusiast.

DESCRIPTION AND COMMENTS Reading *Ulysses* is pretty stringent prep for a museum visit, but knowing the ins and outs of the Dublin of Leopold Bloom will certainly help you make sense of many of the exhibits in this Georgian town house (which, incidentally, is one of the few places in Dublin where Joyce seems never to have lived). *Ulysses* aficionados can spend hours in front of the massive chart diagramming characters, events, and places in the novel, and pay homage at the door to 7 Eccles Street, home to the Blooms and one of the most famous addresses in literature. Those who appreciate Joyce's genius but don't live and breathe his work may be content with what's to be learned about the great man at the nearby Dublin Writers Museum. Exhibits here also chronicle tenement life in Dublin in the 19th and 20th centuries, when the neighborhood went into decline and dozens of families lived in once-grand houses such as this one. The center, devoted to Joyce scholarship, contains a large library of the writer's works, hosts lectures, and provides excellent walking tours through Joyce's Dublin.

TOURING TIPS Walking tours past the pubs, lanes, houses, and other venues of Joyce's works depart from the center from May to August on Tuesday, Thursday, and Saturday at 2 p.m.; fees are €10 adults, €8 seniors and students.

 Kilmainham Gaol ★★★★½

APPEAL BY AGE	PRESCHOOL ★★★	GRADE SCHOOL ★★★★	TEENS ★★★★
YOUNG ADULTS ★★★★	OVER 30 ★★★★½		SENIORS ★★★★½

Inchicore Road, Dublin 8, *Kilmainham;* ☎ **01-453-5984;** **www.heritageireland.ie**

Type of attraction Historic prison. **Buses** 51B, 78A. **Admission** €5.30 adults, €3.70 seniors, €2.10 children and students, €11.50 families. **Hours** April–September, daily, 9:30 a.m.–6 p.m.; October–March, Monday–Saturday, 9:30 a.m.–5:30 p.m., and Sunday, 10 a.m.–6 p.m. **When to go** Try to arrive early in summer, as tours fill up quickly later in the day. **Special comments** The jail has a small tearoom. **How much time to allow** 2 hours.

DESCRIPTION AND COMMENTS This formidable prison opened in 1798 and closed in 1927; today it serves as a testimonial to Irish revolutionary history. A museum, an introductory slide presentation, and a highly informative guided tour provide excellent background on such 18th- and 19th-century revolutionary heroes as Robert Emmet, executed for his role in the Dublin riots of 1803, and Charles Stewart Parnell, the 19th-century nationalist leader and member of the Irish Parliament. Most gripping are the displays and commentaries recounting the 1916 Easter Uprising, when the Irish Republican Brotherhood mounted an armed revolt in Dublin, for which the British executed 15 of the leaders, many of them here at Kilmainham. On the guided tour, among the moving tales you'll hear about this event is the story of young Joseph Plunkett, who married Grace Gifford in the prison chapel shortly before his execution. You will leave Kilmainham knowing a fair amount about Irish national history, and you will also see one of the most impressive rooms in all of Ireland—the elliptical central hall surrounded by tiers of cells.

TOURING TIPS If you leave the museum and walk north a few blocks to the banks of the Liffey, you'll come to the War Memorial Gardens, laid out by the British architect Sir Edwin Lutyens. Ask for directions at the prison admission booth.

Marsh's Library ★★★★

APPEAL BY AGE	PRESCHOOL ★	GRADE SCHOOL ★★★		TEENS ★★★
YOUNG ADULTS ★★★		OVER 30 ★★★★		SENIORS ★★★★

St. Patrick's Close, Dublin 8, *Dublin Castle and the Cathedrals;*
☎ **01-454-3511; www.marshlibrary.ie**

Type of attraction Ireland's first public library. **Buses** 50, 50A, 54, 54A, 65, 65B, 77. **Admission** €2.50 adults, €1.25 students and seniors. **Hours** Monday and Wednesday–Friday, 10 a.m.–1 p.m. and 2–5 p.m.; Saturday, 10:30 a.m.– 1 p.m. **When to go** Anytime. **Special comments** Visitors are welcome to browse the library's catalogs and certain sections of the holdings. **How much time to allow** 1 hour.

DESCRIPTION AND COMMENTS Ireland's oldest public library, founded in 1701, is an atmospheric repository of rare manuscripts and books from the 16th through 18th centuries. Many date from times when books were so rare that scholars were locked into mesh cages to view them; the cages are still in place but no longer used, and visitors are free to roam the library with its fine oak bookcase at leisure and peruse the fascinating exhibits, which are rotated frequently to display the collection's most precious holdings. The library, incidentally, is named for its founder, Archbishop of Dublin Narcissus Marsh (1638–1713), who is buried nearby on the grounds of St. Patrick's Cathedral.

TOURING TIPS The library is set in a cottage garden at the edge of the grounds of St. Patrick's Cathedral, so you may want to combine a visit to both these landmarks of old Dublin.

National Gallery of Ireland ★★★★½

APPEAL BY AGE	PRESCHOOL ★★	GRADE SCHOOL ★★★		TEENS ★★★
YOUNG ADULTS ★★★		OVER 30 ★★★★½		SENIORS ★★★★½

Merrion Square West, Dublin 2, *Georgian Dublin;* ☎ 01-661-5133;
www.nationalgallery.ie

Type of attraction Ireland's premier collection of art. **Buses** 7, 7A, 8, 10, 10A, 44, 47. **Admission** Free. **Hours** Monday–Wednesday and Friday–Saturday, 9:30 a.m.–5:30 p.m.; Thursday, 9:30 a.m.–8:30 p.m.; Sunday, noon–5:30 p.m. **When to go** Thursday evenings, when you'll have galleries to yourself and can spend as much time as you want in front of the canvases. **Special comments** The museum has a well-stocked bookshop where you can pick up postcards of the works that appeal to you, as well as an attractive cafe. The museum's collection of watercolors by Joseph Turner go on view once a year, in January, when the winter light is said to do them the most justice. **How much time to allow** At least 2 hours.

DESCRIPTION AND COMMENTS Ireland's national collection of European art boasts a number of impressive masterpieces, many collected over the years by Sir Alfred and Lady Clementine Belt and displayed in their country manor in County Wicklow. The couple's donation of 17 works in 1987 put the museum on the world map as a serious art museum. The top floor is especially satisfying: Caravaggio's *The Taking of Christ,* Andrea Mantegna's *Judith with the Head of Holofernes,* and Vermeer's *Lady Writing a Letter with Her Maid* hang among works by Degas, Tintoretto, Rembrandt, Poussin, and Verona in a string of pleasant and well-lit galleries. The Caravaggio is the museum's most newsworthy painting of the moment: presumed lost but recently discovered hanging inconspicuously in a rectory, covered with grime, it is the subject of a fascinating book, *The Lost Painting.* A ground-floor gallery houses works by Jack Yeats, Ireland's most famous 20th-century painter and brother of W. B. Yeats; the artist's impressionistic style and vivid palette capture many Irish scenes, including *The Liffey Swim,* still an annual Dublin event. Other Irish paintings make a decent showing too, as do British artists, but none more prominently than Reynolds, whose *First Earl of Bellamont* is an unintentionally mirthful portrayal of Georgian foppery.

TOURING TIPS The museum hosts an excellent lecture program and conducts guided tours; free tours are led Saturdays at 3 p.m. and Sundays at 2 p.m., 3 p.m., and 4 p.m.

National Museum of Ireland– Archaeology and History ★★★★½

| APPEAL BY AGE | PRESCHOOL ★★★ | GRADE SCHOOL ★★★ | TEENS ★★★★ |
| YOUNG ADULTS ★★★★ | | OVER 30 ★★★★½ | SENIORS ★★★★½ |

Kildare Street, Dublin 2, *Georgian Dublin;* ☎ **01-677-7444; www.museum.ie**

Type of attraction Museum of national treasures. **Buses** 7, 7A, 10, 11, 13. **Admission** Free. **Hours** Tuesday–Saturday, 10 a.m.–5 p.m.; Sunday, 2–5 p.m. **When to go** Weekdays, when the museum is less crowded. **Special comments** Guided tours (45 minutes; €2 a person) leave regularly from the information desk and provide a rewarding overview of the collections. **How much time to allow** At least 2 hours.

DESCRIPTION AND COMMENTS Ireland's treasure trove of artifacts dating from 6,000 BC to the 20th century is housed in suitably grandiose quarters, behind an imposing 19th-century facade and beneath a soaring rotunda. Understandably, the crowd-pleaser is the stash of Irish gold: Celtic scepters, jewelry, crosses, a gold boat from the first century AD, a collar from about 700 BC, and other items fill one glittering case after another. Other priceless relics gathered from around Ireland include the Tara Brooch and Ardagh Chalice, both from the eighth century, and the elaborately decorated Cross of Cong, from the 12th century. Remnants of the centuries of Viking occupation fill the upstairs galleries, along with artifacts from medieval Ireland. Collins Barracks, in west Dublin, houses the museum's collection of decorative arts (see following profile), and the natural-history collection is around the block on Merrion Street (see page 143).

TOURING TIPS You may want to combine a visit to the National Museum with one to the nearby National Gallery of Ireland (see preceding profile). The Museum Cafe at the National Museum is a good spot for enjoying lunch.

National Museum of Ireland–Decorative Arts and History (aka Collins Barracks) ★★★★

| APPEAL BY AGE | PRESCHOOL ★★ | GRADE SCHOOL ★★ | TEENS ★★★ |
| YOUNG ADULTS ★★★ | | OVER 30 ★★★ | SENIORS ★★★ |

Benburb Street, Dublin 8, *Kilmainham*; ☎ 01-677-7444; www.museum.ie/decorative

Type of attraction Museum of decorative arts. Buses 34, 70, 80; DART: Museum. Admission Free. Hours Tuesday–Saturday, 10 a.m.–5 p.m.; Sunday, 2–5 p.m. When to go Anytime; the museum does not draw big crowds the way the city-center collections do. Special comments The staff leads highly informative tours, showing off the prizes of the collection that you might otherwise overlook; times vary, so check with the information desk. How much time to allow About 2 hours.

DESCRIPTION AND COMMENTS This eclectic collection includes stunning silver, fine furniture, rustic pieces from Irish country cottages, old maps, and haute couture. Collins Barracks is a handsome example of military architecture dating from the 18th century, and is a distinctive setting for the diverse holdings. In fact, the massive assembly yard proves to be the perfect spot for the Viking ship that has been permanently dry-docked there. As you wander through the recently restored halls, keep an eye out for such off treasures as 14th-century Chinese porcelain and furniture designed by Eileen Gray, an Irish designer who made her mark on the upper echelons of early-20th-century interior design (seeing her swanky designs is worth the trip out here). Several galleries house an in-depth, evocative collection devoted to the Easter Uprising of 1916, paying due homage to the events that led to Irish independence in 1921, with uniforms, posters, and other artifacts.

TOURING TIPS The museum is quite close to the Guinness Storehouse and the Irish Museum of Modern Art.

Number 29 ★★★★

APPEAL BY AGE	PRESCHOOL ★★	GRADE SCHOOL ★★★	TEENS ★★★
YOUNG ADULTS ★★★	OVER 30 ★★★½		SENIORS ★★★½

29 Fitzwilliam Street Lower, Dublin 2, *Georgian Dublin;* ☎ **01-702-6165; www.esb.ie/numbertwentynine**

Type of attraction Historic home. **Buses** 7, 8, 10, 45; DART: Pearse. **Admission** €6 adults, €3 seniors and students, free for children under age 16. **Hours** Tuesday–Saturday, 10 a.m.–5 p.m.; Sunday, 1–5 p.m. **When to go** Anytime. **Special comments** A pleasant cafe on the ground floor serves tea and pastries, and a shop sells a small but good selection of books on history and architecture. The staff here is knowledgeable and most willing to answer questions about the house and other attractions. **How much time to allow** At least 1 hour.

DESCRIPTION AND COMMENTS The guided tour of these posh surroundings begins "below stairs," with a strong dose of egalitarian reality. A 15-minute video, narrated by the ghost of one of the residents of this comfortable 1797 residence, spells out the appalling poverty, class distinctions, and miserable living conditions that prevailed when such elegant Georgian homes were built in Dublin. This puts a bit of perspective on the comforts upstairs, where the National Museum of Ireland has painstakingly restored sitting rooms and bedrooms with authentic detail. Especially notable are the various hidey-holes in which tea, food, jewels, and other valuables were stashed in case the starving servants succumbed to temptation. The fine bones of the old house itself are the standout, though: the huge fanlight and windows and the generous yet sensible proportions speak volumes about the beauties of Irish Georgian architecture.

TOURING TIPS Number 29 sheds light on the prevailing architecture in this section of Dublin. After the tour, with your newly acquired appreciation, walk up Fitzwilliam Street and around Merrion Square to admire the rows of Georgian homes. Also note the hideous concrete building just to the south of Number 29: this is the headquarters of the Electricity Supply Board, which in the 1960s tore down a row of Georgian houses to build the eyesore. ESB underwrites Number 29, and rumors are afoot that the headquarters may be redone to better suit its surroundings.

Old Jameson Distillery ★★

APPEAL BY AGE	PRESCHOOL ★	GRADE SCHOOL ★	TEENS ★★
YOUNG ADULTS ★★★	OVER 30 ★★★		SENIORS ★★★

Bow Street, Dublin 7, *Central Dublin;* ☎ **01-807-2355; www.oldjamesondistillery.com**

Type of attraction Museum in a historic distillery. **Buses** 67, 67A, 68, 69, 79, 90. **Admission** €12.50 adults, €9 seniors and students over 18, €8 students under 18, €25 families of up to 2 adults and up to 4 children. **Hours** Daily, 9:30 a.m.–6 p.m. **When to go** If you're planning on going to the top of the Chimney as well, wait for good weather. **Special comments** The distillery pub serves meals and light snacks, and an attractive restaurant is the setting for Shindig evenings that include a tour, tasting, an excellent four-course meal, and first-rate entertainment. The gift shop sells many varieties of whiskey and a great deal of whiskey-oriented paraphernalia. **How much time to allow** 1½ hours.

DESCRIPTION AND COMMENTS Homage is due this Dublin distillery, which dates from 1791, because it has contributed mightily to the local economy through many hard times. A look at the whiskey-distilling process in this re-created factory entails a slick video presentation and a guided tour past an array of exhibits, housed in an old warehouse and providing a lesson in the steps of the process—from growing grain to filling barrels—and explaining why Irish whiskey is different from Scotch whisky (and spelled with an *e* to boot). Your reward for being an attentive student is a free shot of whiskey in the tasting room, but for this price, you can enjoy two shots and some nice chatter at any pub.

*un*official **TIP**
As you travel around Ireland, you will have the chance to visit whiskey distilleries other than the Old Jameson—in Midleton, outside Cork, and in Bushmills (the only operation that provides a look at a working distillery). Save your hard-earned money and your yearnings to see how Irish whiskey is made for one of those facilities.

TOURING TIPS For a bird's-eye view of Dublin, head next door to the old distillery chimney, where an elevator whisks you up to a viewing tower. (Dubliners, with their gift for verbal play, call the chimney the "flue with a view.") The Chimney is open Monday through Saturday, 10 a.m. to 5:30 p.m., and Sunday, 11 a.m. to 5:30 p.m.; ☎ 01-817-3800 for information. Fees are a steep €5 for adults, €3.50 for children, and €15 for families.

Oscar Wilde House   ★★★★

APPEAL BY AGE	PRESCHOOL ★	GRADE SCHOOL ★★	TEENS ★★★
YOUNG ADULTS ★★★		OVER 30 ★★★	SENIORS ★★★

1 Merrion Square, Dublin 2, *Georgian Dublin;* ☎ **01-662-0281;**
www.amcd.ie

Type of attraction Home of famous author. **Buses** 6, 8, 10, 45; DART: Pearse. **Admission** €5. **Hours** By pre-arranged guided tours. **When to go** Anytime you can; the house is rarely open. **Special comments** Call or check the Web site for updates on opportunities to visit the house. **How much time to allow** 1 hour.

DESCRIPTION AND COMMENTS Oscar Wilde was raised in this house, which, then as now, was one of the finest residences on one of the most elegant squares in Dublin. His eye-surgeon father, Sir William, and socialite-poet mother, Speranza, filled the salons with fine furnishings and a stream of privileged guests, who no doubt provided young Oscar with material for the comedies of manners he would later write. Owned and recently restored by the American College Dublin, the rooms are oddly devoid of personality, given the larger-than-life character the home honors. The reception hall, dining room, Speranza's salon, and Sir William's surgery room have been painstakingly furnished and painted in exacting detail to replicate the styles of the second part of the 19th century. Missing, though, are books and personal effects that might provide some clue to the enormous talent that took root here. Perhaps this patina will come with ongoing restoration efforts.

TOURING TIPS For a more insightful look at domestic life in the Dublin of yesterday, step around the corner to Number 29 (see page 138), a restored Georgian house on Lower Fitzwilliam Street.

Royal Hospital Kilmainham–Irish Museum of Modern Art ★★★½

APPEAL BY AGE	PRESCHOOL ★	GRADE SCHOOL ★★	TEENS ★★★
YOUNG ADULTS ★★★	OVER 30 ★★★½		SENIORS ★★★½

Military Road, Dublin 8, *Kilmainham*; ☎ 01-612-9900; www.modernart.ie

Type of attraction Historic building and art museum. **Buses** 24, 79, 90. **Admission** Free. **Hours** Tuesday–Saturday, 10 a.m.–5:30 p.m.; Sunday, noon–5:30 p.m. **When to go** In good weather, if possible, so you can enjoy the gardens. **Special comments** The galleries often host temporary exhibitions of contemporary art; check the Web site. A small cafe serves light snacks. **How much time to allow** About 2 hours to see the historic rooms and the galleries.

DESCRIPTION AND COMMENTS This building, one of the finest in Ireland and completed in 1684, is a replica of Les Invalides in Paris. Like the more famous landmark, this structure also once housed disabled and retired soldiers. A painstaking restoration has returned the great hall, chapel, staterooms, courtyards, and gardens to their former glory—a magnificent setting for a small but worthy collection of contemporary Irish and European art. You will get a heady dose of visual pleasure here as you admire the glories of the baroque chapel and paneled staterooms, then wander through galleries hung with works by Damien Hirst, Francesco Clemente, and other modern masters. The museum hosts many fine exhibitions.

TOURING TIPS Guided tours are held Wednesday, Friday, and Sunday at 2:30 p.m. Take time to wander through the beautifully restored formal gardens.

St. Patrick's Cathedral ★★★★

APPEAL BY AGE	PRESCHOOL ★★	GRADE SCHOOL ★★★	TEENS ★★★
YOUNG ADULTS ★★★	OVER 30 ★★★★		SENIORS ★★★★

St. Patrick's Close, Dublin 8, *Dublin Castle and the Cathedrals*;
☎ 01-453-9472; www.stpatrickscathedral.ie

Type of attraction Church. **Buses** 50, 50A, 54, 54A, 65, 65B, 77. **Admission** €5 adults, €4 seniors and students, €12 families of up to 2 adults and 2 children. **Hours** March–October, Monday–Saturday, 9 a.m.–6 p.m.; Sunday, 9–11 a.m., 12:45–3 p.m., 4:15–6 p.m.; November–February, Monday–Friday, 9 a.m.–6 p.m.;

Saturday, 9 a.m.–5 p.m.; Sunday, 10–11 a.m., 12:45–3 p.m. **When to go** Plan a visit to coincide with a lunchtime recital or evensong. **Special comments** The cathedral hosts lunchtime recitals throughout the year. The highly acclaimed cathedral choir sings twice on weekdays, during matins at 9:40 a.m. and evensong at 5:30 p.m. **How much time to allow** 1 hour.

DESCRIPTION AND COMMENTS These days, the centuries-long rivalry between Dublin's two neighboring cathedrals, Christ Church and St. Patrick's, seems to have swung in favor of the latter. Both edifices were built in the 12th century, and both were restored in the 19th century with profits gotten from spirits: St. Patrick's benefited from the Guinness brewing fortune, while whiskey magnate Henry Roe was the benefactor for Christ Church. However, while the restoration of Christ Church was heavy handed, that of St. Patrick's left much of the cathedral's medieval magnificence intact and added the magnificently colorful Victorian floor tiles. St. Patrick's, built on the site where its namesake is said to have preached in the fifth century, is now the largest church in Ireland as well as the flagship of the Church of Ireland. In its long and storied past, the church has served as a stable for Cromwell's horses, been ravaged by storms and fire, and been divided with a wall to serve both French Huguenots and Dubliners.

The medieval interior and verdant grounds are littered with the tombs of some of Ireland's greatest sons and daughters. The most famous tomb here is that of the satirist Jonathan Swift, who wrote *Gulliver's Travels* and most of his other great work while he was the dean of St. Patrick's (1713–1745) Swift's companion, Stella (Mrs. Esther Johnson), lies nearby. The author's deanship has endowed the cathedral with many stories of his savage wit and sense of irony. Near his grave is a pulpit on wheels, on which altar boys would push him up and down the aisles on the lookout for the faithful who had nodded off during Sunday afternoon services. "Of all misbehavior," he would allegedly bellow, "none is comparable to that of those who come here to sleep. Opium is not so stultifying to many persons as an afternoon sermon." Another intriguing artifact is the chapter house door, with a hole through it. As legend has it, the Earl of Kildare cornered a supporter of his enemy the Earl of Ormonde, and the fellow took refuge in the chapter house and barred the door. Kildare cut a hole into the door and stuck his arm through, taking a chance on losing it or implementing a truce with a handshake. A handshake it was, giving rise to the expression "To chance your arm."

TOURING TIPS Marsh's Library (see page 135), at the southern edge of the cathedral grounds, is well worth a visit. Adjoining St. Patrick's park is one of Dublin's loveliest green spaces, laid out in the early 20th century on the site of a notorious slum.

Shaw Birthplace ★★★½

APPEAL BY AGE	PRESCHOOL ★★	GRADE SCHOOL ★★★	TEENS ★★★
YOUNG ADULTS ★★★★★		OVER 30 ★★★½	SENIORS ★★★½

33 Synge Street, Dublin 8, *St. Stephen's Green*; ☎ 01-475-0854

Type of attraction Home of famous author. **Buses** 16, 19, 22. **Admission** €7 adults, €5.95 seniors and students, €4.40 children, €18 families. **Hours** May–October, Monday–Tuesday and Thursday–Friday, 10 a.m.–1 p.m., 2–5 p.m.; Saturday–Sunday, 2–5 p.m. **When to go** Anytime. **Special comments** A shop sells postcards, gifts, and copies of the author's work. **How much time to allow** 1 hour.

DESCRIPTION AND COMMENTS Far more evocative than the sparsely furnished Oscar Wilde House, this modest terrace house says more about middle-class life in 19th-century Dublin than it does about young George Bernard Shaw. He would leave Ireland for London at the age of 23 and go on to be one of the greatest playwrights of the late 19th and early 20th centuries, winning the Nobel Prize for Literature for his repertoire of such works as *Pygmalion.* You can feel the claustrophobia of the confines of family life here as you peer into the cramped, overfurnished parlors, the primitive kitchen, and the wee bedroom on the landing where the playwright slept as a youth. The excellent recorded commentary is full of juicy tidbits about his unhappily married parents and his mother's infatuation with another man.

TOURING TIPS The house is just off the South Circular Road, about a ten-minute walk due south of St. Stephen's Green, so it can be added to a tour of that part of Dublin.

OTHER SIGHTS

kids **THE ARK: A CULTURAL CENTRE FOR CHILDREN** Eustace Street, Dublin 2, *Temple Bar;* ☎ 01-670-7788; about €7, depending on activity; open daily, 10 a.m. to 4 p.m., often closed to all but school groups during the week; buses 37, 39, 51, 51B; **www.ark .ie.** With the presence of this wonderful activity center, tourist folks really can honestly say the boozy Temple Bar district is family oriented. Kids sign up for programs to make stained glass, learn about Irish music, watch plays, and otherwise engage themselves in creative and meaningful activities.

CASINO AT MARINO Marino; ☎ 01-833-1618; €2.90 adults, €1.30 seniors, students, and children; €7.40 families; May through September, daily, 10 a.m. to 5 p.m.; October through April, Saturday and Sunday, 10 a.m. to 5 p.m.; DART to Clontarf Road; a few minutes walk from there. Please don't venture out here to the close-in suburbs expecting to have a go at the slots: *Casino* means "Little House." The earl of Charlemont, an avid art collector whose town house on Parnell Square now houses the collections of the Dublin City Gallery–The Hugh Lane, commissioned this delightful garden house on his seaside estate late in the 18th century to mimic the neoclassical splendors he saw on his nine-year Grand Tour of Europe. What from the outside looks like one large space is actually a delightful maze of rooms, decorated inside and out with statuary and carvings. Hours vary, so call before making the trek out here.

DUBLIN EXPERIENCE Trinity College, Davis Theatre, Dublin 2, *Trinity College and Temple Bar;* ☎ 01-608-1688; €4.20 adults, €2.20 children, €3.50 seniors and students, €8.40 families; open late May through late September: daily, 10 a.m. to 5 p.m. on the hour; buses 5, 7A, 8, 15A, 15B, 15C, 46, 55, 62, 63, 83, 84; DART: Tara Street. All you need to know about the history of Dublin, and then some, presented in a snappy multimedia show.

kids **DUBLIN ZOO** Phoenix Park, Dublin 8, Phoenix Park; ☎ 01-677-1425; €13.50 adults, €9 children ages 3 to 16, free for children under age 3, €11 for seniors and students, €38 for families of two adults and two children, €43 for families of two adults and three children, and €47 for families of two adults and four children; open summer, Monday through Saturday, 9:30 a.m to 6 p.m., and Sunday, 10:30 a.m. to 6 p.m., and winter, Monday through Saturday, 9:30 a.m. to dusk, and Sunday, 10:30 a.m. to dusk; buses 10, 25, 26; **www.dublinzoo.ie.** The third-oldest zoo in the world opened in 1830, following the examples set by zoos in London and Paris. Others around the world have long since surpassed this one in size and sophistication, although recent expansion and restoration have made accommodations for the animals much more humane (many of the habitats are cageless). The Dublin zookeepers' big claim to fame is the ability to breed lions in captivity, and they have successfully bred and nurtured 700 lion cubs over the past 150 years; one of the progeny posed for the famed MGM trademark.

GALLERY OF PHOTOGRAPHY Meeting House Square, Dublin 2, *Temple Bar;* ☎ 01-671-4653; **www.irish-photography.com;** free; Monday through Saturday, 11 a.m. to 6 p.m.; Sunday, 1 to 6 p.m. All city-center buses. Airy galleries showcase Irish and international photography and host an ongoing round of excellent exhibitions, many featuring the work of emerging artists. The ground-floor shop is the best place to pick up a photo book of Ireland.

IRISH-JEWISH MUSEUM 4 Walworth Road, Dublin 8, *St. Stephen's Green;* ☎ 01-453-1797; **www.jewishireland.com;** free; May through September, Sunday, Tuesday, and Thursday, 11 a.m. to 3:30 p.m.; October through April, Sunday, 10:30 a.m. to 2:30 p.m.; buses 16, 19, or 122. Ireland's sizable Jewish communities are honored in a former synagogue in what was once one of Dublin's most populous Jewish neighborhoods. Material on view includes photographs, books, and more than a passing reference to Leopold Bloom, the Odysseus-like protagonist of James Joyce's *Ulysses.*

NATURAL HISTORY MUSEUM Merrion Street Upper, Dublin 2, *Georgian Dublin;* ☎ 01-677-7444; free; Tuesday through Saturday, 10 a.m. to 5 p.m.; Sunday, 2 to 5 p.m.; buses 44, 48; DART: Pearse; **www.museum.ie/naturalhistory.** Founded in 1857, this wonderfully old-fashioned collection of bones seems locked in the Victorian era. You'll find more-complete (and more sophisticated) collections elsewhere, but few are as evocative of the great 19th-century age of discovery as Dublin's.

NATIONAL PRINT MUSEUM Haddington Road, Beggar's Bush, Dublin 4, *Ballsbridge;* ☎ 01-660-3770; **www.iol.ie/~npmuseum;** €3.50 adults, €2 seniors, students, and children; €7 families of up to two adults and two children; Monday through Friday, 9 a.m. to 5 p.m.; Saturday and Sunday, 2 to 5 p.m.; DART to Grand Canal Dock. Anyone with an interest in printmaking will want to take the trip to this former chapel that now houses a lovely collection of printing presses, paraphernalia, and, of course, prints and historic newspaper pages, all brought to life by the charmingly loquacious guides.

NEWMAN HOUSE 85–86 St. Stephen's Green, Dublin 2, *St. Stephen's Green;* ☎ 01-706-7422; €5 adults, €4 seniors and students; by guided tour only; June through August, Tuesday through Friday, at noon, 2 p.m., 3 p.m., and 4 p.m.; buses 10, 11, 13, 14, 14A, 15A, 15B. Two sides of Dublin come together in this grand residence, which actually combines two houses: the rococo swirls of plasterwork, grand staircase, ornate Apollo Room (where the sun god is lavishly depicted), and baroque Saloon are the most extravagant examples of Georgian decor in the city. The premises were the original locale of the Catholic University of Ireland, founded by Cardinal John Henry Newman in 1850. The poet Gerard Manley Hopkins was a student here, and his quarters are included in the tour; you'll learn that the nude nymphs that are part of the decor were covered up to protect him and other young men from temptation.

ROYAL HIBERNIAN ACADEMY (RHA) 25 Ely Place, Dublin 2, *St. Stephen's Green;* ☎ 01-661-2558; **www.royalhibernianacademy.ie;** free; Tuesday through Wednesday, Friday, and Saturday, 11 a.m. to 5 p.m.; Thursday, 11 a.m. to 8 p.m.; Sunday, 2 to 5 p.m.; all city-center buses. The esteemed RHA selects the artists who show here, and the galleries are among Ireland's most prestigious showcases for contemporary work.

TEMPLE BAR GALLERY & STUDIOS 5 Temple Bar, Dublin 2, *Temple Bar;* ☎ 01-671-0073; **www.templebargallery.com;** free; Tuesday through Saturday, 11 a.m. to 6 p.m. (until 7 p.m. on Thursday); all city-center buses. Almost as if to prove that rowdy Temple Bar does have a purpose other than entertaining young drinkers, these publicly funded galleries establish the neighborhood as one of Dublin's real art centers, showing the work of Irish artists in all media.

WHITEFRIAR STREET CARMELITE CHURCH Whitefriar Street, Dublin 2, *Dublin Castle and the Cathedrals;* ☎ 01-475-8821; free; open daily, 8:30 a.m. to 6:30 p.m.; buses 16, 16A, 19, 19A, 22. Of Dublin's many places of worship, this one stands out as the repository of the relics of St. Valentine, making the church a popular venue for lovers, those who've been disappointed in love, and those who are simply romantically inclined.

DINING *in* DUBLIN

DINING IN DUBLIN IS A DELIGHT. Even a decade ago, a statement like that would have elicited laughs. But with prosperity comes a taste for fine food, and Dubliners these days have a wide choice of excellent restaurants serving a variety of cuisines. While Dublin chefs are experimenting with international flavors, a few factors remain fairly constant: ingredients are most often seasonally fresh and from local producers; service is, for the most part, excellent; and friendliness, courtesy, and other hallmarks of Irish hospitality are much in evidence. Even in the most formal restaurants, a meal remains a relaxed, comfortable affair; you'll rarely be rushed and, to the contrary, will be encouraged to linger.

Here's another factor you can count on—Dublin restaurants are expensive. You won't spend as much for a good meal here as you will in London or New York, but you will pay quite a bit. A tab of €60 to €80 for dinner for two is pretty common, and it's very easy to pay much more than that (see Part Three, Lodging, Dining, and Shopping). Lunch is usually less expensive than dinner, and many of the finest restaurants in Dublin dish up especially good value for the noon meal, usually on reasonably priced prix-fixe menus. Many restaurants also offer set menus at dinner, but these are often available only before 7 or 7:30 p.m.

unofficial **TIP**
Some Dublin restaurants add a service charge to the tab, but many don't. If the policy isn't stated clearly on the menu, don't be shy about asking. If a service charge is not included, a tip of 10–15% is customary, provided that the service was acceptable. But don't bother to ask if you can light up over your coffee, because the answer will be no: smoking is prohibited in all public spaces in Ireland.

SOME CHOICES FOR A CHEAP MEAL IN DUBLIN

BEWLEY'S CAFÉ 78–79 Grafton Street, Dublin 2, *Grafton Street;* ☎ 01-679-4085; all city-center buses. Dublin's favorite cafe closed a while back (amid much public protest) and reemerged in this new guise that retains several floors of nooks and crannies. Lingering is now only permitted in the ground-floor cafe, where a fairly standard selection of pastries and sandwiches is served; much of the premises houses a sit-down restaurant that serves bland Italian food. Bewley's is still bathed in the mellow light of its tall Arts and Crafts windows, and while the food may be a bit lackluster, the cafe does make a handy stop for a cup of tea while making the Grafton Street rounds. And though much of the old Bewley's ambience has fallen by the wayside, its beloved 45-minute-long lunchtime theatrical productions have been revived. Monday through Saturday, 7:30 a.m. to 7 p.m.; Sunday, 8:30 a.m. to 6 p.m.

ELEPHANT AND CASTLE 18 Temple Bar, Dublin 2, *Temple Bar;* ☎ 01-679-3121; buses 51B, 51C, 68, 69, 70. If you're homesick for a juicy

How Restaurants Compare in Dublin

NAME	CUISINE	OVERALL	QUALITY	VALUE	PRICE
L'Ecrivain	Modern Irish	★★★★½	★★★★½	★★★★	Very exp
The Tea Room	Continental	★★★★½	★★★★½	★★★★	Exp
Chapter One	Modern Irish	★★★★½	★★★★½	★★★½	Very exp
Restaurant Patrick Guilbaud	French	★★★★½	★★★★½	★★★½	Very exp
Jacob's Ladder	Modern Irish	★★★★	★★★★½	★★★★	Mod/exp
Enoteca della Langhe	Wine bar	★★★★	★★★★	★★★★½	Inexp
La Mère Zou	French	★★★★	★★★★	★★★½	Exp
Les Frères Jacques	French/ Continental	★★★★	★★★★	★★★½	Exp
The Winding Stair	Modern Irish	★★★★	★★★★	★★★½	Mod/exp
Chez Max	French	★★★★	★★★★	★★★★	Mod
Dunne and Crescenzi	Italian	★★★★	★★★★	★★★★	Inexp
101 Talbot	Irish/ vegetarian	★★★½	★★★★	★★★★½	Mod
Beshoffs	Fish-and-chips	★★★½	★★★½	★★★★	Inexp
L'Gueuleton	French	★★★½	★★★½	★★★½	Mod
Pearl Brasserie	French	★★★½	★★★½	★★★½	Mod/exp
Halo	French	★★★½	★★★½	★★★	Exp/ Very exp
Mermaid Cafe	Seafood/ modern Irish	★★★½	★★★½	★★★	Exp
Eden	Continental	★★★	★★★	★★★	Mod
Peploe's	Wine bar	★★★	★★★	★★★	Mod/exp

burger or just looking for a quick bite along Temple Bar, you can't go wrong at this dinerlike purveyor of American-style grub. Food is served throughout the day. Monday through Friday, 8 a.m. to 11:30 p.m.; Saturday and Sunday, 10:30 a.m. to 11 p.m.

GRUEL 68A Dame Street, Dublin 2, *Temple Bar;* ☎ 01-670-7119; buses 50, 50A, 54, 56, 77. Jam-packed, noisy, and really not very comfortable, Gruel overcomes its shortcomings (and humble name) with a fine array of soups, salads, and sandwiches, dispensed all day long at very reasonable prices. Monday through Wednesday, 10 a.m.

to 9:30 p.m.; Thursday through Saturday, 10 a.m. to 10:30 p.m.; Sunday, 10 a.m. to 9 p.m.

IRISH FILM CENTRE   6 Eustace Street, Dublin 2, *Temple Bar;* ☎ 01-677-8788; buses 21A, 78A, 78B. Dublin's wonderful screen for serious film (international, classic, documentary) is blessed with a lively cafe and bar that are popular even for those not lining up at show times. The creative, ever-changing menu includes many Mediterranean-inspired and vegetarian dishes, with price tags that hover comfortably around €8 a plate. Monday through Friday, 12:30 to 3 p.m. and 6 to 9 p.m.; Saturday and Sunday, 12:30 to 3 p.m. and 6 to 9 p.m.

LA MAISON DES GOURMETS   15 Castle Market, Dublin 2, *Grafton Street;* ☎ 01-672-7258; all city-center buses. A little bit of Paris brings wonderful pastries to Dublin, along with salads, savory tarts, and charcuterie platters. Daily, 6 a.m. to 6 p.m.

LEO BURDOCK'S   2 Werburgh Street, Dublin 8, *Dublin Castle and the Cathedrals;* ☎ 01-454-0306; buses 21A, 50, 50A, 78, 78A. You'll have to dine standing up, but you'll be in good company—Dubliners come from all over town to feast on what is considered to be the best fish-and-chips in town. Burdock's is almost as sacred as nearby Christchurch and St. Patrick's Cathedral, and a must-stop when visiting this end of town. Monday through Saturday, noon to midnight.

QUEEN OF TARTS   Dame Street, Dublin 2, *Dublin Castle and the Cathedrals;* ☎ 01-670-7499; all city-center buses. Fresh baked goods and scones so light they float off your plate are the main temptations, but you shouldn't indulge in the sweets until you polish off one of the equally excellent sandwiches, salads, or tarts. The surroundings are cramped but aromatic and homey, and the prices most reasonable. Monday through Friday, 7:30 a.m. to 7 p.m.; Saturday, 9 a.m. to 7 p.m.; Sunday, 9 a.m. to 7 p.m. You'll also find an outlet nearby, on Cow's Lane in Temple Bar.

SIMON'S PLACE   George's Street Arcade, Dublin 2, *Dublin Castle and the Cathedrals;* ☎ 01-679-7821; buses 21A, 50, 50A, 78, 78A. A cozy sandwich shop at the entrance to a bazaarlike shopping arcade serves hefty sandwiches and hearty soups.

WAGAMAMA SOUTH   King Street, Dublin 2, *St. Stephen's Green;* ☎ 01-478-2152; all city-center buses. The ubiquitous London chain, a favorite for yummy and inexpensive noodles and other Asian dishes, has arrived in Dublin, bringing with it the communal tables, minimalist surroundings, and very reasonable prices that make it a megahit across the Irish Sea. Monday through Saturday, noon to 10:50 p.m.; Sunday, noon to 9:50 p.m.

YAMAMORI   71–72 South Great George Street, Dublin 2, *Dublin Castle;* ☎ 01-475-5001; buses 21A, 50, 50A, 78, 78A. A Japanese noodle house is a great addition to the Dublin scene, providing a nice alternative to Wagamama when the yen for inexpensive Asian fare hits. The sushi is commendable, and heaping plates of noodles fill the bill for a hearty meal.

Food Halls

Has it come to this? The only way to save money when traveling is to smuggle food into your hotel room? Not quite. But Dublin's food shops do provide an inexpensive alternative to restaurants as well as the opportunity to try exotic fare and the fresh bounty of Irish farms and seas. No need to scurry back to your room—Dublin parks (see page 124) are fine places for a picnic. In addition to these food emporia, also check out the markets that operate around the city on various days of the week (see page 167).

EPICUREAN FOOD HALL Middle Abbey and Lower Liffey streets, Dublin 1, *Central Dublin*; all city-center buses. Dublin's main food hall is a tempting collection of stalls, many with tables and counters where you can grab a quick bite; this is also the place to load up on cheeses, salamis, and other snacks to stuff into the minibar in your hotel room. **Caviston's,** an excellent all-around deli with a superb selection of Irish farmhouse cheeses, is here, as are outposts of world cuisine such as **Istanbul Restaurant** and **Itsabagel.** Daily, 10 a.m. to 6 p.m. (open later on some Thursdays and Sundays).

FALLON AND BYRNE 11–17 Exchequer Street, Dublin 2, *Dublin Castle*; all city-center buses. Dublin's most elegant food store offers aisles of tempting cheeses and deli items, as well as a snazzy cafe with a takeaway counter piled high with sandwiches, tarts, and salads. Monday through Friday, 8 a.m. to 10 p.m.; Saturday, 9 a.m. to 9 p.m.; Sunday, 11 a.m. to 9 p.m.

MARKS AND SPENCER 15–20 Grafton Street, Dublin 2, *Grafton Street*; all city-center buses. The British chain, known for its food halls, stocks the one here with a vast array of high-line groceries as well as an amazing assortment of prepared dishes. Monday through Wednesday, 9 a.m. to 6 p.m.; Thursday, 9 a.m. to 9 p.m.; Friday and Saturday, 9 a.m. to 6 p.m.; Sunday, noon to 6 p.m.

SHERIDAN'S CHEESEMONGERS 21–23 Nassau Street, Dublin 2, *Grafton Street*; all city-center buses. Dublin's best selections of cheeses, right off Irish farms and many that have been flown in from abroad; cheese is the word here, but smoked salmon and other gourmet treats are also on offer. Monday through Friday, 10 a.m. to 6 p.m.; Saturday, 9:30 a.m. to 6 p.m.

Museum Cafes

Most of Dublin's museums are equipped with cafes or tearooms, providing pleasant surroundings for a moderately priced meal. Here are some of the best:

CHESTER BEATTY LIBRARY AND GALLERY OF ORIENTAL ART Clock Tower Building, Dublin Castle, Dublin 2, *Dublin Castle*; ☎ 01-407-0750; buses

50, 51B, 54A, 56A, 77, 77A, 78A, 123. **Silk Road** elevates museum cafes to new heights, serving excellent Middle Eastern fare in the museum's handsome atrium. May through September: Tuesday through Friday, 10 a.m. to 5 p.m.; Saturday, 11 a.m. to 5 p.m.; Sunday, 1 to 5 p.m.; October through April: Tuesday through Friday, 10 a.m. to 5 p.m.; Saturday, 11 a.m. to 5 p.m.; Sunday, 1 to 5 p.m.

DUBLIN CASTLE Dame Street, Dublin 2, *Dublin Castle;* ☎ 01-677-7129; buses 50, 50A, 54, 54A, 65, 65B, 77. A warrenlike series of rooms and a covered garden are pleasant surroundings in which to enjoy a surprisingly wide array of home-cooked meals, along the lines of Irish stew and curries. Sandwiches and salads are also available, as are beer and wine. Monday through Friday, 10 a.m. to 4:45 p.m.; Saturday and Sunday, 2 to 4:45 p.m.

DUBLIN CITY GALLERY–THE HUGH LANE Parnell Square North, Dublin 1, *Central Dublin;* ☎ 01-222-5550; buses 11, 13, 16, 16A, 22, 22A. The downstairs cafe, done up in soothing neutral shades and overlooking a secluded garden, would be a lovely place for lunch—even if a viewing of the sumptuous collection wasn't part of the bargain. Tuesday through Thursday, 10 a.m. to 6 p.m.; Friday and Saturday, 10 a.m. to 5 p.m.; Sunday, 11 a.m. to 5 p.m.

NATIONAL GALLERY OF IRELAND Merrion Square West, Dublin 2, *Georgian Dublin;* ☎ 01-677-7444; buses 7, 7A, 8, 10, 11, 13. The cafeteria—a comfy room facing a cobbled court—is preferable to the pricier, more formal restaurant. The self-service counter is laden with salads, sandwiches, stews, quiches, and other plain fare made fresh daily, which can be enjoyed at leisure in pleasant, laid-back surroundings. Monday through Wednesday, Friday, and Saturday, 9:30 a.m. to 5:30 p.m.; Thursday, 9:30 a.m. to 8:30 p.m.; Sunday, noon to 5 p.m.

NATIONAL MUSEUM OF IRELAND–DECORATIVE ARTS AND HISTORY (AKA COLLINS BARRACKS) Benburb Street, Dublin 8, *Kilmainham;* ☎ 01-677-7444; buses 34, 70, 80; DART: Museum. A meal is hard to find in this part of town, but the cheerful ground floor cafe that spills into the courtyard here more than fills the bill. Tuesday through Saturday, 10 a.m. to 5 p.m.; Sunday, 2 to 5 p.m.

PUB GRUB It won't take you long to discover that it's not the food that draws Dubliners to their pubs. Even so, in many you can dine decently, if not fancily, on sandwiches and other light fare, and in some you can eat very well. Keep in mind that some of the busier, more tourist-oriented pubs draw visitors in with music and feed them mediocre but expensive meals. Some pubs have earned a solid reputation over the years for serving more-modest yet reliable and fairly priced meals. In James Joyce's *Ulysses,* Leopold Bloom stops into **David Byrne's** (21 Duke Street, Dublin 2, *Grafton Street;* ☎ 01-677-5271) for a sandwich and a glass of wine, and you can do the same, or you can dine on one of the daily specials. **O'Neill's** (2 Suffolk

dublin dining

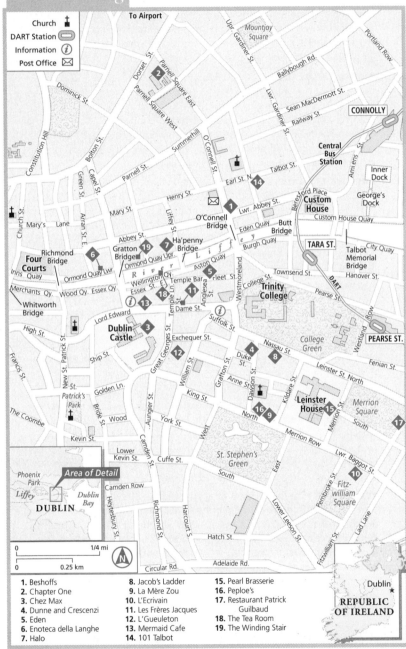

Church ✝
DART Station ⬯
Information ⓘ
Post Office ✉

1. Beshoffs
2. Chapter One
3. Chez Max
4. Dunne and Crescenzi
5. Eden
6. Enoteca della Langhe
7. Halo
8. Jacob's Ladder
9. La Mère Zou
10. L'Ecrivain
11. Les Frères Jacques
12. L'Gueuleton
13. Mermaid Cafe
14. 101 Talbot
15. Pearl Brasserie
16. Peploe's
17. Restaurant Patrick
    Guilbaud
18. The Tea Room
19. The Winding Stair

Street, Dublin 2, *Grafton Street*; ☎ 01-679-3671) has a carvery that packs in a big lunch crowd. Another busy lunch spot is the **Stag's Head** (1 Dame Court, Dublin 2, *Temple Bar*; ☎ 01-679-3701), where you can enjoy sandwiches and hot meals amid Victorian splendor and beneath the enormous eponymous showpiece. **Neary's** (1 Chatham Street, Dublin 2, *Grafton Street*; ☎ 01-677-7371) serves a memorable version of that pub staple, the smoked-salmon sandwich, in comfy Victorian surroundings.

(*Also see pub profiles on page 161.*)

RESTAURANTS IN DUBLIN

 Beshoffs ★★★½

FISH-AND-CHIPS	INEXPENSIVE	QUALITY ★★★½	VALUE ★★★★

6 Upper O'Connell Street, Dublin 1, *Central Dublin*; ☎ 01-872-4181
Westmoreland Street, Dublin 2, *Trinity College and Temple Bar*;
☎ 01-677-8026

Buses All city-center buses. **Reservations** No. **Entree range** €4–€11; full meals from €8.95. **Payment** Cash only. **Bar** Beer and wine only. **Disabled access** Yes. **Hours** Monday–Saturday, 10 a.m.–9 p.m.; Sunday, noon–9 p.m.

MENU RECOMMENDATIONS There's only one reason to eat here.

COMMENTS Dubliners have been stepping into this venerable "chipper" since the early 20th century, when Ivan Beshoff, a Russian-born seaman, decided to try his hand at running a Dublin chipper. No one can say standards have slipped. The freshest salmon, haddock, and sole are served alongside chips made from potatoes grown on the outfit's own farm. The O'Connell Street establishment, the flashier of the two, has recently been done up in a vaguely Edwardian style, but that barely disguises the fact that this is a no-nonsense sort of place where the emphasis is on dispensing an excellent product.

Chapter One ★★★★½

MODERN IRISH	VERY EXPENSIVE	QUALITY ★★★★½	VALUE ★★★½

18–19 Parnell Square, Dublin 1, *Central Dublin*; ☎ 01-873-2266

Buses 11, 13, 16, 16A, 22, 22A. **Reservations** Required. **Entree range** €34–€38; 2-course lunch, €27.50; 3-course lunch, €31; pre-theater menu, Tuesday–Saturday, 6–7 p.m., €37.50. **Payment** AE, MC, V. **Bar** Full service. **Disabled access** Limited. **Hours** Tuesday–Friday, 12:30–2:30 p.m., 6–11 p.m.; Saturday, 6–11 p.m.

MENU RECOMMENDATIONS Selections from the charcuterie trolley, chicken wrapped in pancetta, roasted scallops, and pork belly.

COMMENTS Depending on how you choose to look at it, the cellar of the Dublin Writers Museum is either an odd or an appropriate locale for this bastion of good taste and fine cuisine. Granted, few of the scribes you will encounter in the exhibits upstairs could ever have afforded to dine in a place like this (though the excellent €20 house wine might appeal), but the elegantly modern decor beneath brick arches, the flawless service, and the sublime preparations of chef Ross Lewis will transport you to poetic realms. Many smart innovations make this lovely place all the more appealing: The charcuterie trolley, laden with Irish hams and salamis, provides a fine start to a meal; the lunch menus provide an affordable treat; and a special pre-theatre menu makes an evening at the nearby Gate all the more memorable.

Chez Max ★★★★

FRENCH	MODERATE	QUALITY ★★★★	VALUE ★★★★

1 Palace Street, Dublin 2, *Dublin Castle*; ☎ 01-633-7215

Buses buses 50, 50A, 54, 56A, 77, 77A, 77B. **Reservations** Yes. **Entree range** €14.50–€22.50; 2-course early-bird special served Sunday–Thursday, 5:30–7 p.m., €19. **Payment** MC, V. **Bar** Excellent wine list. **Disabled access** Yes. **Hours** Sunday–Friday, noon–3:30 p.m.; Saturday, noon–4 p.m.; Sunday–Thursday, 5:30–10 p.m.; Friday–Saturday, 5:30–11 p.m.

MENU RECOMMENDATION Veal kidneys in puff pastry, *salade parisienne* at lunch; escargots, stuffed quail, and *cassoulet toulousain* at dinner; *moules frites* anytime.

COMMENTS A bright, wood-floored room on a cobbled lane next to the stone walls of Dublin castle provides all the ambience of the Left Bank, and the crisp, attentive service with a Gallic flair and the excellent renditions of bistro classics do nothing to shake the mood. Cheese and meat platters, available all day, provide the perfect snack when visiting the castle and nearby cathedrals.

Dunne and Crescenzi ★★★★

ITALIAN	INEXPENSIVE	QUALITY ★★★★	VALUE ★★★★

South Frederick Street, Dublin 2, *Grafton Street*; ☎ 01-675-9892

Buses All city-center buses. **Reservations** No. **Entree range** €10–€15 **Payment** AE, MC, V. **Bar** Wine only. **Disabled access** Yes. **Hours** Monday–Saturday, noon–11 p.m.

MENU RECOMMENDATIONS Pasta specials, salads, cheese selections.

COMMENTS Dublin eateries get no more friendly than these large, atmospheric rooms that do double duty as an amply stocked wine cellar. You can graze here on the excellent selections of cheeses and assorted antipasti, but a few deftly prepared pasta, risotto, and meat dishes are always on offer as well. Salads and panini also fill the bill for light meals with flair.

Eden ★★★

CONTINENTAL	MODERATE	QUALITY ★★★	VALUE ★★★

Meeting House Square, Dublin 2, *Temple Bar*; ☎ 01-670-5372

Buses 51B, 51C, 68, 69, 79. **Reservations** Recommended. **Entree range** €20–€29; 2-course lunch, €23; 3-course lunch, €27; pre-theater menu, Sunday–

Thursday, 6–7 p.m., €29. **Payment** AE, DC, MC, V. **Bar** Full service. **Disabled access** Yes. **Hours** Daily, 12:30–3 p.m., 6–10:30 p.m.

MENU RECOMMENDATIONS Scallops, venison, duck breast, vegetarian dishes.

COMMENTS This bright, airy room facing a lovely square is furnished in white vinyl and chrome, a throwback to the 1990s that looks so dated as to be stylishly retro. The overall effect, though, is soothing, especially when tables spill into the square in warm weather, and once the appetizers arrive it soon becomes clear that Eden is not just about trendy appearances. Instead, the emphasis is on creative and truly excellent cooking that brings together fresh seafood, game, and Irish produce; many specials are prepared daily, often including vegetable curries and other meatless dishes. Weekend brunches are popular and an especially good value.

Enoteca della Langhe ★★★★

WINE BAR	INEXPENSIVE	QUALITY ★★★★	VALUE ★★★★½

Bloom's Lane, Dublin 1, *Central Dublin*; ☎ 01-888-0834

Buses 70, 80. **Reservations** Not necessary. **Entree range** €8–€14. **Payment** MC, V. **Bar** Wine only. **Disabled access** Yes. **Hours** Monday–Wednesday, 12:30 p.m.–midnight; Thursday–Saturday, 3:30 p.m.–1 a.m.; Sunday, 3:30 p.m.–midnight.

MENU RECOMMENDATIONS Bruschetta, cheese and salami plates, pastas.

COMMENTS With bright lights and lively chatter, this delightful and serious-minded purveyor of wine by the glass and Italian ambience adds much to the buzz of this North of the Liffey neighborhood filled with new shops and eateries. Many patrons stop by only to sip wine and watch soccer, but you can make a very satisfying meal out of the simple and delicious offerings of cheese, charcuteries, and some simple salads and pastas.

Halo ★★★½

FRENCH	EXPENSIVE/VERY EXPENSIVE	QUALITY ★★★½	VALUE ★★★

Morrison Hotel, Ormond Quay, Dublin 1, *Central Dublin*; ☎ 01-878-2999

Buses 70, 80. **Reservations** Required. **Entree range** €28–€32. **Payment** AE, MC, V. **Bar** Full service. **Disabled access** Yes. **Hours** Daily, noon–3 p.m., 6–10 p.m.; sandwiches and other light fare served 3–6 p.m.

MENU RECOMMENDATIONS Filet of turbot, lamb rump with lamb sausage, short ribs of Irish beef.

COMMENTS Stepping into the exotic dining room of the über-hip Morrison Hotel is a little like entering a circus tent: great swaths of purple fabric, angled mirrors, multiple levels, and a lively buzz create a theatrical environment. Trappings aside, though, dining well is serious business here, and if one Dublin restaurant epitomizes the city's bold new culinary frontier, this might be it—the kitchen sends out French classics with a slight fusion twist. Inventive pricing makes the experience quite accessible—many of the tempting appetizers, such as fresh oysters with an anise glaze and salads laden with Irish produce, are also available as reasonably priced dinner plates.

 ### Jacob's Ladder ★★★★

MODERN IRISH   MODERATE/EXPENSIVE   QUALITY ★★★★½   VALUE ★★★★

4 Nassau Street, Dublin 2, *Trinity College;* ☎ 01-670-3865

Buses 7, 8, 10, 11. **Reservations** Recommended. **Entree range** €30–€33; earlybird dinner, Tuesday–Friday, 5:30–7 p.m., €21 for 2 courses, €26.75 for 3 courses. **Payment** AE, MC, V. **Bar** Full service. **Disabled access** Limited. **Hours** Tuesday–Friday, 12:30–2:30 p.m., 5:30–9:40 p.m.; Saturday, 6–10 p.m.

MENU RECOMMENDATIONS Irish stew, filet of bass.

COMMENTS A ladderlike climb indeed is required to reach these upstairs rooms, but the effort is rewarded with lovely views through high windows over Trinity College. Simple furnishings and plain wood floors don't detract from this pleasant outlook, and the excellent service does nothing to dispel the myth that you're in a special place high above the city. Chef Adrian Roche's careful preparations do homage to the freshest local ingredients, with an emphasis on seafood.

La Mère Zou ★★★★

FRENCH   EXPENSIVE   QUALITY ★★★★   VALUE ★★★½

22 St. Stephen's Green, Dublin 2, *St. Stephen's Green;* ☎ 01-661-6669

Buses 10, 11A, 11B, 13, 20B. **Reservations** Recommended. **Entree range** €20–€28; prix-fixe lunch, €25; early-bird dinner, Monday–Saturday, 6–7 p.m., €26.50. **Payment** AE, MC, V. **Bar** Full service. **Disabled access** Yes. **Hours** Monday–Friday, 12:30–3 p.m., 6–10 p.m.; Saturday, 6–11 p.m.

MENU RECOMMENDATIONS Mussels (prepared any way).

COMMENTS Lacquered orange walls and orange-and-yellow-plaid fabrics brighten the basement quarters of this lovely little outpost of rural France facing St. Stephen's Green. The cuisine, as charmingly country French as the decor, includes reliable old standbys such as mussels (prepared in many different ways) and confit of duck. The set menus are of excellent value, making La Mère Zou especially appealing for a homey early dinner.

L'Ecrivain ★★★★½

MODERN IRISH   VERY EXPENSIVE   QUALITY ★★★★½   VALUE ★★★★

109a Lower Baggot Street, Dublin 2, *Georgian Dublin;* ☎ 01-661-1919

Bus 10. **Reservations** Required. **Entree range** €40–€45; 2-course lunch, €35; 3-course lunch, €45; prix-fixe dinner, €75. **Payment** AE. **Bar** Full service. **Disabled access** Yes. **Hours** Monday–Friday, 12:30–2 p.m., 7–10 p.m.; Saturday, 7–10 p.m.

MENU RECOMMENDATIONS Seared scallops, baked oysters, fillet of Irish Angus beef.

COMMENTS One of Ireland's few restaurants to have earned a Michelin star continually lives up to its reputation as the second-finest dining room in town (after Patrick Guilbaud), and chef Derry Clarke's traditional-yet-innovative approach to meat and seafood classics never fails. The food is sublime, and the two-course lunch special is a relative bargain enjoyed by what seems to be half the business crowd of Dublin. The soothingly toned, peak-ceilinged upstairs dining room is surprisingly casual and welcoming, filled with light during the day and complemented by service that manages to be both adept and casual.

L'Gueuleton   ★★★½

FRENCH	MODERATE	QUALITY ★★★½	VALUE ★★★½

1 Fade Street, Dublin 2, *Grafton Street;* ☎ 01-675-3708

Buses All city-center buses. **Reservations** No. **Entree range** €13–€15.50 at lunch, €15.50–€26 at dinner. **Payment** Cash only. **Bar** Beer and wine only. **Disabled access** Yes. **Hours** Monday–Saturday, noon.–11 p.m.

MENU RECOMMENDATIONS Duck terrine, Toulouse sausages with *choucroute,* duck-leg confit.

COMMENTS Dublin's only contender to Chez Max (see page 152) for a veritable Parisian-style bistro serves hearty and deft renditions of calorific Southwestern French classics—the name, after all, means "gluttonous feast." Many of the dinner entrees are available at lunch for a lower price, making a midday meal all the more appealing.

Les Frères Jacques   ★★★★

FRENCH/CONTINENTAL	EXPENSIVE	QUALITY ★★★★	VALUE ★★★½

74 Dame Street, Dublin 2, *Temple Bar;* ☎ 01-672-7258

Buses 50, 50A, 54, 56, 77. **Reservations** Recommended. **Entree range** €38–€40; prix-fixe menus: 2-course lunch, €19; 4-course dinner, €40. **Payment** AE, MC, V. **Bar** Full service. **Disabled access** Yes. **Hours** Monday–Friday, 12:30–2:30 p.m., 7:30–10:30 p.m.; Saturday, 7–11 p.m.

MENU RECOMMENDATIONS Panfried foie gras and apple tarte Tatin; roast rack of lamb.

COMMENTS This small, plush room that opens right onto busy Dame Street is a welcome retreat and a bastion of old-world service, atmosphere, and cooking that doesn't shy away from decadent treats such as foie gras and rich sauces. One of the best French restaurants in Dublin, this is a top choice for a romantic dinner, but lunchtime prices, among the biggest culinary bargains in town, are the big draw.

Mermaid Cafe   ★★★ ½

SEAFOOD/MODERN IRISH	EXPENSIVE	QUALITY ★★★½	VALUE ★★★

69–70 Dame Street, Dublin 2, *Temple Bar;* ☎ 01-670-8236

Buses 50, 50A, 54, 56A, 77, 77A, 77B. **Reservations** Recommended. **Entree range** €20–€32. **Payment** MC, V. **Bar** Full service. **Disabled access** Yes. **Hours**

Monday–Saturday, 12:30–2:30 p.m., 6–11 p.m.; Sunday, noon–3:30 p.m., 6–9 p.m.

MENU RECOMMENDATIONS Antipasto platter, crab cakes.

COMMENTS You know the food has to be good when diners are willing to pay a lot to crowd into cramped rooms that open unromantically to busy Dame Street through huge windows. Seafood is favored in the kitchen, and many fresh-fish dishes, Maryland-style crab cakes (a concession to the fact that the cuisine is American inspired), and a creamy seafood casserole are standouts. Rib-eye steaks and several lamb dishes are served as well. Mermaid Cafe also serves the best Sunday brunch in Dublin, with pancakes, bagels, and other fare that will remind you of home; the restaurant also has a good traditional Irish fry.

101 Talbot ★★★½

IRISH/VEGETARIAN   MODERATE   QUALITY ★★★★   VALUE ★★★★ ½

101 Talbot Street, Dublin 1, *Central Dublin;* ☎ 01-874-5011

Buses 27A, 31A, 31B, 32A, 32B, 42B, 43, 44A. **Reservations** Recommended. **Entree range** €13.50–€23; 2-course "value menu" dinner, €21.50. **Payment** AE, MC, V. **Bar** Full service. **Disabled access** Limited. **Hours** Tuesday–Saturday, 5–11 p.m.

MENU RECOMMENDATIONS Pasta, fresh fish, daily vegetarian specials, organic Irish steak.

COMMENTS A big yellow upstairs room, floored in red linoleum, is completely devoid of pretension, rightly suggesting that the emphasis here is on warm service and good cooking. Vegetarians and the health conscious will delight in a menu that offers several inventive pasta dishes and choices such as couscous topped with vegetables, but the highest-grade Irish beef and pork, along with market-fresh fish, also appear on the daily-changing menu. The wonderful cuisine, excellent value, location north of the River Liffey (where good restaurants are few and far between), and proximity of the Gate and Abbey theaters draw a loyal crowd of Dubliners.

Pearl Brasserie ★★★½

FRENCH   MODERATE/EXPENSIVE   QUALITY ★★★½   VALUE ★★★½

20 Merrion Street Upper, Dublin 2, *Georgian Dublin;* ☎ 01-661-3572

Buses 10, 11A, 11B, 13, 20B. **Reservations** Recommended. **Entree range** €22–€30; prix-fixe menus: 1-course lunch, €16; 2-course lunch, €21.50; 3-course lunch, €26; dinner, €43 and €51. **Payment** AE, D, MC, V. **Bar** Full service. **Disabled access** Yes. **Hours** Tuesday–Friday, noon–2:30 p.m., 6–10:30 p.m.; Saturday and Sunday, 6–10:30 p.m.

MENU RECOMMENDATIONS Dublin Bay prawns wrapped in smoked duck, pan-fried sea bass, oysters.

COMMENTS A cellarlike downstairs room, warmed by fires and always lively, hits just the right note for a pleasant meal. This is a good place for a long and affordable lunch on a rainy day (lunchtime menus are an excellent value), and a bit of a scene in the evening, when a young, upwardly mobile crowd converges; at this time, the oyster bar is a perfect choice for light grazing and lively chatter.

Peploe's ★★★

WINE BAR	MODERATE/EXPENSIVE	QUALITY ★★★	VALUE ★★★

16 St. Stephen's Green, Dublin 2, *St. Stephen's Green*; ☎ 01-676-3144

Buses 10, 11A, 11B, 13, 20B. **Reservations** Not necessary. **Entree range** €16–€30. **Payment** AE, MC, V. **Bar** Full service. **Disabled access** Yes. **Hours** Daily, noon–midnight.

MENU RECOMMENDATIONS Braised rump of lamb, rabbit stew, smoked-fish cakes.

COMMENTS In theory, this suite of stylish rooms on the ground floor of a Georgian terrace seems like a welcome retreat, as it is for a crowd of well-heeled regulars—an informal yet chic spot for lunch or a snack while shopping on nearby Grafton Street or visiting the nearby museums. But be warned: If it's a casual meal you're after, you can easily end up spending quite a bit on a full meal of the temptingly inventive offerings based on Irish classics.

Restaurant Patrick Guilbaud ★★★★½

FRENCH	VERY EXPENSIVE	QUALITY ★★★★½	VALUE ★★★½

The Merrion Hotel, 21 Merrion Street, Dublin 2, *Georgian Dublin*; ☎ 01-676-4192

Buses 10, 11A, 11B, 13, 20B. **Reservations** Required. **Entree range** €48–€52; 2-course lunch, €38; 3-course lunch, €50; evening tasting menu, €180. **Payment** AE, DC, MC, V. **Bar** Full service. **Disabled access** Yes. **Hours** Tuesday–Saturday, 12:30–2:15 p.m., 7:30–10:15 p.m.

MENU RECOMMENDATIONS Chicken and foie gas, Wicklow venison.

COMMENTS It's easy to feel like a country mouse in Dublin's (and Ireland's) most celebrated restaurant, although the surroundings soon put you at ease. Lovely works by Irish painters enliven the simple and elegant decor, and large windows open onto a terrace and the lush and colorful gardens of the Merrion Hotel. The most economical way to sample the classic French cuisine is at lunch, when relatively economical set menus are served, but if you feel like splurging, try the tasting menu at dinner—an Irish culinary feast that only a Frenchman could devise.

The Tea Room ★★★★½

CONTINENTAL	EXPENSIVE	QUALITY ★★★★½	VALUE ★★★★

Clarence Hotel, 6–8 Wellington Quay, Dublin 2, *Temple Bar*; ☎ 01-407-0813

Buses 51B, 51C, 68, 69, 79. **Reservations** Recommended. **Entree range** €29–€42; 2-course lunch, €26; 2-course dinner, €39. **Payment** AE, DC, MC, V.

Bar Full service. **Disabled access** Yes. **Hours** Monday–Friday and Sunday, 12:30–2:30 p.m.; Monday–Saturday, 7–10:30 p.m.; Sunday 7–9:30 p.m.

MENU RECOMMENDATIONS Daily fresh fish, pheasant and other Irish game.

COMMENTS The main dining room of the Clarence is as chic and cool as the rest of the hotel, awash in light oak and starched linens and bathed in mellow light. But as befits an operation owned by rock band U2, this excellent restaurant pulls off its trendiness without a lot of pretense. An obliging staff and the commodious surroundings (with widely spaced tables and acceptable noise levels) put diners at ease, ready to focus on the deft creations of chef Mathieu Malin. The freshest Irish game, fish, and produce provide the basics, and you can sample the excellent preparations on the good-value lunch menus; Sunday lunch, especially, fills the bill if you feel like treating yourself to a luxurious afternoon without breaking the bank.

The Winding Stair ★★★★

| MODERN IRISH | MODERATE–EXPENSIVE | QUALITY ★★★★ | VALUE ★★★½ |

40 Lower Ormond Quay, Dublin 1, *Central Dublin;* ☎ **01-873-3292**

Buses All city-center buses. **Reservations** No. **Entree range** €19.50–€24.95. **Payment** MC, V. **Bar** Beer and wine only. **Disabled access** No. **Hours** Monday–Saturday, noon–3:30 p.m. and 6:30–10:30 p.m.; Sunday, noon–3:30 p.m. and 6:30–9:30 p.m.

MENU RECOMMENDATIONS Kerry prawns on toast, Irish lamb chops, smoked haddock.

COMMENTS It can't be easy to take over one of Dublin's most beloved lairs, the cafe of the old Winding Stair bookshop. While bibliophiles can no longer linger over tea and Tolstoy, any one with an appetite for the freshest Irish ingredients will savor the flavorful creations, friendly service, excellent wine list . . . and those wonderfully moody views of the Liffey, which have not changed at all. More good news is that the bookshop has reopened downstairs (see page 167).

ENTERTAINMENT *and* NIGHTLIFE *in* DUBLIN

TO KEEP UP WITH WHAT'S HAPPENING in Dublin, check out **www .dublinevents.com** and **www.eventguide.com** for up-to-the-minute entertainment listings, and **www.ireland.com,** the online version of the *Irish Times*. Handy print resources include *In Dublin*, published every two weeks and available at newsstands (€3); the Thursday edition of the *Irish Times* (€0.50); and *Where: Dublin*, handed out free at better hotels. Another place to check out what's happening in Dublin is **www .ticketmaster.ie**—scan the listings, but avoid paying the high per-ticket service charge by purchasing directly from the box offices.

THEATER

DUBLIN, WHICH HAS A LONG TRADITION of staging good theater, can claim Richard Brinsley Sheridan (*The School for Scandal*), George Bernard Shaw (*Major Barbara* and many others), John Millington Synge (*The Playboy of the Western World*), Sean O'Casey (*The Plough and the Stars*), and Samuel Beckett (*Waiting for Godot*) as its own. While the theater scene in Dublin is, naturally, much smaller than those in New York and London, the Abbey and the Gate are among two of the world's great theaters, and Dublin has several excellent smaller stages as well.

ABBEY THEATRE 26 Abbey Street, Dublin 1, *Central Dublin;* ☎ 01-878-7222; **www.abbeytheatre.ie;** most city-center buses to O'Connell Street stops; Luas, Abbey Street; DART: Connolly. Tickets €15 to €30, €9 for seniors and students at some performances; box-office hours Monday through Saturday, 10:30 a.m. to 7 p.m. Ireland's national theater, founded in 1904 by W. B. Yeats, Lady Augusta Gregory (Yeats's patron), and playwright J. M. Synge, is famous for introducing many of the major Irish works of the 20th century. The Abbey continues to stage traditional Irish theater, while its smaller stage, the Peacock, strays into more experimental terrain.

BEWLEY'S CAFÉ 78–79 Grafton Street, Dublin 2, *Grafton Street;* ☎ 086-878-4001; **www.bewleyscafetheatre.com;** all city-center buses. One of Dublin's most beloved institutions is this upstairs stage with its lunchtime presentations of short (less than 1 hour long), often innovative dramas. Performances, accompanied by soup and sandwiches, are Monday through Saturday at 1:10 p.m. and cost €15. The stage also hosts events on some evenings.

THE GAIETY King Street South, Dublin 2, *Grafton Street;* ☎ 01-677-1717; **www.gaietytheatre.com;** all city-center buses; Luas: St. Stephen's Green. Tickets €15 to €80, vary widely by performance. One of Ireland's best-known stages, a Victorian gem, hosts dramas, musicals, and visiting tours, as well as operas and concerts.

THE GATE Cavendish Row, Dublin 1, *Central Dublin;* ☎ 01-874-4045; **www.gate-theatre.ie;** buses 3, 10, 11, 13, 16, 19. Tickets €20 to €25; box-office hours Monday through Saturday, 10 a.m. to 7 p.m. This lovely Georgian hall is the setting for Ireland's "second stage," where the repertoire includes the classics and contemporary works, usually by better-known European and American playwrights.

SAMUEL BECKETT CENTRE Trinity College, Dublin 2, *Trinity College and Temple Bar;* ☎ 01-608-2266; **www.tcd.ie;** all city-center buses. Ticket prices and box-office hours vary. The theater is the stage for Trinity College drama students, whose work can be exceptional, and also hosts visiting theater and dance companies.

CLASSICAL MUSIC, OPERA, AND DANCE

DANCE THEATRE OF IRELAND Bloomfields Centre, Lower Georges Street, Dún Laoghaire; ☎ 01-280-3455; **www.dancetheatreireland .com;** DART: Dún Laoghaire. Ticket prices and box-office hours vary. Innovative choreography set against multimedia backdrops is the hallmark of this troupe.

DUBLIN CITY GALLERY–THE HUGH LANE PARNELL Square North, Dublin 1, *Central Dublin;* ☎ 01-222-5550; **www.hughlane.ie;** buses 11, 13, 16, 16A, 22, 22A. Dublin's exquisite museum of Impressionist and other 19th- and 20th-century art hosts popular Sunday-at-noon concerts, when jazz and classical musical are on tap. The free concerts last one hour. Admission is on a first-come, first-seated basis.

NATIONAL CONCERT HALL Earlsfort Terrace, Dublin 2, *St. Stephen's Green;* ☎ 01-417-0000; **www.nch.ie;** buses 10, 11, 13, 14, 14A, 15A, 15B. Box-office hours Monday through Friday, 10 a.m. to 3 p.m. and 6 p.m. to end of performance. The hall is home to the National Symphony Orchestra and the Concert Orchestra, both linked to RTE, the national broadcast network; also hosted are many visiting orchestras and artists. Tickets for the National Symphony Orchestra and the Concert Orchestra cost €10 to €32.

OPERA IRELAND Gaiety Theatre, King Street South, Dublin 2, *Grafton Street;* ☎ 01-677-1717; **www.gaietytheatre.com;** buses 10, 11A, 11B, 13, 20B. Tickets from €10; box-office hours Monday through Saturday, 10 a.m. to 6 p.m. or when performances start. Ireland's best-known and highly respected opera company presents a varied repertoire from classics to new works in the fall and spring.

OTHER PERFORMING-ARTS VENUES

OLYMPIA 72 Dame Street, Dublin 2, *Temple Bar;* ☎ 01-679-3323; **www.mcd.ie/olympia;** all city-center buses. Ticket prices vary; box-office hours Monday through Saturday, 10 a.m. to 6 p.m. This Victorian music hall is an atmospheric place to see any kind of performance, which here could be anything from a rock concert to a ballet.

THE O2 North Wall Quay, Dublin 1, *Central Dublin;* ☎ 01-676-6144; **www.theO2.ie;** bus 53; DART: Connolly. Ticket prices and box-office hours to be announced; call or visit the Web site for details. Formerly the Point Depot and currently undergoing a complete refurbishment, this is Ireland's premier venue for big-name concerts (Coldplay is the first act confirmed for the arena's reopening in December 2008).

PROJECT ARTS CENTRE 39 Essex Street East, Dublin 2, *Temple Bar;* ☎ 01-881-9613; **www.project.ie;** buses 21A, 50, 50A, 78, 78A, 78B. Tickets €10 to €20; box-office hours Monday through Saturday, 10 a.m. to 6 p.m. Dublin's venue for the cutting edge often features performance art, modern dance, and fringe-theater pieces.

ROYAL DUBLIN SOCIETY (RDS) Merrion Road, Dublin 2, *Ballsbridge;* ☎ 01-668-0866; **www.rds.ie** (go here for event information and ticket prices, and to book online); buses 7, 45, 84. Best known as the setting for the Dublin Horse Show, this huge arena occasionally hosts concerts by really big names.

TIVOLI 135–138 Francis Street, Dublin 8, *Dublin Castle;* ☎ 01-454-4472, **www.tivoli.ie;** buses 50, 78A. With a broad repertoire ranging from Shakespeare to musicals to rock concerts, the Tivoli is one of the venues for the Ulster Bank Dublin Theatre Festival. For more information, go to **www.dublintheatrefestival.com.**

 Pubs

Dublin nightlife, indeed Dublin social life, still revolves around the pub—you'll find one around every corner. Many host sessions of traditional music, often nightly and almost always beginning at about 9:30 p.m. and lasting until 11 or so.

DAVY BYRNE'S 21 Duke Street, Dublin 2, *Grafton Street;* ☎ 01-677-5217. In James Joyce's *Ulysses,* Leopold Bloom pops in for a sandwich, and that fictional repast has put the place on the map forever. Most pleasant for lunch or during the afternoon, and a quiet refuge from nearby Grafton Street.

DOHENY AND NESBITT 5 Lower Baggot Street, Dublin 2, *Georgian Dublin;* ☎ 01-676-2945. Snug, Victorian, and wonderfully quiet on a rainy afternoon, this remnant of old Dublin accommodates a nighttime crush with the grace of an old-timer who's seen it all.

THE LONG HALL 51 South Great George's Street, Dublin 2, *Dublin Castle;* ☎ 01-475-1590. This Dublin pub looks the most like a Dublin pub, slathered in polished wood. The place is frequented by habitués who seem to be permanently affixed to the bar, said to be the longest in town.

THE LORD EDWARD 23 Christchurch Place, Dublin 8, *Dublin Castle and the Cathedrals;* ☎ 01-454-2158. Almost as sacred to Dubliners as the medieval cathedral across the street, the two levels of pubdom here provide relaxed surroundings for a pint and a quiet chat.

KEHOE'S 9 South Anne Street, Dublin 2, *Grafton Street;* ☎ 01-677-8312. The only bad thing to be said about this charming Victorian hidey hole of two small rooms is that too many folks would not think of bending their elbows anywhere else.

NEARY'S 1 Chatham Street, Dublin 2, *Grafton Street;* ☎ 01-677-7371. The hushed and upholstered refuge has been a retreat for performers and patrons at the nearby Gaiety Theatre since Victorian times.

THE STAG'S HEAD 1 Dame Court, Dublin 2, *Dublin Castle;* ☎ 01-679-3701. Smoky mirrors and Victorian stained glass provide atmospheric surroundings for a drink after a performance at the nearby Olympia Theatre.

Music Nights and Pubs with Music

Traditional music is as popular with Dubliners as it is with tourists. Plenty of places around town hosts musicians, and the entertainment, sometimes impromptu, is usually excellent.

THE AULD DUBLINER 24–25 Temple Bar, Dublin 2, *Temple Bar;* ☎ 01-677-0527. The rambling old place caters unabashedly to tourists and young neighborhood inebriates, but the music is excellent.

BRAZEN HEAD 20 Lower Bridge Street, Dublin 8, *Dublin Castle;* ☎ 01-677-9549. Claims to be the city's oldest may well be justified: the cozy, stone-walled establishment just off the River Liffey was licensed in 1661 and operates on the site of a drinking establishment from 1198. Robert Emmet and other rebels once met here to discuss Irish freedom; today crowds gather for nightly traditional music.

HA' PENNY BRIDGE Inn 42 Wellington Quay, Dublin 2, *Temple Bar;* ☎ 01-677-0616. The homey upstairs room is the setting for weekend music sessions.

HARCOURT HOTEL 60–61 Harcourt Street, Dublin 2, *St. Stephen's Green;* ☎ 01-478-3677. Not so much a pub as a barroom, the emphasis here is on traditional Irish music and dance.

JURYS IRISH CABARET Burlington Hotel, Upper Lesson Street, Dublin 4, *Georgian Dublin;* ☎ 01-660-5522. The tour groups pour in, but that doesn't stop everyone from having a good time over a meal and an evening of music, dance, and blarney. May through October, Tuesday through Sunday, 7:15 p.m., €50.

O'DONOGHUE'S 15 Merrion Row, Dublin 2, *Georgian Dublin;* ☎ 01-676-2807. Students, locals, and tourists jostle for elbowroom here, but amid the crowds an impromptu traditional-music session is likely to break out.

OLD JAMESON DISTILLERY Bow Street, Dublin 7, *Central Dublin;* ☎ 01-807-2355. The venerable distiller of Irish whiskey puts on an excellent show at its Shindig nights, which include a tour, tasting, excellent meal, and fine music and dancing. April through October, Thursday through Saturday, 7 p.m., €60.

OLIVER ST. JOHN GOGARTY 57–58 Fleet Street, Dublin 2, *Temple Bar;* ☎ 01-671-1822. The most adult watering hole in Temple Bar—by chronological age, not by behavior—sprawls over several levels and hosts boisterous traditional-music sessions most evenings and on Saturday and Sunday afternoons.

BARS

A FEW WATERING HOLES in Dublin offer a cocktail-lounge atmosphere rather than a pub atmosphere—and there *is* a difference.

BANK 20–22 College Green, Dublin 2, *Temple Bar;* 01-677-0677. A former bank is now Dublin's most opulent place for a drink; the lofty Victorian surroundings don't intimidate the habitués, for whom Bank is not a scene but a wonderfully laid-back choice for a cocktail or a pint.

BRUXELLES 7–8 Harry Street, Dublin 2, *Grafton Street;* 01-677-5362. A bronze statue of famed Dublin rocker Phil Lynott stands out front, an indication that this long-standing favorite is an institution—it's a bit grungy, but that's part of the charm.

CAFÉ EN SEINE 40 Dawson Street, Dublin 2, *Grafton Street;* ☎ 01-677-4567. A slightly decadent fin de siècle atmosphere of Art Deco furnishings seems almost Parisian, and it draws a crowd of upwardly mobile young professionals—as well as Dubliners of every other stripe who enjoy a good natter in the cavernous, laid-back space.

COCOON Royal Hibernian Way, Dublin 2, *Grafton Street;* ☎ 01-679-6259. Fashionable young things find themselves wrapped in soothing tones of cream and beige, paying homage to owner and Formula 1 driver Eddie Irvine.

ELY 22 Ely Place, Dublin 2, *Georgian Dublin;* ☎ 01-676-8986. No one will boot you out if you ask for a Guinness, but what a pity when dozens of excellent wines are available by the glass, accompanied by food that ranges from the light-snack variety to good-value meals. Ely's has branched out—to Ely's CHQ in a converted tobacco warehouse next to the International Financial Centre in the Dockland (☎ 01-672-0100) and to Ely HQ, on Forbes Street, Hanover Quay, Grand Canal Basin (☎ 01-633-9986).

THE LIBRARY CENTRAL HOTEL 15 Exchequer Street, Dublin 2, *Dublin Castle;* ☎ 01-679-7302. A book-lined, fire-warmed room weathers its current spate of popularity to provide a quiet retreat. The food on offer is commendable, too.

THE MARKET BAR Fade Street, Dublin 2, *Dublin Castle;* ☎ 01-613-9094. Cool, cavernous, and adult, this is a fine spot for a quiet conversation and a light meal. No pub grub here for this crowd—first-rate tapas instead.

ICE BAR Four Seasons Hotel, Simmonscourt Road, *Ballsbridge;* ☎ 01-665-4000. All white, chrome, and marble, this is headquarters for the prosperous young Dubliner set.

MORRISON HOTEL BAR Morrison Hotel, Ormond Quay Lower, Dublin 1, *Central Dublin;* ☎ 01-887-2400. Beautiful, comfortable, and with water views—a lovely spot for a cocktail.

OCTAGON BAR Clarence Hotel, 6–8 Wellington Quay, Dublin 2, *Temple Bar;* ☎ 01-407-0800. A little too cool for its own good, Dublin's sleekest, hippest watering hole is nonetheless a treat to experience, and the best place in town to spot a celeb (if you really want to).

GAY AND LESBIAN DUBLIN

THE WINDS OF CHANGE sweeping over Ireland in recent years have brought with them a little more tolerance for gays and lesbians, but this conservative Catholic country, Dublin included, is a lot less gay friendly than much of the rest of Europe. To keep up with the gay scene, buy a copy of *Gay Community News,* usually available in pubs and restaurants in Temple Bar and around Grafton Street (or visit **www.gcn.ie**).

THE GEORGE 89 South Great George's Street, Dublin 2, *Dublin Castle;* ☎ 01-478-2983. Dublin's largest, longest-established gay bar is part pub, part nightclub, always busy, and open until 2:30 a.m.

IRISH FILM INSTITUTE BAR Irish Film Institute, 6 Eustace Street, Dublin 2, *Temple Bar;* ☎ 01-679-5744. Gay friendly, not gay, this is a delightful place to hang out regardless of your sexual leanings and whether or not you're catching one of the excellent films screened here.

OUT ON THE LIFFEY 27 Ormond Quay, Dublin 1, *Central Dublin;* ☎ 01-872-2480. Second fiddle to The George and not nearly as lively, this watering hole welcomes both men and women in pleasant, laid-back surroundings; Saturday night is men-only.

CLUBS

DUBLIN'S CLUB SCENE is fairly new, and, though growing, still small. But, clubgoers here can exude just as much attitude as those in London and New York. When you're ready to switch from cozy pub to trendy club, check out these places.

CrawDaddy

INTIMATE AND RELAXED

35a Harcourt Street, Dublin 2, *St. Stephen's Green;* ☎ **01-478-0225; www.pod.ie**

Cover about €15. **Drink prices** Moderate. **Food available** None. **Hours** Nightly, from 5 p.m.

COMMENTS A relaxed two-floor venue in a music complex that now occupies the old Harcourt Train Station (see Tripod, facing page) presents a wonderfully eclectic selection of world music, from Afro-Cuban drums to flamenco guitar.

Lillie's Bordello

TRENDY PLACE TO BE SEEN

Adam Court, Dublin 2, *St. Stephen's Green;* ☎ **01-679-9204; www.lilliesbordello.ie**

Cover €15. **Drink prices** Expensive. **Food available** None. **Hours** Monday–Saturday, 11 a.m.–2:30 a.m.

COMMENTS The name, inspired by red walls and portraits of nudes, is as slickly ersatz as the posturing among the well-dressed, 20- and 30-something poseurs trying to appear cool. You want to shout over the music (a mix of 1970s and '80s classic rock and disco): "Will everyone just relax and be themselves!"

Rí-Rá

FRIENDLY PLACE TO DANCE

Dame Court, 1 Exchequer Street, Dublin 2, *Temple Bar;* ☎ **01-677-4835; www.rira.ie**

Cover Varies; free entry 11–11:30 p.m. all nights except Friday. **Drink prices** Moderate. **Food available** Snacks. **Hours** Vary; call or check Web site for details.

COMMENTS The name means "uproar" in Gaelic, but this place is a lot tamer than that—just a friendly scene for a 20s, 30s, and even older crowd to hang out and dance to soul, disco, and other hits. On Sunday evenings, you can linger in the adjoining Globe Bar and listen to free jazz.

Tripod

DUBLIN'S SERIOUS MUSIC VENUE

35a Harcourt Street, Dublin 2, *St. Stephen's Green;* ☎ **01-485-0025; www.tripod.ie**

Cover About €15. **Drink prices** Moderate. **Food available** None. **Hours** Nightly, from about 10 p.m.

COMMENTS A large, acoustically perfect space with a huge dance floor and balcony seating brings rock, R & B, reggae, and the full gamut of live music to what was once the Harcourt Street train station.

SHOPPING *in* DUBLIN

SHAMROCK MOTIFS STEAL THE SHOW in many Dublin shops, but these days the wares offered are far more alluring than the souvenirs and booze that were once the mainstays of the city's shopping scene. Shopping in Dublin can be an extremely satisfying experience, all the more so because shopkeepers maintain old-fashioned standards such as courtesy, knowledge of the stock, and helpfulness. In general, shops are open Monday through Saturday, 9 a.m. to 6 p.m., and Sunday, noon to 6 p.m. On Thursday evenings, many shops don't close until 8 or 9 p.m.

WHERE TO SHOP

TO MANY DUBLINERS, **O'Connell Street** is still the city's main shopping avenue, although the venerable and wonderful **Clery's** department store is one of the few old-time establishments to remain. Most Dubliners who find themselves in this part of town head west off of O'Connell onto **Henry Street,** a busy pedestrian zone lined with emporia of the large-chain-store ilk. The most fashionable shopping is south of the river these days, on **Grafton Street** and a cluster of other streets around **St. Stephen's Green. Temple Bar,** more famous for restaurants and bars than for shopping, caters to the neighborhood's brisk tourist trade with many small boutiques, while **Nassau Street,** near the national museums, also caters to tourists with souvenirs and excellent made-in-Ireland goods.

SHOPPING CENTERS

BRINGING NEW LEVELS of sophistication to the shopping-center experience is **Powerscourt Centre** (59 William Street, off Grafton Street, Dublin 2), which occupies the former 18th-century town house of the Viscount Powerscourt. Similarly sophisticated shopping venues in this Grafton Street area are **Westbury Mall,** adjoining the Westbury Hotel, and the Royal Hibernian Way, entered at 49–50 Dawson Street. The **Stephen's Green Centre** (Dublin 2), new but rather grandly Victorian with its glass-roofed, multileveled arcade, is on the west side of the Green. North of the River Liffey are **ILAC Shopping Centre** (Henry Street, Dublin 1) and the **Jervis Centre** (Jervis Street, off O'Connell Street, Dublin 1). One could argue that **George's Street Arcade** (Dublin 2), the city's oldest shopping center, is really a covered market, Dublin's grand bazaar, if you will. The attractive old place between Grafton Street and Dublin Castle is filled with tony shops as well as stalls selling jewelry and bric-a-brac; all and all, it's a down-to-earth retreat from the glitter of nearby Powerscourt.

DEPARTMENT STORES

ARNOTTS 12 Henry Street, Dublin 1, *Central Dublin;* ☎ 01-872-1111; all city-center buses. Dublin's largest department store carries just about everything, as well as a smaller selection, focusing on designer fashion, in a Grafton Street branch.

BROWN THOMAS 88–95 Grafton Street, Dublin 2, *Grafton Street;* ☎ 01-605-6666; all city-center buses. Exclusive, expensive, and a showcase for top designers, including many from Ireland.

CLERY'S O'Connell Street, Dublin 1, *Central Dublin;* ☎ 01-878-6000; all city-center buses. Old-fashioned and as comfortable as an old glove, Clery's is a bastion of traditional clothing and home furnishings.

DUNNES STORES Henry Street, Dublin 1, *Central Dublin;* ☎ 01-671-4629; all city-center buses. This is the flagship of a popular chain that dependably outfits Dubliners in cheap casual clothing.

MARKS AND SPENCER 15–20 Grafton Street, Dublin 2, *Grafton Street;* ☎ 01-679-7855; all city-center buses. The British chain is a hit in

Dublin, too, stocking sensible and sensibly priced fashions and basics (from groceries to undies).

MARKETS

COW'S LANE MARKET Cow's Lane, *Temple Bar;* Saturday, 10 a.m. to 5:30 p.m.; buses 50, 50A, 54, 56, 77. An excellent assortment of high-quality jewelry and clothing, some of it vintage, some of it cutting-edge. In winter months, the market operates around the corner in St. Michael and St. John's Banquet Hall.

LIBERTY MARKET 71 Meath Street, near Christ Church Cathedral, Dublin 8, *Dublin Castle and the Cathedrals;* Friday and Saturday, 10 a.m. to 6 p.m.; Sunday, noon to 5 p.m.; buses 21A, 50, 50A, 78, 78A, 78B. Bric-a-brac, clothing, and crafts.

MEETING HOUSE SQUARE Dublin 2, *Temple Bar;* Saturday and Sunday, 10 a.m.–5 p.m.; buses 50, 50A, 54, 56, 77. Produce, fruits, cheeses, and other goods fresh off the farm.

MOORE STREET MARKET West of O'Connell Street, Dublin 1, *Central Dublin;* daily, 10 a.m.–4 p.m.; buses 25, 34, 37, 38A, 66A, 67A. Local color is abundant in the city's main market, along with fruits, vegetables, flowers, and inexpensive clothing.

TEMPLE BAR SQUARE Dublin 2, *Temple Bar;* Saturday and Sunday, 11 a.m.–4 p.m.; buses 50, 50A, 54, 56, 77. Used and rare books, magazines, and prints are lodestones for browsers.

WHERE TO FIND . . .

Antiques

There are two Dublin stops for any hunter. **Francis Street** (near Christ Church Cathedral) is one long row of antiques shops; buses 21A, 50, 50A, 78, 78A, 78B. **O'Sullivan** (43–44 Francis Street, ☎ 01-454-1143) is internationally known for its fine furniture, and many shops on this street sell similarly exquisite pieces. A large and much-attended **Antiques and Collectibles Fair** draws vendors from throughout Ireland to **Newman House** (85–86 St. Stephen's Green) every second Sunday; buses 10, 11, 13, 14, 14A, 15A, 15B.

Books

The **Winding Stair** (40 Lower Ormond Quay, Dublin 1, *Central Dublin;* ☎ 01-873-3292), a wonderful shop overlooking the River Liffey, is back in business, after a brief closure that sent many Dubliners into deep mourning. The stock concentrates on literature and history, the staff is knowledgeable, and a restaurant of the same name (see page 158) has taken over the upper floor. Some other excellent bookshops around the capital are **Cathach Books** (10 Duke Street, Dublin 2, *Grafton Street;* ☎ 01-671-8676), which is oriented toward rare books and first editions, and **Secret Book and Record Shop** (15a Wicklow Street, Dublin 2,

Grafton Street; ☎ 01-679-7272), good hunting grounds for less-expensive secondhand editions. **Books Upstairs** (36 College Green, Dublin 2, *Trinity College and Temple Bar;* ☎ 01-679-6687) is a large general-interest shop that caters to students at nearby Trinity College, as does the enormous and commendably stocked **Hodges Figgis** (56 Dawson Street, Dublin 2, *Grafton Street;* ☎ 01-677-4754). **Waterstone's,** the British chain, has a commanding presence down the street (7 Dawson Street, Dublin 2, *Grafton Street;* ☎ 01-679-1415), with a fine selection of Irish drama and literature. **Eason's** (40 O'Connell Street, Dublin 1, *Central Dublin;* ☎ 01-858-3800) is a big, brightly lit chain with a fairly unliterary stock of books, but it's a great spot for stationery needs and European magazines. All city-center buses serve these bookstores.

Crystal and China

Brown Thomas department store (see page 166), on Grafton Street, Dublin 2, carries a large line of Irish china and crystal. You'll find another huge selection at the **China Showrooms** (32–33 Abbey Street, Dublin 1, *Central Dublin;* ☎ 01-878-6211; buses 27B, 53A), where Waterford, Belleek, and all the other big Irish names are available.

Heritage

Nassau Street, following the southern walls of Trinity College, provides one-stop shopping for souvenir hounds, and two shops even send visitors home with an Irish pedigree. **House of Names** (26 Nassau Street, Dublin 2, *Trinity College and Temple Bar;* ☎ 01-679-7287) and **Heraldic Artists** (3 Nassau Street, Dublin 2, *Trinity College and Temple Bar;* ☎ 01-679-7020) affix your family name and crest to everything from coasters to sweaters to shields. If you're not sure if you do indeed have a heraldic Irish name, not to worry—Heraldic Artists will help you investigate your Irish heritage. **Knobs and Knockers** (19 Nassau Street, Dublin 2, *Trinity College and Temple Bar;* ☎ 01-671-0288) will send you home with a replica of the gorgeous brass implements that grace Dublin's Georgian doorways. All city-center buses serve these Nassau Street shops.

 ## Knits and Weaves

The **Kilkenny Design Centre** (6–10 Nassau Street, Dublin 2; ☎ 01-677-7066) and **Blarney Woollen Mills** (21–23 Nassau Street, Dublin 2, ☎ 01-671-0068) are both in Trinity College and Temple Bar; all city-center buses; DART: Pearse. Conveniently located just down the street from one another, these shops provide easy shopping for superb handwoven sweaters and other knitwear (especially at Blarney, an outlet of the Cork-based mills), as well as distinctive Irish ceramics and pottery (especially at Kilkenny). Other high-quality woolens and housewares are available just around the corner at **Avoca Handweavers** (11–13 Suffolk Street, Dublin 2, *Grafton Street;* ☎ 01-677-4215; same buses). Another popular neighborhood spot of the same ilk is **House of Ireland** (37–38 Nassau Street, Dublin 2, *Trinity College and Temple Bar;* ☎ 01-671-1111; all city-center buses), carrying tweeds, crystal, and all things Irish. **Monaghan's** (15–17 Grafton Arcade, *Grafton Street;* ☎ 01-679-4451; all city-center buses) outfits men, women, and children in Irish-made cashmeres, Aran sweaters, and other delightful woolens. **Louis Copeland** (18–19 Wicklow Street, Dublin 2, *Grafton Street;* ☎ 01-872-1600; all city-center buses) is Ireland's finest tailor, the place for traditional tweeds as well as sleek contemporary designs.

Irish Crafts

Whichcraft (5 Castlegate, Lord Edward Street, Dublin 2, *Dublin Castle;* ☎ 01-670-9371; buses 50, 54A, 56A, 65, 65A, 77, 77A, 123, 150) features the work of artisans from throughout Ireland, creating a showcase for the latest and finest in pottery, weaving, glass, and more. **Craft Centre of Ireland** (atop the Stephen's Green Centre, Dublin 2; ☎ 01-475-4526; all cross-city buses) also showcases the work of Irish artisans. **Tower Craft Design Centre** (Grand Canal Quay, Dublin 2, *near Georgian Dublin;* ☎ 01-677-5655; bus 2 or 3; DART: Pearse) is an enclave of artisans who work in an old sugar-refining plant, creating everything from cards to carpets. **Louis Mulcahy** (46 Dawson Street, Dublin 2, *Grafton Street;* ☎ 01-670-9311; **www.louismulcahy .com;** city-center buses) is an Irish institution, creating ceramics from his studio on the Dingle peninsula, of which this shop is an outlet. **Weir and Sons** (96–99 Grafton Street, Dublin 2; all city-center buses) is also an Irish institution, selling jewelry, much of it of Irish design, from this atmospheric old shop since 1869.

Irish Music

Most Dublin music shops, even the megastores such as **HMV** (Grafton Street, Dublin 2; ☎ 01-679-5334; all cross-city buses) and **Tower Records** (around the corner at 6–8 Wicklow Street, Dublin 2, *Grafton Street;* ☎ 01-671-3250), sell traditional Irish music, and employees usually know quite a bit about it. **Claddagh Records** (2 Dame Street, Dublin 2, *Temple Bar;* ☎ 01-677-8943; all cross-city buses) stocks the city's largest selection and also posts notices of who's performing where in Dublin and elsewhere in Ireland. At the **Celtic Note** (12 Nassau Street, Dublin 2, *Trinity College;* ☎ 01-670-4157; all city-center buses), you might even hear live music as you browse the extensive stock.

EXERCISE *and* RECREATION *in* DUBLIN

WHO KNEW? Dublin is paradise for the recreation enthusiast.

unofficial **TIP**
A good source of information on sea angling and freshwater fishing around Dublin is the **Irish Tourist Board**'s Web site (**www.discoverireland .ie**), which provides info on guides, where to fish, and other resources.

BEACHES

A DOZEN OR SO ARE WITHIN EASY REACH from the city, many via public transportation. **North Bull Island, Malahide,** and **Howth,** all to the north of the city center, have clean sands and good swimming; bus: 130 from Abbey Street to Bull Island; DART to Howth and Malahide. **Killiney** and **Sandymount,** to the south, also have nice long beaches, although tides at Sandymount can be extremely strong; DART to both.

FISHING

A FISHING TRIP IS JUST A DART ride away to the shores of **Dublin Bay,** to **Howth** or **Malahide** north of the city center, or south to **Dún Laoghaire;** all locations offer fishing from rocks and/or piers. For more information on these places, see "Day Trips from Dublin," page 172.

GOLF

YOU DON'T HAVE TO STRAY FAR from the Dublin city center to experience the links for which Ireland is famous. The course closest to the city center is **Elm Park Golf and Sports Club** (Nutley Lane, Dublin 4, *Ballsbridge;* ☎ 01-269-3438; **www.elmparkgolfclub.ie**), located in a southern residential neighborhood near the Ballsbridge hotels. Greens fees are about €80 weekdays, €100 on weekends. One of the world's leading courses is at **Portmarnock Golf Club,** about 16 kilometers (10 miles) north of the city center and seaside in Portmarnock (☎ 01-846-2968; **www.portmarnockgolfclub.ie**); greens fees of €165 weekdays and €190 weekends. Similarly well known is the **Royal Dublin Golf Club** (☎ 01-833-6346; **www.theroyaldublingolfclub.ie**), located on Bull Island in Dublin Bay; greens fees are about €120.

HORSEBACK RIDING

BY THE WAY, to the Irish this activity is known as "horse riding." Horse trails lace Phoenix Park, where you can rent a horse from **Ashtown Riding Stables** (Ashtown, Dublin 15, *near Phoenix Park;* ☎ 01-838-3807; buses 37, 38, 39, 40). The stables are open daily, 9:30 a.m. to 5 p.m.; guided trail rides and instruction are available, as is independent riding; rates begin at about €30.

JOGGING

YOU'LL SEE JOGGERS running through the center of town, but you will be wise not to follow their example—heavy vehicular and pedestrian traffic make city streets less than ideal for exercise. A far better option is **Phoenix Park,** with its acres of greenery and many paths; from the city center, the quickest routes are on buses 10, 25, and 26.

SWIMMING

ONE OF THE BEST PUBLIC POOLS in Dublin is in the city center, at the **Markievicz Leisure Centre** (Townsend Street, Dublin 2, *near Georgian Dublin;* ☎ 01-672-9121; all cross-city buses; DART: Tara Street). Monday through Friday, 7 a.m. to 10 p.m.; Saturday, 9 a.m. to 6 p.m.; Sunday, 10 a.m. to 4 p.m.; €4.70, €8.50 families. The center also has an excellent gym.

WATER SPORTS

Surfdock (Grand Canal Dockyard, Dublin 4; ☎ 01-668-3945; **www .surfdock.ie;** bus 2 or 3; DART: Grand Canal) is the in-town center for sailing, kayaking, and windsurfing, with 17 hectares (42 acres) of enclosed waterway around the Grand Canal. Equipment rental and instruction are available. **Fingal Sailing School,** north of the city in Malahide (☎ 01-845-1979; **www.fingalsailingschool.com;** DART: Malahide), rents sailboats and other craft for excursions in Dublin Bay.

SPECTATOR SPORTS

FOR SCHEDULES AND OTHER information, check out the city's many entertainment resources (see page 158).

Football

The game Americans know as soccer is as popular in Ireland as it is elsewhere in Europe. Big international matches are played at **Lansdowne Road Stadium** (62 Lansdowne Road, Dublin 4, *Ballsbridge;* ☎ 01-668-4601; DART: Lansdowne Road), while matches of the **Eircom League** usually take place at **Dalymount Park** (Phibsborough, Dublin 7; ☎ 01-868-0923; buses 10, 19, 19A, 121, 122), home turf of the locally popular **Bohemians Football Club.**

Gaelic Football and Hurling

These two games are uniquely Irish, and wildly popular. Gaelic football is a blend of soccer, rugby, and football (the American version), while hurling might be compared to lacrosse. Both games involve getting the ball into a net or through goalposts; in Gaelic football the ball can be played with hands or feet, and in hurling it's propelled down the field with hurley sticks. Both games provide plenty of fast action and engender a great deal of enthusiasm at citywide matches organized by the **Gaelic Athletic Association;** competition comes to a head during the **All-Ireland Championship** in summer. **Croke Park,** the massive 82,000-seat stadium in north Dublin (Clonliffe Road; ☎ 01-855-8176; buses 3, 11, 16), is the venue for all major Gaelic football and hurling events (if asking a Dubliner for directions, be sure to specify that you want the stadium and not nearby Glasnevin Cemetery, often called by the same name). For information about these sports and events, call the Gaelic Athletic Association at ☎ 01-836-3222 or visit **www.gaa.ie.**

Horse Racing

The main Dublin course, and the closest to the city center, is **Leop-ardstown** (Foxrock, Dublin 18; ☎ 01-289-2888). Steeplechases are the main events here, including the **Hennessy Gold Cup** in February, although flats are also run throughout the year. You can reach the track on bus 46A from the city center; for schedules and other information, go to **www.leopardstown.com.**

DAY TRIPS *from* DUBLIN

SOUTH ALONG DUBLIN BAY

Dún Laoghaire, Sandycove, and Dalkey

A BUSY SEASIDE TOWN at the southern edge of Dublin, **Dún Laoghaire** is known to many travelers as the ferry port for the trip across the Irish Sea to and from Holyhead, in Wales. Those who linger here a bit can walk out to the end of **East Pier,** one of a twin set, each extending for 2.5 kilometers (1.5 miles). Another option is to stay closer to shore and follow the harbor south along **Marine Parade** about one kilometer (less than a mile) to the little seaside settlement of **Sandycove.** Dubliners come here to shop for fish at the legendary Caviston's, 59 Glasthule Road (with an adjoining cafe), and to brace the cold waters of **Forty Foot Bathing Pool.** This inlet was reserved for men—few of whom wore suits—until a decade or so ago, when women stormed the waters and staked a claim. Suit or no suit, the pool can be mighty chilly in winter, and in summer, too, for that matter, but that doesn't seem to deter the hardy. Rising above the waters is **James Joyce Tower,** a rounded stone tower built in 1804 to help thwart a Napoleonic invasion of Ireland and now famous for its tenuous, though effective, association with James Joyce.

unofficial **TIP**
All three of these seaside towns are on the DART line, with service from Connolly and other Dublin stations about every 20 minutes.

If you choose to continue by DART to Dalkey, you'll alight at a very pleasant seaside village that was a medieval port for Dublin. Scattered bits of this past remain, and the stony turrets of ruined castles rise above the affluent town's neighborhoods. You can learn a bit about local history in the **Dalkey Heritage Centre,** occupying the tower of Goat Castle and an adjoining church (Castle Street; ☎ 01-285-8366.) Open Monday through Friday, 9:30 a.m. to 5 p.m., Saturday and Sunday, 11 a.m. to 5 p.m.; €6 adults, €5 seniors and students, €4 children. It's a lot more interesting, however, just to have a look around the town itself (rather than paying admission to the Heritage Centre, ask the folks at the desk for one of the free walking maps). Just offshore is a barren outcropping known as **Dalkey Island,** famous for a holy well, the water of which is said to cure rheumatism. If it's summer and you want

dublin day trips

| Balbriggan | *Bernagearagh Bay* |
| R127 | |

St. Patrick's Island

Skerries

Shenick's Island

N1

R127

R128

Lambay Island

R108

R126

Donabate

Irish Sea

Swords

R106 Malahide

R122

N1

R106

Dublin Airport

M1

Portmarnock

Ireland's Eye

N2

R107

R104

Sutton **Howth**

N3

R103

▲ Ben of Howth

R105

North Bull Island

Clontarf

DUBLIN

Dublin Bay

N4

Liffey

N7

R119

Royal Canal

N11

R117

R112

Dún Laoghaire

Sandycove

Dalkey

Dalkey Island

R113

Dalkey Hill ▲

Killiney Hill ▲

To Shankill

Killiney

0 2 1/2 mi
0 2.5 km

Area of Detail

Dublin ★

REPUBLIC OF IRELAND

1. Hill of Tara
2. Howth Castle Rhododendron Gardens
3. James Joyce Tower
4. Malahide Castle
5. National Transport Museum of Ireland
6. Newgrange
7. Powerscourt House and Gardens
8. Glendalough Abbey
9. County Kildare

to test the water's efficacy, you can board an excursion boat in nearby **Coliemore Harbour** (about €25 for the round-trip).

A resemblance to the Bay of Naples (as some 19th-century land developers decided there was) has inspired many Italian names in the area, and you may indeed feel a touch of the Mediterranean when looking down the hill-backed coast from the park in Dalkey's **Sorrento Point.** You can walk along the coast another kilometer (half mile) or so to **Killiney,** home to many Irish celebs. The main attraction, a long stretch of sandy beach, is open to the not so rich and famous as well.

Attraction in Sandycove

James Joyce Tower ★★★★

APPEAL BY AGE	PRESCHOOL ★	GRADE SCHOOL ★★★	TEENS ★★
YOUNG ADULTS ★★★		OVER 30 ★★★	SENIORS ★★★

Sandycove, Dublin; ☎ 01-280-9265; www.dun-laoghaire.com/dir/jjtower.html

Type of attraction Museum in historic tower. **Admission** €6.70 adults, €5.70 seniors and students, €4.20 children, €18 families. **Hours** March–October, Monday–Saturday, 10 a.m.–1 p.m. and 2–6 p.m.; Sunday and holidays, 2–5 p.m. **When to go** Anytime. **Special comments** The museum occasionally hosts readings and other Joyce-related events. **How much time to allow** About 1 hour.

DESCRIPTION AND COMMENTS James Joyce stayed here for a week in August 1904, and that sojourn both inspired the opening scene of *Ulysses* and put this distinctive round martello tower from 1804 on the map as a must-see stop on a James Joyce itinerary. The story behind the visit is the most interesting aspect of the place—that and the spectacular views of Dublin Bay from the tower's weapon platform, installed as defense against a potential invasion by Napoleon. Joyce's host was Oliver St. John Gogarty, another literary figure who appears in his guest's great novel (not flatteringly) as Buck Mulligan. The collection of letters, photographs, and first editions is commendable, but you'll learn and see more about the writer at the Dublin Writers Museum and the James Joyce Centre (see pages 132 and 133, respectively).

TOURING TIPS Don't even think of coming here without taking a walk along the sea, either to and from Dún Laoghaire or both; you might want to take DART to Sandycove, visit the museum, then walk back to the DART station in Dún Laoghaire.

NORTH ALONG DUBLIN BAY
Howth

A SUBURB SOME 13 KILOMETERS (8 miles) north of Dublin, Howth seems more like a seaside village. Pretty old houses surround a lively fishing pier that's usually thronged with Dubliners buying some of the city's freshest seafood, and the fringes of the town meander toward **Howth Head.** An 8.5-kilometer (5-mile) path skirts the flanks of the rugged headland, providing sensational views of the sea, mountains, and the **Eye of Ireland,** a rocky islet just offshore. DART zips out to Howth from Connolly and other Dublin stations, with service about every 15 to 20 minutes; the trip takes about 20 minutes.

Howth's primary appeal is the chance to catch some sea air on a walk around the busy harbor and along the piers past bobbing fishing boats, then, for some real exercise, around Howth Head. In spring and early summer, you may also want to step into **Howth Castle Rhododendron Gardens,** where some 12 hectares (30 acres) of colorful blossoms create a carpet of color beneath the castle walls. The castle is the ancestral home of the St. Lawrence family and closed to the public, but the rhododendron gardens are open April through June, daily, 8 a.m. to sunset; admission is free; ☎ 01-832-2624.

Attraction in Howth

kids National Transport Museum of Ireland   ★★★★

APPEAL BY AGE	PRESCHOOL ★★★★	GRADE SCHOOL ★★★★	TEENS ★★★
YOUNG ADULTS ★★★		OVER 30 ★★★	SENIORS ★★★

Grounds of Howth Castle, Dublin 13; ☎ **01-832-0427; www.nationaltransportmuseum.org**

Type of attraction Museum of commercial and military vehicles. **Admission** €3 adults, €1.25 seniors and children, €8 families. **Hours** June–August, Monday–Saturday, 10 a.m.–5 p.m.; September–May, Saturday, Sunday, and public holidays, 2–5 p.m. **When to go** In good weather, because many of the exhibits are outdoors. **Special comments** Kids love this place. **How much time to allow** About 2 hours.

DESCRIPTION AND COMMENTS An earnest collection tended by transportation buffs is dedicated to preventing buses, trucks, and trams from rusting into oblivion on the junk heap. The 60 vintage vehicles will evoke nostalgia in some, and perhaps a sense of wonderment in visitors accustomed to the comparatively mundane-looking vehicles that clog the road today. Especially appealing is the Pig, an all-purpose truck with a pointed snout that once plied the streets of Dublin and other Irish cities. Even vehicles that look surprisingly like their modern-day descendants, such as the generations of double-decker buses and trams, delight young visitors and may transport their adult companions back to days of yore.

TOURING TIPS If you don't have kids in tow and aren't fascinated by vintage vehicles, spend your time instead walking around Howth Headland.

MALAHIDE

MALAHIDE WOULD BE A PLEASANT TOWN even without its stunning castle and botanical gardens. Attractive lanes run from a green down to the sea, where marinas are cluttered with colorful pleasure craft. Just north of the town center is the vast parkland that surrounds the castle and lends the impression that Malahide is a country town rather than a suburb. DART zips out to Malahide from Connolly and other Dublin stations, with service about every 15 to 20 minutes; the trip takes about 20 minutes.

The 100 hectares (250 acres) of parkland surrounding **Malahide Castle** are laced with walking paths, and within the park is the 8-hectare (20-acre) **Talbot Botanic Garden,** where more than 5,000 species, many from New Zealand and Australia, thrive in well-tended beds, a walled garden, and a conservatory. The garden is open May through September, daily, 2 to 5 p.m.; €3.50, free for students and seniors. Also on the grounds is the **Fry Model Railway Museum,** where dozens of model trains chug through gorgeous, minutely fabricated Irish landscapes. The price of admission also includes **Tara's Dollhouse,** a collection of antique dolls and toys. The museum is open April through September, Saturday through Thursday, 10 a.m. to 1 p.m. and 2 to 5 p.m.; €7 adults, €4.40 children, €5.95 seniors and students, €20 families.

Attraction in Malahide

Malahide Castle ★★★★

APPEAL BY AGE	PRESCHOOL ★★	GRADE SCHOOL ★★	TEENS ★★★
YOUNG ADULTS ★★★		OVER 30 ★★★	SENIORS ★★★

Malahide; ☎ 01-846-2184; www.malahidecastle.com

Type of attraction Medieval castle. **Admission** €7.25 adults, €6.10 seniors and students, €4.55 children under age 12, €21 families. **Hours** October–March, Monday–Saturday, 10 a.m.–5 p.m.; Sunday, 11 a.m.–12:45 p.m. and 2–5 p.m.; April–September, Monday–Saturday, 10 a.m.–5 p.m.; Sunday, 10 a.m.–6 p.m. **When to go** In good weather, so you can spend time in the gardens and other parts of the grounds; you'll also want to explore the town and waterfront. **Special comments** You can save a few euros and buy a ticket for combined admission to the castle and one of the following: Fry Model Railway Museum (on the grounds), Dublin Writers Museum (see page 132), James Joyce Tower in Sandymount (see page 174), and the Shaw Birthplace (see page 141); €12.50 adults, €10.30 seniors and students, €7.70 children, and €35.50 for families **How much time to allow** The better part of a day if you want to visit the gardens, park, and other attractions on the grounds, plus explore the town.

DESCRIPTION AND COMMENTS The Talbots lived at Malahide Castle for close to 800 years, until the last of the clan sold the place in the 1970s to pay estate taxes and then moved to Tasmania. While the turrets and towers bear the mark of medieval builders, first and foremost Malahide stands out as a place to view the domestic manners of the aristocracy. Accompanied by a taped commentary rather intrusively broadcast over loudspeakers, visitors step in and out of the salons and bedrooms, brought up to mid-20th-century tastes and conveniences, and where the family once socialized and spent rainy afternoons writing letters. The castle's masterpiece is a Van Wyck portrait of the clan eating breakfast on a morning in 1690—that happened to be the day of the Battle of the Boyne, from which none of the breakfasters returned.

TOURING TIPS Try to combine a tour of the castle with a visit to the Talbot Botanic Gardens, but note that hours are spotty. Young visitors who deserve a reward for their patience will be delighted with the Fry

Model Railway Museum and Tara's Dollhouse. A cafe on the castle's ground floor is quite gloomy but will take off the chill with hot meals and delicious pastries.

FARTHER AFIELD

The Hill of Tara and Newgrange

Two of Ireland's most important historic sights, both of them associated with the pre-Christian era, are just to the north of Dublin.

The **Hill of Tara,** meeting place of pagan princes and Druid priests, is 33 kilometers (20 miles) northwest of Dublin via the N3; **Newgrange,** one of the world's most extensive prehistoric tombs, is 60 kilometers (36 miles) north on the N2. Public transportation to both is by bus, to Navin for the Hill of Tara and to Slane for Newgrange; for schedules, check with **Dublin Tourism** (see page 96).

Tours of the Hill of Tara and Newgrange

You can also join one of several all-inclusive tours that include transportation and guided tours of both sites. **Mary Gibbons Tours** are excellent, with pickup at major Dublin hotels and a full-day visit to the sites, accompanied by informed commentary; pickups begin at 9:30 a.m., with return about 4:30 p.m.; €35; for more information, call ☎ 01-283-9973; **www.newgrangetours.com.**

Hill of Tara   ★★★½

APPEAL BY AGE	PRESCHOOL ★★	GRADE SCHOOL ★★★	TEENS ★★★
YOUNG ADULTS ★★★		OVER 30 ★★★½	SENIORS ★★★½

North of Dublin, outside Navan; ☎ 046-902-5903

Type of attraction Center of pre-Christian Ireland. **Admission** €2.10 adults, €1 children and students, €1.30 seniors, €5.80 for families. **Hours** Mid-May–mid-September, daily, 10 a.m.–6 p.m. **When to go** In good weather, because you'll be outdoors. **Special comments** A tearoom on the grounds serves snacks and light meals. You might want to lend an ear to ongoing protests over government plans to built a highway through the Tara Valley; check out **www.tarawatch.org** for the latest news as well as updates on UNESCO's plans to designate the Hill of Tara a World Heritage Site. **How much time to allow** At least 1 hour, to walk on the hill and visit the Interpretive Center.

DESCRIPTION AND COMMENTS The seat of the High Kings of Ireland was, through the pre-Christian centuries to as late as the 11th century, home to rulers and an assembly point for tribal and religious leaders from throughout Ireland. It's significant that when St. Patrick defied Druid leaders in the fifth century and lit his famous bonfire on Easter Eve, he did so within sight of the Hill of Tara—making it known to the powerful elite that Christianity had arrived in Ireland and would challenge pagan rites. Wooden assembly halls and any other structures of note have long vanished; what remains is a 90-meter (300-foot) knoll that commands a view of much of central Ireland. The sight is impressive, but to fully comprehend the significance of the site, spend time in the well-done Interpretive Center, where re-creations, timelines, and other exhibits bring pre-Christian Ireland to life.

TOURING TIPS If you're traveling by car, it's easy to continue on from the Hill of Tara to Newgrange; the two are about ten kilometers (six miles) apart.

Newgrange ★★★★★

| APPEAL BY AGE | PRESCHOOL ★★★★ | GRADE SCHOOL ★★★★ | TEENS ★★★★ |
| YOUNG ADULTS ★★★★ | | OVER 30 ★★★★½ | SENIORS ★★★★★ |

Outside Slane; ☎ 041-988-0300; www.knowth.com/newgrange.htm

Type of attraction Prehistoric tomb complex. **Admission** €5.80 adults, €4.50 seniors, €2.90 children over age 6 and students, free for children under age 6, €14 families. **Hours** May and mid–late September, daily, 9 a.m.–6:30 p.m.; June–mid-September, daily, 9 a.m.–7 p.m.; November–February, daily, 9:30 a.m.–5 p.m.; March–April and October, daily, 9:30 a.m.–5:30 p.m. **When to go** Early in spring through summer, to avoid crowds. **Special comments** Admission is by guided tour only, on a first-come, first-served basis; you may have to wait for admission or be turned away. **How much time to allow** At least 1 hour.

DESCRIPTION AND COMMENTS One of the world's most impressive prehistoric sites predates Stonehenge by 1,000 years. Although lacking the drama the tall monoliths impart to that place, Newgrange is just as transporting. It is estimated that a workforce of hundreds labored for at least two decades to construct the passage tombs, covered by a mound 100 meters (330 feet) across and constructed from some 250,000 tons of stones most likely transported overland from the Wicklow Mountains, 80 kilometers (50 miles) south. Newgrange appears to have done double duty as a burial place and an observatory. On each of five days on and around the winter solstice, the main chamber is brilliantly illuminated by sunlight for 20 minutes—thousands apply to witness the illumination, of whom less than 100 are selected by lottery.

TOURING TIPS Tours begin at the Brú na Bóinne Visitors Centre, where you will see exhibits introducing the site. Visitors are taken to the mound by coach from there. The center is also the departure point for tours of nearby Knowth, another passage tomb, at which there is no access to the passage and chambers.

THE WICKLOW MOUNTAINS

MANY DUBLINERS CONSIDER THESE GENTLE, lovely mountains— rising 925 meters (about 3,000 feet) just 30 kilometers (18 miles) to the south—to be among their city's greatest assets. As well they should: dense forests cover the slopes, and rushing streams sprint through valleys into clear mountain lakes. The mountains are all the more appealing because they cradle one of Ireland's grandest estates, **Powerscourt,** and one of the country's most romantic monastic ruins, **Glendalough Abbey.**

The **Wicklow Way** walking path crosses the mountains, passing through rugged country as well as villages. For information on hiking on the way, and the many other outdoor activities in **Wicklow Mountains National Park,** stop in at the Information Office in Glendalough (☎ 0404-45425); May through August, daily, 10 a.m. to 6 p.m.; April and September: weekends only, 10 a.m. to 6 p.m.

Tours of the Wicklows

If you're without a car, the only practical way to see the mountains is on a tour. For a strenuous excursion, set off with **Dirty Boots Treks.** You'll be picked up in front of Trinity College and driven high into the mountains for four- to five-hour hikes through gorgeous scenery. Resting and conversation are allowed, and among the rewards is a pint in a country pub before heading back to Dublin. One-day treks are €50; longer treks are also on the calendar. For more information, call ☎ 01-623-6785 or go to **www.irelandwalkingcycling.com/walking tours/dirtybootstreks.htm.**

Wild Wicklow Tours pack a lot into a day's outing and embellish the Wicklow scenery with smart and witty commentary. Trips include a brief tour of Dublin, a stop at Sandycove, a shopping break at Avoca Handweavers, a guided tour of Glendalough Abbey and hike through the valley, a pub lunch (not included in the price), a drive over Sally Gap (a scenic mountain pass), and a return through Dún Laoghaire. Chances are you'll have a better time on this tour, and see more, than you would on your own in a car. Tours run daily, with pickup in central Dublin beginning at 8:50 a.m., and returning at 5 or 5:30 p.m.; €28 adults, €25 children and students. For more information, call ☎ 01-280-1899 or go to **www.wildwicklow.ie.**

Attractions in the Wicklows

 ## Glendalough Abbey ★★★★½

APPEAL BY AGE	PRESCHOOL ★★★	GRADE SCHOOL ★★★★	TEENS ★★★★
YOUNG ADULTS ★★★★	OVER 30 ★★★★½	SENIORS ★★★★½

About 50 kilometers (30 miles) south of Dublin; ☎ 0404-45325

Type of attraction Ruins of monastery. **Admission** Free; accompanying exhibition with an audiovisual presentation, €5.30 adults, €3.70 seniors, €2.10 students and children under 12. **Hours** March–mid-October, daily, 9 a.m.–6 p.m.; mid-October–mid-March, daily, 9:30 a.m.–5 p.m. **When to go** Out of high season or early in the day to appreciate the setting with a semblance of peace and solitude. **Special comments** The only drawbacks to this remarkable place are the entrance, where vendors sell wares such as souvenirs and postcards, and a modern hotel that intrudes upon the scenery. The fairly expensive exhibition and show do not add enough to the experience to warrant the price of admission. **How much time to allow** At least 2 hours, to allow time for a walk around the lakes.

DESCRIPTION AND COMMENTS Glendalough pleases on so many levels. These stone buildings on the floor of a peaceful valley once composed one of Europe's great centers of learning. Remains of the churches, tower, and other buildings (rendered to ruin by 14th-century British plunderers) present a satisfying look at what Ireland's monastic communities were like. Nestled beneath forested mountain slopes alongside a set of interlocking lakes, the place is incredibly romantic. The founder was St. Kevin, one of Ireland's favorite saints and the son of early Irish royalty, who came here in the sixth century to live like a hermit in a dank, creepy cave now known as St. Kevin's Bed. Kevin probably oversaw the building of the humble Church of the Oratory; a later church, named for him, still shows off its remarkable barrel vaulting. The best-preserved structure is the 11th-century round tower, and from its 100-foot height a lantern once guided the faithful and those hungry for sustenance and learning to the monastery.

TOURING TIPS Follow the shores of the lakes to the Information Office of Wicklow Mountains National Park, where you can stock up on information about the park.

Powerscourt House and Gardens   ★★★★½

| APPEAL BY AGE | PRESCHOOL ★★★ | GRADE SCHOOL ★★★★ | TEENS ★★★★ |
| YOUNG ADULTS ★★★★ | | OVER 30 ★★★★½ | SENIORS ★★★★½ |

25 kilometers (15 miles) south of Dublin on R117; ☎ 01-204-6000; www.powerscourt.ie

Type of attraction Historic home and magnificent gardens. **Admission** *House:* free; *garden:* €8 adults, €7 seniors, €5 children ages 5–16, free for children under age 5, and students; *waterfall:* €5 adults, €4.50 seniors, €3.50 children ages 2–16, free for children under 2. **Hours** *House and garden:* daily, 9:30 a.m.–5:30 p.m.; *waterfall:* January–February and November–December, daily, 10:30 a.m.–4 p.m.; March–April and September–October, daily, 10:30 a.m.–5:30 p.m.; May–August, daily, 9:30 a.m.–7 p.m. **When to go** Spring to see the best blooms, or any summer morning to avoid crowds. **Special comments** A shop and a cafe, both run by Avoca Handweavers, feature excellent woolen goods and good food. **How much time to allow** At least half a day to appreciate the gardens and make the trek to the waterfall.

*un*official **TIP**
To reach Powerscourt by public transportation, take DART to Bray and bus 185 from there; Dublin Bus and other companies offer tours to the estate. For more information, contact **Dublin Bus** (☎ 01-703-2574) or **Dublin Tourism** (☎ 01-605-7700; **www.visitdublin.com**).

DESCRIPTION AND COMMENTS The first viscount of Powerscourt, a favorite of King James I of England, commissioned this Palladian-style house in 1731, hiring the architect Richard Castle. The handsome facades and ballroom are all that remain of what was one of Ireland's finest houses, which was gutted by a fire in 1974. The gardens, a Victorian addition, have fared better. They are the creation of the gout-afflicted, sherry-swizzling Daniel Robertson, who allegedly had to be pushed around the grounds in a wheelbarrow as he brought his vision to magnificent fruition. His lawns, dells, ponds, statuary, and even a pet cemetery create a showcase of European garden design; they're a delight to explore at random, treating you to one vista after another. Untamed nature lends a hand in the magic of the place, too: Powerscourt Waterfall, on the grounds but a hefty 6 kilometers (3.5 miles) from the house, is Ireland's tallest cascade, plummeting 120 meters (400 feet) into the Dargle River.

TOURING TIPS Wear walking shoes, because you'll be covering quite a bit of ground to see the gardens and the waterfall. You might want to forgo the busy and glitzy cafe and bring a picnic to enjoy in a dell.

COUNTY KILDARE

THIS IS IRELAND'S PRIME HORSE COUNTRY, the Irish equivalent of Kentucky's Bluegrass region. The **Irish Derby** is run here, at the **Curragh** (with its own railway stations for easy connection to Dublin on race days), and the region is home to the major Irish stud farms. Unless you're coming to have a flutter on a horse at the Curragh, the main reason for a visit is a pilgrimage to **Irish National Stud.**

Kildare is also famous for a two-legged creature, Saint Brigid, and Kildare's 13th-century **St. Brigid's Cathedral** stands on the site of the monastery that this remarkable woman founded in the fifth century to accommodate both nuns and monks—a highly controversial practice at the time. From the sounds of it, Brigid was not one to back down; when pressed into marriage, she plucked out her eye to demonstrate her conviction not to wed (the eye allegedly reappeared when she took her vows). The handsome church, with its round tower, is open May through September, Monday through Saturday, 10 a.m. to 1 p.m. and 2 to 5 p.m. and Sunday, 2 to 5 p.m.

Irish Rail (☎ 01-836-6222; **www.irishrail.ie**) and **Bus Éireann** (☎ 01-836-6111; **www.buseireann.ie**) provide regular service from Dublin to Kildare.

Attraction in County Kildare

Irish National Stud ★★★★

APPEAL BY AGE	PRESCHOOL ★★★	GRADE SCHOOL ★★★★	TEENS ★★★★
YOUNG ADULTS ★★★★	OVER 30 ★★★★½		SENIORS ★★★★½

Dublin–Limerick Road, Kildare, about 40 minutes from Dublin by car;
☎ 45-522-963; www.irish-national-stud.ie

Type of attraction Stud farm with museum and beautiful gardens. **Admission** House: free; garden: €10.50 adults, €8 seniors and students, €6 children ages 5–16, free for children under age 5, €27 families of up to 2 adults and 4 children under 16. **Hours** Mid-February–late December, daily, 9:30 a.m.–5 p.m. **When to go** Spring, to see the best blooms, or any summer day. **Special comments** If you're dying to go home with a T-shirt emblazoned with the words "National

Stud," the gift shop is the place to get it. The shop is also well stocked with equestrian prints and books on horses, and a self-service restaurant serves lunch. You can also picnic in a wooded area just off the car park. **How much time to allow** At least half a day.

DESCRIPTION AND COMMENTS You don't have to be a horse lover to enjoy a day's outing to Irish horse country, and the acres of emerald greenery, along with the Japanese and woodland gardens on the site, provide a nice, if rarefied, taste of country life. Of course, the horses are beauties, and the mares and foals are the stars of the show.

Admission includes an excellent guided tour of the grounds, and for more enlightenment on the horse business, a museum that pays homage to racing, show jumping, and other equine arts. The Japanese gardens, laid out between 1906 and 1910, are considered to be the finest example of classical Japanese garden design in Europe, and are a wonderful bower of bridges, pools, and pagodas. St. Fiachra's Garden is more rustic, created to celebrate the millennium by showing the Irish landscape to its best advantage, with lakes, rushing streams, and woodlands.

TOURING TIPS Wear walking shoes, because you'll be covering quite a bit of ground to see the gardens. Bus Éireann provides service directly to National Stud, Monday through Saturday, leaving Dublin at 9:30 a.m. and returning at 3:45 p.m., Sunday, leaving Dublin at 10 a.m. and noon and returning at 3 p.m. and 5:30 p.m.; a free shuttle bus runs from the train station to National Stud every 20 minutes during the day.

PART FIVE

The
SOUTH of IRELAND

IF YOU THINK YOU'LL HEAD SOUTH from Dublin into the boon-docks, you're in for a bit of surprise. While the landscape does roll across the greenest farmland you'll ever see, southern Ireland is an amazingly sophisticated part of the world. You'll enjoy lively towns and cities such as **Cork** and **Kilkenny,** remarkable medieval monu-ments (none more haunting than the **Rock of Cashel**), and, in places like **Cobh** and **Kinsale,** a good dose of Irish history served up in sea-side surroundings.

KILKENNY

KILKENNY IS OFTEN DESCRIBED as Ireland's loveliest medieval city—in fact, it might be fairly categorized as Ireland's loveliest city, period. A castle of mellow stone looms, benevolently these days, above the banks of the River Nore, and medieval houses and churches line the streets and lanes.

The city's greatest fame came in the Middle Ages, when the Irish Parliament met in **Kilkenny Castle.** But if you've heard of Kilkenny, you're more likely to associate it with cats. Legend has it that Oliver Cromwell's soldiers, occupying the city in 1650, tied the tails of two cats together. They fought each other to the end, and the term "Kil-enny cats" has come to connote those who fight relentlessly, whatever the cost. The apocryphal incident also inspired a verse that many an Irish schoolchild can recite: "There wanst was two cats of Kilkenny /

the south of ireland

Thurles   N8   Kilkenny City
Milestone
Holycross   N700
Cappamore   Ballingarry   Bennettsbridge
Caherconlish   Cappawhite   Killenaule   Stoneyford
N24   Rock of Cashel   N76   N10
Herbertstown   TIPPERARY   Callan
Tipperary Town   N74   Cashel   Knocktophet
Fethard   Windgap   N697
N688   Slievenamon   N9
Knocklong   Mountain
Glen of Aherlow   Cahir   N24   Ahenny
Galty Mountains   Clonmel
Kilfinane   Ballylanders   Carrick-on-Suir   N24
LIMERICK   Burncourt   R678   Portlaw
R665   Clogheen   R671   R. Suir
N73   Ballyporeen   R676   R677
Mitchelstown   R626   WATERFORD   N25
Kildorrery   N8   Knockmealdown Mountains   Kilmacthomas
N25   Lemybrien   Bunmahon   R675
N72   Ballyduff   R672   Annestown
Fermoy   N72   R666   Cappoquin   Clonea Strand
Rathcormac   R628   Lismore   N72   Dungarvan
Tallow
Ballyknock   R671   Ring
R614   Watergrasshill   R634   N25
N8   R626   R627
Cork   Ardmore
N20   Midleton   Youghal
N22   N25   Cloyne
N71   Cobh   Shanagarry
CORK   Ballycotton

To Swansea →

To St. Malo & Roscoff →

Kinsale

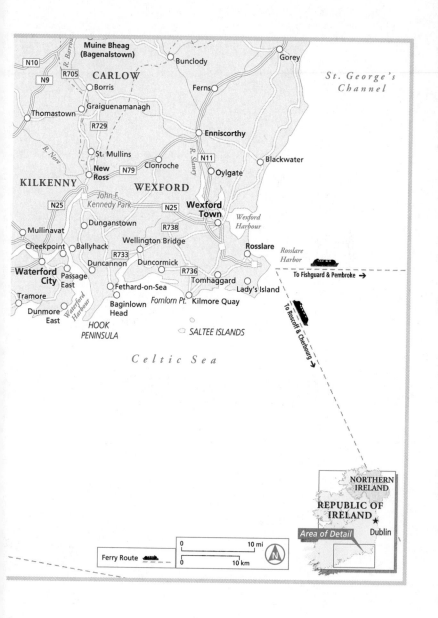

kilkenny

Church †
Information ⓘ
Parking 🅿
Public Toilet 🚻

To Freshford
Troy's Gate
Troy's Ln.
Green St.
Green's Bridge
River Nore
Greensbridge St.
To Castlecomer, Dublin
Castlecomer Rd.
Ballybough St.

Grange Rd.
Church Ln.
Church Ln.
Vicar St.
Inistiown
Coach Rd.
† 8

Thomas St.
Dean St.
Abbey St.
Parliament St.
Wolfe Tone St.
John's Green
Barrack St.
Castlecomer New Rd.

Black Abbey ■
New Building Ln.
Abbey St.
Court House
🅿 🚻
John's Quay
Michael St.
John St. Upper
Dublin Rd.
4

Rothe House
Black Mill St.
Evan's Ln.
To Carlow

James's St.
James's Green
Chapel Ln.
Collier's Ln.
Butler Slip
11
St. Kieran St.
John St. Lower
Maudlin St.

Dominic St.
🅿
Poyntz's Ln.
High St.
12
Guard Ln.
Garden Row
9
William St.
Thdsel ■
St. John's Bridge

Kickham St.
Parnell St.
Friary St.
ⓘ
Rose Inn St.
River Nore
Canal Walk

Stephen's St.
Penne.
father Ln.
3
6
🚻
🅿
The Parade
1
7
10

Gaol Rd.
Upper Walkin's St.
Lower New St.
Ormonde Rd.
Patrick St.
2 **Kilkenny Design Centre**
Castle Rd.

Gaol St.
Old Callan Rd.
College Rd.
Jacob St.
Fr. Hayden's Rd.
Nuncio Road
Archers St.

To Callan, Cork
Coote's Ln.
Patrick St.
Upper New St.
5

NORTHERN IRELAND
To Waterford

REPUBLIC OF IRELAND
Dublin ★
Kilkenny ●
To Thomastown Jerpoint Abbey, & Kells Priory

■ **Accommodations**
1. Butler Court
2. Butler House
3. Kilkenny Ormonde
4. Lacken House
5. Mount Juliet Estate
6. Zuni Townhouse

● **Attractions**
7. Kilkenny Castle
8. St. Canice's Cathedral

◆ **Dining**
9. Café Sol

10. Kilkenny Design Restaurant
11. Kyteler's Inn
12. Pordylos

Each thought there was one cat too many / So they fought and they fit / And they scratched and they bit / 'Til instead of two cats there weren't any." And now you'll understand why cats appear on so many signs around Kilkenny.

PLANNING YOUR VISIT TO KILKENNY

NICELY HOUSED in a 16th-century almshouse on Rose Inn Street (the lower part of Ormonde Street), the **Kilkenny Tourist Office** provides information on places to stay, what to see and do, and where to dine in Kilkenny and the surrounding region. For information, call ☎ 056-775-1500.The center is open April through October, Monday through Saturday, 10 a.m. to 6 p.m.; November through March, Monday through Saturday, 9 a.m. to 1 p.m. and 2 to 5 p.m.

Special Events in Kilkenny

Kilkenny's full roster of events includes the **Carlsberg Kilkenny Rhythm & Roots Festival** in late April or early May, a celebration of what can only be described as an Irish version of country music; **www.kilkennyroots.com**. The **Cat Laughs Comedy Festival,** in late May and/or early June, is one of Europe's leading comedy events; call ☎ 056-776-3837 or visit **www.thecatlaughs.com**. The **Kilkenny Arts Festival** brings music, dance, and theater to town for ten days in August; call ☎ 056-776-3663 or visit **www.kilkennyarts.ie.**

ARRIVING AND GETTING ORIENTED IN KILKENNY

KILKENNY IS ABOUT 120 KILOMETERS (75 miles) south of Dublin. Trains arrive from Dublin and other Irish cities at McDonagh Station, on the east bank of the River Nore. About four trains per day run between Dublin and Kilkenny; the trip takes a little less than two hours, and the fare is about €20 each way. For information, call toll-free ☎ 1850-366-222 or 01-836-6222, or visit **www.irishrail.ie**.

By car, Kilkenny is easy to reach on Ireland's national road network; allow about two hours for the trip down the N9 and N78 from Dublin.

Bus Éireann coaches arrive at the train station from throughout Ireland. Buses leave from Dublin for Kilkenny about every three hours, and the trip takes three and a half hours; the fare is about €10 one-way and €15 for a round-trip. For information, call ☎ 056-776-4933 or visit **www .buseireann.ie.**

unofficial **TIP**
Parking is severely limited in Kilkenny; the best bet is to park immediately in the large car park in the center of town on Ormonde Street for about €1 per hour or €8 per day. Most hotels in town offer free parking for guests.

HOTELS IN KILKENNY

Butler Court   ★★★

| QUALITY ★★★ | VALUE ★★★ | €80–€130 |

How Hotels Compare in the South of Ireland

HOTEL	OVERALL	QUALITY	VALUE	PRICE
KILKENNY				
Zuni Townhouse	★★★★	★★★★½	★★★	€70–€120
Butler House	★★★★	★★★★	★★★	€120–€170
Lacken House	★★★★	★★★★	★★★	€75–€150
Kilkenny Ormonde	★★★	★★★★	★★★	€140–€220
Butler Court	★★★	★★★	★★★	€80–€130
CORK				
Imperial Hotel	★★★★	★★★★	★★★★	From €109
Lancaster Lodge	★★★★	★★★★	★★★★	€96–€125
Lotamore House	★★★½	★★★★	★★★½	€80–€130
Hayfield Manor	★★★½	★★★★	★★½	From €189
Hotel Isaacs Cork	★★★	★★★½	★★★	€80–€150
MIDLETON AND EAST CORK				
Glenview House	★★★★★	★★★★	★★★★	€95–€130
Ballymaloe House	★★★½	★★★★	★★½	€175–€220
Barnabrow Country House	★★	★★★½	★★★	€90–€120
KINSALE				
Old Presbytery	★★★★	★★★★½	★★★★	€110–€170
Chart House	★★★★	★★★★	★★★	€50–€120
Old Bank	★★★½	★★★	★★½	From €200
Friar's Lodge	★★★	★★★	★★★★½	€80–€150
Trident	★★★	★★★	★★½	€110–€190

Patrick Street, Kilkenny; ☎ 056-776-1178; fax 056-779-0767; info@butlercourt.com; www.butlercourt.com

Location City center. **Amenities and services** 10 rooms; hair dryers, Internet connections. **Elevator** No. **Parking** On property, free. **Price** Includes Continental breakfast; off-season rates are available. **Credit cards** AE, MC, V.

JUST AROUND THE CORNER from the castle, John and Yvonne Dalton's ten contemporary-style units are tucked into an attractive courtyard. The arrangement is like that of a motel, and all rooms open to a patio-like lower court or an upstairs balcony. The off-street location ensures plenty of quiet, and the courtyard is especially welcome in good weather for a relaxing break from sightseeing. Guest rooms are furnished in a comfortable but fairly standard hotel style, with a few touches to add a bit of character (such as cherry hardwood floors) and modern conveniences (such as power showers, which use pumps to create stronger water flow).

Butler House ★★★★

QUALITY ★★★★	VALUE ★★★	€ 120–€ 170

16 Patrick Street, Kilkenny; ☎ 056-772-2828; fax 056-776-5626; res@butlerhouse.ie; www.butler.ie

Location City center, near castle. **Amenities and services** 13 rooms; hair dryers, satellite TV, in-room tea and coffee facilities, trouser press. **Elevator** No. **Parking** Nearby, free. **Price** Includes full Irish breakfast; off-season rates and Internet specials are sometimes offered. **Credit cards** AE, MC, V.

IN THE 1970S, the Irish State Design Agency renovated this lovely Georgian mansion that was once the Dowager House of the Kilkenny Castle estate. Marble mantelpieces, tall windows, and sweeping staircases are accented with soft natural fabrics and soothing earth tones for a distinctive, relaxing atmosphere. Many of the guest rooms are enormous, overlooking well-maintained gardens through huge bow windows, and lounge chairs, kilims, contemporary art, and soft lighting add comfort to the remarkable surroundings. Not as stunning are the large but rather spartan bathrooms, although ongoing renovations include improvements such as tub-and-shower combinations. Fresh baked goods and hot breakfasts are served in the Design Centre Café at the end of the garden.

Kilkenny Ormonde Hotel ★★★

QUALITY ★★★★	VALUE ★★★	€ 140–€ 220

Ormonde Street, Kilkenny; ☎ 056-772-3900; fax 056-772-3977; info@kilkennyormonde.com; www.kilkennyormonde.com

Location City center. **Amenities and services** 118 rooms; 2 bars, child care, gym, hair dryers, indoor swimming pool, in-room tea and coffee facilities, Internet connections, irons, minibars, nonsmoking rooms, 3 restaurants, room service, satellite TV, sauna, steam room, trouser press. **Elevator** Yes. **Parking** On property, free. **Price** Includes full Irish breakfast; many special rates and offers available on the Web site. **Credit cards** AE, D, MC, V.

THIS SPRAWLING MODERN HOTEL, handily situated in the center of town, does a large convention and meeting business during the week and caters to family getaways on weekends. The striking contemporary design nicely accommodates the crowds with flowing public spaces, lively bars and restaurants, and a large leisure center. (If you want lodgings that reflect Kilkenny's medieval atmosphere, this is not the place for you.) Guest rooms, decorated in unexciting business-hotel style, are loaded with conveniences such as large writing desks; many are set up to accommodate families and, in addition to having a double and single bed, are linked to an adjacent room through an interconnecting door. Some of the rooms and all of the suites have sweeping views over the castle and the old town.

Lacken House ★★★★

| QUALITY | ★★★★ | VALUE | ★★★ | € 75–€ 150 |

Dublin Road, Kilkenny; ☎ 056-776-1085; www.lackenhouse.ie

Location At the edge of the city center. **Amenities and services** 11 rooms, including 4 family rooms and 2 suites; lounge with open fire, hair dryers, satellite TV, tea and coffee facilities. **Elevator** No. **Parking** On property, free. **Price** Includes full Irish breakfast. **Credit cards** AE, MC, V.

THE VICTORIAN LANDMARK that helped make Kilkenny famous for its cuisine is now doing business solely as a guesthouse—bad news for travelers on the gourmet trail, good news for anyone looking for comfortable lodgings near the sights. The new owners have refurbished the guest rooms in traditional style and have put a great deal of effort into ensuring that the establishment maintains its excellent reputation.

Zuni Townhouse ★★★★

| QUALITY | ★★★★ ½ | VALUE | ★★★ | € 70–€ 120 |

26 Patrick Street, Kilkenny; ☎ 056-772-3999; fax 056-775-6400; info@zuni.ie; www.zuni.ie

Location City center. **Amenities and services** 13 rooms; hair dryers, Internet connections, restaurant, satellite TV. **Elevator** Yes. **Parking** Nearby, free. **Price** Includes full Irish breakfast; many special bed, breakfast, and dinner rates available, from €135 a person for 2 nights. **Credit cards** AE, MC, V.

THE GROUND-FLOOR RESTAURANT is the main business here, and a great deal of care goes into providing memorable meals in stylishly contemporary surroundings. Unlike many establishments that tack on guest rooms as a second thought, Zuni also minds the hotel end of the business, providing some of Kilkenny's nicest accommodations. Smart and hip yet soothing and relaxing, the guest quarters are an oasis of sleek contemporary furniture, brightly painted walls, glamorous fabrics, and high-tech lighting; the welcome amenities include large bathrooms with power showers.

Staying around Kilkenny

Mount Juliet Estate ★★★

| QUALITY | ★★★★ | VALUE | ★★★ | € 300–€ 400 |

Thomastown; ☎ 056-777-3000; fax 056-772-3019; www.mountjuliet.ie

Location City center. **Amenities and services** 46 rooms and suites, 12 apartments; 3 restaurants, bar, indoor swimming pool, gym, spa, tennis courts, golf course, riding stables, trout fishing, room service, minibars, laundry service. **Elevator** No. **Parking** On property, free. **Price** Includes full Irish breakfast; many special rates and offers available on the Web site. **Credit cards** AE, D, MC, V.

IRISH ACCOMMODATION gets no more luxurious than it does at this country estate on the River Nore, where some 1,500 acres encompass gardens, woods, green fields, and a golf course. Accommodations range from manor-house rooms to self-catering apartments, and all are large and sumptuous. Public rooms are grand and have been restored to re-create a lifestyle that no one's been able to afford for the past century or so. Guest rooms in the main house, one of the finest historic homes in Ireland, are the most atmospheric, while rooms in outlying buildings—Hunters Yard, Rose Garden Lodges, and the Paddock—are a little more relaxed and private, with many opening directly onto the grounds. Service is attentive but not obtrusive, and the dining is among the best in Ireland.

EXPLORING KILKENNY

KILKENNY CASTLE DOMINATES ONE END of the medieval city, **St. Canice's Cathedral** the other. Beginning at the castle, a walk down **High Street** leads past the **Tholsel,** built in 1761 as the commodities exchange. The handsome arcaded building, topped with a clock tower, later became the assembly rooms, where dances, meetings, and Kilkenny's other social and civic events transpired. Now it houses the municipal archives. Just beyond is **Butter Slip,** the most appealing of the medieval lanes that lead off High Street. The commerce that once transpired here is remembered in a famous Kilkenny verse: "If you ever go to Kilkenny, look for the hole in the wall, where you get 24 eggs for a penny, and butter for nothing at all."

Slip down the alley to **Kieran Street,** turn left, and you will come to **Kyteler's Inn,** now a pub and the onetime home of Alice Kyteler, who entered the annals of history in 1323 as the subject of Ireland's first witchcraft trial. It's more likely that Alice was simply a crafty poisoner—after doing away with four wealthy husbands, she disappeared during the trial; her lady-in-waiting wasn't so fortunate and was burned at the stake. Kieran Street soon comes to **Parliament Street** and the **Courthouse,** where the ground floor houses dank prison cells. Just across the street is the exquisite **Rothe House,** a merchant's home from 1594 with three wings facing two courtyards. The house, with period furnishings and beautiful wood ceilings, is open January through March and November through December, Monday through Saturday, 1 to 5 p.m.; April through June and September through October, Monday through Saturday, 10:30 a.m. to 5 p.m.; Sunday, 3 to 5 p.m.; and July through August, Monday through Saturday, 10 a.m. to 6 p.m.; Sunday, 3 to 5 p.m. Admission is €3 adults, €1 children, €2 seniors and students; for more information, call ☎ 056-772-2893.

unofficial **TIP**
Tynan's Walking Tours provide an excellent way to survey the city as you walk through the medieval streets with a local historian. Walks depart from the Kilkenny Tourist Office on Rose Inn Street, March–October, Monday–Saturday, 9:15 a.m., 10:30 a.m., 12:15 p.m., 1:30 p.m., 3 p.m., and 4:30 p.m.; November–February, Tuesday–Saturday, 10:30 a.m.,12:15 p.m., and 3 p.m.; €6 adults, €5.50 seniors and students, €3 children, a.m., 12:15 p.m., and 3 p.m.

Black Abbey, just beyond the house at the end of Abbey Street, was founded in 1225 by the Dominican order of monks. Oliver Cromwell more or less destroyed the nave when he occupied Kilkenny in 1650. The (over)restored stone structure once again functions as an abbey; the church is open daily, 8 a.m. to 6 p.m. The name is derived from the black capes the Dominicans once wore or, more darkly, from the fact that so many of them died in the Black Death of 1348. St. Canice's Cathedral is a little farther north, at the end of the medieval city.

ATTRACTIONS IN AND AROUND KILKENNY

 Jerpoint Abbey ★★★★

APPEAL BY AGE	PRESCHOOL ★★	GRADE SCHOOL ★★	TEENS ★★★
YOUNG ADULTS ★★	OVER 30 ★★★★		SENIORS ★★★★

Thomastown, 14 kilometers (9 miles) south of Kilkenny on R700;
☎ **056-772-4623**

Type of attraction Evocative ruins of a medieval abbey. **Admission** €2.90 adults, €2.10 seniors, €1.30 children, €7.40 families of up to 2 adults and 3 children. **Hours** March–May and mid-September–mid-November, daily, 9:30 a.m.–5 p.m.; June–mid-September, daily, 9:30 a.m.–6 p.m.; mid-November–December 1, daily, 10 a.m.–4 p.m. **When to go** In good weather, because the abbey is in ruin and you will be exposed to the elements. **Special comments** Bus service from Kilkenny to Jerpoint Abbey is extremely limited, and a taxi costs about €30 round-trip. If you don't have a day to spare spend your time exploring Kilkenny instead. **How much time to allow** At least 1 hour.

DESCRIPTION AND COMMENTS These remains of a 12th-century monastery, built for the Benedictines but handed over to the Cistercians a century later, are evocative and utterly charming, lost in time in a bucolic setting. The compound's stellar attractions are the Romanesque carvings in the side chapels and on the tombs littering the roofless nave. The rough works are tenderly human in their aspect—clergymen grin while legions of long-forgotten souls look forlorn and vulnerable. Just as impressive, though, is the serenity that surrounds the place. Visit anytime other than the height of summer, and you may have the well-preserved cloisters and peaceful grounds to yourself. At these times, as you look over the surrounding countryside, it's easy to imagine this as an isolated community of about 100 monks and brothers who worked the gardens, ground their own grain in the now-ruined water mill, worshipped in the still-impressive church, and were buried beneath the stones in the cemetery. A small interpretive center adjoining the ruins is well worth a quick visit to learn about the carvings and monastic life; should one of the guardians be on duty and offer to lead a tour, by all means take advantage of the opportunity.

TOURING TIPS The setting is lovely, and the grounds are a nice place to stretch out and relax; bring a bag lunch to enjoy in the picnic area.

How Attractions Compare in the South of Ireland

ATTRACTION	DESCRIPTION	AUTHOR'S RATING
KILKENNY		
Jerpoint Abbey	Evocative ruins of a medieval abbey	★★★★
Kells Priory	Another monastic ruin	★★★★
St. Canice's Cathedral	Second-largest medieval cathedral in Ireland	★★★★
Kilkenny Castle	Castle, family home of the Butler clan	★★★½
CASHEL		
Rock of Cashel	Majestic ruins of an early fortress and medieval church complex atop a massive rock	★★★★★
WATERFORD		
Waterford Crystal Factory	World-famous manufacturer of glass	★★★
CORK		
English Market	A covered food market	★★★★
Church of St. Anne Shandon	A historic and beloved church	★★★½
Crawford Municipal Art Gallery	An excellent small art gallery	★★★½
Cork City Gaol	Former prison, now a museum	★★★
Blarney Castle	One of Ireland's most famous castles	★★
MIDLETON AND EAST CORK		
Fota House	Historic home and grounds	★★★★
Fota Wildlife Park	Zoo	★★★
Old Midleton Distillery	Historic whiskey distillery	★★½
COBH		
Cobh, the Queenstown Story	Exhibit tracing Cobh's dramatic maritime history	★★★½
KINSALE		
Charles Fort	Historic fort overlooking Kinsale Harbour	★★★★

Walks and Drives in the South

The varied landscapes of the South can best be enjoyed on foot and on drives through backwaters and along unspoiled coastlines.

GREAT WALKS

THE BLACKWATER WAY

If you cross the Vee in the **Knockmealdown Mountains** and descend toward Cashel, you'll encounter the Blackwater Way a couple of times. This 188-kilometer (113-mile) route begins in the village of **Clogheen** on the River Tar and crosses the Knockmealdowns into the Blackwater Valley to the town of **Fermoy.** You can get a taste for the walk and enjoy some nice riverside scenery on a short amble out from the village of Clogheen (see the Blackwater Valley drive, at right). For a more strenuous mountain walk, join the way as it passes through the top of the Knockmealdowns. You'll find the way well marked off a parking area in the part of the mountain pass known as the **Gap.** From there, you can climb the way across mountainside moors toward the summit, for stunning views over what seems to be all of central Ireland.

THE SCILLY WALK

One of the pleasures of a visit to **Kinsale** (see page 229) is a seaside stroll along Scilly Walk, a path that begins at the end of **Long Quay** on the east side of the port and follows the harbor for about three kilometers (two miles) to **Charles Fort.** The path passes through several attractive harborside communities and comes temptingly close to two atmospheric pubs, the **Spaniard** and the **Bulman.** Tour the fort on one of the excellent guided tours, and if you are up for more walking, you can continue another five kilometers (three miles) out the peninsula to **Frower Point,** for excellent harbor views.

CORK CITY RIVER WALKS

In addition to the many city walks to be enjoyed in Cork, you can also easily get away from the bustle of the city center. One such walk is along the **Maradyke,** a tree-shaded pedestrian avenue that follows the River Lee west for about 2 kilometers (1.2 miles) from the city center, skirting **Fitzgerald Park.** Near the end of the park, you can cross the **Daly Bridge** and ascend the hill to **Cork City Gaol** (see page 215). Another walk follows the south bank of the River Lee for about five kilometers (three miles) east, along a shaded walkway, toward the village of **Blackrock** near **Cork Harbour.** There's plenty of activity to observe on the wharves along the river, and Blackrock is a pleasant place that retains the air of a fishing port.

GREAT DRIVES

THROUGH THE BLACKWATER VALLEY AND THE KNOCKMEALDOWNS TO CASHEL

The **Rock of Cashel** provides all the sightseeing thrills you might need for a day, but if you visit this medieval monument from Cork City or eastern County Cork, you can add a scenery-filled drive up the Blackwater Valley and through the Knockmealdown Mountains. The route begins at the old port and resort of **Youghal,** on busy N25, 48 kilometers (30 miles) east of Cork City and 74 kilometers (45 miles) south of Waterford.

Youghal, at the mouth of the Blackwater River, once belonged to Sir Walter Raleigh, a gift from Queen Elizabeth I. Allegedly, Raleigh introduced the potato to Ireland in his farmlands here. (Beware: Many other places in Ireland make the same claim.) A long stretch of walls still surrounds part of the old city, built on a natural harbor with a miles of sandy beaches.

From Youghal, follow the Blackwater River north, but note that finding the riverside route takes a bit of alert navigating. Follow N25 north from Youghal about 1 kilometers (1.5 miles), and you'll see a turnoff for the **River Blackwater;** a series of minor roads designated as Scenic Route follows the rushing river north and in about 30 kilometers (20 miles) comes to Lismore.

Lismore Castle, looming high on a cliff above the river, is the Irish seat of the Duke and Duchess of Devonshire. Past residents include the chemist Robert Boyle, who was born in the castle in 1627 and is still known for his Boyle's Law. Adele Astaire, sister of Fred and his onetime dancing partner, gave up Hollywood to marry a Devonshire duke in the 1930s and lived in the castle for many years; her brother was a frequent visitor. You can visit the extensive gardens from May through October, daily, 1:45 to 4:45 p.m.; admission is €4 adults and €2 children under age 16.

From Lismore, R668 climbs through woods and moors as it crosses the Knockmealdown Mountains, passing the summit through a wide natural pass known the **Vee;** the narrow valley leading into the Vee is known as the **Gap.** Pull into one of the turnouts on the north side of the pass for stunning views over the fields that dot the plain below. As you descend into the valley, cross the River Tar at **Clogheen** and follow the river east to **Clonmel,** passing through the pretty villages of **Newcastle** and **Kilmanahan.**

Clonmel, about 35 kilometers (21 miles) from Lismore, is still partially walled and gated. The seat of County Tipperary, it has some serious literary associations: **Laurence Sterne** (1713–1768), author of *Tristram Shandy,* was born here; another novelist, **Anthony Trollope** (1815–1882), was a town postmaster.

Continued on next page

Walks and Drives in the South (continued)

GREAT DRIVES (CONTINUED)

THROUGH THE BLACKWATER VALLEY AND THE KNOCKMEALDOWNS TO CASHEL (CONTINUED)

Cashel, where a giant outcropping of rock is topped with the spectacular remains of a medieval church complex (see page 203), is 25 kilometers (15 miles) northwest on R688. You can make a quick return to Cork City and its surroundings on N8.

ALONG THE COAST OF WEST CORK

The coastline of County Cork is attractive and relatively unspoiled, etched with bays and headlands.

From **Kinsale** (see page 229), follow R600 west for 20 kilometers (12 miles) to **Timoleague,** a pleasant seaside village built around the ruins of a 13th-century Franciscan abbey. Among the stone window-frames and foundations of the chapel and refectory is a most unusual feature: the remains of a wine cellar. **Timoleague's Castle** is long gone, but the palm-shaded gardens remain and are open to the public June through August, daily, noon to 6 p.m.; admission is €2.

Follow R601 from Timoleague around **Courtmacsherry Bay** through the fishing village of the same name to **Butlerstown,** and then around the headlands to the shores of **Clonakilty Bay.** The peninsula that separates these two bays is known as the **Seven Heads,** for its seven headlands; the large peninsula to the east of Courtmacsherry Bay is the **Old Head of Kinsale,** off of which the *Lusitania* was torpedoed by the Germans in 1915, killing 1,198 people. The peninsula is now the grounds of an exclusive golf club (see page 236).

Clonakilty, about ten kilometers (six miles) from Timoleague, is an extremely attractive village with several sandy beaches nearby. About five kilometers (three miles) west of town off N71 is the birthplace of **Michael Collins** (1890–1922), the resistance fighter who was killed in an ambush outside nearby **Macroom.** The house burned to the ground in 1921, and little remains but the foundation.

Beyond **Rosscarbery,** another five kilometers (three miles) down N71, join the coast again on R597; after about three kilometers (two miles), come to **Drombeg Stone Circle,** a ring of 17 standing stones thought to be 2,000 years old. Adjacent to the site is a stone cooking-trough from the fourth through seventh centuries, in which it is believed hot stones were placed to heat water.

Retrace the route back to Kinsale, or if you are returning to Cork, follow N71 northeast.

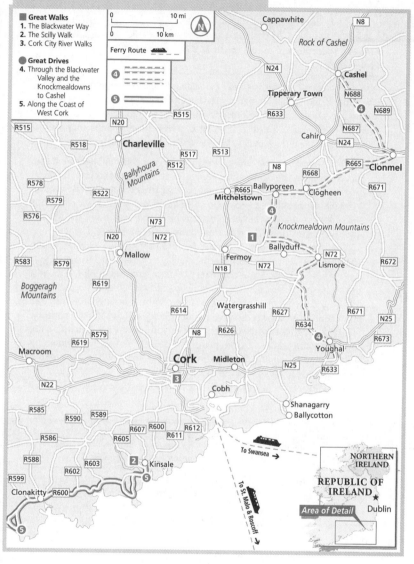

walks and drives in the south

■ **Great Walks**
1. The Blackwater Way
2. The Scilly Walk
3. Cork City River Walks

● **Great Drives**
4. Through the Blackwater Valley and the Knockmealdowns to Cashel
5. Along the Coast of West Cork

0 ____ 10 mi
0 ____ 10 km

Ferry Route

Cappawhite

Rock of Cashel

N8

N24

Cashel

Tipperary Town

N688

N689

R633

Cahir

N687

N24

R515

Clonmel

R665

R671

N20

R515

R518

Charleville

R517

R513

N8

R668

Ballyporeen

Clogheen

R512

R665

Mitchelstown

Ballyhoura Mountains

R578

R522

R579

R576

N73

N20

N72

Mallow

Knockmealdown Mountains

Ballyduff

N72

Lismore

R672

Fermoy

N18

N72

R583

R579

Boggeragh Mountains

R619

Watergrasshill

R627

R671

N25

R614

R626

R634

Youghal

R673

R579

N8

Macroom

R619

Cork

Midleton

N25

R633

N22

Cobh

R585

Shanagarry

Ballycotton

R590

R589

R607

R600

R612

R586

R605

R611

To Swansea →

R588

Kinsale

R603

R599

Clonakilty

R602

R600

To St. Malo & Roscoff →

NORTHERN IRELAND

REPUBLIC OF IRELAND

Dublin

Area of Detail

Kells Priory   ★★★★

APPEAL BY AGE	PRESCHOOL ★★★	GRADE SCHOOL ★★★	TEENS ★★★
YOUNG ADULTS ★★★		OVER 30 ★★★★	SENIORS ★★★★

Kells, 15 kilometers (9 miles) south of Kilkenny on R699;
☎ **056-772-8255**

Type of attraction Evocative ruins of a medieval abbey. **Admission** Free. **Hours** Dawn–dusk; during the summer, a guardian on the site leads tours. **When to go** In good weather. **Special comments** Bus service from Kilkenny to Kells is extremely limited, and a taxi costs about €30 round-trip. The Kilkenny Tourist Office can provide bus schedules. **How much time to allow** At least 1 hour.

DESCRIPTION AND COMMENTS One of Ireland's largest and mightiest medieval ruins rises from the banks of the King's River. A series of six fortified towers rising along the thick walls suggest that this complex, established in 1193, was more than a monastic settlement and place of worship, but with constant warring between various lords and their clans, the Middle Ages were hard times for religious communities in Ireland.

Geoffrey Fitz William, an Anglo-Norman knight, was awarded some 40,000 acres, and he established the village of Kells and this priory as part of his holdings. Soon the priory church, cloisters, belfry, kitchens, and eventually the walls and towers began to sprawl over the 300-acre compound. Kells came to house a large community of monks but, like other monasteries, was dissolved under Henry VIII in the 16th century. The once-mighty complex became a farm and eventually fell into ruin, and sheep still wander through the enclosure. Even so, the remaining stone foundations and fortifications fire the imagination to evoke a great outpost of civilization in medieval Ireland.

TOURING TIPS From the priory, follow the riverside path to Kells.

Kilkenny Castle   ★★★½

APPEAL BY AGE	PRESCHOOL ★★	GRADE SCHOOL ★★	TEENS ★★
YOUNG ADULTS ★★★		OVER 30 ★★★★	SENIORS ★★★★

Center of Kilkenny, ☎ **056-772-1450; www.irishheritage.ie**

Type of attraction Castle, family home of the Butler clan. **Admission** €5.30 adults, €3.70 seniors, €2.10 children and students, €11.50 families of up to 2 adults and 2 children. **Hours** April–May, daily, 10:30 a.m.–5:30 p.m.; June–August, daily, 10 a.m.–7 p.m.; September, daily, 10 a.m.–6:30 p.m.; October–March, daily,10:30 a.m.–12:45 p.m. and 2 p.m.–5 p.m. **When to go** Anytime. **Special comments** Access by guided tour only; includes a 15-minute audiovisual presentation that may make young visitors restless. **How much time to allow** 2 hours (including 1 hour to walk on the grounds).

DESCRIPTION AND COMMENTS Strongbow, an Anglo-Norman warrior and settler, built a wooden fortress here in 1172, and a castle has commanded the bend of the Kilkenny River ever since. As you'll learn on the guided tour (the only way to see the castle), the present structure dates to the

Middle Ages; from 1391 well into the 20th century, it was the home of the Butler family, who were given the title Earls of Ormond. The Butlers were such a force in Irish politics that the Irish Parliament often met at the castle, and clearly the family did well. Improvements went on well into the 19th century, including extensive gardens, a massive stable block (now housing the Kilkenny Design Centre), and elaborate interiors. The drawing room, library, and other family rooms provide a glimpse of the Victorian splendor in which 19th-century landholders lived. The tour ends with a bang in the Long Gallery, where portraits of generations of Butlers hang beneath a hammer-beam ceiling. A humorous endnote in this family legacy: one of the last of the Butlers, a member of the American branch of the family, came to Kilkenny to hand over the keys to the castle and the last claims to ownership; a member of the rock group U2 happened to wander into the ceremonies and steal the show.

TOURING TIPS Cross the street to the former stable block, now housing the Kilkenny Design Centre. Filled with the work of craftspeople from throughout Ireland, the center provides one of Ireland's best shopping experiences, and the Design Centre Café is an excellent spot for lunch.

St. Canice's Cathedral ★★★★

APPEAL BY AGE	PRESCHOOL ★★	GRADE SCHOOL ★★★★	TEENS ★★
YOUNG ADULTS ★★★		OVER 30 ★★★★	SENIORS ★★★★

Dean Street, ☎ 056-776-4971;

Type of attraction Second-largest medieval cathedral in Ireland. **Admission** *Cathedral:* €3 adults, €2 seniors, students, and children; *separate admission to round tower:* €2 adults, €1.50 seniors, students, and children; *combined admission to cathedral and round tower:* €4, €10 for families; *combined admission to cathedral (does not include round tower) and Rothe House:* €3 adults, €2 seniors, students, and children **Hours** April, May, and September, Monday–Saturday, 10 a.m.–1 p.m. and 2 p.m.–5 p.m.; Sunday, 2 p.m.–5 p.m.; June–August, Monday–Saturday, 9 a.m.–6 p.m.; Sunday, 2 p.m.–6 p.m.; October–March, Monday–Saturday, 10 a.m.–1 p.m. and 2–4 p.m.; Sunday, 2 p.m.–4 p.m. **When to go** Anytime, but try to find a slot of fair weather if you plan on climbing the round tower. **Special comments** Take time to wander through the cathedral randomly and enjoy the medieval monuments throughout. **How much time to allow** 30 minutes, 1 hour if you climb the round tower.

DESCRIPTION AND COMMENTS This is one of Ireland's most impressive medieval monuments, completed in the 13th century and, after St. Patrick's in Dublin, the second-largest medieval church in Ireland. Commanding the north end of Kilkenny, the massive Gothic hulk has weathered a number of catastrophes. Part of the roof collapsed in 1332, and it was rebuilt as penance by William Outlaw, who was accused of relations with the alleged witch Alice Kyteler (see Kyteler's Inn, next page). Oliver Cromwell seized the cathedral when he and his troops took Kilkenny in 1650 and did the usual Cromwellian damage, leaving the church walls intact but destroying the monuments. Most of them have been retrieved and effigies of knights in armor, elaborate carvings, and other medieval artifacts are rather haphazardly but charmingly displayed throughout the chilly, dark interior, clad in black Kilkenny marble. For centuries before the cathedral was built, St. Canice's was the center of a large monastic settlement, and the round tower, once a beacon guiding the faithful from miles around, still stands, a little the worse for wear; a climb to the top affords stunning views over County Kilkenny.

TOURING TIPS Combine a visit to St. Canice's with a look at several other nearby remnants of medieval Kilkenny, such as Black Abbey, Butter Slip, and Rothe House (see "Exploring Kilkenny," page 191).

RESTAURANTS IN KILKENNY

Café Sol ★★★★

MEDITERRANEAN	MODERATE	QUALITY ★★★★	VALUE ★★★★★

6 William Street, Kilkenny; ☎ 056-776-4987

Reservations Recommended for dinner. **Entree range** Lunch, €6–€12; dinner, €16–€29; early-bird dinner, Sunday–Friday, 6–7:15 p.m., Saturday, 5:30–6:15 p.m., €22 for 2 courses, €26 for 3 courses. **Payment** AE, MC, V. **Bar** Full service. **Disabled access** Yes. **Hours** Monday–Saturday, 11:30 a.m.–10 p.m.; Sunday, noon–9 p.m.

MENU RECOMMENDATIONS Scones, soups, grilled sausages, pastas for lighter fare; char-grilled Kilkenny beef, char-grilled salmon.

COMMENTS This terra-cotta–colored, light-filled room brightens even the grayest Irish weather, and a welcome air prevails as the wooden tables fill throughout the day. The simple surroundings belie the sophistication of the kitchen, which turns out flavorful variations on salmon, lamb, and other local staples.

Kilkenny Design Restaurant ★★★

BUFFET	MODERATE	QUALITY ★★★½	VALUE ★★★★

Castle Yard, Kilkenny; ☎ 056-772-2118

Reservations None. **Entree range** €13–€17. **Payment** AE, MC, V. **Bar** Full service. **Disabled access** Yes. **Hours** Daily, 9 a.m.–5 p.m. (closed Sunday, January–April).

MENU RECOMMENDATIONS Fresh salmon, home-baked breads and pastries.

COMMENTS Everything is fresh and homemade—soups, breads, meat pies— and served buffet-style in bright, airy rooms above the Design Centre. The views over the gardens of the castle's former Dowager's House enhance the experience.

Kyteler's Inn ★★★

PUB FOOD	MODERATE	QUALITY ★★★	VALUE ★★★★½

St. Kieran's Street, Kilkenny; ☎ 056-772-1064

How Restaurants Compare in the South of Ireland

NAME	CUISINE	OVERALL	QUALITY	VALUE	PRICE
KILKENNY					
Café Sol	Mediterranean	★★★★	★★★★	★★★★★	Mod
Pordylos	Irish	★★★★	★★★	★★★	Mod
Kilkenny Design Restaurant	Buffet	★★★	★★★½	★★★★	Mod
Kyteler's Inn	Pub food	★★★	★★★	★★★★½	Mod
CORK					
Jacobs on the Mall	Continental	★★★★½	★★★★	★★★★	Mod/exp
Farmgate Café	Irish	★★★★	★★★★	★★★★½	Inexp/mod
Nash 19	Modern Irish	★★★★	★★★★	★★★★½	Inexp/mod
Fenns Quay	Continental	★★★★	★★★★	★★★★	Mod/exp
Jacques	Modern Irish	★★★★	★★★★	★★★½	Mod/exp
Café Paradiso	Vegetarian	★★★★	★★★★	★★★	Mod/exp
Les Gourmandises	French/modern Irish	★★★★	★★★★	★★★	Exp
MIDLETON AND EAST CORK					
Farmgate Rest. and Country Store	Irish	★★★★	★★★★	★★★★★	Mod
O'Donovan's	Modern Irish	★★★★	★★★★	★★★★	Mod
Ballymaloe House	Modern Irish	★★★★	★★★★	★★★½	Exp
KINSALE					
Fishy Fishy Café	Seafood	★★★★	★★★★	★★★★★	Mod
The Vintage	Irish	★★★★	★★★★	★★★	Mod
Little Skillet	Irish	★★★½	★★★★	★★★★	Mod
Blue Haven	Pub/Irish	★★★	★★★	★★★★*/ ★★★**	Mod/exp

*pub/**restaurant*

Reservations None. **Entree range** €8–€15. **Payment** AE, MC, V. **Bar** Full service. **Disabled access** Yes. **Hours** *Meals:* daily, noon–3 p.m., 6:30–9 p.m.; *pub:* 11:30 a.m.–1 a.m.

MENU RECOMMENDATIONS Witches' brew (vegetable soup), fish-and-chips (not always available).

COMMENTS The town's most highly touted medieval inn serves up nightly music and plenty of atmosphere with its stone walls, heavy beams, a dark cellar, and even a resident witch, Alice, infamous for allegedly poisoning four husbands. Alice's evil aura doesn't seem to deter legions of diners, who tend to wash down the plain offerings of sandwiches, the occasional curry, and simply grilled salmon and steak with pints of Smithwick's, brewed in Kilkenny for almost 250 years.

Pordylos ★★★★

IRISH	MODERATE	QUALITY ★★★	VALUE ★★★

Butter Slip, Kilkenny; ☎ 056-777-0660

Reservations Recommended for dinner. **Entree range** €19.50–€25; 3-course set menu, €40; early-bird special, Monday–Friday, 5–7 p.m.: 2 courses, €21.95, 3 courses, €26.95. **Payment** AE, MC, V. **Bar** Full service. **Disabled access** No. **Hours** Tuesday–Saturday, 12:30–3 p.m. and 6–10:30 p.m.

MENU RECOMMENDATIONS Lamb, fresh fish.

COMMENTS Comprising candlelit beamed rooms on the upper floor of a medieval building in atmospheric Butter Slip, Pordylos is justifiably popular: the atmosphere is amiable, the service is adept, and the less-elaborate offerings—stews, chops, lobster, fish—are well done.

ENTERTAINMENT AND NIGHTLIFE IN KILKENNY

KILKENNY'S OWN **Smithwick's Brewery** keeps the city's lively pubs well supplied. Taste a Smithwick's (pronounced without the *w*) while enjoying traditional music at **Kyteler's Inn** (St. Kieran's Street; ☎ 056-772-1064) and **Caislean Ui Cuain** (The Castle Inn), a dark-paneled 18th-century coaching inn on the Parade (☎ 056-776-5406). Everyone's favorite Kilkenny pub is the amiable and cozy **Eamon Langton's** (69 John Street; ☎ 056-776-5133), with a fire for winter nights and an airy garden room for the summer. **Marble City Bar** (66 High Street; ☎ 056-776-1143) combines a lively pub scene with an adjoining tearoom, open during the day. If you want to expand beyond the pub scene, check out the **Westgate Theatre** (Parliament Street; ☎ 056-776-1674), which often hosts visiting performers for plays and concerts.

SHOPPING IN KILKENNY

THE FORMER STABLE BLOCK of Kilkenny Castle is now one of Ireland's leading showcases for crafts, the Kilkenny **Design Centre** (Castle Yard; ☎ 056-772-2118). Artisans from all over Ireland assemble here to show a stunning array of ceramics, glassware, pottery, jewelry, and knitwear. Prices are not low, but the quality is about as high as you're going to find. The Design Centre is open year-round, Monday through Saturday, 9 a.m. to 6 p.m.; June through September, Sunday, 11 a.m. to 5 p.m.

Craftspeople at **Nicholas Mosse Pottery,** about ten kilometers (six miles) east of Kilkenny, on the River Nore in Bennettsbridge (☎ 056-772-7505; **www.nicholasmosse.com**), make simple, functional pieces in the style of Irish spongeware, reviving traditional techniques. The studio uses local clay and hydropower from the river to fire the kilns, and each piece is painted by hand, incorporating designs that reflect local plants and animals. The studio and shop are open Monday through Saturday, 10 a.m. to 6 p.m. (Sunday afternoons in the summer). Nicholas Mosse and his wife, Susan, have restored **Kilfane,** an adjoining late-18th-century garden, in a glen surrounding a waterfall. Open July through August, daily, 11 a.m. to 6 p.m., €6; ☎ 056-772-4558; **www.kilfane.com.**

Around **KILKENNY**

CASHEL

RISING ABOVE THE PLAIN OF TIPPERARY some 60 kilometers (38 miles) southeast of Kilkenny, the **Rock of Cashel** may well be Ireland's most imposing sight. Cashel is an easy day trip from Kilkenny, or it's a handy place to stop for a few hours if you're driving west from Kilkenny toward Limerick and the West.

Attraction in Cashel

 Rock of Cashel ★★★★★

APPEAL BY AGE	PRESCHOOL ★★★★	GRADE SCHOOL ★★★★	TEENS ★★★★
YOUNG ADULTS ★★★★		OVER 30 ★★★★½	SENIORS ★★★★½

Cashel, ☎ 062-61437

Type of attraction Majestic ruins of an early fortress and medieval church complex atop a massive rock. **Admission** €5.30 adults, €3.70 seniors, €2.10 children and students, €11.50 families of up to 2 adults and 2 children. **Hours** Mid-March–early June, daily, 9 a.m.–5:30 p.m.; early June–mid-September, daily, 9 a.m.–7 p.m.; mid-September–mid-October, daily, 9 a.m.–5:30 p.m.; mid-October–mid-March, daily, 9 a.m.–4:30 p.m. **When to go** In good weather—with clear skies, the views over the Plain of Tipperary are extensive. **Special comments** The slick 15-minute audiovisual presentation detracts a bit from the romance and sanctity of the surroundings but does a good job of summarizing the Rock's complex history; see it before touring, because the perspective will come in handy. **How much time to allow** 2 hours.

DESCRIPTION AND COMMENTS One of Ireland's most visited attractions is alluring in spite of the crowds it attracts. The giant rock topped with medieval remains is a spectacular sight, even when swept with clouds and rains, and the ruins are richly evocative and telling of the church's onetime power. Early kings settled the Rock as early as the fourth century; virtually impregnable and commanding the countryside for miles around, it's easy to understand the Rock's strategic importance. The Roman Catholic Church took over in the 12th century and remained until the late 18th century; it didn't take long for the harsh elements to render the complex the ruin you'll see today. As befits a gloomy ruin, the Rock of Cashel is well endowed with lore. One of the most popular legends surrounds the 12th-century cross (a replica of the original) that stands near the entrance to the complex. The cross not only commemorates the church's acquisition of the Rock, but also the spot where, in AD 432, St. Patrick baptized King Aengus, Ireland's first Christian ruler. On the same day, Patrick allegedly held up a shamrock to explain the mystery of the Holy Trinity, and the symbol took hold in the hearts of the Irish people.

Begin a tour in the newest building, the restored 15th-century Hall of the Vicars Choral. This timbered hall, warmed by an enormous hearth, served as quarters for vicars who were chosen to sing during services. The largest building on the Rock is St. Patrick's Cathedral, now a roofless ruin marred by the events of 1647, when Cromwell's troops attacked Cashel and set fire to the cathedral where hundreds of townspeople had taken refuge. Weatherworn sculptures and carvings in the transept depict the lives of the saints and other biblical scenes, and gargoyles still surround the window frames. The best-preserved building is Cormac's Chapel, built in 1127 by king and bishop Cormac McCarthy. One of Ireland's finest Romanesque structures—note the rounded arches and twisted columns typical of that style—retains some of its frescoes (a rarity in the moist climate of Ireland). The oldest building is the round tower, 92 feet high and built as a beacon and lookout in 1101. A few souls remain forever, in the gloomy graveyard next to the cathedral walls.

TOURING TIPS In summer, try to avoid visiting the Rock between 11 a.m. and 3 p.m., when visitors arrive by the busload.

WATERFORD

THIS BUSY AND SOMETIMES SHABBY PORT, 50 kilometers (30 miles) south of Kilkenny, was founded by the Vikings 1,200 years ago. Among the industries the town has supported over the years, none is more famous than the **Waterford Crystal Factory,** and a visit to the factory and shop is what draws most visitors here. The **Waterford Tourist Office** (41 The Quay; ☎ 051-875788) provides information about the town and the surrounding county; open April through September, Monday through Saturday, 9 a.m. to 6 p.m., and October, Monday through Saturday, 9 a.m. to 5 p.m.

The town's most striking landmark is **Reginald's Tower,** a circular beacon built by the Vikings more than a thousand years ago and rising from the end of the busy quays on the River Suir. The nearby **Waterford Treasures at the Granary** museum (Merchant's Quay; ☎ 051-304500; **www.waterfordtreasures.com**) puts the tower and the rest of Waterford's long history in nice perspective, with Viking artifacts and a snappy multimedia show. Open June to August, 9:30 a.m.

to 9 p.m.; April to May and September, 9:30 a.m. to 6 p.m.; October to March, 10 a.m. to 5 p.m.; €4 adults, €3 seniors and students, €2 children under 16, free for children under 5, €12 for families of two adults and two children.

Travelers on a quest to discover their Irish heritage should make a stop at the **Waterford Heritage Genealogical Centre** in St. Patrick's Church (Jenkins Lane; ☎ 051-876123), where the staff can help you trace your lineage to ancestors who may have emigrated from County Waterford.

Attraction in Waterford

 Waterford Crystal Factory ★★★

APPEAL BY AGE	PRESCHOOL N/A	GRADE SCHOOL N/A	TEENS ★★
YOUNG ADULTS ★★★	OVER 30 ★★★		SENIORS ★★★

Cork Road; ☎ 051-373311; www.waterfordvisitorcentre.com

Type of attraction World-famous manufacturer of glass. **Admission** Free for audiovisual presentation, gallery, and showrooms; tour: €9 adults, €6.50 seniors and students, free for children under age 12. **Hours** *Tours:* March–October, daily, 8:30 a.m.–4:15 p.m.; November–February, Monday–Friday, 9 a.m.–3:15 p.m.; *Gallery and showrooms:* March–October, daily, 8:30 a.m.–6 p.m.; November–March, Monday–Friday, 9 a.m.–5 p.m. **When to go** Avoid busy weekends if possible. **Special comments** Children under age 10 are not allowed on factory tour. **How much time to allow** 1 hour for audiovisual presentation and tour; as long as you want for shopping.

DESCRIPTION AND COMMENTS One of Ireland's most popular attractions is also the largest crystal factory in the world and modern Waterford's most important industry. That explains the no-nonsense approach to this well-run factory tour and shopping experience. A superb audiovisual presentation explains such chapters in the company's history as the bleak times when the Famine forced it to close; Waterford didn't begin producing again until 1947, and the prestige the company has regained since then says much about the quality of the product. A brief but fascinating factory tour shows off the glassblowing and cooling processes, and then visitors are left on their own to roam through the shop and a gallery showing off historic pieces. Alas, no discounts are to be had in the shop (although the selection is first-rate), and unlike Irish purveyors of beer and whiskey, Waterford does not hand out free samples at the end of the visit.

TOURING TIPS Call ahead to reserve a place on the tours, which fill up quickly. Gatchell's Restaurant, on the premises, serves excellent lunches.

Dining in Waterford

Two of the most atmospheric old Waterford pubs are the **Munster** (Bailey's New Street; ☎ 051-874656), where much of the dark wood comes from the town's old toll bridge, and **T. & H. Doolan** (32 George's Street; ☎ 051-841504), a former coaching inn.

Bodéga ★★★

| WINE BAR | MODERATE–EXPENSIVE | QUALITY ★★★★ | VALUE ★★★ |

St. Kieran's Street, Kilkenny; ☎ 056-772-1064

Reservations None. **Entree range** €8–€15; early-bird dinner, Monday–Friday, 5:30–7 p.m., €21 for 2 courses, €26 for 3 courses. **Payment** AE, MC, V. **Bar** Full service. **Disabled access** Yes. **Hours** Monday–Saturday, noon–10 p.m.

MENU RECOMMENDATIONS Mussels prepared any way.

COMMENTS A touch of the Mediterranean brings a bit of life to Waterford's otherwise fairly low-key urban scene, with earth-toned surroundings and down-to-earth international fare. Duck, Toulousian sausages, and steaks are accompanied by excellent wines and served with warmth.

WEXFORD

ANOTHER DOWN-TO-EARTH port town, 60 kilometers (36 miles) east of Waterford, is best known to many people for the annual **Wexford Opera Festival** in October, one of Europe's major musical events and known for its adventurous programming. For more information on the festival, call ☎ 053-912-2144 or visit **www .wexfordopera.com.** For information on the town and Wexford County, step into the tourist office on Crescent Quay (☎ 053-23111; **www.wexfordtourism.com**; open Monday through Saturday, 9 a.m. to 6 p.m.).

Wexford is also a popular stop for travelers on their way to and from the busy ferry port in Rosslare, and this proximity to the Irish Sea gave the town importance to Vikings in the tenth century and Norman settlers a century later. A few vestiges of this past include mostly ruined **Selskar Abbey,** on Westgate Street, and nearby **Westgate Tower,** a 13th-century tollgate that is much more interesting than the museum of local history it houses (☎ 053-46506; open Monday through Friday, 10 a.m. to 5 p.m.).

The best way to see the rest of the small town is simply to follow Main Street between Redmond Square at the northwest end and Barrack Street at the southeast end, passing through **Bull Ring** in the middle. This central square, named for the gruesome sport of bullbaiting that once took place there, has gone down in Irish history as the site of the signing of the first declaration of the Irish Republic, in 1798. Most the town's commerce is along this street, and on the narrow lanes and alleys that cross it.

North Slob, a stretch of marshland just beyond the industrial port, is protected as the **Wexford Wildfowl Reserve** and is the winter home of 10,000 Greenland geese, as well as many other species of waterfowl (off R742, near Curracloe; ☎ 053-23129; open daily, 10 a.m. to 5 p.m., until 6 p.m. spring and summer; admission free).

CORK

IRELAND'S SECOND-LARGEST city is also one of its oldest, dating to the seventh century, when St. Finbarr founded a monastery in marshy land along the River Lee (*Carcaigh*, the city's Gaelic name, means "marsh"). Today, Finbarr is remembered in a massive Gothic Revival cathedral that looms over an appealing city encircled by two arms of the River Lee, where docks once sent goods all over the world. Alleys and pedestrian streets, many of which were once waterways, bustle with students at **Cork University** and businesspeople working in new buildings going up alongside the river. A noted free-spiritedness made the city a major center of rebellion in the 1919–1921 War of Independence; today. the Rebel City turns its attention to jazz festivals, a lively pub scene, and some of Ireland's finest cuisine. Cork is an excellent jumping-off point to such nearby places as **Cobh, Kinsale,** and **Midleton,** as well as **County Kerry,** just to the south.

PLANNING YOUR VISIT TO CORK

FOR INFORMATION ON PLACES TO STAY, what to see and do, and where to dine in Cork and the surrounding region, contact the **Cork Tourist Office** (Tourist House, 42 Grand Parade; ☎ 021-425-5100, **www.corkkerry.ie**). The center is open Monday through Saturday, 9:15 a.m. to 5:30 p.m.

Special Events in Cork

Cork celebrates Ireland's patron saint with a lively **St. Patrick's Festival** March 17 to 19, featuring poetry readings, traditional-music concerts, and other events; for information and tickets, call ☎ 021-480-2596 or visit **www.corkstpatricksfestival.ie.** The **Cork International Choral Festival,** late April and/or early May, draws singers from around the world for concerts in Cork City Hall; for information, call ☎ 021-421-51255 or visit **www.corkchoral.ie.** The other big musical event is the late-October **Guinness Cork Jazz Festival,** one of the world's most acclaimed jazz fests, attracting more than 1,000 performers to stages around the city; for information, call ☎ 021-427-8979 or visit **www.corkjazzfestival.com.** The **Cork Film Festival** screens features, documentaries, and shorts for one week in late October; for information, call ☎ 021-427-1711 or visit **www.corkfilmfest.org.**

ARRIVING AND GETTING ORIENTED IN CORK

CORK IS 260 KILOMETERS (160 miles) southwest of Dublin. Trains arrive from Dublin and other Irish cities at **Kent Station,** located off MacCurtain Street in the northeast corner of the city. Trains run between Dublin and Cork about ten times a day, and the trip takes about 2 hours and 45 minutes; fare is about €45 each way. For more information, call toll-free ☎ 1850-366222 or 01-836-6222, or visit **www.irishrail.ie.**

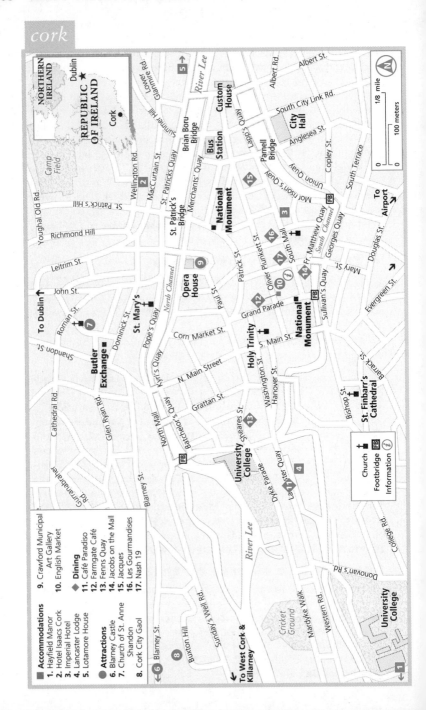

cork

Accommodations
1. Hayfield Manor
2. Hotel Isaacs Cork
3. Imperial Hotel
4. Lancaster Lodge
5. Lotamore House

Attractions
6. Blarney Castle
7. Church of St. Anne Shandon
8. Cork City Gaol
9. Crawford Municipal Art Gallery
10. English Market

Dining
11. Café Paradiso
12. Farmgate Café
13. Fenns Quay
14. Jacobs on the Mall
15. Jacques
16. Les Gourmandises
17. Nash 19

■ Church
🅵🅱 Footbridge
ⓘ Information

By car, Cork is easy to reach on Ireland's national road network; allow about four hours for the trip down the N8 from Dublin. If you're traveling from Shannon Airport or elsewhere in the West, take N20 from Limerick and allow about three hours for the trip. Cork is only about an hour from Killarney and points in County Kerry via N22. Parking is severely limited in Cork, and it is much to the city's discredit that more effort has not been made to restrict city traffic and build municipal garages on the outskirts. You'll find a handy garage near the tourist office on Grand Parade and several others on the eastern end of town, near the bus station and Lapp's Quay. Expect to pay about €1.50 an hour. Street parking is limited, and in most spots you are required to purchase a disc, available at newsstands; these usually are good for only three hours maximum at a cost of about €1.80 an hour. (Scratch off your arrival time, and display the disc on the dashboard.) There are also park-and-ride lots on major approaches to the city; fees of about €3 a day include transportation to and from the city center. If you're staying in Cork, take our advice and don't drive—stash the car and explore the city on foot.

Bus Éireann coaches arrive from throughout Ireland at the bus station on Parnell Place. Buses leave from Dublin for Cork about every 2 hours, and the trip takes 4 hours and 30 minutes; fares are low, about €10 one-way and €15 round-trip. For more information, call ☎ 021-450-8188 or visit **www.buseireann.ie.**

Cork Airport is one of the busiest in Ireland, second only to Dublin for traffic handled. You may fly in directly from London and other European cities on **Aer Lingus, British Airways,** or **Ryanair,** and service is expanding all the time. **Aer Arann** (☎ 081-821-0210; **www.aerarann.com**) flies from Dublin and Belfast to Cork, with fares starting at about €40.

Once you've arrived, you can get around Cork easily via local buses operated by Bus Éireann; the fare is €1.10, and service is frequent from 7 a.m. to 11 p.m., with limited service after that.

HOTELS IN CORK

Hayfield Manor ★★★½

QUALITY ★★★★	VALUE ★★½	FROM €189

Perrott Avenue, Cork City; ☎ 021-484-5900; fax 021-431-5940; sales@hayfieldmanor.ie; www.hayfieldmanor.ie

Location West of city center. **Amenities and services** 88 rooms; bar, beauty salon, business center, cafe, hair dryers, Internet access, minibars, restaurant, room service, satellite TV, sauna, spa, swimming pool, trouser press. **Elevator** Yes. **Parking** On property, free. **Price** Many rates include lavish breakfast; special rates and packages available. **Credit cards** AE, MC, V.

BUILT IN 1996 in the style of a grand Georgian country house, Hayfield Manor dishes up more old-world ambience than many of the genuine country-house hotels it imitates. The drawing room is filled with antiques, heavy paneling lines the hushed library, and a grand staircase sweeps up to the exceptionally large and traditionally furnished bedrooms. While you might feel self-conscious plopping down with a good mystery in any of the public spaces, the bedrooms are genuinely comfortable, with cushy wing chairs, thoughtful lighting, and fine bedding. The modern world intrudes in the form of in-room sound systems, flat-screen TVs, and stunning bathrooms with long, deep tubs, separate power showers, and marble vanities. An attractive leisure complex includes an indoor swimming pool, a sauna, a small gym, and spa facilities. A formal restaurant overlooks a small garden; casual meals are served in a woody bar and an airy conservatory cafe—these amenities are especially welcome, because Hayfield Manor is tucked away in a residential neighborhood about a mile away from shops and restaurants.

Hotel Isaacs Cork ★★★

QUALITY ★★★½	VALUE ★★★	€80–€150

48 MacCurtain Street, Cork; ☎ 021-450-0011; fax 021-450-6355; cork@isaacs.ie; www.isaacs.ie

Location City center. **Amenities and services** 47 rooms, 11 apartments; air-conditioning in some rooms, Wi-Fi, minibars in some rooms, nonsmoking rooms, room service, safes in some rooms. **Elevator** Yes. **Parking** On property, free. **Price** Includes full Irish breakfast. **Credit cards** AE, MC, V.

MUCH ABOUT THIS MEMBER of a small Irish chain is appealing and distinctive, including the location on an up-and-coming commercial street on the north bank of the river that's convenient to all the sights but just enough off the beaten track to give you the feel of a real Cork neighborhood. Shops and restaurants surround the hotel, and in the same 18th-century warehouse are two popular eateries, Greene's and the eponymous Isaacs, both good value and serving solid modern-Irish cuisine in relaxed surroundings. Beyond a cobbled court and garden (enlivened with a waterfall) are busy and welcoming lounges; the comfortable guest rooms upstairs are bright and airy, with wood floors and attractive pine furnishings, and some overlook a waterfall in the garden. Windows are double-glazed to minimize traffic noise from busy MacCurtain Street, and the shiny bathrooms have tubs with power showers.

Imperial Hotel ★★★★

QUALITY ★★★★	VALUE ★★★★	FROM €109

South Mall, Cork; ☎ 021-427-4040; fax 021-427-5375; www.flynnhotels.com

Location City center. **Amenities and services** 88 rooms; restaurant, cafe, bar, spa, room service, hair dryers, in-room tea and coffee facilities, Internet access, nonsmoking rooms, satellite TV, 24-hour desk/concierge, trouser press. **Elevator** Yes. **Parking** On property, €6. **Price** Breakfast about €10; special offers available on Internet. **Credit cards** AE, MC, V.

CORK'S OLDEST HOTEL, in operation since 1813, has just been refurbished, and once again the marble floors and crystal chandeliers are gleaming. It's easy to imagine such noted past guests as Sir Walter Scott and Charles Dickens walking the halls, or Irish revolutionary Michael Collins checking in the night before he was ambushed and killed. Guest rooms have been redone in a comfortably traditional style, with shiny bathrooms and Internet hookups, and the lobby is again one of Cork's favorite gathering spots.

Lancaster Lodge ★★★★

QUALITY ★★★★	VALUE ★★★★	€96–€125

Lancaster Quay, Cork; ☎ 021-425-1125; fax 021-425-1126; info@lancasterlodge.com; www.lancasterlodge.com

Location City center. **Amenities and services** 39 rooms; hair dryers, in-room tea and coffee facilities, Wi-Fi, nonsmoking rooms, safes, satellite TV, 24-hour desk-concierge, trouser press. **Elevator** Yes. **Parking** On property, free. **Price** Includes full Irish breakfast; special offers available on Internet. **Credit cards** AE, MC, V.

THE SURROUNDING CAR PARKS and office blocks give this modern building on the banks of a branch of the River Lee at the southern edge of the city center a forlorn feeling, but just inside the austere entryway are a handsome lounge and breakfast room with light-colored wood floors and striking contemporary furnishings. Guest rooms are likewise appealing: large and relaxing; decorated with care in soothing tones; and fitted out with sleek chairs and sofas, thoughtful lighting, amenities such as wireless broadband access and satellite TV, and spacious bathrooms with counter space and tub/shower combinations (two with Jacuzzis). The best rooms are in the front, facing the river and overlooking the city. Breakfast is traditionally Irish, with an array of cereals and fruits on the buffet, plus eggs and other hot dishes cooked to order. St. Patrick's Street and other places in the city center are within a five-minute walk, and some of Cork's best restaurants, including Fenns Quay (see page 217), are just outside the door. Stash the car in the ample car park and explore Cork on foot.

Lotamore House ★★★½

QUALITY ★★★★	VALUE ★★★½	€80–€130

Tivoli, Cork; ☎ 021-482-2344; fax 021-482-2219; lotamore@iol.ie; www.lotamorehouse.com

Location East of city center. **Amenities and services** 20 rooms; complimentary tea and coffee, hair dryers, honor bar, nonsmoking rooms, satellite TV, trouser press. **Elevator** No. **Parking** On property, free. **Price** Includes full Irish breakfast. **Credit cards** AE, MC, V.

GENERATIONS OF CORK BURGHERS lived in this Georgian mansion atop a grassy knoll on the banks of the River Lee, and although Cork's busy wharves and a highway now lie at the end of the long drive, Lotamore still has the air of a country house. The unspoiled interior has been refurbished with style, and in the lounges and guest rooms, deep-red hues and earth tones cover the walls, cushy old chairs are covered in handsome fabrics, and tables and sideboards are antique. Overstuffed couches surround the hearth in the drawing room, and guests help themselves to coffee, tea, or a drink from the honor bar. A grand staircase leads to large and rather posh bedrooms filled with handsome old armoires, deep reading chairs (a few more reading lamps would be a welcome addition), and good beds dressed with fine linens. Most rooms have nice views down the river to the Cork hills beyond, and several ground-floor rooms overlook the lawns and rhododendron gardens. Bathrooms are modern and have tub-and-shower units. Lotamore is about ten minutes away from the city center and can only be reached easily by car or taxi.

EXPLORING CORK

SURROUNDED BY TWO ARMS of the River Lee, Cork sometimes is called an Irish Venice. That is a bit of an exaggeration, but the quays and alleys leading to the river's arms do give Cork a maritime feel. It's a pleasure to walk through the small center of Cork at random, allowing yourself to get lost—which you inevitably will do, because the streets are poorly marked. Arm yourself with a map from the tourist office and keep your sights set on the steeple of the **Church of St. Anne Shandon,** a conspicuous landmark and handy navigation guide on the north side of the river.

A good place to begin is on the river at **St. Patrick's Bridge,** the city's most famous span. The enormous statue just along **Patrick Street** honors **Father Matthew,** a 19th-century leader of the Temperance Movement who's due some respect, as the fellow must have had a pretty hard time of things in a hard-drinking town like Cork. Patrick Street is Cork's busiest shopping street; rather than letting that take you inland, stick to the river and the quays where the city's commerce bustled until the early 20th century. A walk along **Lavitt's Quay** brings you to the **Opera House** and the **Crawford Municipal Art Gallery** (see page 215). A turn south onto Paul Street takes you into the **French Quarter,** settled by Huguenot refugees from France, and from there to the **Grand Parade.** This wide avenue, once a canal, is graced with two of the city's most revered landmarks: off the Grand Parade is an entrance to the **English Market** (see page 216), Cork's historic food emporium, and the lacy, spirelike **National Monument** at the south end honoring Irish patriots. If you cross the river at the monument and continue south, soon you'll find yourself beneath the hulk of **St. Finbarr's Cathedral,** dedicated to Cork's founding saint and appropriately elaborate, with piles of Gothic Revival stonework and a colorfully painted interior. The cathedral is open daily, 9 a.m. to 6 p.m.; admission is free.

A walk north across St. Patrick's Bridge takes you into the hilly **Shandon Quarter,** where **St. Mary's Dominican Church** faces the river from behind an imposing portico of thick Ionic columns. Just beyond the church, on John Redmond Street, is the **Butter Exchange,** a late-18th-century building that did a lively business grading butter in the days when that was the city's principal commodity, shipped from the Cork wharves to Australia and South America. The small **Butter Museum** chronicles the role of butter in Irish life since the Middle Ages, and the subject is much more intriguing than you might assume (☎ 021-430-0600; open March through October, daily, 10 a.m. to 5 p.m.; July through August, daily, 10 a.m. to 6 p.m.; €3.50 adults, €2.50 seniors and students, €1.50 children under 12). A fitting end to a walk through Cork is a climb up the tower of the **Church of St. Anne Shandon** (see next page) for an aerial survey of the city.

Tours of Cork

You'll get a glimpse into the history and architecture of Cork on the **guided walking tours** that start at 8 p.m., June through August, Monday through Friday, from the tourist office in Grand Parade. The cost is €8, and the tour ends with a pint at a local pub. For more information, check with the tourist office or call ☎ 021-488-5404. An easy way to get around Cork and see the sights is on **Cork Panoramic** buses. The open-top hop-on, hop-off vehicles circuit the major sights, allowing you to get on and off as you wish; this is an especially handy way to see outlying attractions such as **Cork City Gaol.** Buses operate April to October, daily; €12 adults, €10 seniors and students, €4 children; for information, call ☎ 021-430-9090. **Bus Éireann** offers a narrated Cork City tour in July and August for about €9; call ☎ 021-450-8188 for information.

ATTRACTIONS IN CORK

 Blarney Castle ★★

APPEAL BY AGE	PRESCHOOL ★★	GRADE SCHOOL ★★★★	TEENS ★★★★
YOUNG ADULTS ★★★		OVER 30 ★★★	SENIORS ★★★

Route R617, Blarney, about 8 kilometers (5 miles) northwest of Cork City center; ☎ **021-438-5252; www.blarneycastle.ie**

Type of attraction One of Ireland's most famous castles. **Admission** €10 adults, €8 seniors and students, €3.50 children ages 8–14, €23.50 families of up to 2 adults and 2 children. **Hours** May, Monday–Friday, 9 a.m.–6:30 p.m.; Sunday, 9:30 a.m.–5:30 p.m.; June–August, Monday–Friday, 9 a.m.–7 p.m.; Sunday, 9:30 a.m.–5:30 p.m.; September, Monday–Friday, 9 a.m.–6:30 p.m.; Sunday, 9:30 a.m.–5:30 p.m.; October–April, Monday–Friday, 9 a.m.–sundown; Sunday, 9:30 a.m.–sundown. **When to go** Avoid midday in summer, when busloads of visitors arrive. **Special comments** Kissing the stone requires a climb and some uncomfortable positioning; not suitable for visitors with limited mobility. **How much time to allow** 2 hours for the stone and grounds.

DESCRIPTION AND COMMENTS *Blarney* means, basically, nonsense, which you'll encounter a lot of in this ruin of the onetime stronghold of the McCarthy clan. When 16th-century owner Cormac McCarthy hesitated to turn the castle over to Elizabeth I, the English queen referred to his tactics as "blarney." Today a well-worn path leads past crumbling rooms and dark passageways and up a watchtower, where a blasé attendant will hold your legs as you dangle backward to kiss the most famous of Irish emblems, the Blarney Stone. The stone, formally known as the Stone of Eloquence, is allegedly half of an orb presented to McCarthy as a medal of honor for his valor in the Battle of Bannockburn in 1314; kissing it is said to impart the "gift of the gab," something Ireland doesn't need more of.

Essentially, this experience involves waiting (up to half an hour at busy times) to get into an uncomfortable and unflattering position and kiss a slobber-covered chunk of rock. A photographer catches you in the act and offers to sell you a print for €10. These shenanigans are fun for kids, but if you don't have any youngsters with you, skip the blarney. If you insist on engaging in another ritual of superstition, step into the Rock Close, an eerie grotto said to be haunted by ancient spirits and in which several rock outcrops resemble the face and hat of a witch and other such beings. Here, you make a wish, back down the steep and slippery Wishing Stairs to a little pool, and then retrace your steps backward—with your eyes closed the whole time, without stepping into the pool, and without breaking your neck on the steps. Do so successfully and your wish will come true.

TOURING TIPS Be sure to spend some time on the grounds.

kids Church of St. Anne Shandon ★★★½

APPEAL BY AGE	PRESCHOOL ★★★★	GRADE SCHOOL ★★★★	TEENS ★★★★
YOUNG ADULTS ★★★★		OVER 30 ★★★	SENIORS ★★½

Church Street; ☎ 021-450-5906; www.shandonbells.org

Type of attraction A historic and beloved church. **Admission** €3 adults, €2 seniors and students, €8 families of up to 2 adults and 2 children. **Hours** Easter–end of October, Monday–Saturday, 9:30 a.m.–5:30 p.m.; November–Easter, Monday–Saturday, 10 a.m.–3 p.m. **When to go** On a clear day to enjoy the view from the tower. **Special comments** With the tower climb, view, and bell ringing, St. Anne's is a big hit with kids. **How much time to allow** 1 hour.

DESCRIPTION AND COMMENTS Cork's most famous landmark stands on a hill on the north side of the River Lee. The pepper-pot steeple, topped with a salmon-shaped weather vane rising above a neighborhood across the river from the city center, is a handy point of reference as you navigate the alleys and twisting lanes of downtown Cork. This 18th-century structure is so integral to life in Cork that the local football and hurling teams take their colors from the limestone that covers two of the tower's four sides and the red sandstone that covers the other two sides. St. Anne's famous bells are commemorated in "The Bells of Shandon," a piece of sentimental fluff by early-19th-century bard Francis Mahony: "With deep affection and recollection, I often think of those Shandon Bells, whose sound so wild would, in the days of childhood, fling round my cradle their magic spells." The bells will sound wildly throughout your visit to Cork, as visitors are invited to become bell ringers and take a turn at playing a tune on the six-ton monsters. Once you've tried your hand, continue up the steep stairs to the top of the tower for a stunning view of Cork and the hills that surround the city. St. Anne's has yet another name, too. It is blasphemously but affectionately known as the four-faced liar, because until 1986 each of the clock faces on the church tower told a different time.

TOURING TIPS Some climbing is required to ring the bells and enjoy the view, so St. Anne's is not a good choice for visitors with limited mobility.

Cork City Gaol ★★★

APPEAL BY AGE	PRESCHOOL ★★	GRADE SCHOOL ★★★★	TEENS ★★★★
YOUNG ADULTS ★★★		OVER 30 ★★★	SENIORS ★★★

Convent Avenue, about 2 kilometers (1 mile) west of the city center;
☎ 021-430-5022; www.corkcitygaol.com

Type of attraction Former prison, now a museum. **Admission** €7 adults, €6 seniors and students, €4 children, €14 families of up to 2 adults and 3 children. **Hours** March–October, daily, 9:30 a.m.–6 p.m.; November–February, daily, 10 a.m.–5 p.m. **When to go** Anytime. **Special comments** Architecture buffs who otherwise may not be interested in this aspect of Irish history should note that the jail is an important example of early-19th-century public architecture. **How much time to allow** 2 hours.

DESCRIPTION AND COMMENTS Opened in 1824 as a model prison, this assemblage of towers and high walls is remarkably intact, and, despite the grim history of place and the icy chill that still prevails within the stone walls, it is a remarkable piece of architecture. In fact, it's so easy to get carried away with the Victorian beauty of the jail that you might forget the human misery once endured in the tiny cells—that is, if it weren't for the excellent audio tour (included in the admission price) that tells the stories of half a dozen inmates incarcerated here over the years. As you stand in the multistory elliptical compounds and peer into cells containing realistic dummies, you learn that most of the inmates were poor and on the brink of starvation, reduced to crimes such as stealing pieces of cloth, for which they received long terms of hard labor. Even the prison's skimpy gruel and flea-ridden mattresses were an improvement on life in the tenements of Cork. After closing in 1928, the prison stood empty for many years. In the 1950s, part of the compound became headquarters for Radio Éireann. A small museum traces the history of radio and displays a remarkable selection of the device.

TOURING TIPS The tour ends on a false note, with an over-the-top film that summarizes the prison's history, complete with trial scenes—the film doesn't add much to the experience, and you'll be more moved if you make an escape before it starts.

Crawford Municipal Art Gallery ★★★½

APPEAL BY AGE	PRESCHOOL ★	GRADE SCHOOL ★	TEENS ★★
YOUNG ADULTS ★★		OVER 30 ★★	SENIORS ★★★

Emmet Place, off Lavitt's Quay; ☎ 021-490-7855;
www.crawfordartgallery.com

Type of attraction An excellent small art gallery. **Admission** Free. **Hours** Monday–Saturday, 10 a.m.–5 p.m. **When to go** Anytime. **Special comments** The museum's cafe is a destination in itself; operated by the Allen family of Ballymaloe fame (see page 221), the cafe serves an excellent selection of fresh fish, lamb, and vegetarian dishes, with lunch entrees beginning at about €10. **How much time to allow** At least 1 hour.

DESCRIPTION AND COMMENTS One of Ireland's best collections of art fills the 18th-century brick customs house plus a modern extension, and it is all the more enjoyable to view because it is small enough not to overwhelm. A ground-floor gallery is filled with one of the museum's prizes, a collection of casts of Greek and Roman sculptures. This area usually is thronged with art students leaning over their drawing pads. A stroll through the galleries beyond, though, reveals the heart of the collection, a couple dozen or so canvases by 19th- and 20th-century Irish artists. Jack Yeats, brother of the poet W. B. Yeats, is well represented by works such as *Off the Donegal Coast* (1922); Sean Keating's *Men of the South* (1921) is a moving depiction in browns and grays of nationalists during Ireland's War of Independence. Earlier works include canvases by Cork's own James Barry (1741–1806).

TOURING TIPS Occasionally, much of the permanent collection is taken down to make room for special exhibitions; the Greek and Roman casts are almost always on view, as is a small selection of works by Yeats and other artists.

English Market ★★★★

APPEAL BY AGE	PRESCHOOL ★★	GRADE SCHOOL ★★	TEENS ★★
YOUNG ADULTS ★★	OVER 30 ★★★★		SENIORS ★★★★

Off the Grand Parade

Type of attraction A covered food market. **Admission** Free. **Hours** Monday–Saturday, 9 a.m.–6 p.m. **When to go** Morning, when the market is at its liveliest. **Special comments** This is an excellent place to forage for breakfast, especially the pastries from Cork Bakery Company and a cup of coffee from Iago. **How much time to allow** At least 1 hour.

DESCRIPTION AND COMMENTS Every city should have a market like this at its center. You haven't experienced real Cork life until you've taken a leisurely stroll through this vast covered hall dating back to 1881 (rebuilt after a fire in 1980). More than 140 stalls brim with Irish produce, fish, and meat, making it easy to see why Cork is one of Ireland's culinary capitals. Who sells the best of what is a matter of ongoing debate in Cork, but Iago consistently gets nods for Irish cheeses, and O'Reilly's is the place to stop for tripe (cow stomach) and *drisheen* (sausage made with pig's blood). The liveliest spectacle is the ongoing show in the fish aisles, where restaurateurs and nattily attired office workers alike pick over mussels, eels, and other denizens of the deep. Many of the stalls offer free samples, so come prepared to snack, and if you can't resist the hunger pangs, head upstairs to the Farmgate Café, where the kitchen is supplied by the market stalls and a table provides a bird's-eye view of the proceedings below.

TOURING TIPS Because the market is in the city center near the shops and city-center attractions of Patrick Street, consider nipping in more than once during your rounds.

RESTAURANTS IN CORK

Café Paradiso ★★★★

| VEGETARIAN | MODERATE/EXPENSIVE | QUALITY ★★★★ | VALUE ★★★ |

16 Lancaster Quay, Cork City; ☎ 021-427-7939

Reservations Recommended. **Entree range** €13–€25. **Payment** AE, MC, V. **Bar** Full service. **Disabled access** Dining room, yes; restrooms, no. **Hours** Tuesday–Saturday, noon–3 p.m. and 6:30–10:30 p.m.

MENU RECOMMENDATIONS Feta-and-pistachio couscous, roasted-aubergine casserole, red-onion risotto.

COMMENTS It seems only fair that Cork's reputation for fine food should extend to vegetarian, and this Irish temple of meatless cuisine does the city's reputation proud with wonderful preparations that use the freshest ingredients from the city's organic suppliers. The wood-floored room is a pleasant setting for some of Cork's most satisfying meals, accompanied by a glass or two from the excellent wine list and topped off with a selection of farmhouse cheeses.

Farmgate Café ★★★★

| IRISH | INEXPENSIVE/MODERATE | QUALITY ★★★★ | VALUE ★★★★½ |

English Market, Cork City; ☎ 021-427-8134

Reservations None. **Entree range** €8.50–€16. **Payment** MC, V. **Bar** Wine and beer. **Disabled access** Yes. **Hours** Monday–Saturday, 9 a.m.–5 p.m.

MENU RECOMMENDATIONS Lamb stew, fish chowder.

COMMENTS Fresh Irish fare gets no fresher than this: the wooden tables and chairs line a gallery overlooking the English Market, the stalls of which keep the kitchen in steady supply of produce, meat, fish, and cheese. These ingredients appear in some typical, elsewhere-hard-to-find Cork dishes, such as tripe and drisheen, as well as savory tarts and hearty soups. Berry crumbles and other desserts are memorable, too, as is the experience of savoring the buzz of the market from this welcoming perch.

Fenns Quay ★★★★

| CONTINENTAL | MODERATE/EXPENSIVE | QUALITY ★★★★ | VALUE ★★★★ |

5 Sheares Street, Cork City; ☎ 021-427-9527

Reservations Recommended. **Entree range** €16–€25; early dinner, before 7:30 p.m., €22.50 for 3 courses; dinner, €27.50 for 3 courses. **Payment** AE, MC, V. **Bar**

Full service. **Disabled access** Dining room, yes; restrooms, no. **Hours** Monday–Saturday, 10 a.m.–10 p.m.

MENU RECOMMENDATIONS Black pudding with potato pancake, seafood chowder, Irish lamb burger.

COMMENTS In this bright, welcoming space, white-brick walls are covered with splashes of contemporary art, and the kitchen sends out delicious food to keep patrons happy throughout the day. Freshly baked muffins appear at breakfast time; soup and sandwiches are available for quick lunches; and, most notably, innovative twists on Irish beef and lamb, fresh fish, hearty salads with farm cheeses, and pasta dishes made with fresh vegetables appear on the evening menu. The early-dinner menu is small but excellent.

Jacobs on the Mall   ★★★★½

| CONTINENTAL | MODERATE/EXPENSIVE | QUALITY ★★★★ | VALUE ★★★★ |

30A South Mall, Cork City; ☎ 021-425-1530

Reservations Recommended; required on weekends. **Entree range** €17–€29. **Payment** AE, D, MC, V. **Bar** Full service. **Disabled access** Yes. **Hours** Monday–Saturday, 12:30–2:30 p.m. and 6:30–10 p.m.

MENU RECOMMENDATIONS Seared tuna, breast of free-range duck, any daily preparation of fresh local fish.

COMMENTS Cork's most distinctive dining room, a vaulted contemporary space occupying a former Turkish bath, is also arguably the city's best restaurant, serving deceptively simple preparations of local produce, fish, and meat on a menu that changes daily. Asparagus is from nearby Kinsale, the fish from local waters, breads fresh from the kitchen ovens; even the simplest offerings, such as farmhouse cheeses with homemade biscuits, can be sublime. Service is relaxed but adept, and while the airy, light-filled space is quite appealing at lunch, you may want to return for a long evening in these soothing, sophisticated surroundings.

Jacques   ★★★★

| MODERN IRISH | MODERATE/EXPENSIVE | QUALITY ★★★★ | VALUE ★★★½ |

Phoenix Street, Cork City; ☎ 021-427-7387

Reservations Recommended. **Entree range** €19.90–€25.90; early dinner, before 7 p.m., 2 courses, €21.90. **Payment** D, MC, V. **Bar** Full service. **Disabled access** Yes. **Hours** Monday–Friday, 6 p.m.–10 p.m.

MENU RECOMMENDATIONS Warm salad of crispy chicken and watercress, free-range chicken stuffed with Parma ham.

COMMENTS Now serving food for a quarter of a century, sisters Jacqueline and Eithne Barry helped put Cork on the culinary map. They pride themselves on the close relationships established with local suppliers over the years, and these fresh ingredients are transformed into preparations that the Barrys refer to as "simple fresh Cork food," served with care but without fuss in subtly modern surroundings.

Les Gourmandises ★★★★

FRENCH/MODERN IRISH **EXPENSIVE** **QUALITY ★★★★** **VALUE ★★★**

17 Cook Street, Cork City; ☎ 021-425-1959

Reservations Recommended. **Entree range** €25.50–€28; €45 dinner, Tuesday–Thursday all evening, Friday–Saturday 6–7 p.m.; €65 tasting menu. **Payment** D, MC, V. **Bar** Full service. **Disabled access** Yes. **Hours** Tuesday–Saturday, 6–10 p.m.; Friday, noon–2 p.m.

MENU RECOMMENDATIONS Les Gourmandises tasting plate, hot and cold foie gras, duck leg confit with gingerbread.

COMMENTS Chefs-owners Pat and Soizic Kiely trained at top Michelin-starred restaurants in England and Dublin (including the latter city's acclaimed Patrick Guilbaud) before bringing their skills to Pat's native Cork in 2002. Their handsome cream-colored room, warmed by an open fire, is as comfy as a French bistro, as are such bistro classics as beef stews and roast duck. The friendly, low-key service is in perfect keeping with the atmosphere. Any meal here is memorable, but the tasting menu puts a real shine on an evening.

Nash 19 ★★★★

MODERN IRISH **INEXPENSIVE/MODERATE** **QUALITY ★★★★** **VALUE ★★★★½**

19 Princes Street, Cork City; ☎ 021-427-0880

Reservations Not necessary. **Entree range** €8.50–€11.50. **Payment** AE, MC, V. **Bar** Beer and wine. **Disabled access** Yes. **Hours** Monday–Friday, 7:30 a.m.–5 p.m.

MENU RECOMMENDATIONS Scones, soups, warm salads, berry crumbles.

COMMENTS The only complaint you're likely to have about this amiable, bustling city-center gathering spot is that it is not open into the evening hours. Instead, you'll have to settle for a breakfast of hot scones and free-range eggs or one of the casseroles or other sumptuous lunch dishes, all of which chef Claire Nash prepares with fresh ingredients from local suppliers. Daily choices are seen in an open-style pantry near the door; place your order, take a seat in the series of attractive small rooms, and the accommodating servers will bring your meal to you. Lunchtime lines can be long, but the food is well worth the wait.

ENTERTAINMENT AND NIGHTLIFE IN CORK

OFF LAVITT'S QUAY in the city center, the **Cork Opera House** is Cork's major venue for live entertainment, with a lively year-round schedule of opera, drama, and concerts; for information and tickets, call ☎ 021-427-0022 or visit **www.corkoperahouse.ie. Cork Arts Theatre,** on Carroll's Quay, is the city's acclaimed venue for new drama and promotes the work of emerging Irish playwrights; ☎ 021-450-5624; **www.corkartstheatre.com.** The domed **Firkin Crane Cultural Center,** part of the historic Cork Butter Exchange, is dedicated to promoting contemporary Irish dance and often hosts troupes from around Ireland and throughout the world; call ☎ 021-450-7487.

Everyman Palace is a beautifully restored Victorian entertainment hall on MacCurtain Street that stages plays and other performances; call ☎ 021-450-1673.

The heart of Cork nightlife is the city's lively pub scene. At the **Franciscan Well Brew Pub** (North Mall; ☎ 021-421-0130) you can enjoy the house's own brews (including Blarney Blonde and Rebel Red) and soak in the history of the surroundings—the brewery occupies the site of a 12th-century Franciscan monastery. **An Spailpin Fanac** (The Migrant Worker; Main Street; ☎ 021-427-7949) and **An Bodhrán** (42 Oliver Plunkett Street; ☎ 021-427-4544) are Cork's choice spots for live traditional music (a *bodhrán* is a Celtic drum). An Spailpin Fanac dates from 1779, which makes it Cork's oldest pub; the second oldest is the **Mutton Lane Inn** (3 Mutton Lane, off Patrick Street; ☎ 021-427-3471), where an old-world, dark-wood, heavy-beamed aura prevails.

SHOPPING IN CORK

CORK'S MAIN SHOPPING VENUE is **Patrick Street,** and setting the gold standard for the thoroughfare's many shops is **Brown Thomas,** a venerable Dublin-based department store at Number 18 (☎ 021-480-5555). **Paul's Lane,** which cuts a swath through the French Quarter between Patrick Street and the quays, houses a number of antiques shops, including **O'Regan's** (Number 4; ☎ 021-427-2902) and **Mills** (Number 3; ☎ 021-427-3528). The **Living Tradition** (40 MacCurtain Street; ☎ 021-450-2564) stocks a large selection of traditional music and instruments, and the place for books of Irish interest is **Mercier** (5 French Church Street; ☎ 021-427-5040); the shop is run by Mercier Press, Ireland's oldest independent publisher. Irish crafts are on offer at **Crafts of Ireland** (11 Winthrop Street; ☎ 021-427-5864), while the **Shandon Craft Centre** is a co-op where potters, weavers, and other artisans offer distinctive wares (in the Cork Butter Exchange on John Redmond Street; ☎ 021-430-0600). On the grounds of Blarney Castle, **Blarney Woollen Mills** (☎ 021-451-6111) takes advantage of the stone-kissing crowds with a huge store offering one-stop shopping for everything from hand-knit sweaters to fine crystal to key rings.

EXERCISE AND RECREATION IN CORK CITY

CORK IS SURROUNDED by golf courses. Among the top links are the **Cork Golf Club** (on Little Island, eight kilometers [five miles] east of town; ☎ 021-435-3451) and **Douglas Golf Club** (five kilometers [three miles] east in Douglas; ☎ 021-489-5297).

MIDLETON *and* EAST CORK

A PURVEYOR OF FINE IRISH WHISKEY, Jameson's **Old Midleton Distillery** has put the busy market town of **Midleton** on the tourist track. Even without this landmark, however, you would be pleased to find yourself here amid the green fields of rural County Cork, near a stunning seacoast and within easy reach of such places as **Cobh** and **Fota Island.**

Midleton is a good base from which to explore the countryside, coast, and even Cork City, and the town is surrounded by a number of excellent country-house hotels where you can enjoy rural Irish life in comfort.

PLANNING YOUR VISIT TO MIDLETON AND EAST CORK

HOUSED IN THE JAMESON DISTILLERY in the center of town, the **Midleton Tourist Office** provides information on where to stay, what to see and do, and where to dine in the surrounding region. For information, call ☎ 021-461-3702 or visit **www.corkkerry.ie.** The center is open May through September, daily, 9:30 a.m. to 5 p.m.

ARRIVING AND GETTING ORIENTED IN MIDLETON AND EAST CORK

IT'S DIFFICULT TO EXPLORE East Cork without a car. Midleton is within easy reach of Cork City, about 20 kilometers (12 miles) east via N25; the trip takes about 20 minutes. If you opt for public transportation, you're better off using Cork City as a base and traveling by bus or train to Midleton and other places in East Cork from there. **Bus Éireann** coaches travel between Cork City and Midleton about every half hour. One-way fare is about €3; for information, call ☎ 021-450-8188 or visit **www.buseireann.ie.**

HOTELS IN MIDLETON AND EAST CORK

 Ballymaloe House ★★★½

QUALITY ★★★★	VALUE ★★½	€175–€220

Shanagarry, Midleton, County Cork; ☎ 021-465-2531; fax 021-465-2021; res@ballymaloe.ie; www.ballymaloe.ie

Location 23 kilometers (14 miles) southeast of Cork. **Amenities and services** 33 rooms; croquet, gardens, 9-hole golf course, hair dryers, lounges, playground, swimming pool, tennis court, TV room (no in-room TVs). **Elevator** Yes. **Parking** On property, free. **Price** Includes full Irish breakfast; special offers available on the Internet; reduced rates for stays of 3 days and longer. **Credit cards** AE, D, MC.

THE 160-HECTARE (400-acre) estate of the Allen family may be the most famous country-house hotel in Ireland. The patina of fame washes over the place, and you might get the feeling that the old house is the center of the empire—which, actually, it is. Since the dining room opened in 1964, three generations of Allens have become world renowned as restaurateurs, instructors (at the nearby Ballymaloe Cooking School), and authors of books on cooking and entertaining (for sale in the hotel shop). Even so, the Allens remain very hospitable, and they have done a smart job with the guest rooms. Distinctively decorated yet comfortably simple, these occupy the original house, tastefully and seamlessly attached newer wings, and the old farmyard. Accommodations vary considerably in size, and not all are accessible by elevator, so discuss your needs when booking. Some of the nicest rooms are on the ground level, with small patios adjoining the lawns. Rooms in the farmyard are small but cozy, and a few of these are suites with conservatory-like sitting rooms. Ballymaloe offers special mid-week breaks and other cost-saving plans, usually including a meal or two in the acclaimed dining room, so call or visit the Web site to see what's available when you plan to stay.

Barnabrow Country House ★★★

QUALITY ★★★½	VALUE ★★	€90–€120

Cloyne, Midleton, County Cork; ☎ 021-465-2534; fax 021-465-2534; barnabrow@eircom.net; www.barnabrowhouse.ie

Location Countryside, between Cloyne and Ballycotton. **Amenities and services** 21 rooms; babysitting, cots, gardens, hair dryers, restaurant. **Elevator** No. **Parking** On property, free. **Price** Includes full Irish breakfast; children under age 12 stay for €25. **Credit cards** AE, MC, V.

LAMBS, PONIES, AND CHICKENS roam the grounds surrounding the imposing 17th-century farmhouse at the heart of this estate, where guests relax in the extensive gardens and soak in the rural atmosphere. The best rooms are the five in the main house; these are large and light, painted in soothing hues, floored with African teak, and furnished with a pleasing mix of traditional, contemporary, and African pieces; several of the large bathrooms are equipped with claw-footed soaking tubs. Other accommodations are in outbuildings grouped around the farmyard, and while smaller than those in the main house, these can accommodate families and are nicely appointed with casual, handsome furniture. Most rooms open directly to the outdoors, making them ideal for kids to come and go and wander the grounds. Guests enjoy a large breakfast served at a communal table in the main house, as well as excellent lunches and dinners made with local game, fish, and produce grown on the farm, served in a beamed dining room.

Glenview House ★★★★★

QUALITY ★★★★	VALUE ★★★★	€95–€130

Midleton, County Cork; ☎ 021-463-4680; fax 021-463-4680; info@glenviewmidleton.com; www.glenviewmidleton.com

Location 3 miles west of Midleton, off Fermoy Road. **Amenities and services** 4 rooms and 2 apartments; dinner sometimes available upon request; gardens, honor bar, hair dryers, in-room tea and coffee facilities, lounge; guest rooms available March–September, apartments available year-round. **Elevator** No. **Parking** On property, free. **Price** Includes full Irish breakfast; weekly rates for apartments. **Credit cards** AE, MC, V.

KEN AND BETH SHERRARD set the gold standard for a stay in an Irish country house. This hospitable, well-traveled couple are unobtrusively on hand to share advice on exploring the region, and they graciously ensure comfort during your stay in the house and grounds they have lovingly restored over the past 40 years. In 1965, Ken ingeniously salvaged the contents of a row of Georgian town houses on Fitzpatrick Street in Dublin that were slated for demolition, and many of the mantelpieces, floors, cornices, and other architectural details now grace Glenview. Guests relax in the handsome drawing room, where a fire blazes in colder months, and upstairs are three commodious and thoughtfully appointed guest rooms overlooking the rolling countryside. One room on the ground floor is equipped for travelers with disabilities. The coach house has been converted to two comfortable apartments, one with two bedrooms and another with one bedroom; both have pleasant sitting rooms and full kitchens, one of which is designed to be used by guests in wheelchairs. An Irish breakfast is served at the huge family table and includes eggs from Beth's hens as well as fresh fruit and home-baked breads. Beth also prepares exquisite dinners on request.

EXPLORING EAST CORK

TO THE EAST OF CORK, rich farmlands roll down to the sea. The coast is lined with sandy beaches and still-thriving fishing ports such as **Ballycotton, Shanagarry,** and **Youghal.** Midleton and the surrounding countryside are also convenient to **Fota Island** and **Cobh.** You may want to spend a full day exploring the region east of Midleton, and another in Fota and Cobh. From Midleton, Route R629 leads south across farmlands to Shanagarry and Ballycotton, and from there you can follow the coast north and east on R633 to Youghal, a busy port town of which Sir Walter Raleigh was once mayor. To reach Fota and Cobh, simply follow N25 back toward Cork for about ten kilometers (six miles) and take the well-marked exit that leads you first to Fota Island then around the northern shores of Cork Harbour to Cobh.

ATTRACTIONS IN MIDLETON AND EAST CORK

Fota House ★★★★

APPEAL BY AGE			
PRESCHOOL ★★	GRADE SCHOOL ★★		TEENS ★★★
YOUNG ADULTS ★★	OVER 30 ★★★★		SENIORS ★★★★

Fota Island, about 5 kilometers (3 miles) west of Midleton; follow N25 west toward Cork City and take the well-marked exit to Fota Island; if you are driving from Cork, follow N25 east and take the same exit; trains run from Cork to Fota Island and on to Cobh; contact Irish Rail, ☎ 1850-366-222 or 01-836-6222, or visit www.irishrail.ie; Fota House: ☎ 021-481-5543; www.fotahouse.com

Type of attraction Historic home and grounds. **Admission** €5.50 adults, €4.50 seniors and students, €2.20 children, €12.50 families of up to 2 adults and 3 children. **Hours** April–September, Monday–Saturday, 10 a.m.–5 p.m.; Sunday, 11 a.m.–5 p.m.; October–March, Monday–Saturday, 10 a.m.–4 p.m.; Sunday,

11 a.m.–4 p.m. **When to go** In good weather, if possible, to enjoy the grounds. **Special comments** The house is sparsely furnished, which may disappoint some visitors. **How much time to allow** 2 hours to see the house, garden, and arboretum.

DESCRIPTION AND COMMENTS The Smith-Barry clan traces its roots to the 12th-century Anglo-Saxon invasion of Ireland, so they had 900 years in which to amass their vast lands, which at one time encompassed much of the eastern part of County Cork. At the center of these holdings was Fota Island, where the family built a house and planted gardens and an arboretum. The house and grounds had fallen into disrepair by the end of the 20th century, but ongoing restorations have made Fota a show-case that you should go out of your way to visit.

The present house was built in the Regency style in the 1820s, and the 70 rooms (only those on the ground floor can be visited) are an impressive assemblage of columns, friezes, and plasterwork. After tour-ing castles and ornate manor houses, you'll appreciate Fota's clean lines and classical proportions. Some visitors may be disappointed in the sparse furnishings, as much of the family collection was sold off over the years to settle debts. Then again, you may find the absence of fur-niture an asset because it allows the architectural detailing to take center stage. The servants' wing shows off life on the other side of the house. An octagonal larder is equipped with a massive carousel for hanging game and fowl; rows of bells summoned staff to different rooms of the house; a massive charcoal stove and shelves stocked with copper pots were essential parts of everyday life in a great house.

The walled garden is beautiful, but the arboretum is the standout here. The family commissioned plant-collecting expeditions to the far corners of the world, and trees and plants from China, Japan, and South America continue to thrive at Fota. One tall specimen may look familiar to visitors from the western United States—it's a sequoia, one of the first to be planted in Europe, brought back from California in the early 19th century.

TOURING TIPS Videos in each room of the house tell the stories of residents and servants and provide a wealth of information on architecture and period tastes; take the time to view these sophisticated viewing aids. A pleasant cafe serves light meals and snacks.

Fota Wildlife Park ★★★

APPEAL BY AGE	PRESCHOOL ★★★★	GRADE SCHOOL ★★★★	TEENS ★★★★
YOUNG ADULTS ★★★★		OVER 30 ★★★	SENIORS ★★★

Fota Island, about 5 kilometers (3 miles) west of Midleton; follow N25 toward Cork City and take the well-marked exit to Fota Island; if you are driving from Cork, follow N25 east and take the same exit; trains run from Cork to Fota Island and on to Cobh; contact Irish Rail, ☎ 1850-366-222 or 01-836-6222, or visit www.irishrail.ie; park: ☎ 021-481-2744; www.fotawildlife.ie

Type of attraction Zoo. **Admission** €13 adults; €8.50 seniors, students, children under age 16; free for children under age 2; €54 families of up to 2 adults and 4 children. **Hours** Monday–Saturday, 10 a.m.–3:30 p.m. (last admission; gates are locked at 4:30 p.m.); Sunday, 11 a.m.–3:30 p.m. **When to go** In good weather. **Special comments** A visit involves a walk of about 2 kilometers (1.2 miles) along a well-marked route; wheelchairs are available. An open-air tour train is €1 to ride from the entrance to the park's far end, or €2 round-trip. **How much time to allow** About 2 hours.

DESCRIPTION AND COMMENTS The deer and the antelope really do roam free on these 70 acres, along with flamingos, giraffes, and 90 other species of creatures exotic to Ireland. Human admirers watch their antics from a path that for the most part is separated from the grazing grounds only by low electronic fences. Fota is not as spectacular as world-renowned zoos in San Diego and some other North American cities, but it does an admirable job of showing off its inhabitants in natural surroundings. In the past 20 years, the park also has done a much-lauded job of breeding endangered species. The cheetahs (the only denizens confined to an enclosure) now number in the hundreds, and most were born here; Fota also has helped rescue an Irish native, the white-tailed sea eagle, from the brink of extinction.

TOURING TIPS If you want to extend a day in the fresh air, combine a trip to the wildlife park with a visit to the Fota House gardens and arboretum.

 Old Midleton Distillery ★★½

APPEAL BY AGE	PRESCHOOL ★★	GRADE SCHOOL ★★	TEENS ★★
YOUNG ADULTS ★★	OVER 30 ★★		SENIORS ★★

Off Main Street, Midleton; ☎ 021-461-3594; www.whiskeytours.ie

Type of attraction Historic whiskey distillery. **Admission** €12.50 adults, €9 seniors and students, €6 children under age 18, €25 families of up to 2 adults and 2 children. **Hours** March–October, daily, 10 a.m.–5 p.m.; November–February, daily, tours at 11:30 a.m., 1 p.m., 2:30 p.m., and 4 p.m. **When to go** Anytime. **Special comments** Much of this tour is conducted outdoors, so dress warmly and bring rain gear as needed. **How much time to allow** Tour and tasting take about 1½ hours.

DESCRIPTION AND COMMENTS Irish distillers not only make good whiskey but also run a slick business in whisking visitors through the country's three major distilleries: the one here, the Jameson Distillery in Dublin, and the Bushmills Distillery to the north in County Antrim are among Ireland's most popular attractions. The Midleton operation traces its roots to 1825, when James Murphy converted a woolen mill on the banks of the Dungourney River into a distillery that operated until 1975; a new plant adjoins the site. A slick introductory video gives visitors the lowdown on the distillery's history as well as the process of making Irish whiskey, and it also reveals tidbits such as how Paddy and Powers, other mainstays of an Irish pub, joined the Jameson family.

unofficial **TIP**
If you want to have a few extra "drops of the dew," volunteer for the taste test. You may well join many other aficionados in opining that Jameson's is one of the best beverages ever invented.

Another bit of knowledge you'll gain is that *uisce beatha,* Irish for "whiskey," means "river of life." A guided tour of the historic premises shows off the world's largest pot still and explains that Jameson is smooth as silk because it's distilled three times, whereas Scotch whisky (spelled without the *e*) is distilled only twice. You don't see the actual distilling process, which transpires in the modern plant. You do, however, dip into the river of life at a free tasting at the end of the tour, when you can also stock up on premium whiskeys or key chains shaped like whiskey bottles.

TOURING TIPS If you're traveling to Northern Ireland, save your distillery tour until you get to Old Bushmills on the Antrim Coast (see page 417), where you can see distilling and bottling in process—far more interesting than looking at old vats.

RESTAURANTS IN MIDLETON AND EAST CORK

Ballymaloe House ★★★★

MODERN IRISH	EXPENSIVE	QUALITY ★★★★	VALUE ★★★½

Shanagarry, Midleton, County Cork; ☎ 021-427-7387

Reservations Recommended. **Entree range** Lunch, €40; dinner, €70. **Payment** D, MC, V. **Bar** Full service. **Disabled access** Yes. **Hours** Seating times are Monday–Saturday, 1 p.m. and 7–9:30 p.m.; Sunday, 1 p.m. and buffet dinner, 7:30–8:30 p.m.

MENU RECOMMENDATIONS Any fish or seafood from nearby Ballycotton, fresh vegetables and greens from the farm gardens, free-range pork and lamb, farmhouse cheeses.

COMMENTS Ballymaloe, in the capable hands of the Allen family of culinary stars, has a well-deserved reputation for turning the freshest ingredients into masterpieces of modern Irish cuisine and serving them in perfect country-house surroundings. Just about everything on the exquisite menu is from the farm and local suppliers, and these ingredients emerge from the kitchen of chef Rory O'Connell in deftly prepared, simple dishes. Even the potatoes accompanying the roasts are memorable. Service is flawless but not fussy, and the intimate dining rooms are enlivened with reproductions of the Allen family's collection of paintings by Jack Yeats (many of the originals are in the National Gallery in Dublin). Meals can begin and end with drinks in one of the lounges or the conservatory, or maybe a walk in the well-tended gardens.

Farmgate Restaurant and Country Store ★★★★

IRISH	MODERATE	QUALITY ★★★★	VALUE ★★★★★

Coolbawn, Midleton, County Cork; ☎ 021-463-1878

Reservations Recommended for dinner. **Entree range** €12–€25. **Payment** AE,

MC, V. **Bar** Full service. **Disabled access** Yes. **Hours** Monday–Saturday, 9 a.m.–5 p.m.; Thursday–Saturday, 6:45–9:30 p.m.

MENU RECOMMENDATIONS Cheeses, baked goods, Irish stew.

COMMENTS The displays of fresh produce, cheeses, and baked goods in the shop at the front of this popular spot are a good omen of what to expect. Like the outlet in the English Market in Cork City, Farmgate has put Midleton on the culinary map for its fresh-as-can-be, simple-yet-superb renditions of soups and salads, as well as stews and other Irish classics. In fact, you may want to make the effort to come to Farmgate on one of the three evenings dinner is served, because the menu then expands impressively and often includes memorably fresh fish.

O'Donovan's ★★★★

MODERN IRISH	MODERATE	QUALITY ★★★★	VALUE ★★★★

58 Main Street, Midleton, across from Old Midleton Distillery;
☎ **021-463-1255**

Reservations Recommended. **Entree range** €17–€26; €25 2-course early dinner (6–7 p.m.). **Payment** AE, MC, V. **Bar** Full service. **Disabled access** Yes. **Hours** Monday–Saturday, 6–9:30 p.m.

MENU RECOMMENDATIONS Warm salad of lamb kidneys and Ballycotton crab salad.

COMMENTS This former pub remains one of Midleton's most popular gathering spots, with Pat O'Donovan keeping a close eye on the low-key dining room to make sure his guests are content. The menu relies heavily on fresh seafood just off the boats in nearby Ballycotton, as well as produce and meats from Pat's suppliers throughout East Cork.

Around MIDLETON *and* EAST CORK

COBH

WHAT NOW SEEMS LIKE A PLEASANT seaside town of Georgian and Regency terrace-style houses was once Ireland's busiest port. With an excellent position at the end of Great Island in Cork Harbour, Cobh (pronounced "cove," and known as Queenstown for a while under British rule) was a naval base in the Napoleonic Wars. It also served as the point of embarkation for convicts transported to Australia and emigrants sailing for America, as well as the last port of call for the *Sirius* (the first ship to steam across the Atlantic) in 1838 and for the *Titanic* on her first and only voyage in 1912. Survivors from the *Lusitania*, which was torpedoed by a German boat off nearby Kinsale Head in 1915, were brought to Cobh.

Cobh wears this mantle of history well and shows it off in its excellent **Heritage Centre.** The waterfront is littered with a few touching monuments and memorials, including those to the victims of the

unofficial **TIP**

A good way to see Cobh is on Michael Martin's **Titanic Trail tours.** These lively and informative 60- to 70-minute-long walks take in former steamship offices, popular gathering spots for passengers, the quays, and other land- marks. Tours begin at the Commodore Hotel: April– May and September, daily, 11 a.m.; June–August, daily, 11 a.m. and 2 p.m.; October–March, varying times. Cost is €9.50 for adults, €4.75 for children under 12. For more infor- mation, call ☎ 021- 481-5211 or visit **www .titanic-trail.com.**

Lusitania and *Titanic*. Most moving, though, is the statue of Annie Moore and her siblings, who sailed from Cobh in 1891; on January 1, 1892, Annie became the first immigrant to pass through New York's Ellis Island. On a hill behind the waterfront looms massive **St. Colman's Cathedral,** completed in 1915 and topped with a graceful **spire.** The church is open daily from 8 a.m. to 6 p.m., but the best reward of a walk to the entrance is the fine view over the harbor.

Arriving and Getting Oriented in Cobh

Cobh is about 20 kilometers (12 miles) west of Midleton and the same distance east of Cork, and easily visited on a day trip from either. If you are driving from Midleton or Cork, follow the well-marked exit off N25 for Cobh–Great Island. An easy way to reach Cobh from Cork is by rail; the trip takes 25 minutes, affording excellent views of the coast, and ends next to the *Queenstown Story* exhibit. Trains run about every half hour to hour throughout the day, and the round-trip fare is about €6. For more information, call Irish Rail, ☎ 1850-366- 222 or 01 836-6222, or visit **www.irishrail.ie.**

Attraction in Cobh

 Cobh, the Queenstown Story ★★★½

APPEAL BY AGE	PRESCHOOL ★★	GRADE SCHOOL ★★★	TEENS ★★★
YOUNG ADULTS ★★		OVER 30 ★★★½	SENIORS ★★★½

Cobh Heritage Centre, on waterfront in old train station;
☎ **021-481-3591; www.cobhheritage.com**

Type of attraction Exhibit tracing Cobh's dramatic maritime history. **Admission** €7.10 adults, €6 seniors and students, €4 children, €20 families of up to 2 adults and 4 children. **Hours** May–October, daily, 10 a.m.–6 p.m.; November–April, daily, 10 a.m.–5 p.m. (closed Christmas week). **When to go** Weekdays, if possible; the exhibit can be crowded on weekends. **Special comments** The exhibits are informative, but a walk around the town gives more of a sense of place; try to join one of the Titanic Trail tours (see Unofficial Tip above), and don't miss the *Titanic* and *Lusitania* memorials or the emigrants' statue on the waterfront. **How much time to allow** 2 hours.

DESCRIPTION AND COMMENTS Cobh's maritime past is remembered in an extensive exhibit that is quite engaging, not only because it's so well done, but also because Cobh's history is so colorful. The town once was Ireland's major emigration port; millions embarked from here between 1750 and the mid–20th century. Not all went willingly, as Cobh Harbour was filled with "coffin ships" used to transport prisoners to Australia, so called because of the hideous death rates during the long crossing. The Famine of 1844–48 brought millions of eager emigrants desperate to flee starvation and start a new life in the New World. Extensive exhibits, most with lavish audiovisual components, trace conditions in Ireland and life aboard the outgoing ships. Cobh was also the first and last European port of call for transatlantic liners, and other exhibits explore two momentous events in this history. The *Titanic* called here in 1912, just days before hitting an iceberg and sinking, and the *Lusitania* was torpedoed off nearby Kinsale Head by the Germans in 1915, with a loss of 1,198 lives; the attack catapulted the United States into World War I. Survivors were brought to Cobh, and many of the dead are buried in the town cemetery. Other exhibits show off advertising posters and other memorabilia recalling the glory days of ocean liners.

TOURING TIPS If you're of Irish heritage, chances are your ancestors shipped out of Cobh. You can trace your roots at the adjacent genealogy search center, where the staff will lend a hand; the fee for a genealogical profile is €30. The Cobh Heritage Centre also has a gift shop and a good cafe.

KINSALE

SMALL AND UNDENIABLY CHARMING, Kinsale presents visitors with a fascinating history, a beautiful harbor, and excellent restaurants and hotels. The harbor has drawn everyone from Stone Age tribes to British troops seeking an Irish stronghold against invaders to modern-day yachting enthusiasts. Kinsale will easily entertain you for two days, and it is also a handy base from which to visit Cork, Cobh, Fota Island, and other places in County Cork.

PLANNING YOUR VISIT TO KINSALE

FOR INFORMATION ON WHERE TO STAY, what to see and do, and where to dine in Kinsale and the surrounding region, contact the **Kinsale Tourist Office** (Pier Road, ☎ 021-477-2234, **www.cork kerry.ie**, or **www.kinsale.ie**). The center is open March through June, Monday through Saturday, 9:30 a.m. to 5:30 p.m.; July through August, Monday through Saturday, 9 a.m. to 7 p.m.; Sunday, 10 a.m. to 7 p.m.; March to June, Monday through Saturday, 9:30 a.m. to 5:30 p.m.; December through January, limited hours, often weekends only.

unofficial **TIP**
As soon as you arrive, stash your car in the large lot near the harbor next to the tourist-information office (about €1.80 per hour, €10 per day, or €17 overnight), or find a spot on the street (about €0.50 per hour, sometimes with a two-hour minimum; pay at one of the self-service pay stations and display the ticket in the car window). Fortunately, many Kinsale accommodations provide free parking.

Special Events in Kinsale

Kinsale's first big event of the year is a **St. Patrick's Day Parade** on March 17. In late April, the town hosts the **Heineken Kinsale Sevens by the Sea,** one of Europe's largest rugby meets, drawing 80 teams from ten countries; for information and tickets, call ☎ 021-477-2783 or visit **www.kinsalesevens.com.** In early October, the **Kinsale International Festival of Fine Food** offers tastings, special meals, demonstrations, and other events that promote Kinsale as the "Gourmet Capital of Ireland"; for information, call ☎ 021-477-9900. **Kinsale's Jazz and Blues Festival** in late October coincides with the Guinness Cork Jazz Festival; for information, call ☎ 021-477-2135.

ARRIVING AND GETTING ORIENTED IN KINSALE

KINSALE IS 30 KILOMETERS (18 miles) south of Cork; the most direct route by car is on R611. Driving in the town's narrow lanes can be difficult during the busy summer season. If you're traveling between Kinsale and Cobh, the most scenic route takes you via R600, R613, and R610, with a trip across an inlet of Cork Harbour on a small ferry; the fare is €3.50 per car.

Bus Éireann coaches from Cork run about every hour and arrive at the Esso Station on Pier Road near the tourist office. The fare is about €5 one-way or €7 round-trip. For more information, call ☎ 021-450-8188 or visit **www.buseireann.ie.**

Kinsale has no public transportation, but most sights, with the exception of **Charles Fort** (see page 233), are within easy walking distance in the town center; for a taxi, call **Kinsale Cabs** at ☎ 021-477-2642.

HOTELS IN KINSALE

Chart House ★★★★

QUALITY ★★★★	VALUE ★★★	€50–€120

Denis Quay, Kinsale, County Cork; ☎ **021-477-4586; fax 021-477-7907; charthouse@eircom.net; www.charthouse-kinsale.com**

Location City center. **Amenities and services** 4 rooms; hair dryers, Internet connections, irons, satellite TV, sauna, tea and coffee, trouser press. **Elevator** No. **Parking** On street, free. **Price** Includes full Irish breakfast. **Credit cards** AE, MC, V.

MARY AND BILLY O'CONNOR have turned their 200-year-old house, the former home of a sea captain and just steps from the harbor, into Kinsale's most comfortable and luxurious bed-and-breakfast. The four bedrooms, filled with majestic old bedsteads and other fine antiques, are well appointed with modern amenities such as deep whirlpool soaking tubs and power showers. Two of the upstairs rooms are especially spacious and have sitting areas. A snug little single on the ground floor is a great value given that occupants can easily spread out to the charming living room, where a fire glows in colder months and Billy and Mary serve tea and coffee. The couple also serve an excellent breakfast at a highly polished antique table in an elegant dining room.

Friar's Lodge   ★★★

QUALITY ★★★	VALUE ★★★★½	€80–€150

Friar Street, Kinsale, County Cork; ☎ 021-477-7384; fax 021-477-4363; mtierney@indigo.ie; www.friars-lodge.com

Location City center. **Amenities and services** 18 rooms; 3 self-catering apartments also available; DVD players, hair dryers, in-room tea and coffee facilities, Internet connections, irons, laundry service, pillow menus, satellite TV, turndown service. **Elevator** Yes. **Parking** On property, free. **Price** Includes full Irish breakfast; off-season rates and Internet specials sometimes available. **Credit cards** AE, MC, V.

WHEN MAUREEN TIERNEY, a longtime veteran of the hospitality industry and a traveler herself, built her guesthouse a few years ago, she had strong ideas about the sorts of amenities she preferred. Her rooms may not be as atmospheric as those at some of the neighboring inns, but they are extremely large; well furnished in traditional, comfortable style; and loaded with extras including DVD players (films are available at the front desk and at a shop around the corner), turndown service, and even a choice of down or synthetic pillows (for allergy sufferers). Complimentary sherry is on hand in the cozy lounge in the evenings, and a full Irish breakfast is served in an attractive dining room.

Old Bank   ★★★½

QUALITY ★★★	VALUE ★★½	FROM €200

Pearse Street, Kinsale, County Cork; ☎ 021-477-4075; fax 021-477-4296; oldbank@indigo.ie; www.oldbankhousekinsale.com

Location City center. **Amenities and services** 17 rooms; golfer friendly (information on courses, tee times, and more); limited room service, smoke-free accommodations. **Elevator** Yes. **Parking** On property, free. **Price** Includes full Irish breakfast; special offers and off-season rates sometimes available. **Credit cards** AE, MC, V.

MICHAEL AND MARIE RIESE have created a stylish little inn that commands the best spot in Kinsale: facing the harbor at the end of the charming main street. A mix of antiques and fine fabrics adds a touch of luxury to the high-ceilinged guest rooms; beds can be configured as singles or zipped together as kings, and the well-designed bathrooms have tub-and-shower combinations. Nice touches, such as window seats from which to watch the boats and a well-appointed drawing room with an open fire, encourage you to settle in and relax. To get the most out of a stay, request a room at the front of the house (for the best views). If you're up for a splurge, ask for the postmaster's suite—a capacious room with a sitting area and fireplace—or for the sumptuous Collection Suite. Michael is a master chef and prides himself on his elaborate breakfasts, which are served in a stylish dining room.

Old Presbytery ★★★★

QUALITY ★★★★½	VALUE ★★★★	€110–€170

**43 Cork Street, Kinsale, County Cork (closed December 1–February 14);
☎ 021-477-2027; fax 021-477-2166; info@oldpres.com;
www.oldpres.com**

Location City center. **Amenities and services** 6 rooms; 3 self-catering apartments also available; hair dryers, in-room tea and coffee facilities. **Elevator** No. **Parking** On property, free. **Price** Includes full Irish breakfast. **Credit cards** AE, MC, V.

KINSALE'S MOST ATMOSPHERIC accommodations are at the top of the old town in this fine old house, where an alluring warren of alcoves and staircases leads to six attractive and comfortable guest rooms. Phillip and Noreen McEvoy have decorated each tasteful room differently, with a penchant for plain Irish pine antiques (they opt for a more ornate look in the Victorian lounge). Several rooms have balconies, and number six is especially appealing with its glassed-in sitting room and terrace; a penthouse suite is on two levels, with a rooftop bedroom reached via a winding staircase. Phillip is a chef, and his breakfast feasts of smoked and fresh fish, crepes, and fresh pastries provide a memorable start to a day. None of the rooms in the main house are suitable for guests who can't manage stairs, and all guests would be well advised to leave heavy luggage in the car. Easier to reach are the three self-catering apartments in an adjoining house, reached from the rear car park. All of these have two bedrooms and two bathrooms, as well as large sitting rooms with gas fires and well-equipped kitchenettes; they are available for several days or longer periods.

Trident ★★★

QUALITY ★★★	VALUE ★★½	€110–€190

**World's End, Kinsale, County Cork; ☎ 021-477-9300; fax 021-477-4173;
info@tridenthotel.com; www.tridenthotel.com**

Location City center. **Amenities and services** 75 rooms; bar, restaurant, pub, gym, sauna, steam room, whirlpool, hair dryers, in-room tea and coffee facilities, Internet connections, satellite TV. **Elevator** Yes. **Parking** On property, free. **Price** Includes full Irish breakfast; off-season rates and package specials sometimes available. **Credit cards** AE, MC, V.

KINSALE HAS SO MANY SMALL, cozy inns that it seems odd to settle for a large and rather anonymous hotel such as this. That may be the point, though—the large, sleekly appointed rooms are like those in an upscale business hotel and offer comfort and few surprises, with the exception of the best water views to be had from any Kinsale hotel. When booking, request a room in the newer wing closest to the harbor, particularly one of the suites hanging directly over the water—two of these have large terraces. While the long hallways are a bit dispiriting, the Savannah Restaurant is airy, provides refreshing water views, and serves excellent local seafood. The Wharf Tavern, all dark wood and stone, serves excellent pub grub.

EXPLORING KINSALE

KINSALE'S MEDIEVAL LANES climb from the harbor toward **Compass Hill,** and the well-preserved streets are endowed with remnants of the town's long past. The tallest structure in Kinsale is the steeple of **St. Multose Church.** The Dutch-style **Old Courthouse,** at the far end of Church Place, was built in the 17th century. It enjoyed the spotlight in 1915, when officials from around the world gathered in the courtroom for the inquest into the sinking of the *Lusitania* by a German torpedo boat off Kinsale Head. That tragedy and other episodes in Kinsale history are evoked in the small **Regional Museum,** open April through September, daily, 10 a.m. to 6 p.m., and October through March, Monday through Friday, 11 a.m. to 1 p.m. and 3 to 5 p.m.; €2.50 adults, €1.50 seniors and students, free for children under 18; for more information, call ☎ 021-477-2044. **Desmond Castle,** around the corner on Cork Street, houses the **International Museum of Wine**—not as much of a stretch as it may seem in vineyard-deprived Ireland. As you'll learn, Irish emigrants helped establish the wine trade around the world. More interesting are the modest exhibits honoring other events in the building's past: The Spanish quartered here during the thwarted Spanish-Irish attempt to oust the British in the Battle of Kinsale in 1601; the British imprisoned American sailors here during the American Revolution and French soldiers during the Napoleonic Wars; and starving farmers took refuge here during the Famine, when the building served as a workhouse. The castle is open mid-April through mid-June, Tuesday through Sunday, 10 a.m. to 6 p.m.; mid-June through October, daily, 10 a.m. to 6 p.m.; €2.75 adults, €2 seniors and students, €1.25 children, €7 families; for more information, call ☎ 021-477-4855.

ATTRACTION IN KINSALE

Charles Fort ★★★★

APPEAL BY AGE	PRESCHOOL ★★★	GRADE SCHOOL ★★★★	TEENS ★★★★
YOUNG ADULTS ★★★★		OVER 30 ★★★★	SENIORS ★★★★

Summercove; on the harbor, about 3 kilometers (2 miles) south of Kinsale; ☎ 021-477-2263

Type of attraction Historic fort overlooking Kinsale Harbour. **Admission** €3.70 adults, €2.60 seniors, €1.30 children under age 12, €8.25 families of 2 adults and up to 2 children. **Hours** Mid-March–October, daily, 10 a.m.–6 p.m.; November–mid-March, daily, 10 a.m.–5 p.m. **When to go** In good weather. **Special comments** Even if you're not a military-history buff, this place is fascinating, and the views over the harbor and headlands from the ramparts are worth the price of admission alone. **How much time to allow** 2 hours (1 hour for guided tour, 1 hour to wander on your own).

DESCRIPTION AND COMMENTS The British began work on this mighty star-shaped bastion overlooking Kinsale Harbour in 1677, still feeling vulnerable after British forces had successfully thwarted a joint invasion of Irish and Spanish forces in the Battle of Kinsale in 1601. Consider the fort's strategic position at the entrance to the harbor to understand its military importance—the extent and thickness of the walls seem to make it impregnable. Ironically, it was attacked only once, and despite its mighty defenses, the fort failed the test and was taken. You can walk the ramparts and wander through the fort on your own, but be sure to take one of the frequent tours included with the admission price. The resident historians are gold mines of information, and you'll get an hour-long earful, all of it illuminating and most of it true. (You be the judge of the veracity of the tale about the officer's bride whose ghost can still be seen taking an evening stroll on the ramparts.) Several buildings within the massive complex have been renovated, and one of them houses an excellent exhibition that chronicles the long history of the fort and includes a brief film reenacting the life of an Irish soldier.

TOURING TIPS If the weather cooperates, venture out to the fort on the Scilly Walk, which follows the harbor through little hamlets and parklike groves; a stop for a pint at the Bulman, just below the fort in the village of Scilly, is mandatory.

RESTAURANTS IN KINSALE

THE FIRST CHOICE FOR A CASUAL MEAL is **Mother Hubbard's** (Market Street; ☎ 021-477-2440), a popular breakfast spot that bakes memorable pastries and serves soup and sandwiches into the afternoon.

Blue Haven ★★★

PUB/IRISH   MODERATE/EXPENSIVE   QUALITY ★★★   VALUE ★★★★ (PUB),
★★★ (RESTAURANT)

3 Pearse Street, Kinsale, County Cork; ☎ 021-477-7858

Reservations Recommended for restaurant. **Entree range** *Pub:* €10–€18; *restaurant:* €20–€37; 3-course early dinner, €35. **Payment** AE, MC, V. **Bar** Full service. **Disabled access** Yes. **Hours** *Pub:* daily, 12:15–3 p.m. and 6:30–10 p.m.; *restaurant:* daily, 7–10 p.m.

MENU RECOMMENDATIONS *Pub:* Fresh oysters, beer-battered haddock and fries, banana banoffi pie; *restaurant:* crab linguine, caramelized scallops, grilled filet of sea bass.

COMMENTS This friendly old hotel in the center of Kinsale serves food to suit any mood and appetite, in a woody pub, an airy daytime cafe, or an elegant conservatory-style restaurant. You'll find good food and service in all, but the pub is especially appealing in that it offers that hard-to-find good-but-light evening meal. The more-elaborate restaurant menu is appealing, too, laden with excellent preparations of seafood and game. You may want to settle in next to the fire or on the patio with a pint and take a look at the different menus to see what suits your fancy.

Fishy Fishy Café ★★★★

| SEAFOOD | MODERATE | QUALITY ★★★★ | VALUE ★★★★★ |

Guardwell, Kinsale, County Cork; ☎ 021-477-4453

Reservations None. **Entree range** €10–€15. **Payment** AE, MC, V. **Bar** Wine and beer. **Disabled access** Yes. **Hours** Daily, noon–3:45 p.m.

MENU RECOMMENDATIONS Grilled prawns, seafood chowder, smoked salmon on brown bread.

COMMENTS Seafood doesn't come any fresher than it does at this fish market with a scattering of indoor and outdoor tables. The menu is small and hinges on what's fresh off the boats—crab and scallops are often available, as are John Dory and other local fish. You should see no need to stray from the listed offerings, but if you do the kitchen will prepare any fish in the cases as you like it. Little wonder Fishy Fishy has a devoted lunchtime following, so arrive early or late.

Little Skillet ★★★½

| IRISH | MODERATE | QUALITY ★★★★ | VALUE ★★★★ |

Main Street, Kinsale, County Cork; ☎ 021-477-4202

Reservations Recommended for dinner. **Entree range** €16–€20. **Payment** MC, V. **Bar** Full service. **Disabled access** Yes. **Hours** Daily, 12:30–2:30 p.m. and 6–10:30 p.m.

MENU RECOMMENDATIONS Seafood chowder, Irish stew.

COMMENTS The stone-walled room with open hearth and simple furnishings has the feel of a country kitchen, and the offerings do nothing to dispel the feeling that you're enjoying a knowledgeably prepared home-cooked meal. Seafood offerings are made from the freshest fish, and the vegetables are chosen carefully from local suppliers. The charms of the place are well known, so plan on enjoying a pint in the little bar across the street while you wait for a table. Anne and Richard Ennos offer likewise-engaging accommodations upstairs.

The Vintage ★★★★

| IRISH | MODERATE | QUALITY ★★★★ | VALUE ★★★ |

50 Main Street, Kinsale, County Cork; ☎ 021-477-2502

Reservations Recommended for dinner. **Entree range** €10–€20. **Payment** AE, MC, V. **Bar** Full service. **Disabled access** Yes. **Hours** Mid-February–mid-April and mid-October–December, Tuesday–Saturday, 6:30–10 p.m.; Sunday,12:30–4 p.m. and 6:30–10:30 p.m.

MENU RECOMMENDATIONS Dublin lawyer (a flaming lobster), oven-roasted duck, fresh fish prepared any way.

COMMENTS An oak-beamed, stone-walled room is the setting for an excellent meal based on ingredients that change with the seasons. The cozy surroundings are especially well suited to the fowl and game dishes that prevail in the colder months, and the freshest seafood is always on the menu. An excellent selection of wines is available, and the service is highly polished yet friendly.

ENTERTAINMENT AND NIGHTLIFE IN KINSALE

TWO OF KINSALE'S MOST POPULAR and atmospheric pubs are on the harbor outside of town. **The Bulman** (just below Charles Fort in Summercove; ☎ 021-477-2131) has cozy rooms warmed by fires and a seawall-cum-terrace across the road from which to watch the sun set. **The Spaniard** (Scilly; ☎ 021-477-2436), on a hillside above the harbor closer to town, sports a maritime-themed interior beneath a thatched roof and packs in an evening crowd with live music. In town, **The Shanakee** (from *seanachai*, or "storyteller" in Gaelic; Market Street; ☎ 021-477-7077) is the best of the pubs offering live music.

EXERCISE AND RECREATION IN KINSALE

WATER-SPORTS ENTHUSIASTS should make a beeline for **Oyster-haven Holiday and Activity Centre,** which rents sailboards, kayaks, wet suits, and more; the center also has tennis courts. Oysterhaven is eight kilometers (five miles) outside of town; call ☎ 021-477-0738. Sailboats can be chartered from **Sail Ireland Charters** at the Trident Hotel; call ☎ 021-477-2927 or visit **www.sailireland.com.** Bicycles are available for rent at the **Hire Shop** (18 Main Street; ☎ 021-477-4884), providing an excellent way to explore the paths around Kinsale Harbour; the shop also rents rods and other fishing equipment. The most famous golf course in the area is the **Old Head Golf Links on Kinsale Head,** with a fine reputation and greens fees to match; for information, call ☎ 021-477-8444 or visit **www.oldheadgolflinks.com. Kinsale Golf Club,** five kilometers (three miles) to the north, is also well regarded and much less expensive; call ☎ 021-477-4722. Walkers can set out on the maintained paths following the shores of Kinsale Harbour. The much-trod **Scilly Walk** (see page 194) provides a scenic route from the town center to Charles Fort.

PART SIX

THE SOUTHWEST *of* IRELAND

EASYGOING, DEEPLY RURAL, RUGGED, beautiful, friendly, fun-loving—it's pretty easy to see why this corner of Ireland is, for many visitors, what Ireland is all about. You won't find much here to grouse about, except maybe the weather, and even then the locals will tell you to wait five minutes and that will change. Settle into **Kenmare** or **Dingle Town,** hike across the magnificent mountain-and-lake scenery of **Killarney National Park,** inch along on cliff-hugging coastal roads, and you'll see why the people who live here are in no rush to see things change in these parts. Of course, things do change, and you'll run into some hard-core tourism in places such as **Killarney Town** and some spots along the **Ring of Kerry.** When you do, take a cue from the locals—just take a turn off the beaten path.

KENMARE

ONE OF THE MOST LOVELY TOWNS in Ireland is tucked neatly into the hills at the head of the Kenmare River. The river, as you'll soon notice, is actually a bay, dividing the Beara and Iveragh peninsulas. British settlers, including Sir William Petty, surveyor general for Oliver Cromwell in the 17th century, found it more convenient to call the

the southwest of ireland

bay a river because by law fish-farming was allowed only in rivers and not in open waters. The name lives on, to the confusion of visitors, who are nevertheless much taken with the sight of the purple mountains of the peninsulas rising across the gleaming waters.

Kenmare is a cheerful place of brightly colored houses and storefronts, a remnant of a 19th-century overhaul when the town was tidied up as part of the sprawling Lansdowne Estates. Another aspect of Kenmare's heritage is also much in evidence—lace. In the wake of the Famine, the nuns of the order of the Poor Clares taught young women lace making, and Kenmare lace soon became the rage of Victorian English society. A member of the order, Sister Mary Francis Clare Cusack, known as the "Nun of Kenmare," is famous for her stance against the indifference of the British during the Famine.

With a number of fine hotels and restaurants, Kenmare is an excellent base for exploring much of County Kerry, and even County Cork, just to the north. From here, you easily can make excursions northwest to the **Ring of Kerry, Killarney National Park,** and the **Dingle Peninsula,** or northeast to Cork City and its environs. Kenmare makes a far more pleasant base than busier Killarney, just to the north (see page 255).

PLANNING YOUR VISIT TO KENMARE

THE KENMARE TOURIST OFFICE is handily located in the town square and is open from mid-April to late October, Monday through Saturday, 9 a.m. to 6 p.m. If you're visiting outside of those dates, try to stock up on info at other Cork/Kerry tourist offices, such as those in Cork City or Dingle Town. When you're in the Kenmare office, be sure to drop by the free **Kenmare Heritage Centre** in the back room; small but earnest displays do an excellent job of explaining the town's history. Also on the premises is the **Kenmare Lace and Design Centre,** where you can see demonstrations of Kenmare lace making, which follows a technique similar to the craft practiced in Venice. For more information, call ☎ 064-41233 or visit **www.corkkerry.ie.**

unofficial **TIP**
If you're in town in late May, you can enjoy some pleasant treks into the surrounding countryside organized by the **Kenmare Walking Festival;** ☎ 064-42639. In mid-August, Kenmare celebrates an old-fashioned Irish Fair, with livestock and crafts exhibits; for information, call ☎ 064-42653 or go to **www.kenmare.com.**

ARRIVING AND GETTING ORIENTED IN KENMARE

KENMARE IS ABOUT 65 KILOMETERS (40 miles) southwest of Cork, an easy trip by car along N22, with a turn west on R569. **Bus Éireann** coaches run between Kenmare and Killarney, about 40 kilometers (25 miles) northwest, once a day; in Killarney you can continue to Dublin or other Irish cities by bus or train. For more information, call ☎ 064-34777 or visit **www.buseireann.ie.**

HOTELS IN KENMARE

O'Donnabhain's ★★½

QUALITY	★★★★	VALUE	★★★★	€50–€80

**Henry Street Kenmare, County Kerry; ☎ 064-42106; fax 064-41799;
info@odonnabhain-kenmare.com; www.odonnabhain-kenmare.com**

Location Center of town. **Amenities and services** 10 rooms; pub downstairs.
Elevator No. **Parking** On street or behind the pub. **Price** Includes full Irish
breakfast. **Credit cards** MC, V.

EVEN WITHOUT THE FRIENDLIEST PUB in town downstairs, these large and
airy guest rooms would be an excellent choice while exploring Kenmare
and the surroundings. A central, in-town location, excellent service, and a
pleasant lounge and breakfast room add to the appeal of the extremely
spacious and quiet rooms. These are decorated in a pleasingly traditional
style and are bright and airy, with large windows and skylights, and have
excellent modern bathrooms. Jer, the proprietor, is usually on hand and
gladly dispenses advice about the best way to explore the Beara and Iveragh Peninsulas. Several cottages in the nearby countryside are also
available for rental.

Park Hotel Kenmare ★★★½

QUALITY	★★★★	VALUE	★★★	€225–€360

**Kenmare, County Kerry; ☎ 064-41200; fax 064-41402;
info@parkkenmare.com; www.parkkenmare.com**

Location The edge of town overlooking the Kenmare River. **Amenities and
services** 46 units; restaurant, bar gardens, lounges, golf, tennis, croquet, spa, pool,
private theater, room service, in-room tea and coffee facilities. **Elevator** Yes.
Parking Free, on grounds. **Price** Includes full Irish breakfast. **Credit cards** MC, V.

THE HEARTH GLOWING in the hallway sets the tone for one of Ireland's
finest hotels, and what may be the most welcoming of all them all. The
emphasis here is on comfort, not pretense, just as the 19th-century
building, built as a grand railway hotel, is appealing and not overwhelming. All rooms are spacious and have sitting areas, most face the sea, and
many have private terraces. Lush gardens open to Kenmare's Reenagross
Park, creating the impression that you are in the middle of the countryside, even though the center of town is just outside the gates. The
excellent in-house dining room serves set menus from about €50 that
lean toward seafood.

Sallyport House ★★★½

QUALITY	★★★★	VALUE	★★★	€90–€150

**Sound Road, Kenmare, County Kerry (closed mid-November–March 1);
☎ 064-42066; fax 064-42067; port@iol.ie; www.sallyporthouse.com**

Location The edge of town near the mouth of the Kenmare River. **Amenities
and services** 5 rooms; gardens, in-room tea and coffee facilities. **Elevator** No.

How Hotels Compare in the Southwest of Ireland

HOTEL	OVERALL	QUALITY	VALUE	PRICE
KENMARE				
Shelburne Lodge	★★★★½	★★★★	★★★★	€80–€100
Sea Shore Farm	★★★½	★★★★	★★★½	€65–€130
Sallyport House	★★★½	★★★★	★★★	€90–€150
KILLARNEY				
Cahernane House	★★★★	★★★★	★★★	€150–€250
Arbutus Hotel	★★★★	★★★	★★★★	€90–€140
DINGLE				
Castlewood House	★★★★	★★★★½	★★★	€100–€130
Greenmount House	★★★★	★★★★	★★★★	€110–€170
Gorman's	★★★★	★★★★	★★★	€120–€170
Milltown House	★★★★	★★★★	★★★	€100–€150
Captains House	★★★★	★★★	★★★★	€60–€100
Heaton's Guesthouse	★★★	★★★½	★★★★	€60–€150
Old Pier	★★★	★★★	★★★★	€50–€100

Parking Free, on grounds. **Price** Includes full Irish breakfast. **Credit cards** MC, V. *Note:* Not suitable for children under age 13.

JANE AND JOHN ARTHUR, a brother-and-sister team, have converted their family home into an extremely comfortable five-bedroom guesthouse that overlooks the gardens and estuary waters of the Kenmare River on three sides. The handsome downstairs lounges are filled with old family furniture, and one chimney contains stone salvaged from a workhouse that once stood on the site. Extremely large bedrooms are individually decorated with antiques and extras such as sofas and window seats, and one of the rear rooms has a separate sitting room; all have queen- and king-size beds (with orthopedic mattresses and fine linens) as well as lavish bathrooms. The center of town is an easy ten-minute stroll away through parkland.

Sea Shore Farm ★★★½

QUALITY ★★★★	VALUE ★★★½	€65–€130

Tubrid, Kenmare, County Kerry (closed November 15–March 1);
☎ **064-41270; fax 064-41270; seashore@eircom.net;**
www.seashorekenmare.com

Location On the bay, about 1.5 kilometers (1 mile) outside of town. **Amenities and services** 6 rooms; beach, gardens, hair dryers, in-room tea and coffee facilities. **Elevator** No. **Parking** Free, on grounds. **Price** Includes full Irish breakfast. **Credit cards** MC, V.

THE APTLY NAMED HOME of the O'Sullivans is on the shores of the Kenmare River amid the rich farmlands that co-owner Patricia O'Sullivan's grandfather settled almost a century ago. In good weather, chairs and tables are set out on the patio and lawns overlooking the sea; you can fish from the pier or, if you don't mind the frigid seawater, swim from a small beach on the property. In colder months, a fire burns in the pleasant lounge. Guest rooms are comfortable, bright, and extremely large; all have views of the sea and fields and new baths with power showers. Furnishings are eclectic, and rooms are sprinkled with 19th-century armoires, Art Deco tables, and other pieces that Patricia picks up at flea markets. Two ground-floor rooms open to patios, while the upstairs rooms have large floor-to-ceiling windows that slide open. One of the downstairs rooms is unusually large and, with three exposures, exceptionally bright, and one of the upstairs units has a small adjoining bedroom and is well suited for guests with children. A refrigerator and microwave in the upstairs hallway are among the thoughtful touches that make a stay here extremely comfortable. A nice walk of about 20 minutes along a little-traveled country lane brings you to town.

Shelburne Lodge   ★ ★ ★ ★ ½

QUALITY ★★★★	VALUE ★★★★	€ 80–€ 100

Cork Road, Kenmare, County Kerry (closed December 1–March 1);
☎ **064-41013; fax 064-42135; shelburnekenmare@eircom.net;**
www.shelburnelodge.com

Location About 0.5 kilometers (one-fifth of a mile) outside the city center on the Cork Road (R569). **Amenities and services** 9 rooms; gardens; tea, coffee, wine, and other drinks available; tennis **Elevator** No. **Parking** Free, on grounds. **Price** Includes full Irish breakfast. **Credit cards** MC, V.

MAURA FOLEY HAS LONG BEEN in the hospitality business (she created the Lime Tree and Packie restaurants in town), and now she and her husband Tom extend their amazing talents to making guests feel welcome in their stylish, 18th-century stone manor house at the edge of town. The grounds are stunning, with gardens, lawns, a grass tennis court, and fine old trees, and throughout the house, fine kilims and carpets are scattered on highly polished floors, bold but soothing colors and artwork cover the walls, and a drawing room and smaller sitting room are stocked with books and furnished with comfortable couches and chairs. Welcoming, attractive guest rooms contain a mix of antique and classic furnishings and have excellent beds and large bathrooms that are as tastefully done as the rest of the house; a large unit in the rear of the house is well suited to families. Maura shows off her culinary skills with a breakfast in which breads, preserves, cheeses, and hot entrees are all fresh and delicious. It's worth a stop in Kenmare just to stay in this guesthouse, and you might want to consider settling into Shelburne Lodge for a long stay as you explore the many nearby Southwest attractions.

How Restaurants Compare in the Southwest of Ireland

NAME	CUISINE	OVERALL	QUALITY	VALUE	PRICE
KENMARE					
The Purple Heather	Cafe	★★★★	★★★★	★★★★½	Inexp
Packie's	Bistro	★★★★	★★★★	★★★★	Mod
Lime Tree	Seafood/ modern Irish	★★★★	★★★★	★★★	Exp
KILLARNEY					
Gaby's Seafood Restaurant	Seafood	★★★★	★★★★	★★★★	Exp
Treyvaud's	Irish	★★★★	★★★★	★★★★	Mod
DINGLE					
Global Village	Modern Irish	★★★★	★★★★	★★★★½	Mod
Chart House	Modern Irish/ seafood	★★★★	★★★★	★★★★	Exp
Goat Street Café	Modern Irish	★★★½	★★★★	★★★★	Inexp
Out of the Blue	Seafood	★★★	★★★★½	★★★½	Exp
Lord Baker's	Irish	★★★	★★★	★★★★	Mod/inexp
Fenton's	Modern Irish	★★★	★★★	★★★	Mod

EXPLORING KENMARE

YOU CAN TOUR THE TOWN on a fairly short stroll because most shops and restaurants are concentrated in a small triangle between **Henry, Main,** and **Shelbourne streets.** Just to the north is the leafy town square, including the tourist office, the **Kenmare Heritage Centre,** and **Kenmare Lace and Design Centre.** A **Druid stone circle** is just to the south of the town center off Market Street (more than 100 such stone circles dot the remote landscapes of Counties Cork and Kerry). The 15 stones here surround a center dolmen (perhaps used for rituals) and were put in place at least 3,000 years ago, perhaps to plot solstices. The Marquis of Lansdowne began planting rare specimens on the banks of the Kenmare River at the southern edge of town some 200 years ago, and now the gardens, woodlands, and estuaries comprise **Reenagross Park.** Trails crisscross this extensive parkland, providing some excellent waterside walks and bird-watching.

RESTAURANTS IN KENMARE

YOU'LL FIND ANY NUMBER of great spots for a picnic on the shores of Kenmare River and along the Beara Peninsula (Healy Pass would be a prime choice) and a good place to stock up is the **Truffled Pig** (The Square; ☎ 064-42953). The selection of cheeses, meats, spreads, and prepared food is temptingly excellent.

Lime Tree ★★★★

SEAFOOD/MODERN IRISH	EXPENSIVE	QUALITY ★★★★	VALUE ★★★

Shelburne Street, Kenmare; ☎ 064-41225

Reservations Recommended. **Entree range** €18–€27. **Payment** AE, MC, V. **Bar** Full service. **Disabled access** Yes. **Hours** Daily, 6:30–10 p.m.

MENU RECOMMENDATIONS Blue-cheese tartlet, smoked-salmon-and-fennel risotto, roast Kerry lamb.

COMMENTS A 19th-century stone schoolhouse that also did duty for officials doling out passage to famine-stricken farmers now serves some of Kenmare's best fare and its most atmospheric dining experience. Stone floors and handsome country furnishings set a rustic tone, and French doors open to the flowery terraces that surround the building; an upstairs art gallery sells works by local artists. This place isn't all show, though—the cooking is down-to-earth, with an emphasis on the freshest local ingredients. Kerry lamb is oven-roasted to perfection, and wild salmon done on an oak plank elevates this Irish staple to new heights.

Packie's ★★★★

BISTRO	MODERATE	QUALITY ★★★★	VALUE ★★★★

Henry Street, Kenmare; ☎ 064-41508

Reservations Recommended. **Entree range** €14–€28. **Payment** AE, MC, V. **Bar** Full service. **Disabled access** Yes. **Hours** Tuesday–Sunday, 6–10 p.m.; closed January–mid-March.

MENU RECOMMENDATIONS Sole stuffed with prawns, roast duck, Irish lamb stew.

COMMENTS If you're staying in Kenmare for more than a few days, return to this cozy, candlelit, center-of-town bistro a couple of times to dine your way through the tempting menu. Seafood plays a large part in the preparations, but not exclusively so, and you may want to sample the diverse and creative offerings to make a meal of starters, many of which you won't see on a lot of menus: seafood sausages, a salad of warm duck livers, smoked cod cakes. Main courses, too, are innovative, and sole and other fish caught just hours earlier are accompanied by vegetables from the restaurant's own kitchen garden.

The Purple Heather ★★★★

CAFE	INEXPENSIVE	QUALITY ★★★★	VALUE ★★★★½

Henry Street, Kenmare; ☎ 064-41016

How Attractions Compare in the Southwest of Ireland

ATTRACTION	DESCRIPTION	AUTHOR'S RATING
KENMARE		
Bantry House	Historic home in a magnificent setting	★★★½
KILLARNEY NATIONAL PARK		
Muckross House and Traditional Farms	Victorian home and grounds	★★★★
Ross Castle	Medieval stronghold	★★★
IVERAGH PENINSULA		
Skellig Experience	Museum of life on the Skellig Islands	★★★★
Derrynane House	Historic home of Daniel O'Connell	★★★
DINGLE		
The Blasket Centre	Museum of life on the Blasket Islands	★★★★

Reservations Not necessary. **Entree range** €6–€16. **Payment** Cash only. **Bar** Full service. **Disabled access** Yes. **Hours** Monday–Saturday, 10:45 a.m.–5:30 p.m.

MENU RECOMMENDATIONS Salads, toasted open-faced sandwiches.

COMMENTS It's hard not to consider this bar and cafe the center of Kenmare social life. Drop into the appealing room of dark wood and deep hues anytime during the day for informal fare that helped put Kenmare on the gourmet map—heavenly omelets, salads full of local produce and farmhouse cheeses, excellent pâtés and hearty soups, all of it accompanied by homemade dark bread.

ENTERTAINMENT AND NIGHTLIFE IN KENMARE

SEVERAL KENMARE PUBS woo customers with traditional music, nightly in summer, in the off-season less frequently, usually one or two nights a week at most. **Foley's** and **Davitt's,** both on Henry Street, are the most likely to have music year-round; in summer, just stroll along Henry and Main streets, and let your ears lead you into the pub with the music that appeals most to you.

Around **KENMARE**

THE BEARA PENINSULA

SOUTHWESTERN IRELAND stretches into the Atlantic in a string of craggy peninsulas. The **Iveragh Peninsula** (christened the "Ring of Kerry" by tourist authorities) and the **Dingle Peninsula** are well

walks and drives in the southwest

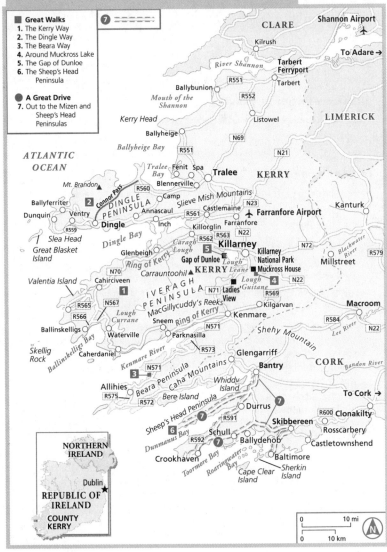

Great Walks
1. The Kerry Way
2. The Dingle Way
3. The Beara Way
4. Around Muckross Lake
5. The Gap of Dunloe
6. The Sheep's Head
   Peninsula

A Great Drive
7. Out to the Mizen and
   Sheep's Head
   Peninsulas

known and well traveled, but the **Beara Peninsula** remains remote, at least relatively so. You needn't travel far out of Kenmare (west on R571) before you find yourself with the **Kenmare River** on your right and the purple spine of the heather-covered **Caha Mountains** on your left. At the far western tip of Beara, a creaky cable car with room for "three passengers and one cow" swings across the sea to **Dursey Island,** where colonies of seabirds nest amid the ruins of a medieval castle. At **Castletownbere,** the main town on the peninsula, fleets of foreign fishing trawlers anchor in a harbor that once sheltered the ships of smugglers who traded Irish fish for French brandy.

It isn't necessary to venture all the way out to the end of the peninsula to enjoy spectacular scenery. **Gleninchaquin Park,** about 12 kilometers (7.5 miles) out of Kenmare, is blessed with a remarkable array of beautiful scenery that you can explore on trails that cross a glacial valley through glens and meadows, follow the shores of lakes and stream, and climb the face of a waterfall. The park is privately owned and charges €5 for a day's visit; ☎ 064-84235; **www.gleninch aquin.com.** At the village of **Lauragh,** about 16 kilometers (10 miles) from Kenmare, R574 heads south into the mountains and across one of the most thrilling routes in all of Ireland, **Healy Pass.** This narrow road traverses the mountainous border between Cork and Kerry, where the backdrop of desolate moors and purple peaks looks more like a stage set than a real place. Just to the south of the peninsula, facing the windswept expanses of Bantry Bay, is one of the greatest of Irish great houses, **Bantry House** (see below).

Attraction around the Beara Peninsula

Bantry House   ★ ★ ★ ½

APPEAL BY AGE	PRESCHOOL ★★	GRADE SCHOOL ★★★	TEENS ★★★
YOUNG ADULTS ★★	OVER 30 ★★★		SENIORS ★★★

Outside Bantry on N71, County Cork; ☎ **027-50047; www.bantryhouse.ie**

Type of attraction Historic home in a magnificent setting. **Admission** *Houses, gardens, and French Armada Centre: €10; gardens and French Armada Centre: €5.* **Hours** March–October, daily, 10 a.m.–6 p.m. **When to go** Try to find a break in the rain showers so that you can spend time in the gardens. **Special comments** Bantry House provides a good break in the journey if you're traveling between Cork and Kenmare, and the tearoom is a decent spot for a sandwich or other refreshments. **How much time to allow** About 2 hours for the house, gardens, and French Armada Centre.

DESCRIPTION AND COMMENTS The White family came to Bantry Bay in the 17th century and ingratiated themselves with the British a century later. In 1795, Richard White raised the alarm when an armada of French ships, in an alliance with Irish nationalist Wolfe Tone, attempted an invasion of Ireland. Tone's plan was to land 50 ships laden with 15,000 troops at Bantry Bay; White heard rumor of the fleet's arrival and posted lookouts. Irish weather proved more effective than British bravado and forced the ships to turn back to France, but White was made the First Earl of Bantry for his loyalty. Set amid terraced gardens overlooking Bantry Bay, the house has been richly

Walks and Drives in the Southwest

While it wouldn't be quite fair to other regions to say the Southwest is Ireland's most scenic region, let's just say that in the Southwest an amazing amount of beautiful scenery is compressed into a relatively small area. It's no accident that many of Ireland's most traveled walking paths and favorite drives crisscross the Southwest.

GREAT WALKS

THE KERRY WAY

Some of Ireland's finest scenery unfolds along this 214-kilometer (128-mile) route that passes through **Killarney National Park** and circles the **Iveragh Peninsula** (aka the Ring of Kerry). You can pick up the way at any number of spots as you explore the park (for instance, it skirts the shores of Muckross Lake) and drive around the peninsula. A very nice and relatively easy way to enjoy some of the Kerry Way's best coastal scenery is around **Derrynane,** on the southern side of the Iveragh Peninsula. In addition to views of the sea, mountains, and Skellig Islands, this segment of the way also provides a bit of historical insight—it begins in **Derrynane National Historic Park** (see page 251), which preserves the birthplace of Daniel O'Connell, known as the Liberator for his efforts on behalf of independence and against the oppression of Catholics. The route first follows the trails of the **Derrynane Dunes Nature Trail** to the Coomnahorna River estuary, where you're likely to see many shorebirds. From the estuary you can follow a lovely stretch of beach for one kilometer (one-half mile) east to the beginning of a mass path, one of the rough tracks common in the countryside that were once used for funeral processions and other religious rites. The path follows a rugged coastal hillside, affording views of headlands and offshore islands, and comes to another small beach. By the time you've retraced your steps to Derrynane from here, you will have covered about seven kilometers (four miles).

embellished through the years, most lavishly by Richard White, the second earl. He scoured Europe for treasures, bringing back furnishings that include Gobelin and Aubusson tapestries (those in the Rose Room are said to have been commissioned by Louis XV for Marie Antoinette) and portraits of George III and Queen Charlotte by Allan Ramsay, the celebrated 18th-century Scottish portraitist. The small French Armada Centre next to the house details the events of 1795 with excellent exhibits accompanied by sound effects. Most interesting are a model of the frigate *Surveillante*—which the French were forced to scuttle off the coast—and the artifacts found on board when it was recovered in 1982.

TOURING TIPS Leave at least one hour to explore the gardens, which are spread across seven terraces above the bay. Formal plantings include the first earl's Rose Garden and the second earl's Italian Garden, but most

THE DINGLE WAY

This 153-kilometer-long (92-mile-long) walking route circumnavigates one of Ireland's most scenic peninsulas and is one of the country's most popular long-distance routes. Casual walkers can pick up the well-marked way anywhere along the peninsula for a short trek. In fact, the most scenic stretch, around **Slea Head,** is easily accessible and only about seven kilometers (five miles) west of **Dingle Town** (see page 261). If you're traveling by public transportation, you can take the bus from **Dingle to Ventry** and begin the walk from there; if you're traveling by car, follow the coast road west and pick up the way where it crosses the road about three kilometers (two miles) east of Slea Head. As you walk west, you'll pass some of the Dingle Peninsula's many early ruins, including 2,500-year-old **Dunbeg Fort** (see page 270), with thick earthenwork ramparts rising precariously above the sea, as well as groupings of *clocháns,* beehive-shaped huts built without mortar by early-Christian hermits. As you approach Slea Head, the views over the sea, adjoining **Dunmore Head** (the westernmost point in Ireland) and the **Blasket Islands,** are stunning.

THE BEARA WAY

Another of County Kerry's walking circuits circles the **Beara Peninsula,** covering 196 kilometers (118 miles). One stretch, from the village of **Castletown Bearhaven** on the southern side of the peninsula, introduces you not only to spectacular scenery but also to some fascinating archaeological remains. From the village, follow the signs for **Derreena Taggart Stone Circle,** about 2 kilometers (1.2 miles) west; this ring of 12 standing stones is about 2,000 years old. From here the path continues across bogs where peat was once cut and over beautiful moors for about three kilometers (two miles) to another remnant of early life on the peninsula, the **Teernahilane Ring Fort.**

Continued on next page

exhilarating are the views over the mountains and bay from the top terrace, reached by stone stairs known as the "Staircase to the Sky."

 ## THE IVERAGH PENINSULA (RING OF KERRY)

NATURE BESTOWED THIS LONG PENINSULA with more than its fair share of shadowy mountains and rugged coastlines, and where nature slacked off, advertising flacks picked up the slack. The so-called Ring of Kerry is Ireland's most publicized national attraction, and fleets of tourist buses heed the call in summer. The scenery is captivating, but no more so than in many other parts of Ireland (the adjoining Beara and Dingle peninsulas are more appealing), and if you've already visited Killarney National Park, you won't find scenery to top those glorious mountains and lakes.

Walks and Drives in the Southwest (continued)

GREAT WALKS (CONTINUED)

THE BEARA WAY (CONTINUED)

Another good walk follows the Beara Way as it skirts **Coulagh Bay** from the village of **Eyeies,** on the north side of the peninsula. Leaving this colorful village to the east, follow the Way as it winds along the rugged coast of Coulagh Bay for about 4 kilometers (2.5 miles). Tides permitting, you can walk part of this route on nearly deserted beaches. Near the headland at the northern end of the bay, follow a well-marked path inland to the **Ballycrovane Ogham Stone,** one of some 300 such stones in Ireland, most of them in Counties Cork and Kerry, that are inscribed with a pre-Christian Celtic script known as Ogham. This stone and many others like it are thought to mark burial grounds.

AROUND MUCKROSS LAKE

A half-day walk, about 11 kilometers (8 miles) around this lake in the heart of **Killarney National Park** (see page 258), exposes you to the varied and delight-ful scenery of one of Ireland's six national parks: waterfalls, rugged mountains, bubbling streams, and, of course, the lake itself. As you follow the well-marked **Lake Shore Path** south from **Muckross House,** you pass through lovely wood-land to a short path into **Torc Waterfall,** where flights of rough stone steps lead to viewpoints over the 20-meter (60-foot) cascade and, to the north, the peaks of **MacGillycuddy's Reeks,** Ireland's tallest mountains. The path then skirts the southern shores of the lake and comes to a beautiful spot called **Meeting of the Waters,** where the waters of Muckross Lake, Lough Leane, and a small river flow together beneath the **Old Weir Bridge,** then to **Dins Cottage** (no public access), set amid lovely gardens of azaleas, magnolias, and eucalyptus. As you proceed north, then east, the path skirts the shores of Lough Leane as well as Muckross Lake. You'll come to small **Doo Lough,** a relatively secluded spot sur-rounded by woodlands, then **Reenadinna Wood,** Europe's largest yew forest, before the path crosses beneath a stand of magnificent oaks and returns to the grounds of Muckross House. You may well want to take time at the end of the walk to join a tour of one of Ireland's finest homes (see page 260).

If you approach from the south, the first stop is the pretty and much-visited village of **Sneem,** full of gaily painted cottages. Set on a forlorn hillside beyond Sneem is **Staigue Fort,** a well-preserved, circu-lar Iron Age stone enclosure that probably functioned as a fortified homestead some 2,500 years ago, providing protection to farmers and their cattle. The fort is open Easter through September daily, 10 a.m. to 9 p.m.; free (although you'll pay a €1 fee to cross private land to reach the fort); €3 for the small museum, where drawings and artifacts will enlighten you on theories about the fort's function.

The next village along the coast is **Caherdaniel,** where **Derrynane House** was the home of Daniel O'Connell, the "Liberator," who won

THE GAP OF DUNLOE

No signage is necessary to guide yourself through this gorgeous boulder- and lake-laced gorge—simply follow the crowds who partake in one of Ireland's most popular outings. The 6.5-kilometer (4-mile) trek between **MacGilly-cuddy's Reeks** and **Purple Mountain** is all the more appealing because of the noticeable absence of motorized traffic. If you're coming from Killarney and other points in the Southwest, it's most convenient to begin the walk at the north end of the gap, **at Kate Kearney's Cottage,** once the home of a maiden who sold *poteen* (moonshine) and now a lively pub. Should you be worried about having the stamina to walk the length of the gap, you can rent a jaunting car to take you halfway in. The walk, however, is quite comfortable and relatively easy, combining so many views of mountains and lakes that you won't mind the summertime crowds. If you want to get away from the crowds and add quite a bit more exertion to the walk, you can climb out of the Gap about halfway through and make the climb to the summit of Purple Moun-tain, 830 meters (2,700 feet) high. Another pub, **Lord Bandon's Cottage,** is at the south end of the gap, the so-called **Head of the Gap.** From there you can retrace your steps back to Kate Kearney's Cottage or board a boat for a cruise across the Upper Lake and Lough Leane to **Ross Castle** (see page 261), near Killarney Town.

THE SHEEP'S HEAD PENINSULA

One of the least-visited peninsulas on the Southwest Coast stretches west from **Bantry.** The 88-kilometer (53-mile) **Sheep's Head Way** takes full advantage of the rural settings of the peninsula's interior and the rugged coastlines. You can get a nice taste of the way at its most dramatic point, a 4-kilometer (2.5-mile) loop around **Sheep's Head.** Begin in the parking area at the end of the road along the south side of the peninsula. From there, a well-marked path leads across rocky headlands to the **Sheep's Head Lighthouse** and then follows the tops of sea cliffs high above Bantry Bay on the return loop.

Continued on next page

equal rights for Irish Catholics in 1828. The house is now a fascinat-ing museum (see profile on next page), and the grounds compose the 128-hectare (320-acre) **Derrynane National Historic Park,** a nice place to stroll on the beach. Just beyond is one of the most scenery-filled stretches of the Ring, the **Coomakista Pass,** where pulling off the road affords stunning views up and down the coast.

Just beyond Waterville you will have the option to make the 32-kilometer (20-mile) loop around **Skellig Ring** at the tip of the pen-insula; do so, because the views of crashing surf and the conical **Skellig Islands** (see page 254) are fantastic, the best part of the Ring of Kerry circuit. The largest island, **Skellig Michael,** rises more than

Walks and Drives in the Southwest (continued)

GREAT DRIVES

The peninsulas of the Southwest are ringed by some of Ireland's most popular driving routes. The **Iveragh Peninsula** (see page 249), christened the Ring of Kerry by the tourism powers, is the most traveled, though more-rewarding drives can be enjoyed on the **Dingle Peninsula** (see page 270), the **Beara Peninsula** (see page 245), and on the relatively unknown **Mizen** and **Sheep's Head peninsulas.**

OUT TO THE MIZEN HEAD AND SHEEP'S HEAD PENINSULAS

A trip out to Mizen Head begins in **Skibbereen,** about 85 kilometers (53 miles) west of Kinsale on N71. This lively town hosts two markets, one of cattle on Wednesdays and one for farm-fresh vegetables, local seafood, cheeses, and other local produce on Fridays. **Lough Hyne,** about six kilometers (four miles) southwest of town, is a saltwater lake and much warmer than the sea, providing a habitat for sea anemones and a wide variety of other marine species. Skibbereen is also graced with the lovely lakeside gardens of the **Liss Ard Foundation,** which you can visit from May through October, daily, 10 a.m. to dusk; admission is €5.

A detour of 12 kilometers (8 miles) southwest from Skibbereen on R595 brings you down to **Baltimore,** a beautiful fishing village and pleasure port; ferries connect the town with **Sherkin Island,** where only 90 residents live

230 meters (700 feet) out of the Atlantic surf; for six centuries it sheltered a colony of early-Christian monks. You can learn more about this settlement and the islands' wildlife at the **Skellig Experience** (see page 255).

Attraction on the Iveragh Peninsula

 Derrynane House ★★★

APPEAL BY AGE	PRESCHOOL ★	GRADE SCHOOL ★★★	TEENS ★★★
YOUNG ADULTS ★★		OVER 30 ★★★	SENIORS ★★★

Off N70 outside Caherdaniel, County Kerry; ☎ 066-947-5113; www.heritageireland.ie

Type of attraction Historic home of Daniel O'Connell. **Admission** €2.90 adults, €2.10 seniors, €1.50 children and students, €7 families of up to 2 adults and 2 children. **Hours** May–September, Monday–Saturday, 9 a.m.–6 p.m.; Sunday, 11 a.m.–5 p.m.; April and October, Tuesday–Sunday, 1–5 p.m.; November–March, Saturday–Sunday, 1–5 p.m. **When to go** Anytime, but wait for coach tours to leave before entering the house. **Special comments** A small tearoom serves sandwiches and pastries. **How much time to allow** About 45 minutes.

among the ruins of medieval **Dún na Long Castle** and **Sherkin Abbey,** and with **Cape Clear Island,** the southernmost point in Ireland and well positioned for excellent bird-watching and sightings of whales and dolphins.

From Skibbereen, follow N71 west along the River Ilen and the shores of Roaringwater Bay to the attractive village of **Ballydehob;** then follow R592 out to the port of **Schull.** From there, continue around Toormore Bay to **Goleen,** then past sandy beaches and spectacular seascapes where waves crash into the high cliffs of **Mizen Head.**

After returning to Toormore, follow R591 along the north side of the Mizen Peninsula to **Durrus,** at the head of Dunmanus Bay and the Sheep's Head Peninsula. A narrow road leads west out to the village of **Kilcrohane** and beyond that to **Sheep's Head** (see the Sheep's Head Peninsula walk, page 251). The drive out to the head is adventurous enough, but you should also head north from Kilcrohane on the steep, narrow road aptly named the **Goat Path** over Seefin Mountain. At the summit, get out and make the easy walk to the viewpoint on the mountaintop to see the remarkable views over Bantry Bay and the Beara Peninsula to the north and Dunmanus Bay and the Mizen Peninsula to the south.

Follow the Goat Path down to the shores of Bantry Bay, and then drive east to **Bantry,** from which you can continue north on N71 toward **Kenmare** (see page 237) or east toward **Kinsale** (see page 229).

DESCRIPTION AND COMMENTS In this old house, once the center of a small estate, you'll learn about the man known as the Liberator and a fascinating period in Irish history. O'Connell was educated in France because Catholics were not entitled to schooling in Protestant-governed Ireland, but he returned home and ran for Parliament in 1828, becoming the first Irish Catholic to be sent to Westminster. He won Catholics full rights of citizenship in 1829, and he founded the grassroots Catholic Association to promote education and representation. O'Connell is very much a presence in the old rooms, many of which he remodeled with his own hands and filled with family portraits and artifacts such as the pistol with which he won a duel.

TOURING TIPS Take one of the guided tours if available; if not, ask for one of the handouts that explain the contents of each room.

unofficial **TIP**
The northern flank of the Ring is not as dramatic as the southern side. If you don't mind twists and turns and a little fancy clutch work, you might want to consider returning east on one of the inland roads, which follow isolated valleys and rugged mountainous terrain. If you do follow the northern coastal road, stop at **Glenbeigh,** a pleasant resort with palm trees and a nice beach.

THE SKELLIGS

YOU'LL SEE THESE THREE conical-shaped islands as you round the Iveragh Peninsula. Learn about the early-Christian monastic community that flourished on one of them, **Skellig Michael,** at the **Skellig Experience** on Valentia Island (see facing page). A visit to that excellent exhibit also includes a two-hour sea cruise around the islands. Even so, it's well worth the time and energy to visit the islands, about 14 kilometers (8 miles) offshore, where the beehive cells that housed monks for many dark centuries still remain and colonies of seabirds roost on the rock faces. A community lived on Skellig Michael (the largest of the islands, and the only one that can be visited) from about AD 600 to 1100. Life must have been austere even by monkly standards, given that the monks' diet consisted almost entirely of fish, birds, and eggs, save for grains or other foodstuffs they might have obtained from passing ships. Viking raiders and other passersby were not always friendly, though one Viking, Olav Trygvasson, lingered in friendly fashion long enough to be baptized on the island in AD 956; this future king of Norway later introduced Christianity to his country. Just east of Skellig Michael is **Little Skellig,** noted not for monks but for huge colonies of an estimated 45,000 gannets and other seabirds, as well as gray seals, which laze around the base of the island on huge rocks. A third Skellig is known for its shape as **Washerwoman's Rock.**

Planning Your Visit to the Skelligs

The first stop for anyone planning to visit the Skelligs is the **Skellig Experience** on Valentia Island (see facing page). The next step is to contact one of the outfits that run excursions to **Skellig Michael,** usually for about €40 a person. From Valentia Island, these include **Des Lavelle** (☎ 066-947-6124) and from Portmagee, **O'Keefe's** (☎ 066-947-7103), **Murphy's Sea Cruise** (☎ 066-947-7156), and **Joe Roddy** (☎ 066-947-4628); you'll see plenty of signs for Skellig cruises at this far end of the Iveragh Peninsula, but make sure that the outfit you deal with actually goes ashore—some just circumnavigate the islands. You'll also need to wait for good weather, because boats can land at the narrow concrete pier on Skellig Michael only when seas are relatively calm. Weather permitting, boats leave at about 10:30 a.m. for the hour-long crossing to Skellig Michael and give passengers about two hours to explore before the return trip, which usually includes a spin around the base of Little Skellig to see the birds and other sea life. Government guides often meet the boats on Skellig Michael and give an informative talk before letting visitors wander on their own. Bring your lunch for a picnic in a memorable setting, because food is not available on the island.

Exploring the Skelligs

A visit to Skellig Michael begins at the foot of the steep and slippery steps that ascend the flank of the rock 180 meters (600 feet) to the monastic colony. Six beehive-shaped huts and two cavelike oratories and a church seem barely habitable, but they are little different now than they were through the six centuries when they housed a devout community, members of which spent their days in prayer and hunting and fishing for their meager sustenance. Pilgrims have been coming to the island for centuries, too, many of whom used to crawl out to a cross (no longer there) on a precipitous outcropping near the summit of the peak as an act of death-defying penitence.

Attraction around the Skelligs

Skellig Experience ★★★★

APPEAL BY AGE	PRESCHOOL ★★★	GRADE SCHOOL ★★★★	TEENS ★★★★
YOUNG ADULTS ★★★★		OVER 30 ★★★★	SENIORS ★★★★

Valentia Island, off causeway from the mainland; ☎ 066-947-6306; www.skelligexperience.com

Type of attraction Museum of life on the Skellig Islands. **Admission** Exhibit: €5 adults, €4 seniors and students, €3 children, €14 families of up to 2 adults and 2 children; exhibit and cruise: €27.50 adults, €24.50 seniors and students, €14.50 children, €71.50 families of up to 2 adults and 2 children. **Hours** April–May, daily, 10 a.m.–6 p.m.; June–August, daily, 10 a.m.–7 p.m.; September–November, daily, 10 a.m.–6 p.m. **When to go** Visit the exhibit anytime, but the experience is much more rewarding when the cruises are operating. **Special comments** Sea cruises do not operate in rough weather; call ahead; the museum also offers a "mini-cruise" around Valentia Harbour, but you should spend the extra money on the Skelligs cruise; if that's full or not running, spend your time and money elsewhere. **How much time to allow** 3 hours with sea cruise, 1 hour without.

DESCRIPTION AND COMMENTS These innovative exhibits re-create life on the Skellig Islands, the rocky outcroppings in the Atlantic just southwest of the Ring of Kerry, with models and audiovisual effects. Replicas of the stone oratories and cells of the early-Christian monastic community that flourished on Skellig Michael, light effects demonstrating the Skellig Lighthouse, and models of storm petrels and other seabirds pay due homage to the islands and their rare habitats. More thrilling, though, is the two-hour sea cruise around the base of the islands, where you'll see seabirds, gray seals, the Skellig Lighthouse, and the rocky remains of the monastic settlement.

TOURING TIPS If you take the sea cruise, you won't have time to dally elsewhere on the Ring of Kerry.

KILLARNEY

SOME TIME AGO, this former farming village decided that visitors to Killarney National Park yielded a lot more bounty than any bumper crop ever would. It's harsh to say the town has sold its soul to tourism, but there is not a lot of soul in evidence: in summer the streets are jammed with tourists, and in winter the many shops and restaurants that serve tourists are empty and forlorn. The best thing going for

Killarney is its prime location as a launching pad for explorations into Killarney National Park. With an airport and bus and train stations, you may well make your first landfall in the Southwest in Killarney. If you do, take heart: the park's green expanses and a network of walking trails come right to the edge of the ubiquitous shopping arcades, making it easy to get out of town and plunge right into the natural beauty that probably drew you to this part of Ireland.

PLANNING YOUR VISIT TO KILLARNEY

THE **Killarney Tourist Office,** on Beech Road in the center of town, is open June through September, daily, 9 a.m. to 6 p.m., and October through May, Monday through Saturday, 9:15 a.m. to 5:15 p.m. The staff dispenses information about the town as well as the park. For more information, call ☎ 064-31633 or visit **www.corkkerry.ie.**

ARRIVING AND GETTING ORIENTED IN KILLARNEY

KILLARNEY IS ABOUT 40 KILOMETERS (25 miles) northwest of Kenmare and 100 kilometers (60 miles) southwest of **Limerick**. **Bus Éireann** coaches link Killarney with Dublin, Cork, Galway, Limerick, and other points in Ireland. The trip to Dublin takes almost six hours, involves a change in Limerick, and costs about €20 one-way, €35 round-trip; for information, call ☎ 066-712-3566 or visit **www .buseireann.ie.** Killarney is one of the few towns in the region with rail links, with service to and from Dublin, Limerick, and other Irish cities. The trip to Dublin costs about €40; for more schedules and information, contact Irish Rail, ☎ 064-31076; **www.irishrail.ie.**

HOTELS IN KILLARNEY

Arbutus Hotel ★★★★

QUALITY ★★★	VALUE ★★★★	€90–€140

College Street, Killarney, County Kerry ☎ 064-31037; fax 064-34033; stay@arbutuskillarney.com; www.arbutuskillarney.com

Location Center of town. **Amenities and services** 14 rooms; restaurant, bar, in-room tea and coffee facilities, satellite TV. **Elevator** No. **Parking** On street, free. **Price** Includes full Irish breakfast. **Credit cards** AE, CB, D, DC, JCB, MC, V.

IF KILLARNEY HAS A HEART AFTER ALL, it lurks in this wonderfully old-fashioned hotel right in the center of town, where hearths glow, salons are handsomely decorated, and the rooms are large and comfortable. The Buckley family has been running the place since the 1920s and continues to provide attentive service and go out of their way to ensure everything is in top form. Several rooms are set up for families, with multiple beds, and others are done in a lavish traditional style, with four-posters and armchairs, but even the standard rooms are extremely comfortable and quiet. The downstairs pub serves an excellent pint and keeps a welcoming fire glowing in the hearth.

Cahernane House   ★ ★ ★ ★

QUALITY	★ ★ ★ ★	VALUE	★ ★ ★		€ 150–€ 250

Muckross Road, Killarney, County Kerry ☎ 064-31895; fax 064-34340; info@cahernane.com, www.cahernane.com

Location On the shores of Lough Leane **Amenities and services** 33 rooms; restaurant, bar, fishing, horseback riding, in-room tea and coffee facilities, satellite TV. **Elevator** No. **Parking** On property, free. **Price** Includes full Irish breakfast. **Credit cards** AE, CB, D, DC, JCB, MC, V.

KILLARNEY IS SURROUNDED BY several sumptuous country-house hotels, and this family-run manor reached down a long private drive is one of the most attractive and most comfortable. The lounges and guest rooms in the manor house and a garden wing are traditionally furnished and luxurious, and service is remarkably attentive and extends to advice on how to best enjoy the national park. The greatest amenity, however, is the setting—most rooms overlook the lake and the mountains behind it, and the lawns and terraces provide a private getaway in which to enjoy all this natural beauty.

EXPLORING KILLARNEY

THE DRAW HERE, OF COURSE, is the park, and you won't feel the need to spend much time exploring Killarney proper. In fact, the one truly noteworthy in-town attraction is actually on national-park lands—**Knockreer Estate.** The house burned down years ago, but the gardens are lovely and afford sweeping views over the Lough Deenagh and the mountains. Admission is free, open daily, dawn to dusk. From here you can continue exploring the park on a series of paths that lead around the lake and to **Ross Castle** (see page 261).

RESTAURANTS IN KILLARNEY

Gaby's Seafood Restaurant   ★ ★ ★ ★

SEAFOOD	EXPENSIVE	QUALITY	★ ★ ★ ★	VALUE	★ ★ ★ ★

27 High Street, Killarney; ☎ 064-32519

Reservations Recommended. **Entree range** €27–€44; gourmet tasting menu, €50. **Payment** AE, MC, V. **Bar** Full service. **Disabled access** Limited. **Hours** Monday–Saturday, 6–10 p.m.; closed Sunday–Tuesday from January to mid-March.

MENU RECOMMENDATIONS Kerry seafood platter, lobster prepared any way.
COMMENTS Belgian Gert Maes has brought continental flare to Killarney and established one of Ireland's top seafood restaurants. A glowing hearth near the entrance and simple furnishings in the several rooms provide a warm setting in which to enjoy seafood just off the boats that day and enhanced with the kitchen's elixir-like sauces. Lobster, the house specialty, is done with Cognac and cream, but even the freshest oysters, unadorned, taste better here than they do almost anywhere else.

Treyvaud's ★★★★

IRISH	MODERATE	QUALITY ★★★★	VALUE ★★★★

62 High Street, Killarney; ☎ 064-33062

Reservations Recommended. **Entree range** €14–€24; 10% discount on dinners 5–7 p.m.; 4-course Sunday lunch and early dinner, €22; gourmet tasting menu, €75. **Payment** AE, MC, V. **Bar** Full service. **Disabled access** Yes. **Hours** Daily, noon–10:30 p.m.

MENU RECOMMENDATIONS Brothers Paul and Mark Treyvaud operate Killarney's most popular place for a meal, combining friendly service, pleasant contemporary decor, and an appealing menu that ranges from Irish stew, chowders, fish cakes, and sandwiches to such substantial choices as braised Kerry beef and seafood dishes. This is one of the few places in town where locals outnumber the tourists, and it's easy to understand why.

EXERCISE AND RECREATION IN KILLARNEY

THE PATHS OF KILLARNEY NATIONAL PARK run right up to the edge of town, inviting anyone with a bent for **cycling** to start pedaling. **O'Sullivan's** (Lower New Street; ☎ 064-26927), the largest of several outfits that rent bikes, also sells hiking gear and other outdoor equipment. The staff is knowledgeable and on occasion leads bike tours of the park; the shop is open seven days a week from 8:30 a.m. to 6 p.m. (later in summer), and bikes rent for about €15 a day.

Fishing enthusiasts will find many remote spots for salmon and brown trout throughout the park. Licenses are required, and prices vary with where you are fishing and what you are angling for, from about €10 for trout and €25 for salmon. **O'Neill's** (Plunkett Street; ☎ 064-31970) dispenses licenses, gear, tackle, and advice; plus, they can help you hire a "gillie" (fishing guide).

Killarney Golf and Fishing Club (Killorglin Road; ☎ 064-31034; **www.killarney-golf.com**) offers **golfers** their choice of three 18-hole courses, all set against a backdrop of spectacular scenery; greens fees begin at about €80 for 18 holes.

Around KILLARNEY

KILLARNEY NATIONAL PARK

ONE OF THE MOST BEAUTIFUL CORNERS of Ireland, this wilderness of heather-covered mountains, lush forests, and shimmering lakes has been popular with tourists since the middle of the 19th century. The huge expanse of natural beauty is now protected as a 10,000-hectare (25,000-acre) national park, much of which can only be explored on foot and by boat. You'll see enough from the roads that skirt the park to whet your appetite to get out of the car and explore the park further.

Approaching from Kenmare, N71 passes through a cleft in the mountains known as **Moll's Gap,** affording the first views over the park's lake-filled valleys and sheltering mountain ranges. Continue on a few miles to the even-better spectacle from **Ladies' View,** so named for Queen Victoria's ladies-in-waiting, who enjoyed the outlook when the Queen was a guest at **Muckross House** (see next page). The **Torc Waterfall** cascades down a nearby mountainside, but any sense of wilderness comes abruptly to an end as N71 enters Killarney. On the other side of town, though, the romantic ruins of the seventh-century monastery that once flourished on Innisfallen Island rise out of the lake, and beyond lies the **Gap of Dunloe,** accessible only on foot, horseback, or bike. Here is some of the park's most enchanting scenery, where enormous boulders litter a pass that cuts through MacGillycuddy's Reeks, Ireland's highest mountains, and ends at one of the park's most remote expanses of water, Upper Lake.

Exploring Killarney National Park

Hiking trails crisscross the park, and many of the trailheads are on or around the grounds of Muckross House. Even a quick hike up the Old Boathouse Nature Trail along a peninsula in Muckross Lake or up the Blue Pool Trail to the pretty eponymous lake will introduce you to the park's beauty. For more information on the park and its attractions, visit the **Killarney National Park Visitor Centre,** on the grounds of Muckross House.

Tours of Killarney National Park

One of the easiest ways to see the park is in a horse-drawn jaunting car, an open carriage that accommodates up to four passengers; about €25 per person, per hour; tours are available at Muckross House and other points within the park. **Adventure Tours** offers a scenery-filled excursion in a jaunting car through the Gap of Dunloe, followed by a boat trip across three of the park's lakes; for more information, call ☎ 064-30200 or visit **www.gapofdunloetours.com.** For a rougher trek, horses can be rented at **Muckross Riding Stables,** Mangerton Road, Muckross; call ☎ 064-32238. The scenery is especially beautiful when viewed from one of the lakes. Board the *Lily of Killarney* or *Pride of the Lakes* on the pier at Ross Castle. Hour-long cruises operate April through October every hour and a half or so, beginning at 10:30 a.m.; €8 for adults, €4 for children, €20 for families; for reservations on the *Lily of Killarney,* call ☎ 064-31068; for *Pride of the Lakes,* call ☎ 064-32638.

Attractions around Killarney National Park

Muckross House and Traditional Farms ★★★★

| APPEAL BY AGE | PRESCHOOL ★★★ | GRADE SCHOOL ★★★★ | TEENS ★★★★ |
| YOUNG ADULTS ★★★★ | | OVER 30 ★★★★ | SENIORS ★★★★ |

In Killarney National Park, about 5 kilometers (3 miles) south of the town of Killarney, County Kerry; ☎ 064-31440; www.muckross-house.ie

Type of attraction Victorian home and grounds. **Admission** *Muckross House:* €5.75 adults, €4.50 seniors, €2.35 children and students, €14.50 families of up to 2 adults and 3 children; *Traditional Farms:* €6.50 adults, €5 seniors, €3 children and students, €17.50 families of up to 2 adults and 3 children; joint ticket: €10 adults, €8 seniors, €5 children and students, €27.50 families of up to 2 adults and 3 children. **Hours** *Muckross House:* July 1–August 31, daily, 9 a.m.– 7 p.m.; September 1–June 30, daily, 9 a.m.–5:30 p.m.; *Traditional Farms:* March– April and October, Saturday–Sunday, 1–6 p.m.; May, daily, 1–6 p.m.; June– September, daily, 10 a.m.–6 p.m. **When to go** The house tour is a good refuge when the skies open up, but try to find a break in the weather so you can explore the grounds; the Traditional Farms are not enjoyable in the rain, especially if you are accompanied by children. **Special comments** The Muckross Walled Garden Centre is a glass-fronted complex facing the walled Victorian gardens that houses a self-service restaurant and shops selling local crafts. **How much time to allow** At least 1 hour if you're visiting only the house, 3 hours to include the grounds and Traditional Farms.

DESCRIPTION AND COMMENTS Much of the lands that now compose Killarney National Park were part of the Welsh-Irish Herbert family estate, a fortune made through copper mining on the Muckross Peninsula. Henry Arthur Herbert and his wife, the watercolorist Mary Balfour, built this Victorian mansion at the heart of the estate on the shores of Lough Leane, completing it in 1843 and furnishing the 20 rooms much as they appear today. Queen Victoria spent a few days at Muckross in 1861, and the expense of bringing the house up to snuff for the royal visit is said to have contributed to the family's financial woes. They lost the house in 1898; a member of the Guinness family bought it in 1899; and William Bowers Bourn, an American who made his millions in California gold mines, presented the house as a wedding gift to his daughter, Maud, and Arthur Rose Vincent, in 1910. Muckross is filled with heavy furniture, antlers, portraits, and elaborate silver services, but it has the feel of a family home. Even Queen Victoria's suite, spe- cially fitted out for the visit, is not particularly grandiose. Note its ground-floor location—the queen was terrified of fire and never slept in an upstairs room. Downstairs is a warren of pantries and kitchens that show how the other half spent their days at Muckross House.

So, too, do the Traditional Farms, where authentic-seeming replicas of three working farms from the 1930s and 1940s depict rural life in those not-so-long-ago days in Ireland when machinery was still horse drawn and cottages were lit by kerosene lamps.

TOURING TIPS Take one of the free house tours if available; guides are a font of gossipy background.

Ross Castle   ★ ★ ★

APPEAL BY AGE	PRESCHOOL ★★★★★	GRADE SCHOOL ★★★★★	TEENS ★★★★★
YOUNG ADULTS ★★★★★		OVER 30 ★★★★½	SENIORS ★★½

On Lough Leane, 2 kilometers (about 1 mile) south of Killarney off N17, County Kerry; ☎ 064-35851; www.heritageireland.ie

Type of attraction Medieval stronghold. **Admission** €5 adults, €2 children and students, €3.50 seniors, €11 families of up to 2 adults and 2 children. **Hours** Mid-March–May, daily, 9:30 a.m.–5:30 p.m.; June–August, daily, 9 a.m.–6:30 p.m.; September–mid-October, daily, 9:30 a.m.–5:30 p.m.; mid-October–mid-November, daily, 9:30 a.m.–4:30 p.m. **When to go** Anytime, but it's best in spring or fall when the crowds thin out and you can get a better sense of the place. **Special comments** In the busy summer months, you may have to wait to enter. **How much time to allow** About 1 hour.

DESCRIPTION AND COMMENTS The O'Donoghue Ross clan of Irish chieftains built this castle on the shores of Lough Leane in the 15th century. Substantial portions of the fortification walls and two of the round towers remain intact. Though today the castle makes an incredibly romantic appearance, with its tall walls and towers rising from the misty waters of the lake, this positioning, with most of the castle protected by the water from land attack, was purely defensive—and ineffective. In 1652, inhabitants held off an invasion by more than 2,000 Cromwellian troops for days, until the British floated batteries onto the lake and bombarded the beleaguered castle from two sides. Somewhat ironically, this defensive stronghold is rather charmingly, even cozily fitted out with some splendid 16th- and 17th-century furniture.

unofficial **TIP**
If you can't resist doing the Ring, keep in mind that a complete circuit covers a slow 180 kilometers (112 miles) on route N70, more if you want to make the dramatic **Skellig Loop** at the western tip of the peninsula, and will take the better part of a day.

TOURING TIPS After touring the castle, take a walk along one of the paths that follow the lakeshore, or board one of the boats that depart from the castle pier (see page 259).

DINGLE TOWN

AT HEART A FISHING PORT but also a popular seaside getaway for ordinary Irish folks and foreign visitors alike, Dingle is an agreeable place to settle in for a few days. A number of really good guesthouses and many excellent restaurants make it all the more appealing. Don't expect to find yourself completely off the beaten path, though. The town is still small, at about 1,500 year-round residents, but holiday bungalows march across the green hillsides and smart shop windows line the cobbled streets—signs that Dingle is no longer the quaint, out-of-the-way village it was even 30 years ago.

PLANNING YOUR VISIT TO DINGLE

LOCATED ON THE WATERFRONT near the center of town, the **Dingle Tourist Office** is open mid-April through October, Monday through Sunday, 9 a.m. to 5 p.m.; November through March, Tuesday through Saturday, 9 a.m. to 5 p.m. The office is really nothing but a souvenir shop, but the staff can be helpful regarding accommodations and local sights. For more information, call ☎ 066-915-1188 or visit **www .corkkerry.ie**.

ARRIVING AND GETTING ORIENTED IN DINGLE

DINGLE IS ABOUT 70 KILOMETERS (42 miles) west of Killarney, and by car the most direct route is via N22 and R561. **Bus Éireann** coaches link Dingle with Dublin, Cork, Galway, and other points in Ireland, but a trip just about anywhere involves a transfer in Tralee to the north or Killarney to the south. The trip to Dublin takes almost eight hours; about €20 one-way, €35 round-trip; for information, call ☎ 066-712-3566 or visit **www.buseireann.ie**. Buses arrive and depart from the Quay, in front of the supermarket.

HOTELS IN DINGLE

Captains House ★★★★

QUALITY ★★★	VALUE ★★★★	€60–€100

**The Mall, Dingle, County Kerry (closed December 1–March 15);
☎ 066-915-1531; fax 066-915-1079; captigh@eircom.net;
homepage.eircom.net/~captigh**

Location Center of town. **Amenities and services** 8 rooms; in-room tea and coffee facilities, satellite TV. **Elevator** No. **Parking** On street, free. **Price** Includes full Irish breakfast. **Credit cards** AE, CB, D, DC, JCB, MC, V.

SNUG IS THE WORD FOR THIS OLD HOUSE (actually, two narrow town houses joined together) in the center of town, where Jim Milhench, a retired sea captain, and his wife Mary run a tight ship. Downstairs is a cozy parlor filled with mementos of Jim's travels and warmed by a turf fire in colder months, as well as a conservatory, where a large breakfast is served. A long garden at the rear of the house runs down to the River Mall; it's a delightful place to relax after a day of sightseeing. Guest rooms, reached via steep stairs and twisting hallways full of nooks and crannies, vary considerably in size. Although most rooms are quite small and not unlike cabins on a ship, they are extremely comfortable, with good beds and tidy little bathrooms, and the best are in the rear of the house overlooking the garden. This is not a good choice for anyone who has a hard time with stairs, and all guests would be well advised to leave heavy bags and, given the tight quarters, superfluous belongings in the car.

Castlewood House ★ ★ ★ ★

QUALITY ★ ★ ★ ★ ½	VALUE ★ ★ ★	€ 100–€ 130

The Wood, Dingle, County Kerry; ☎ 066-915-2788; fax 066-915-2788; castlewoodhouse@eircom.net; www.castlewooddingle.com

Location West edge of town. **Amenities and services** 12 units; hair dryers, in-room tea and coffee facilities, Internet access, minibars, DVD players. **Elevator** Yes. **Parking** Free, on property. **Price** Includes full Irish breakfast. **Credit cards** AE, MC, V.

LITTLE WONDER THAT THIS beautifully appointed house at the edge of Dingle Bay has the feel of a luxury hotel: owners-managers Brian Heaton and Helen Woods Heaton trained at some of Ireland's finest hotels before returning to Dingle to open their own guesthouse next to Heaton's, the well-known inn run by Brian's parents. In fact, the two houses look like a matching set of McMansions, and both live up to the family's reputation for hospitality. The 12 individually decorated and tasteful rooms at Castlewood are all oversize; the largest are set up like suites and have welcoming sitting areas overlooking the bay and king-size beds covered in fine linens. The individually decorated bathrooms are large, with expanses of marble, long vanities, deep whirlpool tubs (in many), and separate power showers. Over-stuffed couches surround a hearth in the handsome lounge, and a large breakfast is served in a sunny room overlooking the bay. Treats include porridge made with Irish Mist or Baileys and made-to-order omelets.

Gorman's ★ ★ ★ ★

QUALITY ★ ★ ★ ★	VALUE ★ ★ ★	€ 120–€ 170

Ballydavid, Dingle Peninsula; ☎ 066-915-5162; fax 066-915-5162; info@gormans-clifftophouse.com; www.gormans-clifftophouse.com

Location On the sea of the Slea Head Drive. **Amenities and services** 9 units; restaurant, lounge, room service, hair dryers, in-room tea and coffee facilities, garden, some Jacuzzi baths. **Elevator** No. **Parking** Free, on property. **Price** Includes full Irish breakfast. **Credit cards** AE, MC, V.

PERCHED DRAMATICALLY AT THE EDGE of the sea on the northwest end of the Dingle Peninsula, this stone house is the perfect retreat for anyone who wants to get away from it all and enjoy unbroken views of crashing surf. Handsome pine furnishings, pottery hand-thrown in the nearby workshops of Louis Mulcahy, and glowing fires create a luxuriously cozy atmosphere from which to watch the drama from almost every window. The restaurant is superb, making a return from a long walk or bike ride along the Dingle Way all the more appealing. Set dinners are €32 to €38, and a day begins with a lavish Irish breakfast served in a seaside lounge.

Greenmount House ★★★★

QUALITY ★★★★	VALUE ★★★★	€110–€170

Gortonara, Dingle, County Kerry; ☎ 066-915-1414; fax 066-915-1974; info@greenmount-house.com; www.greenmount-house.com

Location East edge of town. **Amenities and services** 14 units; garden, in-room tea and coffee facilities, turndown service. **Elevator** No. **Parking** Free, on property. **Price** Includes full Irish breakfast. **Credit cards** MC, V.

A HILLSIDE PERCH OVERLOOKING the town and bay is only part of the appeal of John and Mary Curran's legendary B&B; for many visitors it's the highlight of a tour around Ireland. The Currans have been welcoming guests for almost 30 years in their expanded family bungalow, and they never seem to tire of improving the property. Most rooms are really suites, with comfortable sitting areas, large windows filled with views over the town, bay, and surrounding hills, and many with terraces or patios. Furnishings in the guest rooms and the lounges are tasteful, colors and fabrics throughout are soothing, and bathrooms are continually being refurbished. The day begins with breakfast in the conservatory, and the buffet table is so laden with homemade cakes, breads, and farmhouse cheeses—augmented with a large selection of cooked dishes—that few guests manage to leave Greenmount without gaining a pound or two. The center of town is an easy walk down the hill.

Heaton's Guesthouse ★★★

QUALITY ★★★½	VALUE ★★★★	€60–€150

The Wood, Dingle, County Kerry (closed late November–early February); ☎ 066-915-2288; fax 066-915-2324; heatons@iol.ie; www.heatonsdingle.com

Location West edge of town. **Amenities and services** 16 rooms; garden, in-room tea and coffee facilities. **Elevator** No. **Parking** Free, on property. **Price** Includes full Irish breakfast. **Credit cards** AE, MC, V.

THIS HOUSE ACROSS THE ROAD from Dingle Bay is another favorite with return visitors to Dingle who enjoy the comfortable and low-key surroundings, the extremely comfortable rooms overlooking the water and lawns, and Cameron and Nuala Heaton's almost legendary hospitality. Guest rooms are furnished individually and stylishly, with comfy touches such as lounge chairs and sofas. Cameron and Nuala are on hand to see to the needs of their guests and provide advice on what to see and where to eat, and they take special pride in a lavish breakfast served in a sunny front room that overlooks the bay. Heaton's is next door to Castlewood (see previous page), run by the Heatons' son Brian and his wife, Helen Woods Heaton; the properties are at the edge of town, about a ten-minute walk away.

Milltown House ★★★★

QUALITY ★★★★	VALUE ★★★	€100–€150

Dingle, County Kerry (closed November 15–April 15); ☎ 066-915-1372;
fax 066-915-1095; info@ milltownhousedingle.com;
www.milltownhousedingle.com

Location On the bay, just west of town. **Amenities and services** 10 rooms;
garden, hair dryers, in-room movies, in-room tea and coffee facilities, trouser
press. **Elevator** No. **Parking** Free, on property. **Price** Includes full Irish breakfast.
Credit cards AE, MC, V.

THIS FINE OLD HOUSE, set amid lawns on the shores of Dingle Bay, is a
countrylike getaway only about 1 kilometer (0.5 miles) from the center of
town. This is the sort of place that guests return to often and think of
fondly. Robert Mitchum stayed here when he was filming *Ryan's Daughter,*
and his room, number ten, is one of several oversize doubles that have
large bay windows furnished with easy chairs facing the bay and town.
Geared for relaxing, all of the rooms have sitting areas, and while the furnishings are old-fashioned, they include firm beds and modern amenities
such as flat-screen TVs. *Ryan's Daughter* and *Far and Away,* also set on the
Dingle Peninsula and starring Tom Cruise and Nicole Kidman, are aired on
the in-house movie system. While many hotels try to create as many reve-
nue-producing rooms as possible, the Kerry family takes the opposite
approach, continually enlarging rooms to make them more comfortable.
Two of the ground-floor rooms open to private patios, and another, number eight, has its own entrance to the gardens that surround the house. A
lavish breakfast, which always includes fresh fish, is served in a delightful
conservatory; other public rooms include a large lounge, and tables and
chairs are set out in the lawn next to the bay in good weather.

Old Pier ★ ★ ★

| QUALITY ★ ★ ★ | VALUE ★ ★ ★ ★ | € 50–€ 100 |

Feothanach, Ballydavid, County Kerry; ☎ 066-915-5242;
info@oldpier.com; www.oldpier.com

Location On the north side of Dingle Peninsula, about 15 kilometers (9 miles)
outside of Dingle Town. **Amenities and services** 5 rooms; hair dryers, in-room
tea and coffee facilities. **Elevator** No. **Parking** On property. **Price** Includes full
Irish breakfast. **Credit cards** MC, V.

THE SURF CRASHES INTO THE ROCKS just steps from the front door of this
five-room guesthouse in a tiny fishing village on the north side of the
Dingle Peninsula, setting the stage for a scenery-filled seaside getaway.
Rooms are large and snug, with wood floors, nice pine furniture, and tasteful fabrics. Most have wonderful views of the sea. A family room is equipped
with extra beds for children, who will enjoy the expansive grounds and
nearby beaches. The best part of staying at the Old Pier is the proximity of
the dining room downstairs, which serves some of the freshest and best-
prepared seafood in the region. This is where locals come for a good
seafood meal, and guests can arrange very attractive dinner and bed-and-
breakfast deals.

EXPLORING DINGLE

DINGLE IS COMPACT, wedged between the bay and the mountains, and the town's few sights are within easy walking distance. The **Chapel of St. Joseph's Convent,** off Green Street, is lit with the heavenly light from 12 stained-glass windows by Harry Clark, one of Ireland's leading 20th-century artisans. Completed in 1922, the windows charmingly depict scenes from the life of Christ and are nicely documented in a free audio-guide tour; Monday through Friday, 9:30 a.m. to 1 p.m. and 2 to 5 p.m. Dingle's flashiest attraction is the rather modest **Oceanworld Aquarium,** on the harbor, call ☎ 066-915-2111 or visit **www .dingle-oceanworld.ie.** Skip this unless it's raining and the kids are restless. The effort to show native fish is sincere, and there are plenty of chances to pet starfish and other creatures, but the experience pales if you've visited more-ambitious aquariums elsewhere. Open daily, 10 a.m.–5 p.m.; €12 adults; €9 seniors and students; €6 children; €32 families of up to two adults and four children. Dingle's most famous attraction can be hard to pin down, is often out of sight, and is prone to getting you wet—this, of course, is **Fungie,** a bottlenose dolphin who swam into the harbor in 1983 and, much to the delight of local entrepreneurs, decided to stay. Boat operators charge €12 for adults and €6 for children for the cruise out to see Fungie, who appears with such regularity that the trip comes with a money-back guarantee if the star is a no-show. Boats leave from the pier near the tourist office every half hour in the summer, less frequently off-season.

unofficial **TIP**
Besides the boat tours, another way to see Fungie is to walk out along the east side of the harbor, following the seashore path beyond the Coast Guard Station to the lighthouse; Fungie often frolics just offshore.

RESTAURANTS IN DINGLE

A COUPLE OF CHARMING CAFES are tucked away on Dingle's cobbled streets; most are open only during the day. **An Café Liteartha** (☎ 066-915-2204), behind the bookstore of the same name on Dykegate Street, serves soup, sandwiches, and freshly baked scones; open Monday through Saturday, 9 a.m. to 6 p.m., this is a delightful place to sit for a spell and read.

Chart House ★★★★

MODERN IRISH/SEAFOOD	EXPENSIVE	QUALITY ★★★★	VALUE ★★★★

The Mall, Dingle; ☎ 066-915-2255

Reservations Recommended. **Entree range** €17–€24; three-course menu, available all evening, €35. **Payment** MC, V. **Bar** Full service. **Disabled access** Yes. **Hours** June–September: daily, 6–10 p.m.; limited hours at other times.

MENU RECOMMENDATIONS Roasted cod, peppered filet of pork.

COMMENTS This handsome stone building near the bay provides the most pleasant dining experience in town, with sophisticated yet informal surroundings in a wood-floored, rose-hued room overlooking the water. Friendly but polished service pairs with superb preparations of seafood from the local waters and meats from Kerry farms. Sauces are perfectly flavored, while interesting risottos and vegetable concoctions accompany the main courses. Several vegetarian dishes are served every evening as well—a warm polenta tartlet, perhaps, or simple homemade ravioli stuffed with spinach and brie. Desserts include homemade ice creams and a wonderful selection of Irish cheeses.

Fenton's ★★★

MODERN IRISH	MODERATE	QUALITY ★★★	VALUE ★★★

Green Street, Dingle; ☎ 066-915-2172

Reservations Recommended. **Entree range** €28–€30; early-bird dinner, until 7 p.m., €29.95 for 2 courses. **Payment** MC, V. **Bar** Full service. **Disabled access** Yes. **Hours** Tuesday–Sunday, 6–9:30 p.m.; closed November–March.

MENU RECOMMENDATIONS Hot buttered lobster, black sole à la meunière, roast rack of lamb with rosemary and thyme, apple and berry crumble.

COMMENTS When locals want a relaxed evening out, they often come to this cozy old house in the center of town, where Patricia Fenton makes her guests feel at home in a cheerful wood-floored room warmed by a fire in an old stone hearth. A small menu sticks to local produce—lamb reared on the family farm, lobster and other seafood from Dingle Bay, and homegrown vegetables, all deftly prepared.

Global Village ★★★★

MODERN IRISH	MODERATE	QUALITY ★★★★	VALUE ★★★★½

Main Street, Dingle; ☎ 066-915-2325

Reservations Recommended. **Entree range** €17–€24; early-bird menu, 5–7 p.m., €19.50 for two courses, €23.50 for three courses. **Payment** MC, V. **Bar** Full service. **Disabled access** Yes. **Hours** Daily, 5–9:30 p.m.; closed mid-November–February.

MENU RECOMMENDATIONS Thai curry, duck, fresh fish of the day.

COMMENTS Chef Martin Bealin claims to have been inspired by his world travels—hence some interesting spices and the appearance of a curry dish or two on the menu—but he has not forgotten his Irish roots. His cooking is honest and down-to-earth, with an emphasis on the freshest fish from Dingle waters as well as prime Irish beef and lamb. His excellent presentations are served with great warmth and attention to guests; the pleasant, relaxed tile-floored room features works by local artists.

Goat Street Café ★★★½

| MODERN IRISH | INEXPENSIVE | QUALITY | ★★★★ | VALUE ★★★★ |

Goat Street, Dingle; ☎ 066-915-2770

Reservations None taken. **Entree range** €9–€10. **Payment** AE, MC, V. **Bar** Wine and beer. **Disabled access** Yes. **Hours** Sunday–Wednesday, 10 a.m.–5 p.m.; Thursday–Saturday, 6–9 p.m.

MENU RECOMMENDATIONS Lamb tagine, pasta with smoked salmon.

COMMENTS This modest little place has just a few tables and makes no attempt at decor, but the kitchen is much more ambitious than the surroundings suggest. The menu changes daily and usually includes such simple fare as homemade soups and farm-fresh salads. But the more sophisticated fare, including a salad of warm duck confit, is such a surprising treat that it would be a shame to miss.

Lord Baker's ★★★

| IRISH | MODERATE/INEXPENSIVE | QUALITY ★★★ | VALUE ★★★★ |

Main Street, Dingle; ☎ 066-915-1277

Reservations Recommended. **Entree range** €15–€25; early-bird dinner, €16.50; prix-fixe menu, €24.95; lunches and light evening meals, about €9–€14. **Payment** AE, MC, V. **Bar** Full service. **Disabled access** Yes. **Hours** Friday–Wednesday, 12:30–2 p.m. and 6:30–10 p.m.

MENU RECOMMENDATIONS Seafood chowder, rack of lamb, lobster.

COMMENTS More Dingle restaurants—which tend to serve full meals only at dinnertime—should take their cue from the oldest pub in town, where you can choose from a bar menu and enjoy a lighter, less expensive evening meal or opt for a full dinner. Certainly, the lighter option—maybe a bowl of seafood chowder or lobster bisque followed by crab claws or a crab sandwich—is a satisfying meal in itself. The best place to enjoy your meal is the handsome old stone-walled barroom warmed by a turf fire; a more formal dining room and walled garden are just beyond.

Out of the Blue ★★★

| SEAFOOD | EXPENSIVE | QUALITY ★★★★½ | VALUE ★★★½ |

Waterside, Dingle; ☎ 066-915-0811

Reservations Required. **Entree range** €18–€32. **Payment** MC, V. **Bar** Beer and wine only. **Disabled access** Yes. **Hours** Thursday–Tuesday, 12:30–3 p.m. and 6–9:30 p.m.

MENU RECOMMENDATIONS Fresh catch of the day.

COMMENTS This simple, brightly covered shack is the talk of Dingle these days, and the basic room has far fewer seats than can accommodate diners eager to eat here. The menu depends entirely upon what's available from the boats that dock just outside the door, and chef Seamus MacDonald prepares the catch simply but interestingly, with a dash of spices and skillful sauces, accompanied by delicious soups and chowders, fresh vegetables, and homemade breads. It's not all smooth sailing here: the premises are far too small for the crowds of appreciative patrons, and long waits, cramped seating, and rushed service are common.

ENTERTAINMENT AND NIGHTLIFE IN DINGLE

THINK PUBS, with which Dingle is well endowed. Many offer live traditional music a couple of evenings a week, some more often, and the musicians are usually in tune and ready to begin by 9:30 p.m., winding down around 11:30 p.m. This means that if you want to enjoy some pub grub, you'd better order by 8:30 p.m., because most pubs stop serving at 9 p.m. to accommodate the heavy-drinking music crowd. Two of the best pubs for music are **An Driochead Beag** (The Small Bridge) and **O'Flaherty's,** both on Bridge Street. In the old days, pubs doubled as shops, and this tradition lives on in Dingle. **Dick Mack's,** on Green Street, is still part leather- and shoe-repair shop, and the smell of leather mingles nicely with that of beer. **Foxy John's,** on Main Street, is also a hardware store, and **O'Currain's,** across the street, does double duty as a clothing shop. Dingle's other nighttime entertainment is the **cinema** on the Mall, where a first-run film, often British, usually is showing.

SHOPPING IN DINGLE

SHOPPERS WITH AN EYE for good craftsmanship will be pleased to find some high-quality work in Dingle's shops. **Gaileari Beag** (18 Main Street; ☎ 066-915-2976) is a showplace for local artisans, with excellent pottery and other works on display, including fused-glass jewelry and lamps by Fiona and Jazz Wood. **Greenlane Gallery** (Green Street, ☎ 066-915-2018) shows works by local painters and sculptors. The **Weaver's Shop** (also on Green Street, ☎ 066-915-1688) features scarves, shawls, tablecloths, and distinctive decorative pieces by Lisbeth Mulcahy, one of Ireland's most noted weavers.

EXERCISE AND RECREATION IN DINGLE

DINGLE IS A GOOD BASE for active visitors. The peninsula is skirted by some excellent beaches, the best being the five-kilometer-long (three-mile-long) strand at Inch, backed by dunes; much of David Lean's film *Ryan's Daughter* was shot on the beach. Inch is about ten kilometers (six miles) east of Dingle on R561. **Mountain Man** (Strand Street; ☎ 066-915-2400) rents bikes and equipment and dispenses a lot of advice on where to ride. Most cyclists head out to Slea Head at the eastern tip of the peninsula. You can golf at the **Dingle Golf Club,** about 16 kilometers (10 miles) north of Dingle Town in Ballyferriter; ☎ 066-915-6255; about €60 for 18 holes. If you want to explore the mountains or trot along a beach on horseback, rent a mount at **Dingle Horse Riding** (Ballinaboula House; ☎ 066-915-2199). Walkers can choose a stretch of the **Dingle Way,** which circles the peninsula for 150 kilometers (90 miles); the tourist office in Dingle sells guides to walking the path.

Around **DINGLE**

 THE DINGLE PENINSULA

THE WESTERNMOST TIP of Ireland stretches some 50 kilometers (30 miles) from the mainland into the Atlantic surf—a spine of rugged mountains, rocky cliffs, and soft sands. Remnants of prehistoric and early-Christian cultures litter the hilly countryside, where farmers still speak Irish, and fishing boats set out from tidy harbors along the coast. None of these charms are lost on the visitors who crowd the peninsula in summer, but the empty landscapes accommodate them well. Besides, the Dingle Peninsula is far enough off the beaten track that for much of the year the towns and villages settle back into their quiet ways, and the sense of otherworldliness is enhanced by thick mists, good stout, and the ever-present traditional Irish tunes.

Exploring the Dingle Peninsula

The most dramatic scenery on the peninsula lies to the west of Dingle Town, and you can enjoy the sights on a well-marked 50-kilometer (30-mile) loop from the west end of town. Be prepared to drive slowly (roads are twisting, often one lane, and shared more often than not with sheep) and to stop frequently, as there's much to see, from Iron Age forts to early-Christian settlements to spectacular scenery.

About 13 kilometers (8 miles) beyond Dingle Town the road comes to 2,500-year-old **Dunbeg Fort,** with thick, earthen ramparts rising precariously above the sea. In fact, much of the enclosure has already crashed into the waves, but enough remains to show the defensive strength of the enclosure and its strategic position on a wave-washed promontory; entrance is free, but you'll pay €2 to cross private land to reach the fort. About 1 kilometer (0.5 miles) or so down the road is a colony of stone beehive huts said to have been built by early Christians; you'll pay another €2 to get to them. After you ford a stream, the road comes to **Slea Head,** where you should pull over next to the stone crucifixion scene to enjoy views of the wild surf racing ashore and the Blasket Islands looming in the near distance. Just beyond is another scenic spot, **Dunmore Head,** the westernmost point in Europe, and the village of Dunquin, where the ruins of stone cottages abandoned during the Famine years litter the hillside around a small harbor and boats depart for the Blasket Islands. Life in this bleak outpost is chronicled in the nearby **Blasket Centre** (see facing page). **Ballyferriter,** about eight kilometers (five miles) down the road, is the largest village at this end of the peninsula. It's dominated by the glossy operations of the Louis Mulcahy Pottery studios; sophisticated pottery and dinnerware made from local clay is displayed in a large shop daily, from 10 a.m. to 6 p.m.; ☎ 066-915-6229.

Several more early-Christian settlements are clustered on this part of the northern coast. At **Reasc,** a 6th- to 12th-century monastery enclosure includes remnants of an early church and an intricate cross carved into a Celtic stone pillar from 500 BC. More intact, though, is the nearby **Gallus Oratory,** a beautiful, remarkably well-preserved 1,300-year-old church resembling the keel of a boat, constructed with dry-stone corbeling developed by prehistoric tomb builders; daily, 10 a.m. to 5 p.m. (hours vary in off-season); €3 includes a film introduction to Ireland's prehistoric and early-Christian cultures. Running into a cove just down the coast is **Brandon's Creek,** a landing stage for fishing boats. St. Brendan the Voyager is said to have set out from here sometime in the middle of the sixth century and sailed across the Atlantic to the New World in a *currach,* a fragile little vessel of hide stretched over a wood frame. In 1976, an adventurous scholar who embarked on the same voyage from this spot in a similar boat made it all the way to Newfoundland.

Return to Dingle Town over the **Connor Pass,** a view-a-minute ride (in good weather, that is) through a breach in the spine of mountains that runs the length of the peninsula.

Tours of the Dingle Peninsula

Tim and Michael Collins, a father-and-son team, introduce visitors to the peninsula's prehistory and early-Christian cultures on their fact-filled **Sciuird Archaeology Tours,** which depart from Dingle Town. These guys know all the back roads, and they will show you tombs and forts you'd never find on your own, while giving you an earful about life in these parts. Tours last about two and a half hours; May through September, 10:30 a.m. and 2 p.m.; call for times in the off-season; ☎ 066-915-1606; €20.

Attraction on the Dingle Peninsula

 The Blasket Centre ★ ★ ★ ★

APPEAL BY AGE	PRESCHOOL ★ ★	GRADE SCHOOL ★ ★ ★	TEENS ★ ★ ★
YOUNG ADULTS ★ ★		OVER 30 ★ ★ ★ ★	SENIORS ★ ★ ★ ★

Dunquin, tip of Dingle Peninsula, about 16 kilometers (10 miles) west of Dingle Town on R559; ☎ 066-915-6444; www.heritageireland.ie

Type of attraction Museum of life on the Blasket Islands. **Admission** €3.70 adults, €2.60 seniors, €1.30 children and students, €8.70 for families. **Hours** Easter–June and September–October, daily, 10 a.m.–6 p.m.; July–August, daily, 10 a.m.–7 p.m. **When to go** Anytime. **Special comments** A stop here is mandatory before visiting the islands. **How much time to allow** About 1 hour.

DESCRIPTION AND COMMENTS The remote Blasket Islands were home to several hundred inhabitants until the early 1950s, when the last of the islanders went to the mainland. For centuries the only contact an islander had with the rest of the world was to row across 12 miles of open ocean in a *currach* (a boat made of animal hide) to this end of the Dingle Peninsula. It's not surprising that the islanders developed their own ways—their own dialect, musical variations, and a small body of literature (referred to as the Blasket Library). This well-designed museum preserves the Blasket culture with fascinating photographs, manuscripts, and models of island houses; a 20-minute video contains rare footage of the last days of life on the islands, as well as some lyrical readings of poetry. Large windows at the front of the museum overlook the islands.

TOURING TIPS If you're inspired to see the islands, board the Blasket ferry in nearby Dunquin Harbour. Boats run hourly in the summer, but not at all from mid-October to March, and not in bad weather, when rough seas make it foolhardy to dock at the tiny landing stage on Great Blasket; €20 round-trip. You'll learn a lot more about the islands on a visit to the museum than you will to the islands.

PART SEVEN

The LOWER SHANNON

THE SHANNON, THE LONGEST RIVER in the British Isles, flows into the Atlantic Ocean through a wide estuary in County Limerick. While many travelers, who know the region only as a gateway to Ireland through Shannon Airport, rush through on their way to other places, the green landscapes that roll away from the estuary merit a visit of several days or more. The countryside is littered with castles, pretty towns and villages, and some of Ireland's grandest hotels. One of Ireland's largest cities, **Limerick,** is here, too. You might want to settle down for a spell upon first arriving in Ireland, or perhaps enjoy the region as a last taste of the country before taking off.

NOT TO BE MISSED IN THE LOWER SHANNON

■ ADARE

ADARE IS A PICTURE-BOOK PLACE that is the self-proclaimed "prettiest village in Ireland." Who's to say if that is really true in this country with so many pretty villages, but Adare is certainly attractive. The thatch-roofed cottages lining its main street look as if they were built solely for the pleasure of photographers. Actually, the Earls of Dunraven built the rose-covered village cottages and houses in the middle of the 19th century for tenants on their estate, which straddles the banks of the River Maigue at the edge of town. The estate's parklands are a delight for walkers, and the Dunravens' Gothic Revival

unofficial **TIP**
The Lower Shannon region is tucked conveniently between Kerry and Galway, so it makes a nice stopover when traveling between places in those two counties.

the lower shannon

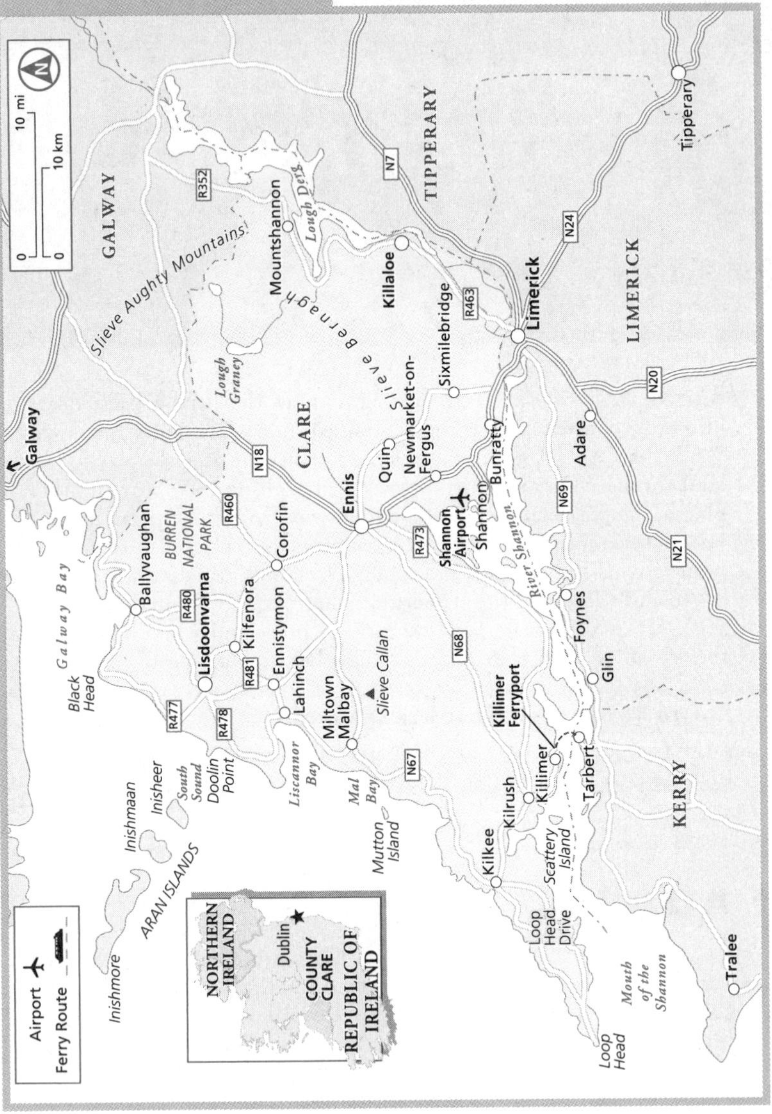

manor house is one of Ireland's most luxurious hotels.

Just 40 kilometers (25 miles) south of Shannon Airport, Adare is a good choice for a first or last stop in Ireland. Comfortable hotels plus good restaurants and many activities and attractions add to the appeal.

PLANNING YOUR VISIT TO ADARE

YOU'LL FIND INFORMATION on Adare and the surrounding region at the **Adare Heritage Centre** on Main Street; it's open May through September, Monday through Saturday, 9 a.m. to 7 p.m., Sunday 9 a.m. to 6 p.m.; and October through April, Monday through Saturday, 9:30 a.m. to 5:30 p.m.; call ☎ 061-396666 or visit **www.adareheritagecentre.ie**. The information desk is not always staffed, especially around lunchtime. The Heritage Centre galleries present displays, a model of the town, and an audiovisual presentation highlighting Adare's history.

ARRIVING AND GETTING ORIENTED IN ADARE

ADARE IS JUST 20 KILOMETERS (12 miles) southwest of Limerick City; the trip is a quick 15 minutes by car on N20. If you're coming

unofficial **TIP**
Admission to the **Adare Heritage Centre** (€5 adults, €3.50 children, €15 families) is steep for what you'll see. You can learn just about all you really need to know about Adare on the historical placards in front of the building or in one of the free handouts from the information desk.

How Hotels Compare in Lower Shannon

HOTEL	OVERALL	QUALITY	VALUE	PRICE
ADARE				
Adare Manor	★★★★	★★★½	★★★	From €295
Dunraven Arms	★★★★	★★★★	★★★★	€125–€190
Glin Castle	★★★★	★★★★	★★★	From €310
Adare Country House	★★★	★★★½	★★★★½	€50–€80
LIMERICK				
Jurys Inn Limerick	★★★	★★★	★★★★	From €79
ENNIS				
Dromoland Castle	★★★★½	★★★★–★★★★½	★★★½	From €250
The Old Ground	★★★★	★★★	★★★	€120–€170
KILRUSH				
Hillcrest View Bed and Breakfast	★★★½	★★★½	★★★★	€50–€70

from **Shannon Airport,** follow N18 to Limerick and continue from there on N20 to Adare. If you're coming from County Kerry, follow N21 north, which will bring you right to Adare, as will N20 north from Cork; from Dublin, take N7 through Limerick and N20 from there. **Bus Éireann** buses run frequently throughout the day between Limerick and Adare, and the fare is about €3 each way; from Shannon Airport, take the coach to Limerick (€5.20; service about every hour throughout the day, more frequently during morning and evening rush hours), and continue from there to Adare. Limerick will also be the transfer point if you're traveling to Adare by train or coach from most other parts of Ireland. For more information on Bus Éireann service, call ☎ 061-313333 or go to **www.buseireann.ie.**

HOTELS IN AND AROUND ADARE

Adare Country House ★★★

QUALITY	★★★½	VALUE	★★★★½	€ 50–€ 80

Adare Village, County Limerick; ☎ 061-395986; adarecountryhouse@eircom.net; www.adarecountryhouse.com

Location At the edge of Adare. **Amenities and services** 12 units; garden, hair dryers, in-room tea and coffee facilities. **Elevator** No. **Parking** Free, on property. **Price** Includes full Irish breakfast. **Credit cards** MC, V.

DENIS AND EILEEN MORONEY'S appealing bed-and-breakfast is located on a country lane amid fields and gardens at the edge of Adare, about a five-minute walk from pubs and shops. The rooms are quite large, with wide-planked floors and handsome pine furnishings, and the oversize modern bathrooms are equipped with deep bathtubs. The Moroneys serve a good breakfast in a handsome dining room, and they have set aside a small lounge and a sunny terrace for guests to use.

 Adare Manor ★★★★

QUALITY	★★★½	VALUE	★★★	FROM	€ 295

Adare Village, County Limerick; ☎ 061-396566; fax 061-396124; reservations@adaremanor.com; www.adaremanor.com

Location At the edge of Adare. **Amenities and services** 63 units; bar, beauty salon, bicycling, business center, fireplaces in some rooms, fishing, gardens, golf, gym, hair dryers, horseback riding, in-room tea and coffee facilities, Internet connections, restaurant, room service, safes, shop, spa, swimming pool, tennis, turndown service, walking. **Elevator** Yes. **Parking** On property, free. **Price** Full Irish breakfast, €23; many special offers available; apartments and houses on the grounds rent from about €400 a night. **Credit cards** AE, DC, MC, V.

THE EARLS OF DUNRAVEN built their neo-Gothic manor house on the banks of the River Maigue, fitting it out with intricately carved woodworking, acres of leaded glass, dozens of chimneys, and fine furnishings. The house has been a hotel since the 1980s, one of Ireland's finest, and the stone walls, winding stairs, glowing hearths, and even a gallery lined with elaborate choir stalls (ask to see the risqué carvings) provide plenty of color. With two staff members for every guest, service is exceptionally attentive and professional, enhancing the feeling that guests are in a private home. The best accommodations are the so-called staterooms in the old house, enormous and luxuriously appointed suites—some even have fireplaces in the cavernous marble bathrooms—that have hosted many heads of state and celebrities. Rooms in a new wing are disappointing; they're comfortable but strung out along dispiriting hallways and furnished in a dull, conventional style. Most rooms throughout the hotel have nice views over the river, boxwood gardens, and the fairways of a Robert Trent Jones golf course. The grounds also include the romantic ruins of a castle and monastery, as well as a cluster of self-catering villas.

Dunraven Arms ★★★★

QUALITY	★★★★	VALUE	★★★★	€ 125–€ 190

**Adare Village, County Limerick; ☎ 061-396633; fax 061-396541;
reservations@dunravenhotel.com; www.dunravenhotel.com**

Location In the village center. **Amenities and services** 88 units; bar, beauty salon, bicycling, fireplaces in some rooms, fishing, garden, gym, hair dryers, horseback riding, hunting, in-room tea and coffee facilities, Internet connections, 2 restaurants, room service, safes, swimming pool, walking. **Parking** On property, free. **Price** Includes full Irish breakfast; many special offers available, some of exceptional value. **Credit cards** AE, MC, V.

THIS HANDSOME MUSTARD-COLORED inn not only retains a friendly small-town-hotel atmosphere, it also offers a great deal of luxury. The paneled bar is the most popular gathering spot in town, and several snug, fire-warmed guest lounges are to the rear of the reception area. The high-ceilinged guest rooms at the front of the hotel retain a solid, old-fashioned air, but Dunraven Arms breaks the older-is-better rule—a new wing that extends through gardens at the rear of the hotel is, despite the long hallways, just as attractive. The rooms in this new wing are large, handsomely furnished with traditional pieces (including four-poster beds in many), and outfitted with spacious bathrooms and separate dressing rooms; several rooms have fireplaces. Aside from offering a beautiful indoor pool and well-equipped gym, the hotel arranges fishing, golf, horseback riding, shooting, and other recreational activities.

Glin Castle ★★★★

QUALITY	★★★★	VALUE	★★★	FROM	€ 310

**Glin, County Limerick; ☎ 068-34173; fax 068-34364; knight@iol.ie;
www.glincastle.com**

Location On the banks of the River Shannon, about 40 kilometers (25 miles) west of Adare. **Amenities and services** 15 rooms; sitting room, library, drawing room, extensive gardens, tea, dinner served nightly. **Parking** On property, free.

Price Includes full Irish breakfast; the castle sleeps 30 comfortably and can be rented, with staff, in its entirety. **Credit cards** AE, MC, V.

THE FITZGERALDS HAVE BEEN the Knights of Glin since the 14th century. Their current castle dates only from 1785 and, in a dash of retrofitting, was adorned with crenellations and other medieval-looking adornments in the 19th century. The current knight is the noted art historian Desmond FitzGerald, who has filled the castle with a stunning collection of 18th-century Irish furniture. Neoclassical columns and elaborate plasterwork provide a suitable setting for these wonderful pieces, and the centerpiece of the castle is a flying staircase, with a double set of stairs that rises to a central flight for the final ascent. The magnificent gardens are a sea of color in spring and summer. All this grandeur is the setting for one of Ireland's most charming manor hotels, with huge and opulently appointed bedrooms and baths and an excellent staff to see to all your needs. Dinner, featuring local seafood, produce, and meats, is served nightly in a dining room that is as grand as the rest of the castle, and several lounges invite you to relax in style and feel, quite appropriately, like lord and lady of the castle. That right actually belongs to Sir Desmond (who prefers to go by "Knight") and Madame FitzGerald, who are sometimes in residence and pleased to speak about the ancestral home.

EXPLORING ADARE

ADARE IS GEARED TO WALKING, and your route should begin on **Main Street,** a postcard vision of brightly colored thatch-roofed cottages with roses climbing around the doorways. A more somber presence is that of the **Trinitarian Abbey,** built in the 13th century by a French order of monks whose raison d'être was to raise ransom money for Christians taken captive by the Moors during the Crusades. The stone compound was enlarged after English troops under King Henry VIII severely damaged such monasteries throughout Ireland in a campaign to wipe out Catholicism; it now serves as a Catholic church. The placid **Wishing Pool** across the street, backed by a double-arched stone bridge, once did double duty as a communal laundry and a watering hole for horses.

Main Street ends at the ornate gates that mark the entrance to the vast, beautiful, and emerald-green parklands surrounding **Adare Manor,** the ancestral home of the Earls of Dunraven. The manor is now a hotel (see profile on page 276), and the links of its golf course wind through the grounds, but visitors are welcome to stroll the paths and lanes shaded by majestic old trees. The ruins of **Desmond Castle,** begun in the early 13th century within an ancient ring fort, rise from the banks of the River Maigue near the manor; the towers and Great Hall are discernible among the terribly romantic piles of stone rubble. Nearby, a 25-meter (75-foot) tower looms over the ruins of a **Franciscan monastery** founded in the 15th century by the Friars of the Strict Observance. Another monastery, this one in good repair, is the **Augustinian Priory** just to the north; a fascinating example of

How Restaurants Compare in the Lower Shannon

NAME	CUISINE	OVERALL	QUALITY	VALUE	PRICE
ADARE					
Wild Geese	Modern Irish	★★★★	★★★★	★★★½	Exp
Inn Between	Modern Irish	★★★	★★★	★★★★	Mod
LIMERICK					
Green Onion	Modern Irish	★★★★	★★★½	★★★	Mod
ENNIS					
The Cloister	Modern Irish/ seafood	★★★½	★★★½	★★★½	Mod
Durty Nellie's	Pub fare	★★½	★★½	★★★	Mod/inexp
KILRUSH					
Kelly's	Pub food	★★★★	★★★½	★★★★	Inexp

medieval architecture, it now serves as a Protestant church. A good vantage point from which to enjoy the **River Maigue** is the nearby **village bridge,** built of stone in the 14th century and, although widened over the centuries, still medieval in appearance.

RESTAURANTS IN ADARE

THE DUNRAVEN ARMS'S woody bar is a good choice for sandwiches, snacks, and other light fare. (See hotel profile on page 277.)

Inn Between ★★★

MODERN IRISH   MODERATE   QUALITY ★★★   VALUE ★★★★

Inn Between, Main Street, Adare; ☎ 061-399-6633

Reservations Recommended. **Entree range** €13–€22. **Payment** AE, MC, V. **Bar** Full service. **Disabled access** Yes. **Hours** Tuesday–Sunday, 6:30–10:30 p.m.; lunches available in summer.

MENU RECOMMENDATIONS Wild salmon, caught locally; burgers.
COMMENTS This airy bistro with warm-hued, skylit rooms and a pleasant patio occupies one of Adare's famed thatch-roofed cottages. You can dine lightly (the homemade soups and juicy burgers are excellent) or a little more elaborately, choosing from a range of meat dishes and locally caught fish.

Wild Geese ★★★★

MODERN IRISH   EXPENSIVE   QUALITY ★★★★   VALUE ★★★½

Rose Cottage, Main Street, Adare; ☎ 061-396451

Reservations Recommended. **Entree range** €30; early menu, 6:30–7:30 p.m. Monday–Friday, 6:30–7 p.m. Saturday, €35 for 2 courses. **Payment** AE, MC, V. **Bar** Full service. **Disabled access** Yes. **Hours** May–September, Tuesday–Saturday, 6:30–10 p.m.; Sunday, 5:30–10 p.m; October–April, Tuesday–Saturday, 6:30–10 p.m.

MENU RECOMMENDATIONS Roasted Adare lamb, wild pheasant stuffed with rosemary, any fresh fish.

COMMENTS Diners come to Adare just to enjoy a meal in these country-style dining rooms. Chef David Foley is a local man—well, almost. He trained at Tralee, over the border in County Kerry, and worked at several restaurants in Southwest Ireland before moving on to London and Dublin, returning to the region in 1999 to open his own restaurant. Foley uses the freshest local game, seafood, and produce in preparations that are creative but sensible—fresh crab appears in soufflés; Adare lamb is enhanced only with fresh herbs; monkfish is enlivened with tempura vegetables. The service, like the food, is down-to-earth but polished.

EXERCISE AND RECREATION IN ADARE

HEADQUARTERED NEAR ADARE in Ballingarry, **Celtic Angling** offers fly-fishing excursions (with equipment and instruction) to local streams and lakes as well as salmon-fishing outings on the River Shannon; call ☎ 069-68202 or go to **www.celticangling.com.** The 18-hole golf course at **Adare Manor,** designed by Robert Trent Jones, meanders through woodlands, around the shores of three lakes, and along the banks of the River Maigue; for greens fees and other information, call ☎ 061-395044 or go to **www.adaremanor.com.** Horseback riding is available at **Clonshire Polo and Equestrian Centre** (☎ 061-396770; **www.clonshire.com**).

Around **ADARE**

ALONG N69

A SHORT DRIVE NORTH from Adare brings you to the **Forest of Curraghchase,** which is laced with trails, and then to Route N69, which follows the wide estuary of the River Shannon west through old river towns such as **Foynes** (see below). At **Tarbert,** you can board a ferry to cross the river to **Killimer** and **Kilrush** (see page 299). N69 continues south from Tarbert into County Kerry to **Tralee,** the county capital, and from there you can continue on to the nearby **Dingle Peninsula** (see page 270).

Attractions along N69

Foynes Flying Boat Museum ★ ★ ★

How Attractions Compare in the Lower Shannon

ATTRACTION	DESCRIPTION	AUTHOR'S RATING
ADARE		
Foynes Flying Boat Museum	Aviation museum	★★★
TRALEE		
Kerry County Museum	Exhibits highlighting the history and scenic beauty of County Kerry	★★½
LIMERICK		
Hunt Museum	Museum of art and antiquities	★★★★
King John's Castle	Restored medieval castle	★★★½
ENNIS		
Bunratty Castle and Folk Park	Restored medieval castle and re-creation of Irish rural life	★★★★½
Ennis Friary	Ruins of monastic complex	★★★
Craggaunowen	A re-creation of prehistoric Ireland	★★
KILRUSH AND THE WEST CLARE PENINSULA		
Dolphinwatch Carrigaholt	Boat trip in the Shannon Estuary	★★★★
Vandeleur Walled Garden	Garden	★★★

Foynes, County Limerick; ☎ 069-65416; www.flyingboatmuseum.com

Type of attraction Aviation museum. **Admission** €8 adults, €6 seniors and students, €4 children under age 14, free for children under age 5, €25 for families of up to 2 adults and 4 children. **Hours** March–October, daily, 10 a.m.–6 p.m.; November, daily, 10 a.m.–6 p.m. **When to go** Anytime; the museum is indoors. **Special comments** Children may find the film and exhibits a bit dull, and visitors with limited vision may find it difficult to view the print-heavy exhibits. **How much time to allow** About 1 hour.

DESCRIPTION AND COMMENTS In the late 1930s, the little harbor town of Foynes on the Shannon Estuary became the port for the first trans-atlantic air-passenger service, Pan American's "flying boats." Foynes's fame was short-lived because longer-distance aircraft introduced during

walks and drives in the lower shannon

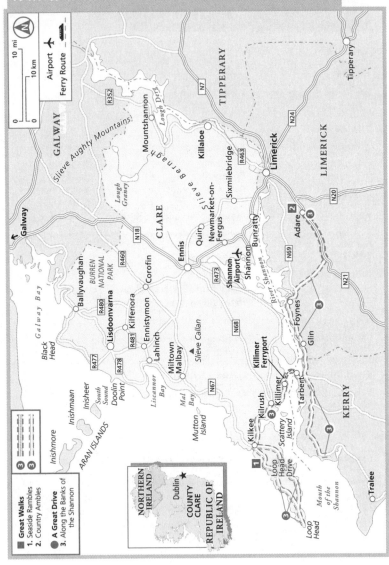

Great Walks
1. Seaside Rambles
2. Country Ambles

A Great Drive
3. Along the Banks of the Shannon

10 mi
10 km

Airport
Ferry Route

NORTHERN IRELAND
Dublin
COUNTY CLARE
REPUBLIC OF IRELAND

World War II made the flying boats obsolete, but the town's prominence in aviation history is remembered in this earnest little museum in what was once the terminal building. An excellent film, as well as photographs, news clippings, and radio equipment, muster exciting nostalgia for the era. You'll learn that the Foynes–New York journey took 25 hours, passage came with a bed and seven-course meals, and there was a fifty-fifty chance the plane would have to turn back at the point of no return when it became clear there wasn't enough fuel to get to the next stop. Among the early passengers was Eleanor Roosevelt, who traveled under the alias "Mrs. Smith"; and one of the flying-boat pioneers was Captain Charlie Blair, who married the Irish actress Maureen O'Hara. A full-scale model of one of the craft, complete with luxurious quarters, is docked just outside; while you'll never travel by air in such style, you can take a seat in the terminal canteen and order an Irish coffee, invented here on a wet winter's night in 1942.

TOURING TIPS Foynes is a handy rest stop if you're following the Lower Shannon between the Dingle Peninsula and other places in County Kerry, and places in County Limerick and County Clare.

TRALEE

THE CAPITAL OF COUNTY KERRY, about 80 kilometers (50 miles) south of Adare, is an attractive yet unassuming workaday place where inhabitants are much more in evidence than tourists. During the last week of August, though, Tralee becomes frivolous as it stages the **Rose of Tralee International Festival,** with events that include a beauty contest to nominate the "Rose of Tralee" (a namesake of the popular Irish song), live music, and a horse race. Tralee is also home to **Siamsa Tire,** the **National Folk Theatre of Ireland,** with a permanent home next door to the Kerry County Museum (see page 286) in the Town Park. Performances bring folktales and traditional rural ways to life through music, dance, and mime. Shows are seasonal, from May to October, with the most performances in July and August. For more information, call ☎ 066-712-3055 or visit **www.siamsatire.com.**

Exploring Tralee

A popular excursion from Tralee is aboard the **Tralee–Blennerville Steam Train,** a mere three kilometers (two miles) along narrow-gauge track to Blennerville, where the largest working windmill in Ireland, 20 meters (60 feet) tall and built in 1800, is once again in operation after standing idle for decades. The train leaves from Ballyard Station in Tralee, with departures every 30 minutes from May through October, 10:30 a.m. to 6 p.m.; round-trip fare is €6 adults, €4 seniors and students, €3 children, and €12 for families of up to two adults and two children; for more information and to check on schedules, which can vary, call ☎ 066-712-1064. Guided tours of the **Blennerville Windmill** explain the flour-making process, and a small exhibit covers the bases from windmill operations to the fate of Kerry farmers during

Walks and Drives in the Lower Shannon

River and ocean scenery dominate the lush land surrounding the estuary of Ireland's longest river.

GREAT WALKS

SEASIDE RAMBLES

You can walk the entire **Loop Head Drive** (see page 302), east of **Kilrush,** in a couple of days, and almost any segment offers a thrilling shorter walk. Especially scenic is the section just south of **Kilkee,** where the narrow road hugs the tops of high cliffs battered relentlessly by enormous waves. **Ballybunion** is also a prime walking spot, with vista-filled cliff-top walks along the sea.

COUNTRY AMBLES

You'll find especially pleasant, path-laced parklands at **Adare Manor** in Adare (see page 276), the former estate of the Earls of Dunraven, where the scenery includes the ruins of a castle and monastery and the rushing waters of the River Maigue. The **Forest of Curragchase,** just north of Adare off N69, shelters beautiful formal gardens as well as a vast arboretum planted with fine specimens of native Irish trees.

A GREAT DRIVE

ALONG THE BANKS OF THE SHANNON

A good place to begin this drive along the shores of the **Shannon** to the coast of the Atlantic is the pretty village of **Adare.** If you're staying in or around **Ennis** or elsewhere north of Limerick, you can easily reach Adare via the N20.

Adare (see page 273) is a pleasure to explore on foot, with a pleasing number of thatch-roofed cottages, the ruins of a castle, and several monasteries and abbeys. Especially inviting are the tree-shaded lanes that crisscross the parklands of **Adare Manor.**

From Adare, follow N20 west for about eight kilometers (five miles) to **Rathkeale,** where Sir Walter Raleigh and the poet Sir Edmund Spenser stayed at **Castle Matrix** in 1589. Legend has it that Sir Walter planted Ireland's first potatoes, imported from the Carolinas, at Rathkeale, but that claim is one you'll encounter frequently throughout Ireland. The headquarters of the Irish Heraldry Society, the castle houses some fine period furnishings and a famous set of documents pertaining to the Wild Geese, Irish mercenaries who served in Continental armies in the 17th and 18th centuries. It's open mid-May

the Famine years; also on the grounds are a restaurant and a crafts shop. The Windmill complex is open April through October, daily, 10 a.m. to 6 p.m.; €6 adults, €4 children over age 5. For more information, call ☎ 066-712-1064. To learn more about local attractions and through mid-September, Saturday through Thursday, 11 a.m. to 5 p.m.; admission is €5.

Leaving Rathkeale, follow R518 north for ten kilometers (six miles) to **Askeaton.** Ruins dominate this appealing town on the River Deel. **Desmond Castle,** a stronghold that the Desmond clan built on an island in the river in the 15th century, fell to the British in 1580, though the banqueting hall and chapel remain in ruined splendor. A 15th-century Franciscan abbey, of which only the cloisters remains, is on the nearby shore of the Deel.

A drive of another ten kilometers (six miles) west on N69 brings you to the banks of the Shannon at **Foynes.** The views of the river are sweeping, and the **Foynes Flying Boat Museum** (see page 280) pays homage to the town's service as the European terminus for transatlantic Flying Boat service.

Glin, 13 kilometers (8 miles) west on N69, is the riverside domain of the Knights of Glin, whose current castle, dating from 1785, is now a luxurious guesthouse (see page 277); ask at the desk if you might be able to take a stroll through the gardens.

Tarbert, six kilometers (four miles) farther west, is the port for ferry service across the Shannon to **Killimer** in County Clare. Before embarking, time permitting, make a jaunt west for 25 kilometers (15 miles) to the mouth of the river at **Ballybunion.** This attractive little resort offers some fine beaches and bracing cliff-top walks above the Atlantic.

From Tarbert, ferries run year-round, daily, with departures every hour. (The fare is €20 one-way, €30 round-trip, for one car and passengers). Board a boat for the 20-minute crossing, and, once in Killimer, make the short drive east to **Kilrush** (see page 299).

After exploring Kilrush, follow the **Loop Head Drive** (see page 302) through the seaside resort of **Kilkee.** From there, follow the well-marked route along the high cliffs of the Atlantic coast southwest to **Loop Head Lighthouse,** then along the mouth of the **Shannon.** The entire loop covers about 50 kilometers (30 miles).

If you're staying in or around Ennis, the quickest return is on N68; Ennis is only about 40 kilometers (24 miles) from Kilrush on this route. If you're staying in Adare or somewhere else south of Limerick, you'll save considerable time by taking the ferry back across the Shannon to Tarbert and traveling east from there on N69.

events, visit the **Tralee Tourist Office,** which also houses the **Kerry County Museum** (see profile on next page). The office is open Monday through Friday, 9 a.m. to 1 p.m. and 2 to 5 p.m., and on some weekends in the summer.

Attraction in Tralee

Kerry County Museum ★★½

APPEAL BY AGE	PRESCHOOL ★★★	GRADE SCHOOL ★★★★★	TEENS ★★★★
YOUNG ADULTS ★★★★		OVER 30 ★★½	SENIORS ★★½

Ashe Memorial Hall, Denny Street; ☎ 066-712-7777; www.kerrymuseum.ie

Type of attraction Exhibits highlighting the history and scenic beauty of County Kerry. **Admission** €8 adults, €6.50 seniors and students, €5 children, €22 families of up to 2 adults and 3 children. **Hours** January–April and November–December, Tuesday–Friday, 9:30 a.m.–5 p.m.; May–October, daily, 9:30 a.m.–5:30 p.m. **When to go** Anytime; the museum is a good rainy-day excursion with kids. **Special comments** This is one museum that kids are likely to enjoy more than their parents—the video presentations and medieval re-creations are especially popular with young visitors. **How much time to allow** About 2 hours.

DESCRIPTION AND COMMENTS Three exhibits present an overview of County Kerry. The least imaginative of these is "Kerry in Colour," a slide presentation in which scenic images are projected onto a large screen to the accompaniment of traditional Irish music. The museum's greatest asset, a treasure trove of Celtic crosses, Norman pottery, and other artifacts, is displayed in "The Story of Kerry," but the big extravaganza is "Geraldine Tralee," a reconstruction of the medieval town complete with sounds and smells; an audio guide explains what's transpiring in the various tableaux. (The Geraldines are the Anglo-Norman family that more or less ruled Counties Kerry and Limerick for centuries.) The showmanship is a bit amateurish, but fun, and the kids will have a ball.

TOURING TIPS The tourist office is in the same building, so stock up on touring info while you're here; a cafe serves a tasty lunch selection of soups, other hot dishes, and sandwiches.

▌▐ LIMERICK

THIS INDUSTRIAL PORT CITY at the mouth of Shannon Estuary has thrived on its terrible portrayal in Frank McCourt's international best seller, the Pulitzer Prize–winning *Angela's Ashes*. Fans of the memoir flock to Limerick to see for themselves the scenes of the author's grim, impoverished childhood, though the "gray place with a river that kills" is fairly tame these days. Rows of elegant Georgian houses clustered around the city center are being restored, and even the once-grimy Shannon quays have been spruced up a bit.

You won't want to allot too much of your valuable travel time to Limerick, and you'll probably want to stay in more-appealing places such as Adare or Ennis, but a half day here is well spent.

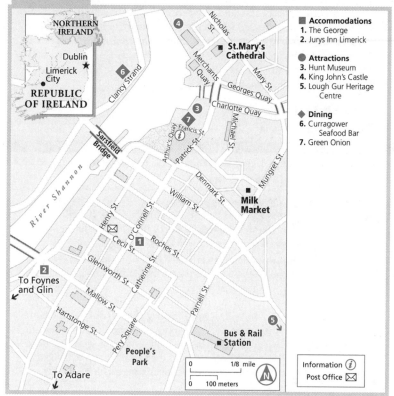

limerick

NORTHERN IRELAND

Dublin

Limerick City ★

REPUBLIC OF IRELAND

Clancy Strand

Sarsfield Bridge

River Shannon

To Foynes and Glin

To Adare

Nicholas St.

St. Mary's Cathedral

Merchants Quay

Georges Quay

Mary St.

Charlotte Quay

Michael St.

Arthur's Quay

Francis St.

Patrick St.

Denmark St.

William St.

Mungret St.

Milk Market

Henry St.

O'Connell St.

Cecil St.

Roches St.

Glentworth St.

Catherine St.

Mallow St.

Hartstonge St.

Pery Square

Parnell St.

People's Park

Bus & Rail Station

■ **Accommodations**
1. The George
2. Jurys Inn Limerick

● **Attractions**
3. Hunt Museum
4. King John's Castle
5. Lough Gur Heritage Centre

◆ **Dining**
6. Curragower Seafood Bar
7. Green Onion

0   1/8 mile
0   100 meters

Information (i)
Post Office ✉

PLANNING YOUR VISIT TO LIMERICK

ON ARTHUR'S QUAY, the **Limerick Tourism Centre** provides information on attractions in the city and throughout the Shannon region and also helps arrange accommodations. Call ☎ 061-317522 or visit **www.discoverireland.ie/shannon.aspx**.

ARRIVING AND GETTING ORIENTED IN LIMERICK

LIMERICK IS JUST 25 KILOMETERS (15 miles) southeast of Shannon Airport, one of the two major international gateways to Ireland (see page 56). If traveling by car, follow route N18, one of the few four-lane highways in Ireland, which connects the city with the airport. From County Kerry, N21 leads north into Limerick; from County Cork, N20 leads to Limerick; and from Dublin, N7 crosses the center of the country to Limerick. **Bus Éireann** buses run frequently throughout the day between Limerick and Shannon Airport; the fare is about €5.40, and service runs about every hour, more frequently during morning and evening rush hours. Bus Éireann also provides service between Limerick and all other parts of Ireland. For more on Bus Éireann service, call ☎ 061-313333 or go to **www.buseireann.ie.** Limerick is on a rail line, and **Irish Rail** provides service from Dublin, Cork, Killarney, and other cities; the trip from Dublin's Heuston Station takes about two and a half hours, and the fare is about €41. For more information, call ☎ 061-315555 or visit **www.irishrail.ie.**

HOTELS IN LIMERICK
The George ★ ★ ★

QUALITY	★ ★ ★	VALUE	★ ★ ★ ★	FROM	€ 89

O'Connell Street, Limerick; ☎ 061-460400; fax 061-460410; www.thegeorgeboutiquehotel.com

Location Center of Limerick. **Amenities and services** 119 units; restaurant, bar, hair dryers, in-room tea and coffee facilities, Wi-Fi, laundry, use of pool and gym at nearby facility. **Elevator** Yes. **Parking** In nearby car park, free for overnight. **Price** Breakfast available from à la carte menu. **Credit cards** AE, MC, V.

DESCRIPTION AND COMMENTS An escalator sweeps guests from the street up to the invitingly dramatic lobby, a sure sign that lodging in Limerick has taken an upturn. The fact that Limerick now has a hotel like this at its center shows that the city is on the upswing. Public areas and guest rooms are contemporary and elegant, and large flat-screen TVs and rainforest showers that create a gentle spray from multiple nozzles are wonderful modern amenities that you would never find at this price anywhere else. Other traditional elements are in place, too, including fine linens and relaxed service that reflects old-fashioned Irish hospitality.

Jurys Inn Limerick ★ ★ ★

QUALITY	★ ★ ★	VALUE	★ ★ ★ ★	FROM	€ 79

Lower Mallow Street, Limerick; ☎ 061-207000; fax 061-400966; www.jurysdoyle.com

Location Center of Limerick. **Amenities and services** 151 units; bar, hair dryers, in-room tea and coffee facilities, laundry. **Elevator** Yes. **Parking** In nearby car park, €7.50 a day. **Price** Breakfast available from à la carte menu. **Credit cards** AE, MC, V.

DESCRIPTION AND COMMENTS This outlet of a well-known Irish chain provides some of Limerick's most comfortable lodging, right in the city center and very well priced, too. No-nonsense business hotel–style rooms, some with views of the River Shannon, are large and comfortable, and unlike rooms in most Irish hotels, rent for a flat rate regardless of the number of guests. Most rooms sleep three adults or two adults and two children, making Jurys a good value for families. What the hotel lacks in character it makes up for with location—Arthur's Quay shopping, the Hunt Museum, and the castle are all an easy walk away.

EXPLORING LIMERICK

O'CONNELL STREET, a row of unimposing but serviceable shops, runs through the center of Limerick. The city's flashier shopping quarter is now **Arthur's Quay,** at the northern end of O'Connell, and just north of that is the **Hunt Museum** (see below), an excellent collection of art and antiquities housed in the city's old Custom's House that no visitor to Limerick should miss. Just north, on **King's Island,** rise the city's two most famous landmarks, **King John's Castle** (see next page) and **St. Mary's Cathedral.** The cathedral dates to 1172, but only an exquisite Romanesque doorway and parts of the nave survive intact from that time. The church is open June through September, Monday through Saturday, 9 a.m. to 5 p.m.; October through May, Monday through Saturday, 9 a.m. to 1 p.m.; €1.30 donation.

Tours in Limerick

A community-boosting organization, **St. Mary's Integrated Development Programme** leads excellent walking tours that introduce visitors to historic sights in Limerick as well as points of interest from Frank McCourt's *Angela's Ashes.* All tours cost €4, €7.50 families, and depart from St. Mary's Action Centre (44 Nicholas Street on King's Island). The 90-minute historic tours depart Monday through Friday, 11 a.m. and 4 p.m.; *Angela's Ashes* tours depart daily at 2:30 p.m.

ATTRACTIONS IN AND AROUND LIMERICK

A REWARDING SIDE TRIP from Limerick takes you north about 16 kilometers (10 miles) to the village of **Kilahoe.** This appealing village on the border of County Tipperary is also at the southern tip of a large, crystal-clear lake, **Lough Derg.** A well-marked 150-kilometer (90-mile) drive takes you around the lake, which is quite unspoiled, excellent for freshwater swimming, and surrounded by rolling green countryside. If you have roots in County Clare, follow the west side of the lake for about 16 kilometers (10 miles) from Kilahoe to Tuamgraney, where the **East Clare Heritage Centre** (☎ 061-921135) will help you trace your ancestry. The center is open June through September, daily, 10 a.m. to 6 p.m., and admission to exhibits that highlight the region's history is €4 adults, €2 seniors and students, and €1.50 for children. You can also board a boat here (€8) for the brief crossing to **Inishcealtra,** a seventh-century monastic settlement.

Hunt Museum ★★★★

| APPEAL BY AGE | PRESCHOOL ★★ | GRADE SCHOOL ★★★ | TEENS ★★★★ |
| YOUNG ADULTS ★★★ | OVER 30 ★★★★ | SENIORS ★★★★ |

Rutland Street, Limerick; 061-312833; www.huntmuseum.com

Type of attraction Museum of art and antiquities. **Admission** €7.75 adults, €6.25 seniors and students, €4 children, €17.50 families of up to 2 adults and 2 children. **Hours** Monday–Saturday, 10 a.m.–5 p.m.; Sunday, 2 p.m.–5 p.m. **When**

to go Anytime. **Special comments** The museum hosts Sunday-evening concerts and frequent lectures; the ground-floor Du Cartes Café is an appealing spot for lunch or, if you want an early dinner after a museum visit, try the Green Onion, across the street (see page 292). **How much time to allow** About 2 hours.

DESCRIPTION AND COMMENTS Barely a decade old, this handsome museum occupies Limerick's elegant 18th-century Customs House. On display are the amazing collections of the late John and Gertrude Hunt, avid collectors themselves and advisers to noted collectors such as William Randolph Hearst and the Aga Khan. The Hunts' wide-ranging tastes and vast knowledge are what make the excellent displays in this museum so fascinating. The couple amassed a trove of Celtic and medieval artifacts second only to those on display at the National Museum in Dublin, along with 18th-century ceramics, 19th- and 20th-century paintings by Renoir and Picasso, and other decorative arts spanning the centuries. Three of the most stunning artifacts are a shield from the eighth century BC, a ninth-century-AD cross from County Antrim in Northern Ireland, and a bronze horse believed to have been crafted by Leonardo da Vinci. But the pleasure of visiting this eclectic and charming collection—small enough not to overwhelm—is simply to wander and come upon the many unexpected treasures that most attract your notice.

TOURING TIPS Take advantage of one of the free guided tours often available; these show off the highlights or focus on one period, such as medieval artifacts, or one topic, such as jewelry.

King John's Castle ★ ★ ★ ½

APPEAL BY AGE	PRESCHOOL ★★★	GRADE SCHOOL ★★★★	TEENS ★★★★
YOUNG ADULTS ★★★★	OVER 30 ★★★★		SENIORS ★★★★

King's Island, Limerick; ☎ 061-360788; www.shannonheritage.com

Type of attraction Restored medieval castle. **Admission** €9 adults, €6.65 seniors and students, €5.25 children, €20.60 for families of up to 2 adults and 2 children. **Hours** January–February and November–December, daily, 10 a.m.–4:30 p.m.; March–April and October, daily, 9:30 a.m.–5 p.m.; May–September, daily, 9:30 a.m.–5:30 p.m. **When to go** In good weather, if possible, to enjoy the ramparts and courtyard. **Special comments** Try to be in Limerick at some point after dark to see the castle illuminated by floodlights. **How much time to allow** About 2 hours.

DESCRIPTION AND COMMENTS This imposing 13th-century fortress, built by order of King John of England on an island in the heart of the city, is especially impressive when viewed from across the rivers that surround it, with the long, high walls and round towers rising above the water. The castle is one of Ireland's most intact medieval monuments, and massive restorations and ongoing archaeological excavations ensure a rich and informative visit that includes a heady mix of Viking houses, a reconstructed medieval courtyard where costumed craftspeople and merchants ply their trades, and rampart walks. An excellent audiovisual presentation brings to life events such as the siege of 1642, which all but destroyed the castle and the rest of Limerick. Much of what is known about the siege was brought to light by a soldier's diary that is among some 1,000 artifacts unearthed in the castle to date. The city and castle repelled another siege, this one by William of Orange, when Irish troops retreated to the castle after the Battle of the Boyne in 1690.

TOURING TIPS Kids probably will get bored with some of the archaeological displays, in which case you might want to let them enjoy the medieval courtyard while you tour the galleries. Combine a visit to the castle with a look at St. Mary's Cathedral, also on the island.

Lough Gur Heritage Centre ★★★

APPEAL BY AGE	PRESCHOOL ★★	GRADE SCHOOL ★★	TEENS ★★★
YOUNG ADULTS ★★★	OVER 30 ★★★		SENIORS ★★★

Near Croom, off R20 about 20 kilometers (12 miles) east of Limerick; ☎ 061-385086, www.loughgur.com

Type of attraction Ancient site **Admission** €5 adults, €3 seniors, students, and children, €12.75 for families of up to 2 adults and 2 children. **Hours** May–September, daily, 10 a.m.–6 p.m. **When to go** In good weather, if possible. **Special comments** The center sponsors a summer-solstice festival and a fall storytelling festival. **How much time to allow** About 1 hour.

DESCRIPTION AND COMMENTS This peaceful site, a small valley sheltering a lake and surrounded by limestone hills, has been inhabited for the past 5,000 years. In fact, some of Ireland's most important archaeological treasures have been unearthed here—these include a Bronze Age shield that is now on display in the National Museum in Dublin. While there is little on the site to indicate the presence of so much history except the remains of a ninth-century farmstead and a reconstruction of a lake dwelling, the thatch-roofed visitors center does an excellent job of re-creating the various communities that thrived here with models, replicas of important finds, and a well-produced slide show. You will also learn a bit about Honey Fitzgerald, the father of Rose Fitzgerald Kennedy, the matriarch of the famous American political clan.

TOURING TIPS If you are inspired to see more of archaeological Ireland, continue on to Craggaunowen (see page 296), where Irish prehistory is brought to life with elaborate re-creations of dwellings. John Hunt, the archaeologist and art historian whose collection of art now hangs in Limerick's Hunt Museum (see page 289), did much of the excavation at Lough Gur and was inspired to create Craggaunowen.

RESTAURANTS IN LIMERICK

MANY OF LIMERICK'S historic pubs serve decent meals and pour a fine pint. Especially atmospheric is the 300-year-old **Locke Bar & Restaurant** (2A–3 George's Quay; ☎ 061-413733), where you'll find fresh seafood along with traditional Irish music on Sundays and Tuesdays. **Du Cartes Café** in the Hunt Museum (see page 289) is a good spot for lunch.

Curragower Seafood Bar ★★★★

SEAFOOD	MODERATE	QUALITY ★★★★	VALUE ★★★★

Clancy's Strand, Limerick; ☎ 061-321788

Reservations Not taken. **Entree range** €10–€22. **Payment** MC, V. **Bar** Full service. **Disabled access** Yes. **Hours** Daily, noon–11 p.m.

MENU RECOMMENDATIONS Seafood chowders, fresh oysters.

COMMENTS A traditional Irish city like Limerick should have a landmark like this: an old-fashioned pub that overlooks St. John's Castle and dispenses remarkably fresh seafood from a series of tiny rooms. Fresh oysters in season, hearty seafood stews, and even staples like wild salmon taste better here than they do almost anywhere else. While you shouldn't expect elaborate preparations or fancy sauces, you can count on freshness and a friendly welcome from the staff and patrons alike.

Green Onion ★★★★

MODERN IRISH	MODERATE	QUALITY ★★★½	VALUE ★★★

Old Town Hall Building, Rutland Street, Limerick; ☎ 061-400710

Reservations Recommended for dinner. **Entree range** €13–€22. **Payment** AE, MC, V. **Bar** Full service. **Disabled access** Yes. **Hours** Monday–Saturday, noon–10 p.m.

MENU RECOMMENDATIONS Daily salad specials, wild-mushroom-and-garlic soup, steak-and-Guinness stew.

COMMENTS Limerick's most talked-about restaurant hasn't changed with the justifiable fame it's earned over the years—the softly lit two-level dining room still has an informal air to it, augmented with jazz in the background. This is the sort of place where you'll want to linger awhile. The cafe is crowded most evenings, about as close to a scene as Limerick stages, but it is especially mellow in the afternoon and early evening.

SHOPPING IN LIMERICK

THE CITY'S SMART NEW shopping complexes are **Arthur's Quay** and **Cruises Street Shopping Centre,** both in the city center. These malls have done much to revitalize downtown Limerick, although travelers looking for a slice of old Ireland may be disappointed to discover that, with some exceptions, they provide a fairly generic blend of find-them-anywhere shops. More authentic are the locally crafted sweaters and other garments at 100-year-old **Irish Handicrafts** (26 Patrick Street; ☎ 061-415504). **Milk Market,** east of the city center at Ellen and Wickham streets, houses a decent Saturday-morning food market, when wonderful produce and cheeses from throughout central Ireland fill the stalls; on Fridays, arts and crafts take over the premises.

ENNIS

MANY TRAVELERS SPEED RIGHT PAST Ennis en route to County Kerry, Galway, and other better-known places to the north and south, but don't do the same. The seat of County Clare boasts only one great monument, **Ennis Friary,** but it's an appealing place of medieval appearance, with narrow lanes and attractive old houses along the banks of the River Fergus.

unofficial **TIP**
Ennis is a good place in which to alight after arriving at Shannon Airport or to enjoy a last night before flying home (**Dromoland Castle** is well geared to a splurge).

PLANNING YOUR VISIT TO ENNIS

THE ENNIS TOURIST OFFICE is on Arthur's Row, O'Connell Square; ☎ 065-682-8366; it is open from May to September, Monday through Saturday, 9:30 a.m. to 5:30 p.m.; Sunday, 9:30 a.m. to 1 p.m. and 2 p.m. to 5:30 p.m.

Special Events in Ennis

Ennis is known for its traditional music, performed at pubs around the town and at the **Glór Irish Music Centre** on Friar's Walk. For a week in late May, the **Fleadh Nua** brings together musicians and dancers for one of Ireland's largest festivals of traditional music; ☎ 065-686-7777. The **Ennis Trad Festival** in early November also showcases traditional music as well as jazz and bluegrass; ☎ 065-684-4522.

ARRIVING AND GETTING ORIENTED IN ENNIS

ENNIS IS 25 KILOMETERS (15 miles) north of Shannon Airport and 37 kilometers (20 miles) north of Limerick, connected to both by N18. **Bus Éireann** buses connect Ennis with many cities in Ireland, although many connections are through Limerick. For more on Bus Éireann service, call ☎ 061-313333 or go to **www.buseireann.ie.** For more information on **Irish Rail** service, call ☎ 061-315555 or visit **www.irishrail.ie.** Bus Éireann also provides service throughout the day between Shannon Airport and Ennis; the fare is about €5 and buses run about every hour, more frequently during morning and evening rush hours.

HOTELS IN AND AROUND ENNIS

 Dromoland Castle   ★★★★½

QUALITY ★★★★–★★★★½	VALUE ★★★½	FROM €250

Newmarket-on-Fergus, County Clare; ☎ **061-368144; fax 061-363355; sales@dromoland.ie; www.dromoland.ie**

Location Outside the village of Newmarket, at Dromoland exchange off N18, about 16 kilometers (10 miles) north of Shannon Airport. **Amenities and services** 100 units; 2 bars, beauty salon, bicycling, business center, fishing, gardens, golf, gym, hair dryers, horseback riding, in-room tea and coffee facilities, Internet connections, nonsmoking rooms, 2 restaurants, room service, safes, shop, spa, swimming pool, tennis, walking. **Elevator** Yes. **Parking** Free valet. **Price** Includes full Irish breakfast; many special offers available. **Credit cards** AE, DC, MC, V.

ONE OF IRELAND'S BEST-KNOWN castle hotels is a delightful warren of finely paneled galleries and twisting stone passageways that manages to be both grandly impressive and comfortably welcoming. The staff works very hard to make guests feel at ease, and the relatively few public rooms are nicely outfitted with cushy chairs and sofas custom-tailored for long hours of reading in front of a fire. Many of the guest rooms, especially those in the older part of the hotel, are luxuriously large and supremely appointed with firm king-size beds, cozy arrangements of couches and armchairs, and double sinks and separate tubs and showers in the commodious bathrooms. Rooms in a relatively unobtrusive new addition across the entrance court match the hotel's high standards, but even their grand size and such amenities as luxurious marble baths can't conceal the smack of cookie-cutter newness. Ask about the various styles of accommodations when booking, and if you want genuine character, request a room in an older part of the hotel. Dromoland is just minutes from Shannon Airport, so the hotel is ideally situated for a grand introduction to Ireland or a treat-yourself last-night splurge. With a world-famous golf course, an indoor pool overlooking a walled garden, and miles of walking paths crisscrossing the grounds, the castle offers plenty of diversions, so don't overbook on sightseeing excursions.

The Old Ground ★★★★

| QUALITY | ★★★★ | VALUE | ★★★ | € 120–€ 170 |

O'Connell Street, Ennis, County Clare; ☎ 065-682-8127; fax 065-682-8112; reservations@oldgroundhotel.com; www.flynnhotels.com

Location Center of Ennis. **Amenities and services** 114 units; bar, cafe, hair dryers, in-room tea and coffee facilities, restaurant, room service, trouser press, turndown service. **Elevator** Yes. **Parking** Free, on grounds. **Price** Includes full Irish breakfast; many special offers available. **Credit cards** AE, DC, MC, V.

THIS IVY-COVERED HOUSE in the center of Ennis, dating from the 18th century, has served as a town hall and jail at various times in its long history. The recently restored guest rooms are stylish, with contemporary furnishings, excellent lighting, and rich fabrics. The lounge, library, and other public rooms are especially atmospheric and welcoming, with genuine antiques, open fires, and charming bow windows. A cozy bar, the Poets Corner, hosts live music sessions in the evenings, and the delightfully airy Town Hall Café is a nice place for a cup of coffee or light meal.

EXPLORING ENNIS

THE RIVER FERGUS surrounds the old center of Ennis, giving the town its name—*inis* means "island" in Irish—and riverside walks follow the torrent. From the riverbanks, narrow streets, connected by arches known as bow-ways, twist and wind through the town's medieval layout, although many of the handsome, brightly colored houses are from the 19th century. The finest remnant of medieval Ennis is the Friary, founded in 1240 by Donnchadh Cairbreach O'Brien, King of Thomond, and now in ruin (later generations of Thomonds built nearby Bunratty Castle; see profile below). Two of the town's greatest heroes are commemorated with statues. Daniel O'Connell (1775–1847), whose Derrynane House can be visited in County Kerry (see page 252), was known as "The Liberator" for his efforts on behalf of Catholic emancipation, and he represented County Clare in Parliament from 1828 to 1831. Éamon De Valera (1882–1975) was born in the United States but returned to his ancestral County Clare and served as prime minister of Ireland from 1937 to 1959 before becoming president.

ATTRACTIONS IN AND AROUND ENNIS

kids Bunratty Castle and Folk Park ★★★★½

| APPEAL BY AGE | PRESCHOOL ★★★★½ | GRADE SCHOOL ★★★★★ | TEENS ★★★★★ |
| YOUNG ADULTS ★★★★★ | OVER 30 ★★★★½ | SENIORS ★★★★½ | |

**Off N18, Bunratty, County Clare; ☎ 061-360788;
www.shannonheritage.com**

Type of attraction Restored medieval castle and re-creation of Irish rural life. **Admission** €15 adults, €6.50 seniors, €10 students, €9 children, €32 for families of up to 2 adults and 2 children. **Hours** *Castle:* daily, 9:30 a.m.–4 p.m.; *Folk Park:* January–March and November–December, daily, 9:30 a.m.–5:30 p.m.; April–May and September–October, daily, 9 a.m.–5:30 p.m.; June–August, daily, 9 a.m.–6 p.m. **When to go** Try to avoid weekends, when the castle and park can be especially crowded. **Special comments** Bunratty is not to be missed for families with younger children; the park staff makes young visitors feel especially welcome, and craft demonstrations, grazing animals, and cottage visits will keep them amused for hours. **How much time to allow** At least half a day.

DESCRIPTION AND COMMENTS Ireland's most intact medieval castle is also one of the country's most visited tourist attractions, known to busloads of visitors as the scene of nightly banquets. Home to the O'Briens, Earls of Thomond, from around 1500, the tall fortress has been beautifully restored down to its last medieval timber and is filled with stunning 15th- to 17th-century furnishings. Despite the crowds and the commercial buzz, the castle is a pleasure to visit (forgo the banquet, though, unless you think you might enjoy eating mediocre food with hundreds of strangers as wenches sing "When Irish Eyes Are Smiling"). Even when the castle is jammed with visitors, rooms such as the Great Hall and the paneled guest apartments manage to evoke life in a medieval castle.

The adjoining Folk Park is a serious undertaking that manages to be fun and educational at the same time. A re-creation of a complete village is pleasant but the least successful element of the park—many authentic villages await you on your Irish travels. Far more interesting are the laborers', farmers', and fishing families' cottages, some moved intact from other locales and all authentically furnished. Some, such as the Byre dwelling, are extremely humble cottages in which families and livestock shared one earthen-floored room. Golden Vale is the well-furnished home of a prosperous farmer, and the Victorian-era, stuffily comfortable Hazelbrook House was the home of a manufacturer of a popular brand of Irish ice cream. A walled garden flourishes, yielding a healthy amount of fresh produce, and water mills continue to function. During the summer the grounds are abuzz with blacksmiths, millers, and other costumed craftspeople demonstrating the old ways, but even without them the Park does an admirable job of portraying a way of life that endured in Ireland until not too many decades ago.

TOURING TIPS Mac's Pub, in the re-created village, serves light meals and a good pint of Guinness.

Craggaunowen ★★

| APPEAL BY AGE | PRESCHOOL ★★ | GRADE SCHOOL ★★★★★ | TEENS ★★★★ |
| YOUNG ADULTS ★★★★ | | OVER 30 ★★ | SENIORS ★★ |

Near Quin, County Clare, about 30 kilometers (18 miles) north of Bunratty; ☎ 061-360788; www.shannonheritage.com

Type of attraction A re-creation of prehistoric Ireland. **Admission** €8.50 adults, €6.20 seniors and students, €5 children, €19.50 for families of up to 2 adults and 2 children. **Hours** April–mid-October, daily, 10 a.m.–6 p.m. **When to go** In good weather, if possible, because many attractions are outdoors. **Special comments** Kids will probably enjoy this place more than their parents will; for an outing the whole family will enjoy, Bunratty Castle and Folk Park is a much better choice. **How much time to allow** About 2 hours.

DESCRIPTION AND COMMENTS What will they think of next? Craggaunowen is a prehistoric theme park, with re-creations of ring forts, dolmen, and other fragments of Ireland's long past. Before you fork over the admission fee, you may well want to consider visiting the real prehistoric monuments that are so thick on the ground in Ireland. Kids may fall for the neat-looking *crannog*, a fortified island dwelling, and the costumed Celts and Iron Age farmers, but their parents might be reminded of Fred Flintstone and Barney Rubble. One of the most interesting artifacts here is the leather-hulled boat in which Tim Severin sailed across the Atlantic to re-create St. Brendan's alleged sixth-century voyage to the New World.

TOURING TIPS Adjoining Craggaunowen Castle, the real McCoy and built in 1550, towers over the park. Also nearby is Kannpogue Castle, in Quinn (see facing page).

 **Ennis Friary** ★★★

APPEAL BY AGE	PRESCHOOL ★★	GRADE SCHOOL ★★	TEENS ★★★
YOUNG ADULTS ★★★	OVER 30 ★★★		SENIORS ★★★

Abbey Street, town center; ☎ 065-682-9100; www.heritageireland.ie

Type of attraction Ruins of monastic complex. **Admission** €1.50 adults, €1 seniors, €0.75 children and students, €4.25 families. **Hours** April–May and mid-September–October, daily, 10 a.m.–5 p.m.; June–mid-September, daily, 10 a.m.–6 p.m. **When to go** Anytime. **Special comments** When the friary is closed, you can get a decent view of the ruins through the gates. **How much time to allow** About 30 minutes–1 hour.

DESCRIPTION AND COMMENTS Founded in 1240 and one of Ireland's great medieval centers of learning, this large, now-ruined monastic complex once housed 350 monks and as many as 600 students. The old moss-covered stones still evoke the friary's great wealth and importance. Among the many carvings that litter the ruins are an endearingly primitive statue of St. Francis and the alabaster MacMahon tomb. An elegant stone window frame still graces the chancel.

TOURING TIPS After touring the friary, step into Cruise's Pub, in a 17th-century house next door, for a drink or a light meal; the low ceilings, beams, and open hearths seem much in keeping with the medieval atmosphere of the friary, and the patio overlooks the ruins.

Knappogue Castle and Walled Gardens ★★★

APPEAL BY AGE	PRESCHOOL ★★★	GRADE SCHOOL ★★★	TEENS ★★★
YOUNG ADULTS ★★★	OVER 30 ★★★★		SENIORS ★★★★

Near Quin, County Clare, about 30 kilometers (18 miles) north of Bunratty; ☎ 061-360788; www.shannonheritage.com

Type of attraction Historic castle. **Admission** €7 adults, €3.30 seniors, €3.25 students, €3.35 for children, €15 families of up to 2 adults and 2 children. **Hours** May–September: daily, 9:30 a.m.–5 p.m. **When to go** Anytime, since this place is not nearly as crowded as Bunratty. **Special comments** Architecture and fine-furniture buffs will probably enjoy Knappogue, with its fine restoration and collection of antiques, as much as they do Bunratty, but the absence of the Folk Park might make this outing less fun for kids; you may want to tack on a trip to nearby Craggaunowen for them. **How much time to allow** About 1 hour.

DESCRIPTION AND COMMENTS Texans Mark and Lavern Andrews lovingly restored the 15th-century home of the McNamara clan, and their fine attention to detail shows in the remarkable collection of medieval furnishings and even the intricate stonework. The Andrews had a sound structure with which to work because Oliver Cromwell based himself here and spared the castle from pillage, and well into the 19th century, subsequent owners cared for the original structure and added two wings and a beautiful walled garden.

TOURING TIPS From May to September, Knappogue hosts medieval banquets that are based on traditional recipes using ingredients from the castle garden and end with a pageant of song and dance; about €50.

RESTAURANTS IN AND AROUND ENNIS

Medieval castles are popular dining spots in these parts. The experience doesn't have a lot to offer aside from the thrill of feasting in a genuine banqueting hall: food and entertainment are generally bland, and your entertainment budget will go a lot further if you opt for a more authentic experience, such as enjoying a pint and some traditional music in a pub. Banquets are staged year-round at 5:30 p.m. and 8:45 p.m. at **Bunratty Castle and Folk Park,** €50; and May through September at 7 p.m. at **Knappogue Castle,** €50. Call ☎ 061-360788 for more information and to make reservations.

The Cloister ★★★½

MODERN IRISH/SEAFOOD	MODERATE	QUALITY ★★★½	VALUE ★★★½

Club Bridge, Abbey Street, County Clare; ☎ 065-682-9262

Reservations Recommended. **Entree range** €14–€23. **Payment** AE, DC, MC, V. **Bar** Full service. **Disabled access** Yes. **Hours** Daily, 12:30–3 p.m. and 6–9:30 p.m.

MENU RECOMMENDATIONS Fresh mussels, oysters, and other seafood.
COMMENTS The scent of turf fires permeates these beamed rooms built into the remains of a 13th-century church, overlooking the monastery gardens. Part of the premises are given over to a publike room where excellent lunches are served and traditional music is often played, but evening dining is a serious business, too, with an emphasis on local seafood and game.

Durty Nellie's ★★½

PUB FARE	MODERATE/INEXPENSIVE	QUALITY ★★½	VALUE ★★★

Next to Bunratty Castle, Bunratty, County Clare; ☎ 061-364861

Reservations Not accepted. **Entree range** €8–€20. **Payment** AE, MC, V. **Bar** Full service. **Disabled access** Yes. **Hours** Daily, 11:30 a.m.–10 p.m.

MENU RECOMMENDATIONS Sandwiches and other light meals.
COMMENTS Given the hordes of visitors who pass through the doors, this character-filled 400-year-old pub—once a drinking spot for the guards at the adjacent Bunratty Castle—does a commendable job of preserving some atmosphere, serving passable food, and even offering live music on occasion. Keep your menu choices simple, and don't even think of darkening the doorway if you're looking for an authentic Irish-pub experience—this is an unabashed tourist trap.

ENTERTAINMENT AND NIGHTLIFE IN ENNIS

AT THE EDGE OF THE OLD CITY on Causeway Link, the **Glór Irish Music Centre** is a strikingly designed theater that stages traditional music and dance concerts as well as drama and other events. Check the schedule to see what's on tap when you're in Ennis: call ☎ 065-684-3103 or visit **www.glor.ie.** Ennis keeps more than 60 pubs in business, many of which host traditional-music sessions. Some of the most atmospheric, and the ones where you'll find the best music, are **Brandon's** (O'Connell Street; ☎ 065-682-8133, **Ciaran's** (1 Francis Street; ☎ 065-684-0180), **Paddy Quinn's** (7 Market Street; ☎ 065-682-8148), and **Cruise's** (Abbey Street; ☎ 065-684-0180).

SHOPPING IN AND AROUND ENNIS

AN IMPRESSIVE ARRAY of Irish china and crystal can be found at **Giftvenue** (36 Abbey Street; ☎ 065-682-9607); selections include lines from Belleek, Waterford, and other big-name European producers. **Custy's** (2 Francis Street; ☎ 065-682-1727) does the town's musical heritage proud with a good selection of music by traditional artists, as well as instruments. Bunratty Castle, not surprisingly, adds shopping to its tourist-oriented activities. **Bunratty Village Mills** (on the castle grounds; ☎ 061-364321) is a collection of shops housed in quaint cottages that sell crystal, tweeds, and other Irish products, many of high quality. **Avoca,** the well-known Irish woolen mill, has an outlet nearby on Route N18 that sells a full line of beautiful handwoven blankets and clothing, as well as china, crystal, and other fine items from other Irish manufacturers (☎ 061-364029).

EXERCISE AND RECREATION IN AND AROUND ENNIS

ONE OF MANY 18-HOLE golf courses in the region, the **Ennis Golf Club** (Drumbridge Road; ☎ 065-682-4074), charges a modest €25 to €35 for a round; **Dromoland Golf Club,** on the grounds of the castle hotel (see page 293) and one of the most famous courses in Ireland, charges €100. Walkers have a choice of several well-marked routes through the County Clare countryside, including the **Mid-Clare Way,** which leads to the **East Clare Way,** providing almost 300 kilometers (180 miles) of walks along paths and country lanes through spectacular scenery; ask for maps and information at the tourist-information office in Ennis.

▌ KILRUSH

THIS ATTRACTIVE TOWN on the West Clare Peninsula is deceptively grand at first appearance. The wide streets and large central square, which give the impression that Kilrush is more prominent than it really is, are part of an improvement scheme by 18th-century landlords, the Vandeleurs, who attempted to put Kilrush on the map as a model estate town. For most travelers the real appeal of Kilrush is its off-the-beaten-track location and proximity to rugged, little-visited coastal scenery. Kilrush is a good place to stop for a day or two as you travel north to County Galway or south to County Kerry; you'll get a nice glimpse of an Irish country town that's relatively unconcerned with tourism.

PLANNING YOUR VISIT TO KILRUSH

THE **Kilrush Tourist Information Centre** (in the center of town on Moore Street) is open June through September, Monday through Saturday, 10 a.m. to 1 p.m. and 2 to 6 p.m., and Sunday, 10 a.m. to 2 p.m.; ☎ 065-905-1577. Outside of these hours, you can consult information boards in the town square for listings of hotels, restaurants, and services.

ARRIVING AND GETTING ORIENTED IN KILRUSH

KILRUSH IS ABOUT 45 KILOMETERS (27 miles) west of Ennis on N68, about a 45-minute trip by car. **Bus Éireann** buses connect Kilrush with Ennis, where you can make connections to Galway, Dublin, Cork, and other parts of Ireland; buses run about every three hours (more frequently during the summer), and the trip takes a little less than an hour; fare is about €10. For more information, call ☎ 061-313333 or go to **www.buseireann.ie.**

If you're approaching County Clare from the south, you might want to cross the Shannon Estuary on the car ferry that runs between Tarbert, in County Limerick on the south side of the estuary, and Killimer, on the north side near Kilrush. If you're traveling, say, from the Dingle Peninsula, and want to see the sights of West Clare, the 20-minute ferry crossing saves you the 130-kilometer (80-mile) loop around the Shannon Estuary through Limerick. Ferries run year-round, daily, with departures every hour. The fare is €17 one-way, €28 round-trip, for one car plus passengers. For more information, call ☎ 065-905-3124 or visit **www.shannonferries.com.**

HOTEL IN KILRUSH

Hillcrest View Bed and Breakfast ★★★½

QUALITY ★★★½	VALUE ★★★★	€ 50–€ 70

Doonbeg Road, Kilrush, County Clare; ☎ 065-905-1986; fax 065-905-1900; ethnahynes@eircom.net; www.hillcrestview.com

Location At the edge of Kilrush. **Amenities and services** 6 units; garden, hair dryers, in-room tea and coffee facilities, lounge, Wi-Fi. **Elevator** No. **Parking** Free, on grounds. **Price** Includes full Irish breakfast. **Credit cards** MC, V.

ETHNA AND AUSTIN HYNES show great prowess as innkeepers at their stylish and comfortable bed-and-breakfast, the nicest lodging in Kilrush. The couple began by hosting guests in two tidy bedrooms in the front of the family home. In the late 1990s, they built an attractive addition with four new rooms designed to their specifications, two upstairs and two on the ground floor. These new rooms are especially comfortable, large, and sunny, with polished-pine floors, firm beds, attractive yet unobtrusive furnishings, thoughtful lighting, and windowed bathrooms equipped with excellent showers. Austin cooks a delicious breakfast (including home-made porridge) that Ethna serves in a conservatory overlooking a walled garden that is a wonderful place to relax after a day of sightseeing.

EXPLORING KILRUSH AND THE WEST CLARE PENINSULA

TWO EXHIBITIONS IN KILRUSH plot the region's history. The **Kilrush Heritage Centre,** in the Town Hall on Market Square, concentrates on the local landlords, the Vandeleurs, and how they developed Kilrush as an estate town. The exhibit tells you a little more than you ever thought you wanted to know about Kilrush, but the detailed explanation of estate towns, common throughout Ireland, is revealing, as are the sad details of the plight of the tenants during the Famine. The center is open June through August, daily, 10 a.m to 6 p.m.; admission costs €4 adults, €1.50 children, €7 families; ☎ 065-905-1047. The **Scattery Island Centre,** on Merchants Quay, tells the story of the monastic community founded by St. Senan in the sixth century on an island just offshore from Kilrush; it is open from June to mid-September, daily, 10 a.m. to 6 p.m.; admission is free; ☎ 065-905-2139. From the harbor you can see the stark and spooky ruins of the round tower and several churches. In the summer, fishermen make extra cash ferrying the curious who want a close-up look at the island (beware, though, as one of St. Senan's accomplishments was slaying an enormous sea monster out there); boats run irregularly, depending on demand, and the fare is about €15 round-trip.

Kilrush is at the edge of the West Clare Peninsula, a finger of land that juts into the mouth of the Shannon and the Atlantic. The peninsula is far off the well-beaten tourist track, so you'll feel as if you have the rugged coastal scenery to yourself. The well-marked **Loop Head Drive** begins in the seaside town of Kilkee, follows the high cliffs of the Atlantic coast southwest to Loop Head lighthouse, and then heads back to Kilkee on the south side of the peninsula, along the mouth of the Shannon.

Kilkee, 12 kilometers (8 miles) west of Kilrush, might seem alien to Americans who have a preference for long, deserted beaches and easygoing seaside towns. The Victorian-era bathing resort is a tidy and densely packed collection of brightly colored row houses that have been the summer quarters of generations of Irish families. An air of gentility hangs over the town, and a long seaside promenade follows a sheltered, sandy strand on a bay that provides safe swimming. Pools in the rocks at the edge of the bay, known as the

unofficial **TIP**
The **Loop Head Drive** covers only about 50 kilometers (30 miles), but with stunning scenery or a nice village to explore around nearly every bend in the road, you may want to spend a full day on the drive.

Pollock Holes, teem with fish and plant life and are especially popular with snorkelers.

Kilkee is the starting point of the **Loop Head Drive,** a thrilling route along the rugged and unspoiled coast. The loop is much less traveled than more famous scenic coastal drives on the Ring of Kerry and Dingle Peninsula, imparting a sense that you've found a corner of wild Ireland. The scenery just south of Kilkee along the Atlantic is especially dramatic. Here, a narrow road hugs the tops of high cliffs, surf crashes through blowholes, and enormous waves charge relentlessly against rocky headlands. At the **Bridges of Ross,** a natural arch spans two rocky outcroppings, providing a dizzying look at the sea crashing beneath your feet; the sense of adventure may be heightened by the fact that a second bridge crashed into the sea not too long ago. The lighthouse at the tip of the peninsula is not open to the public, but a path leads to land's end, one of many such headlands in the west of Ireland where the green landscape drops into the Atlantic surf. Just inland, along the southern coast of the peninsula, is the village of **Kilbaha.** The modern village church shelters the **Little Ark of Kilbaha,** a relic of mid-19th-century Catholic persecution. The British, and therefore Protestant, local landlords refused to allow their Catholic tenants to build a church. When the village priests held mass in workers' cottages, the landlords had the cottages torn down. One enterprising priest, or so the story goes, went to Kilkee and saw the portable bathing boxes that were pulled, with costumed swimmers inside, to the water's edge, allowing bathers to immerse themselves without exposing themselves immodestly. The priest built a chapel in the same style, had it wheeled to the beach on Sundays, and there preached to his faithful, who knelt in the sand. At **Carrigaholt,** farther east along the peninsula, forbidding MacMahon Castle overlooks the Shannon. A "murder hole" over the entrance reveals a lot about the no-nonsense purpose of the tall fortress, the inhabitants of which once dropped burning oil and heavy objects through the hole onto the heads of would-be invaders.

ATTRACTIONS IN KILRUSH AND THE WEST CLARE PENINSULA

Dolphinwatch Carrigaholt ★★★★

APPEAL BY AGE	PRESCHOOL ★★★	GRADE SCHOOL ★★★★	TEENS ★★★★
YOUNG ADULTS ★★★★		OVER 30 ★★★★	SENIORS ★★★★

Carrigaholt, on the Loop Head Peninsula outside Kilrush; ☎ 065-905-8156; www.dolphinwatch.ie

Type of attraction Boat trip in the Shannon Estuary. **Hours** April 1–October 31: daily, call for schedule. **Admission** 2-hour trips: €24 adults, €12 for children ages 4–16, free for children under age 4; 4-hour sunset trips: €30. **When to go** Anytime. **Special comments** The M/V *Discovery,* another dolphin-watching vessel, operates out of the Kilrush Marina, with as many as 3–4 excursions per

day April–October; call ☎ 065-905-1327 or visit **www.discoverdolphins.ie.**
How much time to allow 2 hours.

DESCRIPTION AND COMMENTS The mouth of the River Shannon is home to a
school of bottlenose dolphins, and they are well accustomed to daily
visits from the Dolphinwatch boat. But the antics of the playful creatures are just part of the show. It's a pleasure to be out in the brine-
scented air of the wide Shannon Estuary where it meets the Atlantic,
and the water-level views of rugged cliffs and green pasturelands are
stunning. Sightings of grey seals are also common, and many species of
seabirds populate the waters and surrounding shores. Commentary is
intelligent, amusing, and salty at times, although it's hard to top the
sound of the dolphins communicating with one another, heard through
underwater microphones.

TOURING TIPS Don't rush away from Carrigaholt once the boat docks; allow
some time to take a look at the 15th-century castle that once protected
the port and, weather permitting, to enjoy a pint on the patio of one of
the village pubs overlooking the Shannon.

Vandeleur Walled Garden ★★★

| APPEAL BY AGE | PRESCHOOL ★★ | GRADE SCHOOL ★★★ | TEENS ★★★ |
| YOUNG ADULTS ★★ | OVER 30 ★★★ | | SENIORS ★★★ |

Killimer Road, Kilrush; ☎ 065-905-1760

Type of attraction Garden. **Admission** €5 adults, €3 seniors and students, €2
children ages 6–18, €10 families of up to 2 adults and 3 children. **Hours**
Summer, 10 a.m.–6 p.m.; winter, 10 a.m.–4 p.m. **When to go** Best in spring and
summer. **Special comments** A stone building at the entrance to the garden
houses a pleasant coffee shop. **How much time to allow** 30 minutes–1 hour.

DESCRIPTION AND COMMENTS The Vandeleur clan came to Kilrush in 1687 and
built a 400-acre estate that is still surrounded by the formidable walls
you pass as you head south out of town. The house long ago fell into
ruin, but a walled garden built nearby to nurture rare plantings has
been beautifully restored. You might not think so when a gale blows in
off the Atlantic, but Kilrush enjoys a fairly mild climate, which is
enhanced by the tall walls surrounding this two-acre garden. Banana
trees, hydrangeas, ferns, and roses grow in profusion, and the colorful
beds are laid out along well-tended paths. Vandeleur is not the grandest garden in Ireland, but it's a delightful spot and a surprising oasis in
the fairly rugged terrain of West Clare.

TOURING TIPS Much of the rest of the Vandeleur estate is set aside as a forest
park, and from the garden you can follow paths through lush woods.

RESTAURANT IN KILRUSH

Kelly's ★★★★

| PUB FOOD | INEXPENSIVE | QUALITY ★★★½ | VALUE ★★★★ |

Henry Street, Kilrush; ☎ 065-905-1811

Reservations Not necessary. **Entree range** €7–€15. **Payment** MC, V. **Bar** Full service. **Disabled access** Yes. **Hours** Monday–Saturday, 11 a.m.–9:30 p.m.; Sunday, 12:30–9:30 p.m.

MENU RECOMMENDATIONS Fresh seafood.

COMMENTS This friendly place looks like old Ireland, with a handsome oak bar and small tables grouped around a fire up front, and snug booths in the tile-floored dining room. Half the clientele comes in for a pint and gossip, the other half for the best food in town. Delicious open-faced prawn sandwiches on homemade brown bread are served throughout the day, and evening specials often include grilled fish fresh from the sea that day.

EXERCISE AND RECREATION IN KILRUSH

THE WATERSIDE GOLF LINKS at the **Kilrush Golf Club** on Ennis Road afford views over the Shannon Estuary; a round costs €30 weekdays, €35 weekends; ☎ 065-905-1138. The **Doonbeg Golf Club,** designed by Greg Norman, is a somewhat controversial course in the village of Doonbeg, north of Kilkee—the links carpet beautiful coastal dunes and hills that many locals thought should have been preserved as parkland. Greens fees are about €185; ☎ 065-905-5600.

PART EIGHT

The *WEST* of IRELAND

IT DOESN'T MATTER if you're traveling from Kerry and Dingle to the south or Sligo and Donegal to the north. Just when you think the scenery couldn't get any better, you discover the rugged sea, mountain, bog, and moorland landscapes of the real West of Ireland. These lands west and north of the River Shannon, parts of the province once known as Connaught, are so wild—and until recently unknown—that Oliver Cromwell would condemn those who would not conform to his hard rule "to Hell or Connaught." Little wonder that the independent and uncivilized West resisted outside influences for centuries, and is still *Gaeltacht* (Irish speaking) in many parts. Do not be put off by the foreignness of this part of Ireland. The West is amazingly hospitable, relatively unspoiled, and home to a city that all Irish love, **Galway.**

unofficial **TIP**
The best way to see the Cliffs of Moher is on a boat trip—you will avoid the crowds, and the perspective from the bottom of the towering rock faces is far more dramatic than it is from the top. Hour-long Cliffs of Moher cruises depart April–October, daily, from the pier in Liscannor at 9 a.m. and from the pier in Doolin at 1:30 p.m. and 5:30 p.m.; €20, with discounts for families and students. For more information and to book (strongly recommended), call ☎ 065-707-5949 or go to **www .mohercruises.com.**

CLIFFS *of* MOHER

THE CLIFFS OF MOHER, 40 kilometers (25 miles) west of Ennis on N85 and R478, rise some 230 meters (700 feet) out of the sea in an eight-kilometer (five-mile) swath of spectacular scenery. Puffins and other seabirds nest and roost on shelves of black shale and sandstone, the **Aran Islands** float in a cloud of mist in the distance, and the surf rushes ceaselessly ashore. A path follows the top of cliffs to vantage points such as **O'Brien's Tower,** a viewing platform built during the Victorian tourist days, and **Hag's Head,** a rock formation about an hour's walk south

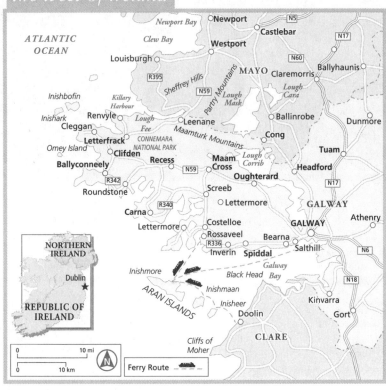

the west of ireland

that resembles a woman looking out to sea. Be advised that human visitors far outnumber seabirds at the cliffs, and the former pay €8 to park at the **Atlantic Edge Visitor Centre** (see below).

Atlantic Edge Visitor Centre ★★

APPEAL BY AGE	PRESCHOOL ★★★★	GRADE SCHOOL ★★★★	TEENS ★★★★
YOUNG ADULTS ★★★★		OVER 30 ★★★	SENIORS ★★★

Cliffs of Moher, County Clare; ☎ 065-708-6141; www.cliffsofmoher.ie

Type of attraction Viewpoint. **Admission** €8 per car. **Hours** November–February, daily, 9 a.m.–5 p.m.; March and October, daily, 9 a.m.–6 p.m.; April, 9 a.m.–6:30 p.m.; May, 9 a.m.–7 p.m.; June, 8:30 a.m.–7:30 p.m.; July and August, 8:30 a.m.–8:30 p.m.; September, 8:30 a.m.–6:30 p.m. **When to go** Anytime. **Special comments** The center has a tearoom and a shop filled with every tacky Irish souvenir ever fabricated. **How much time to allow** About 1 hour.

DESCRIPTION AND COMMENTS This controversial new complex is buried within the cliff face, providing a James Bond–like stage set from which you

NOT TO BE MISSED IN THE WEST OF IRELAND

The Burren (page 310)   Cong (page 338)

Connemara (page 332)   Connemara National Park (page 332)

Galway (page 319)   Kylemore Abbey and Garden (page 334)

Westport (page 340)

view the sea and length of the cliffs without going outdoors and, to ensure you will be further protected from enjoying this place in its natural glory, sit in a theater to watch a film. Yes, this is a decidedly unnatural way to enjoy one of Europe's great natural wonders, nothing short of a sad defilement, and you should do what you can to avoid this horrible place. You will get a much greater sense of the grandeur of the cliffs from the sea or by following trails through the grasslands and heath atop the cliff. Your options, then, are to take a Cliffs of Moher cruise (see page 305); to park a distance from the visitors center and walk along the cliff tops; or to plan a visit for the very early morning or late evening, when the center is closed.

TOURING TIPS Parking is prohibited in many places along the road near the center; observe the signs carefully, and plan on parking a kilometer or so away and walking along the cliffs.

▌ DOOLIN

THIS SMALL VILLAGE on the rugged coast of north Clare, six kilometers (four miles) north of the Cliffs of Moher on coastal road R479, is famous throughout the world for traditional Irish music, drawing droves of enthusiasts. The irony is, the crowds who come to enjoy a small Irish coastal town all but obliterate the small-village ambience. However, the music—although increasingly performed by musicians from throughout Europe—is generally first-rate. For a bit of authentic village atmosphere, head out to **Doolin Pier,** where fishermen bring in a bounty of lobster, salmon, and other fresh catches; for a bit of exercise and some stunning scenery, walk south along the Cliffs of Moher.

HOTEL IN DOOLIN

Atlantic Coast ★★★

QUALITY ★★★	VALUE ★★★	€ 60–€ 90

The Pier, Doolin, County Clare; ☎ 065-707-4189; atlanview@eircom.net

Location On coast, near Doolin Pier. **Amenities and services** 12 rooms; garden, in-room tea and coffee facilities, lounge. **Elevator** No. **Parking** Free, on property. **Price** Includes full Irish breakfast. **Credit cards** MC, V.

DOOLIN IS REALLY JUST ONE long string of bed-and-breakfasts. This one manages to stand out because of its overall quality and its edge-of-the-sea

How Hotels Compare in the West of Ireland

HOTEL	OVERALL	QUALITY	VALUE	PRICE
DOOLIN				
Atlantic Coast	★★★	★★★	★★★	€60–€90
GALWAY				
Hotel Meyrick	★★★★	★★★★	★★★½	€135–€165
Glenlo Abbey	★★★★	★★★	★★★	€170–€190
Park House Hotel	★★★	★★★★	★★★	€155–€185
Jurys Inn Galway	★★★	★★★	★★★★	From €94
CLIFDEN				
Ballynahinch Castle	★★★★★	★★★★½	★★★★	€160–€240
Foyles Hotel	★★★½	★★★½	★★★★½	€80–€130
Abbeyglen Castle Hotel	★★★	★★★	★★★	€110–€145
CONG				
Ashford Castle	★★★★	★★★½	★★★	€280–€450
WESTPORT				
Delphi Mountain Resort and Spa	★★★★	★★★★	★★★	From €99
Carlton Atlantic Coast	★★★	★★★½	★★★	€140–€160

location near the pier, handy for a trip to the Aran Islands or a cruise past the base of the Cliffs of Moher, and to Doolin's famous music pubs. Nearly all the rooms in the rambling two-story gabled house have views over Galway Bay to the Aran Islands and down the coast to the Cliffs of Moher; a couple of rooms on the ground floor open to a seaside lawn. The large rooms contain unobtrusive pine furniture, and the bathrooms, most with showers only, are spacious; many rooms have multiple beds for families. The upstairs hallway opens to two pleasant alcoves that are well equipped with couches and books, providing cozy places for guests to relax outside their rooms.

Half Door ★★★

QUALITY ★★★½	VALUE ★★★★	€60–€70

Doolin, County Clare; ☎ 065-707-5959; www.halfdoordoolin.com

Location In village. **Amenities and services** 5 rooms; garden, lounge, hair dryers. **Elevator** No. **Parking** Free, on property. **Price** Includes full Irish breakfast. **Credit cards** MC, V.

How Restaurants Compare in the West of Ireland

NAME	CUISINE	OVERALL	QUALITY	VALUE	PRICE
DOOLIN					
McGann's	Pub fare	★★★★	★★★½	★★★★	Inexp
GALWAY					
Nimmo's	Continental	★★★★½	★★★★	★★★★	Mod
McDonagh's	Seafood	★★★★	★★★★	★★★★	Inexp/mod
Malt House	Modern Irish	★★★★	★★★★	★★★	Exp
K C Blakes	Modern Irish	★★★★	★★★½	★★★½	Mod
The Quays	Pub fare	★★★★	★★½	★★★	Inexp/mod
CLIFDEN					
Owenmore Restaurant	Modern Irish	★★★★	★★★★	★★★	Exp
Marconi Restaurant	Modern Irish	★★★½	★★★½	★★★★	Mod
WESTPORT					
Quay Cottage	Seafood	★★★★	★★★★	★★★½	Mod

DOOLIN LOST A MUCH-NEEDED good restaurant but gained a wonderful place to stay when Anne Hughes closed her Lazy Lobster and turned the premises into this pleasant little inn. The Half Door is many cuts above the B&B standard: The sun-filled lounge is a welcoming place to linger, and the large guest rooms are decorated in a warmly contemporary style, with tasteful fabrics and prints. Several rooms accommodate families or multiple families, and a few units can be combined for extra space and privacy. Anne is on hand with advice about visiting the Burren, the Aran Islands, and other nearby attractions, adding much to the appeal of one of the great places to stay in the West.

RESTAURANT IN DOOLIN

McGann's ★★★★

PUB FARE   INEXPENSIVE   QUALITY ★★★½   VALUE ★★★★

Main road, near the bridge, Doolin; ☎ 065-707-4133

Reservations Not necessary. **Entree range** €10.50–€12.50. **Payment** MC, V. **Bar** Full service. **Disabled access** Yes. **Hours** Daily, food served noon–9 p.m.

MENU RECOMMENDATIONS Seafood chowder, mussels with garlic.

COMMENTS Doolin's other music pubs serve food, too, but this small, cozy room hits just the right note. A turf fire takes off the chill in the cooler months, service is always friendly, the seafood is fresh from the pier, and the place is full of local chatter. Plan to arrive around 7 or 7:30 p.m. for dinner so you'll have a table when the music starts at 9:30 p.m.

ENTERTAINMENT AND NIGHTLIFE IN DOOLIN

DOOLIN'S CULTURAL LIFE—and fame—centers on three pubs. All offer nightly music (but not every evening in the winter; schedules vary), and the entertainment is generally first-rate but best if the music is traditional. The largest and most famous of the pubs is **Gus O'Connor's** (Fisher Street; ☎ 065-707-4168); the music is usually pretty good and decent meals are served, but the place is geared to tourists. **McDermott's** (☎ 065-707-4328) and **McGann's** (☎ 065-707-4133), across the road from each other near the bridge on the main road, are local hangouts with a feel of authenticity that's lacking at O'Connor's. Pop into all three during an evening to see what sort of music is on tap. Music usually begins at 9:30 p.m. and continues until midnight.

The BURREN

THE BURREN (derived from *boireann,* Gaelic for "rocky land") is a plain of limestone that covers some 1,600 hectares (4,000 acres) of western County Clare, a portion of which is protected as **Burren National Park.** The land is not conducive to farming, to say the least; as one of the surveyors for Oliver Cromwell put it, this is "a savage land, yielding neither water enough to drown a man, nor tree to hang him, nor soil enough to bury." While the Burren is not hospitable to human habitation, it's a natural wonderland, home to rare butter-flies, puffins and other seabirds, and goats and hares. For most of the summer, the Burren becomes a sea of color as plants flower in profu-sion from cracks in the limestone. The Burren was more welcoming, even forested, when prehistoric and early-Christian settlers built forts and tombs here, hundreds of which still dot the stark landscape.

EXPLORING THE BURREN

IF YOU'RE COMING FROM THE SOUTH, you would do well to make the village of **Kilfenora** your first stop, because the **Burren Centre** (see page 313) does a good job of introducing the region's geology, botany, and history. From there, head east on R476, and at **Leamaneh Castle** turn north into the barren landscape. Leamaneh Castle, not open to the public, is a 15th-century fortified manor house, not much of which remains but the tall walls. At **Caherconnell,** a stone enclosure is one of the Burren's many ring forts; just north along the road is the well-marked path to the **Poulnabrone Dolmen,** a slablike tomb that dates from 2500 to 2000 BC. Another tomb, a wedge-shaped slab, is at nearby **Gleninsheen;** a neck collar found near the tomb dates to around 700 BC and is in the National Museum in Dublin. **Cahermore Stone Fort,** continuing north, was probably inhabited well into the Middle Ages. **Ballyvaughan,** the largest town in the region, is a pleasant little crossroads and fishing village on the shores of Galway Bay. The **Burren Exposure** (see page 316) is another exhibit that captures the uniqueness of the region.

One of the region's most charming settlements is **Lisdoonvarna,** a pretty, old-fashioned Victorian spa town that seems a world removed from the bleak landscapes of the rest of the Burren. Lisdoonvarna is famous for it mineral springs (which still attract legions of soakers) and also for love. Yes, that's right—old-fashioned love, which also attracts legions of visitors, many of them single, when the town celebrates with a weeklong Matchmaking Festival in late summer. Dances, music sessions, and dinners provide ample opportunity for lonely hearts to find the perfect someone. For more information, visit **www.matchmakerireland.com.**

unofficial **TIP**
You won't miss much if you skip **Aliwee Caves,** the Burren's outpost of grossly commercialized tourism: cheese shops, a "potato bar," and other such enterprises surround the entrance to a warren of rather dull caverns. If you must visit, expect to pay a hefty fee to enter: €12 adults, €9 seniors and students, €5.50 children, €29 for families; the caves are open daily, 10 a.m.–6:30 p.m., but intermittently in December and January.

How Attractions Compare in the West of Ireland

ATTRACTION	DESCRIPTION	AUTHOR'S RATING
THE BURREN		
Kilmacduagh	Ruins of monastic complex	★★★½
The Burren Centre	Exhibits with multimedia displays	★★★
The Burren Exposure	Exhibits with multimedia displays	★★★
GALWAY		
Galway Irish Crystal Heritage Centre	Crystal factory with a history museum	★★
CONNEMARA		
Kylemore Abbey and Garden	Manor house	★★★★
WESTPORT		
Westport House	Historic home and amusement park set in gardens	★★½

Walks and Drives in the West

Some of Ireland's most spectacular scenery is in the West, where the landscapes encompass the soaring **Cliffs of Moher,** the stony expanses of the **Burren,** and the craggy mountains and moors and bogs of **Connemara.**

GREAT WALKS

THE BURREN

The 3.5-kilometer-long (2-mile-long) **Green Road** traverses **Burren National Park,** providing an easy way for walkers to get a close-up view of the limestone plateaus and other geological features unique to this region. The Burren Way begins in **Ballyvaughan,** on Galway Bay, and makes a 35-kilometer (22-mile) trek through the region; the southern terminus is the coastal village of **Doolin** (see page 307). The way follows some remote country tracks into the heart of the limestone plateau, where in spring and summer you'll be surrounded by exotic wildflowers growing from fissures in the limestone. Burren National Park does not have a visitors center, but you can find information on walks in this region at the **Burren Centre** and the **Burren Exposure** (see pages 313–317).

CONNEMARA NATIONAL PARK

Nature trails within the park (see page 332) are short and easy; the longest, **Sruffaunboy,** is only 1.5 kilometers (1 mile) long but shows off a section of bog and comes to an observation point over the moors where Connemara ponies graze. You may also spot some of the red-tailed deer that have been reintroduced to the park, and you can observe the lichens, moss, and orchids that flourish in the region. The most popular walk in Connemara is up the flanks of **Diamond Hill,** rising some 450 meters (1,500 feet) from the northeastern corner of the park and affording wonderful views over moors, bogs, and the **Twelve Bens Mountains.** A path to the top (not always open; check with the park's visitors center) crosses boardwalks and climbs wooded steps in many parts to prevent erosion and protect the fragile bogland environment.

TOURS IN THE BURREN

WHILE THE ONLY EASY WAY to see the Burren is by car or on an extensive walking trip, in spring and summer you can see the region on one of **Bus Éireann**'s day tours from Galway. Tours take in a good swath of the region and the Cliffs of Moher and operate from early April to late September; the cost is €25 adults, €18 seniors and students, €13 children, and €55 for families. Tours depart from the train/bus station in the city center at 10 a.m. and return at about 6 p.m. For more information, call ☎ 091-562000 or go to **www.buseireann.ie.**

UP CROAGH PATRICK

One of the most popular walks in Ireland follows the well-worn **Pilgrims' Path** up the flanks of this 760-meter-tall (2,500-foot-tall) mountain rising above **Clew Bay.** You see this conical-shaped peak from miles away as you make the drive between **Leenane** and **Westport.** Legend has it that St. Patrick retreated to the mountaintop for 40 days during Lent in AD 441, and while there lured all the serpents in Ireland to the side of a precipice and commanded them to slither off—and that's why you never see a snake in Ireland. As many as 25,000 pilgrims make the climb to a chapel at the summit every year; in fact, some of them crawl to the top, rendered all the more uncomfortable by all the stones and boulders that strew the steep path. The official date for the pilgrimage is the last Sunday in July, though the faithful and those who simply want to enjoy the views of Clew Bay and the mountains of Connemara make the climb year-round. The path begins in the small village of **Murrisk,** eight kilometers (five miles) south of Westport on R335, and the walk to the top and back takes a little more than two hours.

GREAT DRIVES

FROM THE CLIFFS OF MOHER INTO THE BURREN

The Cliffs of Moher provide a dramatic starting point for a drive through one of Ireland's most striking landscapes, the Burren.

The **Cliffs of Moher** (see page 305) are a spectacular 8-kilometer (5-mile) swath of sea cliffs that rise some 230 meters (700 feet) out of the surf. You can view from many different angles on a cliff-top walk (see above).

From the cliffs, follow R478 inland through a bleak, stony landscape for about ten kilometers (six miles) to **Lisdoonvarna,** a pretty little spa town once famous for its sulfurous springs. You can still plunge into a sulfur bath at the Lisdoonvarna Spa and **Bath House.** If you roll into town in late August or early September, you can also partake in the **Matchmaking Festival,** a holdover

Continued on next page

ATTRACTIONS IN AND AROUND THE BURREN

The Burren Centre ★ ★ ★

APPEAL BY AGE	PRESCHOOL ★★	GRADE SCHOOL ★★	TEENS ★★
YOUNG ADULTS ★★	OVER 30 ★★★		SENIORS ★★★

Kilfenora; ☎ 065-708-8030; www.theburrencentre.ie

Type of attraction Exhibits with multimedia displays. **Admission** €5.50 adults, €4.50 seniors and students, €3.50 children, €15 families. **Hours** March–May and October, daily, 10 a.m.–5 p.m.; June–September, daily, 9:30 a.m.–6 p.m.

Walks and Drives in the West (continued)

GREAT DRIVES (CONTINUED)

FROM THE CLIFFS OF MOHER INTO THE BURREN (CONTINUED)

from the days when farmers would come to town around harvest time looking for wives; marriages may still develop from the festivities, which include a great deal of lively music and dancing.

A trip of about ten kilometers (six miles) up to **Ballyvaughan** on coast road R477 provides sweeping views over **Galway Bay,** as well as a chance to visit the **Burren Exposure** (see page 316), an exhibit that celebrates the unique flora, geology, and human history of this region in high-tech displays.

The **Burren** (from *boireann*, Gaelic for "rocky land"), a plain of limestone that covers some 1,600 hectares (4,000 acres), unfolds as you travel south from Ballyvaughan on R480 and R476. If you're making the trip in summer, the Burren will be a sea of color as plants flower in profusion from cracks in the limestone. Many rare flowers, including Mediterranean and Arctic species, take root in fissures in the Burren's limestone.

Just outside Ballyvaughan you can visit **Aliwee Cave,** but the region's above-ground topography and prehistoric and early-Christian remains are far more interesting.

You will encounter both as you travel south, coming to such well-posted sights as **Gleninsheen** and **Poulnabrone Dolmen** stone tombs, as well as **Cahermore** and **Caherconnell,** two of the Burren's many ring forts (see pages 310 and 311).

At **Corofin,** 23 kilometers (15 miles) south of Ballyvaughan, the **Dysert O'Dea Castle Archaeology Centre** does a good job of putting the Burren's archaeological heritage into perspective with excellent displays. The castle itself is a fascinating relic; built in 1480, this imposing tower house is now filled with Bronze Age to medieval artifacts from eighth-century St. Tola church and 24 other nearby historic monuments, all of which are within a three-kilometer (two-mile) radius of the castle and can easily be reached on foot. It's open

When to go Anytime. **Special comments** The center has a good tearoom, and its shop sells crafts that are a cut above the wares found in most tourist spots, including beautiful handmade Aran sweaters and eerily lifelike porcelain dolls made in the region. **How much time to allow** About 1 hour.

DESCRIPTION AND COMMENTS The snazziest exhibit in this modest museum is a three-dimensional map of the region, a high-tech and sophisticated piece of gadgetry that allows visitors to trigger video and audio shows with a touch of a button and learn whatever they want to know about flora, fauna, or geology. Meanwhile, a 25-minute film tells the fascinating story of how this limestone wasteland came to be some 300 million years ago and why so many unique plants, many of

May 1 to mid-October, daily, 10 a.m. to 6 p.m.; admission is €4.50 adults, €3.50 seniors and students, €10 families, free for children under age 5; ☎ 065-683-7401.

You will see more of the stark Burren landscape as you travel the 16 kilometers (10 miles) west to **Kilfenora** on R476. The **Burren Centre** (see page 313) is another well-done exhibit of the Burren's geology and human history.

From Kilfenora you can make the ten-kilometer (six-mile) trip back to the Cliffs of Moher on R476 and R478.

INTO CONNEMARA

A scenery-filled circuit of **Lough Corrib** provides a taste of medieval abbeys and castles, as well as the bog-and-mountain scenery of Connemara. For a longer circuit of Connemara, see the following pages.

From **Galway City,** N84 follows the western shores of **Lough Corrib** to **Cong.** The lake, the second largest in Ireland, is one of the country's best spots for freshwater angling, a beautiful expanse of water that is especially appealing when it reflects a blue sky. About 15 kilometers (9 miles) north of Galway you'll come to **Annaghdown Priory,** founded by St. Brendan the Navigator in the sixth century.

Another religious ruin, that of **Ross Errilly Abbey,** stands next to the Black River about eight kilometers (five miles) up the road, near the town of **Headford.** This Franciscan community dates from the 14th century.

Cong (see page 338), another 12 kilometers (7.5 miles) north, is tucked between Lough Corrib and **Lough Mask,** just to the north. It's famous as the setting for the 1952 film *The Quiet Man,* starring John Wayne and Maureen O'Hara, and for its ruined Augustine monastery in the village center, on Abbey Street (free, always open). The monastery's famous relic, the **Cross of Cong,** is now in the National Museum in Dublin, though some structures embellished with wonderful Romanesque carvings and archways remain.

Continued on next page

Mediterranean origin, flourish in cracks in the rocks. Other exhibits focus on the history of human habitation in the region, explaining the significance of the many ring forts and tombs. If you are interested in knowing about this unique region, you'll find these earnest, well-done displays to be highly informative; some young travelers and those eager to hurry on to Galway and other places may be bored stiff, however.

TOURING TIPS Step next door to the 12th-century Kilfenora Cathedral, a fairly humble place that's partly in ruin. By an ecclesiastical fluke, the Pope is the absentee bishop of the cathedral and its diocese. Five high crosses grace the graveyard.

Walks and Drives in the West (continued)

GREAT DRIVES (CONTINUED)

INTO CONNEMARA (CONTINUED)

From Cong you can begin a circuit of Lough Mask on R345. Not only will you be treated to lovely lake views, but in the village of **Ballinrobe,** 9 kilometers (5.5 miles) north of Cong, you can admire stained-glass windows by Harry Clarke, the 20th-century artisan who also fashioned the windows of the Chapel of St. Joseph's Convent in Dingle Town (see page 266).

A circuit of Lough Mask on R330 and R345 brings you, in about 40 kilometers (25 miles), back to the northern shores of Lough Corrib around the villages of **Maam** and **Maam Cross.** You're now in a typical Connemara landscape, where brown moors and bogs extend to craggy mountains. If you arrive in Maam Cross during one of the town's frequent cattle fairs, you encounter a real slice of rural Ireland. A detour of 16 kilometers (10 miles) west on N59 to brings you to **Recess** and, just beyond, **Ballynahinch Castle** (see page 336), a delightful hotel where you can have a sandwich and a pint in front of the fire in the handsome pub or take a stroll along the banks of the Ballynahinch River.

About 15 kilometers (9 miles) south of Maam Cross on N59 is the attractive village of **Oughterard,** a low-key resort on the shores of Lough Corrib.

Galway City is 27 kilometers (17 miles) southeast on N59.

ALONG THE GALWAY COAST INTO CONNEMARA

You can enter Connemara the traditional way, north along N59 past the shores of Lough Corrib, or by the back door, but what a back door it is—the relatively unspoiled coast west of Galway City.

From **Galway City,** follow R336 west and north through a string of appealing seaside villages: **Spiddle, Rossaveel, Scrib,** and **Roundstone.** In all of

The Burren Exposure ★★★

APPEAL BY AGE	PRESCHOOL ★★	GRADE SCHOOL ★★★	TEENS ★★★
YOUNG ADULTS ★★★		OVER 30 ★★★	SENIORS ★★★

4 kilometers (2.5 miles) north of Ballyvaughan; ☎ 065-707-7277

Type of attraction Exhibits with multimedia displays. **Admission** €6 adults, €3.50 seniors and students, €14 families. **Hours** One week before Easter–October, daily, 10 a.m.–6 p.m. **When to go** Anytime. **Special comments** Kids probably will find the slide shows at the Burren Exposure to be more of a thrill than the rather staid exhibits at the Burren Centre. **How much time to allow** About 90 minutes.

DESCRIPTION AND COMMENTS Like the Burren Centre (see page 313), the Burren Exposure tells the story of this unique region with the help of these villages you'll find a smattering of thatch-roofed cottages, as well as a large contingent of Irish speakers.

After about 40 kilometers (25 miles) you'll come to **Clifden** (see page 335), an appealing town that seems especially well endowed by nature, surrounded as it is by the sea, a rocky coastline, and such typical Connemara features as bogs and mountains.

Leave Clifden to the north on the **Sky Road,** a thrill-a-minute, 14-kilometer (9-mile), cliff-hugging coast road that drops you in **Letterfrack,** about 15 kilometers (9 miles) north of Clifden. The town houses the headquarters of **Connemara National Park** (see page 332), where trails cross bogs and moors in the shadows of the Twelve Bens Mountains.

Just seven kilometers (four miles) beyond Letterfrack, N59 enters the **Kylemore Valley,** between the Twelve Bens to the south and the Dorruagh Mountains to the north and the beautiful setting of **Kylemore Abbey** (see page 334).

About 15 kilometers (9 miles) west of Kylemore Abbey, N59 comes to **Leenane,** famous for playwright Martin McDonagh's *Leenane Trilogy* but notable too for its setting on the shores of fjordlike **Killary Harbour.** This inlet carved by a glacier, extends inland for 16 kilometers (10 miles). **Mweelrea** and other Connemara peaks rise from the shores of the harbor, in which waters plunge to depths of 150 meters (495 feet). A visit to the **Leenane Sheep and Wool Museum** will give you more information than you ever realized you might want on shearing, weaving, and dyeing, as well as about the breeds that graze just outside the door. The museum is open April through October, daily, 9:30 a.m. to 7 p.m., and admission is €4; ☎ 095-42231.

The return to Galway City is direct but scenery filled. Follow R336 south to Maam Cross, and from there take N59 to Galway, passing through the lake, bog, and moor scenery that is typical of Connemara.

sophisticated technology. Here, the exhibits are a lot slicker than those at the Burren Centre, and three slide shows cover the region's flora, geology, and human history. You will come away from either exhibit with more or less the same knowledge. It's important, though, that you make a stop at one or the other before touring the area, because your appreciation of the landscape will be much greater after having had such an introduction. If you're coming from the south or the west (Doolin, the Cliffs of Moher, or Ennis), stop at the Burren Centre; if you're coming from the north (Galway), stop at the Burren Exposure.

TOURING TIPS The Whitehorn Café, next to the center, is worth a stop in itself and offers good lunches and stunning sea views.

walks and drives in the west

0   10 mi
0   10 km

Ferry Route ⚓ - - -

Newport Bay   ○Newport   N5
Castlebar   N17
Clew Bay   Westport
Louisburgh○   N60   Ballyhaunis○
R395   **3**   MAYO   ○Claremorris
Sheffrey Hills   N59   Lough Cara
Inishbofin Kylemore   Killary   Lough Mask   ○Ballinrobe   Dunmore
Abbey   Harbour
Inishark   Renvyle   Lough   Leenane   ○Cong   ○
Cleggan   Fee   Maamturk Mountains   Lough   R334 ○Ross Errilly ○Tuam
Letterfrack   CONNEMARA   **2** **6** Maam   Corrib   Abbey
Omey Island   NATIONAL PARK   Cross   Headford
○Clifden   Oughterard○   N17
Ballyconneely **6**   Recess   N59   Screeb   Annaghdown
R342   ○Lettermore Priory **5** ■GALWAY
Roundstone   R340   Carna○   Costelloe   **5** GALWAY   Athenry
Lettermore○   Rossaveel   Bearna
R336   Inverin Spiddal Salthill   N6
Galway
Inishmore   Black Head Bay   N18
Ballyvaughan
Inishmaan   Kinvarra
Inisheer   Gort○
ARAN ISLANDS   Doolin   Lisdoonvarna
Cliffs of   The   **1**   Corofin○
Moher   **4**   Burren
Kilfenora
CLARE

NORTHERN
IRELAND

Dublin
★

REPUBLIC OF
IRELAND

——— **4**
⊙⊙⊙⊙ **5**
⊙⊙⊙⊙ **6**

■ **Great Walks**
1. The Burren
2. Connemara National
   Park
3. Up Croagh Patrick

● **Great Drives**
4. From the Cliffs of Moher
   into the Burren
5. Into Connemara
6. Along the Galway Coast
   into Connemara

Kilmacduagh ★★★½

**About 5 kilometers (3 miles) outside Gort on the road to Corrofin; no
phone; www.irelandmidwest.com**

Type of attraction Ruins of monastic complex. **Admission** Free. **Hours** Sunrise–
sunset. **When to go** In good weather; you'll spend much of your time here
walking through fields and crouching over stones to interpret carvings. **Special
comments** If you're driving from the Burren to Galway, it's easy to reach Gort
and Kilmacduagh on a short detour; at Kinvarra, head south off N67 to the
monastery. **How much time to allow** About 1 hour.

DESCRIPTION AND COMMENTS Of Ireland's many ruined monasteries, Kilmacduagh stands out because of its eerie isolation on a plain at the edge
of the Burren. Enough remains of the stone complex to impart a sense of
the importance of Kilmacduagh, which, founded in AD 610, flourished for

almost a thousand years—give or take, that is, a couple of centuries of Viking raids between AD 900 and 1100. Signage is scarce, and visitors are left to pick their way across pastures littered with old stones and clusters of graves. Much of what remains dates from the peaceable centuries that followed the Norman occupation of Ireland. A round tower from the 11th century leans a bit but is remarkably intact, as are the walls of the now-roofless cathedral.

TOURING TIPS Kilmacduagh is a nice spot for a picnic; you can get supplies in Gort or other towns in the Burren.

GALWAY

ONE OF IRELAND'S MOST CHERISHED CITIES is an agreeable place that fans out from a cluster of medieval lanes running down to the River Corrib and Galway Bay. Anglo-Normans settled the city as a trading post, and their medieval descendants—the Tribes, as the original 14 merchant families were called—established a lively commerce with far-flung ports in Spain and elsewhere around the globe that continued well into the 19th century. Given its geographic isolation in the West, Galway long remained a land apart from the rest of Ireland, allowing Irish culture to take a strong hold here. You'll still hear Irish in the streets and cafes, and many of the Irish speakers are young students at the university. The sense of ease you're likely to feel in Galway may be bolstered by the fact that there's not a lot to see. Attractiveness is the city's main attraction, and you can spend a pleasant day simply following the many pedestrian lanes and riverside and bayside walks.

PLANNING YOUR VISIT TO GALWAY

REALLY JUST A BIG TOURIST SHOP, the **Galway Tourist Office** is handily located off Eyre Square, near the train and bus stations on Forster Street; it is open from May to June and September, daily, 9 a.m. to 5:45 p.m.; July and August, daily, 9 a.m. to 7:45 p.m.; October to April, Monday through Friday, 9 a.m. to 5:45 p.m., Saturday, 9 a.m. to 12:45 p.m. You'll have to stand in line to speak to someone, but the staff tends to be very helpful. If you don't want to wait, look for a copy of the *Galway Tourist Guide* or one of the other free handouts available. For more information, call ☎ 091-537700 or visit **www.discoverireland.ie/west.aspx.**

Special Events in Galway

Galway's full roster of events includes the **Galway International Rally** in early February, one of Ireland's major car races; **www.galwayinternational.com.** The **Early Music Festival** in mid-May presents a week of medieval, Renaissance, and baroque dance and music concerts in theaters and churches; for more information, call ☎ 087-930-5506 or visit **www.galwayearlymusic.com.** More than 150 musicians fill Galway pubs for **Galway Sessions,** a week of traditional-music and jazz concerts in June; ☎ 087-243-2644 or **www.galwaysessions.com.** The **Galway Film Fleadh Festival** screens Irish and international films, showing more than 70 features, in July; ☎ 091-751655 or **www .galwayfilmfleadh.com. Galway Cathedral Recitals** presents more than a month of concerts from mid-July to mid-August; **www.galwaycathedral .org/recitals.** The **Galway Races** attracts thousands of horse-racing enthusiasts the first week of August, with other meets in the fall; ☎ 091-753870 or **www.galwayraces.com.** The **Galway International Oyster Festival,** held in the outlying seaside villages of Clarenbridge and Kilcolgan, is a five-day party in late September with music, dancing, oyster-shucking contests, and other festivities; ☎ 091-587992 or **www.galwayoysterfest.com.** A season of classical music, **Music for Galway** presents concerts from September through April; ☎ 091-705962 or **www.musicforgalway.ie.**

ARRIVING AND GETTING ORIENTED IN GALWAY

GALWAY IS ABOUT 90 KILOMETERS (54 miles) north of Shannon Airport, an easy trip by car along N18. If you're coming from Doolin or the Burren, the quickest route takes you along N67 to its junction with N18 south and east of Galway. You'll enter the city through a series of busy but well-marked roundabouts; simply follow the CITY CENTRE signs. Good train service runs six times a day between Dublin and Galway. The trip takes about three hours; one-way fares begin at €29. For more information, call toll-free ☎ 1850-366222 or ☎ 01-836-6222, or visit **www.irishrail.ie. Bus Éireann** coaches arrive from Dublin, Limerick, and other points in Ireland, with about 15 buses a day to and from Dublin; the trip takes about three and a half hours, and the fare is about €15 one-way. For more information, call ☎ 064-34777 or visit **www.buseireann.ie.** The train and bus stations are near Eyre Square and the tourist-information office on Forster Street. You can also reach Galway by plane on one of the flights that **Aer Arann** operates from Dublin, London, and other cities. The airport is 16 kilometers (10 miles) east of the city center off N6.

HOTELS IN AND AROUND GALWAY
Glenlo Abbey ★★★★

QUALITY ★★★	VALUE ★★★	€ 170–€ 190

Bushypark, Galway; ☎ 091-526666; fax 091-527800;
info@glenloabbey.ie; www.glenlo.com

Location 5 kilometers (3 miles) north of Galway on N59. **Amenities and services** 46 units; bar, garden, golf course, hair dryers, in-room safes, room service, shoe shine, trouser press, 2 restaurants. **Elevator** Yes. **Parking** Free, on property. **Price** Includes full Irish breakfast; many special offers available. **Credit cards** AE, DC, MC, V.

GALWAY'S FAMOUS COUNTRY-HOUSE hotel is a 58-hectare (138-acre) estate on the shores of Lough Corrib, where an abbey, a manor house, and a tasteful new wing provide the feeling of an exclusive retreat. Glenlo, though, is not necessarily about getting away from it all: the abbey now serves as a small conference center, and two old rail cars on the property house the distinctive Pullman restaurant that is frequently booked for weddings and other events. In the atmospheric lounges in the old house, fine old furniture surrounds the large fireplaces, while guest rooms, most of which are in the new wing, have a bit less character. Even so, they are extremely large, very well appointed with ultratraditional furnishings that often include four-poster beds, and a good value for the amenities and luxuries offered.

Hotel Meyrick ★★★★

QUALITY ★★★★	VALUE ★★★½	€135–€165

Eyre Square, Galway; ☎ 091-564041; fax 091-566704; res@galway-gsh.com; www.gshotels.com

Location City center, on Eyre Square. **Amenities and services** 99 units; bar, restaurant, fitness center, sauna, hair dryers, in-house movies, in-room tea and coffee facilities, Internet access, irons, laundry and dry cleaning, nonsmoking rooms, room service, shoe shine. **Elevator** Yes. **Parking** In nearby car park, about €10 a day. **Price** Some rates include full Irish breakfast; many special offers available. **Credit cards** AE, DC, MC, V.

GALWAY'S GRANDEST CITY-CENTER hotel faces Eyre Square and, like that space, has recently undergone extensive renovations to emphasize the structure's Victorian opulence. The marble-floored entry and sunny, hearth-warmed lounges are especially appealing—grand enough to let all those who enter know that this is still the best address in town. Many of the oversize guest rooms have been redone to capture the hotel's 1870s affluence, while others reflect a crisp yet soothing contemporary style. The top floor houses suites with their own exclusive lounge and a state-of-the-art spa facility. Tariffs vary wildly and can be quite high on weekends, when the hotel is booked by Irish visitors enjoying a couple of days in Galway, but room rates often come down considerably midweek.

Jurys Inn Galway ★★★

QUALITY ★★★	VALUE ★★★★	FROM €94

Quay Street, Galway; ☎ 091-566444; fax 091-568415; jurysinngalway@jurysdoyle.com; www.jurysinn.com

Location City center. **Amenities and services** 128 rooms; bar, cafe, hair dryers, in-room tea and coffee facilities. **Parking** In nearby car park, about €10. **Price** Breakfast not included. **Credit cards** AE, MC, V.

LOCATION IS THE GREATEST APPEAL of this outlet of a respected chain. Rooms look upon the rushing River Corrib or out to Galway Bay, and the pedestrian streets of the city's charming city center, with their many pubs and restaurants, are just outside the door. The hotel's airy public areas

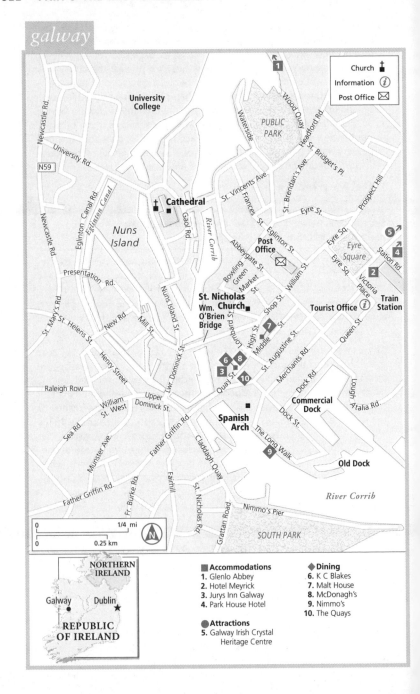

galway

Church ✝
Information ⓘ
Post Office ✉

University College

Newcastle Rd.

University Rd.

N59

Newcastle Rd.

Eglinton Canal Rd.

Eglinton Canal

Presentation Rd.

Newcastle Rd.

St. Mary's Rd.

St. Helens St.

New Rd.

Mill St.

Henry Street

Raleigh Row

William St. West

Sea Rd.

Munster Ave.

Father Griffin Rd.

Fr. Burke Rd.

Fairhill

Father Griffin Rd.

Claddagh Quay

St. Nicholas Rd.

Grattan Road

Nimmo's Pier

SOUTH PARK

✝ **Cathedral**

Gaol Rd.

River Corrib

Nuns Island

Nuns Island St.

Lwr. Dominick St.

Upper Dominick St.

Spanish Arch

Waterside

PUBLIC PARK

Wood Quay

Headford Rd.

St. Bridget's Pl.

St. Brendan's Ave.

Prospect Hill

St. Vincents Ave.

Frances St.

Eglinton St.

Eyre St.

Eyre Sq.

Eyre Square

Eyre Sq.

Station Rd.

Victoria Place

Train Station

5 ↗

4 ↗

2

Abbeygate St.

Bowling Green

Market St.

St. Nicholas

Wm. Church ■

O'Brien

Bridge

Lombard St.

High St.

Middle St.

Shop St.

William St.

Post Office ✉

Tourist Office ⓘ

7

6 **8**

3

10

Quay St.

St. Augustine St.

Merchants Rd.

Queen St.

Dock Rd.

Lough Atalia Rd.

Commercial Dock

Dock St.

The Long Walk

9

Old Dock

River Corrib

0 _____ 1/4 mi
0 _____ 0.25 km

Ⓝ

NORTHERN IRELAND

Galway   Dublin ★

REPUBLIC OF IRELAND

■ **Accommodations**
1. Glenlo Abbey
2. Hotel Meyrick
3. Jurys Inn Galway
4. Park House Hotel

● **Attractions**
5. Galway Irish Crystal Heritage Centre

◆ **Dining**
6. K C Blakes
7. Malt House
8. McDonagh's
9. Nimmo's
10. The Quays

include a contemporary bar and cafe, and the guest rooms are large, immaculate, and uniformly but pleasantly furnished in an unobtrusive standard business style. Jurys is especially well suited to families or those traveling in pairs or groups, because the hotel has a "one room, one price" policy, by which a flat rate applies to rooms no matter how many guests use them. Most rooms sleep three, either with a double and a single bed, or with a double bed and a pullout sofa. Rates vary with the demands of the season and days of the week, but always represent a good value for the standard of comfort.

Park House Hotel ★ ★ ★

QUALITY ★ ★ ★ ★	VALUE ★ ★ ★	€ 155–€ 185

Forster Street, Eyre Square, Galway; ☎ 091-564924; fax 091-569219; parkhousehotel@eircom.net; www.parkhousehotel.ie

Location City center, off Eyre Square. **Amenities and services** 57 units; hair dryers, in-room safes, in-room tea and coffee facilities, Internet access, laundry service, nonsmoking rooms, satellite TV, trouser press, turndown service. **Elevator** Yes. **Parking** Free valet. **Price** Includes full Irish breakfast. **Credit cards** AE, MC, V.

JUST STEPS FROM EYRE SQUARE, this large hotel seems to be perpetually busy, and the lively lobby and adjacent bar are some of the town's most popular meeting spots. The Park House couples its prime location with unusually spacious rooms that are much more sedate and relaxing than the bustling public areas. Deluxe rooms are the size of suites, with separate sitting areas, and the junior suites comfortably sleep four with plenty of extra room for lounging and working. Even the standard rooms are large; while they face an interior courtyard and don't have city views, these rooms are extremely comfortable, and many provide a combination of queen-size and single beds to suit families. Rates vary considerably, and special offers (check the hotel Web site) provide especially good value.

EXPLORING GALWAY

YOU'LL PROBABLY FEEL IMMEDIATELY at home in Galway on account of the soft gray stone; narrow, twisting streets on which the only traffic is two legged; and homely sensations that combine the tang of salt air from Galway Bay with the sound of rushing water from the River Corrib. Galway is compact, wedged as it is between the river and bay, and invites a leisurely stroll. In fact, a walk through the town is an attraction in itself: while Galway does not have major museums and other such sights—not yet, anyway—you'll find plenty to do just soaking in the local color.

The center of town is **Eyre Square,** a pretty patch of cobblestones and trees from which radiate any number of pedestrian-only lanes. The main thoroughfare, which begins on the north side of Eyre Square and runs to the River Corrib, changes its name from William Street to Shop Street to High Street to Quay Street.

You could probably find all the sustenance and goods you might ever need for your stay in Galway without ever straying from this series of streets, but the alleyways and lanes that twist away in various directions tempt you into the depths of the **Latin Quarter.** The medieval heart of the old city gets its name from the brisk trade that once transpired from here with Spain. On the corner of Abbeygate Street is **Lynch's Castle,** a sturdy 16th-century fortified house made necessary by raids from other Irish tribes. The gloominess of this structure, home to the prominent Lynch family, foretells the fate of one of its residents. Judge Lynch FitzStephen was forced to hang his own son after the lad was found guilty of murdering a Spanish sailor who had stolen his girlfriend. The so-called Lynch Memorial Window, an elaborate carved frame embedded in a medieval stone wall around the corner from the castle and next to the **Collegiate Church of St. Nicholas,** marks the spot where the deed transpired. St. Nicholas, which dates to the 14th century, does honor to its ranking as one of Ireland's best-preserved medieval churches with many fine carvings and gargoyles.

A more recent episode in Galway's history comes to light just around the corner, opposite the church clock tower, in the **Nora Barnacle House.** On June 16, 1904, James Joyce had his first date with Nora, the daughter of a Galway baker. The two married, and Joyce set his epic novel *Ulysses* on this date, which he calls Bloomsday. The modest dwelling is filled with a touching collection of the couple's photos, letters, and other memorabilia. It is open mid-May through mid-September, Monday through Saturday, 10 a.m. to 5 p.m.; €1.50; ☎ 091-564743.

The banks of the River Corrib are just a block away, and you can follow the rushing torrent on the **Corrib River Walkway.** From spring into early summer, a spectacle unfolds in the waters beneath the **Salmon Weir Bridge,** when salmon climb upstream to their spawning grounds in Lough Corrib. On an island at the western end of the bridge rises the imposing **Cathedral of Our Lady Assumed into Heaven and St. Nicholas,** completed in 1965 and said to be the last major stone structure to be completed in Ireland.

Now a pub, **Tigh Neachtain,** near the intersection of High and Cross streets, was the 18th-century home of Richard "Humanity Dick" Martin, a local politician who promoted animal-rights legislation and patrolled the streets looking for mistreated beasts. He was also known as "Hair Trigger Dick" because of his dueling acuity. Quay Street ends near the Spanish Arch and the old docks at the juncture of the River Corrib and Galway Bay, where Spanish ships once unloaded their goods of wine and brandy. The waterfront neighborhood just to the west of the arch is **Claddagh,** a collection of thatch-roofed fishing cottages until the middle of the 20th century, when more-conventional housing and worldly ways replaced the close-knit, independent community.

One tradition that persists is the **Claddagh ring,** in which a pair of hands encloses a heart topped with a crown to symbolize love, friendship, and loyalty. If you buy a Claddagh ring in one of Galway's many souvenir shops, be careful how you wear it. When worn with the heart facing inward, the ring indicates the wearer is spoken for; with the heart facing outward, the ring tells the world that the wearer is available.

Tours in Galway

Kay Davis, a local woman who knows Galway like the back of her hand, leads two-hour walking tours through the old city from late June to September, Monday, Wednesday, and Friday, 11:30 a.m.; €8. Tours depart from the tourist-information office. For more information or for a private tour throughout the year, call ☎ 091-792431. **Lally Tours** is one of several outfits that offer bus tours of Galway. (Actually, Galway is so compact and easy to navigate on foot that only visitors with limited mobility might require a bus tour.) Fare is €10; for schedules and other information, visit the offices at 19–20 Shop Street, call ☎ 091-562-2905, or go to **www.lallytours.com.**

Corrib Princess cruises take 90-minute trips from Galway Bay up the River Corrib into Lough Corrib, providing a nice look at the city and the pastoral shoreline beyond; May through June and September, daily, 2:30 p.m. and 4:30 p.m.; July through August, daily, 12:30 p.m., 2:30 p.m., and 4:30 p.m.; €12 adults, €11 seniors and students, €7 children. You won't see much of interest on the cruise, but the trip up the river is pleasant and provides a nice way to get off your feet and relax while enjoying a pint and a snack from the onboard bar.

ATTRACTION IN GALWAY

Galway Irish Crystal Heritage Centre ★★

APPEAL BY AGE	PRESCHOOL ★★	GRADE SCHOOL ★★★	TEENS ★★★
YOUNG ADULTS ★★		OVER 30 ★★★	SENIORS ★★★

Dublin Road, Galway; ☎ 091-757311; www.galwaycrystal.ie

Type of attraction Crystal factory with a history museum. **Admission** €4 adults, €3 seniors and students, €2 children, €10 families. **Hours** Monday–Friday, 9 a.m.–5:30 p.m.; Saturday, 10 a.m.–5 p.m.; Sunday, 11 a.m.–5 p.m. When to go Anytime. **Special comments** The center has a cafeteria and, of course, an excellent shop. **How much time to allow** 1 hour.

DESCRIPTION AND COMMENTS Galway's only real pack-'em-in tourist trap is this factory, shop, and history museum. It seems every bus tour in the land makes a potty stop here, so expect big crowds. If you can, turn your back on the general bustle and immerse yourself in the exhibits, most of which are quite well done. Especially engaging are the displays that highlight the old way of life in Claddagh, the Irish-speaking fishing enclave on the bay at the edge of the old town (see left). Beware, though, that the photos of thatch-roofed cottages and fisher folk mending nets will instill in you a sad nostalgia for life the way it was until the middle of the 20th century. Other displays will help you make sense of the confusing hierarchy of 14 Irish tribal families that held a grip on Galway for many centuries. *Fiona,* a nifty hooker (as the broad-hulled, thick-masted boats that sail Galway Bay are known), is preserved in all her glory. The main business at hand, though, is making and selling crystal, and guided tours will steer you through the work areas to the fancy shop.

TOURING TIPS Paid admission is for a guided tour; you can see the history exhibits and visit the shop on your own at no charge.

RESTAURANTS IN GALWAY

YOU'LL PROBABLY NOTICE the **Goya** name as you dine your way through Galway—this wonderful bakery supplies bread and desserts to many restaurants. To experience the baked goods at the source, step into the delightful bakery and cafe on Kirwan's Lane (☎ 091-567010). **Sheridans** (☎ 091-564829), also on Kirwan's Lane, is well stocked with a tempting array of Irish cheeses, plus olives, sausages, and other treats for a hotel-room snack. **G.C.B.,** or **Galway City Bakery** (7 Williamsgate Street; ☎ 091-563087), is a handy stop for baked goods or a sandwich, and the upstairs restaurant serves salads and other light fare.

K C Blakes ★ ★ ★ ★

MODERN IRISH	MODERATE	QUALITY ★ ★ ★ ½	VALUE ★ ★ ★ ½

10 Quay Street, Galway; ☎ 091-561826

Reservations Recommended. **Entree range** €12–€23. **Payment** AE, MC, V. **Bar** Full service. **Disabled access** Limited. **Hours** Daily, 5–10:30 p.m.

MENU RECOMMENDATIONS Beef-and-Guinness stew, pasta, seafood.

COMMENTS This stone-tower house is a remnant of medieval Galway, although the two dining rooms, one on each floor, are strikingly contemporary lairs with dark polished floors, soothing lighting, and colorful art. In the kitchen, the emphasis is on the freshest local ingredients, which appear at the table in deft and creative preparations, some of which are quite casual, such as open-faced sandwiches, and others are more elaborate and often pair unusual spices with the freshest sole, salmon, and other seafood.

Malt House ★ ★ ★ ★

MODERN IRISH	EXPENSIVE	QUALITY ★ ★ ★ ★	VALUE ★ ★ ★

High Street, Galway; ☎ 091-567866

Reservations Recommended. **Entree range** €14–€25; early dinner 6–7:30 p.m., €26 for 2 courses. **Payment** AE, MC, V. **Bar** Full service. **Disabled access** Yes. **Hours** Monday–Saturday, 12:30–3 p.m. and 6:30–10:30 p.m.

MENU RECOMMENDATIONS Honey-glazed duckling, rack of lamb with parsley crust, panfried scallops.

COMMENTS A quiet courtyard off busy High Street sets the welcoming tone for this cozy hideaway, where hearty traditional fare is served in a beamed dining room. In a nod to the old-fashioned surf-and-turf concept, the menu offers steak and other meat from the land (in this case, often from the farms around Galway) and fresh-that-day seafood from local markets. Service is gracious and unhurried, and you can polish off an evening here with an after-dinner drink in the attractive bar.

McDonagh's ★★★★

SEAFOOD	INEXPENSIVE/MODERATE	QUALITY ★★★★	VALUE ★★★★

22 Quay Street, Galway; ☎ 091-565001

Reservations Not necessary. **Entree range** €8–€30. **Payment** AE, MC, V. **Bar** Full service. **Disabled access** Yes. **Hours** Daily, noon–10 p.m.

MENU RECOMMENDATIONS Fish-and-chips, fresh oysters.

COMMENTS Galway's one-stop shop for the freshest seafood is part old-fashioned fish-and-chips restaurant, part restaurant, and part fish market. Fish-and-chips—fried to perfection—are made with mackerel and other fish caught that day. In the more formal restaurant you can eat simply but divinely on a heaping plate of mussels, fresh oysters on the half shell, or crab claws, washed down with a selection from the excellent wine list.

Nimmo's ★★★★½

CONTINENTAL	MODERATE	QUALITY ★★★★	VALUE ★★★★

Long Walk, Spanish Arch, Galway; ☎ 091-561114

Reservations Recommended. **Entree range** €12–€24. **Payment** MC, V. **Bar** Full service. **Disabled access** Limited. **Hours** Tuesday–Sunday, 12:30–3 p.m. and 7–10 p.m.

MENU RECOMMENDATIONS Fish soup, beef bourguignonne.

COMMENTS One of the most romantic restaurants anywhere occupies an old stone house on a quay beside the River Corrib. The torrent rushes right beneath the windows of the rustic, heavily timbered wine bar on the ground floor and the charming candlelit restaurant upstairs. Dinner is served in both sections; a menu of daily specials often includes a hearty fish soup and succulent roast lamb. Even the desserts, "imported" from Galway's best bakery, Goya, add to the feeling that an evening here is a special night out.

The Quays ★★★★

PUB FARE	INEXPENSIVE/MODERATE	QUALITY ★★½	VALUE ★★★

11 Quay Street, Galway; ☎ 091-568347

Reservations Not necessary. **Entree range** €8–€16. **Payment** MC, V. **Bar** Full service. **Disabled access** Limited. **Hours** Daily, 12:30–9 p.m.

MENU RECOMMENDATIONS Poached salmon, burgers.

COMMENTS One of Galway's most popular and atmospheric pubs incorporates carvings, pews, and arches from a medieval French church. The several levels of dining rooms are lively spots for lunch or an early dinner, when it seems that much of the working population of Galway packs in for salads, sandwiches, and hot meals that often include a nice selection of seafood. In late evenings, The Quays stages live music.

ENTERTAINMENT AND NIGHTLIFE IN GALWAY

THE WOODY, CARVED INTERIOR of **The Quays** (11 Quay Street, ☎ 091-568347) was salvaged from a medieval French church, making this multilevel space an especially atmospheric place to hear music; not all of it, unfortunately, is traditional Irish—or particularly good. **Tigh Neachtain,** or **Naughton's** (17 Cross Street; ☎ 091-568820), is the favorite hangout of many locals and visitors, partly because the old interior has not changed in more than 100 years and also because the nightly sessions of traditional music are reliably first-rate. The Rabbitts have run their family pub, appropriately named **Rabbitt's** (23–25 Forster Street; ☎ 091-566490), since the 1870s, and the old place has changed little during their tenure. **Au Pucan** (11 Forster Street; ☎ 091-561528), just down the street from Rabbitt's, is hard to miss with its thatched roof, beneath which a loyal cadre of locals gathers for good traditional-music sessions.

Galway supports a lively theater scene. **Siamsa,** the **Galway Folk Theatre,** stages a summer-only show of dance, music, and folk drama that calls to mind the step-dancing format of *Riverdance*. The theater is in **Claddagh Hall,** Nimmos Pier, and operates June through August, Monday through Friday, 8:45 p.m.; €20; ☎ 091-755479 or **homepage .tinet.ie/~siamsa. Taibhdhearc Theatre** focuses on Irish-language plays, and summer brings an excellent program of song, dance, and folk drama in a handsome theater on Middle Street; performances run July through August, Monday through Friday, 8:45 p.m.; €10 to €12; ☎ 091-563600. **Druid Theatre** presents Irish drama as well as Anglo-Irish and other works from the international repertoire; year-round, 8 p.m.; €11 to €20; ☎ 091-568617 or **www.druidtheatre.com.**

In summer, if you have a car, consider an evening drive south along Galway Bay to the village of **Kinvarra.** There, **Dunguaire Castle,** a fortified medieval tower house is an imposing presence above the rocky shore. The old vaulted banquet hall is the scene of nightly feasts that are a cut above the tourist pageants staged at several other castles. Seating is limited to 55, sparing participants the bus-tour crush; the food is quite good, and entertainment includes spirited readings of works by Yeats and other Irish poets. Banquets are staged April through October, nightly, at 5:30 p.m. and 8:30 p.m., and cost €50. For information and reservations, call ☎ 061-360788 or visit **www.shannonheritage.com.** Kinvarra is about 25 kilometers (15 miles) south of Galway via N18 and N67.

SHOPPING IN GALWAY

A HUGE SELECTION of Claddagh rings in silver and gold is on offer at **Claddagh and Celtic Jewellery Company** (next to Jurys Inn at 1 Quay Lane; ☎ 091-534494; **www.claddaghandceltic.com**). **Mulligan's** (5 Middle Street; ☎ 091-564961) stocks a large selection of traditional Irish music, while **McCambridges** (38–39 Shop Street, ☎ 091-562259) is a good place to stock up on Irish cheeses and chocolates, as well as delicatessen-type fare for a picnic. **O'Maille** (16 High Street; ☎ 091-562696) carries a fine selection of Irish knits and tweeds, and **Treasure Chest** (William Street at Castle Street; ☎ 091-563862; **www.treasure chest.ie**) is well stocked with lines of high-quality Irish china and crystal. The **Galway Crystal Heritage Centre** (Dublin Road; ☎ 091-757311) is a strange combination—glass-blowing studio, shop, and heritage center with decent exhibits on Galway's history. The fine crystal produced on the premises is beautiful, and Belleek china and other high-line Irish crafts are also sold; note, though, that prices here are about the same as they are in any other shop.

EXERCISE AND RECREATION IN GALWAY

GOLF COURSES SURROUND GALWAY. Especially scenic links can be enjoyed at the **Galway Bay Golf and Country Club** (in Renville; ☎ 091-790503) and the **Galway Golf Club** (in Blackrock; ☎ 091-522033); greens fees at both are about €50 weekdays, €60 weekends. To explore the town and countryside by bicycle, stop in at **Celtic Cycles** (Queen Street; ☎ 091-566606), where you'll pay about €20 per day for a rental. Anglers should step into the offices of the **Western Regional Fisheries Board** (Weir Lodge, Earl's Island; ☎ 091-563118) for info on where to fish, what flies to use when, and other advice.

The ARAN ISLANDS

THESE THREE ISLANDS—**Inishmore, Inishmaan,** and **Inisheer**—some 48 kilometers (30 miles) out to sea off the West Coast—retain their rugged beauty, if no longer their rugged way of life. For more than 1,000 years, fishermen and farmers on the once-remote outposts eked a meager livelihood from the rough sea and stony soil; you may have seen the hard way of life here depicted in Robert Flaherty's classic documentary, *Man of Aran* (1934). Among the illustrious visitors who have sought solitude on the islands in the past is the Irish playwright J. M. Synge (1871–1909), who set his *Riders to the Sea* here. These days, some 1,500 islanders subsist mainly on the proceeds of some 200,000 annual tourists, but they maintain their independence from mainlanders, a distinctly simple way of life, and an adherence to the Irish language, spoken unless otherwise necessary. The islands have managed to escape the worst incursions of modern life and retain their beautiful landscapes, in which emerald-green fields sweep down to the sea and such fabled mainland sights such as the **Twelve Bens in Connemara** and the **Cliffs of Moher** at the edge of the Burren are within view on a clear day.

PLANNING YOUR VISIT TO THE ARAN ISLANDS

BY BOAT, you can reach the islands from Doolin (see page 307) on service from **Doolin Ferry Company;** several boats sail daily from the Doolin pier from mid-April through September; round-trip fare is €27 to and from Inishmore and €25 to and from Inishmaan; for more information, call ☎ 065-707-4455 or visit **www.doolinferries.com.**

Aran Island Ferries sail from Rossaveel, 37 kilometers (23 miles) west of Galway City, and from Galway during high season. You can count on three a day from April through October, at 10:30 a.m., 1 p.m., and 6 p.m., and two a day the rest of the year, at 10:30 a.m. and 6 p.m.; shuttle buses run from Victoria Place (near Eyre Square) in Galway to the Rossaveel dock. Sailings take about 45 minutes, but count on two hours for a trip that includes connections on the shuttle bus. Round-trip fares are about €20 adults, €15 seniors and students, and €10 children. The shuttle bus costs €6 extra round-trip. In summer, you can travel directly from Galway Dock for an extra €6.50 per ticket. You can purchase tickets at the **Galway Tourist Office** (see page 319) and at the Aran Island Ferries Office on Victoria Place. There is also a ticket office on the dock in Rossaveel. For more information, call ☎ 091-568903 or visit **www.aranislandferries.com.**

You can reach the islands by air on **Aer Arann Islands,** with ten-minute flights from Connemara Airport, 32 kilometers (20 miles) west of Galway City, to the three islands. Service departs almost hourly from April through September and three times a day out of season, at 9 a.m., 10:30 a.m., and 3 p.m. A shuttle service connects the airport and Victoria Place in Galway. Round-trip fares are €45, €25 for children; the bus is an additional €6. For more information, call ☎ 091-593034 or visit **www.aerarannislands.ie.**

ARRIVING AND GETTING ORIENTED IN THE ARAN ISLANDS

A SMALL TOURIST-INFORMATION OFFICE near the docks on Inishmore distributes a useful map of the islands and other information. The office is open June through August, daily, 10 a.m. to 5 p.m., and less frequently in the off-season.

You will probably be met in Kilronan on Inishmore by a fleet of minibuses with drivers offering tours of the island. For about €10, you get a nice intro to the lay of the land in about two and a half hours. Other modes of transportation are your own feet; jaunting car (a horse-drawn carriage; an island tour for two costs about €40); and bicycle. Bikes are available from any number of outfits near the docks, including **Aran Bicycle Hire** (☎ 099-61132). The only easy way to see the other islands, which are considerably smaller, is on foot.

Accommodations on the islands are provided by B&Bs. Arrange reservations in advance at the **Galway Tourist Office** (see page 319); the office in Inishmore can also help you find a bed, often in the home of a family with an extra room.

EXPLORING THE ARAN ISLANDS

THE BUSIEST AND LARGEST of the islands is **Inishmore**, eight kilometers (five miles) long and three kilometers (two miles) wide; most of its 800 or so residents live in the little settlement of **Kilronan**. While the island has some attractions to draw your interest, the greatest pleasure of being on any of the Arans is to get away from it all and walk or bike through meadows and the small, stone-wall-enclosed fields and along the coasts.

The **Island Heritage Centre** in Kilronan introduces you to the island's traditional ways, as well as its unique limestone geology and accompanying flora—the Arans are in many ways an extension of the Burren, and many of the same Mediterranean flowers that blossom there in spring and summer also sprout in the Arans. Take a seat in the Centre's theatre for one of the frequent daily showings of the hour-long *Man of Aran* for a good look at how harsh life here was not so very long ago. The Centre is open April through June, daily, 10 a.m. to 5 p.m.; July and August, daily, 10 a.m. to 7 p.m.; and September through October, daily, 10 a.m. to 5 p.m. Admission is €3.50 for the museum only, €2 extra for the film.

Inishmore's big attraction is **Dún Aenghus,** one of Europe's best-preserved prehistoric monuments, dating to about 2,000 BC. The fort, surrounded by walls that are 4 meters (13 feet) thick and 3 meters (10 feet) high, was built by Celts. This mighty enclosure now sits precariously at the edge of a 100-meter (330-foot) cliff that drops to the crashing surf, which occasionally claims sections of the ramparts. The fort is open April through October, daily, 10 a.m. to 6 p.m.; and November through March, daily, 10 a.m. to 4 p.m. Admission is €2. In high season, guides occasionally give excellent tours.

Inishmaan, with a population of about 300, is the most remote-seeming of the islands and a pleasure to explore on foot. Trails and country tracks will lead you to a smattering of sights, including the stony ruins of early-Christian churches and **Conor Fort,** an earthen fortress that is a smaller-scale Dún Aenghus.

Inisheer, the smallest of the islands, is relatively flat and especially well suited for walking. You can hike around the island in an afternoon, taking in the flower-filled meadows and sights such as the early-Christian Church of St. Kevin. This sturdy little structure is buried in sand every winter and dug out in time to celebrate St. Kevin's Day on June 14.

CONNEMARA

JUST NORTH OF GALWAY begins the vast and empty landscape known as Connemara. From Galway, the main road into Connemara is N59, a scenic route around the shores of Lough Corrib to the town of **Clifden,** and from there into **Connemara National Park.**

Connemara is mountainous in parts, covered with prairielike moors in others, and dotted with forests of pine and fir that surround rushing streams and glittering lakes. The largest of the lakes—in fact, the second-largest lake in Ireland—is the 175-square-kilometer (65-square-mile) **Lough Corrib,** one of the country's best spots for freshwater angling. You might be tempted to compare this rugged terrain to that of the American West, but Connemara is really like no place else. Its dark, brooding mountains and brown bogs create a uniquely Irish landscape that is quite desolate. Even in summer, you're likely to have parts of this wild region to yourself.

Twelve craggy mountains—the **Twelve Bens,** also known as the **Twelve Pins**—rise from the center of the region. The tallest, **Benbaun,** reaches 730 meters (2,400 feet). Bogs cover one-third of the landscape, and you'll see the long, dark trenches left by turf cutters who dig turf, or peat, from the bogs, dry it, and sell it for fuel. All over Ireland you'll smell the sweet scent of turf fires dug from landscapes like this, but the supply is quickly dwindling.

Some 2,000 hectares (4,942 acres) of the region is preserved as **Connemara National Park,** which spreads across bogs and moors up the flanks of the Twelve Bens. The park's visitors center is in the village of **Letterfrack,** about 95 kilometers (57 miles) north of Galway on N59. Earnest, fairly engaging displays point out the area's geology and ecology. You'll learn about peat and how it is harvested; meadowlarks, merlins (small falcons), and other birds that inhabit the park; and the famous Connemara ponies, said to have descended from stock grounded when the Spanish Armada was wrecked offshore. Enthusiastic staffers dispense maps of hiking trails and copious advice on what to see and how best to enjoy this beautiful place. In summer, rangers guide hikes and conduct nature programs for kids. The park is open year-round, but the visitors center (☎ 095-41054) is open seasonally, April through May and September through mid-October, 10 a.m. to 5:30 p.m.; June, 10 a.m. to 6:30 p.m.; July through August, 9:30 a.m. to 6:30 p.m.; €2.75 adults, €2 seniors, €1.25 children and students, €7 families.

Major towns that surround the Connemara wilderness are **Clifden,** on the coast in the west; **Cong,** on the shores of Lough Corrib to the east; and **Leenane,** on the shores of Killary Harbour to the north. **Westport,** on the other side of fabled Crough Patrick from Leenane, is an appealing town on the shores of Crew Bay.

EXPLORING CONNEMARA

YOU CAN GET A NICE TASTE of Connemara in a day's outing from Galway. A good loop tour would take you out of Galway on N59, with your first stop in **Oughterard,** about 25 kilometers (15 miles) west. In this fishing village and resort you can get a good look at Lough Corrib, take advantage of some of Ireland's best freshwater angling, or embark on a lake cruise. A string of lakes lies to either side of N59 as you continue north into scenery that becomes starker and more dramatic as the peaks of the Twelve Bens begin to rise above moors and bogs. At **Maam Cross** you have the option to head north toward Leenane and Cong, but unless you are in a hurry to get to Cong, continue west. At **Recess** you might want to make a slight detour to **Ballynahinch Castle** (see page 336), a delightful hotel where you can have a sandwich and a pint in front of the fire in the handsome pub or take a stroll along the banks of the Ballynahinch River. The road then passes through some of the region's most beautiful landscapes as you skirt the Twelve Bens and drop into **Clifden** (see page 335). After stretching your legs around the jaunty town square, get a taste of Connemara's seascapes on the **Sky Road.** At the end of that scenic route, N59 heads east to Letterfrack and the visitors center at Connemara National Park. Just down the road is spectacular **Kylemore Abbey** (see next page), and in the village of Leenane you'll pick up route R336 and drop south to **Cong** (see page 338). From Cong, it's 35 kilometers (21 miles) back to Galway on R334 and N84. If you're continuing to Westport, head north from Leenane on N59 or R335.

Tours in Connemara

The easiest way to visit Connemara is by car, but if you're not driving, consider one of several tours that operate out of Galway. These include summer tours from **Bus Éireann,** the national bus network (☎ 091-562000 or **www.buseireann.ie**), and from **Lally Tours** (☎ 091-562905 or **www.lallytours.com**). Both provide a full day of sightseeing with stops at Clifden, Kylemore Abbey, and other points of interest. Fares are €25 adults; €18 for seniors, students, and children; and €55 families of up to two adults and three children. At the village of Oughterard, you can board a **Corrib Cruise** from May to September, daily, for sailings in Lough Corrib that last 90 minutes or half a day and include a stop at the village of Cong; the longer cruise also includes a quick stop to see the ruined monastic complex on Inchagoil Island. You can also board the boats in Cong. Short cruises from Oughterard: 11 a.m. and 2:45 p.m.; €12 adults, €6 children, €25 families. Long cruise: 11 a.m.; €16 adults, €7 children, €32 families. For more information, call ☎ 092-460029 or visit **www.corribcruises.com.**

ATTRACTION AROUND CONNEMARA

Kylemore Abbey and Garden   ★★★★

APPEAL BY AGE	PRESCHOOL ★★★	GRADE SCHOOL ★★★★	TEENS ★★★★
YOUNG ADULTS ★★★★		OVER 30 ★★★★	SENIORS ★★★★

Outside Letterfrack, off N59; ☎ 095-41146; www.kylemoreabbey.com

Type of attraction Manor house. **Admission** €10 adults, €6.50 seniors and students. **Hours** Abbey and grounds: daily, 9 a.m.–5 p.m.; walled garden: mid-March–October, daily, 10 a.m.–4:30 p.m. **When to go** In good weather to enjoy the grounds. **Special comments** A pottery workshop, a shop selling high-line crafts and clothing, and a cafeteria are on the grounds. **How much time to allow** About 2 hours.

DESCRIPTION AND COMMENTS Kylemore is the home of the order of Irish Benedictine nuns and an exclusive boarding school for girls, but the allure of the faux-Gothic castle and its lavish grounds is primarily secular: Kylemore was for many decades a pleasure dome for wealthy and entitled residents. From 1867 to 1871, Mitchell Henry, heir to a Manchester, England, cotton fortune, built the house and landscaped the 5,500-hectare (13,000-acre) estate at the base of the Twelve Bens for his wife, Margaret. She had admired the spot, with its lake and glens, on a carriage ride during their honeymoon. Margaret died in 1874, but Mitchell remained on the estate for 30 years, representing Galway in the House of Commons; in 1903, he sold Kylemore to the Duke and Duchess of Manchester. The noble couple's elaborate lifestyle came to an end when the duchess's wealthy American father, who bankrolled the enterprise, died in 1914. The nuns, bombed out of their convent in Ypres, Belgium, during World War I, took over the estate in 1920, and ever since have paid the bills by educating the daughters of Ireland's elite. In the abbey you'll see a few opulent reception rooms that are furnished in a fairly humdrum style (most of the original furnishings have been removed, so you really don't get a sense of the house as a wealthy residence). More impressive are the lovely grounds, a small chapel that's built like a cathedral in miniature, and an elaborate stream-laced garden in which exotic fruits and flowers flourish behind thick limestone walls.

TOURING TIPS A shuttle bus runs between the abbey and the walled garden, in a sheltered vale about 1.6 kilometers (1 mile) from the house, but walk at least one way to enjoy the lakeside and valley scenery.

EXERCISE AND RECREATION IN CONNEMARA

A ONE-STOP SHOP for land- and water-based activities is **Delphi Adventure Holidays,** located next to the Delphi Mountain Resort north of Leenane. The center makes use of the surrounding mountains for hill walking, mountain biking, and mountaineering, and **Killary Harbour** is well suited to waterskiing, kayaking, and many other water sports. For more information, call ☎ 095-42307 or go to **www .delphiadventureholidays.ie. Connemara Walking Centre** caters to walkers with half- and full-day hikes throughout the spring and summer in many different parts of Connemara. Walks take place March through October, costs begin at about €20, and groups assemble at Island House on Market Street in Clifden for bus transportation to the different starting points; ☎ 095-21379 or **www.walkingireland .com.** Lough Corrib is known as some of Ireland's best angling waters; an excellent source for information on renting boats and tackle, advice on flies to use, and more, is **Angling West** (Rushveala Lodge, Oughterard; ☎ 091-557933 or **www.anglingwest.com**). **Irish Cycling Tours** in Leenane rents bicycles and other equipment and leads tours; ☎ 095-42276 or **www.irishcyclingtours.ie.** Golf courses include the **Connemara Golf Club** (outside Clifden in Ballyconneely; ☎ 095-23502) and the **Oughterard Golf Club** (outside Oughte-rard; ☎ 091-552131).

CLIFDEN

BACKED BY THE PEAKS of the **Twelve Bens,** Clifden seems almost like an Alpine village, but the bogs and the rocky coastline that surround the town remind you that you are indeed in Connemara. The year-round population barely tops

> *unofficial* **TIP**
> With lively pubs and shops in the compact town center, Clifden is a good place to stop for a break from touring or for an overnight stay.

1,000, but Clifden is by far the largest town in Connemara as well as the region's self-proclaimed capital. Clifden is also the start of the **Sky Road,** a scenic drive along Clifden Bay.

Arriving and Getting Oriented in Clifden

Clifden is 80 kilometers (48 miles) northwest of Galway on N59. A drive here from Galway takes you through some stunning Connemara scenery that includes the shores of Lough Corrib and the craggy, heather-covered Twelve Bens. A tourist-information office, on the Galway Road (N59) at the entrance to the town center (☎ 095-21163), is open May through September, daily, 9 a.m. to 6 p.m. If you're heading into Connemara in other seasons, you can stock up on the same info at the **Connemara National Park Headquarters** or at the **Galway Tourist Office** (see pages 332 and 319).

Special Events in Clifden

From June through August, Clifden stages a show of traditional dancing and music in the town hall on Tuesday and Thursday evenings. In late July, you can see Connemara ponies at the **Claddaghduff Pony Show;** these handsome beasts make a reappearance during the **Festival of the Connemara Pony** in mid-August.

Hotels in and around Clifden

Abbeyglen Castle Hotel ★★★

QUALITY ★★★	VALUE ★★★	€110–€145

Sky Road, Clifden; ☎ 095-21201; fax 095-21797; info@abbeyglen.ie; www.abbeyglen.ie

Location Just outside Clifden's city center. **Amenities and services** 38 rooms; bar, garden, hair dryers, helipad, in-room tea and coffee facilities, irons, pitch-and-putt golf, restaurant, swimming pool. **Elevator** Yes. **Parking** Free, on property. **Price** Many special offers available, including low-season packages that include dinner, bed, and breakfast at very reasonable rates. **Credit cards** AE, DC, MC, V.

THIS 175-YEAR-OLD CASTLELIKE manor house, complete with turrets and crenellations, is set in a sheltered glen laced with streams and lovely gardens. Abbeyglen has all the trappings of a romantic getaway and is beloved by many repeat visitors. A comfortable, informal atmosphere permeates a series of lounges and a game room, while a parrot jabbers at the reception desk. You can enjoy a drink or complimentary afternoon tea in front of a peat fire or relax for hours in one of the armchairs in the lounge. The lawns and pleasant swimming pool are inviting without being fussy. A recent refurbishment scheme has ensured that the rooms and large bathrooms, most with big tubs, are comfortable, but—much to the delight of many regular guests—the place still has the look of a much-used, slightly run-down country manor.

Ballynahinch Castle ★★★★★

QUALITY ★★★★½	VALUE ★★★★	€160–€240

Recess, County Galway; ☎ 095-31006; fax 095-31085; bhinch@iol.ie; www.ballynahinch-castle.com

Location About 15 kilometers (9 miles) east of Clifden off N59. **Amenities and services** 40 rooms; cycling, fishing, gardens, nonsmoking rooms, room service, tennis, walking; closed at Christmas and part of February. **Elevator** No. **Parking** On property, free. **Price** Includes full Irish breakfast; many special offers available; lower rates for longer stays. **Credit cards** AE, DC, MC, V.

ONE OF IRELAND'S MOST NOTED country-house hotels occupies an 18th-century manor on the banks of the Ballynahinch River, surrounded by 450 acres of woodlands and mountain pastures. Former residents of the estate include Grace O'Malley, the "Pirate Queen" of Connemara; "Humanity Dick" Martin, founder of the Royal Society for the Prevention of Cruelty to Animals; and HRH the Maharajah Ranjitsinji, also known as "Ranji, Prince of Cricketeers." Even without this colorful provenance, Ballynahinch is an utterly delightful place that doesn't miss a beat in providing a memorable retreat. Open fires and Persian carpets grace the welcoming public rooms, where guests seem to spend many contented hours sitting quietly and reading; when the urge strikes, fishing, walking, and many other activities await just outside the front door. The woody pub is a popular gathering spot for guests and locals alike, and the Owenmore Restaurant is the best dining room in Connemara. Forest trails, riverside walks, and gardens grace the grounds. Delightful guest rooms are situated in the old house and in thoughtful, light-filled new extensions strung out above the river, which can be viewed through floor-to-ceiling windows. The furnishings are airily Georgian; excellent beds are covered with fine linens; and bathrooms are new, large, nicely outfitted, and often reached through dressing rooms. The attentive service caps off the feeling that guests are enjoying a casually elegant country house—which they are.

Foyles Hotel ★★★½

| QUALITY | ★★★½ | VALUE | ★★★★½ | €80–€130 |

Main Street, Clifden; ☎ 095-21801; fax 095-21458; foyles@anu.ie; www.foyleshotel.com

Location Town center. **Amenities and services** 30 rooms; hair dryers, in-room tea and coffee facilities. **Elevator** No. **Parking** On street. **Price Includes** full Irish breakfast. **Credit cards** MC, V.

THE IN-TOWN LOCATION, just steps away from Clifden's shops and pubs, is one of the many appeals of this nicely old-fashioned hotel. A sunny lounge filled with oversize armchairs faces the town square, and a small patio surrounded by a flowery garden is at the rear of the reception area. Upstairs, the high-ceilinged guest rooms are well done, with solid, beautifully maintained old furniture, including handsome chests and armoires and firm beds. Color schemes are restful, and the decor is appealingly traditional without being overbearingly so; bathrooms have been updated with large basins, deep bathtubs, and good showers. Rooms in the front of the hotel afford entertaining views of the town's comings and goings, but those on the side and at the rear of the hotel are completely free of traffic noise.

Restaurants in and around Clifden

Marconi Restaurant ★★★½

| MODERN IRISH | MODERATE | QUALITY ★★★½ | VALUE ★★★★ |

In Foyle's Hotel, Main Street, Clifden; ☎ 095-21801

Reservations Recommended in summer. **Entree range** €14.95–€18.95. **Payment** MC, V. **Bar** Full service. **Disabled access** Yes. **Hours** Daily, 6:30–9:30 p.m.

MENU RECOMMENDATIONS Fresh Connemara oysters, Connemara lamb, fresh Atlantic salmon.

COMMENTS The dining room of Foyle's Hotel is, like the rest of the establishment, slightly formal and old-fashioned; these surroundings impart the feeling that a meal is a special occasion. The service can be rushed when staff is short, but the kitchen reliably prepares fish and seafood fresh off the boats. A good light meal for seafood lovers might begin with oysters, washed down with a glass of white from the decent wine list and followed by one of the other excellent seafood appetizers, such as calamari, crab cakes, or mussels steamed in white wine. (Incidentally, Guglielmo Marconi, Italian inventor of the radio and the restaurant's namesake, was part Irish.)

unofficial **TIP**
For lunch or a snack, drop into the daytime-only **Two Dog Café** (Church Street; ☎ 095-22186), where the baked goods are delicious.

Owenmore Restaurant ★★★★

| MODERN IRISH | EXPENSIVE | QUALITY ★★★★ | VALUE ★★★ |

Ballynahinch Castle, Recess; ☎ 095-31006

Reservations Recommended, as is smart attire. **Entree range** €45, prix-fixe dinner. **Payment** AE, DC, MC, V. **Bar** Full service. **Disabled access** Yes. **Hours** Daily, 7–10 p.m

MENU RECOMMENDATIONS Poached wild Atlantic salmon, rack of roasted Connemara lamb.

COMMENTS This elegant dining room in Ballynahinch Castle hotel is the finest restaurant in Connemara. Chef Robert Webster takes inspiration from the surrounding landscapes as he artfully prepares local lamb, seafood, and produce. The room does much to enhance the pleasure of a meal here: huge windows overlook the Ballynahinch River, and the lovely atmosphere is augmented by smooth, attentive service that makes guests feel welcome and pampered.

Shopping in Clifden

Clifden caters to its many visitors with shops selling goods of unusually high quality. These stores include an outlet of the noted Irish chain **Avoca Handweavers,** which showcases its excellent tweeds, along with carvings and other Connemara souvenirs, in a bright shop set next to the sea about ten kilometers (six miles) outside town on the Clifden–Leenane Road; ☎ 095-41058. Right in town is **Millars Connemara Tweed Ltd.** (Main Street, ☎ 095-21038), justifiably famous for its wool from local sheep; you can buy it by the yard or woven into hats, blankets, and other attractive apparel and household items.

CONG

THIS LITTLE VILLAGE, tucked between Lough Corrib to the south and Lough Mask to the north, would be noteworthy in its own right, but Cong is still resting on the fame it garnered as the setting for the 1952 film *The Quiet Man*. John Wayne and Maureen O'Hara got star billing, but the green countryside and pretty cottages—still much in evidence—steal the show.

Arriving and Getting Oriented in Cong

Cong is about 35 kilometers (21 miles) north of Galway on N84 and R334. A longer but slightly more scenic route takes you out of Galway on N59, with a turn north on R336 at Maam Cross, from which it's about another 20 kilometers (12 miles) to Cong. The busy **Cong Tourist Office** (in the town center near the abbey; ☎ 094-954-6542) is open March through June and September through November, daily, 10 a.m. to 6 p.m., and July through August, daily, 10 a.m. to 7 p.m.

Hotel in Cong

Ashford Castle ★★★★

| QUALITY ★★★½ | VALUE ★★★ | €280–€450 |

Cong, County Mayo; ☎ 094-954-6003; fax 094-954-6260; ashford@ashford.ie; www.ashford.ie

---

Location At edge of village. **Amenities and services** 83 rooms; bicycles, boating, fishing, 9-hole golf course, health club, horseback riding, nonsmoking rooms, shooting, tennis. **Elevator** Yes. **Parking** Free, on property. **Price** Includes full Irish breakfast; many special offers available. **Credit cards** AE, DC, MC, V.

ONE OF IRELAND'S MOST ACCLAIMED hotels gives credence to the old real-estate maxim that location—and, in this case, a breathtaking one—is everything. The 19th-century castle, built with its many turrets and towers around a 13th-century manor, is nestled stunningly between Lough Corrib and the River Cong. Inside, oil paintings glimmer on paneled and stone walls, and suits of armor stand sentry beneath grand staircases. Despite the grandeur, though, there's a certain lack of authenticity to the place. Ashford can seem more like an American resort hotel than an Irish castle; service can be brusque (so atypical of Ireland); and some of the public areas seem to have had their last bit of life polished out of them. The guest rooms are furnished to a very high level of traditional comfort and offer every amenity, but some, especially those in the newer wing, are actually a bit dull. Most rooms, however, have wonderful outlooks, and because the castle is surrounded by water, there is no need to pay extra for a lake view. Many guests, who include a long roster of celebrities, would not think of staying elsewhere and extol virtues such as the hotel's two excellent restaurants, the Connaught Room and the George V; two atmospheric bars; a state-of-the-art spa; and a wealth of activities. But if you're looking for a relaxed retreat where you'll feel like a guest in an Irish country house, set your sights instead on nearby Ballynahinch Castle (see page 336).

Exploring Cong

Cong's most august monument is the ruined **Augustine monastery** in the village center, on Abbey Street (free, always open). The monastery's famous relic, the **Cross of Cong,** a processional object emblazoned with gems and enamel, is now in the National Museum in Dublin. What remains here are some wonderful Romanesque carvings and archways, a chapter house, and a charming and ingenious fishing hut, raised above the river on stone pilings. The crafty monks would lower a basket on a rope with a bell attached; when a fish swam into the basket, the bell would ring.

Many visitors still come to Cong in search of the region's Technicolor beauty made famous by *The Quiet Man.* The village caters to these film buffs with the **Quiet Man Cottage,** a replica of the dwelling used in the film. It's hard to imagine anyone actually plunking down hard-earned cash to see the grainy production photos and dusty costumes, but if you can't resist this bit of Hollywood memorabilia, you'll pay €4 to indulge yourself; open mid-March through October, daily, 10 a.m. to 5 p.m.; ☎ 094-954-6089. If you are such an ardent fan of the Duke that you need to see more, **Paddy Rock** leads tours of the locations used in the film; you can contact him at ☎ 094-954-6155.

Shopping in Cong

Step into **Kate Luskin's shop** at the edge of town near the entrance to Ashford Castle for a wonderful selection of handmade Aran knitwear, made from the wool of local sheep and colored with natural dyes. You can select a sweater from the shelf, or Kate will make one to order. Prices are extremely reasonable for the quality of the materials and craftsmanship, beginning at €125. If Kate's not there, just ring the bell and she'll come over from her house nearby; ☎ 094-954-6757.

WESTPORT

THIS ATTRACTIVE TOWN of wide streets and gracious squares, designed by architect James Wyatt in the 1770s, is to the north of Connemara, on the other side of the Doolough Valley and Croagh Patrick, a conical-shaped peak close to the hearts of the devout. In the fifth century, St. Patrick spent the 40 days of Lent atop the mountain, fasting, praying, and ringing a bell to expel all snakes from Ireland; a small white oratory marks the site of his hermitage. Thousands of pilgrims, some of them barefoot, still make their way up a wide path to the summit, as do hikers devoted more to exercise than to Ireland's patron saint.

Westport is one of Ireland's most appealing towns, though its current prosperity is fairly recent—the town fell into a 200-year-long stretch of hard times when British mills supplanted the local linen industry around the turn of the 19th century.

PLANNING YOUR VISIT TO WESTPORT

THE WESTPORT TOURIST OFFICE (James Street; ☎ 098-25711) is open May through October, Monday through Saturday, 9 a.m. to 7 p.m.; November through January, Monday through Friday, 9 a.m. to 6 p.m. and Saturday, 9 a.m. to 1 p.m. At the **Heritage Centre,** downstairs, you can learn all you need to know about Westport House, the Pirate Queen, Crough Patrick, and other people, places, and episodes in local history; €3.

unofficial **TIP**
Walking tours of Westport depart from the clock tower on nearby Bridge Street at 8 p.m. in July and August; cost is €5.

ARRIVING AND GETTING ORIENTED IN WESTPORT

WESTPORT IS ABOUT 20 KILOMETERS (12 miles) north of Leenane on N59. A slightly longer and much more scenic route takes you out of Leenane on N335 through the **Doolough Valley** and along the southern shores of **Clew Bay.** This route first takes you just outside Leenane around **Killary Harbour,** a fjordlike body of water carved by a glacier. Near the entrance to the Doolough Valley, **Aasleagh Falls,** reached by a short trail from the road, cascades down a hillside where ferns and wild rhododendron flourish. The valley is beautiful, though the remote landscapes were the setting for the Famine Walk, one of many gruesome episodes during the Great Potato Famine of the 1840s. Some 600 tenants walked through the valley to ask their land-lord at Delphi Lodge, south of the village of Louisburgh, for food and were turned back; most died of starvation on the side of the road. Archbishop Desmond Tutu is one of many pilgrims who have retraced their steps on an annual commemorative walk.

HOTELS IN AND AROUND WESTPORT

 Carlton Atlantic Coast ★★★

QUALITY ★★★½	VALUE ★★★	€130–€160

The Quay, Westport, County Mayo; ☎ 098-29000; fax 098-29111; info@atlanticcoasthotel.com; www.atlanticcoasthotel.com

Location Facing Westport harbor, about 1 mile from town center. **Amenities and services** 85 rooms; bar, cafe, hair dryers, in-room tea and coffee facilities, nonsmoking rooms, restaurant, satellite TV, swimming pool, spa. **Elevator** Yes. **Parking** Free, on property. **Price** Includes full Irish breakfast; many special offers and family rates available. **Credit cards** AE, DC, MC, V.

BEHIND THE FACADE of an 18th-century mill on the old Quay facing West-port's harbor, the Atlantic Coast is strictly contemporary, with light and airy public spaces and large guest rooms facing the sea through big win-dows. While the atmosphere throughout is more functional than cozy, any feeling of anonymity is offset by the friendly service and the presence of many families who come here for short getaways, especially on weekends. Many of the rooms have a double bed and a single bed; folding beds can be wheeled in for no extra charge; babysitting is available; and the hotel is equipped with an indoor swimming pool—all attractions for travelers with children. Adults are catered to with a spa and an excellent top-floor restau-rant, while the ground-floor bistro serves casual meals well suited to young guests. Westport House (see page 343), with its many kid-friendly attractions, is nearby, a pleasant walk along the Quay and through the estate parklands.

Delphi Lodge ★ ★ ★ ★ ½

QUALITY ★★★★	VALUE ★★★★	€130–€200

Leenane, County Galway; ☎ 095-42296; fax 095-42296; www.delphilodge.ie

Location In a secluded valley near Leenane. **Amenities and services** 12 units; dining room, bar, library, billiards room, garden, fishing, horseback riding, walking, golf nearby, in-room tea and coffee facilities. **Elevator** No. **Parking** Free, on property. **Price** Includes full Irish breakfast; special offers available. **Credit cards** AE, MC, V.

ONE OF IRELAND'S FAVORITE COUNTRY retreats overlooks its own lake and the Connemara mountains, providing informal but sophisticated lodgings in a stunningly beautiful setting. The house that the Marquis of Sligo built as a sporting retreat in the early 19th century still seems like a private home, and attentive but relaxed hospitality lends the air of house party in which guests may or not participate; five cottages on the estate provide even more of private retreat. An excellent dinner is served at a communal table nightly, and by day guests can engage in many outdoor activities—or just soak in the beauty of one of the most beautiful corners of Ireland.

Delphi Mountain Resort and Spa ★ ★ ★ ★

QUALITY ★★★★	VALUE ★★★	FROM €99

Leenane, County Galway; ☎ 095-42208; fax 095-42223; delphigy@iol.ie; www.delphiescape.com

Location Above Killary Harbour, south of Westport. **Amenities and services** 22 units; bar, bicycles, fishing, hair dryers, horseback riding, in-room tea and coffee facilities, nonsmoking rooms, restaurant, spa, walking. **Elevator** Yes. **Parking** Free, on property. **Price** Includes full Irish breakfast; many special offers and spa-treatment packages available. **Credit cards** AE, MC, V.

YOU WILL FALL UNDER THE SPELL of this lovely retreat, which promises to offer an escape from the stresses of modern life, the moment you step inside—or perhaps as you approach, because the stone-and-timber building blends so unobtrusively with the mountain landscape that surrounds it. Inside, a turf fire burns in a stone hearth in the lobby, color schemes are soothingly neutral, and walls of glass bring the outdoors inside. Guest rooms are simply but comfortably decorated with natural fabrics, hardwood floors, and appealing contemporary furnishings; many are suites with loft bedrooms, and all have large tiled bathrooms and either patios or small balconies. The spa is especially restful, and guests have access to a large Jacuzzi overlooking the mountains, a sauna and other facilities, and a full range of pay-as-you-go treatments. Even the dining room, which specializes in Irish seafood but also serves meat and vegetarian dishes, is extremely relaxing. The cocktail bar caters to the broad tastes of guests, serving smoothies and fruit juices as well as beer and cocktails. Delphi offers a range of multiday spa and outdoor-activity packages but is open to overnight guests as well.

EXPLORING WESTPORT

WESTPORT WARRANTS A LEISURELY STROLL to take in the harmony and elegance of the 18th-century town plan. All streets converge on the **Octagon,** architect James Wyatt's innovative take on a town square. A gurgling river rushes past one side of the appealing space, and a riverside walk is shaded by lime trees. Westport's harbor is about 1 kilometer (0.5 miles) west of the town center on Clew Bay. The 17th-century mills lining the Quay now house shops, apartments, and a hotel (the **Carlton Atlantic Coast,** page 341), though there's still a salty tang to the place. **Westport House** (see below) elegantly commands a green hillside just above the bay.

TOURS FROM WESTPORT

FROM JUNE 19 THROUGH SEPTEMBER 4, **Bus Éireann** operates tours from Westport to Connemara, with stops at Kylemore Abbey and Cong. Tours depart from the tourist office at 10:30 a.m. and return at 5 p.m., and the cost is €22 adults, €18 students, 15 children, and €55 for families of up to two adults and three children. For more information, call ☎ 096-71800 or go to **www.buseireann.ie.**

ATTRACTION IN WESTPORT

kids **Westport House** ★ ★ ½

APPEAL BY AGE	PRESCHOOL ★★★★	GRADE SCHOOL ★★★★★	TEENS ★★★★
YOUNG ADULTS ★★★★		OVER 30 ★★½	SENIORS ★★½

Outside Westport; ☎ 098-27766; www.westporthouse.ie

Type of attraction Historic home and amusement park set in gardens. **Admission** *House and gardens only:* €11.50 adults, €7.50 seniors, €9 students, €6.50 children; *house, gardens, and attractions:* €21 adults, €12 seniors, €20 students, €16.50 children, €75 families of up to 2 adults and 4 children. **Hours** *House, gardens, and attractions:* daily, 11:30 a.m.–5:30 p.m. **When to go** Avoid Sundays, when every child in the West of Ireland descends upon the place. **Special comments** If you've been dragging your young companions through museums and historic homes, the rides, zoos, and other commercial attractions of Westport House will be a welcome treat for them. **How much time to allow** About 1 hour for the house, and as long as the kids want for the rides and other attractions.

DESCRIPTION AND COMMENTS This stately home on the shores of Clew Bay is the work of two of Ireland's leading architects: Richard Cassels (Powerscourt [see page 180] is his masterpiece), and James Wyatt, who laid out the handsome streets and squares of Westport. Cassels began the house in 1730 on the site of an earlier castle, of which some dungeons remain, and Wyatt completed the job in 1788. Stately touches such as the grand staircase and elegant dining room are Wyatt's. The collections of paintings, Waterford crystal, and fine silver are the family treasures of the Browne family, owners of Westport House and descendants of Grace O'Malley, the infamous 16th-century "Pirate Queen" who made her fortune raiding ships off the coast of western Ireland. Parts of the grounds, including some formal gardens, are indeed lovely, but, sadly, the estate has become a money-generating theme park with intrusive and unstately amusements that include swan-boat rides, a log flume, and a mock farmyard.

TOURING TIPS If you want to enjoy a slice of Irish history without commercial intrusions, limit your tour to the house.

RESTAURANTS IN WESTPORT

THE TOP CHOICE FOR A CASUAL MEAL in Westport is **McCormack's** (Bridge Street, ☎ 098-25619), a casual cafe that shares its premises with an art gallery and a deli–butcher shop. Chowders, stews, and baked goods are sublime; cheese and other foods are available for take-out in the shop downstairs. A mandatory evening stop is **Matt Malloy's** (Bridge Street, ☎ 098-26655), a down-to-earth pub owned by Matt Malloy of the Chieftains; traditional music is on tap many evenings.

Quay Cottage ★★★★

SEAFOOD	MODERATE	QUALITY ★★★★	VALUE ★★★½

The Harbour, Westport; ☎ 098-26412

Reservations Recommended. **Entree range** €18–€27; prix-fixe dinners, €25 and €35. **Payment** AE, MC, V. **Bar** Full service. **Disabled access** Yes. **Hours** May–October, daily, 6–10 p.m.; November–April, Tuesday–Saturday, 6–10 p.m.

MENU RECOMMENDATIONS Fish chowder, garlic grilled oysters.

COMMENTS A stone cottage at one end of Westport's historic quay reflects the gentrification that has turned what was once a working port into a leisure district, but there's nothing casual about the approach to food here. Many of the dishes that arrive at the pine tables in the nautically themed room are based on seafood from Clew Bay just outside the front door, though duckling and other land-based choices are available, too. Service is adept, and a view of the bay gleaming in the moonlight awaits when you emerge at the end of a meal.

NORTH *of* WESTPORT

NORTHERN COUNTY MAYO is wild and windswept, a landscape of moors, isolated farms, and a rugged coastline. Among the reasons to linger here—and to simply enjoy rural Ireland is a big one—is the opportunity to visit **Achill Island** and **Céide Fields,** a 5,000-year-old Stone Age site.

ACHILL ISLAND

THE LARGEST IRISH ISLAND comprises 147 square kilometers (57 square miles) of bogs, moors, and wild coasts and is only 6 meters (20 feet) off the coast, about 60 kilometers (36 miles) north of Westport via N59 and R319, which crosses a causeway to the island. In good weather, Achill Island is incredibly beautiful, remote, and wild, with wonderful walks along sea cliffs, some of which rival those at Slieve League (see page 371) in height. Conversely, when mist and fog set in for days on end, as they often do, the island can seem like the bleakest place on earth.

You can drive around the island on well-marked **Atlantic Drive,** coming to beautiful beaches, small villages, and ascending, on the north coast, around the bases of **Croaghaun,** 688 meters (2,270 feet) tall, and **Slievemore,** topping off at 671 meters (2,214 feet). One of the most haunting spots on the island is **Slievemore Village,** where more than a hundred ruined, overgrown cottages are reminders of the Famine, when villagers left in search of food, and of evictions by landlords seeking higher rents. **Heinrich Boll,** the Nobel Prize–winning German novelist and essayist, lived in the village of **Doogort** during the 1950s and based his *Irish Diary* on his experiences. Doogort isn't much more than a small collection of houses backed by the flanks of Slievemore, next to a beautiful beach.

CÉIDE FIELDS

THIS MODEST-LOOKING SITE some 80 kilometers (50 miles) north of Westport seems like an outpost at the end of the world, which indeed it was when a Stone Age settlement flourished here 5,000 years ago. Boglands covered the houses and farm plots millennia ago, beautifully preserving the stone foundations of houses and the fences that parceled off fields. It takes a little imagination, and some time in the excellent visitors center, to appreciate the significance of the place, which is also enhanced on one of the guided walks. The site is on coast road R314, near Ballycastle; ☎ 096-43325. Open mid-March through May and October, daily, 10 a.m. to 5 p.m.; June through September, daily, 10 a.m. to 6 p.m.; and November, daily, 10 a.m. to 4:30 p.m. Admission is €3.50 adults, €2.50 seniors, €1.25 students and children, and €8.25 for families.

The drive to Céide Fields from Westport is especially scenic if you follow the coast north through **Castlebar** and **Ballina** to the pleasant seaside village of **Killala** and around **Downpatrick Head,** where the sea erupts in plumes through a string of blowholes.

PART NINE

The **NORTHWEST** of **IRELAND**

NORTHWEST IRELAND IS LIKELY to hit you like a big gust of salty sea breeze: the rugged landscapes are never far from the wild North Atlantic, and they're as wild as the sea. A string of maritime peninsulas jut in and out of the sea; inland, brown and purple heaths and moors climb the sides of craggy mountains. The British settled so-called Plantation Towns throughout the region and still control the lands just across the border in Northern Ireland; however, much of the rural, desolate Northwest is Irish speaking, and even the signs are in Gaelic. The major towns of the Northwest, **Sligo** and **Letterkenny,** are boomtowns these days, but even so their populations are less than 20,000 each. Most of your travels here will be on country roads where the only traffic you might encounter for miles is four-legged.

SLIGO TOWN

AN OLD-FASHIONED CHARM still prevails in this sturdy commercial town spanning the banks of the River Garavogue near Sligo Bay, but there's quite a buzz in the air, too. New shops, a new riverside walk along the Garavogue, and new prosperity might bring to mind the often quoted line by William Butler Yeats, "All changed, changed utterly." Yeats, incidentally, is Sligo's most famous son. Though born in Dublin, the poet and his brother, the painter Jack Yeats, had *the northwest of ireland*

IRISH SEA

Greencastle

Moville

Lough Foyle

Malin

Limavady

A37

A6

DERRY

A505

NORTHERN IRELAND

Derry

A6

A2

Malin Head

Ballyliffin

Clonmany

INISHOWEN PENINSULA

Fort Dunree

Buncrana

Fahan

A5

A38

A5

Carrowkeel

Rathmullan

Inch Island

Rathmelton

N13

N14

N15

TYRONE

Lough Swilly

Fanad

Carrigart

R247

Millford

N56

Rathmelton

Letterkenny

N56

Rossguill

Horn Head

Dunfanaghy

Creeslough

N56

Glenveagh National Park

Docharry

Fintown

Glenties

R250

DONEGAL

DONEGAL

N15

Mountcharles

N15

ATLANTIC OCEAN

Tory Island

Bloody Foreland

Gola Island

Bunbeg

R259

Gweedore

Dunglow

N56

N56

Glencolumbkille

R263

Ardara

N56

Killybegs

Inver Bay

Rossnowlagh

Owey Island

Arranmore Island

Burtonport

ATLANTIC OCEAN

10 mi

10 km

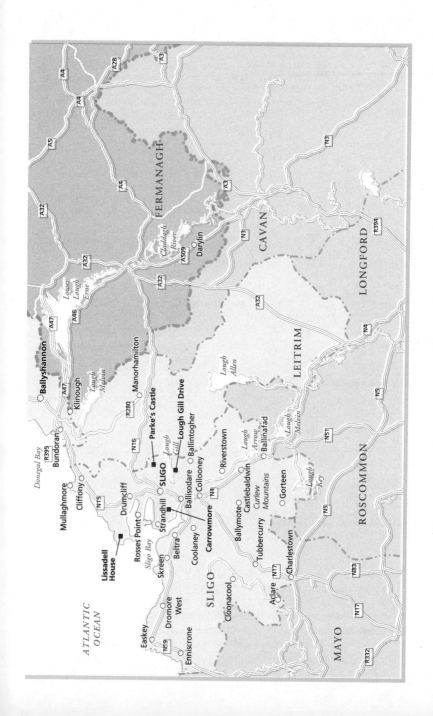

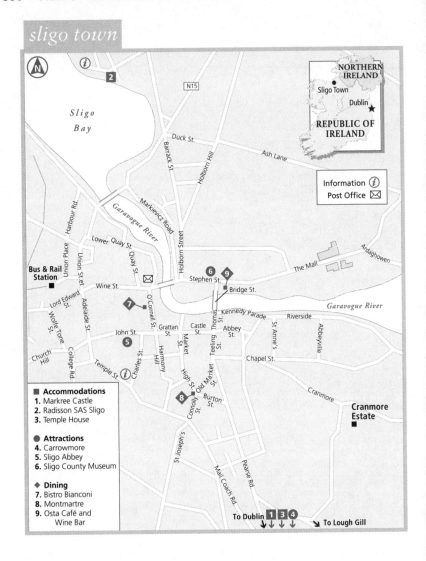

sligo town

their roots in Sligo and spent much of their lives here. Those for whom the name Yeats recalls the poet's famous line "I will arise and go now, and go to Innisfree" will be inspired by **Yeats Country,** as the countryside around Sligo is known. Part of the route skirts **Lough Gill** and affords views of the "Lake Isle of Innisfree" that Yeats made famous. **Sligo Abbey,** in ruin, is the sole reminder of the town's prominence as a trading center in the Middle Ages—and of a savage attack on the town by the British, under Sir Frederick

Hamilton in 1642, in which the abbey and most of the rest of Sligo were destroyed. Most of the handsome town center dates from the 19th century, when in the pre-Famine days the docks and warehouses along the Garavogue and Sligo Bay brought wealth and prominence to Sligo.

PLANNING YOUR VISIT TO SLIGO TOWN

SERVING THE NORTHWEST REGION, the **Sligo Tourist Office** provides information on the town as well as the rest of Counties Sligo and Donegal. Located at the edge of the city center on Temple Street, the office is open Monday through Friday year-round, 9 a.m. to 5 p.m., and on some summer weekends; ☎ 071-916-1201; **www .irelandnorthwest.ie.**

Special Events in Sligo Town

Sligo's most famous annual event is the **Yeats International Summer School,** for two weeks in July and/or August, when lectures, readings, and other events honor the town's famous poet; for information, call ☎ 071-69802 or visit **www.yeats-sligo.com.** The **Scriobh Literary Festival** in September attracts writers from throughout Ireland, as well as international literary figures, for readings and workshops; for more information, contact the Model Arts and Niland Gallery; ☎ 071-914-3694. Several musical festivals include the **Yeats Country Music Festival** in June, with country-music performers from throughout Ireland and the United States; ☎ 01-605-7707, **www.showtours .ie;** and the **Sligo Feis Ceoil,** also in June, with choral singing, sessions of traditional music, and more; ☎ 087-960-2866, **www.sligofeis ceoil.com.** In October, the **Sligo Festival of Baroque Music** focuses on music from the 16th to 18th centuries; ☎ 071-914-1405, **www.model art.ie.** November's **Sligo International Choral Festival** brings together choristers from around the world; ☎ 086-259-2290, **www.sligo choralfest.org.**

ARRIVING AND GETTING ORIENTED IN SLIGO TOWN

SLIGO IS ABOUT 138 KILOMETERS (85 miles) northeast of Galway and 217 kilometers (135 miles) northwest of Dublin. By car, follow N3 across Ireland from Dublin to Sligo; from Galway, take N59 north. **Irish Rail** runs five trains per day between Dublin and Sligo, and the trip takes about three hours. Standard one-way fare is €27. The Sligo train station is on Lord Edward Street; for more information, call ☎ 071-916-9888 or go to **www.irishrail.ie.** About six **Bus Éireann** buses travel between Dublin and Sligo daily. The trip takes about four hours and costs €18; call ☎ 071-916-0066 or go to **www .buseireann.ie.** The Sligo bus station is near the train station on Prince Edward Street.

How Hotels Compare in the Northwest of Ireland

HOTEL	OVERALL	QUALITY	VALUE	PRICE
SLIGO TOWN				
Temple House	★★★★½	★★★★	★★★★	€105–€160
Markree Castle	★★★★	★★★	★★★	€100–€165
Radisson SAS Hotel Sligo	★★★	★★★★	★★★	From €99
DONEGAL TOWN				
St. Ernan's House	★★★★	★★★★	★★★	From €240
NORTH DONEGAL				
Frewin	★★★★½	★★★★	★★★★	€75–€130
Rathmullan House	★★★★	★★★★	★★★	€130–€260
Castle Grove Country House Hotel	★★★★	★★★½	★★★	€80–€160

HOTELS IN AND AROUND SLIGO TOWN

Markree Castle ★★★★

QUALITY ★★★	VALUE ★★★	€100–€165

Collooney, County Sligo; ☎ 071-916-7800; fax 071-916-7840; markree@ iol.ie; www.markreecastle.ie

Location 13 kilometers (8 miles) south of Sligo Town, outside the village of Collooney. **Amenities and services** 30 rooms; bar, fishing, gardens, horseback riding, nonsmoking rooms, restaurant. **Elevator** Yes. **Parking** Free, on property. **Price** Includes full Irish breakfast. **Credit cards** AE, MC, V.

BUILT IN 1640, this rather ominous, fortresslike castle is the ancestral home of Charles Cooper, who operates the 400-hectare (1,000-acre) estate as a hotel providing some of the most charmingly idiosyncratic lodgings in all of Ireland. You'll know the place isn't run-of-the-mill from the moment you enter the front doors and climb the stone staircase to the paneled and gal- leried Great Hall, where a roaring fire burns in a great hearth. In the guest rooms, tucked into corners and towers and reached by a labyrinth of stair- ways and passages, furnishings are sometimes mismatched and a bit worn, but for the castle's long roster of loyal devotees, that's beside the point— overall, they're comfortable and oozing with character. (The elevator serves only some levels, so be sure to mention any accessibility needs you may have when booking.) Public rooms include a sunny double-length drawing room with a mismatched pair of fireplaces, a cozy bar, and an ele- gant rococo dining room where an excellent prix-fixe dinner is served with delightful old-world formality. The River Unsin sprints past the front door, while paths crisscross the wooded grounds to the estate's own lake. If you want a break from the ordinary, this is the place.

Radisson SAS Hotel Sligo ★★★

QUALITY ★★★★	VALUE ★★★	FROM €99

Ballincar, Rosses Point Road, County Sligo; ☎ 071-914-0008; fax 071-914-0006; info.sligo@radissonsas.com; www.radissonsas.com

Location About 3 kilometers (2 miles) north of Sligo Town in direction of Rosses Point. **Amenities and services** 132 units; restaurant, bar, spa, in-room safes, in-room tea and coffee facilities, Wi-Fi, irons, minibars, nonsmoking rooms, restaurant, room service. **Parking** Free, on property. **Price** Includes full Irish breakfast; special Internet rates available. **Credit cards** AE, MC, V.

SLEEK OUTLETS OF THIS CHAIN have opened in towns around Ireland, and in places such as Sligo, which have a dearth of inner-city hotels, they provide a high standard of comfort not readily available. This business-oriented hotel may not reflect the character of this colorful town and region, but service is friendly and professional and the clean lines, contemporary decor, and warm hues are soothing—as are all the standard hotel comforts and an added perk, views over Sligo Bay. Be sure to request a room with this view, and for extra space and comfort, upgrade yourself to a business-class room or a junior suite.

Temple House ★★★★½

QUALITY ★★★★	VALUE ★★★★	€105–€160

Ballymote, County Sligo (closed December–March); ☎ 071-918-3329; fax 071-918-3808; enquiry@templehouse.ie; www.templehouse.ie

Location Outside the village of Ballymote, about 20 kilometers (12 miles) south of Sligo Town, off N17. **Amenities and services** 5 rooms; bird-watching, boating, dinner available on request (€45), fishing, gardens, high tea for children, nonsmoking rooms, shooting, walking, Wi-Fi. **Elevator** No. **Parking** Free, on property. **Price** Includes full Irish breakfast. **Credit cards** AE, MC, V.

THE PERCEVAL FAMILY HAS LIVED in this grand Georgian mansion, one of Ireland's largest homes still in private hands, since 1665; the estate rolls across more than 400 hectares (1,000 acres), and Perceval predecessors at Temple House built the Knights Templar castle, now in ruin on the grounds. Today, Roderick and Helena Perceval oversee the guesthouse operation Roderick's parents undertook almost 40 years ago, and they have made many sensible changes, such as updating bathrooms and heating, while leaving all the wonderful qualities of Temple House intact. Guests make themselves at home in country-house surroundings that are delightfully lived-in—Temple House is a real home, not a polished hotel. The marble-floored hall features cases displaying stuffed game birds and fish landed on the estate; a grand staircase is lined with Perceval family portraits; a handsome sitting room, warmed by a fire in winter, opens to a terrace overlooking the lough; and Wellingtons wait by the door for those who want to wander through the wooded grounds or down to the dock for a row. Guest rooms—huge and filled with old family armoires, canopied beds, and writing desks—remain outfitted much as they were a century ago, with the exception of stylish new bathrooms with power showers. A wonderful breakfast and evening meals (the latter on request and featuring local produce) are served in a beautiful dining room. Children are most welcome at Temple House, and all guests enjoy the warm attention of Roderick and Helena, who are gracious and gifted hosts.

EXPLORING SLIGO TOWN AND ITS ENVIRONS

SLIGO'S CITY CENTER STRADDLES the **River Garavogue,** but most commerce transpires south of the river. The main shopping district is on and off **O'Connell Street,** a lively thoroughfare that climbs away from the river toward the ruins of Sligo Abbey (see lower right). At the foot of O'Connell Street, alongside Hyde Bridge, is the **Yeats Memorial Building,** home to the Yeats Society and the venue for the popular annual Yeats International Summer School. Despite the academic-sounding name, the "school" is actually a festival that celebrates the poet's work. Readings, musical performances, and other events round out the workshops and other scholarly undertakings. Yeats is remembered on the north side of the bridge with an impressionistic and beloved statue; just beyond, up Stephen Street, the **Sligo County Museum** (see page 361) houses a small selection of letters and other Yeats memorabilia.

Copious remnants of the neolithic peoples who inhabited the region some 7,500 years ago litter the hills that surround the center of Sligo. The most striking remains are those at **Carrowmore** (see below).

ATTRACTIONS IN SLIGO TOWN

Carrowmore ★★★★

APPEAL BY AGE	PRESCHOOL ★★	GRADE SCHOOL ★★★	TEENS ★★★
YOUNG ADULTS ★★★	OVER 30 ★★★★		SENIORS ★★★★

Southern edge of Sligo Town, marked off N4; ☎ 071-916-1534; www.heritageireland.ie

Type of attraction Megalithic cemetery. **Admission** €2.10 adults, €1.30 seniors, €1.10 children and students, €5.80 families of up to 2 adults and 2 children. **Hours** Mid-March–October, daily, 10 a.m.–6 p.m. **When to go** Try to visit in good weather, because you'll spend most of your time outdoors. **Special comments** Rising above Carrowmore is Knocknarea, a mountain that crowns a promontory in Sligo Bay. You can walk to the summit, a moderately difficult 45-minute climb, to enjoy the views. A huge stone mound, known as a cairn, is said to be the tomb of Maeve, the first-century-BC Celtic queen; more likely, archaeologists say, the stones cover another large passage tomb. **How much time to allow** At least 1 hour.

How Attractions Compare in the Northwest of Ireland

ATTRACTION	DESCRIPTION	AUTHOR'S RATING
SLIGO TOWN		
Carrowmore	**Megalithic cemetery**	★★★★
Lissadell House	**Historic home**	★★★½
Parke's Castle	**Historic home**	★★★½
Sligo County Museum	**Museum of local history**	★★★½
Sligo Abbey	**Medieval abbey and friary**	★★½
DONEGAL TOWN		
Old Abbey	**Monastic ruins**	★★★½
Donegal Castle	**Castle and fortified house**	★★½
NORTH DONEGAL		
Glebe House	**Historic home and art gallery**	★★★★
Glenveagh Castle	**Historic home**	★★★★

DESCRIPTION AND COMMENTS These passage tombs (burial chambers dug into the hillside, with entrances constructed of stone) span several prehistoric centuries. Most date from around 5,000 BC, making them even older than Stonehenge in England. One of the tombs, from about 5,500 BC, is believed to be the oldest piece of freestanding stone architecture in the world. Quarrying in the not-so-distant past destroyed many of the tombs, which once numbered in the hundreds, although the 40 or so that remain still comprise the largest collection of prehistoric tombs in the British Isles. Most importantly, standing on this windy hillside—one of the world's great ancient sites—and staring into the tombs so carefully constructed millennia ago is a haunting experience. Exhibits in a small stone cottage help illuminate the significance of Carrowmore.

TOURING TIPS Another prehistoric grave site, Carrowkeel, lies to the east of Carrowmore, high above the shores of Lough Arrow outside the town of Castlebaldwin. Carrowkeel is much more remote than Carrowmore, and much less visited and developed, so you may find yourself alone on the hillside exploring the 14 tombs. To reach Carrowkeel, follow the well-marked single-lane road up the hill from Castlebaldwin.

 Sligo Abbey   ★★½

APPEAL BY AGE	PRESCHOOL ★★	GRADE SCHOOL ★★	TEENS ★★
YOUNG ADULTS ★★	OVER 30 ★★½		SENIORS ★★½

Abbey Street, Sligo Town; ☎ 071-914-6406; www.heritageireland.ie

walks and drives in the northwest

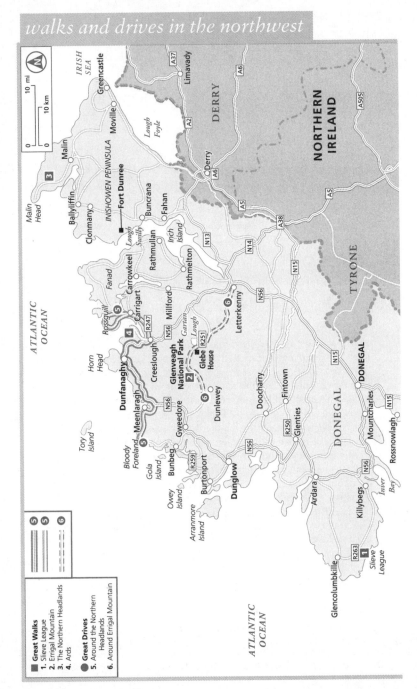

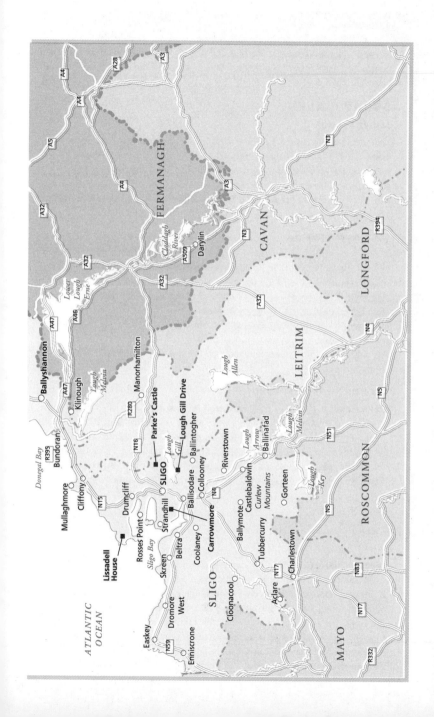

Walks and Drives in the Northwest

Rugged and often desolate, Northwest Ireland is graced with wild moors, rocky coasts, and stark mountains that are among some of the most beautiful landscapes in Ireland.

GREAT WALKS

SLIEVE LEAGUE

Hands-down, the most dramatic walk in Ireland is along these soaring sea cliffs (see page 371) about 50 kilometers (30 miles) west of **Donegal Town.** A short but unforgettable walk begins in the small village of **Bunglass** and follows the tops of the cliffs for three kilometers (two miles), traversing Eagle's Nest and other heights before reaching the **Slieve League** summit via **One Man's Pass,** an aptly named narrow ridge with dizzying drops on either side.

ERRIGAL MOUNTAIN

A scramble up this distinctively shaped mountain, 752 meters (2,476 feet) tall and the highest peak in Donegal, is one of Ireland's most scenic hikes. The most popular, and least demanding, ascent covers about eight kilometers (five miles) and begins at a well-marked turnoff on R251 three kilometers (two miles) east of the village of **Dunlewey.** Soon after you cross the grassy lower slopes of the peak, you will be rewarded with views across the surrounding mountains, moors, and glens and from the summit, extending all the way to the Inishowen Peninsula to the north and Slieve League to the south and east.

THE NORTHERN HEADLANDS

Malin Head, at the tip of the **Inishowen Peninsula,** is officially the northernmost tip of Ireland. A view-filled walk begins at **Malin Well Beach,** about 1 kilometer (0.5 miles) east of the town of Malin Head and follows cliff tops east along the peninsula to **Black Hill.** The round-trip trek is 12 kilometers (7.5 miles), but even a short walk affords wonderful views of the **Antrim Coast** in Northern Ireland (see page 413) and the **Kintyre Peninsula** in Scotland.

Type of attraction Medieval abbey and friary. **Admission** €2.10 adults, €1.30 seniors, €1.10 children and students, €5.80 families of up to 2 adults and 2 children. **Hours** Mid-March–October, daily, 10 a.m.–6 p.m.; November–mid-December, Saturday and Sunday, 9:30 a.m.–4:30 p.m. **When to go** Anytime; the ruins are especially evocative in the rain. **Special comments** If you are traveling north to Donegal and are pressed for time, you may want to give Sligo Abbey a quick glance and tour the more dramatic abbey ruins in Donegal Town. **How much time to allow** About half an hour.

ARDS

Ards Forest Park, about 30 kilometers (18 miles) northwest of **Ramelton** on Sheephaven Bay, encompasses more than 600 hectares (1,000 acres) of woodlands and beaches, as well as lakes, bogs, and even a few prehistoric stone circles. A network of trails follows the shores of **Lough Lilly** and the bay, crossing terrain that seems barely touched. An especially scenic walk (three kilometers or two miles round-trip) leads from the main parking area (where a sign shows trails within the park) to **Black Strand** on Clonmass Bay. Follow the dune-backed beach to a path that leads east through woodlands to **Binnagorm Point,** for stunning views of the bay and surrounding hills.

GREAT DRIVES

AROUND THE NORTHERN HEADLANDS

Northwest Ireland meets the sea in a string of mountainous peninsulas, most of which can be circumnavigated on scenery-filled drives.

Carrigart, some 14 kilometers (9 miles) north of Ramelton on R245, is the start of **Atlantic Drive** around the Rosguill Peninsula. You might want to linger a little while on **Rosapenna Beach,** just to the north of town, before following the signs onto the 15-kilometer (9-mile) circuit.

Atlantic Drive passes bays on one side and mountains on the other, coming to beaches at **Downings** and **Tranarossan Strand.** As you round the tip of the peninsula, you'll have spectacular views of the coast, with **Horn Head** to the west, **Fanad Head** to the east, and **Errigal Mountain** to the south.

At the southern end of the peninsula, pass through Carrigart again, and then continue 11 kilometers (7 miles) south on R245 to the town of **Creslough,** on Sheephaven Bay. Just outside of town, on a promontory at the southern end of the bay, is **Doe Castle,** not much more than a stone tower surrounded by thick walls. In the 15th century, the castle was the residence of MacSweeney Doe, a *gallowglass* (foreign mercenary) hired by the O'Donnell clan; the site is not attended but is usually open, and you can visit the stark, damp rooms daily, 10 a.m. to 5 p.m.; admission is free.

Continued on next page

DESCRIPTION AND COMMENTS Modern-day Sligo bustles just outside the walls, but the significant remains of a once-important religious community are a reminder of the role this medieval settlement played. Maurice Fitzgerald, a Norman baron and one of the founders of Sligo, brought the Dominicans to Ireland and built this elaborate complex for the friars. They taught, studied, and worshipped here, and the friary also served as a place for public worship. Among the remains is a wealth of elaborate stonework, including the framework for 13th-century lancet

Walks and Drives in the Northwest (continued)

GREAT DRIVES (CONTINUED)

AROUND THE NORTHERN HEADLANDS (CONTINUED)

Also near Creslough is **Ards Forest Park,** where the wonderfully varied landscapes include slat marshes, wooded valleys, and long, sandy beaches and are crisscrossed with excellent hiking trails (see previous page); ☎ 074-53271; open daily, 8 a.m. to dusk; free admission, parking fees.

From Creslough, follow N56 north 11 kilometers (7 miles) to **Dunfanaghy,** on the western shore of Sheephaven Bay. The tides here are extreme, so the town's **Killyhoey Beach** becomes a vast tidal flat at some times and is completely submerged at others. A small road to the north of town rounds **Horn Head,** which drops to the sea in steep cliffs where gulls, puffins, and other seabirds roost.

Once back in Dunfanaghy, you can retrace your steps east to Carrigart or continue west into more-rugged scenery. If you opt for the latter, follow N56 west for 11 kilometers (7 miles) through stony, barren terrain to **Falcarragh,** then another 13 kilometers (8 miles) to **Meenlaragh.** Weather permitting— and it's often not—boats sail from this scrappy little village to desolate, treeless **Tory Island,** inhabited by a few hearty fishermen.

The mainland is not much more hospitable, and as you head west on R257 you won't see much but stone-studded moors and stark mountains. This is the **Gweedore Headland,** where Irish is the first language in the tiny villages and lonely farms. The singer Enya comes from Gweedore, and it's easy to see a connection between the barren landscapes and her soulful music. The western edge of the headland, about 30 kilometers (18 miles) south of Meenlaragh, is **Bloody Foreland,** named for the color of the rocky seaside cliffs as they catch the rays of the setting sun.

AROUND ERRIGAL MOUNTAIN

A short drive west from **Letterkenny** brings you into some of Ireland's wildest and most spectacular mountain scenery. Here, the slopes of the **Derryveagh**

windows, one of the few sculpted altars to remain from a medieval Irish church, an elaborate rood screen, and lovely cloisters. Tombstones gloomily litter the ruins, as the abbey was destroyed during the British sacking of Sligo in 1642 and became the town burial ground. Among the tombs are medieval markers above the graves of princes and princesses of Sligo, and their presence here amid the rest of the ruins is a comment on the fleeting nature of earthly might.

TOURING TIPS You can learn more about Sligo's long history at the Sligo County Museum (see right).

Mountains are covered with moors, bogs, stands of birch, and carpets of ferns.

From Letterkenny, follow R250 and R251 for 16 kilometers (11 miles) to **Gratan Lough,** a large lake surrounded by forested slopes. The lakeside village of Church Hill is said to have been the birthplace of St. Colomba in the sixth century. **Glebe House,** on the northwest shores of the lake, is an oasis of civilization—the 19th-cenutry manor is filled with a fine collection of 19th- and 20th-century art and surrounded by beautiful gardens (see page 375).

Gratan Lough is at the edge of **Glenveagh National Park.** These 10,000 hectares (24,000 acres) of moors, mountains, and lakes compose what may just be the most beautiful and wild scenery in Ireland, and the park is an enchanting place to spend as much time as you can manage. Within the park the summits of the Derryveagh Mountains rise; the lush valleys of the River Owenbeagh are filled with stands of oak; and Lough Veagh cuts a shimmering blue swath through the northeast corner. The **Derrylahan Nature Trail** is one of many paths that traverse the wilderness. You can get information on walks and other activities in the park at the visitors center, just outside Church Hill; open mid-April through October, daily, 10 a.m. to 6 p.m.; ☎ 074-913-7090. Not all of the charm of Glenveagh is natural: **Glenveagh Castle** (see page 376) is a lavish home reflecting 20th-century tastes and comforts, surrounded by well-tended gardens.

For close-up views of **Errigal Mountain** or a trek to its 752-meter (2,476-foot) summit (see above), follow R251 around the northern fringes of the park to the little village of **Dunlewey,** beautifully perched between the shores of Dunlewey Lough and the flanks of the mountain. A trail to the summit begins from a roadside trailhead three kilometers (two miles) east of the village on R251. The **Lakeside Centre** in Dunlewey, occupying a 19th-century weaver's home, aptly features demonstrations of old weaving techniques and also provides short boat trips on the waters of Dunlewey Lough; ☎ 075-31699; open April through May, Saturday and Sunday, noon to 6 p.m., and June through September, daily, noon to 6 p.m.; admission is €5.

Sligo County Museum   ★ ★ ★ ½

APPEAL BY AGE	PRESCHOOL ★★	GRADE SCHOOL ★★		TEENS ★★
YOUNG ADULTS ★★		OVER 30 ★★★½	SENIORS ★★★½	

Stephen Street, Sligo Town; ☎ 071-42212

Type of attraction Museum of local history. **Admission** Free. **Hours** June–September, Tuesday–Saturday, 10 a.m.–noon and 2–4:50 p.m.; October–mid-December and mid-March–May, Tuesday–Saturday, 2–4 p.m. **When to go** Anytime. **Special comments** For fans of William Butler Yeats, the manuscripts and other memorabilia are fascinating; all visitors will be entranced by the paintings of Jack Yeats. **How much time to allow** At least 1 hour.

DESCRIPTION AND COMMENTS This small museum houses two collections. One shows earnest-but-humdrum exhibits of artifacts that pertain to local history but comes to life with regard to the works of William Butler Yeats, who is lovingly remembered with first editions, letters, and other memorabilia—a gold mine for Yeats fans. The adjoining Niland Gallery is devoted to the works of the poet's brother, Jack Yeats, who was one of the most important painters of 20th-century Ireland and whose colorful canvases evoke many local scenes. Portraits by John Yeats, the father of William and Jack, are also on view. The family had its roots in Sligo, and this is the largest collection of paintings by Jack and John outside of the National Gallery in Dublin.

TOURING TIPS If you are continuing north, you will encounter more works by Jack Yeats at the art gallery of Glebe House near Letterkenny (see page 375).

> *unofficial* **TIP**
> For a picnic, step into aromatic **Cosgrove and Son** (32 Market Street; ☎ 071-42809), which offers a tempting array of Irish cheeses and soda breads, or **Kate's Kitchen/Hopper & Pettit** (24 Market Street; ☎ 071-43022), which sells a wide assortment of deli selections.

RESTAURANTS IN AND AROUND SLIGO TOWN

Bistro Bianconi ★★★

ITALIAN	MODERATE	QUALITY ★★★★	VALUE ★★★

O'Connell Street, Sligo; ☎ 071-914-7000

Reservations Not necessary. **Entree range** €13–€28. **Payment** AE, MC, V. **Bar** Full service. **Disabled access** Yes. **Hours** Daily, 12:30–2:30 p.m., 5:30–midnight.

MENU RECOMMENDATIONS Pizza.

COMMENTS Some of the best pizza in Ireland comes out of the wood-fired ovens here, and carryout is available for those wishing to indulge in summertime pizza on the beach. A full menu of Italian specialties, as well as some delicious appetizers (including a baguette decadently topped with many different cheeses) and hefty salads, is served in a handsome room of white tile and light-colored wood.

Montmartre ★★★★½

FRENCH	MODERATE	QUALITY ★★★★	VALUE ★★★★½

Market Yard, Sligo; ☎ 071-916-9901

Reservations Recommended. **Entree range** €14–€23; early dinner, €15; prix-fixe dinner, €35. **Payment** AE, DC, MC, V. **Bar** Full service. **Disabled access** Yes. **Hours** Tuesday–Sunday, 5–11 p.m.

MENU RECOMMENDATIONS Fish soup, roast rabbit.

COMMENTS Chef Stéphane Magaud does credit to the airy and charming bistrolike surroundings in an old building at the top of the city center.

How Restaurants Compare in the Northwest of Ireland

NAME	CUISINE	OVERALL	QUALITY	VALUE	PRICE
SLIGO TOWN					
Montmartre	French	★★★★½	★★★★	★★★★½	Mod
Bistro Bianconi	Italian	★★★	★★★★	★★★	Mod
DONEGAL TOWN					
The Weaver's Loft	Irish	★★★	★★★½	★★★★	Inexp
KILLYBEGS					
Kitty Kelly's	Seafood/Irish	★★★★	★★★★	★★★★	Mod
NORTH DONEGAL					
Weeping Elm	Modern Irish	★★★★½	★★★★½	★★★½	Exp
Green Room	Continental	★★★★	★★★★	★★★★	Exp
Bridge Café	Seafood	★★★½	★★★	★★★★	Mod

Excellent preparations of French classics are made modern with many imaginative twists. Service has a twist, too, as the French waitstaff are as friendly and accommodating as their Irish counterparts. The wine list is exceptional, with many exciting choices available by the glass and half bottle.

Osta Café and Wine Bar   ★★★★½

MODERN IRISH	MODERATE	QUALITY ★★★★	VALUE ★★★★½

Garavogue Weir View, off Stephen Street, Sligo; ☎ 071-914-4639

Reservations Not necessary. **Entree range** €5–€10. **Payment** No credit cards. **Bar** Wine. **Disabled access** Yes. **Hours** Monday–Wednesday, 9 a.m.–8:30 p.m.; Thursday–Saturday, 9 a.m.–9:30 p.m.

MENU RECOMMENDATIONS Soups, sandwiches on homemade brown bread.
COMMENTS This pleasant room overlooking the river is an exciting presence in downtown Sligo, a sign of the town's renaissance. A meal can be quick and simple, but from the selection of Irish cheeses, homemade baked goods, and the freshest salads, it is clear that the emphasis is on the highest-quality ingredients.

ENTERTAINMENT AND NIGHTLIFE IN SLIGO TOWN

SLIGO'S MOST ATMOSPHERIC PUB is **Hargadon Brothers** (4 O'Connell Street; ☎ 071-917-0933), a dark and welcoming place of paneled walls, stone floors, cozy little alcoves, and crackling fires.

Shoot the Crows (Castle Street; ☎ 071-916-2554) is the best place in town to hear traditional music. **Hawk's Well Theatre** (Johnston Court; ☎ 071-916-1526) is Northwest Ireland's leading theater, hosting top companies from throughout the country, while the **Blue Raincoat Theatre** is Sligo's resident theater company and often presents plays by Yeats and other local artists in its theater on Lower Quay Street (☎ 071-917-0431).

EXERCISE AND RECREATION IN AND AROUND SLIGO TOWN

EXCELLENT BEACHES RING THE SHORES of Sligo Bay (beware, though: the water is cold), the most popular being those at **Rosses Point** and **Strandhill.** If you tire of the beach and fancy a round of golf, head inland to the **Strandhill Golf Club** (Strandhill; ☎ 071-916-8188; **www.strandhillgc.com**) or the **County Sligo Golf Club** (Rosses Point, ☎ 071-917-7134; **www.countysligogolfclub.ie**).

Around **SLIGO TOWN**

ENGAGING SCENERY surrounds Sligo Town, from rugged maritime landscapes to green glens and mist-shrouded mountains littered with prehistoric remains.

 LOUGH GILL

THIS SERENE BODY OF WATER (the name aptly means "Lake Beauty"), shimmering beneath green hills, is endowed with a great deal of romance. The lake lies at the center of what the tourist industry has termed "Yeats Country," referring to the prominence of this region in the poetry of William Butler Yeats. Although the poet and playwright was born in Dublin and raised in London, he held these landscapes close to his heart and wrote of them often. Another romantic notion associated with the lake is the legend of the bell of Sligo Abbey. The story goes that when Sir Frederick Hamilton sacked Sligo in 1642 and demolished the abbey, his soldiers sank the silver bell in the lake. Unlikely as the tale is (the plunder would no doubt have been carted off), it's said still today that the pure of heart and deed can hear the bell tolling.

An extremely popular route, and a must-do for Yeats fans, is the **Lough Gill Drive.** This well-marked circuit follows R287, R288, and R286 around the lake, affording wonderful views. From the south end of the route, a lane leads to a landing stage where a boatman may or may not be waiting to ferry visitors to the **Isle of Innisfree.** For Yeats fans, the island may recall such lines as "I hear lake water lapping with low sounds by the shore." Others may experience slight disappointment upon seeing the nondescript little islet. Even so, this island, the subject of Yeats's "The Lake Isle of Innisfree," summoned for the poet all the nostalgia he felt for Sligo. On the lake's eastern shore stands formidable **Parke's Castle** (see below). The suburbs of Sligo appear a bit farther along R286 and dispel the romantic aura of Lough Gill.

Attraction along Lough Gill

Parke's Castle ★ ★ ★ ½

APPEAL BY AGE	PRESCHOOL ★★★	GRADE SCHOOL ★★★★	TEENS ★★★
YOUNG ADULTS ★★★★		OVER 30 ★★★½	SENIORS ★★★½

Eastern shore of Lough Gill, ☎ 071-916-4149

Type of attraction Historic home. **Admission** €2.75 adults, €2 seniors, €1.25 children and students, €7 families. **Hours** April–May, Tuesday–Sunday, 10 a.m.–5 p.m.; June–September, daily, 9:30 a.m.–6:30 p.m.; October, daily, 10 a.m.–5 p.m. **When to go** Anytime. **Special comments** From the castle, you can make an easy walk to the remains of Creevelea Abbey, founded by the Franciscans in 1508; the remains include a charming cloister and carvings depicting the life of St. Francis of Assisi. **How much time to allow** 1 hour, 2 hours to also explore the lakeshore and nearby Creevelea Abbey.

DESCRIPTION AND COMMENTS The O'Rourkes, a clan of local rulers, built a fortress on the shores of Lough Gill in the Middle Ages, but the present structure dates from the 17th century. That's when Captain Robert Parke, a British planter, arrived, confiscated the surrounding lands from Irish Catholics, and used materials from the original structure to build a fortified castle that would offer him protection from the hostile populace. Despite this tumultuous history and the injustices of the Plantation system, by which King James I of England meant to supplant the native Irish and subject them to British rule, you can't help but notice that Parke's Castle is a beautiful place—a tall, handsome house of light stone and sturdy timbers. Beyond the enclosed courtyard is a massive great hall and several other drafty rooms that overlook the lake through tall windows.

TOURING TIPS In good weather, board one of the boats that depart from the dock below the castle for a tour of Lough Gill.

ROSSES POINT AND DRUMCLIFF

A DRAMATIC HEADLAND at the entrance to Sligo Harbour, **Rosses Point,** about eight kilometers (five miles) northwest of Sligo, is ringed with long, golden beaches that are especially attractive in the low light of the sun setting over the Atlantic Ocean. William Butler Yeats and his brother, painter Jack Yeats, spent their boyhood summers at Rosses Point. The former Yeats and his wife, Georgina, are buried nearby in the churchyard at **Drumcliff.** The poet's simple tombstone is engraved with words he penned himself: "Cast a cold eye / On life, on death. / Horseman, pass by!" Behind the graves rises the dramatic, flat-topped summit of **Ben Bulben.** From Sligo, R291 leads out to Rosses Point, and N4 leads seven kilometers (four miles) north from Sligo to Drumcliff.

Attraction around Drumcliff
Lissadell House ★★★½

APPEAL BY AGE	PRESCHOOL ★★	GRADE SCHOOL ★★	TEENS ★★
YOUNG ADULTS ★★	OVER 30 ★★★½		SENIORS ★★★½

**On Drumcliff Bay, 3 kilometers (2 miles) west of Drumcliff on N15;
☎ 071-916-3150; www.lissadellhouse.com**

Type of attraction Historic home. **Admission** *House, gardens, and special exhibitions:*
€12 adults, €6 children. **Hours** Daily, 10:30 a.m.–6 p.m. **When to go** Try to find a
patch of good weather so you can enjoy the grounds. **Special comments** Tours
are unusually enlightening; they provide fascinating details of the house's history
and its past inhabitants, as well as ongoing restoration efforts such as refurbishing
the original wall coverings and gas fixtures. **How much time to allow** 1 hour for
the house, an additional half-day to tour the gardens and grounds.

DESCRIPTION AND COMMENTS This neoclassical Georgian mansion of local
limestone is not only lovely, but it also has witnessed some remarkably
colorful history. For most of its history, the house has been home to the
Gore-Booth family, the most famous member of which is best known
as the Countess Markievicz (the title that Constance Gore-Booth
acquired when she married a Polish count). Constance was a prominent
figure in the 1916 Easter Rising, for which she was imprisoned and
sentenced to death (the sentence was reversed), and she became the
first female member of the British House of Commons and the Dáil
Éireann, or Irish Parliament. The count's family portraits grace pilasters
in the dining room. Constance's forebear Sir Robert Gore-Booth distinguished himself as an enlightened landlord when he mortgaged
Lissadell House to raise funds to save his tenants from starvation during
the Famine; Constance's brother, Josslyn, carried on this tradition, selling more than 28,000 acres to his tenants at affordable rates and
instituting vast agrarian reforms. William Butler Yeats, a frequent visitor to the house, became close friends with Constance and her sister,
Eva; he wrote, "The light of evening, Lissadell, / Great windows open
to the south, / Two girls in silk kimonos." Edwin Walsh and his wife,
Constance Cassidy, have recently purchased Lissadell House, where
they are raising their seven children. Several rooms as well as the gardens are open to the public on guided tours.

TOURING TIPS The woods surrounding Lissadell House are home to the largest colony of barnacle geese in Ireland, as well as many other wildfowl
and birds.

DONEGAL TOWN

DONEGAL TOWN IS A FRIENDLY PLACE, nestled into a valley of the
River Eske near its mouth in Donegal Bay. Even the proud 15th-century
castle that dominates the town center is a benign presence these days,
and a convivial atmosphere prevails in the Diamond, the triangular

marketplace upon which major streets converge. The name Donegal derives from *Dún na nGall*, or "Fort of the Foreigners"—a reference to the Vikings, who sailed in and out of Donegal Bay and in the ninth century set up a garrison here as a handy base for raiding and pillaging the north. The O'Donnell clan drove out the Vikings and built the fortified house that has become **Donegal Castle** (see next page), and soon a colony of scholarly monks flourished at Donegal's now-ruined abbey. A monument in the Diamond commemorates the Franciscan friars who painstakingly preserved the history of Gaelic Ireland in their *Annals of the Four Masters,* which traces the history of Ireland up to 1618. It is easy to understand why the monks found it necessary to preserve Gaelic culture: the British took over the town in the 17th century, drove out Catholic landholders, and gave their properties to Protestant colonists from England.

ARRIVING AND GETTING ORIENTED IN DONEGAL TOWN

DONEGAL IS ABOUT 66 KILOMETERS (40 miles) northeast of Sligo Town; the direct route by car is on N4 and N15. At least six **Bus Éireann** buses travel between Donegal and Sligo daily; the trip takes about 1 hour and costs €3.50. Buses stop on the Diamond, the Donegal marketplace. For information about the town and surrounding region, step into the **Donegal Tourist Office** on Quay Street; ☎ 074-972-1148, **www.donegaltown.ie;** Easter through September, Monday through Friday, 9 a.m. to 5 p.m.; Saturday, 10 a.m. to 6 p.m.; Sunday, noon to 4 p.m.; October through Easter, Monday through Friday, 9 a.m. to 5 p.m.

EXPLORING DONEGAL TOWN

YOU'LL FIND IT A PLEASURE to spend an hour or two walking through Donegal, strolling on and off the Diamond, visiting the town's two sights of note (see profiles following), and eyeing the many woolen goods that fill the shop windows.

HOTELS IN DONEGAL TOWN

Ard Na Breatha ★★★★

QUALITY ★★★★	VALUE ★★★★	FROM €55

Drumrooske, Donegal, County Donegal; ☎ **074-972-2288**

Location In Donegal Bay. **Amenities and services** 6 units; lounge, garden, hair dryers. **Elevator** No. **Parking** On property, free. **Price** Includes full Irish breakfast. **Credit cards** AE, MC, V.

DESCRIPTION AND COMMENTS A welcoming little guesthouse on the edge of town introduces you to the best of Donegal-style hospitality, with a warm and friendly atmosphere, the attentions of owners Theresa and Albert Morrow, and pleasantly furnished rooms. A lounge with an open fire and a garden are perfect places to relax, and breakfast is delicious. The Morrows also offer dinner on occasion; the meal is one of the best around and is served with style.

St. Ernan's House ★★★★

QUALITY ★★★★	VALUE ★★★	FROM €240

Donegal, County Donegal; ☎ 074-972-1065; fax 074-972-2098; www.sainternans.com

Location In Donegal Bay. **Amenities and services** 12 units; boating, dining room, garden, lounges, swimming. **Elevator** No. **Parking** On property, free. **Price** Includes full Irish breakfast. **Credit cards** AE, MC, V.

DESCRIPTION AND COMMENTS This remarkable retreat occupies its own island in Donegal Bay, providing magnificent water views along with a great deal of luxury and a real sense of escape from the world. Guests make themselves at home in a series of handsome, fire-warmed lounges and retreat upstairs to rooms that vary considerably in size but attain the same level of taste and comfort. Donegal Town is only 2 kilometers (1.25 miles) away from the end of the causeway that connects the island to the mainland, but it would be easy to hole up here for a couple of days—especially since superb prix-fixe dinners (from €55) are served in a dining room as tasteful as the rest of the house.

ATTRACTIONS IN DONEGAL TOWN

 Donegal Castle ★★½

APPEAL BY AGE	PRESCHOOL ★★	GRADE SCHOOL ★★	TEENS ★★
YOUNG ADULTS ★★	OVER 30 ★★½		SENIORS ★★½

Castle Street, Donegal Town; ☎ 074-972-2405, www.heritageireland.ie

Type of attraction Castle and fortified house. **Admission** €3.70 adults, €2.60 seniors, €1.30 children and students, €8.70 families. **Hours** Mid-March–October, daily, 10 a.m.–5:15 p.m.; November–mid-March, Thursday–Monday, 9:30 a.m.–4:30 p.m. **When to go** Anytime. **Special comments** After visiting the castle, take a good look at the Diamond, the marketplace that Sir Basil Brooke also designed as part of his efforts to make Donegal a model British Plantation Town. **How much time to allow** About 45 minutes for castle and grounds.

DESCRIPTION AND COMMENTS Standing mightily in the center of town, Donegal Castle is partly in ruin, but it incorporates the splendid and beautifully restored 15th-century fortified house that was once the residence of the O'Donnells, a ruling clan who were ousted by the British in 1607. The O'Donnells did not leave without a fight—Hugh Roe O'Donnell managed to fend off at least one onslaught of British troops and died not in battle but of fever in Spain, where he had gone to muster a force to fight a British invasion. When Englishman Sir Basil Brooke finally took possession in 1610, he added the turrets and gables that lend the castle its distinctive appearance. You can wander the pleasant grounds, enclosed behind high walls, and visit the Great Hall and a few other rooms on informative (and blessedly short) 25-minute guided tours. All in all, though, as far as Irish castles go, this one is fairly dull.

TOURING TIPS From the castle, walk across the Diamond, the center of Donegal, and from there follow Quay Street south to the Old Abbey. This route will give you a nice sense of the town.

Old Abbey ★ ★ ★ ½

APPEAL BY AGE	PRESCHOOL ★★★	GRADE SCHOOL ★★★	TEENS ★★★
YOUNG ADULTS ★★★	OVER 30 ★★★½		SENIORS ★★★½

The Quay, Donegal Town

Type of attraction Monastic ruins. **Admission** Free. **Hours** Always accessible. **When to go** In good weather, if possible. **Special comments** If you're traveling on to Dublin, be sure to seek out the facsimile of *Annals of the Four Masters,* compiled here and on view at the National Library. **How much time to allow** 45 minutes.

DESCRIPTION AND COMMENTS The O'Donnells, the ruling clan of this region, established a monastery for the Franciscan Order in 1474, at about the same time that they constructed their castle. The two centuries that followed were unusually tumultuous for what had been intended to be a quiet religious community on the banks of the River Eske. The abbey was important enough to attract a gathering of clergy, scholars, and political leaders in 1539, but it soon was torn asunder by the fierce fighting that ensued as the British stepped up their attempts to dominate this part of Ireland. Attacks in 1593, 1601, and 1607 all but destroyed the complex, though the friars remained. From 1632 to 1636, four resident scholars endeavored to preserve the Celtic culture in *Annals of the Four Masters,* a compilation of old Gaelic manuscripts that trace Irish history and mythology from the earliest times; a facsimile of this precious work is on view at the National Library in Dublin. What remains today are the choir and other portions of the church, as well as two walls of the cloisters, all romantically perched above the river near its mouth at Donegal Bay.

TOURING TIPS The abbey ruins are particularly impressive from the water; look for them as you enter Donegal Bay on a Waterbus tour (see Unofficial Tip, page 367).

RESTAURANT IN DONEGAL TOWN

The Weaver's Loft ★★★

IRISH	INEXPENSIVE	QUALITY ★★★½	VALUE ★★★★

Above Magee's, the Diamond; ☎ 074-972-2660

Reservations Not necessary. **Entree range** €6–€10. **Payment** AE, MC, V. **Bar** Beer and wine only. **Disabled access** No. **Hours** Monday–Saturday, 10 a.m.–5 p.m.

MENU RECOMMENDATIONS Fresh seafood from Donegal Bay.

COMMENTS This pleasant cafeteria above Magee's, Donegal's famous woolen-goods shop, is a handy place for a meal before or after sightseeing and shopping. Hot meals change daily but often include Irish stew and fish chowder, both made with care. Hefty salads, sandwiches, and pastries are always available.

SHOPPING IN DONEGAL TOWN

ANYONE LOOKING FOR HANDWOVEN Donegal tweeds need look no farther than **Magee of Donegal** (☎ 071-972-1526), famous throughout the land for its handsome jackets and coats, as well as a fine array of woolen goods and fabrics. Magee's, in fact, is one of Donegal's main attractions, and it commands pride of place on the Diamond. The **Donegal Craft Village,** about two kilometers (one mile) south of town on Ballyshannon Road, brings together weavers, jewelers, and other local craftspeople to sell their wares; while here, step into the **Aroma Café** (☎ 074-972-3222) for a cup of delicious soup or a salad.

Around DONEGAL TOWN

KILLYBEGS

BUSY AND FAR MORE BUILT-UP than other places on this relatively remote stretch of North Donegal coast, Killybegs is made picturesque by its harbor full of vessels from around the world. The town is one of the major fishing ports in Ireland, and huge trawlers from as far afield as Eastern Europe unload their catches at sundown, when the town is especially lively. Killybegs is 28 kilometers (17 miles) west of Donegal Town on R293.

Restaurant in Killybegs

Kitty Kelly's ★★★★

SEAFOOD/IRISH	MODERATE	QUALITY ★★★★	VALUE ★★★★

Largy, Killybegs; ☎ 074-973-1925

Reservations Recommended. **Entree range** €8–€10. **Payment** MC, V. **Bar** Full bar. **Disabled access** Yes. **Hours** Daily, 7–9:30 p.m.

MENU RECOMMENDATIONS Fresh fish and seafood.

COMMENTS This pink-toned cottage on the coast road five kilometers (three miles) west of Killybegs is hard to miss, and not just because of its distinctive paint job—it seems that most of Killybegs heads here for dinner. The cozy, old-fashioned interior can be a Tower of Babel as crews from the many foreign ships that dock in town settle in for a meal of mussels from Bruckless and other delicious homemade fare.

♩ SLIEVE LEAGUE

PERHAPS THE MOST DRAMATIC VIEW in all of Ireland—and that is saying quite a lot—is the prospect of these multihued ocean cliffs rising some 600 meters (2,000 feet) out of the raging surf. The tallest sea cliffs in Europe, they are much more thrilling to behold than even the Cliffs of Moher (see page 305) near Galway. The remote location is no small part of the appeal, and you may find yourself alone standing on a precipitous ledge regarding the spectacle of the majestic cliff face, framed by sea and mountains.

From the village of Carrick, follow the signs to Bunglas and Slieve League. At the tiny village of Teelin, signs will direct you to the road that precipitously climbs the slopes of Slieve League, passing stunning (if hair-raising) views of the sea far below and the cliffs ahead. After about three kilometers (two miles), the road comes to a ledge that affords dead-on views of jagged cliffs. From here you can walk to the summit on **One Man's Pass,** not recommended for those who suffer from vertigo or for anyone when the path is slippery. The apt name derives from the fact that at one point the path is wide enough for only one walker to pass through the sheer drop-offs on both sides of the narrow track.

NORTH DONEGAL

THE MOST NORTHERLY REACHES of Ireland meet the sea in a series of rugged headlands. The interior is a rugged landscape of mountains, lakes, and forests, where many of the villages of whitewashed cottages are *Gaeltacht,* or Irish speaking.

The major town in the far north is **Letterkenny,** which is said to be the fastest-growing place in Ireland. Unfortunately, it may soon also be the least attractive: town planners are taking their cues from the worst sort of development, and Letterkenny these days is an unappealing collection of parking lots, shopping malls, and megastores. Don't linger here—**Ramelton** and **Rathmullan,** a bit farther north on the shores of Lough Swilly, are much more pleasant places to spend your time and to use as a base.

ARRIVING AND GETTING ORIENTED IN NORTH DONEGAL

LETTERKENNY, ABOUT 115 KILOMETERS (70 miles) northeast of Sligo Town, is the main hub of the North Donegal region. If you are traveling by car, follow N15 from Sligo through Donegal Town and north to Stranoriar, where the road continues north as N56. **Bus Éireann** buses travel between Letterkenny and Dublin four times a day; the trip takes about four hours and costs €10. The bus station is at the end of a shopping-center parking lot at the north end of town. Keep in mind, though, that the only easy way to explore the often lonely countryside is by car. Letterkenny is also the place to stock up on information. The **Tourist Information Office** occupies a flashy new building rather inconveniently located outside the town center, on a roundabout on the Derry Road; ☎ 074-21160; **www.discoverireland .ie/northwest.aspx.** The office is open September through May, Monday through Friday, 9 a.m. to 5 p.m.; June, Monday through Saturday, 9 a.m. to 6 p.m.; and July through August, Monday through Saturday, 9 a.m. to 8 p.m., and Sunday, 10 a.m. to 2 p.m.

HOTELS IN NORTH DONEGAL
Castle Grove Country House Hotel ★ ★ ★ ★

QUALITY ★★★½	VALUE ★★★	€80–€160

Letterkenny, County Donegal; ☎ 074-915118; fax 074-915118; reservation@castlegrove.com; www.castlegrove.com

Location Off R245, about 3 kilometers (2 miles) north of Letterkenny. **Amenities and services** 14 rooms; bar, boats, disabled access, laundry service, hair dryers, nonsmoking rooms, restaurant, walking. **Elevator** No. **Parking** Free, on property. **Price** Includes full Irish breakfast. **Credit cards** AE, MC, V.

THOUGH THE SPRAWL OF LETTERKENNY encroaches, this delightful estate remains intact, tucked away on the shores of Lough Swilly on grounds laid out by the great British landscape designer Capability Brown in the 18th century. Sheep graze beneath magnificent old oaks as the sea glimmers in the distance, and the house merges old-world elegance with thoughtful attention to comfort and amenities. Guest rooms are located upstairs and in an adjoining carriage house; all are large and furnished with comfy old pieces (including the occasional four-poster bed), and come with some nice touches—some rooms on the ground floor open to the beautifully maintained gardens, and those at the front of the house have wonderful views of the grounds and sea. The hotel's restaurant, the Green Room, offers the best dining in the region (see page 377).

Frewin ★ ★ ★ ★ ½

QUALITY ★★★★	VALUE ★★★★	€75–€130

Ramelton, County Donegal; ☎ 074-915-1246; fax 074-915-1246; flaxmill@indigo.ie; www.frewinhouse.com

Location Outside Ramelton, 11 kilometers (7 miles) north of Letterkenny off R245. **Amenities and services** 4 units plus a housekeeping cottage; garden, lounges, nonsmoking rooms. **Elevator** No. **Parking** Free, on property. **Price** Includes full Irish breakfast. **Credit cards** MC, V.

THOMAS AND REGINA COYLE restored a Victorian rectory and filled it with their collection of antiques, memorabilia, books, Persian carpets, and old prints—all handsomely displayed in the warm, uncluttered lounges and private rooms of this wonderful guesthouse. The Coyles' fine taste and the good bones of the old house are a winning combination, and guests soon feel at home in an airy sitting room as well as a small library where a fire burns in colder months. A shady garden on a bluff above the River Swilly is a perfect summer retreat. Guest accommodations have sitting areas with snug armchairs and cushy couches, and firm beds in the sleeping alcoves are dressed in fine linens. Rich cream-colored tones and soft lighting are notably relaxing, and three of these suitelike rooms have large soaking tubs in their well-equipped bathrooms. Regina's full Irish breakfast is accompanied by home-baked breads and delicious preserves; dinners can be arranged for €40. A beautifully restored cottage on the grounds is available for about €500 per week.

Rathmullan House ★★★★

QUALITY ★★★★	VALUE ★★★	€130–€260

Rathmullan, County Donegal; ☎ 074-915-8188; fax 074-915-8200; info@rathmullanhouse.com; www.rathmullanhouse.com

Location On Lough Swilly at the village's edge. **Amenities and services** 30 units; bar, beach, disabled access, gardens, nonsmoking rooms, restaurant, swimming pool, tennis court. **Elevator** Yes. **Parking** Free, on property. **Price Includes** full Irish breakfast; good-value special offers available at Web site. **Credit cards** AE, MC, V.

THIS FINE 19TH-CENTURY MANSION, built for a Belfast banker, faces a two-mile-long beach that's perfect for long strolls. The Wheeler family has owned and operated Rathmullan House for four decades, and they supply their guests, many of whom return year after year, with a great deal of easygoing comfort. The hotel is quietly luxurious but relaxed, and social life centers on the inviting drawing room, library, lounge and bar, and restaurant, as well as an indoor swimming pool and leisure center. Accommodations vary considerably in size and price, but all are comfortable and full of character. Unlike many owners of vintage hotels who have tacked on characterless modern extensions, the Wheelers have expanded with great taste, adding a wing of enormous, bright, and appealing rooms that open directly to the gardens. Glamorous bathrooms are equipped with deep soaking tubs and freestanding showers. The old-fashioned bedrooms at the front of the house, which face the sea with huge bay windows, have all the modern amenities, including updated bathrooms. Four family-friendly rooms tucked under the eaves can accommodate up to six.

EXPLORING NORTH DONEGAL

AN ATTRACTIVE SETTLEMENT on the River Lennon, about 12 kilometers (7.5 miles) north of Letterkenny on R245, **Ramelton** is a so-called Plantation Town, settled by British Protestant colonists brought to Ireland to displace Catholic landowners and to establish a British presence. Many of the fine houses date from the early 17th century, and near the town center is the oldest Presbyterian church in Ireland. Francis Makemie (1658–1708) emigrated from Ramelton to the United States, where he founded the American Presbyterian church.

Rathmullan, today a pleasant beach town 11 kilometers (7 miles) north of Ramelton on R247, was the scene of the Flight of the Earls in 1607, when the last of the noble Irish chieftains fled by ship, ensuring British dominance of Ireland. This momentous event is very well chronicled in the **Flight of the Earls Heritage Centre,** which overlooks the harbor (☎ 074-915-8131; **www.flightoftheearls.com**); open June through September, Monday through Saturday, 10 a.m. to 6 p.m., and Sunday, 12:30 p.m. to 6 p.m.

A drive north of Rathmullan on R247 and R246 takes you out to **Fanad Head,** one of the many dramatic headlands that jut into the Atlantic from the northernmost reaches of Ireland. On these peninsulas, spines of rugged mountains drop down to the rocky coast and often violent surf. An excellent place to explore these coastal landscapes is **Ards Forest Park,** situated about 30 kilometers (18 miles) northwest of Ramelton via a circuitous route through valleys and over mountain passes (a more direct route takes you north from Letterkenny on N56). Crisscrossed with hiking paths, the park encompasses more than 600 hectares (1,000 acres) of woodlands and beaches, as well as lakes, bogs, and even a few prehistoric stone circles.

The largest of the northern peninsulas is **Inishowen,** the tip of which, **Malin Head,** is officially the northernmost tip of Ireland and affords stunning views of the sea. Views are also spectacular from the **Gap of Mamore,** a mountain pass on the western coast that climbs to 250 meters (820 feet) and is crowned with a strategically placed viewpoint. Some of the peninsula's attractions are man-made rather than natural. **Grianan Ailigh,** at the southwestern tip of the base of the peninsula 30 kilometers (18 miles) northeast of Letterkenny on N13, is a 3,500-year-old ring fort that until the 12th century served as the fortress of the region's ruling clan, the O'Neill chieftains. Unfortunately, the aura of the historic place was diminished severely by an aggressive 19th-century restoration. Another fort, about 20 kilometers (12 miles) up the western edge of the peninsula at **Dunree Head,** was built in 1798 to repel a possible invasion

unofficial **TIP**
You can circumnavigate the **Inishowen Peninsula** on a well-marked 160-kilometer (100-mile) driving route, but to see the peninsula in its entirety requires a lot of driving to enjoy scenery that's not as pleasing as that of more-accessible headlands such as **Fanad Head.** If you've had your fill of coastal scenery elsewhere in North Donegal, limit your visit to a stop at **Grianan Ailigh.**

by Napoleon's forces. The fort now houses a museum of military history, in which the most interesting exhibits trace the use of bases and ports in Northern Ireland during World War I. The museum is open June through September, Tuesday through Saturday, 10:30 a.m. to 6 p.m.; Sunday, 12:30 to 8 p.m.; October through May, Tuesday through Saturday, 10:30 a.m. to 4:30 p.m. Admission is €4 adults, €2 seniors and students.

The heaths and woodlands of **Glenveagh National Park,** 27 kilometers (17 miles) northwest of Letterkenny on R251, climb the slopes of the Derryveagh Mountains, presenting some of the most beautiful and dramatic landscapes in Ireland. Most of the 10,000 hectares (24,000 acres) were amassed by an unusually notorious landlord, John George Adair, who evicted hundreds of tenants and destroyed their cottages in order to create the estate. Glenveagh passed through the hands of several owners before becoming a national park in 1984. Deep in the heart of the estate is the charming **Glenveagh Castle** (see next page). The most popular landmark in and around the park, though, is **Errigal Mountain,** with a pyramid-shaped peak that is covered with snow for much of the year.

ATTRACTIONS IN NORTH DONEGAL

Glebe House ★★★★

APPEAL BY AGE	PRESCHOOL ★★	GRADE SCHOOL ★★★	TEENS ★★★
YOUNG ADULTS ★★★	OVER 30 ★★★★		SENIORS ★★★★

Church Hill, 18 kilometers (11 miles) northwest of Letterkenny on R251; ☎ 074-37071

Type of attraction Historic home and art gallery. **Admission** *Gallery:* free; *house:* €2.90 adults, €2.10 seniors, €1.30 children and students, €7.40 families of up to 2 adults and 2 children. **Hours** June–late September, Saturday–Thursday, 11 a.m.– 6:30 p.m. **When to go** Anytime. **Special comments** If you are pressed for time, skip the house tour and see the gallery only; however, try to see both, as the house is extraordinary. **How much time to allow** About 2 hours.

DESCRIPTION AND COMMENTS An 1820s rectory surrounded by gardens was the home of the 20th-century English landscape painter and portraitist Derek Hill, who donated the house and his remarkable collection of art to the Irish nation in 1981. The house, visited by guided tour only, is a delight, filled with Islamic and Japanese art, William Morris wallpapers, Regency chairs, and other eclectic furnishings. A converted stable now houses a light-filled gallery hung with works by Oskar Kokoschka, Pierre Bonnard, Jack Yeats, and others; each piece is a gem, and browsing this lovely assemblage is a treat you would not expect to find in the remote reaches of North Donegal.

TOURING TIPS Glebe House is at the edge of Glenveagh National Park, so it can easily be included as part of a visit.

Glenveagh Castle ★★★★

APPEAL BY AGE	PRESCHOOL ★★★★★	GRADE SCHOOL ★★★★★	TEENS ★★★★★
YOUNG ADULTS ★★★★★		OVER 30 ★★★★½	SENIORS ★★½

Glenveagh National Park; ☎ 074-913-7090; www.heritageireland.ie

Type of attraction Historic home. **Admission** €3 adults, €2 seniors, €1.50 children and students,. **Hours** Daily, 10 a.m.–6 p.m. **When to go** Early enough in the day to allow time for a hike in the park before or after touring the castle. **Special comments** A minibus runs from the parking lot to the castle; the fare is about €1, and tickets can be purchased at the park's visitors center. You might want to make one leg of the 3-kilometer (2-mile) trip on foot, as the walk along the lakeshore is delightful. A tearoom in the former stable block serves excellent salads and hot meals, which you can enjoy on the terrace in good weather. **How much time to allow** At least 2 hours to see the house and gardens.

DESCRIPTION AND COMMENTS One of the most appealing historic homes in Ireland is perched on the shores of Lough Beagh in the midst of Glenveagh National Park. Woodlands, moors, and heath-covered mountainsides surround the castle, creating a sense of remoteness. The rugged landscapes are welcoming, with their shades of purple and russet reflected in the lake waters, and the Italian and English gardens surrounding the house add a note of civility. The castle was the creation of John George Adair, a notorious landlord who ruthlessly evicted his tenants in 1861 to create the 14,000-hectare (35,000-acre) estate that now comprises Glenveagh National Park. His widow, Cornelia, planted the elaborate gardens. The pleasing, refined rooms, swimming pool, and terraces are largely the work of an American, Henry P. McIlhenny, heir to the Tabasco sauce fortune and president of the Philadelphia Museum of Art. McIlhenny spent part of every year at Glenveagh from 1937 to 1983, entertaining such guests as Greta Garbo. You can visit the house only on a 45-minute guided tour that's filled with anecdotes and shows off the inviting and extremely livable rooms; it's easy to fall under the spell of Glenveagh.

TOURING TIPS You can spend a very pleasant full day at Glenveagh. Stroll through the castle gardens, and then turn your attention to the rest of the enormous park. Follow the maps available at the visitors center to explore the park on one of the many trails.

RESTAURANTS IN NORTH DONEGAL

Bridge Café ★★★½

SEAFOOD	MODERATE	QUALITY ★★★	VALUE ★★★★

End of bridge, Ramelton; ☎ 074-51119

Reservations Recommended. **Entree range** €14–€25. **Payment** MC, V. **Bar** Full service. **Disabled access** No. **Hours** Monday–Saturday, 7:30–10 p.m.

MENU RECOMMENDATIONS Oysters, wild salmon.

COMMENTS The Bridge Café is Ramelton's most popular pub, perched romantically beside the River Swilly and often bathed in fog. The downstairs barroom is warmed by a roaring fire and local chatter; dinner is served upstairs in several nicely lit, low-ceilinged rooms with wood floors. Sit by the fire downstairs and have a pint or a cocktail while regarding the menu; then place your order and wait to be called to your table upstairs. The pub often hosts sessions by local musicians, a pleasant way to end an evening here.

Green Room ★★★★

CONTINENTAL	EXPENSIVE	QUALITY ★★★★	VALUE ★★★★

Castle Grove Country House Hotel, Letterkenny; ☎ 074-915-1118

Reservations Recommended. **Entree range** €18–€30; prix-fixe lunch, €15 and €22; prix-fixe dinner, €30 and €48. **Payment** AE, MC, V. **Bar** Full service. **Disabled access** Yes. **Hours** Monday–Saturday, 12:30–2 p.m. and 6:30–9 p.m.; Sunday, 6:30–9 p.m.

MENU RECOMMENDATIONS Fried fillet of beef, fresh fish and seafood.

COMMENTS A handsome, light-filled extension to this old country house is quite stunning—suitably fancy surroundings for the accomplished cuisine of chef Pascal Desnet. Meals are served with polish and flair, making even a light lunch a memorable occasion. To take full advantage of a meal here, stroll through the well-maintained gardens and enjoy coffee and an after-dinner drink in one of the welcoming lounges.

Weeping Elm ★★★★½

MODERN IRISH	EXPENSIVE	QUALITY ★★★★½	VALUE ★★★½

Rathmullan House, Rathmullan; ☎ 074-915-8188

Reservations Recommended. **Entree range** €18–€35. **Payment** AE, DC, MC, V. **Bar** Full service. **Disabled access** Yes. **Hours** Daily, 7:30–8:45 p.m.

MENU RECOMMENDATIONS Crab and other local seafood, Rathmullan lamb.

COMMENTS The dining room of Rathmullan House is as inviting as the rest of the hotel. Innovative preparations of mostly local ingredients are served in an exciting dining room beneath sweeping tentlike ceilings. The floor-to-ceiling windows, which open to a stunning garden, lend the impression that you are eating outdoors, whatever the weather. Lunches and light early dinners are served in the hotel's Cellar Bar in summer.

PART TEN

NORTHERN IRELAND

THE VERY NAME OF THIS REGION connotes political unrest and violence, but with peace has come a discovery for 21st-century visitors—this is one of the most beautiful and rewarding corners of Ireland.

British and Scottish settlers began flooding into the North in the 17th century, as the British sought to establish a strong footing here and keep the lands out of Catholic (Irish) hands. The six counties of Northern Ireland, often called **Ulster,** remain under British rule, as established in the Anglo-Irish Treaty of 1921, under which the remaining 26 counties of Ireland became independent. Many present-day impressions of Northern Ireland were formed in the 1970s and 1980s, when violence erupted in Belfast and Derry as a groundswell gathered behind the Irish Republican Army (IRA), demanding independence and, with it, better conditions for the often oppressed Catholic population in the North. A cease-fire, inaugurated in 1994 and confirmed by the Good Friday Peace Agreement of 1998, has held, and Northern Ireland is a relatively peaceable kingdom these days. Its complex politics and turbulent past are not to be ignored, but to be accepted along with the many other attributes of the North—natural beauty, architectural treasures, and a great deal of warmth. The North is still off the well-beaten tourist path, and the sense of discovery adds considerably to the pleasure of a visit.

northern ireland

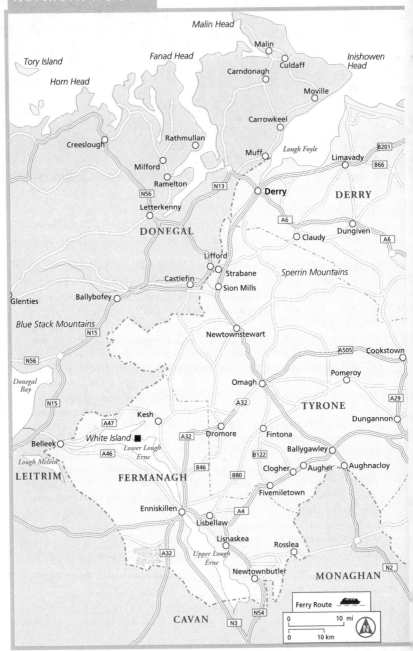

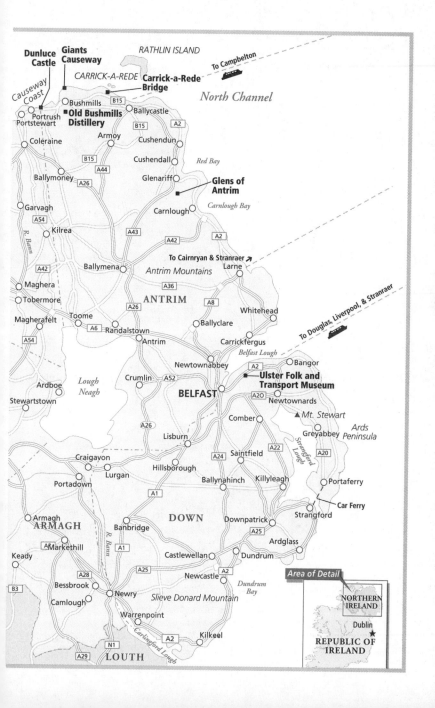

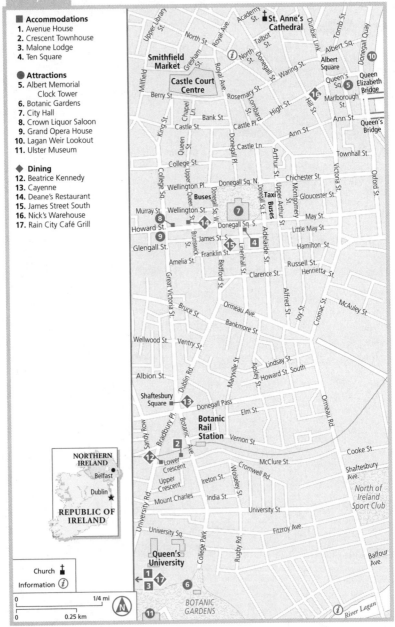

belfast

■ Accommodations
1. Avenue House
2. Crescent Townhouse
3. Malone Lodge
4. Ten Square

● Attractions
5. Albert Memorial
   Clock Tower
6. Botanic Gardens
7. City Hall
8. Crown Liquor Saloon
9. Grand Opera House
10. Lagan Weir Lookout
11. Ulster Museum

◆ Dining
12. Beatrice Kennedy
13. Cayenne
14. Deane's Restaurant
15. James Street South
16. Nick's Warehouse
17. Rain City Café Grill

BELFAST

BELFAST HAS HAD A LOT OF BAD PRESS to overcome—after all, no other city in Western Europe, with the possible exception of Derry, has been as war torn in recent decades. The talk in Belfast these days is about rebirth, and peace has brought with it the pleasure of enjoying a beautiful, fascinating, and often overlooked city of fine avenues, ornate architecture, appealing neighborhoods, and, surprisingly, perhaps, a crop of outstanding restaurants. The whole city seems to be caught up in rebirth, with new hotels and shops opening all the time and streets taking on a gentrified air. Step into the pubs (some of the friendliest in the land), and you'll feel a sense of pride, a notion that Belfast has always been a fine place to be—it's just that now visitors can feel comfortable learning this firsthand.

Belfast is a busy metropolis, as it has been since the late 18th century, when French Huguenots imported linen weaving, British settlers established shipyards and factories, and immigrants came from throughout Ireland to find work. The city is home to some 300,000 souls, about one-third of the population of Northern Ireland.

PLANNING YOUR VISIT TO BELFAST

STAFFERS AT THE **Belfast Welcome Centre** work hard to ensure that visitors get the most out of a visit to Belfast and other places throughout Northern Ireland. You will receive maps and a wealth of helpful information about accommodations, attractions, walking, and other activities. You'll want to head for the office when you get to town (47 Donegall Place, ☎ 028-9024-6609; **www.gotobelfast .com;)** open June through September, Monday through Saturday, 9 a.m. to 7 p.m., and Sunday, noon to 5 p.m.; October through May, Monday through Saturday, 9 a.m. to 5:30 p.m.

Special Events in Belfast

November's Belfast Festival at Queen's University is the city's big cultural bash of the year, staging plays, concerts, dance performances, film screenings, and many other events; for more information, contact the festival office at ☎ 028-9066-6321.

ARRIVING AND GETTING ORIENTED IN BELFAST

BELFAST IS ABOUT 170 KILOMETERS (105 miles) north of Dublin, an easy trip by car along N1 and A1. You'll take the A6, M22, and M2 from Derry; connect to these routes at Derry if you're traveling from Donegal and Letterkenny. If you're traveling into the North from Sligo, you'll take the A4. Good train service runs eight times a day between Dublin and Belfast Monday through Saturday, with five trains on Sunday. The trip takes about two hours; one-way fares begin at €36 (about £28). For information, call **Irish Rail** toll-free at ☎ 1850-366222 or

☎ 01-836-6222, or visit **www.irishrail.ie**; you can also contact **Northern Irish Railways** at ☎ 888-BRITRAIL or 028-9024-6485. Trains arrive and depart from Belfast's Central Station. **Ulsterbus** coaches arrive from Dublin and many other points in the Republic, with about seven buses a day to and from Dublin Monday through Saturday and three trains on Sunday; the trip takes about three hours and the fare is about €20 (about £15) one-way. For more information, call ☎ 028-9033-3000 or visit **www.translink.co.uk.**

Belfast is also served by air, with many flights from the United Kingdom, other parts of Europe, and North America. Ferries also connect Belfast and the North with the U.K. For more information on air and boat service to Northern Ireland, see Part Two, Arriving.

HOTELS IN BELFAST

Avenue House ★★★

QUALITY ★★★	VALUE ★★★★	£45–£55

**23 Eglantine Avenue, Belfast, County Antrim BT9 6DW;
☎ 028-9066-5904; fax 028-9029-1810; info@avenueguesthouse.com;
www.avenueguesthouse.com**

Location University area, south of city center. **Amenities and services** 4 units; hair dryers, in-room tea and coffee facilities, Internet access, nonsmoking rooms. **Elevator** No. **Parking** Free, on street. **Price** Includes full Irish breakfast. **Credit cards** MC, V.

THE TOP CHOICE AMONG the many bed-and-breakfasts in the Eglantine Avenue area occupies a nicely refurbished terrace house and provides a wonderfully convenient base—the lively Malone shops and cafes, Queen's University, the Botanic Gardens, and the Ulster Museum are all within a five-minute walk, and the city center is easily reached just ten minutes away on foot. Stephen and Mary Kelly will tell you how to go about enjoying the local attractions and will engage you in delightful and topical conversation as well. Rooms are large and more comfy—beds are firm, reading chairs are adjacent to large bay windows, and there is plenty of room to spread out. Bathrooms are small but new and nicely equipped. The Avenue is a good base for families because three of the rooms are triples; the top-floor triple is especially large and homey.

Crescent Townhouse ★★★½

QUALITY ★★★½	VALUE ★★½	£90–£110

**13 Lower Crescent, Belfast, County Antrim BT7 1NR; ☎ 028-9032-3349;
fax 028-9032-0646; info@crescenttownhouse.com;
www.crescenttownhouse.com**

Location Off Botanic Avenue, just south of city center. **Amenities and services** 17 rooms; bar, business services, Internet access, nonsmoking rooms, restaurant,

How Hotels Compare in Northern Ireland

HOTEL	OVERALL	QUALITY	VALUE	PRICE
BELFAST				
Ten Square	★★★★★	★★★★★	★★★★	From £175
Crescent Townhouse	★★★½	★★★½	★★½	£90–£110
Malone Lodge	★★★	★★★★	★★★	£110–£1120
Avenue House	★★★	★★★	★★★★	£45–£55
DERRY				
Merchants House	★★★★	★★★	★★★	£45–£55
Tower Hotel Derry	★★★	★★★	★★★★	£59–£75
ANTRIM COAST				
Bushmills Inn	★★★★½	★★★★½	★★★	From £160
Maddybenny Farmhouse	★★★★	★★★★	★★★★	£37–£65

trouser press. **Elevator** Yes. **Parking** Free, on street. **Price** Weekend rates available. **Credit cards** AE, MC, V.

MANY BELFAST RESIDENTS know this handsome old building mainly for its Metro Brasserie (especially popular for lunch, with a good-value early-dinner menu) and Bar 12, a rather posh hangout that hosts cabaret shows and other live entertainment. (Given late-night comings and goings from this popular club, ask for a room far from the entrance.) Upstairs are large and handsome guest rooms, nicely done in varying styles, some traditional and others soothingly contemporary; baths are new, with state-of-the-art fixtures that include, in many rooms, large power showers. Photocopying and other business services, as well as meeting rooms and the proximity of the city center, make the Crescent popular with business travelers, but the hotel is also gracious and laid-back, a nice base for a leisure visit to Belfast, too. The surrounding neighborhood, near the Botanic Gardens and Queen's University, is one of the most pleasant in Belfast.

Malone Lodge ★★★

QUALITY ★★★★	VALUE ★★★	£110–£120

**60 Eglantine Avenue, Belfast, County Antrim BT9 6DY;
☎ 028-9038-8000; fax 028-9038-8088; info@malonelodgehotel.com;
www.malonelodgehotelbelfast.com**

Location University area, south of city center. **Amenities and services** 80 rooms; bar, gym, hair dryers, in-room tea and coffee facilities, Internet access, restaurant, sauna, 2 telephones in each room. **Elevator** Yes. **Parking** Free, on

Walks and Drives in Northern Ireland

Spectacular coastal scenery, some of Europe's best cruising waters, and windswept mountains are among the diverse, and little explored, landscapes of Northern Ireland.

GREAT WALKS

GLENARIFF FOREST PARK

In the most beautiful of the Glens of Antrim, you can follow the Inver and Glenariff rivers as they cascade through forests and mossy valleys. The visitors center (open daily, 9 a.m. to 4:30 p.m.) provides maps of the many trails in the park. The most popular walk, on the **Waterfall Trail** (4.5 kilometers/3 miles), follows a series of cascades on the Glenariff River, and the **Nature Trail** (2.5 kilometers/1.5 miles) follows the Inver River.

THE CAUSEWAY COAST WAY

A well-maintained and well-used walking path follows the Causeway Coast for 52 kilometers (31 miles), from **Portstewart** in the east to **Ballycastle** in the west. The most scenic part is the section around the **Giants Causeway** (see page 416), although the route passes rocky sea cliffs, green mountains, and lush inland valleys along its entire length.

THE MOUNTAINS OF MOURNE

This moor-covered seaside range of 600-meter (2,000-foot) summits, just 50 kilometers (30 miles) south of Belfast, is little traveled and makes for beautiful walking country. An easy place to get a taste of the mountain scenery is **Tollymore Forest Park,** 6 kilometers (3.5 miles) west of the town of **Newcastle.** Four well-marked trails crisscross forests and follow the valley of the River Shimna; the longest trail, the **Long Haul,** covers 13 kilometers (8 miles); trail maps are available at the park entrance, and the park is open daily, 10 a.m. to dusk.

property and on street. **Price** Includes full Irish breakfast; weekend rates and special offers available. **Credit cards** AE, MC, V.

UNEXPECTEDLY TUCKED AWAY amid the terrace houses and B&Bs along Eglantine Avenue, this smart, well-run business hotel is spacious and comfortable. Public spaces include Macklins Bar, extremely popular for its lunchtime carvery, and seem to be perennially busy. Guest rooms, though, are unusually restful; most are enormous, twice the size of most modern hotel rooms, and face the avenue through bay windows fitted with handy arrangements of tables and chairs. Earth tones and unobtrusive furnishings are soothing, while bathrooms are large and updated, many with corner tubs and separate showers. The Malone Lodge is a far better choice than the better-known Wellington Park around the corner.

GREAT DRIVES

ALONG THE CAUSEWAY COAST

Travelers who make it to the North discover that some of Ireland's most spectacular scenery, and one of its most scenic drives, is on the **Causeway Coast,** between the resort of Portush and the Glens of Antrim.

The route follows narrow, winding A2 west from **Portrush,** a faded Victorian resort town. Almost as soon as you leave town, though, you find yourself among green hills and a rocky seacoast that stretches for miles. Just eight kilometers (five miles) outside Portrush is **Dunluce Castle** (see page 415), a ruined 13th-century fortress perched on the edge of a cliff high above the sea.

After another eight kilometers (five miles) comes an even more spectacular sight: **Giants Causeway** (see page 416), where some 35,000 basalt columns extend into the sea, dramatic evidence of volcanic activity 60 million years ago.

Just two kilometers (one mile) south of Giants Causeway is **Bushmills,** an attractive village put on the map by the fame of its local industry, the **Old Bushmills Distillery** (see page 417), the oldest licensed distillery in the world.

Carrick-a-Rede Bridge, 13 kilometers (8 miles) east of Giants Causeway, is another memorable sight, albeit man-made (see page 415). Here, a rope bridge connects the mainland and an island of the same name, swaying in daredevil fashion above the turbulent surf far below.

Ballycastle, eight kilometers (five miles) east, is a delightful seaside town with fine old pubs and shops, a long beach, and docks that bustle with the hubbub of the local fishing fleet. The town is the gateway to the **Glens of Antrim,** nine wooded valleys that etch the mountains along the coast from here for 66 kilometers (40 miles) to Glenariff.

From Ballycastle, continue east along the coast on the narrow road around Murlough Bay to **Fair Head,** a barren headland that affords sweeping views up and down the coast.

Continued on next page

Ten Square ★★★★★

| QUALITY ★★★★★ | VALUE ★★★★ | FROM £175 |

10 Donegall Square South, Belfast, County Antrim BT1 5JD;
☎ **028-9024-1001; fax 028-9024-3210; reservations@tensquare.co.uk;
www.tensquare.co.uk**

Location City center. **Amenities and services** 22 rooms; bar, DVDs, in-room tea and coffee facilities, Wi-Fi, minibars, nonsmoking rooms, room service, safe, trouser press, 2 restaurants. **Elevator** Yes. **Parking** Nearby car park, £8 overnight. **Price** Includes full Irish breakfast; many specials available. **Credit cards** AE, MC, V.

Walks and Drives in Northern Ireland (continued)

GREAT DRIVES (CONTINUED)

ALONG THE CAUSEWAY COAST (CONTINUED)

Cushenden, 26 kilometers (16 miles) east and south of Ballycastle, is an orderly arrangement of squares and terraces that came into being two centuries ago when the local nobility, Lord Cushenden, married a Cornish woman and commissioned the architect Clough Williams-Ellis to create a village that would remind his bride of her native Cornwall.

Cushendall, ten kilometers (six miles) south, is notable for **Turnley's Tower,** built in 1820 as a jail for "idlers and rioters"; you can't miss the red-stone structure, sitting in the middle of a crossroads at the center of the village.

Glenariff, another 11 kilometers (7 miles) farther south, faces Red Bay and lies at the entrance to some of the most magnificent scenery in the Glens, which you can enjoy as you explore the woods and valleys of **Glenariff Forest Park,** open daily, 8 a.m. to dusk; £1 admission fee per car.

AROUND LOUGH ERNE

Just south of **Derry** lies Northern Ireland's so-called **Lakelands,** comprising the waters, shores, and islands of Lough Erne.

From Derry, it's a fairly quick drive through pretty countryside down the River Foyle along B48 to **Omagh,** 50 kilometers (30 miles) south. This ordinary market town in the stark Sperrin Mountains would be unremarkable if it weren't for an IRA bombing in 1998 that killed 29 people.

Omagh's main attraction is about five kilometers (three miles) north, the **Ulster-American Folk Park.** Exhibits here trace the contributions that Irish from the north have made to American culture. The ancestral home of industrialist **Andrew Mellon** (1855–1937) is a simple whitewashed cottage, all the more poignant given the millions that Mellon made in the steel business. Recreations include a log settlement like those where emigrants settled in the New World two centuries ago and a ship that took them there. Castletown, Camphill, Omagh, County Tyrone; ☎ 028-8224-3292. Easter through September: Monday through Saturday, 10:30 a.m. to 6 p.m.; Sunday, 11 a.m. to 6:30 p.m. October through Easter: Monday through Friday, 10:30 a.m. to

BELFAST BOASTS A NEW CROP of small, stylish hotels (the nearby Malmaison, **www.malmaison.com,** and Merchant, **www.themerchanthotel.co .uk,** also fall into this category), but Ten Square holds its own as the first and best. While it might be easy to be put off by the self-conscious trendiness of the place, you're likely to soon see past this attitude—Ten Square is lovely, luxurious, and comfortable, and hospitality is taken very seriously. One of the most delightful spots is the handsome alcove off the reception area, where a fire is always burning. The ground-floor Grill Room is a

5 p.m. Admission: £4.50 adults, £2.50 seniors and children ages 5 to 16, £11 for families of up to two adults and two children.

A drive of 40 kilometers (24 miles) southwest of **Omagh** on A32, B4, and A47 brings you around the northern shores of Lower Lough Erne, surrounded by green hills, to **Belleek.**

Lough Erne, divided into lower and upper lakes (the "lower" lake is the northern section) is considered one of Europe's finest cruising locales, with miles of open water and many inlets and islands.

About halfway between Omagh and Belleek, visible from the lakeshore, is **Boa Island,** connected to the mainland by two bridges. In the island's Caldragh cemetery you'll encounter two pagan stone idols, one double faced.

Belleek is a factory town famous for its handmade china, often created in a distinctive basket weave. You can tour **Belleek Pottery Ltd.** (on weekdays, tours every half hour; ☎ 028-6865-8501) and shop in the showroom, where you'll find a lot of quality and few discounts. Belleek, by the way, is a border town, so you can easily slip west from here to the Republic and zip down or up the N15 to Sligo or Donegal.

From Belleek, follow the shores of Lough Erne on A46 about 35 kilometers (21 miles) to **Devenish,** a ruined monastic community. About three kilometers (two miles) before reaching Devenish, though, make a short, well-marked detour off the highway to **Monea,** a ruined 17th-century castle built by Planters, as colonists from Britain who settled in Ireland were called.

Devenish is on a island just off the mainland and reached by ferry (see page 411). St. Molaise founded a monastery on the island in the sixth century, and medieval remains, including a 12th-century round tower visible for miles around, now litter the marshy terrain.

Enniskillen, six kilometers (four miles) south, is a resort town wedged on a spit between the lower and upper lakes (see page 410). Local attractions include **Castle Coole,** one of the grandest homes in Ireland (see page 411).

From Enniskillen, follow the east side of the lake north for 12 kilometers (7.5 miles) to **Castle Archdale,** a busy resort with several marinas. From there take B4 30 kilometers (18 miles) to Omagh, and then return to Derry.

relaxed place for a good-value meal or snack; Porcelain, upstairs, is a dark, upholstered, modern hideaway in which to enjoy a fine meal. Guest rooms manage to be both showy and peaceful—tall windows graced with shutters of milky glass bring to light creamy whites and neutrals, and the modern furnishings are unobtrusive and comfortable amid excellent lighting and appealing art. Bathrooms are outfitted with deep tubs, oversize sinks, power showers, and other amenities. These rooms pass the ultimate test—they are so relaxing and enjoyable that you will want to stay put.

walks and drives in northern ireland

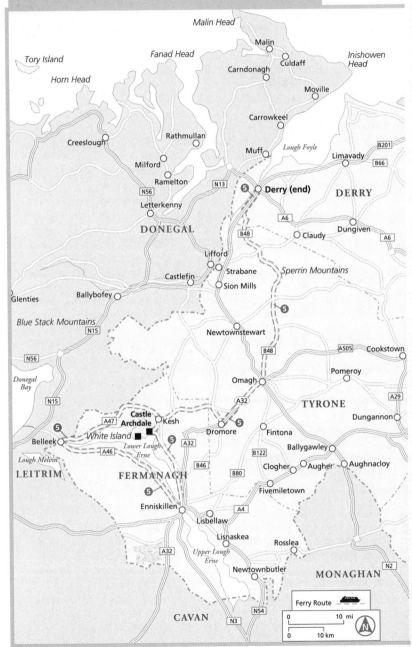

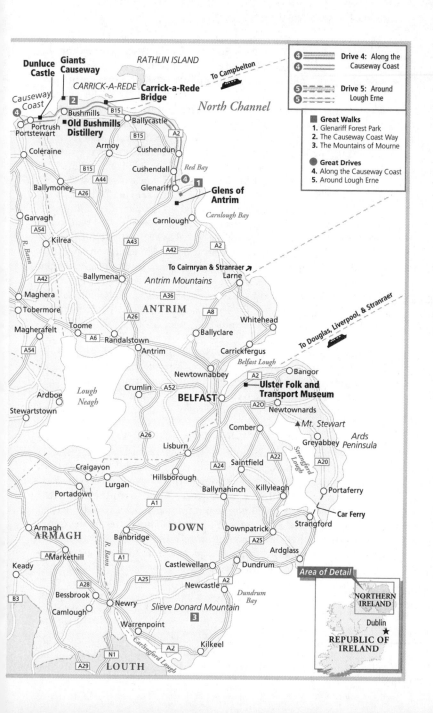

EXPLORING BELFAST

DECADES OF INDUSTRIAL WEALTH in compact central Belfast have bestowed the city with broad avenues and many grand public buildings. **Donegall Square** is the city's central hub; the main avenues converge at the square, and the domed **City Hall** dominates one side. The square is a good departure point for a walk around the city center; a longer trek or short bus ride takes you south to such sights as **Queen's University,** the **Ulster Museum,** and the **Botanic Gardens.** The best way to see **Falls** and **Shankill roads**—respectively, the main streets of the Catholic and Protestant neighborhoods that were for years the epicenters of the Troubles—is on a guided tour (see facing page).

Monuments in **Donegall Square** provide a quick overview of great moments in the city's past; especially worth seeking out are those commemorating the *Titanic* (the doomed luxury liner was built in the city's vast shipyards) and honoring the U.S. Army forces that made first landfall in Europe here in early 1942. You can step inside the main hall of **City Hall,** completed in 1906 and modeled on St. Paul's Cathedral in London; crane your neck to look up the heights of the ornately decorated dome, and take the time to join one of the free guided tours that show off the reception halls and council chambers, all wonderfully grandiose; the foyer is open Monday through Saturday, 9 a.m. to 5 p.m.; guided tours take place Monday through Friday at 2:30 p.m., more frequently June to September. The other monumental structure on the square is **Linen Hall Library,** founded in 1788 and these days the world's largest repository of materials relating to the Troubles; political posters and other fascinating materials relating to the city's turbulent past hang in one of the galleries; ☎ 028-9032-1707; open Monday through Friday, 9:30 a.m. to 7:30 p.m. and Saturday, 9:30 a.m. to 4 p.m.

Two other remnants of Belfast's Victorian heyday are just to the west of Donegall Square. Follow Howard Street to Great Victoria Street and the **Grand Opera House,** an elaborate 1895 structure that, like most other buildings in Belfast, was bombed (as recently as 1991) and then rebuilt in all its extravagance. These days the hall is the venue for some rather mediocre entertainment, such as traveling road shows of big musicals, that doesn't always do justice to the surroundings. The Grand Opera House never fails to steal the show; the box office is open Monday through Friday, 8:30 a.m. to 9 p.m., and Saturday, 8:30 a.m. to 6 p.m. The **Crown Liquor Saloon,** just down the street at Number 46, is an august assemblage of carved wood, colorful tiles, and gilded mirrors that is now owned by the National Trust; business goes on as usual, so sit down in a snug and enjoy a pint. Just across the street is a Belfast landmark of more recent vintage: the nondescript **Europa Hotel,** which has the dubious distinction of being Europe's most bombed hotel, having survived 11 IRA blasts, but has quickly gotten back to business as usual after each one.

St. Anne's Cathedral, a somber, forbidding edifice, is north of the square, on Donegall Street; the cavernous interior is brightened somewhat by the presence of delightful mosaics. A far more appealing piece of architecture is the **Albert Memorial Clock Tower,** at the end of High Street on Victoria Square; the elaborate tower, a tribute to Queen Victoria's husband, Prince Albert, is made all the more interesting by a distinct tilt and the background presence of huge cranes in the shipyards along the River Lagan. You can take in the scene from the **Lagan Weir Lookout,** on Donegall Quay just beyond the square; if you think you might enjoy displays documenting the control of tides in Belfast harbor, you can fork over £2 to step inside the **Lagan Lookout Visitors Centre;** April to September, Monday through Friday, 11 a.m. to 5 p.m.; Saturday, noon to 5 p.m.; Sunday, 2 to 5 p.m.; October to March, Tuesday through Friday, 11 a.m. to 3:30 p.m., Saturday, 1 to 4:30 p.m., Sunday, 2 to 4:30 p.m. Far more enjoyable is a walk through the old riverside warehouse neighborhood between the cathedral and the clock tower, laced with narrow alleyways known as entries.

Tours in Belfast

The most compelling reason to take a tour in Belfast is to see **Falls Road** and **Shankill Road,** epicenters of the Troubles. Whether you tour by cab or bus, you can count on two things: the commentary will be highly informative (and despite the gravity of recent events here, entertaining), and you'll most likely begin with a drive through the Catholic neighborhood around Falls Road, close to the city center. You'll pass the **Sinn Féin** offices and endless murals, then go through the so-called peace wall to **Milltown Cemetery,** where hunger striker Bobby Sands and other IRA members are buried, then into the Protestant Shankill Road neighborhood, where murals include Union Jack motifs and even elaborate portrayals of the victory of the Protestant William of Orange over the Catholic King James II in the Battle of the Boyne in 1690.

Black taxis run by several companies ply this route regularly, charging about £25 for one or two passengers, £8 a person for up to six passengers. You can also arrange with the drivers to travel farther afield to see sights such as the **Harland and Wolff Shipyard,** where the *Titanic* was built and which is now slated for development as a huge commercial district aptly named the Titanic Quarter (although the nomenclature is bound to launch endless jokes about sinking fortunes and businesses that can't stay afloat). Among the taxi companies are **Belfast Black Taxi** (☎ 08081-271125), **Belfast City Black Taxi Tours** (☎ 028-9030-1832), and **Black Taxi Tours** (☎ 028-9064-2264; **www .belfasttours.com**). You can also see Falls and Shankill roads, along with sights in the city center and outlying neighborhoods, on a **Belfast City Sightseeing** tour bus. Departing from Castle Place, these 90-minute tours, accompanied by intelligent commentary, operate daily from May to September, 9:30 a.m. to 4:30 p.m., and October to

April, 10 a.m. to 4 p.m.; £11 adults, £9 seniors and students, £5 children; ☎ 028-459-042; **www.belfastcitysightseeing.com.**

Belfast Safaris provide a look at the city through the eyes of residents, who lead guided walks—either along established routes (£8) that explore different neighborhoods and historic sights or on a route you design (£21); ☎ 028-9031-0610; **www.belfastsafaris.com. Belfast Pub Tours** depart from the Crown Liquor Saloon and take in historic pubs around the city center; May through October, Thursday, 7 p.m.; Saturday, 4 p.m.; £6; ☎ 028-9268-3665; **www.belfastpubtours.com.**

ATTRACTIONS IN AND AROUND BELFAST

Belfast Botanic Gardens and Palm House ★★★★

APPEAL BY AGE	PRESCHOOL ★★★★	GRADE SCHOOL ★★★★	TEENS ★★★★
YOUNG ADULTS ★★★★		OVER 30 ★★★	SENIORS ★★★

Stranmillis Road, ☎ 028-9032-4902

Type of attraction Victorian gardens. **Admission** Free. **Hours** Daily, dawn–dusk; *Palm House and Tropical Ravine:* April–September, Monday–Friday, 10 a.m.–5 p.m.; Saturday–Sunday, 1–5 p.m.; October–March, Monday–Friday, 10 a.m.–4 p.m.; Saturday–Sunday, 1–4 p.m. **When to go** When the Palm House and Tropical Ravine House are open. **Special comments** One of the advantages of staying in the Stranmillis neighborhood is the opportunity to pay frequent visits to these delightful gardens, a pleasure even in bad weather, when the glass houses provide tropical refuge; kids will welcome the chance to be outdoors. **How much time to allow** At least 1 hour.

DESCRIPTION AND COMMENTS Dating from 1827, these gardens sloping down to the banks of the River Lagan are as much a part of Victorian Belfast as the ornate buildings in the city center. Plantings throughout the gardens come from every corner of the globe; the most exotic are the trees and blossoms in the enormous Palm House, a glass-and-wrought-iron greenhouse completed by Belfast architect Charles Lanyon in 1839, and the junglelike foliage of the Tropical Ravine House. Many of the beds surrounding these glass houses are beautifully planted with roses and other flowering plants that thrive in Ireland, enlivening the garden from early spring through fall.

TOURING TIPS If you're up for a walk, follow the gardens to the River Lagan and take the towpath back to the city center. Or you can continue south through the outer reaches of the city. After about five kilometers (three miles), the path comes to the Giant's Ring, a 2,000-year-old stone circle that's 200 meters (600 feet) wide and was used in part for burials; you can also reach the Ring on bus 13 from the city center.

kids Ulster Folk and Transport Museum ★★★★

APPEAL BY AGE	PRESCHOOL ★★★★	GRADE SCHOOL ★★★★	TEENS ★★★★★
YOUNG ADULTS ★★★★		OVER 30 ★★★★	SENIORS ★★★★

How Attractions Compare in Northern Ireland

ATTRACTION	DESCRIPTION	AUTHOR'S RATING
BELFAST		
Belfast Botanic Gardens and Palm House	Victorian gardens	★★★★
Ulster Folk and Transport Museum	Museum of social history	★★★★
Ulster Museum	Museum and art gallery	★★★½
DERRY		
Tower Museum Derry	Museum of local history	★★★★
Workhouse Museum	Museum that chronicles the Famine and Derry's role in World War II	★★★★
ENNISKILLEN		
Castle Coole	One of Ireland's finest country estates	★★★★
ANTRIM COAST		
Giants Causeway	One of Europe's most unusual natural phenomena	★★★★★
Carrick-a-Rede Bridge	Hair-raising rope bridge	★★★★
Dunluce Castle	Castle ruins	★★★★
Old Bushmills Distillery	Whiskey-making factory	★★★★

Cultra, 11 kilometers (7 miles) northeast of Belfast on the A2; ☎ 028-9042-8428; www.uftm.org.uk

Type of attraction Museum of social history. **Admission** *Folk Museum:* £5.50 adults, £3.50 seniors, students, and children ages 5–16, free for children under age 5, £15 for families of up to 2 adults and 3 children, £11 for families of 1 adult and up to 3 children; *Transport Museum:* £5.50 adults, £3.50 seniors, students, and children ages 5–16, free for children under age 5, £15 for families of up to 2 adults and 3 children, £11 for families of 1 adult and up to 3 children. *Combined museum visits:* £7 adults, £4 seniors, students, and children ages 5–16, free for children under age 5, £19 for families of 2 adults and up to 3 children, £13 for families of 1 adult and up to 3 children. **Hours** March–June, Monday–Friday, 10 a.m.–5 p.m.; Saturday, 10 a.m.–6 p.m.; Sunday, 11 a.m.–6 p.m.; July–September, Monday–Saturday, 10 a.m.–6 p.m.; Sunday, 11 a.m.–6 p.m.; October–February, Monday–Friday, 10 a.m.–4 p.m.; Saturday, 10 a.m.–5 p.m.; Sunday, 11 a.m.–5 p.m. **When to go** Much of the folk park is outdoors, so try to find a day when showers are at least infrequent. **Special comments** The museum is a wonderland for kids, who will delight in the cottages, the demonstrations of spinning and other crafts, the trains, and the attractive grounds. **How much time to allow** A full day to do both the folk and the transport museums, half a day for each.

DESCRIPTION AND COMMENTS The two sections of this vast 70-hectare (176-acre) museum compound, one a collection of old structures and the other showcasing cars, planes, and other modes of transportation, all built in Ireland, are seemingly disparate, but together they provide a fascinating and touching look at Irish social history. The folk park is an ambitious assemblage of about 20 structures, ranging in size and grandeur from humble farm cottages to Cultra Manor, an early-20th-century estate house on whose grounds the park is built. The earthen floors and crude furnishings in many of the dwellings speak volumes about the hardships that led so many Irish to emigrate. Even so, the simple farmhouses, workers' cottages, and rudimentary public buildings such as the school are more satisfying to visit than the more refined manor house and lavish reconstruction of a town. Superb exhibits in the Folk Galleries show off artifacts from the rural past and explain social norms and customs that prevailed in many parts of Ireland until only a few decades ago. Locomotives, horse-drawn carts, and some genuine surprises—such as the car that General Motors maverick John DeLorean had built in a Belfast factory—fill the airy galleries of the Transport Museum. The *Titanic* was also built in Ireland, in Belfast shipyards, and a fine exhibit provides an in-depth look at the liner's design, manufacture, and doomed maiden voyage.

TOURING TIPS Plan on breaking up a visit with a meal or tea; the main tearoom is in Cultra Manor, where a lavish Sunday lunch is also served. Refreshments are available at kiosks around the grounds, and many picnic sites are on the grounds.

Ulster Museum ★★★½

APPEAL BY AGE	PRESCHOOL ★★	GRADE SCHOOL ★★★	TEENS ★★★
YOUNG ADULTS ★★★	OVER 30 ★★★½		SENIORS ★★★½

Botanic Gardens, Stranmillis Road; ☎ 028-9038-3000; www.ulstermuseum.org.uk

Type of attraction Museum and art gallery. **Admission** Free. **Hours** Monday–Friday, 10 a.m.–5 p.m.; Saturday, 1–5 p.m.; Sunday, 2–5 p.m. **When to go** Anytime. **Special comments** The museum publishes an excellent guidebook, available free at the information desk, which is most helpful given the wideranging nature of the exhibits. The museum has a small cafe, but Stranmillis Road, just outside the doors, boasts a nice row of cafes and shops. **How much time to allow** About 2 hours.

DESCRIPTION AND COMMENTS The most comprehensive museum in Northern Ireland is devoted to history, the natural sciences, and art. While it might be easy to assume that a collection this far-flung is not going to excel in any arena, the 19th-century neoclassical building in a corner of the Botanic Gardens is filled with a remarkably worthy mix of treasures, displayed in well-designed galleries. It is a pleasure simply to wander and come upon a mummy, mask, or painting that catches your eye. A collection of African arts and crafts from the 19th and 20th centuries is unmatched. Several galleries thoughtfully explain the history of Ireland with an unflinching look at the Troubles and the developments that led to the formation of the North as a separate entity; the painting galleries are hung with masterpieces by Gainsborough, Reynolds, and the late-20th-century American abstract painter Morris Louis. Some of the most exquisite treasures are Spanish gold, salvaged when the Spanish galleon *Girona* sunk off the northern coast in 1588.

TOURING TIPS Take advantage of a visit to the museum to see the Botanic Gardens and the rest of this appealing neighborhood, which lies approximately two kilometers (one mile) south of the city center and includes the handsome campus of Queen's University, modeled on Oxford's Magdalen College.

RESTAURANTS IN BELFAST

Beatrice Kennedy   ★ ★ ★ ★

MODERN IRISH	MODERATE/EXPENSIVE	QUALITY ★ ★ ★ ★	VALUE ★ ★ ★ ½

44 University Road, Belfast; ☎ 028-9020-2290

Reservations Recommended. **Entree range** £14–£17; 2-course express menu, 5–7 p.m., £12. **Payment** AE, MC, V. **Bar** Full service. **Disabled access** Yes. **Hours** Tuesday–Saturday, 5–10:15 p.m.; Sunday, 12:30–2:30 p.m. and 5–8:15 p.m.

MENU RECOMMENDATIONS Seared salmon with cabbage and bacon, Peking duck breast.

COMMENTS The onetime residence of the eponymous genteel lady provides relaxed and refined surroundings, warmed by fires and accented with a few pieces of Victoriana. Meals here never fail to surprise—for their unfailing quality, outstanding presentation, and unexpected touches such as hints of Thai curry and other exotic ingredients that add a great deal of zest to the deft cooking. Even the homemade dessert chocolates are memorable.

Cayenne   ★ ★ ★ ½

FUSION	MODERATE/EXPENSIVE	QUALITY ★ ★ ★ ★	VALUE ★ ★ ★ ½

7 Ascot House, Shaftesbury Square, Belfast; ☎ 028-9033-1532

Reservations Recommended. **Entree range** £11–£18. **Payment** AE, DC, MC, V. **Bar** Full service. **Disabled access** Yes. **Hours** Monday–Friday, noon–2:15 p.m.; Monday–Thursday, 6–10 p.m.; Friday and Saturday, 6–11 p.m.; Sunday, 5–8:45 p.m.

MENU RECOMMENDATIONS Crispy duck salad, char-grilled calamari with chorizo, fresh fish.

COMMENTS Chef-owner Paul Rankin is one of Ireland's most beloved food celebs and has several Belfast restaurants. None disappoint, although

How Restaurants Compare in Northern Ireland

NAME	CUISINE	OVERALL	QUALITY	VALUE	PRICE
BELFAST					
James Street South	Modern Irish	★★★★	★★★★	★★★★	Mod/exp
Beatrice Kennedy	Modern Irish	★★★★	★★★★	★★★½	Mod/exp
Deane's Restaurant	Modern Irish/ fusion	★★★★	★★★★	★★★	Very exp
Nick's Warehouse	Modern Irish	★★★★	★★★	★★★★½	Mod/exp
Cayenne	Fusion	★★★½	★★★★	★★★½	Mod/exp
Rain City Café Grill	Modern Irish	★★★½	★★★½	★★★★	Mod
DERRY					
Mange 2	Irish/ international	★★★★	★★★★	★★★★	Mod
Badger's	Pub fare	★★★	★★★	★★★★	Inexp
ENNISKILLEN					
Blake's of the Hollow	Pub fare/ Modern Irish	★★★★	★★★★	★★★★	Inexp/mod
THE ANTRIM COAST					
Ramore Wine Bar	Pub fare	★★★	★★★	★★★	Inexp

some are better than others: Cayenne earns high marks for creative use of the freshest ingredients in innovative preparations with a spicy Asian twist. Many who've been dining on standard Irish fare think they've died and gone to heaven when they walk into these sleek, restful surroundings of rich wood, contemporary art, and subdued lighting to enjoy one of Rankin's innovative creations. The superb service is both polished and welcoming. At another nearby Rankin restaurant, Roscoff Brasserie (7–11 Linehall Street, ☎ 028-9031-1150), classic dishes are served in a restrained, contemporary dining room.

Deane's Restaurant   ★★★★

MODERN IRISH/FUSION   VERY EXPENSIVE   QUALITY ★★★★   VALUE ★★★

38–40 Howard Street, Belfast; ☎ 028-9033-1134

Reservations Required. **Entree range** £17–£24. **Payment** AE, MC, V. **Bar** Full service. **Disabled access** Yes. **Hours** Monday–Saturday, noon–3 p.m. and 6–10 p.m.

MENU RECOMMENDATIONS Ravioli of lobster, roasted scallops, filet of Irish beef.

COMMENTS One of Ireland's finest restaurants—and the only dining room in Northern Ireland ever to have earned a Michelin star—has been merged with a brasserie on the premises and completely made over to present a memorable dining experience with less formality than was once its hallmark. Michael Deane trained in Bangkok, and subtle spices work their way into simple local ingredients such as squab, fresh fish, and seafood. The results are stunning. There is nothing outlandish about dishes such as mashed potatoes infused with lemongrass or carpaccio of salmon with sticky rice—dish after dish, you wonder why no one has thought of doing this before.

James Street South ★★★★

MODERN IRISH	MODERATE/EXPENSIVE	QUALITY ★★★★	VALUE ★★★★

21 James Street, Belfast; ☎ 028-9043-4310

Reservations Required. **Entree range** £12–£20; lunch menu, £13.50 for 2 courses, £15.50 for 3 courses, pre-theatre menu, £15.50 for 2 courses, £17.50 for 3 courses. **Payment** AE, MC, V. **Bar** Full service. **Disabled access** Yes. **Hours** Monday–Friday, noon–2:45 p.m.; Monday–Saturday, 5:45–10:45 p.m.

MENU RECOMMENDATIONS Roast loin of duck with artichoke and peppers, organic salmon with prawns.

COMMENTS A few pieces of colorful art, polished wood floors, crisp linens, and dramatic but warm lighting create just the right contemporary atmosphere in this refined room facing narrow James Street through arched windows. The minimalist environs strike the right note in suggesting that the emphasis here is on the expertly served exquisite preparations of chef Niall McKenna—lunch or dinner in this accomplished place is always a special occasion.

Nick's Warehouse ★★★★

MODERN IRISH	MODERATE/EXPENSIVE	QUALITY ★★★	VALUE ★★★★½

35–39 Hill Street, Belfast; ☎ 028-9043-9690

Reservations Recommended. **Entree range** £8.50–£17.50. **Payment** AE, MC, V. **Bar** Full service. **Disabled access** Yes. **Hours** Monday–Friday, noon–3 p.m.; Tuesday–Saturday, 6–9:30 p.m.

MENU RECOMMENDATIONS Shepherd's pie, roast chump of lamb (the portion between the leg and loin), grilled filet of salmon.

COMMENTS Chef Nick Price was a pioneer when he opened his warm and welcoming eatery in a warehouse district on an alley near St. Anne's

Cathedral. The neighborhood is booming these days, but Nick remains the local star, serving in a lively ground-floor wine bar, Anix, and an upstairs dining room. A meal downstairs tends to be a lot less formal, with a menu of innovative sandwiches and salads and a lot of animated chatter among the regulars. (Note that the downstairs room is open for lunch on Monday, but the upstairs room is not, and that only the downstairs room serves in the evening).

Rain City Café Grill ★★★½

MODERN IRISH	MODERATE	QUALITY ★★★½	VALUE ★★★★

33–35 Malone Road, Belfast; ☎ 028-9068-2929

Reservations Recommended. **Entree range** £8.95–£15. **Payment** AE, DC, MC, V. **Bar** Full service. **Disabled access** Yes. **Hours** Daily, 9 a.m.–10 p.m.

MENU RECOMMENDATIONS Rain City burger, fish-and-chips, grilled Irish steak.

COMMENTS In this informal bistrolike outlet of the Paul Rankin empire near Queen's University, the emphasis is on casual fare and good value. Cream-colored brick walls and pine tables set just the right mood for an easy meal of a burger or a plate of sausages, while more-substantial fare—including some excellent fish preparations—is also available. The service is friendly and attentive, and kids are most welcome.

ENTERTAINMENT AND NIGHTLIFE IN BELFAST

NOT SURPRISINGLY, pub life is no less active here in the North than it is in the Republic. Belfast's most celebrated watering hole is the **Crown Liquor Saloon** (Great Victoria Street; ☎ 028-9027-9001), a wonderfully atmospheric Victorian showcase of mirrors and carved wood; the Crown is protected as part of the United Kingdom's National Trust, but this museum-like status and the place's popularity on the tourist trail do not detract from the pleasure of enjoying a pint and a plate of oysters or other light fare in these ornate surroundings. Atmosphere is also on tap at the pubs on the narrow lanes of the **Cathedral Quarter.** At **White's Tavern** (2–4 Winecellar Entry; ☎ 028-9033-0988), business goes on beneath brick arches pretty much as it has since 1630, with great conversation and traditional music some nights. The **Spaniard** (3 Skipper Street; ☎ 028-9023-2448) is a snug little place that serves soups and tapas into the early evening, and then pints of excellent Guinness are poured for a crowd of regulars who crowd around the long bar and cozy tables. For a taste of Belfast student life, head out to the "Bot" (the **Botanic Inn**) or the "Egg" (the **Eglantine)**—across Malone Road from one another and attracting throngs of thirsty scholars who pass many an evening in one or the other (Botanic Inn: 23–27 Malone Road; ☎ 028-9066-0460; Eglantine: 32–40 Malone Road: ☎ 028-9038-1994).

For traditional music, settle into the **Fountain Bar** (16–20 Fountain Street; ☎ 028-9032-4769) on Friday evenings; **Maddens** (74 Berry

Street; ☎ 028-9024-4114) on Monday, Friday, and Saturday evenings; **McHughs** (29–31 Queens Square; ☎ 028-9050-9990) on Thursday and Friday evenings; and **Fibber Magee's,** behind the Crown Liquor Saloon, every evening. For disco, R & B, and other (often live) entertainment, check out **La Lea** (43 Franklin Street; ☎ 028-9023-0200) and **Milk** (10–14 Tomb Street; ☎ 028-9027-8876).

The two major performing arts venues in Belfast are the **Grand Opera House** and **Waterfront Hall.** The former, located on Great Victoria Street, is a beautifully restored Victorian music hall that hosts road shows and other visiting companies, with a penchant toward smash musicals from London and New York; for tickets and information, call ☎ 028-9024-1919 or visit **www.goh.co.uk.** Waterfront Hall, the city's main stage, hosts symphonic concerts, dance, traditional Irish music performances, rock concerts, and other big events; to check out what's scheduled during your stay in Belfast, call ☎ 028-9033-4400 or visit **www.waterfront.co.uk. Kings Hall Exhibition and Conference Centre** (☎ 028-9066-5225; **www.kingshall.co.uk**), in Balmoral, also hosts concerts, along with trade shows and other events. **Ulster Hall** (Bedford Street; ☎ 028-9032-3900; **www.ulsterhall.co.uk**) is home to the Ulster Orchestra and the Northern Ireland Symphony Orchestra. Belfast's leading stage for plays is the **Lyric Theatre** (Ridgeway Street; ☎ 028-9038-1081; **www.lyrictheatre.co.uk**).

Odyssey, on Queen's Quay, is a one-stop spot for sports and entertainment. The huge arena is home to the **Belfast Giants,** an ice-hockey team, and is yet another venue for major concerts. The complex also has a bowling alley, IMAX theatre, and 12-screen cinema complex, the best place in town to catch a major new release; for general information, call ☎ 028-9045-1055 or visit **www.theodyssey.co.uk.**

SHOPPING IN BELFAST

THE MAIN SHOPPING VENUES in the city center are **Donegall Place, Royal Avenue,** and **High Street.** Belfast is at best a serendipitous place for the shopper, though, with many outlets of the typical British chains, including a **Marks and Spencer** on Donegall Place (☎ 028-9023-5235). Two places worth seeking out are **Smyth's Irish Linens** (65 Royal Avenue; ☎ 028-9024-2232) and **St. George's Market** (May and Oxford streets; ☎ 028-9043-5704), a colorful piece of 19th-century Belfast that hosts food and crafts vendors every Tuesday and Friday morning, starting at 8 a.m.

Around BELFAST

LOCATED 37 KILOMETERS (23 miles) southeast of Belfast, **Downpatrick** claims a close association with Saint Patrick, who allegedly landed here in AD 432 and soon converted the local clans to Christianity. From here, Patrick traveled across Ireland making conversions, and many Irish pay the saint homage by making pilgrimages here to Downpatrick Cathedral, open Monday through Saturday, 9:30 a.m. to 5 p.m. and Sunday, 2 to 5 p.m.

Patrick is also closely associated with **Armagh,** 65 kilometers (40 miles) southwest of Belfast, where he is said to have built a church that is now incorporated in St. Patrick's Church of Ireland Cathedral, open daily, 10 a.m. to 5 p.m. (closes earlier in some winter months).

DERRY

IN KEEPING WITH ITS COMPLEX NATURE, this appealing and underrated city has two names—those in favor of British rule still call the city Londonderry, an understandably controversial appellation that Catholics have over the years rejected in favor of simply Derry. The city is still officially labeled Londonderry, though the city council and other political bodies within the city often use Derry. So what the city is called depends on to whom you are speaking.

Derry commands a lovely and strategic position on the banks of the River Foyle, and given the possibilities for shipping, British and Scottish Protestants settled the city in the early 17th century and surrounded their stronghold with thick walls that still stand—some of the most intact medieval walls in Europe. The city repelled a siege by the forces of the Catholic King James II in 1688–89, and for its impregnability has earned yet a third name, the Maiden City. The strong Protestant presence and large Catholic population made Derry rife with conflict during the Troubles: beginning in the late 1960s the city saw considerable violence, with daily bombings and horrible bloodshed, including the murder of 14 innocent civilians during the Bloody Sunday protests of January 30, 1972. You'll never be far from the palpable presence of the Troubles in Derry, though these days they make themselves known by colorful, politically charged murals rather than violence.

PLANNING YOUR VISIT TO DERRY

HOUSED IN A HANDSOME PAVILION near the banks of the River Foyle, the **Derry Visitor and Convention Bureau and Tourist Information Centre** (44 Foyle Street, ☎ 028-7126-7284; **www.derryvisitor .com**) is at the south end of town across from the Foyleside Shopping Centre. The extremely helpful staff is full of advice on what to see and do in Derry and the surrounding region (stock up on info about the Antrim Coast here, too), arranges accommodations, and leads excellent walking tours. Open mid-March through June and October, Monday through Friday, 9 a.m. to 5 p.m.; Saturday, 10 a.m. to 5 p.m.; July through September, Monday through Friday, 9 a.m. to 7 p.m.; Saturday, 10 a.m. to 6 p.m.; Sunday, 10 a.m. to 5 p.m.

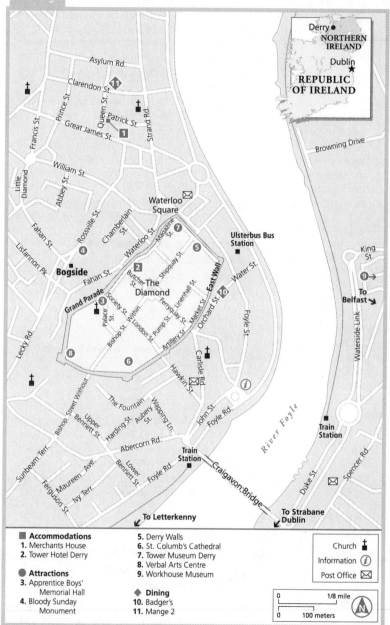

derry

Asylum Rd.

Clarendon St.

Prince St.

Francis St.

Queen St.

Patrick St.

Strand Rd.

Great James St.

1

William St.

Little Diamond

Abbey St.

Fahan St.

Lisfannon Pk.

Rossville St.

Chamberlain St.

Waterloo Square

Waterloo St.

Magazine St.

Ulsterbus Bus Station

7

5

Water St.

Bogside

4

Fahan St.

Butcher St.

Shipquay St.

The Diamond

2

Grand Parade

Society St.

Palace St.

Bishop St. Within

London St.

Linenhall St.

Ferryquay St.

Pump St.

Market St.

Orchard St.

East Wall

10

Foyle St.

3

8

6

Artillery St.

Carlisle Rd.

Hawkin St.

The Fountain

Bishop St. Without

Upper Bennett St.

Harding St.

Wapping Ln.

Aubery St.

John St.

Foyle Rd.

Abercorn Rd.

Sunbeam Terr.

Ferguson St.

Maureen Ave.

Lower Bennett St.

Ivy Terr.

Foyle Rd.

Train Station

Craigavon Bridge

River Foyle

To Letterkenny

To Strabane Dublin

King St.

9

To Belfast

Waterside Link

Train Station

Duke St.

Spencer Rd.

Browning Drive

Derry ●
NORTHERN IRELAND

Dublin ★

REPUBLIC OF IRELAND

■ **Accommodations**
1. Merchants House
2. Tower Hotel Derry

● **Attractions**
3. Apprentice Boys' Memorial Hall
4. Bloody Sunday Monument

5. Derry Walls
6. St. Columb's Cathedral
7. Tower Museum Derry
8. Verbal Arts Centre
9. Workhouse Museum

◆ **Dining**
10. Badger's
11. Mange 2

Church ✝
Information ⓘ
Post Office ✉

0 _____ 1/8 mile
0 _____ 100 meters

N

Special Events in Derry

Derry stages several major cultural events throughout the year. The **City of Derry Drama Festival** in early March is Ireland's most acclaimed showcase for amateur drama (☎ 028-7126-4455). Irish music is celebrated at the **Feis Doire Cholmcille** during March and April, while the **Celtronic Festival** in late June and early July is a festival of Irish dance (☎ 028-7126-4455). The **City of Derry Jazz Festival** in early March to late April brings together an international roster of jazz and big-band enthusiasts (☎ 028-7137-6545; **www.cityofderryjazz festival.com**). Derry's most famous—and notorious—event is the **Relief of Derry Celebration** (held on the Saturday that falls closest to August 12), which commemorates the 1688–89 siege during which Protestants loyal to William of Orange kept the forces of the Catholic King James II at bay for 100 days. In a ceremony that has stirred up violence over the years, members of the Protestant all-male Apprentice Boys organization walk the walls in remembrance of those who lost their lives during the siege.

unofficial **TIP**

The only easy way to see Derry is on foot. If you're driving, stash the car as soon as you get to town. The most convenient car park is at **Foyleside Shopping Centre,** across from the tourist office. The massive parking area is open daily, from 8 a.m. into the evening hours; expect to pay about £2.50 to park for most of the day. From here it's an easy walk to sights, shops, and restaurants.

ARRIVING AND GETTING ORIENTED IN DERRY

DERRY IS ABOUT 110 KILOMETERS (70 miles) north of Belfast and 230 kilometers (145 miles) northwest of Dublin. By car, follow the A6 motorway across Northern Ireland from Belfast to Derry, which takes a little more than an hour. **Northern Ireland Railways** runs eight trains per day between Belfast and Derry, and the trip takes about two hours. Standard one-way fare is £6. Derry's Northern Ireland Railways station is on the east side of the River Foyle on Duke Street. Bus service is faster and much more frequent, with about 16 buses a day making the trip in one and a half hours. The bus station is conveniently located next to the tourist-information office on Foyle Road. For information on both train and bus service, go to **www.nirailways.co.uk**.

HOTELS IN DERRY

Merchants House   ★★★★

QUALITY ★★★	VALUE ★★★	£45–£55

16 Queen Street, Derry, County Londonderry BT48 7EQ;
☎ **028-7126-4223; fax 028-7126-6913; saddlershouse@btinternet.com;**
www.thesaddlershouse.com

Location 5-minute walk from city center. **Amenities and services** 5 units, 1 with private bath; in-room tea and coffee facilities, sitting room. **Elevator** No.

Parking Free, on street. **Price** Includes full breakfast. **Credit cards** Not accepted.

IF EVER A HOTEL WAS SO APPEALING that you'd be willing to forgo a private bath, this lovely old house—a rare Georgian gem—might be the place. The atmosphere of a private home really does prevail here: The sitting room will tempt you to linger for hours and read, guest rooms are commodious and charming with their eccentric but comfortable furnishings, and breakfasts are memorable; shared baths are plentiful, spotless, and just steps from the rooms. Joan and Peter Pyne, who run this delightful guesthouse, also operate the Saddler's House a few blocks away. That, too, is a historic home lovingly restored, featuring seven rooms, three with private bathrooms. Both establishments provide character-filled accommodations in one of Ireland's most distinctive cities.

Tower Hotel Derry ★ ★ ★

QUALITY ★ ★ ★	VALUE ★ ★ ★ ★	£59–£75

Butcher Street, Derry BT48 6HL; ☎ 028-7137-1000; reservations@thd.ie; www.towerhotelderry.com

Location City center. **Amenities and services** 93 rooms; bar, gym, hair dryers, restaurant, room service, wireless Internet access. **Elevator** Yes. **Parking** £5, on property. **Price** Includes full Irish breakfast; special weekend rates available. **Credit cards** AE, MC, V.

THE ONLY HOTEL WITHIN the city walls of Derry can barely make that claim—the walls soar past one end of the hotel, creating a dramatic view from the ground-floor bistro and some of the guest rooms. Other than this location, the Tower can make few claims to distinction but provides standard hotel amenities at a good price. The busy public areas include the pleasant Lime Tree Bar, where sandwiches and other light fare are available throughout the day, and the Bistro, an airy restaurant serving Mediterranean-influenced cuisine (including many pasta dishes). Guest rooms are amply sized and warmly decorated in a safe, traditional style; those at the rear of the hotel offer views over the River Foyle and sections of the city walls.

EXPLORING DERRY

TAKE IN A NICE OVERVIEW of Derry and its history, past and recent, on a fairly easy walk along the medieval walls that still surround the central city, and then into the once-strife-torn **Bogside** neighborhood. You will get a lot more out of a visit to Derry if you make this walk in the company of a knowledgeable guide; see "Tours in Derry," page 407.

The completely intact **Derry Walls,** built by British settlers between 1614 and 1618, are the only such set in Ireland and one of the few in Europe. A walkway of a little more than 2 kilometers (1.25 miles) follows the tops of the walls, affording wonderful views over the historic city within the enclosure, as well as the metropolis that has sprung up over the centuries outside the walls. Frequent stairways lead off the walls, providing access to the places you will want to visit in the city center. If you mount the walls near the **Tourist Information Centre** at Bridge Street and walk in a clockwise direction, you will soon come to **St. Columb's Cathedral,** built in 1633 and a powerful symbol of Protestant Derry. Among the many relics from the 1688–89 siege is a 270-pound mortar ball that the Catholic forces of King James II of England lobbed over the walls with conditions of surrender attached. Legend has it that the citizenry of the besieged and starving city rushed to the walls and shouted "No Surrender!"—a popular chant during the Troubles. Find the Stars and Stripes in the forest of flags and banners that hang in the church; this was the flag brought to Northern Ireland by the American troops who used Derry as their first entry point into the European theater of World War II.

A little farther along is another edifice that's almost as sacred to the Protestant hearts of Derry, the **Apprentice Boys' Memorial Hall.** Built in 1867 in a faux-Gothic manor, this imposing bastion serves as headquarters of the all-male, all-Protestant Apprentice Boys Society, which was formed in 1715 to honor the 13 young apprentices who in 1688 closed the city gates on the advancing troops of King James II, setting in motion Derry's great siege. Members of the organization still meet within the bar and lounges of this ornate structure, where some 20,000 members have been sworn in over the years in the initiation chamber. The Society sometimes opens its doors to nonmembers (check with the Tourist Information Centre), and members make a great showing every year on the Saturday closest to August 12 when they march on the city walls. Violence frequently flared up when thousands of Protestant marchers allegedly flaunted their might to Catholics in the Bogside neighborhood beneath the walls; since the Good Friday Peace Accords of 1998, in a gesture of peace, only a small contingent of the Society is allowed to march past the Catholic precincts.

From this section of the walls you can look down into **Bogside,** so called for the marshy, less-desirable ground upon which this neighborhood took shape around the 1840s Famine, when starving peasants from Donegal came to Derry looking for work. The violence that erupted in this neighborhood during the Troubles accounts for the presence of the British military lookout tower on this section of the walls; much of the installation has been dismantled, and next to the tower is the **Verbal Arts Centre,** a peace-promoting concern that encourages the development of local literary efforts. From the walls you can pick out some of the murals depicting the heated political climate of the past decades (walk into the neighborhood later for a closer look; see below). You can also see the **Bloody Sunday Monument,** which honors the 14 civilians shot by British soldiers during a march on Sunday, January 30, 1972, because they were protesting laws that allowed imprisonment without trial.

Just outside the north end of the walls is the **Guildhall,** an 1890 mock-Gothic fortress and the seat of city government; a bomb blast ripped through the building in 1972, a time when bombings were a daily occurrence in Derry. Like most other damaged structures, the Guildhall was rebuilt, and the magnificent stained-glass windows were remade to the original designs still on file at the glassmaker's studios in Belfast. One of the convicted bombers, Gerry Doherty, took a seat in the council chamber when he was elected to the City Council in the 1980s. The excellent city museum, **Tower Museum Derry,** is just inside the walls here.

Bogside

The Catholic neighborhood beneath the walls has been largely rebuilt since the violence of the past decades, but political murals are stunning reminders. While those promoting the British cause have appeared in Protestant neighborhoods since the division of Ireland in the 1920s, they were outlawed in pro-independence Catholic neighborhoods but began to reappear during the Troubles of the 1970s. The murals one sees today are recent—from the 1990s—and vivid statements of the ideologies that emerged from the strife. If you leave the walled city through Butcher's Gate and turn west (left) toward Rossville Road, you'll soon encounter the murals, usually painted along the gable ends of buildings. Most commemorate significant events in clashes between the IRA and the police and military: *Death of Innocence* portrays Annette McGavigan, a 14-year-old killed in crossfire between police forces and the IRA in 1971; *Rioter* shows a youth armed only with a stone facing a British military vehicle; *Operation Motorman* depicts a British soldier attempting to demolish the neighborhood barricades with which Bogside residents once surrounded themselves. One of the most poignant reminders of the neighborhood's past is the huge sign painted on the end of a building: YOU ARE NOW ENTERING FREE DERRY, capturing the quest for independence that ignited the Troubles.

Tours in Derry

The **Derry Visitor and Convention Bureau** conducts an excellent walking tour that more or less circumnavigates the walls, with stops at St. Columb's Cathedral and other landmarks along the way; you look down on the Bogside neighborhood from overlooks on the walls while your guide explains the murals and monuments, but for a close-up look you'll need to head down there on your own. Tours, which last an hour and a half, depart from the **Tourist Information Centre;** July through August, Monday through Friday, 11:15 a.m. and 3:15 p.m.; September through June, Monday through Friday, 2:30 p.m.; £6 adults, £4 seniors and students. For an in-depth look at the murals, consider joining one of the hour-long walks offered by **Bogside Artists;** for times and fees, call ☎ 028-7129-0371 or visit **www.bogsideartists.com.**

ATTRACTIONS IN DERRY

Tower Museum Derry ★★★★

APPEAL BY AGE	PRESCHOOL ★★	GRADE SCHOOL ★★★	TEENS ★★★
YOUNG ADULTS ★★★	OVER 30 ★★★		SENIORS ★★★

**Union Hall Place, Derry; ☎ 028-7137-2411;
www.derrycity.gov.uk/museums/tower.asp**

Type of attraction Museum of local history. **Admission** £4 adults; £1.50 students and children. **Hours** July–August, Monday–Saturday, 10 a.m.–5 p.m.; Sunday, 11 a.m.–3 p.m.; September, Monday–Saturday, 10 a.m.–5 p.m.; October–June, Tuesday–Saturday, 10 a.m.–5 p.m. **When to go** Weekdays, if possible, because the museum can be quite crowded on weekends, making it harder to enjoy the exhibits. **Special comments** The museum is an essential stop on a trip to Northern Ireland, in that it is probably a visitor's best source of information on the Troubles and the complex conditions that fostered the conflict. **How much time to allow** At least 2 hours.

DESCRIPTION AND COMMENTS Derry's civic museum, which occupies a reconstructed tower house from the 17th century, is a fascinating place, not simply because Derry is such an interesting city, but also because the exhibits are superb. If you've come to Derry thinking the city is simply a blighted war zone, this museum will go a long way toward convincing you otherwise and leave you with a much greater appreciation for the town's architecture, strategic importance, and colorful forebears. The latter include—as you'll learn in the galleries—characters such as Frederick Augustus Hervey, the high-living late-18th-century bishop, and aviator Amelia Earhart, who once landed in a field outside Derry. Multimedia exhibits dramatically reenact the siege of 1688–89 and sensitively explain the historic roots and many tragedies of the Troubles. A new wing shows off one of Northern Ireland's greatest treasures: loot found in the wrecks of Spanish galleons that sank off the coast in 1588.

TOURING TIPS Budget at least half your time to explore the exhibits dealing with the Troubles, because they deserve time and concentration.

 ### Workhouse Museum ★★★★

APPEAL BY AGE	PRESCHOOL ★	GRADE SCHOOL ★	TEENS ★★★
YOUNG ADULTS ★	OVER 30 ★★★½		SENIORS ★★★★

**23 Glendermott Road; ☎ 028-7131-8328;
www.derrycity.gov.uk/museums/workhouse.asp**

Type of attraction Museum that chronicles the Famine and Derry's role in World War II. **Admission** Free. **Hours** Saturday–Thursday, 10 a.m.–5 p.m. **When to go** Anytime. **Special comments** The grim nature of the workhouse and the fate of children here can make a visit unsuitable for young visitors. On the other hand, the section devoted to Derry's role in World War II is of enormous interest to veterans of that conflict and others interested in the war. **How much time to allow** About 1 hour.

DESCRIPTION AND COMMENTS The sense of misery is almost palpable here, and a floor of exhibits movingly depicts the fate of many impoverished victims of the Famine of the 1840s, who had no choice but to throw themselves at the mercy of institutions such as these. The workhouse was essentially a forced labor camp in which families were separated forever. Untold numbers died of hunger and disease. Derry was the North's major port of emigration; many of the inhabitants of the Derry workhouse walked to the city from rural counties hoping to find passage on ships bound for America. Sadly, many could never scrape together the fare and essentially had no choice but to die in the grim dormitories here. Part of the museum chronicles the Battle of the Atlantic, especially the role of the U.S. troops who arrived in 1942 and, three years later, oversaw the surrender of the German U-boat fleet in Derry Harbour.

TOURING TIPS The museum is across the Foyle from the city center, about a ten-minute walk; if you're traveling by car, consider stopping on your way into or out of the city.

RESTAURANTS IN DERRY

Badger's ★★★

PUB FARE	INEXPENSIVE	QUALITY ★★★	VALUE ★★★★

16–18 Orchard Street, Derry; ☎ 028-7136-0763

Reservations Not necessary. **Entree range** £5–£10. **Payment** MC, V. **Bar** Full service. **Disabled access** Yes. **Hours** Monday, noon–3 p.m.; Tuesday–Thursday, noon–7 p.m.; Friday–Saturday, noon–9:30 p.m.

MENU RECOMMENDATIONS Beef-and-Guinness stew, sandwiches.

COMMENTS What may well be the most popular pub in Derry attracts neighborhood locals as well as a highly talkative crowd of journalists and artists (let them do the talking—you don't want to voice an unpopular political opinion in these parts). The Guinness is excellent, and a satisfying meal of a sandwich or a savory pie is easy to come by.

Mange 2   ★★★★

IRISH/INTERNATIONAL	MODERATE	QUALITY ★★★★	VALUE ★★★★

2B Clarendon Street, Derry; ☎ 028-7136-1222

Reservations Recommended. **Entree range** £10–£17. **Payment** MC, V. **Bar** Full service. **Disabled access** Yes. **Hours** Monday–Sunday, 11:30 a.m.–3 p.m. and 5:30–11 p.m.

MENU RECOMMENDATIONS Fresh fish.

COMMENTS Simple, straightforward preparations here are almost always satisfying, and meals are served with care in an unpretentious but pleasing cafelike setting of pine tables and uncluttered walls. Don't let the lack of pretense fool you, though—this is one of Derry's most respected kitchens and most pleasant dining experiences.

SOUTH *of* DERRY

RISING JUST SOUTHEAST OF DERRY, the **Sperrin Mountains** reach their peak at **Sawel**, 661 meters (2,204 feet) tall. For the most part these are gentle mountains, covered with moors and woodlands above valleys parceled into small farms.

South of the Sperrins, green hills run down to the shores of **Lough Erne.** The Ernes are actually two lakes, Upper and Lower Lough Erne, and they compose one of Ireland's most popular spots for boating. Monasteries flourished on the lakeshores in the Middle Ages. Some of Ireland's greatest estates were built in the region in the 18th century, while a pleasant, low-key resort atmosphere prevails today.

ENNISKILLEN

ABOUT 100 KILOMETERS (60 miles) south of Derry, Enniskillen is beautifully lodged between Lower Lough Erne to the north and Upper Lough Erne to the south; the River Erne runs through town, connecting the two. Enniskillen, the capital of County Fermanagh, has the look of a prosperous county seat, with rows of redbrick Georgian houses running down to the river and the lakeshore.

Arriving and Getting Oriented in Enniskillen

Ulsterbus runs daily coach service to and from Enniskillen, with several trips a day; one bus departs from Derry at 9 a.m. and returns at 5:30 p.m., allowing plenty of time for a day's outing. The two-plus-hour trip requires a change in Omagh and costs about £7. The trip is all the more pleasant if you travel by car, allowing yourself time to meander south through Belleek on A47 and from there around the lakeshore (see page 389) to Enniskillen and the attractions that surround the town.

Exploring Enniskillen and the Region

Enniskillen's charms are greatly enhanced by the green hills and blue waters that surround the attractive town, as well as by the hulking presence of **Enniskillen Castle.** This mighty fortress began to take shape in the early 15th century, when the Maguire clan established a foothold in the region to protect the passes that led into the rest of the North. The castle's most prominent feature is the **Watergate,** a tall, turreted, fortified structure that rises on the banks of the River Erne. Watergate, oddly, contains no gate but is near a breach in the castle's thick walls. Much the appearance of the present-day castle is the work of Sir William Cole (1576–1653), a Londoner by birth who was responsible for overseeing boat traffic on Lough Erne and who was eventually given the lease to the castle and the land on which the town took shape. The castle houses a fairly dull collection of local history and wildlife, as well as weapons and uniforms of the Royal Inniskilling Fusiliers. Open year-round, Monday, 2 to 5 p.m.; Tuesday through Friday, 10 a.m. to 5 p.m.; also open Saturday, May through September, 2 to 5 p.m., and Sunday, July and August, 2 to 5 p.m. Admission is £2.75 adults, £2.20 students and seniors, and £1.65 children. For more information, call ☎028-6632-5000 or visit **www.enniskillencastle.co.uk.**

Enniskillen's **Portora Royal School,** established by King James I in 1608, educated Samuel Beckett, Oscar Wilde, and several other noted alumni. The town's other attractions include two of Ireland's finest houses, **Castle Coole** (see below) and **Florence Court,** 13 kilometers (8 miles) southeast off A32. The latter, an appealing manor set on extensive grounds in the Cullcagh Mountains, was built in the 18th century and is richly embellished with elaborate rococo plasterwork. The grounds, laced with hiking trails, are open year-round, daily, dawn to dusk. The house is open late March and July and August, daily, noon to 6 p.m.; April and May, Saturday and Sunday, 1 to 6 p.m.; June, Monday and Wednesday through Sunday, 1 to 6 p.m.; and September, Saturday and Sunday, 1 to 6 p.m. Admission to the house and grounds is £5.50 adults, £2.50 children, and £10.50 for families of up to two adults and two children; admission to the grounds is £3 per car. For more information, call ☎028-6634-8249 or visit **www.nationaltrust.org.uk.**

Devenish Island, in the lake just southeast of Enniskillen, is graced with the best-preserved round tower in Ireland, built in the 12th century as protection against Viking raids. St. Molaise founded a monastery on the island in the sixth century, and the Augustine order of monks built the Abbey of St. Mary here in the 12th century. Chapels and convents lie in picturesque ruins, with the tower rising above them and the lake glimmering in the background. Ferries sail to the island from Trory Point, 6.5 kilometers (4 miles) south of Enniskillen, April through September, £2.25 round-trip. Call ☎ 028-6862-1588 for schedules and information.

Attraction around Enniskillen

Castle Coole ★★★★

APPEAL BY AGE	PRESCHOOL ★★	GRADE SCHOOL ★★★	TEENS ★★★
YOUNG ADULTS ★★★	OVER 30 ★★★★		SENIORS ★★★★

2.5 kilometers (1.5 miles) southeast of Enniskillen off the A4;
☎ **028-6632-5665; www.nationaltrust.org.uk**

Type of attraction One of Ireland's finest country estates. **Admission** £5.50 adults, £2.50 for children under 12, £13.50 for families of up to 2 adults and 2 children. **Hours** June, Friday–Wednesday, 1–6 p.m.; July and August, daily, noon–6 p.m.; September and April–May, Saturday and Sunday, 1–6 p.m.; grounds are open year-round, daily, dawn–dusk. **When to go** Midweek and early in the day, when you are likely to have the grounds to yourself. **Special comments** The house is often used for weddings and other functions, so check to make sure your visit does not coincide with an event that takes over parts of the estate. **How much time to allow** 3 hours for the house and grounds.

DESCRIPTION AND COMMENTS The starkly elegant neoclassical facade of this manor, built for the Earl of Belmore at the end of the 18th century, is one of the most stunning architectural sights in all of Ireland. The earl served in the Irish Houses of Parliament and was one of the wealthiest landowners in Ireland; accordingly, he hired the finest architect of the day, James Wyatt, to build his estate here in the remote wilds of County Fermanagh. The earl more or less retired here when the Act of Union dissolved the Irish Parliament in 1800, and the family remained in residence until the seventh earl of Belmore sold Castle Coole to the National Trust in 1951. The staterooms include several salons furnished in Regency style, a great hall, and a bedroom prepared for a royal visit from King George IV in 1821 (the king never showed up). Just as intriguing are the servants' quarters and a tunnel that connected them to the house, the only entrance help and tradesmen were allowed to use—eliminating the unsightly blemish of a service door on any of the house's four facades.

TOURING TIPS Plan on spending time walking in the beautiful grounds.

Restaurant in Enniskillen

Blake's of the Hollow   ★★★★

PUB FARE/MODERN IRISH   INEXPENSIVE/MODERATE   QUALITY ★★★★   VALUE ★★★★

6 Church Street, Enniskillen; ☎ 028-6632-0918

Reservations Not required. **Entree range** £6–£14; early-dinner menu in Café Merlot daily, 5:30–7:30 p.m., 2 courses £12. **Payment** AE, MC, V. **Bar** Full service. **Disabled access** Yes. **Hours** Daily, 12:30–2:30 p.m. and 5–9:30 p.m.; pub, daily, 11 a.m.–midnight.

MENU RECOMMENDATIONS Aged filet of beef, any fresh-fish preparation.

COMMENTS Enniskillen's most venerable pub, one of the most legendary in all of Ireland, retains all the Victorian grandeur that was in vogue when it opened in 1887, perhaps because the place has been in the same family since then. The operation has expanded and now offers, aside from pub grub in the woody old bar, a formal dining room, Number Six, and the informal Café Merlot. The old bar is still the most atmospheric place in town to drink and dine.

Exercise and Recreation in Enniskillen

Understandably, many visitors come to Enniskillen with the single-minded intention of getting out onto the waters of Lough Erne. **Lakeland Canoe Centre,** on Castle Island just west of town (☎ 028-6632-4250), rents canoes, sailboats, and windsurfers, as well as bikes for a land-based excursion. Should you wish to enjoy the lake without physical exertion, you can cruise the lake, with a stop at Devenish Island, on scheduled two-hour sailings from May to September with

Erne Tours Ltd. (Brook Park, near town center; call ☎ 028-6632-2882 for schedules and fares).

▌ *The* **ANTRIM COAST**

TO THE NORTH AND EAST of Derry lies some of the most spectacular scenery in all of Ireland, along the Antrim Coast. You can explore this coastline on a scenic road, A2, that hugs the green hills dropping down to the sea. Any reluctance you might feel toward leaving this beautiful coastline behind is offset by the pleasures of exploring the **Glens of Antrim,** nine densely wooded river valleys etched out of the mountain terrain along the sea.

ARRIVING AND GETTING ORIENTED ON THE ANTRIM COAST

THE ANTRIM COAST BEGINS outside the resort town of **Portrush,** about 60 kilometers (36 miles) northeast of Derry. Not surprisingly, the easiest and most satisfying way to tour the region is by car, although in summer open-top buses run along the coast from Portrush to the Old Bushmills Distillery and the Giants Causeway; for more information, contact **Translink,** ☎ 028-9066-6630; **www.translink.co.uk.** You'll find an excellent **tourist-information center** at Giants Causeway, ☎ 028-2073-1855; open year-round, Monday through Friday, 9:30 a.m. to 5 p.m., Saturday, 10 a.m. to 4 p.m., and Sunday, 2 to 4 p.m. You will also find reams of information on the Antrim Coast and the Glens at the tourist-information office in Derry.

HOTELS ON THE ANTRIM COAST

Bushmills Inn   ★★★★½

QUALITY ★★★★½	VALUE ★★★	FROM £160

9 Dunluce Road, Bushmills, County Antrim BT57 8QG;
☎ 028-2073-3000; fax 028-2073-2048; mail@bushmillsinn.com;
www.bushmillsinn.com

Location In the village of Bushmills, near the historic distillery and Giants Causeway. **Amenities and services** 32 rooms; bar, hair dryers, nonsmoking rooms, restaurant. **Elevator** Yes. **Parking** Free, on property. **Price** Includes full Irish breakfast. **Credit cards** AE, MC, V.

ONE OF IRELAND'S MOST BELOVED inns maintains its character and high level of comfort year after year and in the midst of ongoing improvements. Guests are greeted by turf fires and old beams, setting the stage for the traditional style admirably and tastefully maintained throughout the hotel, which occupies an old coaching inn and an adjacent mill house. Lounges and a circular library, reached through a secret panel, along with a woody pub and attractive restaurant, are among the appealing public spaces.

Guest rooms are continually being upgraded to a very high standard; these are attractive in a country-house style and not overdone—with fine old beds and armchairs, plus nicely equipped baths. All the attractions of the Antrim Coast are within easy reach; some, such as the Giants Causeway (see page 416), can be reached via an exhilarating hike.

Maddybenny Farmhouse ★★★★

QUALITY ★★★★	VALUE ★★★★	£37–£65

Loguestown Road, Portrush, County Antrim T52 2PT;
☎ 028-7082-3394; accommodation@maddybenny22.freeserve.co.uk;
www.maddybenny.com

Location Outside Portrush. **Amenities and services** 5 units; garden, hair dryers, in-room tea and coffee facilities, lounges, riding, walking. **Elevator** No. **Parking** Free, on property. **Price** Includes a lavish breakfast. **Credit cards** MC, V.

THE LATE ROSEMARY WHITE, one of Northern Ireland's most celebrated innkeepers, extended her 17th-century farmhouse many times over the years, but always with the comfort of her guests in mind. Her family now runs the operation with the same attention to detail. The front of the house, overlooking gardens and lawns, is a series of delightful and sunny lounges, behind them a snug parlor warmed by a fire in colder months. With the exception of a small single, the guest rooms are suitelike arrangements that extend into sitting areas that also double as extra sleeping accommodations for families. Rooms are furnished with quaint old family pieces and equipped with thoughtful touches such as alarm clocks and, in the hall, a refrigerator for guests to use. The enormous breakfasts are part of Rosemary's legacy. Several housekeeping cottages and a famous riding school are also on the property.

EXPLORING THE ANTRIM COAST

YOUR FIRST IMPRESSION OF THE COAST—the faded resort town of **Portrush**—may be a bit disappointing. A few terraces of Victorian houses and a busy harbor are pleasant enough, but continue east on A2 for just five kilometers (three miles) to the first of many spectacular sights, this one man-made: the ruins of **Dunluce Castle** perched on a rocky headland (see facing page). Just down the road is another man-made attraction that's well worth a stop: the **Old Bushmills Distillery,** a venerable institution that is the oldest licensed distillery in the world. If you do enough elbow bending in the tasting room, you will fall for the local blarney that the sea of rocks down the road—the marvelously strange natural phenomenon known as **Giants Causeway**—is the work of a likeable giant named Finn MacCool. Whatever the lore that surrounds the causeway, the sweep of cylindrical basalt outcroppings extending far out to sea toward Scotland is remarkable, all the more enticing because of the many hiking trails that lace the green hillsides around it.

The Glens of Antrim begin to grace the landscape around the small port and resort town of Ballycastle. **Glenariff,** the most beautiful of the glens with its dense woodlands and cascading cataracts, is also the most accessible, on the road and trails lacing **Glenariff Forest Park;** open daily, 8 a.m. to dusk; £1 per car.

ATTRACTIONS ON THE ANTRIM COAST

kids Carrick-a-Rede Bridge ★★★★

| APPEAL BY AGE | PRESCHOOL ★★ | GRADE SCHOOL ★★★★ | TEENS ★★★★ |
| YOUNG ADULTS ★★★★ | | OVER 30 ★★★ | SENIORS ★★★ |

8 kilometers (5 miles) west of Ballycastle; ☎ 028-2073-1582; www.nationaltrust.org.uk

Type of attraction Hair-raising rope bridge. **Admission** £3.70 adults, £2 children, £9.40 for families of up to 2 adults and 2 children. **Hours** March–May and September–November, daily, 10 a.m.–6 p.m.; June–August: daily, 10 a.m.–7 p.m. **When to go** Only in good weather, because the bridge is closed when conditions are windy and wet. **Special comments** Do not even think of stopping if you're afraid of heights; kids have a ball crossing the bridge. **How much time to allow** ½ hour.

DESCRIPTION AND COMMENTS For some 200 summers, fishermen have been putting up a rope bridge to make the short crossing to Carrick-a-Rede Island, where they set out nets to snare salmon that swim toward the rivers to spawn. In recent years, the savvy fisherfolk have figured out that they can net more than some big fish—tourists by the busloads are willing to fork over money to timorously cross the rope-and-plank concoction swaying a dizzying height above the sea. So what if you're falling prey to gimcrack tourism? Crossing the bridge is a heck of a lot of fun, provided you don't suffer from vertigo, and the view of the surf and seabirds is exhilarating; this is one of those experiences you'll be telling the folks back home about.

TOURING TIPS If you see tour buses in the parking lot, try to come back another time—the experiences loses its appeal when the bridge is mobbed.

Dunluce Castle ★★★★

| APPEAL BY AGE | PRESCHOOL ★★★ | GRADE SCHOOL ★★★ | TEENS ★★★ |
| YOUNG ADULTS ★★★ | | OVER 30 ★★★ | SENIORS ★★★ |

On a headland on the coast; ☎ 028-2073-1938; www.northantrim.com/dunlucecastle.htm

Type of attraction Castle ruins. **Admission** £2 adults, £1 seniors and children under age 16. **Hours** April–September, daily, 10 a.m.–6 p.m.; October–March, daily, 10 a.m.–5 p.m. **When to go** Try to avoid a visit during a rain shower; the site can be muddy. **Special comments** Although it's easy to pass by the castle for more-noted attractions such as Giants Causeway and Bushmills Distillery, take the time to stop—a visit to these evocative and poetically perched ruins is a memorable experience. **How much time to allow** About ½ hour.

DESCRIPTION AND COMMENTS The elaborate castle complex, incorporating two 14th-century Norman towers, was the stronghold of the powerful MacDonnell clan, the Counts of Antrim. It wasn't rival clans that did them in, but the forces of nature—the sea churned relentlessly away at the precipitous cliffs on which the castle sits, and on a dark and stormy night in 1639 half the kitchen wing, and part of the staff, plunged into the surf. Over the ensuing centuries, surf and storms completed the job, leaving the castle basically a shell; even so, the ruins romantically evoke life in a medieval castle at the edge of the sea. An engaging staff gives short tours, during which they fill in the architectural gaps with colorful stories of the MacDonnells, life in the castle, and ongoing restoration efforts.

TOURING TIPS Tours do not follow a set schedule, so ask at the entry gate whether someone is available to show you around—a guide adds a lot to the experience.

kids Giants Causeway ★★★★★

| APPEAL BY AGE | PRESCHOOL ★★★★ | GRADE SCHOOL ★★★★★ | TEENS ★★★★★ |
| YOUNG ADULTS ★★★★ | | OVER 30 ★★★★★ | SENIORS ★★★★ |

Near Bushmills; ☎ 028-2073-1582;
www.giantscausewayofficialguide.com

Type of attraction One of Europe's most unusual natural phenomena. **Admission** Free; parking, £5. **Hours** March–October, daily, 10 a.m.–5 p.m.; November–February, daily, 10 a.m.–4:30 p.m. **When to go** In good weather. **Special comments** Take time to watch the 12-minute film in the visitors center for a good roundup of the legends surrounding the Causeway and a concise explanation of the equally compelling geologic forces that formed it; exhibits in the small museum are also well done. **How much time to allow** Several hours, more if you want to spend time hiking along the coast.

DESCRIPTION AND COMMENTS Legends concerning the formation of these pillars of basalt that litter the coast and sea for about six kilometers (four miles) of the coast are as plentiful as the stones themselves. Most concern a giant named Finn MacCool, who allegedly laid down the stepping stones to reach his beloved across the sea in Scotland. The only reason mortals can't also use the stones to get to Scotland is that a rival giant, the lady giant's boyfriend, came to Ireland to settle the score. The story goes that he was terrified when he heard how big and fierce Finn was, and he tore up the stepping stones while beating a quick retreat. Just as awesome, actually, is the science-based theory that the stones were formed when lava erupted from underground fissures some 60 million years ago and crystallized in the cooler seawater. Begin a tour of this fascinating natural phenomenon, administered by the National Trust, at the visitors center. From there you can take a shuttle bus down to the causeway or walk the 2 kilometers (1.5 miles) along a delightful path that sticks to high ground for some wonderful views before descending past bizarre rock formations to the sea via stairways.

TOURING TIPS Unless you really want the exercise, consider walking down the Causeway to enjoy the views as you approach, and then take the minibus back. You can walk the length of the Antrim Coast on the Ulster Way hiking path, so you might consider walking to the Giants Causeway from Bushmills or from the Giants Causeway to the Carrick-a-Rede Bridge.

Old Bushmills Distillery ★★★★

| APPEAL BY AGE | PRESCHOOL ★ | GRADE SCHOOL ★ | TEENS ★★ |
| YOUNG ADULTS ★★★ | OVER 30 ★★★½ | | SENIORS ★★★½ |

Main Street, Bushmills; ☎ 028-2073-1521; www.bushmills.com

Type of attraction Whiskey-making factory. **Admission** £6 adults, £5 seniors and students, £3 children, £17 for families of up to 2 adults and 2 children. **Hours** April–October, Monday–Saturday, 9:15 a.m.–5:30 p.m.; Sunday, noon–5 p.m. (first tour at 11:30 a.m. Sunday, July–September); **When to go** During the week when the plant is in operation; it's actually quite interesting to see bottles being filled and set into boxes. **Special comments** If you've visited the Old Midleton Distillery (page 225), consider bypassing the tour here and settling for a visit to the shop; aside from actually seeing the operation at work, you won't learn anything new; the coffee shop–pub is a good stop for lunch while touring the coast. **How much time to allow** About 1 hour for the tour and tasting and a visit to the gift shop.

DESCRIPTION AND COMMENTS When King James I granted a whiskey-making license to Bushmills in 1608, the locals were already old hands at distilling—allegedly, a distillery has stood on this site since the 13th century. By the time you reach Bushmills, you too may be an old hand at touring distilleries if you've already paid visits to the Jameson operations in Dublin and Midleton. What sets Bushmills apart is the quality of the product, generally regarded as the best Irish whiskey, and the fact that this is a working plant—you actually see workers mashing and bottling, which adds a bit of veracity to the guides' lectures on how whiskey is made. As at other distilleries, the tour ends with a bang, in the tasting room, and you exit the premises through an enormous gift shop.

TOURING TIPS During the busy summer months, call in advance to reserve a place on one of the tours, which fill up fast.

RESTAURANT ON THE ANTRIM COAST
Ramore Wine Bar ★★★

| PUB FARE | INEXPENSIVE | QUALITY ★★★ | VALUE ★★★ |

The Harbour, Portrush; ☎ 028-7082-4313

Reservations Not necessary. **Entree range** £6.50–£8. **Payment** AE, MC, V. **Bar** Full service. **Disabled access** Yes. **Hours** Monday–Friday, 12:15–2:15 p.m. and 5–10 p.m.; Saturday, 4:45–10:30 p.m.; Sunday, 12:30–3 p.m. and 5–9 p.m.

MENU RECOMMENDATIONS Burgers, lamb steaks, grilled fish.

DESCRIPTION AND COMMENTS Ramore is a big presence on the harbor in Portrush, with several restaurants and bars The informal and lively Wine Bar, really more of a family-oriented bistro, serves decent, wide-ranging casual fare in relaxed surroundings with sweeping harbor views. Coast, a pizza parlor, is just down the street, and the nicest part of the operation is the adjacent Harbour Bar, a cozy pub that retains its century-old character.

INDEXES

ACCOMMODATIONS INDEX

Note: Page numbers of accommodation profiles are in **boldface** type.

RESTAURANT INDEX

Note: Page numbers of restaurant profiles are in **boldface** type.

SUBJECT INDEX

Unofficial Guide Reader Survey

If you would like to express your opinion in writing about Ireland or this guidebook, complete the following survey and mail it to:

> *Unofficial Guide* Reader Survey
> P.O. Box 43673
> Birmingham, AL 35243

Inclusive dates of your visit:_____

Members of your party:

	Person 1	Person 2	Person 3	Person 4	Person 5
Gender:	M F	M F	M F	M F	M F
Age:					

How many times have you been to Ireland? _____

On your most recent trip, where did you stay?_____

Concerning your accommodations, on a scale of 100 as best and 0 as worst, how would you rate:

The quality of your room? _____ The value of your room? _____
The quietness of your room?_____ Check-in/checkout efficiency?_____
Shuttle service to the airport?_____ Swimming pool facilities? _____

Did you rent a car? _____ From whom? _____

Concerning your rental car, on a scale of 100 as best and 0 as worst, how would you rate:

Pickup-processing efficiency?_____ Return-processing efficiency?_____
Condition of the car? _____ Cleanliness of the car?_____
Airport-shuttle efficiency? _____

Concerning your dining experiences:

Estimate your meals in restaurants per day? _____
Approximately how much did your party spend on meals per day? ____
_____

Favorite restaurants in Ireland: _____
_____

Did you buy this guide before leaving?____ while on your trip?____

How did you hear about this guide? (check all that apply)

Loaned or recommended by a friend ☐ Radio or TV ☐
Newspaper or magazine ☐   Bookstore salesperson ☐
Just picked it out on my own ☐   Library ☐
Internet ☐

What other guidebooks did you use on this trip? _____

_____

_____

_____

On a scale of 100 as best and 0 as worst, how would you rate them?

_____

_____

_____

Using the same scale, how would you rate the *Unofficial Guide*(s)?

_____

Are Unofficial Guides readily available at bookstores in your area? _____

Have you used other *Unofficial Guides*? _____

Which one(s)? _____

_____

_____

Comments about your Ireland trip or the *Unofficial Guide*(s):

_____

_____

_____

_____

_____

_____

_____

_____

_____

_____

_____

_____

_____

_____

_____

_____

_____

_____

_____